THE CHANCELLORS

Political Responsibility and Industry
Report on European Institutions (with Barend Biesheuvel and Robert Marjolin)
The Politics of Economic Interdependence
A Hard Pounding: Politics and Economic Crisis, 1974–6
The Schuman Plan and the British Abdication of Leadership in Europe

THE CHANCELLORS

Edmund Dell

A HISTORY OF

THE CHANCELLORS OF

THE EXCHEQUER

1945–90

HarperCollins*Publishers*

HarperCollins*Publishers*
77–85 Fulham Palace Road,
Hammersmith, London W6 8JB

Published by HarperCollins*Publishers* 1996
1 3 5 7 9 8 6 4 2

Copyright © Edmund Dell 1996

The Author asserts the moral right to
be identified as the author of this work

A catalogue record for this book
is available from the British Library

ISBN 0 00 255558 1

Set in Linotron Janson by
Rowland Phototypesetting Ltd,
Bury St Edmunds, Suffolk

Printed and bound in Great Britain by
Caledonian International Book Manufacturing Ltd, Glasgow

FOR SUSI

Acknowledgements

The material from the Public Record Office listed among the references is Crown copyright and is reproduced with the permission of the Controller of Her Majesty's Stationery Office. Material from House of Commons debates is subject to parliamentary copyright and that from White Papers to Crown copyright. I am grateful to the Master and Fellows of University College Oxford for permission to quote copyright material from the papers of Lord Attlee held in deposit from University College in the Bodleian Library catalogued as MS Attlee.

Contents

List of Illustrations

Hugh Dalton (*Hulton Deutsch Collection*)

Sir Stafford Cripps (*Hulton Deutsch Collection*)

Hugh Gaitskell (*Hulton Deutsch Collection*)

R. A. Butler (*Hulton Deutsch Collection*)

Harold Macmillan (*Hulton Deutsch Collection*)

Peter Thorneycroft (*Popperfoto*)

Derick Heathcoat Amory (*Popperfoto*)

Selwyn Lloyd (*Hulton Deutsch Collection*)

Reginald Maulding (*Popperfoto*)

James Callaghan (*Camera Press*)

Roy Jenkins (*Hulton Deutsch Collection*)

Iain Macleod (*Hulton Deutsch Collection*)

Anthony Barber (*Hulton Deutsch Collection*)

Denis Healey (*Popperfoto*)

Sir Geoffrey Howe (*Hulton Deutsch Collection*)

Nigel Lawson (*Hulton Deutsch Collection*)

John Major (*Hulton Deutsch Collection*)

Preface

IT MAY REASONABLY BE ASKED how far the argument of this book reflects the views I myself held during my fifteen years as a Member of Parliament, nine of them spent as a Minister. I did not, when I entered Parliament in 1964, advocate devaluation though I did repeatedly question the logic of the Wilson government's policies. Hesitant deflation combined with inadequate export incentives seemed to me to be leading nowhere. My background when I entered Parliament in 1964 was principally that of an industrial manager in Imperial Chemical Industries (ICI) though I had held two academic posts, at Oxford and Manchester Universities, for brief periods. My experience as an industrial manager made me sceptical of the claims made for Labour's industrial policy and for economic planning. I knew how long it can take, in a major company, for decisions of significance to be made, let alone implemented. My scepticism led me to clash with George Brown about the National Plan. I claimed that it was an illusion to imagine that, so far as economic growth was concerned, Labour could do better than the Tories.* My experience in the 1960s at the Ministry of Technology, the Department of Economic Affairs, and the Board of Trade, did nothing to persuade me that Labour had discovered the secret of success through industrial policy and economic planning.

By 1970 the Labour Party and the public were thoroughly disenchanted and I was beginning to question my own role in politics. Certainly by the time I was appointed to the Treasury in March 1974, my views as expressed in this book were fully formed. In 1991, I published *A Hard Pounding: Politics and Economic Crisis 1974–6*. I have told there, in greater detail than has been possible in this book, the story of my experiences during the two and a half years from 1974 to the IMF crisis in the autumn of 1976. For the first two years, I was at the Treasury as Paymaster General and deputy to the Chancellor of the Exchequer, Denis Healey. In April 1976 I became Secretary of State for Trade.

* The story is told in Dell (1991) 26.

I am indebted to a number of people, not all of whom are aware of it. First, there is Sir Alec Cairncross who kindly allowed me to read before publication his immensely valuable and informative diary of his time as Economic Adviser to HM Government and Head of the Government Economic Service. Unfortunately his diary has had to be cut for publication. My references are to the original. I am also grateful to him for his own extensive work on the economic history of the postwar period without which the writing of this book would have been much more difficult. I am grateful to Mark D. Harmon for permitting me to read an early draft of his book *Ties that Bind: The British Labour Government and the 1976 IMF* Crisis.

I am indebted to all those former Ministers, and particularly those former Chancellors, who have written memoirs about their periods in office. Their memories of the time when they bore responsibility have provided me with valuable guidance. Though memory is unreliable, many of them have refreshed their own through the access to government documents permitted to former Cabinet Ministers. Under the thirty-year rule, government sources beyond 1965 are not yet available. In the absence of government sources, memoirs by authors who have had access to government papers, have been invaluable. I myself have the advantage of having personal knowledge of the period leading up to the IMF crisis, and of having played a full part in the Cabinet discussions in 1978 on whether sterling should join the ERM.

In writing the chapter on Butler, I was fortunate in being able to persuade the Rt Hon. David Hunt MP, then Chancellor of the Duchy of Lancaster, to open two files, T236/3241 and T236/3244, which otherwise would have remained closed until the year 2003. My work on Robot (see p. 166) is the first to benefit from the public availability of these files.

I am grateful to my agent, Jennifer Kavanagh and to Michael Fishwick, Publishing Director at HarperCollins, for their readiness to accept from me the idea of a book like this and for their subsequent advice and encouragement.

EDMUND DELL
November 1995

INTRODUCTION

THE TREASURY

The Treasury is the ancient office of the Lord High Treasurer. When a Commission was established to exercise the office of Lord High Treasurer, the person first named in the patent of appointment was described as the First Lord of the Treasury. The Chancellor of the Exchequer was only the Second Lord of the Treasury.[1] For many years now, the Prime Minister of the day has held the post of First Lord of the Treasury. It would be too burdensome if he also acted as the Treasury's Ministerial head. Therefore the management of Treasury business has devolved upon the Chancellor of the Exchequer although he is only the Second Lord. However, few things are more important to the Second Lord than his relations with the First. For this there are two reasons. The first is that Prime Ministers generally have the keenest interest in the work of the Treasury; their support in Cabinet is vital to the Chancellor and when it is absent the Chancellor is unlikely to have his way. The second is that the Prime Minister, as First Lord, *is* a Treasury Minister. Harold Wilson, when he found some lesser Treasury Minister opposing one of his expensive projects, was fond of pointing out that he, too, was a Treasury Minister.

In addition to the First and Second Lords of the Treasury, there are various other Lords Commissioners of the Treasury. These days, the other Lords Commissioners are government whips of various degrees of seniority. They do not signify in serious Treasury business except that two of them constitute a quorum of the Treasury Board. They are asked to sign certain formal documents such as Statutory Instruments in order to relieve the Prime Minister and the Chancellor of the Exchequer, the First and Second Lords, of so tedious a chore. The Parliamentary Secretary to the Treasury is the Government Chief Whip.

The Chancellor has, at the Treasury, a number of Ministerial colleagues who together constitute the collective concept of 'Treasury

Ministers' referred to in many government documents. All Treasury Ministers, other than the Prime Minister, are subordinate to the Chancellor. The Ministerial establishment of the Treasury includes a Financial Secretary who normally supervises the activities of the revenue departments. There may also be an Economic Secretary and a Minister of State. The Paymaster General is sometimes an additional Treasury Minister. The Ministerial establishment at the Treasury will depend on the workload or alternatively on the Prime Minister's wish to exercise additional patronage. Additional Ministers mean additional patronage.

Treasury Ministers are advised by Treasury officials, the principal of whom is the Permanent Secretary. The Treasury's official establishment and organization have changed over the years, but there has always in modern times been a Permanent Secretary and he has always been one of the most senior civil servants in Whitehall. Reference is often made, including in this book, to the 'Treasury'. It is sometimes unclear whether the reference is to the Chancellor of the Exchequer and Treasury Ministers or to the official Treasury. In this book, references to the Treasury are to the official Treasury except where the context indicates otherwise.

Early in the 1960s, it was decided that the Chancellor needed the assistance of a senior Minister in the control of public expenditure. The Chancellor at the time was Selwyn Lloyd. He was very tired and certainly needed some relief. On 9 October 1961, Prime Minister Macmillan appointed Henry Brooke to the new post of Chief Secretary to the Treasury. An announcement said that the Chief Secretary should 'under the general direction of the Chancellor, deal with the whole range of public expenditure, both current and prospective, including the scrutiny of departmental Estimates and the framing of forward surveys'.[2] The Chief Secretary is now a normal part of the Treasury's Ministerial establishment.[3] He usually acts as deputy to the Chancellor and is probably, though not invariably, a member of the Cabinet. When the Chief Secretary *is* a member of the Cabinet, the Chancellor has one colleague on whose support he can usually rely. When the Chief Secretary is not a member of the Cabinet, it is an indication that the government of which he is a member does not attribute the first importance to the control of public expenditure.[4] Twice in recent history the Paymaster General rather than the Chief Secretary has acted as deputy to the Chancellor. This demotes the Chief Secretary to third in seniority. Maurice Macmillan in the dying days of the Heath government, and this author between March 1974 and April 1976 held the appointment of Paymaster General and deputy to the Chancellor.

THE SECRET OF FULL EMPLOYMENT

In 1944, the Churchill coalition government made a major commitment to the people of Britain. The Employment Policy White Paper, published in May 1944, committed it and its successors to maintain a high and stable level of employment. It was a pledge that the high unemployment of the 1930s would not recur. It was universally interpreted as a pledge of full employment, and was not a commitment that governments of either Party could disregard. However, the coalition government made the commitment without knowing how to discharge it. The principal instruments for managing the economy were fiscal policy and monetary policy, and it was hoped that through their use, domestic demand could be managed to ensure full employment. Keynes encouraged this impression. His reputation had been built largely on the belief that he had discovered how to guarantee full employment. In the Labour Party, socialist planning was thought to be another instrument for ensuring full employment. But the Labour Party had no idea what socialist planning might involve, except in so far as it might be modelled on wartime controls and restrictions.

It was not clear what full employment meant. It did not mean that everyone was to be in a job. A legitimate interpretation was that everyone wanting a job should be able to find one without excessive delay. In other words, full employment permitted transitional unemployment, the unemployment of people moving from one job to another. Economies cannot become fixed for ever in a single pattern of production or employment; some people must move from job to job. But to what figure could transitional unemployment be permitted to grow? There was disagreement among economists. To some it seemed sensible to allow unemployment to rise to 3 per cent or about 750,000; that would enable the economy to respond, by redeploying the workforce, to new demands, for example from export markets. To politicians, however, that figure seemed far too high. Postwar British governments behaved as though they knew how to manage the economy in such a way as to keep unemployment below 2 per cent, and do it without imperilling the flexibility necessary to meet the new demands of a changing world.

It was the official Treasury whose anxieties were reflected in the limitation of the commitment to high and stable rather than to *full* employment. The Treasury might have saved itself the trouble of its equivocations – governments were still popularly believed to be committed to full employment. There was, however, a rather important prohibition inserted in the White Paper at the insistence of the Treasury. It knew enough of politicians to wish to safeguard the country against one obvious risk. Paragraph 74 said, 'None of the main proposals contained in this Paper involves deliberate planning for a deficit in the National Budget in years of subnormal trade activity.' Keynes himself, though an advocate of demand management, understood perfectly well that the right to run Budget deficits could be an irresistible temptation to profligate Chancellors. Nevertheless, the prohibition was abhorrent to his 'Keynesian' followers and they spent a great deal of energy trying to persuade Chancellors to ignore it. In practice, during the 1950s when demand remained strong, large Budget deficits were unnecessary for the maintenance of full employment. Indeed, Chancellors should have budgeted for larger surpluses in order to restrain domestic demand.

The Treasury was aware that the fulfilment of a commitment to high and stable employment would require a difficult balancing act and was dependent on circumstances beyond the shores and the control of the UK. As a minimum it depended on a favourable international economic environment. As world markets opened, and became increasingly competitive, the level of employment would depend also on maintaining a competitive economy. The management of demand to secure full employment would have implications for the price level and hence for competitiveness and the balance of payments. Full employment would carry inflationary dangers if the employed, and their trade unions, exploited unwisely the monopoly power that it placed in their hands. They could use the power given to them by full employment to force up wages and hence costs and prices. But the answer, it was at first hoped, lay in public education; workers in employment would have to learn to put the public interest in stable prices ahead of their own private interest. Within the Labour Party especially, it was hoped that appeals to the public interest would carry weight both with workers in employment, and their trade unions. This was an attractive if somewhat naive conviction. The thought that one worker might see his interests in conflict with those of others of his class was a heresy to which socialists would not easily be converted. A common expectation at the time dimmed anxiety about this question: during the war, the foreboding was that the danger in the immediate postwar years would be deflation rather than inflation. That had been the experience after the First World War.

This time that apprehension turned out to be wrong. The problem remained inflation.

When exhortation was found to be failing, numerous devices were employed by governments of both Parties in an attempt to make full employment consistent with a non-accelerating and internationally competitive price level. The devices included incomes policies, sometimes voluntary, sometimes statutory, price controls, subsidies to nationalized industries to induce them to restrain their prices, and legislation to limit the freedom of trade unions. Under Labour in the 1970s, a 'Social Contract' was negotiated between the government and the trade unions which granted trade union leaders rights of consultation at the highest level in return for a rather vague commitment to avoid inflationary wage claims. As trade union leaders do not as a profession believe that wage settlements are a source of inflation, the Social Contract proved a disappointment to the government. Some of these devices brought short-term relief, but long-term reliance could not be placed upon any of them. British prices became uncompetitive, the UK share of trade in manufactured goods declined, and sterling repeatedly came under pressure. During the fixed exchange rate regime of Bretton Woods, there were two devaluations, in 1949 and 1967. When sterling floated, the decline in the pound's value continued with no bottom in sight.

In the 1950s and 1960s the international economic environment was favourable to full employment. Governments could therefore reap the electoral benefits of full employment even if they had not, in truth, the power to ensure full employment. Labour certainly benefited in the 1950 and 1951 elections from the comparison it was able to make between full employment under Labour after the war and mass unemployment under the Tories before the war. Then, with the Tories' narrow victory in 1951, it was found that the Conservatives shared in the secret of full employment. Indeed it was not a secret at all – the method was open to anyone who read Keynes. The reputation of economics soared. The high tide of optimism about a government's ability to maintain full employment lasted from the early 1950s until the early 1970s. Tony Crosland, economist and Labour politician, reflected it as early as 1952 in the *New Fabian Essays*:

> The trend of employment is towards a high level, and a recurrence of chronic mass unemployment is most unlikely. The Keynesian techniques are now well understood, and there is no reason to fear a repetition of the New Deal experience of a government with the will to spend its way

out of a recession, but frustrated in doing so by faulty knowledge. The political pressure for full employment is stronger than ever before; the experience of the inter-war years bit so deeply into the political psychology of the nation that full employment, if threatened, would always constitute the dominant issue at any election, and no right-wing Party could now survive a year in office if it permitted the figures of unemployment which were previously quite normal.[5]

The conviction, reinforced by happy experience, that governments, guided by economists, could guarantee full employment carried political consequences and, possibly, consequences for behaviour, which were damaging to the maintenance of international competitiveness. If full employment could be guaranteed by government, why worry about competitiveness? The 1970s provided a shock to premature optimism. Unemployment rose substantially, and by the 1980s it was beginning to be realized that governments had overestimated their power and deceived their electorates. When circumstances turned unfavourable, and unemployment rose, politicians suddenly discovered the external world and its influences. Governments had gained politically from an impression of economic omnipotence until it became only too obvious that, if indeed they were omnipotent, they must be very ill-intentioned to allow the misery of unemployment to fall on so many of their fellow-citizens. Then their more sophisticated explanations and excuses were the less believed because of their earlier claims.

THREE PERIODS

The period 1945–90 can be divided into three. First there was the time, extending perhaps as far as 1955, when western Europe, devastated by war, was rebuilding its economy and its infrastructure and looked to the USA for the help that would ease recovery and enable it to navigate the political hazards created by extreme postwar shortages. The American response was, first, *ad hoc* aid to individual countries including Britain, and then the more coordinated programme of Marshall Aid which was combined with pressure for European integration. Then, secondly, came the high-water mark of the Bretton Woods system lasting to just after 1970. Once the traumas of the early postwar years had passed, and Marshall Aid had done its work for western Europe, the Bretton Woods system provided a period of relatively benign international economic regulation under American hegemony. The dollar was king, the value of other currencies fixed in relation to it. Trade barriers were reduced in response to American pressure manifested in successive rounds of international trade negotiations conducted under the auspices of the General Agreement on Tariffs and Trade (GATT).

It had been anticipated that if there was to be stability in international economic relationships it could not just be left to the market. Two new institutions had been created after the war, the International Monetary Fund (IMF), and the International Bank for Reconstruction and Development (IBRD), known as the World Bank and concerned primarily with the developing world. These new institutions, often known as the Bretton Woods institutions, stood ready to assist and discipline countries that had fallen on hard times due sometimes to their own mistakes, sometimes for reasons beyond their control.[6] Developed countries knew, or if they did not know they soon learnt, that recourse to IMF for assistance could involve subjection to severe conditionality. British governments became regular supplicants for aid from the IMF. The problem that repeatedly took them to the IMF's door in Washington was pressure on sterling; the reserves available to British governments were never sufficiently large to repel a serious attack on sterling without assistance. It was a problem in principle within the control of British governments but one which, for political reasons, they seemed unable to control.

The third period followed from the collapse of the Bretton Woods system during the years 1971–3. The USA had become concerned about its balance of payments and about the outflow of dollars that had been crucial to Europe's success in achieving full employment. The dollar had ceased to be a reliable store of value and European currencies no longer operated fixed rates against it: thus the principal characteristics of the third period were that currencies were floating, and that, in the absence of American leadership, there was no effective international economic coordination. Keynes had looked to the USA, and to what he believed to be its commitment to full employment, as a guarantee of full employment in Britain. But this was to be a more competitive world, not one designed to ensure full employment. The great new economic powers, Germany and Japan, looked first to their own interests and spurned any suggestion, whether from Britain or the USA, that their behaviour was selfish and uncooperative. The IMF and the World Bank survived as purveyors of aid, accompanied as necessary by the medicine of conditionality.

In Europe, the collapse of Bretton Woods provoked attempts to create a regional substitute. If it was no longer possible to regulate currencies internationally, there were those in European capitals who felt that there should at least be currency stability within Europe even though any purely European system would continue to float against the dollar and the yen. Currency stability within Europe was valued because of the high proportion of trade conducted by European countries with each other. From 1972 there was the 'snake' within which a small, and varying, group of European currencies was tied to the Deutschmark (DM). Then, from 1979, began a more inclusive and, for a time, quite successful era of fixed, but adjustable, exchange rates within the Exchange Rate Mechanism (ERM) of the European Monetary System (EMS). The EMS included France and Italy but still with the DM at its core. Sterling which, in 1972, had been expelled from the 'snake' six weeks after joining it, did not adhere to the ERM until September 1990. Mrs Thatcher's reluctant agreement to membership of the ERM was followed, almost at once, by her downfall. Two years later sterling was ejected from the ERM as unceremoniously as Mrs Thatcher had been from No. 10 Downing Street.

ECONOMIC PERFORMANCE

Taking the period as a whole, the economy of the UK has lagged in growth rate behind that of other developed countries, not to mention the faster-growing economies of the developing world. Slower growth has been accompanied by balance of payments crises, relatively high inflation and depreciation in the exchange rate of the pound sterling. During the period the pound sterling depreciated from $4.03 to about $1.50, and comparable figures could be shown for sterling's relationship to other major currencies. Britain's share of world manufacturing exports was falling fast: in 1951, Britain's exports exceeded the combined total of France, Germany and Japan; by 1991 British exports were only one-sixth of that total and below those of Italy. This decline was accompanied by an increasing deficit in trade in manufactured goods, which by 1989 had reached nearly £19 billion.[7] Britain had become an economic laggard, a stagnant society. After the war it had been the richest western European country; now it was being passed by its neighbours. Britain's decline relative to its European neighbours was nothing new – it had begun at least as early as 1870. But by the 1960s its causes had become a matter of political controversy. Whatever the merits of Keynes's teachings, and whatever their contribution to the management of demand, Keynesianism failed to animate British industry with those animal spirits that the master considered to be the essence of entrepreneurial drive. It became the ambition of successive British governments to reverse the decline, but never their achievement. British Chancellors have been left to contemplate the contrast between the ostensible richness of their intellectual inheritance from Keynes and the poverty of their country's economic performance.

THE SOURCES OF THE UK'S POOR ECONOMIC PERFORMANCE

The sources of the UK's poor economic performance are a matter of controversy. A host of more or less persuasive explanations is given. The problem with many of them is that it is impossible to be confident, far less certain, whether they are causes of poor performance or symptoms of poor performance. Is a weak balance of payments a symptom or a cause? Is lack of investment a cause or a symptom? Are poor labour relations a cause or a symptom? The reasons for poor performance may lie in a combination of all or some of them, though in what proportions they contribute to the problem and whether that contribution is unchanging or varies over time, remains a matter of speculation, not science. Wisest are those who profess ignorance of the answers, but this is a form of wisdom which is as hard to accept as it is to learn. It is of no use to the state unless in encouraging the perception that it is better not to interfere with what is not understood. It is hardly open to Chancellors of the Exchequer, except in retirement, and it is hardly open to historians not to make some attempt at an explanation.

Therefore, although wisdom dictates hesitation about any explanation of poor economic performance, and although there can be no certainty, the study of this history leads the present author to suggest a cause. It lies in the failure of successive British governments, in the first thirty years after the war, through cowardice or misguided conviction, to leave in the economy sufficient by way of spare resources to ensure a reasonable prospect of price stability and balance in its overseas payments. Important elements of overstrain have arisen from the commitment to a definition of full employment which left governments sweating with anxiety if unemployment approached 2 per cent, from the weight of defence expenditure on the balance of payments, and from the creation of a welfare state which was too expensive too soon, and too often, and unnecessarily, free at the point of delivery of services. A further, and continuing, factor has been the optimism of governments, which experience could never educate, about their power to stimulate non-inflationary growth. This optimism has led to repeated inflationary booms. It had its effect on the level of public expenditure. It became a tradition of British politics that governments would make optimistic estimates of growth by way of justification for their expenditure commitments. The estimates of future public expenditure tended to be too low and the estimates of economic growth tended to be too high. Inevitably it was much more difficult to reverse public expenditure commitments when the economic growth failed to materialize than to enter into them in the first place. Much should have been learnt from the IMF crisis of 1976, a turning-point in the history here recounted, but any lessons learnt had not, within the period covered by this book, manifested themselves in better economic management. The story told in this book is of relative decline, frequent crises, and repeated humiliations. A country as rich as the UK should have been able to avoid the crises and the humiliations even if it could not avoid the relative decline.

THE LESSON OF EXPERIENCE

In writing a history of postwar Chancellors of the Exchequer, as in writing any history, the historian must, if he is critical, beware of hindsight. But he should not be too frightened – a great deal that can be seen today could also be seen yesterday. Fear of exploiting the benefit of hindsight is a great, but often unjustified, protector of reputations. Experience can be shattering and educative but many of the lessons that can be learnt from experience should have been learnt before. It is no comfort that so many Chancellors have to learn from their own experience certain enduring lessons that they should have brought to the office with them. Some of these enduring lessons will emerge in the course of this history. One can be stated right away.

Economic management is an art, not a science. It is an art which, in this country, is usually practised in unprepossessing circumstances. Information, the raw material of the art, is late and unreliable. Economic theory provides no comfort, only controversy, and may be a distraction. Scepticism is to be encouraged but, on the other hand, is not in itself creative. Politics is an inevitable presence with its demanding questions and its partisan answers too often pressing the Chancellor against his better judgement, or at least that of the Treasury. At the centre of political attention, he will be subject to a spate of criticism from many people, all of whom will consider themselves better equipped to define policy than he. There are no secure stepping-stones to a more prosperous future – all are at least slippery, some are merely mirages. In the absence of anything better, he may watch the market. It is self-opinionated, short-sighted, often passionate rather than rational, but it may nevertheless provide his best anchor. His essential judgement should be whether his policy is robust; robust against the market, robust against errors in economic forecasting. He should not, whatever he does, claim more for his policies than that they seem optimal in the circumstances as he understands them. He should, so far as he can, avoid risk. Such a pragmatic conclusion is not the happiest *conceivable* outcome to so many years of experience, but it is the happiest *possible*.

We start with Hugh Dalton, the first postwar Chancellor. He was Chancellor for a little over two years. But during that brief period the course was set.

PART I

SHALLOW FOUNDATIONS

1945–55

ONE

Dalton under Keynes

Attlee's was an experienced Cabinet. Attlee, Bevin, Morrison, Cripps and Dalton had been prominent members of Churchill's coalition government, Attlee as Deputy Prime Minister. Many of them, including Dalton, had served in junior ranks in Ramsay MacDonald's government of 1929–31 and some even in his 1924 government. But their most recent experience was in the conduct of war, not in the conduct of economic policy. The Attlee government, despite its extensive experience of Ministerial office, inevitably had no valid experience and few qualifications which would help it cope with the problems of the postwar world. The government had a massive majority in the House of Commons, 146 over all other parties, but the size of their majority was accompanied by the usual costs. It made them feel ironclad. It was Hartley Shawcross who announced that they were the masters for the moment and for a very long time to come.[1] This sentiment expressed an attitude not just in relation to the dispossessed Opposition but to the tasks of government. In fact they were far from being masters of the economy, either for the moment or in time to come.

Attlee was now leading a Parliamentary Labour Party (PLP) of 393 members. Of these, 263 were new to the House.[2] Dalton proclaimed that, at the General Election, 'Youth has come in . . . on a flood tide.'[3] Some of the new MPs would in due course become Cabinet Ministers. Four, Harold Wilson, Patrick Gordon Walker, Hugh Gaitskell and Alf Robens, were to become Cabinet Ministers during the life of the Attlee government. Two, Gaitskell and James Callaghan, would become Chancellors of the Exchequer. Two, Wilson and Callaghan, would become Prime Minister. But, in July 1945, they were untried, and were not available for any but the most junior offices. One of Attlee's failures as Prime Minister was that, given the paucity of talent among the older

Members, he was so slow to exploit the talent available among the new Members. Of the 130 MPs who had served in the previous House of Commons, something like half were sponsored by trade unions. Some of these would not have sought Ministerial responsibilities of any kind, let alone a senior appointment. It was a very limited field from which to select a government. Attlee was fortunate to have in that field men of the calibre of Herbert Morrison, Stafford Cripps, Aneurin Bevan and, above all, Ernest Bevin. Bevin was there by the accident of war, for it was the war that had brought Bevin into the Commons – he had been elected when appointed to the coalition Cabinet in 1940. Bevin's availability made credible a government that would have looked unimpressive without him.

From this limited field of selection Attlee appointed a government which, by modern standards, was rather old. In 1945, Attlee was 62, Bevin 64, Morrison 57 and Dalton almost 58. Cripps, who was later to join this top echelon, was 56. The problem, however, was not that they were old in years, but rather that they suffered frequent ill-health. This was not a minor difficulty during the ensuing years. The energy with which in earlier times they might have conducted themselves, was now largely spent. Partly as a consequence, it was a government that found it exceedingly difficult to take decisions under conditions of crisis and it was, only too often, under conditions of crisis that it had to take decisions. An active young Treasury official like Otto Clarke, one of Britain's most creative public servants, was driven to distraction by the inability of Ministers to make up their minds. Keynes's prejudiced view was that 'the Cabinet is a poor, weak thing'.[4] Of the top echelon of the government, Dalton was the fittest. None of his leading colleagues could have accompanied him on his long walks striding through the hills, dales and forests of England. But, at times of crisis, even he had his health problems; boils would appear in notably uncomfortable locations, and he even took to sustaining himself on drugs.[5] At such moments, he was liable to lose his temper and shout, both at his Ministerial colleagues and his civil servants. It was this government that was to lead Britain into the new world promised in the Labour Manifesto, *Let us face the future*. To later generations of the Labour Party, it appeared that those who had served in senior positions in the Attlee government were giants; Bevin *was* a giant, though often mistaken. For the rest, the record hardly confirms their reputation.

DALTON NOT BEVIN

In his selection of Chancellor, Attlee had little choice. The field consisted of Bevin, Morrison and Dalton. Stafford Cripps was not, at that stage, a competitor. Morrison wanted the Foreign Office but Attlee did not consider him right for that job or for the Treasury. Instead he became Lord President of the Council and effectively, if not constitutionally, Deputy Prime Minister.[6] With Morrison thus deployed, the choice for the Treasury lay between Bevin and Dalton. If one went to the Foreign Office, the other would go to the Treasury. Bevin was the member of Attlee's government commanding the widest public and Parliamentary confidence. His would have been as uncontroversial an appointment as Chancellor as Party politics would permit; indeed, it was expected. Dalton had been virtually promised the Foreign Office and it was what he wanted. It was, according to some reports, the King who influenced Attlee to appoint Bevin to the Foreign Office rather than to the Treasury.[7] The King disliked Dalton. Though he may have been influenced, Attlee's own account suggests that he was concerned by a problem of political management. During the war, oversight and coordination of economic policy had been moved from the Treasury and charged to an interdepartmental committee chaired by the Lord President of the Council and therefore known as the Lord President's Committee. Attlee himself had been Lord President from 23 September 1943 and therefore had experience of its working. The Committee had been serviced by the Cabinet Office, including the Economic Section of the Cabinet Office.[8] Attlee planned to continue the arrangement. Herbert Morrison, as Lord President in the new Labour government, would be in the chair. Attlee, claiming no special expertise in economic policy, did not intend to take the chair of this senior economic committee of the Cabinet, great as were the economic problems facing his government. The Lord President's Committee included the Chancellor. Attlee feared that Bevin could not work harmoniously with Morrison.[9] There was too much bad feeling between them, especially on Bevin's side.

This was the explanation of the change that Attlee gave to Dalton.[10] Morrison himself may not have been anxious to partner Bevin on the home front, though they had worked together during the years of war under a different Prime Minister.[11] Attlee may also have wished that the appointment to the Foreign Office should be one carrying the widest confidence, including of the Opposition. Foreign policy is national policy; the tasks of Chancellor are more naturally controversial. Government departments have also been known to exert influence on the selection of their political bosses. The Foreign Service was likely to prefer Bevin, clearly a man who would get his way in Cabinet – departments want Ministers who get their way in Cabinet. Dalton, on the other hand, was disliked among those who would be serving him in the Foreign Office.[12]

Whether Dalton, old Etonian, son of a Canon of Windsor with close links to the Royal Family, was likely to make a good Chancellor was another question. In the coalition government he had first been Minister of Economic Warfare and then President of the Board of Trade. Dalton had graduated from his Tory background, via the Fabian Society at Cambridge, to academic posts in economics at the London School of Economics, and hence to the House of Commons. The Labour Party, as the prospect of office approached, felt itself short of people with the capacity to discharge Ministerial responsibilities, and a recruit such as Dalton was therefore very welcome. He had been a pupil of Keynes at Cambridge, though Keynes clearly did not think much of him. Nevertheless, he could be counted as a qualified economist, and in the long-distant past he had written a book about public finance.[13] Dalton's technical qualifications for the job were not strong, but no weaker than those of many others who have held the post. The City would in due course claim that, like most Chancellors coming to office, he knew little about the workings of the monetary system. According to Pimlott, writing in 1984, Dalton was 'the most economically literate of modern Chancellors apart from his protégé Hugh Gaitskell'.[14] It is a less than striking claim because of the lack of competition. Even if it was true, his readings in economics did not seem to help him; his *curriculum vitae* was in no way a preparation for the responsibilities he would now carry. His narcissistic memoirs and diaries tell more about the man than he may have wished to reveal. He assures us that, on appointment, he was 'with our supporters . . . one of the most popular Ministers, and, with our opponents, one of the most disliked, or even hated'.[15] He evidently found satisfaction in both reactions. He was eloquent in the House of Commons and loved waving *Let us face the future* at his diminished opponents on the other side of the Chamber. 'I convinced and pleased my own side, and reduced the other side to silence . . .'[16]

The country, and more immediately officials in the Treasury, could only suspend judgement. They would find that, though with many attractive characteristics, and some less so, he lacked the exceptional combination of humility and strength which goes to the making of good Chancellors. Humility is required to ensure that a Chancellor listens to advice he would prefer not to hear. Strength is needed to ensure that decisions are made, carried through Cabinet where necessary, and implemented. Dalton was not exceptional in lack of humility – leading figures in Parties which have just won overwhelming victories in General Elections seldom exhibit much humility. For Dalton the principal problem was that the postwar world was a new world, and particularly a new world for Britain. The responsibilities eventually overwhelmed him. Dalton's lack of inner strength, despite an extrovert personality, was to be revealed at the time of the convertibility crisis in the summer of 1947 when the world intervened decisively and destroyed his credibility. His weakness was not obvious on appointment; nor could it be. How can one forecast how a particular human being will respond to such a crisis and such a humiliation?

Dalton's appointment failed by an even more important criterion. Unlike Bevin, he could not get his way in Cabinet, nor could he exercise comparable influence with the Prime Minister. Bevin had the strength of character and the political base from which, if he had absorbed the facts about the country's economic predicament, which the Treasury would certainly have pressed upon him, he could have insisted on bringing the government's policies into line with the UK's resources. Instead the most powerful man in the Cabinet was absorbing Foreign Office briefs designed to maintain Britain's great-power status at a cost which the UK could not begin to afford. Dalton against Bevin was a battle lost before it began. Moreover it is possible that Bevin, the great trade unionist, would have been able to take a more realistic view of the speed at which welfare services could be developed, and of their acceptable cost, than Dalton, the old Etonian. Thus the last-minute substitution of Dalton for Bevin as Chancellor was a tragedy for the conduct of economic policy. The switch of Bevin to the Foreign Office was the first, and among the most disastrous, mistakes of Attlee as Prime Minister.

VICTORIOUS BRITAIN?

It took a great deal of courage or, alternatively, ignorance, for Dalton to contemplate his future as Chancellor with a song in his heart, a phrase which, heartlessly, history has hung around his neck.[17] The problems were immense, enough on a sober estimate to dim the euphoria at Labour's election victory. The war had devastated the country's overseas assets, and it was on the income from these that it had relied before the war to cover a sizeable proportion of its imports.[18] Those assets had declined in value before the war, partly due to the world recession, partly because they were being sold off to cover a balance of payments deficit.[19] Invisible income had suffered further from the loss of shipping during the submarine war in the Atlantic. Exports, which had been allowed to decline in order that manpower could be moved to war production and the services, made a fraction of their pre-war contribution. Britain had emerged from the war deeply indebted, the most indebted country in the world.[20] This was not the weakening through war of an economy that had been strong pre-war, it was the weakening of an economy that had already been weak pre-war. The immediate tasks were formidable. The country and its industries had to be converted from war to peace. Its industry was run down due to lack of investment. Demobilization had to be carried through without creating unemployment. The size of the problem was increased by the government's domestic policies; for example, keeping food cheap by subsidy added to the demand. The housing programme depended on imports of raw materials.

Then there were the British pretensions to global status. They implied extensive commitments overseas in the defence of the West's interests in various parts of the world. Britain was to be the partner of the USA in ensuring the security of the world, if not an equal partner, at least a significant partner. In some parts of the world, in Greece, Turkey and the Middle East, it would take the lead. The commitments were both of men in the services and of resources. As though all this was not enough, Labour had inherited from the coalition government the cost, including the dollar cost, of the British occupation zone in Germany.

The international economic environment in the aftermath of war was fragmented and frightening. Dollars were short because it was difficult to earn them through exports and yet supplies from the USA were a key component of economic recovery. The Americans were running a payments surplus with the rest of the world of about $8 billion per annum.[21] They would only accept, in payment for their products, dollars or currencies convertible into dollars. As other currencies generally were not convertible into dollars, an export surplus with non-dollar suppliers was no help in purchasing dollar supplies. Except at a continuing cost to the reserves, Dalton could not, without drastic cuts in imports, command the liquid resources with which to pay the nation's dollar import bill. The drastic cuts that would have been required to come near to balancing the country's trade with the USA would have been damaging to recovery and politically unpalatable.[22] They would have implied that the end of war was to be celebrated by a major deterioration in the nation's standard of living. Food consumption would have been the first, and most immediate, victim of such cuts. Keynes expected that the deficit in the balance of payments would continue for at least three years during which a cumulative liability of £1,250 million was likely to be incurred. He referred to the possibility of a 'financial Dunkirk'.[23] Yet it would have required political courage to have rewarded the British people by forcibly reminding them that victory had left them well-nigh destitute and that further, and even greater, efforts would be required of them to create the new Britain and the new life for which some of them had fought.

THE CANCELLATION OF LEND-LEASE

Lend-Lease had been a lifeline extended to Britain by President Roosevelt during the war. It had been praised for its generosity, and had provided the UK with roughly two-thirds of the funds needed to finance a total external deficit of £10 billion over 6 years of war.[24] It had been expected that victory over Japan would take a further eighteen months after the end of the war in Germany. This would give Britain time to begin its reconversion to a postwar economy, still, it was hoped, assisted by Lend-Lease, but the atomic bombs dropped on Japan brought much speedier victory and ended such hopes. Now, with the war ended, Lend-Lease was cancelled by Roosevelt's successor, Truman, despite opposition from the US Treasury and State Department.[25] It was the law as passed by Congress. It was entitled 'An Act for the defence of the United States'. It had been drawn in the interests primarily of the USA, not of the UK, and Truman could not dispense with the law.[26] According to Washington, the UK would now have to pay even for goods then afloat.

The cancellation of Lend-Lease should have been a surprise only to those in London determined to be surprised. The situation was certainly serious enough to make the British government feel rather sorry for itself. The cry was that the UK had been at war from the first day to the last, and it had suffered bombardment and destruction. While the

USA grew even richer, the UK had expended its treasure. Despite the UK's sacrifices and the bonds of alliance, it had evidently not won credit in the USA sufficient to stop the cancellation. While the cancellation should not have been a surprise, there was a lesson in it for those in London who imagined that there would be appreciation in the USA for what Britain considered its exceptional services to victory.

The price which Britain had been forced to pay for Lend-Lease exacerbated its problems as it emerged from the war. During the war, American pressure was exerted on the British government to reduce its gold and dollar reserves, to restrict exports, especially those that might compete with American exports, and transfer yet more men into the services and into war production.[27] Washington had also shown itself intent on employing Lend-Lease to constrain Britain's freedom of action after the war. Britain committed itself to cooperate in the planning of a non-discriminatory postwar trade regime which, it was thought, would be advantageous to American commerce. Article VII of the 1942 Mutual Aid agreement governing Lend-Lease said:

> In the final determination of the benefits to be provided to the United States of America by the Government of the United Kingdom in return for aid . . . the terms and conditions . . . shall include provision for agreed action . . . directed to . . . the elimination of all forms of discriminatory treatment in international commerce, and to the reduction of tariffs and other trade barriers.[28]

Such a non-discriminatory trade regime would call into question the future of imperial preference, the system of tariff preferences under which the Commonwealth other than Canada discriminated against the products of other countries, including the USA.

Despite this wartime experience of American economic diplomacy, despite also the abrupt cancellation of Lend-Lease, the predominant view in London remained optimistic as to the assistance that could be expected from the USA, after the defeat of Germany, in promoting the recovery of the British economy. A British government was about to demonstrate, not for the first or last time, its naive faith in American benevolence. Thus was made what should have been one of the most influential discoveries of the postwar world. The discovery was that the USA is not a charitable institution, certainly not one that regards charity to Britain on British terms as a high priority. The Americans had their own ideas on what was good for Britain and for Europe. These ideas had much in common with their assessment of what was good for the

USA and, as it was their money, they were not to be deterred from exploiting their opportunities for influence. Dalton had the privilege of being the first Chancellor to whom this truth was revealed in the postwar world. His successors would rediscover the same truth in their turn, whenever crises loomed or whenever some bright spirit in London identified a problem that might be more easily solved if only the American taxpayer or his representatives in Congress could be persuaded to be generous. Rediscovery was necessary because the lesson was never really learnt. Among those destined to make this discovery was Keynes.

THE ANGLO-AMERICAN FINANCIAL AGREEMENT

Roy Harrod summarized the situation facing the new Labour government. It was 'that happy period when we should be fighting neither Germans nor Japanese, and merely facing economic ruin'.[29] Harrod was Keynes's friend and biographer. Keynes was a central figure in the first nine months of Dalton's tenure of the Treasury. Harrod's assertion that the UK was facing economic ruin magnified the role of Keynes as the saviour of the British economy. The UK was not facing economic ruin. But the problems were serious enough.

The urgent question was whether the Americans should be asked for help. If help was requested, what would be the terms? The solution to this conundrum, chosen by the government on the advice of Keynes, but with insufficient consideration of alternatives, was to solicit a massive grant or an interest-free loan from the USA. Dalton describes Keynes as being 'almost starry-eyed'. 'He told us', says Dalton, that 'he thought he could get £1500 millions (six billion dollars) as a free gift, or "grant in aid". There would be no question of a loan to be repaid, or of a rate of interest on a loan.'[30] It was remarkable that Keynes had remained so innocent of the realities of American policy given his experiences in negotiating in Washington during the war. Moreover, in August 1945, Keynes had been warned by William L. Clayton, Under Secretary of State, during a visit to London, that the most US public opinion would support by way of aid to the UK was a $3 billion credit. It might be on liberal terms, but it would certainly only be available if there was a satisfactory overall commercial agreement. There was no room for doubt that, for the Americans, a satisfactory commercial agreement meant, as Clayton put it in a memorandum to Fred Vinson, shortly to be US Treasury Secretary, on 25 June 1945, cooperation from the UK 'immediately in the creation of a world economy based on fair trade and currency practices and a minimum of restrictions in the flow of world commerce'.[31] That meant no discrimination against American exports. Clayton added that American opinion would also expect a reduction in the transitional period before sterling became convertible into dollars.[32] Article 14 of the Bretton Woods Agreement had provided for a transitional period of at least five years. Now Clayton was demanding, as the price of assistance, convertibility at the earliest possible date at least for sterling earned in current transactions. There were angry exchanges between Clayton and Keynes. Keynes questioned whether the UK could honourably concede so much for so little. According to one American witness, Keynes 'hit the ceiling'. 'He poured forth his eloquence on the appalling difficulties that would beset Britain for a number of years and on the dangers of premature convertibility.'[33] But Clayton's words should have been no surprise. The US Treasury was always going to demand convertibility and was not to be inhibited in exploiting the difficulties in which the UK found itself. The exchanges that August ended with Clayton asserting that he would be frank and repeat that the British people should not expect to obtain assistance in the form of free grants.[34] Even if he had not understood before, Keynes had now been told enough to know that there was no realistic prospect of Britain securing from the USA more than, say, $4 billion. If such a sum was to be available at all, it would be by way of credit, at interest, on conditions acceptable to the USA.[35]

There would come a point at which commercial credits without any other than commercial terms would become preferable to an inadequate government loan burdened with impossible conditions. Keynes's principal critic in the Treasury was Richard Clarke. Known as 'Otto' because of his Germanic stature, he was a *Financial News* journalist by training. Edwin Plowden says of Clarke, 'he certainly made the Treasury a brighter and more interesting place'.[36] The interest arose, in major part, from Clarke's ability to provoke controversy. Clarke was a member of the Finance Division of the Treasury. It was a division that had expanded enormously since before the war in part in contemplation of the economic problems that would face Britain in its international relationships at the end of the war.[37] In June 1945, Clarke presented a plan alternative to that put forward by Keynes. He wanted to defer an approach to the Americans for a government to government loan for two years until the nature of the postwar world was more clearly seen. The Bank of England had always felt that, while it would not be possible to avoid borrowing, it would be better to borrow without strings at commercial rates on the New York market rather than through the political apparatus in Washington.[38] Washington and politics meant political conditions, possibly inappropriate political conditions. That was also Clarke's view. He argued further that 'the basic fact is that a large part of the world will be short of dollars and will for some time remain short of dollars, except on unacceptable terms'.[39] Keynes's response was: 'I do not think there is any serious risk of an overall shortage of gold and dollars in the first three years.'[40] It was a view shared by the Americans.[41] But Keynes's understanding of the international economic conjuncture was supposed to be exceptional. Britain was to find itself committed by Keynes to American policies on the basis of a hypothesis about the future that rapidly proved to be unfounded.

Keynes remained invincibly optimistic that he could get his $6 billion grant-in-aid or, at worst, an interest-free loan. A massive grant or interest-free loan, if available, would certainly be more advantageous than credit from US suppliers on commercial terms. Bevin at least was sceptical. 'When I listen to Lord Keynes talking', he is reported to have said, 'I seem to hear the coins jingling in my pocket; but I cannot see that they are really there.'[42] The Bank of England never believed it could be done.[43] Keynes was warned by the UK Treasury Office in Washington, which included Frank Lee, later Permanent Secretary to the Treasury, that it could not be done.[44] Dalton, as President of the Board of Trade, had had enough wartime experience of American economic diplomacy to be on his guard. Yet, despite all the evidence to the contrary, Dalton and the Cabinet put their trust in Keynes's powers of persuasion.[45] The thought that they might be missing out on 6 billion free dollars was enough to dull their scepticism. The Labour government conceded to Keynes's pressure and to his optimism and sent him to Washington to perform his miracle. Not merely did they send him, they sent him virtually as a plenipotentiary rather than as a representative of the Chancellor and the Treasury. The task proved to be beyond even Keynes's wit, eloquence, persuasiveness and intellectual prowess.

KEYNES AS NEGOTIATOR

The negotiations should have been seen as carrying major political implications. They required the presence of the Chancellor in Washington, not the whole time but at the most important moments. Yet, though the negotiations for the loan fell primarily within his departmental responsibilities, he took no direct personal part. He seemed singularly reluctant to appear in Washington in the role of a mendicant waving a begging bowl. He preferred the more dignified aspects of overseas representation. If he had been there at the beginning, Dalton would have seen at once that a grant or an interest-free loan were out of the question. If he had been there it would also have given him an opportunity, at the highest Ministerial level, to underline three points. The first would have been that the British government did not wish to enter into an agreement which it might not be able to implement. The second would have been that no guarantee could be given that convertibility in the near future would be possible. The third would have been that the UK must reserve the right to discriminate in trade until the shape of the postwar world became clearer. In a world in which dollars, despite Keynes, might well be short, Britain could not denude itself of the right to discriminate against dollar supplies. British interests could lie in the creation or restoration of non-dollar supplies, especially from the sterling area. This process could be encouraged by discrimination against dollar supplies in favour of supplies from non-dollar sources. Such an opening statement might have made agreement with the Americans impossible. The fact that it was not made suggests that, from the beginning, the real intention in London was to accept the best terms it could get even if there was considerable doubt whether they could be honoured. If capitulation rather than negotiation was the strategy from the beginning, it does help to explain the choice of Keynes as negotiator. Let Keynes who was so confident in his powers of persuasion bring back the best terms he could.

To supervise the negotiations in so far as that was possible from London, Attlee presided over almost daily meetings with Bevin, Dalton, Morrison and Cripps. In these meetings the Ministers were joined by Sir Edward Bridges, Permanent Secretary to the Treasury, Head of the Civil Service, and also, until 1946, Secretary to the Cabinet, and also by other officials.[46]

The official leader of the delegation was the British Ambassador in Washington, the Marquis of Halifax. Halifax had been a major figure in British politics. In 1940, at the downfall of Neville Chamberlain, he had been a strong candidate for Prime Minister. Now he was representing a Labour government. As is so frequently characteristic of ambassadors, he was submissive to the pressures of the government to which he was accredited. If an injection of British backbone into the negotiations was required, Halifax was unlikely to brandish the syringe. In practice, however, the negotiations were conducted by Keynes assisted by a team of officials and economists. Even though the government had accepted Keynes's analysis of Britain's economic predicament, it was a serious error to entrust to him a negotiation of such importance, even on the assumption that the government did not believe his optimism and was simply seeking the best terms it could extract.

There were many reasons why he should not have been sent, enough of them known to Dalton. He was far from well. His optimism about his ability to secure unconditional largesse from the Americans was absurd. It was evidence more of hubris than of cool judgement. He believed that, as a matter of justice due to Britain's sacrifices during the war, the Americans should supply the help he wanted on the terms he specified.[47] There was no such sentiment in Washington and his emphasis of the point was to prove humiliating and counter-productive. Like Halifax, Keynes had always shown himself weak in the face of American pressure. He was likely to be fazed by American toughness and to be unprepared to meet that toughness with toughness. Because he was so optimistic, he was insufficiently equipped with the necessary contingency planning. He negotiated incompetently; indeed, it is difficult to think of a major Anglo-American negotiation that was more ineptly handled. Heading the American side in the negotiations were Secretary of the Treasury Fred M. Vinson[48] and Will Clayton from State. The incompatibility between the lawyer and politician, Vinson, and Keynes, the brilliant, articulate, witty English economist, became ever more pronounced. Wit at which everyone laughed except Vinson did not help the negotiations.[49] Robert Hall, from 1947 Director of the Economic Section in the Cabinet Office, was later to comment: 'Roy [Harrod] has no conception of the damage Keynes did us in the US by his arrogance.'[50]

But, above all, Keynes had his own agenda which was not just to negotiate assistance for Britain but to bring into effect at the earliest possible date the Bretton Woods system which he had elaborated together with the American Harry Dexter White. The Americans were insisting that it was to be a condition of the loan that the UK accepted the Bretton Woods settlement and its institutions. They required that Britain should also accept and support the American proposals for an International Trade Organization (ITO). Keynes saw no problem in Britain's accepting the Bretton Woods system and the ITO once it had obtained the necessary help from the USA. Bretton Woods was, in his mind, in large part his property, his bequest to the world. It would be the foundation of world prosperity. The Bretton Woods system, in Keynes's mind, reconciled the primacy which he allotted to full employment with the free international commerce which would follow from the establishment of the ITO. To achieve this major goal, he, at least, was prepared to belittle the risks to immediate British interests.[51] What was more, he did not appear to notice that if the Americans wanted something from Britain, he had at least some cards in his hands if he was prepared to play them. Otto Clarke later commented:

> To see sterling convertible at an early date was a major objective – perhaps, apart from getting the money, his most important objective. He could not tolerate that after he had overcome for three years all the obstacles which were intrinsic in the task, the edifice [of Bretton Woods] would collapse – and because the British had not played their part.[52]

To lead the British side in the negotiations required not a collaborator but a sceptic.

When Keynes died in April 1946, Clarke noted in his diary, 'The pity of it all is that he negotiated the US Loan, this is what killed him, and he did it with great brilliance, but badly, overcomplicating and finessing against London and against himself.'[53]

THE NEGOTIATIONS

Keynes rapidly discovered that a free gift of $6 billion or, failing that, an interest-free loan, was not on offer. He found that his attempt to trade on Britain's sacrifices during the war was counter-productive.[54] As he explained to the House of Lords on 18 December 1945 in what proved to be his last speech to that assembly:

> It was not very long before the British delegation discovered that a primary emphasis on past services and past sacrifice would not be fruitful. The American Congress and the American people have never accepted any literal principle of equal sacrifice, financial or otherwise, between all the allied participants ... The Americans ... find a post-mortem on relative services and sacrifices amongst the leading allies extremely distasteful and dissatisfying.[55]

It was to be expected that the Americans would find a comparison between their role in the war and that of Britain 'distasteful and dissatisfying'. It was bad tactics, as well as damaging to pride, that the British delegation should have approached the negotiation in this way. Keynes's only excuse was his own strong feeling that, because of Britain's exceptional sacrifices, it did deserve special treatment. Once it was clear that the Americans felt no claim on their gratitude and were prepared to disregard Keynes's cry for justice, his whole negotiating strategy fell to pieces and the great retreat was on.

In his memoirs, Dalton recalls:

> As the talks went on, we retreated, slowly and with bad grace and with increasing irritation, from a free gift to an interest-free loan, and from this again to a loan bearing interest; from a larger to a smaller total of aid; and from the prospect of loose strings, some of which would be only general declarations of intention, to the most unwilling acceptance of strings so tight that they might strangle our trade and, indeed, our whole economic life.[56]

Though indicative of the atmosphere in London, this quotation exemplifies the total ignorance among British Ministers as to the actual possibilities. If there was a retreat, it was only from a position that was from the beginning not negotiable. On 27 October, when it was clear to British Ministers, and even to Keynes, that his original ideas were not negotiable, Dalton sent new instructions. In the expectation that the Americans would be generous, Keynes had offered convertibility of sterling within a year and some arrangements to scale down the wartime accumulated sterling balances. He had failed to tie these concessions to the amount and conditions of the loan.[57] Dalton's new instructions required that, as $5 billion was clearly not available either as a grant-in-aid or an interest-free loan, the concessions which Keynes had prematurely made were to be withdrawn. The UK position on matters such as convertibility and the ratification of Bretton Woods was now to depend on what assistance the US *was* ready to make available and on what terms. Depending on the amount of the assistance and on the terms, there might be no convertibility and ratification of Bretton Woods might be postponed. Dalton's message ended that Keynes's premature concessions 'might have been safely undertaken with $5 billion grant in cash or possibly on an interest-free basis, but they are neither safe nor a good bargain for $4 billion at 2%. The difference between that situation and the original plan is in our judgement not one of degree but of kind.'

This was, at last, the basis on which such a negotiation should have been conducted, not that propounded by Keynes in his belief that the USA would render the UK 'justice'. Keynes was furious on the receipt of this message and he considered resignation. Unfortunately he did not resign and the negotiation did not restart on this new basis. Keynes despatched a dismissive response, and Dalton and his Ministerial colleagues, having made this *pro-forma* attempt to recapture control of a negotiation that was clearly going badly, submitted their own opinions and the fate of their country to an emissary who had already, by his own standards, failed.[58]

As the negotiations proceeded, the need for a visit to Washington by the Chancellor became ever more apparent. On 1 November 1945, Dalton noted in his diary; 'the Washington talks have now dragged on for seven weeks, and we are not yet in sight of a tolerable outcome. Keynes is becoming rather sulky and it is clear that, as must always be the case, following such long negotiations, those who represent us out there and we here at home have drifted into a state of mutual incomprehension.'[59] He did not see the implication that he himself should go. Attlee did visit Washington on 9 November for talks with Truman on atomic matters. But Attlee preferred the negotiations to be conducted vicariously by Keynes, not directly by himself, though the ability of his government to implement its policies depended on the outcome.

There is no suggestion that the outcome of the negotiations was affected by the election of a Labour government. Certainly it caused comment. Congress, especially Republicans in Congress, took no pleasure in subsidizing a socialist government. Socialism of any flavour, democratic or authoritarian, has never been to the taste of those responsible for the US Treasury. Suspicions of Labour's intentions led Attlee, during his visit to Washington, to make a humiliating speech to Congress in which he felt it necessary to assure his audience that the new Labour government in Britain was not opposed to freedom of the press and of religion. On the contrary the Labour Party was 'in the tradition of freedom-loving movements which have always existed in our country . . . We in the Labour Party declare that we are in line with those who fought for Magna Carta, and Habeas Corpus, with the Pilgrim Fathers and the signatories of the Declaration of Independence.' The evidence for these assertions was the number of journalists and even ministers of religion in the PLP. This apologia is unlikely to have stilled criticism, but at least Attlee did not take one piece of infelicitous advice proffered by Halifax. 'A reference to the fact that it was His Majesty's Government and not Laski who were responsible for British policy would go well if you felt like making it.'[60] The advice was prompted by the effect on Republican opinion in the USA of Harold Laski's syndicated column in some American newspapers, by-lined 'Chairman of the British Labour Party', in which he wrote of Britain's 'revolution by consent'. Some Republicans argued that as the USA was being asked to provide the funds for the revolution, the US Congress should be among those asked for its consent.[61] Evidently Attlee did not feel like apologizing for Laski before the US Congress. But something more robust was required from a British Prime Minister than a proclamation of the democratic virtues of British socialism. It might have been provided by Labour's Chancellor of the Exchequer if he had been prepared to make himself present in Washington. He was always prepared to be robust in the House of Commons.

The Conservatives did not believe that they would have found themselves entitled to any more favours from the Americans than Labour. Conservatives as well as Labour were devoted to the sterling area and to imperial preference. Both, therefore, favoured policies in the field of international economic relations objectionable to the US Administration. The tough American negotiating position had been prepared at a time when Churchill was still Prime Minister and was expected to remain so.[62] Sir John Anderson, leading for the Opposition in the debate on the Agreement, while commenting that 'we have had to accept a very hard bargain', added that 'I, for my part, do not doubt that His Majesty's Government have secured the best terms that were open to them in existing circumstances.'[63] For the Conservatives as for Labour, the only hope of doing better in the negotiation would have been to send a senior Minister, to be less compliant, and to take the risk that the negotiations would fail. There was no suggestion in anything emerging from the Conservative front bench that they would have been tougher or better negotiators.

It was not in American interests to allow political prejudices to become too influential; Britain, even under a Labour government, was still an ally, and could still have its uses for American policy. The US Administration did not attempt, in the Loan Agreement, directly to influence the *domestic* policies of the Labour government though some members of Congress would not have been averse to it. Governments that solicit support from foreign administrations or international institutions cannot ignore the likelihood that their domestic policies *will* come under scrutiny.

In the final stage of a long and difficult negotiation, when the British government suspected that Keynes was, as Dalton put it in his diary, 'completely spun out', and Lionel Robbins, one of Keynes's chief aides, had become 'hysterical', the government decided to send Sir Edward Bridges.[64] By the time Bridges arrived, the Americans had extracted from Keynes all the concessions they wanted and the arrival of another negotiator seemed to them inappropriate. According to Harrod, they resolved to make no further concessions to Bridges because that would have been a slur on the negotiating ability of Keynes and Halifax.[65] This is nonsense. The Americans made no concessions to Bridges because they already had extracted what they wanted from Keynes. It was natural that they would not want a new negotiator to reopen questions already settled with Keynes. In fact Keynes had extracted no reciprocal concessions from the Americans other than at the margin. Dalton confesses, 'Bridges got no new specific concessions out of the Americans but, at the end, some most important clarifications.'[66] One 'clarification' was that convertibility would be required not from the end of 1946, as had been suggested, but from one year after the Agreement became operative.[67] The only prospect of rescuing the situation would have been the despatch not of an official, however distinguished, but of a major political figure.

TREASURY AND STATE

The US Treasury has always been highly ideological, in this case too ideological for its own good. It has never had much time for British governments that come soliciting loans, and has always been particularly critical of Labour governments and their alleged profligacy. Often the US Treasury has been right – British governments have brought their problems upon themselves. But the US Treasury, more blinkered even than usual, was not right on this occasion in seeking the commitments on which it insisted in this Agreement.

From time to time in postwar history, British governments have attempted to bypass the US Treasury by means of an appeal to the State Department. The State Department has more regard than the US Treasury for America's international relations. This was not an occasion on which the British government could have looked to the State Department for help. The State Department was fully involved in the negotiations. When the time came to decide the amount of the loan, the US Treasury suggested $3.5 billion and the State Department $4 billion. That was the measure of the greater helpfulness of the State Department. At a meeting in Washington on 8 November, a motion to offer $4 billion was defeated with the State and Commerce Departments in favour and the Treasury and the Federal Reserve Board against. Truman split the difference, which made it $3.75 billion.[68]

To the US Administration and Congress, the value of western Europe was a function of the state of its relations with the Soviet Union. During the winter of 1945–6, hopes were still high in Washington that friendly relations with the Soviet Union would survive the peace. With the passage of time, Washington became increasingly aware of its need for friends in Europe. It was the Secretary of State, General George Marshall, who launched the Marshall Plan, not the US Treasury.[69] He did so just ten months after the US Congress had ratified the Loan Agreement and before the UK government faced the holocaust of sterling that followed the implementation of sterling convertibility. By that time American optimism about relations with the Soviet Union had largely evaporated. But Keynes and Bridges were negotiating this Agreement in the autumn of 1945. The State Department was unlikely, at the end of 1945, to allow a delegation of British officials, even one as high-powered as this, to bypass the US Treasury. And even if the State Department had been convinced, approval of the loan would still have lain with the Congress. The US Treasury may well have made a correct political judgement of what would prove acceptable at that time to Congress.

THE TERMS

In some respects the terms were acceptable. $3.75 billion was a great deal less than asked, and gave little margin for contingencies taking into account the estimates of the UK's dollar deficit in the ensuing years.[70] But it was a sizeable sum. Keynes's comment in the House of Lords debate was that the amount 'In my own judgement . . . is cut somewhat too fine and does not allow a margin for unforeseen contingencies. Nevertheless the sum is substantial. No comparable credit in time of peace has ever been negotiated before . . . it may not prove altogether a bad thing that there should be no sufficient margin to tempt us to relax . . . On a balance of considerations . . . I think that under this heading we should rest reasonably content.'[71] Moreover the Agreement included a settlement of all American claims on the UK arising out of Lend-Lease. This was calculated as being an additional credit of $650 million on the same terms as the $3.75 billion, making a total credit

33

from the USA of \$4.4 billion. Dalton, in the House of Commons, described the Lend-Lease settlement as 'one of the most satisfactory features of the Agreement'.[72] Keynes apostrophized about the Lend-Lease settlement. 'Has any country ever treated another country like this, in time of peace, for the purpose of rebuilding the other's strength and restoring its competitive position?'[73] The interest rate of 2 per cent was not ideal. Keynes commented: 'I shall never so long as I live cease to regret that this is not an interest-free loan . . . The amount of money at stake cannot be important to the United States . . .'[74] But 2 per cent was not extortionate, especially taking account of the fact that nothing would have to be paid until the sixth year and that there was provision for waiving interest if life was proving too difficult for the UK. The repayment period was fifty years after the five-year repayment holiday. Other supplicants for American aid, Keynes emphasized to their Lordships, were getting far worse terms.[75] Canada, which had been very generous to the UK with its unconditional grant aid during the war, later raised the total of North American loans to the UK to \$5 billion, after negotiations in early 1946 made more difficult by Canada's refusal after the war to accept terms inferior to those conceded to the USA.[76]

The blow lay in American insistence that the UK must, as a condition of the loan, rejoin the international trading community without discrimination against the USA. Despite the dollar shortage, despite the world's thirst for dollars, anyone holding sterling earned in current transactions must be permitted to convert it into dollars. The Americans did not relish the idea of a sterling world separate from, and discriminating against, the dollar world. That might be in British interests, at any rate while its economy was recovering and if dollars were scarce. The US Treasury thought it inconsistent with American interests. So did Clayton of the State Department. As the historian of Marshall Aid puts it, 'Clayton had an aversion that bordered on mania when it came to the sterling area and the system of imperial preferences.'[77] Dalton later wrote, 'We fancied that they wished, in effect, to take over the sterling area themselves, and make it a dependency, or colony, of the United States . . .'[78] Keynes explained to the Lords, 'Those on the American side wanted to be able to speak definitely and in plain language to their own business world about the future arrangements in regard to commerce between the United States and the sterling area . . .'[79] Hence the loan agreement laid down that twelve months after Congress approved the loan, sterling earned in current transactions must become freely convertible into dollars. Congress approved the loan in July 1946, the House of Representatives voting 219 to 153. This meant that sterling must become convertible by July 1947. The twelve months breathing space was intended to give Britain time to prepare. Before the war, sterling had, of course, been convertible into dollars. In this sense, convertibility meant, as Dalton put it, 'reverting ... to the pre-war situation. We are not doing something fresh and new.'[80] But what had been possible in 1939, before the war began, would not necessarily be possible in July 1947 for a country that the war had impoverished and left with enormous debts in the form of sterling balances held overseas. The Americans were not alone in wanting sterling convertible. However premature sterling convertibility might seem to the British government, there was, as Dalton confessed to the Commons, 'a considerable desire for [the convertibility of sterling] within the sterling area ...'[81] There was nothing surprising about this; sterling area countries wanted their sterling earnings freed so that they could spend them as dollars if they so desired. Their attitude provided some additional warning of what might happen if sterling was made convertible too soon.

Under Article 14 of the recently concluded Bretton Woods settlement, the UK could have deferred sterling convertibility through a transitional period of five years. The Bank of England had all along been sceptical of Keynes's ideas for the reconstruction of the world economy and of the alternative ideas emanating from the US Administration.[82] It considered them at best premature. It was the Bank that had insisted on writing into the Bretton Woods settlement a transitional period before convertibility. The Bank had been fearful lest the British authorities should undertake external monetary commitments, in particular the early resumption of external convertibility at a fixed rate of exchange, which they would find that they were unable to honour.[83] Indeed it was provided in the settlement that the five years could be extended after consultation with the IMF. The Americans argued that, because of the loan they were extending to the UK, it did not need five years for the transition to convertibility. In his memoirs, Dalton comments that the Americans were forcing Britain to accept the Bretton Woods settlement without its safeguards.[84] In the debate in the House of Commons he said, 'to my regret and after hard bargaining and under heavy pressure in the Washington talks, we had to agree to a certain modification of this arrangement', adding that 'it looked at one stage as though, on this point, negotiations might break down'.[85] He somewhat undermined his own argument by adding, 'I think that [the American argument] has cogency. The transitional period is going to be easier and our difficulties in that period are undoubtedly going to be less severe, because we shall have the dollar credit available . . .'[86] Unfortunately the fact that there had been hard bargaining and heavy pressure and that the government, supposedly, had considered breaking off the negotiations on this point, even though the American position had 'cogency', in no way diluted the commitment. It had been accepted by the government and was being recommended to Parliament.

By accepting the commitment, the UK government proclaimed its view that implementation by due date would be possible. It was relieving the US Treasury of responsibility for the consequences. Yet the Americans should have considered far more carefully whether it was a commitment that the UK was really in a position to make. The Americans were not well served in making a loan for the purposes of achieving sterling convertibility when, as was rapidly proved, sterling convertibility was unsustainable at that time.

The probability was very high that those managing the British economy would be unable by so early a date as July 1947 to overcome the natural preference of those holding sterling to exchange it, if they could, for dollars at the prevailing exchange rate of $4.03 to the pound. They would fail however much they cut their overseas commitments, which the Americans did not want them to do, however limited their social expenditures, however liberal and non-socialist their economic policies. Apart from any other consideration, success would depend on factors far beyond Britain's control, for example on economic recovery among Britain's other trading partners. Dalton had frequently emphasized to the delegation in Washington that the British government must refuse any obligation that it did not feel reasonably certain of being able to implement.[87] Although the American side agreed that it would be undesirable for the UK to accept a commitment that it would be unlikely to be able to honour, the temptation in Washington to use the loan to force convertibility was too great. Even if the miracle of sterling convertibility by July 1947 was conceivable, the risk of failure was too great for such a commitment to be imposed on the UK by a supposedly friendly government. It was likely to lead only to the humiliation of an ally.

The best that Keynes could secure by way of mitigation was Article 12 providing for postponement of convertibility after consultation and with the agreement of Congress. Harrod defends Keynes's judgement in recommending acceptance of the eventual agreement by criticizing the British government for not availing itself of this clause when the time for convertibility came.[88] But the Article was not much of a concession. The agreement of Congress could not have been obtained without much public debate and might well have been refused. The Article was deceptive – it encouraged acceptance of the Agreement in the belief that there could be a way out of convertibility. Sir John Anderson, leading for the Opposition, said that if convertibility proved impossible on the due date, 'We shall then have to bring Clause 12 into play and ask for a modification, and I believe confidently that . . . such a request will be received with good will.'[89] The quantity of good will evident during the negotiations did not in fact encourage any confidence that the American Administration or Congress would grant a deferral in advance of an actual catastrophe such as occurred during the convertibility crisis of July/August 1947.

CONVERTIBILITY AND THE STERLING BALANCES

The sterling balances had been built up during the war. They were sterling debts owed by Britain for the use of local stocks and services. In London it was considered unfair that Britain, that had fought so long and so hard, should emerge from the war so indebted. This feeling was expressed by Dalton himself in his speech in the House of Commons recommending the eventual Anglo-American Financial Agreement. This 'great load of debt, which we are bringing out of the war, is, indeed, a strange reward for all we, in this land, did and suffered for the common cause . . .'[90] Two-thirds of the sterling balances were owed to India, Palestine, Egypt and Eire.[91] Both the Americans and Keynes were thinking of the convertibility of sterling used in current transactions, not of the sterling balances. Keynes assured the Lords that the convertibility commitment

> does not relate to the balances accumulated before the spring of 1947. We are left quite free to settle this to the best of our ability. What we undertake to do is not to restrict the use of balances we have not yet got and which have not yet been entrusted to us . . . the main purpose of a loan of this magnitude was for the precise object of liberating the future earnings of the sterling area, not for repaying their past accumulations.[92]

The question was how to avoid holders of the sterling balances converting them into dollars when given the opportunity. Before travelling to Washington for the American Loan negotiations, it had been

Keynes's view that the UK should cancel, say, one-third of the sterling balances held by the countries in the sterling area. It would be unjust for the British people to accept a burden in the form of the sterling balances which no other combatant country, including the defeated enemies, was expected to carry.[93] After the negotiations, with terms much harsher than he had anticipated, it was Keynes's view that the sterling balances should be blocked or written off.[94] The US Administration shared Keynes's view that Britain could take a cavalier approach to the sterling balances. They were, after all, debts accumulated by Britain in defending India and Egypt and the other holders – something surely was owed to Britain in return for its efforts. Washington could not see why major holders of the sterling balances such as India, Egypt and Ceylon should not be as willing to aid British recovery as it was itself. Britain would be entitled unilaterally to freeze the balances, write them down and fund the residue so that there would be no danger of their becoming liquid and hence convertible into dollars on convertibility day. Against British wishes, the Americans had been adamant that no part of the loan was to be used for settling sterling debts built up during the war. Dalton told the Commons: 'At an early stage of the negotiations, we thought it was particularly desirable that part of the loan should be set aside for this purpose; but . . . the American representatives took the view that Congress would not look kindly upon proposals to apply any part of the dollar credit to reducing our debt to the sterling area.'[95] Article 6 (1) of the Agreement said in terms that no part of the credit was to be used for repayment of the UK debt to the sterling area. The Americans wished to take part with the British in negotiating a settlement of the sterling balances with the holders. The British, naturally, thought that that was their business and won that point. So the British were left with the unpleasant task of trying to deny the holders the benefit of their sterling balances.

It proved a great deal more difficult than Keynes expected. In January 1946, Keynes wrote to Dalton, 'Unless we are sunk altogether, I cannot seriously conceive that we shall have difficulty in meeting our obligations; provided, that is, we make a reasonable settlement with the Sterling Area countries.'[96] But he had persuaded the government to enter into the Agreement before any such settlements had been concluded. Strong-arm methods with the UK's creditors were more easily talked about than implemented. The strongest negotiating weapon in UK hands was that it could block the balances, but the holders of the sterling balances knew perfectly well that the use of that weapon would badly damage the credibility of sterling as an international trading currency. The Bank of England had repeatedly warned that the problem of the sterling balances could only be dealt with, if at all, in negotiation, case by case, not in the broad-brush fashion favoured by Keynes, who preferred not to clutter his mind with detail.[97] Dalton told the Commons what he proposed to do about the sterling balances once he had the American loan:

> We propose to ask each of the Governments concerned to discuss and settle with us, on the broad basis . . . that part of the accumulated balances should be set free forthwith, for current expenditure anywhere in the world; part shall be gradually set free . . . over a term of years; and the balance should be adjusted, perhaps, in some cases, adjusted downwards, as a contribution by the sterling area countries to a reasonable settlement of this war debt problem . . . It is only because the American loan contributes to the solution of this problem that we can afford . . . to take these further steps. That is why the loan is an indispensable preliminary.[98]

The largest amount outstanding was due to India. With India there had to be a negotiation, not a unilateral act by Britain depriving the Indians of the benefit of their property. The UK was in receipt of what would appear to countries such as India a munificent loan from the USA and Canada. It was attempting to negotiate a political settlement with India. How, in such circumstances, could the UK say to India that not merely had it extracted a forced loan from India during the war but that now, in peacetime, the terms of repayment were to be decided by the debtor? And if this could not be said to India, how could it be said to any other holders of the sterling balances? James Meade made this point in a letter to Dalton dated 1 July 1959. How, he asked, could the UK have secured a political settlement with India if at the same time it had been saying:

> For years you have been in debt to us and you have paid up: our political control of you has ensured that. Now the wheel of fortune has turned full circle; we are indebted to you. It is true that you are poor and we are rich and that you need our funds for your economic development. But I am afraid we are not going to pay up.[99]

A strong moral argument regarding the sterling balances influenced policy for many years. It discouraged devaluation of the pound even when the UK's domestic circumstances strongly suggested it. Morality deplored the repudiation of debts. It was an argument that was particularly strong because, so far as the main holders were concerned, the sterling balances *had* been a forced loan to Britain. After the war it was in some minds a sufficient answer to this argument that the holders of the sterling balances *ought* to help the UK which had carried such a burden during the war. They *ought* to have been prepared to allow a write-down of their sterling balances, at least in part. But these were British minds – the idea was a great deal less present in the minds of those to whom the sterling balances were owed. The result was a long negotiation with the individual holders of the sterling balances in which the UK had to be satisfied with the best outcome it could get.

Cancellation of the Indian sterling balances was tried by the British as an opening gambit in negotiations in Delhi in 1947. But there was never any possibility of the Indians agreeing or of the UK persisting in the face of an adamant Indian refusal.[100]

Dalton later recounted:

> We worked out . . . our programme for the sterling balances. We contemplated that rather less than half of these, in the total, should be written off or cancelled, as a result of voluntary negotiations, conducted separately with each of the holders. Rather more than half would be made available to the holders by instalments for current purchases in any country without discrimination. At this time [summer 1945] we hoped for a relief, through the writing-off of sterling balances, of about £1250 millions, to add to the £1250 millions, or $5 billion dollars, which we hoped to obtain from the United States. The first of these hopes were [sic] completely disappointed. No creditor was willing to write off a cent; with the two shining exceptions of New Zealand and Australia, who in 1947 made us gifts from their sterling balances of £10 millions and £20 millions respectively, both from Labour Governments and both Prime Ministers, Peter Fraser and Ben Chifley, personal friends of mine.[101]

Australian generosity should not be exaggerated, though Attlee saw fit to pay tribute to it in his speech to the House on 6 August 1947. It could be regarded as a sensible investment in the future of the sterling area from which Australia at the time was a significant beneficiary. Its drawings from the sterling area dollar pool were to cause anxiety in London repeatedly over the years. In fact the best deal on the sterling balances was obtained from President Peron of Argentina, not a sterling area country.[102] But that agreement was made, as were others, in anticipation of sterling convertibility.

Harrod, while conceding that for once Keynes, his hero, was not entirely without fault, criticizes the government for not freezing the sterling balances.

Keynes may have tended in Washington to underrate the difficulty of negotiating satisfactory settlements. In the immediately following period the British authorities should have strongly held in mind that, if they were unable to reach perfectly watertight agreements with all our creditors before the date of sterling convertibility, they would freeze all the balances so as to make it totally impossible for them to be drawn down when convertibility was established. If, owing to unavoidable delays, it appeared that the freezing operation could not be carried out in time, Britain should have asked the United States to agree to postpone the date of convertibility in accordance with the Agreement, with a view to this freezing being carried out as quickly as possible . . . [103]

But unilateral freezing was inconceivable except to the Americans, and to Keynes and his followers, and it would have been no easier to get Congress to agree a postponement of convertibility on the ground that the UK had been too sensitive in its international relations than on any other grounds. The UK was left with a commitment to convertibility based on an unrealistic hypothesis that a significant part of the sterling balances could be unilaterally frozen, funded, or written off.

FLOATING STERLING

The idea of freeing the British economy from its problems by floating sterling would be a subject of debate throughout the Bretton Woods epoch. But it was never done. In 1945 it could be ruled out as inconsistent with Bretton Woods. Dalton was an advocate of stable exchange rates; this had been his view as President of the Board of Trade during the war and during the discussions that led up to Bretton Woods and now, like so many Chancellors who followed him, he held the same view. He was an advocate of exchange rate stability achieved by international agreements such as Bretton Woods and by government intervention, where necessary, on the exchanges. He looked back at the inter-war years and attributed the poverty and misery of the period to competitive devaluations. As a result of these competitive devaluations in the inter-war years, 'British industry, and British exports in particular, suffered grievous damage.'[104] Therefore he wanted stability. The fear of competitive devaluations arose from a misinterpretation of the pre-war experience. It was far too influential on policy then and subsequently. Devaluation has the immediate effect of reducing a country's standard of living. If competitive devaluations occur, it is because economic crisis is forcing the hands of governments. But if economic crisis is forcing the hands of governments, it is an illusion to imagine that they will not devalue whatever the requirements of Bretton Woods. Whether or not sterling floated, the government might have asked itself how long it could hope to sustain exactly the same value of sterling against the dollar, $4.03, as had obtained pre-war. Stability certainly did not necessarily imply the margin of 1 per cent either side of parity required under Bretton Woods. Dalton himself, although he favoured stability in exchange rates in order to avoid competitive devaluations, also wanted a degree of flexibility in exchange rates.[105] It was precisely this flexibility that the Bretton Woods Agreement denied him. The mandatory 1 per cent margin placed an enormous strain on Britain's scarce reserves of gold and dollars, which were always far smaller than the sterling balances overhanging the market.

There were arguments against floating sterling other than its inconsistency with Bretton Woods. First, there was the moral argument. As sterling would certainly have depreciated, it would have amounted to a repudiation of part of the sterling balances. But this argument was not available to Keynes, who was prepared to write down the sterling balances in any case. It may have been available to Dalton, who wished to proceed by agreement with the holders of the sterling balances. But what would happen to the pound sterling after the war must always have been a matter of considerable doubt. There could have been no certainty that it would be possible to fix sterling, after the war, at the exchange rate of $4.03 to the pound that had been established in 1939. Secondly, there was the probability that, in the short term, sterling depreciation would have worsened the UK's balance of payments position. The capacity did not yet exist to supply the additional exports that greater competitiveness might have made possible and yet imports, in sterling terms, would have been more expensive. The relations with a soon to be independent India could have been another legitimate consideration. In the years to come British governments would frequently dream of an escape to floating rates, as we will see, not always for the best of motives. The balance of the argument always seemed to be against it right up to 1972, when sterling did at last float. After 1945, probably the best opportunity before 1972 came in 1958 when non-resident sterling became convertible.

Without Bretton Woods, floating could have been an option in 1945 or in the years immediately following, provided only that the British government did not regard it as a soft option and intended to conduct economic policy with a view to reasonable stability in the sterling exchange rate.

AN AGREEMENT MADE FOR DEFAULT – TO ACCEPT OR NOT

The outcome of the bruising Washington negotiations was thus an offer of credit conditional on a seriously weakened Britain agreeing to face the future burdened by three severe handicaps: fixed exchange rates with the pound sterling at $4.03, premature commitments to sterling convertibility, and non-discrimination in trade. Added to this was the inescapable weight of the sterling balances, and, by Britain's own choice, unsustainable overseas defence commitments.

If Keynes had not negotiated the deal himself, he would certainly have subjected it to scorn and criticism as violent as that he directed against the Treaty of Versailles and the return to the Gold Standard in 1925. He delivered his defence of the Agreement in his last speech in the House of Lords when he had only four months to live. The speech demonstrated great eloquence and conviction; in it he argued that the terms were, on balance, acceptable. It was he that, while the war was still in progress, had argued repeatedly both in London and Washington that the UK would need dollars after the war but would not, to start with, be able to earn them. Here were the dollars. Certainly, there was much in the agreement he disliked. He told the Lords that he had 'striven every day for three months to improve these proposals so as to lay them less open to . . . criticism . . .'[106] He confessed that 'we accepted in the end more cut-and-dried arrangements in some respects than we ourselves believed to be wise or beneficial, as we explained in no uncertain terms and with all the force at our command'.[107] He spoke as a man apologizing for admitted inadequacies in the agreement but nevertheless as its advocate. The Tory, Viscount Swinton, following him in the debate, commented: 'I am sure [Lord Keynes] will not mind if I say that his dialectic was most brilliant where he was skating over the thinnest ice.' He added, 'these terms are harsh'.[108]

Sir Hubert Henderson, leading economist and frequently a critic of Keynes, wrote a letter to *The Times* published on 12 December 1945, the day of the debate on the Agreement in the House of Commons:

The financial agreement with the United States is for a loan upon conditions which are calculated to ensure default ... all incentive to other countries to buy from us because we buy from them will be removed in about a year from now. Moreover, any part of the large accumulated sterling balances which countries in the sterling area are allowed to spend at all must be made equally available for dollar as for sterling purchases.[109]

The Bank of England was unequivocal in its opposition. It was yet unnationalized. But whether nationalized or not it would want sterling to be once more convertible so that it could resume its status as an international trading currency. The status of the Bank and its Governor had once been high. It had supervised the operations not merely of an international trading currency but of the *predominant* international trading currency. That status had been threatened by the 1931 devaluation and lost, at least temporarily, by the war. A currency not convertible into dollars was not an international trading currency, whatever purposes it fulfilled within the sterling area and elsewhere. Six years later, it would recommend R. A. Butler to restore convertibility so that sterling could once more be an international trading currency. But it advised Dalton that convertibility was not currently a practical objective. The Bank of England thought the commitment to convertibility very ill-advised or even 'sheer madness'.[110] The Bank would have been unwilling to accept a commitment to convertibility on the American timescale even if a $5 billion grant had been available.[111] On 4 December 1945, the Governor of the Bank of England, Lord Catto, deeply worried by the terms being imposed on the UK, particularly in relation to convertibility, begged Dalton to get Attlee to intervene with Truman.[112]

The fact that an institution with such an interest in convertibility had advised against accepting the terms should have been influential. It was not – Keynes thrust the Bank's objections aside. Despite his vigorous reaction to the American demand for convertibility during the discussion with Clayton the previous August, he felt able to tell the Lords that 'I do not regard this particular condition as a serious blot on the loan, although ... I would have preferred it less precise, as I would have preferred many other points to be less precise ...'[113] He added, 'The way to remain an international banker is to allow cheques to be drawn on you; the way to destroy the sterling area is to prey upon it and to try to live on it ...'[114] Part of the Bank's trouble was that its reputation had been marred by pre-war experience. It was held to have been largely responsible for the pre-war recession. In 1925, it had recommended Churchill to return sterling to the Gold Standard at the pre-war sterling-dollar parity of $4.86 to the pound. On the other hand, Keynes was held to have been right in his pre-war opposition to Bank policies. He had revealed to the world new and comforting economic truths. In the light of experience, who would take the Bank's advice when Keynes was so dismissive of it?

The terms of the Anglo-American Financial Agreement faced Dalton and the Labour government with a stark choice. Despite the anxiety about convertibility, the loan was accepted, but only because the alternative in terms of the standard of living of the British people appeared so dire. Bevan and Shinwell, not the country's greatest economists, argued in Cabinet that the terms should be rejected. These were Labour's radicals. Careful men saw things differently. Whatever his own private doubts, Dalton, too ready to be led by Keynes although he had no great liking for him, strongly advocated the agreement in Cabinet. On 6 December, the Cabinet authorized the signing of the Agreement in Washington and, a week later, the House of Commons accepted the decision by 347 to 100 with most Conservatives abstaining. Dalton saddled himself with an obligation which he had persuaded the Cabinet and Parliament to endorse although the probability was that he would not be able to implement convertibility without disaster on the American timescale. By then it would be too late to complain that it was an impossible obligation that should never have been imposed. It had been imposed, and he, the confident voice of British economic policy, had accepted the imposition.

Certainly it was easier to take the American money and run with it. Who could know how things would stand in July 1947? A year is a long time in politics. Many elements entered into the decision to accept the terms. The first, and most important, was clearly the shock effect on the country's standard of living if the loan was rejected, a shock for which the British people were totally unprepared. Lend-Lease had concealed from them the extent of Britain's economic sacrifices during the war, and therefore the consequences for their standard of living once Lend-Lease was withdrawn. The political costs of refusing the loan on the terms offered might certainly have been heavy. This was eighteen months before Marshall's speech at Harvard which brought relief to Europe. Yet if the government had to face the British people with further sacrifices, there was no better time than this. There were four years to go before the next election and the government had a massive majority in the House of Commons. Instead, to justify the Loan, there was a great deal of oratorical exaggeration. Dalton told the House of Commons:

Our people would be driven down once more into the dark valley of austerity from which we thought we were beginning to struggle out . . . we should have to undergo greater hardships and privations than even during the war; and all those hopes of better times, to follow in the wake of victory, would be dissipated in despair and disillusion . . . we should have less food of every kind, excepting bread and potatoes. We should have very much less cotton. We should no longer be able to buy American cotton. The Lancashire cotton industry would be dislocated. Many of the mills can run only on American cotton, and could not switch over to Egyptian cotton, even if Egyptian cotton were forthcoming in sufficient quantities. We should have very much less cotton, and, therefore, fewer clothes, even fewer than we have now, and fewer hopes of exports of cotton textiles . . . we should have only a very small fraction of our present supplies of tobacco. Eighty per cent of our tobacco comes from dollar sources . . . the whole conversion of our industry would be slowed up . . . because we could no longer afford to buy machinery and capital goods from the United States.[115]

Writing years later, Dalton commented, 'Worst of all, from the point of view of public morale, practically no smokes, since eighty per cent of our tobacco cost dollars . . . The Tories would exploit all the inevitable privations.'[116] This contribution to public morale was expensive both in dollars and, probably, in health. By 1947, Britain was smoking one-third more tobacco than before the war. In his Budget speech of 15 April 1947, Dalton gave an indication of the cost: 'It is hardly to be believed, but the whole total of our exports to the United States at this time barely exceeds, in value, our own consumption of American tobacco.'[117]

What Dalton did not explain is how it was that he had ever contemplated breaking off the negotiations if the result would have been so terrible. In fact, this picture was an exaggeration of the actual effects of the denial of an American loan. Robert Boothby, arguing against the Agreement in the House of Commons, asked the very relevant question, what would American cotton suppliers do without the British market.[118] The same could be asked of the suppliers of Virginia tobacco. Credit on commercial terms would certainly have been available. Otto Clarke wrote in a minute of 12 February 1946, at a time when it appeared that Congress might rescue the British government from the Agreement by turning it down, 'I think we should pull through without having to embark on such austerity as would reduce the British economy to a standstill.'[119] Keynes had earlier exaggerated the dramatic consequences of Britain denying itself this American assistance. Now he himself conceded that:

It comes out in the wash that the American Loan is primarily required to meet the political and military expenditure overseas. If it were not for that, we could scrape through without excessive interruption of our domestic programme if necessary by drawing largely on our reserves. The interruption of our domestic programme which is politically and economically possible so long as the military and political expenditure goes on on its present scale is strictly limited. The main consequence of the failure of the loan must, therefore, be a large-scale withdrawal on our part from international responsibilities.[120]

Keynes was highly critical of these overseas commitments in the then state of the British economy and encouraged withdrawal though he accepted that that would take time. But if dollars were required only to meet the costs of gradual withdrawal, they could certainly have been found on commercial terms without entering into unsustainable commitments to the US government. The loan he had negotiated gave the British government the illusion that it could sustain its overseas commitments, whereas it should have begun withdrawal immediately at the end of the war if the only assistance it could get was on the terms now dictated from Washington.

The second reason for acceptance was the damage rejection could have done to the UK's relationship with the USA. It could have triggered a crisis. No one could say how rejection would be received in Washington. The agreement Keynes had negotiated with the Americans served an even higher and longer-term purpose than feeding Britain with dollars. It was a paving measure for Bretton Woods. Keynes had been prepared to accept the inadequacies in the Agreement for the sake of Bretton Woods and so that the UK could satisfy what he described as the Americans' 'urgent desire to see this country a strong and effective partner in guiding a distressed and confused world into the ways of peace and economic order'.[121] Britain was to be alongside the Americans in persuading the world to accept the Bretton Woods settlement. Britain was not to be deprived of its greatness or of its leadership. Dalton said in the House:

There would be a trade war between us, and a great deal of pressure would be used to coax away members of the sterling group . . . Finally, and perhaps most serious of all, the rejection of these Agreements would mean the disruption of all hopes of Anglo-American cooperation in this dangerous new world into which we have moved.[122]

Such fears were exaggerated. So far as the sterling area was concerned, only the independent members could be coaxed away. The independent holders of the sterling balances had a strong interest in the UK sustaining an exchange rate for sterling of $4.03 even if it did reject the loan. This was an incentive to be helpful. If some were coaxed away, it was not at all clear that the UK would be damaged thereby. The relationship with the USA, such as it was, was based on a mutuality of interest, not, as was only too clear, on US generosity. On the British side it embodied contradictory sentiments. It was a relationship publicly prized, privately resented. On the one hand there was a keen desire for the continuation of the transatlantic alliance; Europe was thought to be at risk from Soviet aggression, and American power was the only effective deterrent. On the other hand, intermingled with gratitude for American help during the war, was resentment at the manner in which Britain's weakness had been exploited by the USA for its own economic advantage. After the war, the resentment was compounded by Britain's dependence on the USA, by its emergence as a superpower at the expense of British power, and by the continuing attack of American business and government on such elements of commercial advantage in the UK's relationship with the Commonwealth as had survived the war. If the Anglo-American relationship survived these tensions, it was because it was in the interests of both parties, not just of one, that it should survive.

Too much was made at the time of American generosity. It was almost as though American terms had to be accepted, however damaging, because the Americans, at least in intention, were so generous. Keynes was clearly influenced by such sentiments. There had been a great deal of criticism in Britain of the harsh terms of the Agreement. To this Keynes replied, 'I feel sure that serious injustice is being done to the liberal purposes and intense good will towards this country of the American people as represented by their Administration . . .'[123] Generosity is not a factor which enters readily into the behaviour of states. The USA, like other countries, had its own interests. It entered the war not a day earlier than it was forced to. In the years after 1945, it had a keen interest in the survival of democracy in western Europe. It was an interest that could have been exploited earlier to better effect.

Thirdly, the British government felt that its negotiators had done reasonably well on the question of trade, which had not been handled by Keynes. Sir Stafford Cripps had always been ready to accept the principle of a multilateral world order on condition. The conditions were that any modifications of imperial preference must be part of a bargain embracing reductions of tariffs and other obstacles to trade; that the right to state trading was protected; that the UK could 'programme our imports so that we can spend our foreign resources on what is necessary for our recovery'; and that the development of UK agriculture was not prohibited. In a paper to the Cabinet in September, he noted wryly that 'our negotiators should be in a strong position since the suggestions which have been made to us by the Americans are most clearly designed to provide carefully chosen safeguards for their own agricultural policy . . . our negotiators should make it clear to the Americans that they really cannot have their cake and eat ours.' Further, he wanted to limit American subsidies to their shipping.[124] Now, it was Cripps who presented to the House the US proposals for an ITO which the UK had had to agree to support as a condition of the loan. Cripps claimed that the UK had put up a great and successful battle against American pressure. The case he presented was an embarrassed mixture of economic multilateralism, imperial preference, and national planning. He told the House that 'we must make up our minds as to whether we are to deal with these problems as isolationists or as internationalists'.[125] 'We are quite certain that if a multilateral agreement could be come to between the principal trading nations of the world along the lines suggested, we should find our own situation in international commerce far easier than it ever was in the chaotic time between the two wars.'[126] But he was able to assure his backbenchers, anxious that the rights of the UK to plan its own economy were not being prejudiced, that the UK's interests were being protected. The government, he said, was satisfied that it would be able to carry out the agricultural policy announced by the Minister of Agriculture.[127] The attack in the US proposals on quantitative restrictions did not affect UK rights to support agriculture, impose import quotas, or engage in state trading. Subsidies were only prohibited where they affected international trade, for example export subsidies. British trade had in the past suffered from others' export subsidies and therefore this provision was of benefit to the UK.[128]

He acknowledged that there had been some conflict with the interests of the USA with which the UK had been forced to compromise.

> We have . . . in the course of arriving at the terms of this document, done our utmost to see that our particular interests as a country are not prejudiced unduly, that our special relationships within the Commonwealth and Empire are not affected seriously, and that our own domestic decisions as regards national planning of our agriculture and industry are not made too difficult; but we have had to meet the quite different views and requirements of the United States of America arising out of their own political theories and their industrial necessities.[129]

Cripps informed the House that 'The proposal is that members of [the ITO] should enter into arrangements in order, ultimately, to achieve, if they can, this end, that is the reduction of tariffs and the elimination of preferences.'[130] But he explained that it was all a matter of bargaining and negotiation and that reference to the elimination of preferences did not constitute a *commitment* to the elimination of preferences. 'Nobody can compel anyone to reduce a preference.'[131] There were then a number of interventions in his speech from MPs who wished to know why the wording spoke of the 'reduction' of tariffs but the 'elimination' of preferences.[132] It was quite obvious that the wording was part and parcel of the American attack on imperial preferences. Cripps responded testily to these enquiries: 'One has to recall that the Administration of the United States of America has to get this through Congress just as we have through the House of Commons, and whether they think there is some particular attractiveness in those words or not, I could not say.'[133]

In the end it would be an increasingly protectionist American Congress that decided against ratifying the ITO to which Britain had been forced to commit itself. The result was that for nearly fifty years, the supervision of international trade, and the negotiation of greater openness to the goods and services of other nations, would be promoted by the General Agreement on Tariffs and Trade (GATT), continuing a provisional existence until its member states could make up their minds that the time was ripe to make it, or some comparable body, a permanent feature of the world trading scene.

The temptation to gamble and accept the Agreement was reinforced by the fact that, in the immediate aftermath of the war, exports were doing well. Germany and Japan were occupied by the allied armies and their severely damaged industries were, momentarily, out of the competitive game. In this situation British exports rose rapidly, though still leaving a significant trade gap. Such was the optimism generated by this achievement that Douglas Jay minuted Attlee in April 1946 that by July 1947, exports should be paying for all the UK's foreign commitments.[134] This did not imply anything like balance in the UK's dollar accounts. But, if it was in fact accomplished, perhaps the convertibility commitment could be implemented without disaster. A further implication of this success was that the UK had had a far stronger bargaining position in its negotiations with Washington than Keynes had ever deployed.

THE GOLD STANDARD

The Bank of England, which had always disliked Keynes's vision of the postwar world, its dependence on American support, on premature convertibility, and on non-discrimination, also thought that the Bretton Woods system would have too great a resemblance to the Gold Standard. On 1 March 1944, Cameron Cobbold, then an executive director of the Bank, warned Lord Beaverbrook, a member of a Ministerial Group chaired by the Chancellor of the Exchequer, that the proposed legal obligation of fixed-rate convertibility would resemble a return to the rigidities of the Gold Standard.[135]

Dalton was intensely sensitive to the accusation that in committing the UK to Bretton Woods, he was in effect returning it to a system comparable to the Gold Standard. The Labour Party, in a pamphlet of 1944, had declared 'There must be no return to the Gold Standard.' However, the idea of stability in exchange rates recalled both the Gold Standard and the overvalued pound sterling which, on the Keynesian hypothesis, shared the guilt for the pre-war depression.[136] Dalton replied to the criticism that Bretton Woods amounted to a return to the Gold Standard by devoting to it a major part of his speech in the House of Commons on 12 December 1945. The ideal which he believed Bretton Woods to have achieved was a combination of stability and flexibility. He found justification for his claim that Bretton Woods was in no way comparable with the Gold Standard in the provisions permitting adjustment of exchange rates, some with, some without the agreement of the IMF, and in the ultimate right to resign from the IMF without penalty. This right to resign, he argued, had been no part of the Gold Standard system and, therefore, when the UK had departed from it in 1931 it had been charged, perhaps justifiably, with a breach of faith. There was also the concept of 'fundamental disequilibrium' in the balance of payments. Within the Articles of the Fund, fundamental disequilibrium would permit the adjustment of exchange rates and he intended to get an interpretative declaration from the executives of the Fund indicating that where pressure on the balance of payments threatened full employment, that would be regarded as an example of fundamental disequilibrium.

However comforting Dalton found these arguments, they omitted the political factor. Whether or not the Gold Standard system permitted devaluation, there was no doubt that the sovereign rights of nation states permitted it. 1931 had proved that. In that respect the differences were in words rather than in substance. A real difference was that the IMF had resources with which, with different degrees of conditionality, it could assist a country to get out of temporary trouble. But the resources available to the Fund were not large and, in any case, where there was fundamental disequilibrium, it would, in the end, have to be resolved by an adjustment to the exchange rate or by deflationary domestic policies or by both.

Bretton Woods may have been in words more sophisticated than was the Gold Standard, but the difference can be easily exaggerated. The political factor remained – adjustment of the exchange rate could become a political defeat. To avoid the appearance of defeat, governments might allow exchange rates to become increasingly unrealistic. Fundamental disequilibrium might arrive only by stages but it would arrive. In his condemnation of the return to the Gold Standard, Keynes had written of 'its dependence on pure chance, its faith in "automatic adjustments", and its general regardlessness of social detail'.[137] Once the political factor is brought into account, one can say much the same of Bretton Woods. Experience over the last few decades has raised greater questions about fixed rate systems than Dalton or Keynes acknowledged in their defence of Bretton Woods.

FULL EMPLOYMENT

The government had to be satisfied that nothing in the Agreement or in Bretton Woods prejudiced full employment. Sir Stafford Cripps assured the House of Commons that the Americans proposals for an ITO were designed to protect full employment. He pointed out that Section B of the US proposals

> makes clear that a high and stable level of employment in all individual countries is vital to the success of any scheme of international commercial cooperation . . . Nor must the full employment be created by exporting unemployment from one country to another to the detriment of the other country . . . We now have the suggestion that it should be formally recognised that every country is responsible to all other countries to see that it does not create international difficulties by permitting in its own territories large scale unemployment or by merely exporting that unemployment to the detriment of other countries.[138]

This recommendation was further evidence of the importance attached by the USA to full employment. It no doubt represented an advance in international cooperation. It required, however, some naiveté to believe that it could be implemented in all circumstances or that effective sanctions would be available against any country, the USA in particular, that decided that perhaps the time had come to export its unemployment.

Given Keynes's extraordinary influence on the government, it was important that he too should be satisfied that British adhesion to Bretton Woods and the ITO was consistent with full employment. Keynes's views had been autarkic. In a famous statement he had written:

> I sympathise ... with those who would minimise, rather than those who would maximise, economic entanglement among nations. Ideas, knowledge, science, hospitality, travel – these are things which should of their nature be international. But let goods be homespun whenever it is reasonably and conveniently possible, and, above all, let finance be primarily national.[139]

In advocating Bretton Woods and the ITO, Keynes had obviously undergone a conversion. He had been persuaded by the miseries of the 1930s to turn his mind to the problem of unemployment. It was a problem that he thought he had solved in *The General Theory of Employment, Interest and Money*. But he had solved it, if at all, on the assumption that goods would be homespun. Yet in the open international trading system that Keynes was now recommending, goods would not necessarily be homespun. Harrod, the economist, knew Keynes well and was sufficiently sympathetic to Keynes's views to provide the explanation for Keynes's dramatic change of view:

> The Americans were being extraordinarily cooperative. Large new vistas opened up. We need no longer be content with a nationalist experiment in Keynesian autarky, but could take the better path of an experiment in Keynesian economics on a world scale and not forgo the full benefits which flow from international trade. His mind reverted to Adam Smith and to the great truths which he had preached. Of course they were truths; but for him they had been submerged in recent years by what seemed to be the more urgent problem of mass unemployment and trade depression. So long as the present-day followers of Adam Smith refused to recognise these new problems, he would not preach their gospel. Yet he would be far happier preaching that gospel; and these conversations during the Loan negotiations convinced him that he could now do so without sacrificing any of his cherished principles relating to employment and trade depression. The Americans seemed to be as fully convinced as

he that a nation should not be compelled by her open trading commitments to take action likely to lead to domestic slump.[140]

Evidence of the importance the Americans were now attributing to full employment was to be found in the determination of the Administration to secure from Congress legislation committing the US government to full employment. Indeed, in 1946, Congress passed the Employment Act. It had started life as a Full Employment Bill but by the time Congress had finished with it, scepticism as to the practicality and desirability of such a commitment had diluted the machinery supposedly necessary to ensure it. The words 'full employment' were removed from the bill and replaced by 'maximum employment, production and purchasing power'. Herbert Stein has commented: 'Congress rejected an overly ambitious, inflationary definition of the goal, rejected exclusive reliance on deficit financing as the means and reaffirmed its devotion to the free enterprise system.'[141] As we have seen, similar doubts about a commitment to 'full' employment influenced the drafting of the Employment Policy White Paper in Britain. The only lasting achievement of the US Employment Act was the creation of the Council of Economic Advisers of which Stein was, at one time, chairman.

On the flimsy ground that the USA was now committed to full employment, Keynes abandoned his autarkic views and persuaded the British government to follow him into a world of non-discrimination in trade. He had been wrong in his autarky and now he was premature in his advocacy of non-discrimination. It was this naive faith in American economic leadership as a guarantee of full employment that made him unsuitable as a negotiator with Washington. To bring Bretton Woods and the ITO rapidly into operation was the policy of the Americans. It would mean the end of discrimination against their trade. As would be demonstrated only too soon, it was not a British interest.

The world, in due course, learnt that Bretton Woods could not provide a guarantee of full employment. In so far as full employment was assured during the Bretton Woods period, it was more likely to have been because of pent-up demand left unsatisfied during the war, because of the needs of reconstruction, and because of the outflow of American capital rather than because of Bretton Woods. Thus, in the years after the war, the Western World was saved, if that is not too much of an exaggeration, by American money, not by Keynes and not by Bretton Woods. There was nothing in Bretton Woods from which could be derived the comfort found both by Dalton and Keynes in advocating acceptance of the convertibility condition and non-discrimination. If the Americans wanted Bretton Woods, they should have been told to drop sterling convertibility and non-discrimination for the time being. Keynes was imposing on his own country an inflexibility comparable with that of the Gold Standard and, in the not too distant future, all the political difficulties and economic embarrassments of an increasingly overvalued currency. There was not enough in the Bretton Woods settlement, or in the resources available to its institutions, to free Keynes of the charge, which he deeply resented, that, under the influence of the Americans, he had, contrary to his earlier convictions, converted himself to *laissez-faire*.[142] He was unhappily aware that there were many who were making this charge, including Robert Boothby in his speech in the Commons on 12 December. The emotional climax of Keynes's speech to the Lords came when he cried out against such critics:

> It is not easy to have patience with those who pretend that some of us, who were very early in the field to attack and denounce the false premises and false conclusions of unrestricted *laissez-faire* and its particular manifestations in the former Gold Standard and other currency and commercial doctrines which mistake private licence for public liberty, are now spending their later years in the service of the State to walk backwards and resurrect and re-erect the idols which they had played some part in throwing out of the market place. Not so.[143]

THERE IS NO ALTERNATIVE

Keynes was the negotiator and the adviser. It was Dalton who carried the responsibility. Dalton had ended his speech on 12 December by issuing a challenge, 'to those who are critical of these arrangements, I venture, in conclusion, to put one blunt question: What is your alternative?'[144] Dalton received no answer from the official spokesman for the Opposition, Sir John Anderson. He could only indicate that the Opposition intended neither to oppose nor to support the Motion before the House. This invited the House to welcome the three elements in the Washington agreement negotiated by Keynes. The first element was the Lend-Lease settlement with which Dalton was totally satisfied. The second was the $3.75 billion loan which was subject to the worrying convertibility condition. The third was adherence before 31 December 1945 to Bretton Woods. Anderson referred to the word 'welcomes' in the Motion and said that it seemed 'to import . . . a note of enthusiasm that goes far beyond anything we really feel'. The most substantial answer to Dalton's challenge came, in a speech of great brilliance, from Robert Boothby. 'This is our economic Munich', he proclaimed.[145] He would divide the House 'because I conscientiously believe that this country is not, and will not be, in a position to discharge the obligation she is being invited to undertake by the Government.'[146] Exchange rates could not vary from official parities by more than 1 per cent. 'I confess I think that to anchor ourselves to gold at this parity of exchange [$4.03], at this juncture in world affairs, is an act of absolute insanity.'[147]

He summarized his case in the following words:

> There are two main objectives underlying the agreement which we are being asked to approve. The first is to get back as quickly as possible to the economic system of the 19th century – the system of *laissez-faire* capitalism. The second is to break up, and prise open, the markets of the world for the benefit of the United States of America ... If this is not so ... why did they not give us a commercial loan to enable us to get through the next year or two, without conditions attached, as they did to France? Were they asked to do so? Did they refuse to do so? The rate offered to France, without any conditions attached, was only five-eighths per cent more than the rate we are being charged under the Loan Agreement.'[148]

There was a great deal of truth in this analysis. Indeed the government in essence admitted it. The Americans were launching an attack on the sterling area and on imperial preference. But while the British Empire was to be under attack, the Americans, said Boothby, were not conceding entry into their own enormous market on comparable terms. 'The elimination of Imperial preference breaks up the economic unity of ... the British Empire, but the Customs Union of the United States of America ... remains absolutely untouched.'[149] He took exactly the right point against the commitment to make sterling convertible. 'It is no use [Dalton] drawing this tremendous distinction between letting capital out and letting money out for current transactions. That distinction is extremely difficult to draw; and many people will be able to evade it.'[150] And he perceived in the Bretton Woods Agreement a characteristic that would in the course of the next half-century attract criticism to all fixed rate systems including, eventually, the European Monetary System. 'In the Bretton Woods Agreement ... the onus is put upon the debtor nations to re-establish equilibrium in the balance of trade; and there is no onus at all on the creditor nations.'[151] He ended his attack by turning Dalton's reference to tobacco against him. The government might have a mandate to nationalize gas but 'there is one mandate His Majesty's Government never got from the people of this country, and that was to sell the British Empire for a packet of cigarettes'.[152]

Where Boothby's speech lacked realism was in his alternative. He was right in arguing that the government should have gone for a commercial loan, not for a government loan which had enabled the US Administration to extract such damaging concessions. But beyond that, Boothby believed in the Empire. He offered as his alternative 'the sterling bloc based upon the British Empire, and fortified by the countries of Western Europe'.[153] It was a pity indeed that this government was not prepared to look more closely at the possibilities offered by alliance with the neighbouring countries of western Europe. But the sterling bloc offered no real alternative. The interests of its members were too diverse. Those that were feeding dollars into the sterling area dollar pool wanted the use of them as dollars.[154] They would not accept for any length of time that those dollars should accrue to the benefit of the UK. Boothby was an advocate of a planned economy. 'The *laissez-faire* economy of the 19th century, I would remind the Chancellor of the Exchequer, who used to think this himself, has now to give way to the planned economy of the 20th century.'[155] But Boothby had no more idea than the British government how to plan the economy in peacetime, whether it was the economy of the UK, the economy of the Empire, or the economy of the world which, he thought, *laissez-faire* would reduce to 'anarchy'. Boothby's attack had been magnificent. But his alternative was not a real option.[156]

What would have been much better would have been to attempt a different strategy as described by Richard Clarke:

The simplest plan, which had much to commend it ... was to abandon the concept of a 'Grand Design' negotiation in autumn 1945, for several years' money, sterling balances, convertibility, non-discrimination. We could easily have said 'We are willing to sign the Bretton Woods Agreement and participate in the International Commercial Policy conference; but we are not willing to accept any prior commitments at all until we know how the new world develops: we would be willing to negotiate in 1947.' We would have borrowed, say $1,000 million (some from the Export-Import Bank and some, no doubt, also from Canada), and would have undertaken to accept a loan for the residue of Lend-Lease at the rate of any ultimate major loan ... After the abrupt end of the war and the cessation of Lend-Lease, the Americans could not have refused or tried to impose strings. In fact the events of 1947 showed that the multilateral theologians' concepts of the course of events had been utterly wrong, and that the doctrines of the 1945 negotiations had fallen into the background of US policy except as a far-ahead (and useful) ideal.[157]

The Clarke strategy having been rejected, there was only one alternative to approval of the Loan Agreement, and that was to inform the US Administration that the UK government could not in honour accept a commitment to the convertibility of sterling and that therefore, if that requirement was unnegotiable, it would be forced to reject the loan. That would mean accepting the risk that the UK would once more be fighting on its own, this time not for political but for economic survival. What is certain is that it was not just rejection of the loan terms that involved risks. The risks of accepting were also very grave. In accepting, the Cabinet was taking greater risks than it appeared to realize.

The American credit was open to be drawn upon up to 31 December 1951. Whether it would last that long could only be a matter of guess-work. As things turned out, there was a serious deterioration in the UK balance of payments in 1947, almost all of it in dollars.[158] The drain in dollars was exhausting the loan much more rapidly than forecast. The consequences of the loss of overseas income due to the disposal of overseas assets was exacerbated by the unfavourable turn in the UK's terms of trade.[159] The virtual monopoly of the USA as supplier of many essential goods enabled it to charge high prices, thus increasing the burden of imports on the UK economy. Not merely were American prices high – they were rising. Dalton calculated that between December 1945 and March 1947, American wholesale prices rose in dollar terms by 40 per cent.[160] It is a matter for speculation how far this increase in prices was encouraged by the fact that the US Congress had lent Britain the money with which to pay them.

Accepting the loan was a gamble with the credibility of the British government. It was a gamble not merely on convertibility but on the hope that it would safeguard the recovery of the British economy until it could pay its way without American help. The gamble was too great. It would have been better to have had the showdown at the beginning of 1946. The cost of the unsuccessful gamble was the humiliating departure from convertibility five weeks after it was introduced in July 1947. There was also a cost in continuing mistrust in Washington as to the value that could be placed on British assurances. It was only after the agreement was sealed that Dalton began to wonder whether he should not have attempted to talk the Americans out of the condition. The problem preyed on his mind, a constant source of anxiety when so much else seemed to be going well.[161]

There was a long debate in Congress as to whether it should approve the Agreement. It was not a debate helpful to the UK's reputation. Dalton records: 'Many congressmen . . . deployed lengthy, ill-informed, unfriendly and even spiteful criticism of Britain . . . Much of the criticism . . . was not merely of Britain, but of the actual British Labour Government and its policies.'[162] According to Keynes, Churchill was a helpful influence on Washington opinion. In a memorandum of March 1946 Keynes noted that Churchill had 'told all his friends that he was in favour of the Loan, that we needed it, and that the argument against lending to a Socialist Government was a wrong and invalid argument, with which he would have nothing to do.'[163] The government could not be certain for at least three months that Congress would approve the loan, yet little was done to prepare for such a contingency. The debate was turned in Britain's favour by the increasing concerns in Washington about Soviet policy. But it was not the kind of debate that would encourage the UK government to apply for a waiver of the convertibility commitment when the balance of payments turned seriously adverse in 1947.

Many years later, Richard Clarke, who had opposed the whole strategy of the Keynes Loan, reflected:

> It may be that in real difficulties, free of the US 'strings', and with no moral obligation to help them with their military obligations, it might have been easier. Thirty years later, when one sees the relative success of Germany, Japan, France, which were forced to make great social and economic changes, one cannot be absolutely sure that our right long-term course was to display remarkable ingenuity to retain the status quo.[164]

After the conclusion of the loan negotiations, Dalton noted in his diary, 'my secret reflection on the American loan is that we shall be able to make good use of the dollars – though we wish there were more – but that it is quite certain that the conditions will have to be revised long before AD 2001 and that, even in the next year or two, circumstances may require a large revision, which might even be "unilateral".'[165] He seems to have been proud of this entry because he quoted it in his memoirs. It demonstrated his foresight. In fact it shows a Chancellor of the Exchequer taking his dollars under false pretences. The gods certainly watched with a smile of satisfaction when his default on his commitments under the Anglo-American Financial Agreement destroyed Dalton's reputation and made him so accident-prone that he was, shortly thereafter, driven from office.

TWO

Dalton: *Annus Mirabilis and Annus Horrendus*

THE US TREASURY had become the bountiful parent of the British welfare state. During the eighteen months before the convertibility commitment exploded in Dalton's face, the foundations of the welfare state were laid. It was socialism on credit. The government, moreover, had the satisfaction of knowing that the socialism would not be repossessed by the lender if it defaulted on the terms of the credit. During the negotiations Keynes had warned Dalton that 'There is no way out remotely compatible with the present domestic policy of the Government except on the basis of substantial American aid.'[1] The implication was that, with substantial American aid, the domestic policy of the government could be implemented. Keynes should have supplemented his warning with the further advice that there was no way, in the current economic situation, that the domestic policy of the government could be implemented without grave economic costs. The welfare state, as it stood in 1951, could not have been created without the American loan. It could not have been created with it if the Attlee government had had the least intention of respecting its commitments under the Loan Agreement. By those prepared to take a cavalier attitude to those commitments, the Attlee government is sometimes, these days, seen with rose-tinted spectacles. Pimlott justifies the acceptance of the American loan on the terms negotiated by arguing that 'What the Loan provided was an opportunity for Labour to do the things it had always wanted, and which it had promised in its manifesto. Would social security, the National Health Service, extensive nationalisation, have been possible without it?'[2] But the purpose of the loan was the rehabilitation of the British economy, not the creation of a welfare state.

Dalton told the House of Commons that 'acceptance of the Agreements does not mean a life of ease and plenty for all ... This dollar credit only gives us a breathing space ...'[3] There was no sign at all that the Cabinet itself understood the message. It is questionable whether Dalton understood it himself. The message could indeed have been conveyed more emphatically than by reference to such unlikely outcomes of the loan as a life of ease and plenty for all. There was a breathing space and the question now was how the government would use it. Sir Wilfrid Eady, head of the Finance Division in the Treasury, had always feared that the government would, in exchange for debilitating commitments, end up with a loan that was large enough to engender a false sense of security but not large enough to finance the expected transitional deficit in the balance of payments, let alone the extra strain of convertibility. At best the loan would interpose an expensive false dawn before reality had to be tackled.[4] If there had been no loan, delay in fulfilling the government's electoral promises would have been inevitable.

The convertibility obligation was the Damocles sword hanging over Dalton's future. By accepting the obligation, Dalton knew that he had exposed himself to judgement by the market not later than one year from Congressional ratification. Yet did his colleagues realize how devastating that judgement could be? Cabinet Ministers can put impending economic crises out of their minds with extraordinary ease. Though they are, supposedly, collectively responsible, economic policy is someone else's responsibility, at least until there is dissatisfaction with the flow of money to departments, or major problems of solvency are dumped on the Cabinet table and have to be addressed. In Dalton also, the availability of dollars under the two credits encouraged complacency and irresponsibility. $5 billion was a great deal of money. It generated in the Chancellor the confidence to make many triumphant speeches in the House of Commons. At that he was, as he knew, exceedingly good. He did suffer an occasional nightmare when he recalled that the crunch date, 15 July 1947, the day on which sterling would become convertible, would actually arrive.

The inescapable lesson of the convertibility commitment was that the country must cut unnecessary foreign currency outgoings and build up exports. It was just possible that if foreign currency outgoings were cut and exports were built up sufficiently, the Damocles sword would not fall. To build up exports, the government must divert more of the workforce into the production of goods and services which could be sold abroad. So serious was the situation that everything else must take a lower priority. All those promises made in the manifesto must be postponed until they could be funded not out of foreign borrowings but out of British earnings. How could a default on those promises be explained to the electorate? It could not be explained. Everything of any importance about the economic situation of the country had been known to the leading members of the Labour government before the election. They had, nevertheless, made their election promises without any security that they would have the capacity to fund them. Whatever the political embarrassments, the country should have been told that it would now have to devote itself to building up its exports and stopping the outflow from the reserves before the government could fund more than the beginning of the additional social expenditures promised by the manifesto. It might not have been good for morale either in the Party or in the country. But if a choice has to be made, it is better to default on promises to an electorate than on promises to a foreign lender whose help may once more be required. Foreign lenders have parted with cash and have long memories. The electorate have only parted with their votes.

Although the Attlee government did not have the political courage to postpone its electoral commitments, it might have served it better in the end. If there had been less euphoria, more attention to economics rather than politics, there would have been less disillusion. Given the rapid approach of convertibility, it is unlikely that, whatever it did, the government and its Chancellor could have kept their reputations for competence. But the country might well have been better off, and more capable of sustaining effective social services, if in the short term it had been compelled to exert itself once again. As it was, the enactment of the government's programme, made possible only by the loans from the USA and Canada, diverted resources from exports and ensured that the political demand for standards of welfare which Britain could not yet service out of its own earnings became deeply entrenched in the life of the country at the expense of its economic rehabilitation. Meeting the demand became a political necessity, not just for this government but for subsequent governments.

Dalton was entirely at one with the government's intention to press ahead with its programme. The commitments were lapidary, engraved in the unequivocal form of a political manifesto. He set out to be a political Chancellor, a Chancellor who helped his colleagues to get things done, not a Chancellor who brought with him to Cabinet only a string of negatives and anxieties. He believed his Party's commitments should be met and, now that he had the dollars, he believed that they could be met. He was dedicated to the construction of the British

Socialist Commonwealth and to an extension of public ownership sufficient to make possible socialist planning and full employment. Pimlott describes Dalton as 'the most socialist Chancellor of the Exchequer Britain has ever had'.[5] Unfortunately, while foreign borrowing can empower socialist Chancellors, it can also destroy them.

A SOCIALIST CHANCELLOR

The Beveridge Report had been published in November 1942. Dalton, as a socialist Chancellor, accepted that the state was to provide its citizens with protection, as Churchill put it in a broadcast of 21 March 1943, 'from the cradle to the grave'. But, as Beveridge himself records, whatever Churchill said in public, he had the gravest doubts whether the country should commit itself to the expenditure implied by the Report whereas Dalton believed it, and more, felt it should be implemented at once.[6] Maternity, sickness, retirement, and death, were to be covered together with other contingencies. A national health service had to be created and funded. Estimates of its cost could only be speculative but they would certainly be high. The nation demanded not just a country fit for heroes but homes fit for heroes.[7] Priority was given to subsidized public housing at great cost to the Exchequer and to the balance of payments. The 1944 Butler Education Act awaited implementation. Implementation would not be cheap. A system of national insurance was introduced and, in the euphoric atmosphere of the moment, introduced in the most expensive possible way with provision made for all pensioners at once. Beveridge had recommended a long transition period for pensions as of right.[8] Politics was held to deny the option of phasing over a period of years.[9] Local government could not survive without central government grants. Family allowances were to be paid at the rate of five shillings a week for every child after the first. Food was kept cheap by an expensive system of subsidies. Together with subsidies to agriculture, they amounted to one-fifth of consumers' expenditure on food, about 4 per cent of GNP. This exceeded total expenditure on national insurance and was also greater than expenditure on the health services.[10]

Not all of this expenditure was directed to help the poorest in society. Many who benefited could have afforded the economic cost. Given the economic situation, not everything had to be done at once. Nor was there any need to create services that, being free at the point of delivery, appeared to be manna from heaven. There could have been more overt emphasis on costs as well as on rights. A speculation that might have entered Dalton's calculations would be that if a vote in a General Election is sufficient contribution of effort to secure great benefits, little more is likely to be offered. In his Budget speech of 15 April 1947 Dalton claimed: 'We are entitled to say that the new Britain, represented by this House of Commons, has taken the cost of social security in its stride; the measures have been passed, the money has been found, and the benefits are being enjoyed by those entitled to them.'[11] This may have sounded a little ungrateful to Dalton's American benefactors. Yet, for those who wished to justify socialism on credit, there was an economic argument. In 1945, and in the subsequent years, there was in the economy already an excess of demand and the risk of inflation.[12] Following the parallel of 1918 there was an expectation that these early inflationary pressures would be replaced by deflation bringing unemployment. That inflationary pressures would persist indefinitely was not expected. Those who see the need for higher public expenditure, and in this case that included the Chancellor, can always find economic arguments. It was convenient for colleagues with expenditure programmes to emphasize the deflationary danger that was hanging over the country together with that Damocles sword. This Chancellor needed no persuading. There was, however, no deflationary danger.

Dalton, in his memoirs, refers repeatedly to his enjoyment of his first eighteen months as Chancellor and to his successes in that period. Much of the legislation promised in the election manifesto was passed. His own speeches in the House were well received by his Party. American money helped with many aspects of policy. For example, in an inflationary situation, the loan, which, for the first five years amounted to a grant, helped to keep inflation down. Dalton deserves all the credit due to a poor man gambling with borrowed money. 1946 was, says Dalton, an *annus mirabilis*.[13] Even the *annus mirabilis* was not without its nagging worries. In February 1946 Dalton warned his colleagues about the balance of payments prospects. In October 1946, he warned them that the American and Canadian credits were being used up much too fast.[14] Warnings were, obviously, quite insufficient. The colleagues were too occupied with their own affairs to concern themselves with the country's solvency. No Minister could have had a stronger incentive than Dalton to bring the facts home to his colleagues. He knew he would be more likely to sustain the necessary confidence in sterling and survive the critical appraisal of the market, if the balance of payments was stronger, and if he was seen to be acting against the strong inflationary pressure which existed throughout his period as Chancellor, and indeed throughout the Attlee government. This inflationary pressure would itself have a negative effect on exports by diverting production to the home market. Much of this Dalton did understand and, indeed, argued in Cabinet. But when Cabinet turned him down, he appeared to believe that his ultimate duty was to allow himself to become the scapegoat for their irresponsibility. He was insufficiently forceful in bringing home to his Cabinet colleagues the critical state of the country's economy and its implications both for policy and for the commitment into which the government had entered with the USA. They might be blind to the realities but, if they did not understand, it was he that was primarily to blame. No Chancellor is entitled to take refuge in the incomprehension of his colleagues. He must get his way on fundamentals or he must resign.

Labour Chancellors exhibit one strong professional deformation – they feel they must show their colleagues that they have wide horizons. Though they may see a need to control public expenditure, they see also an obligation to apologize for their need to control it. The requirement to make such demonstrations of socialist virtue was less in the case of Dalton than of some of his Labour successors. Dalton exuded socialist sentiments. Nevertheless, one of his first actions in arriving at the Treasury was to act on his conviction that the growing of trees represented a good investment for the country. He lavished £20 million over five years on the Forestry Commission. This was substantially more than had been spent between the wars. He then made a practice of 'taking to the woods' before each of his budgets and inspecting his 'socialist trees'. It was a consolation to the spirit. But it was also a speculation on the price of wood. The money was not, of course, his.

Another example was his insistence on the needs of the depressed areas of which he had heartrending experience as MP for Bishop Auckland, a Durham constituency. As President of the Board of Trade Dalton had pushed through the Distribution of Industry Act 1945. The intention was to prevent excessive concentration of industry in the south-east and to create employment in the 'development areas' of Scotland, Wales, the North-East and North-West. In his Budget speech of 9 April 1946, Dalton announced that one of his first instructions on becoming Chancellor was that as regards constructive plans for the Development Areas, the Treasury was henceforth to be no longer a curb but a spur. He would find the necessary money with 'a song in my heart'. The Treasury had been a curb because regional policies have their costs not just in money but often in industrial efficiency. Regional policy was yet one more addition to the escalating costs of Labour's social and welfare policies. If there had been a selection of priorities within an acceptable total cost instead of a desperate attempt to do everything at once, a regional policy based on incentives might have ranked high and the Treasury might not have wished to be a curb. But there was another practical objection to Dalton's enthusiastic pursuit of regional policy. However admirable, it is an inescapable feature of Cabinet government that Cabinet colleagues will allow the Chancellor to sing his own favourite songs only if their own voices are not drowned in consequence. The Chancellor should be a judge, assessing priorities, not an advocate of particular desirable causes. This is one of the hardest lessons for warmhearted Chancellors to learn.

Even excluding the food and agricultural subsidies the increase in expenditure resulting mainly from the social services was very large. Cairncross calculates that 'In 1950, before the rearmament programme had made much of a start, public expenditure on goods and services had roughly quadrupled in money terms and doubled in real terms since 1935.'[15] Excluding debt charges and defence expenditure, the total for all civil purposes rose from £1650 million in 1946–7, before the expansion of social services had got very far, to £2060 million in 1949–50 when the main changes had been made.[16] Although this may exaggerate the resource costs of these developments, a matter which economists would debate, market confidence would certainly be affected by plans which would lead to such large increases in public expenditure.

The Treasury found itself in the position that it has repeatedly occupied since the war, the provider of funding for projects which it doubted the nation could afford and whose validity it questioned. It might be assured by its political masters that the welfare state was good for the economy. The Treasury is normally disinclined to give idealistic interpretations of human conduct the benefit of the doubt. If, as a result of its advice being ignored, economic policy failed, it would carry the responsibility. Neither Ministers nor the public would then remember that the Treasury had whinged and whined at the burdens put upon the economy. Although denied the possibility of accommodating the government's demands to what it considered was the utmost that the country could afford, it would be the Treasury that had failed. Because of the euphoria generated by Labour's election victory, because of the opportunity created for social improvements by this first Labour victory with an overall majority in the House of Commons, Dalton's task was undoubtedly more difficult than would be that of his successors. Right up to the convertibility crisis, only three months before his resignation, the political pressures on him were very great and may have appeared to him not to permit much by way of hesitancy in providing what his colleagues demanded. Was this not a government devoted to socialist planning and would not socialist planning resolve all these Treasury doubts about what the nation could afford by stimulating economic growth?

DEFENCE EXPENDITURE

The one area where it might have been expected that a Labour government would be willing to cut to the bone was in defence expenditure. Defence expenditure could be cut without detriment to the government's socialist ideals. It was, therefore, on defence expenditure that Dalton wished to concentrate his pressure. Government military expenditure overseas, running at over £700 million in 1945, accounted for the whole of the 1945 financial deficit of £800 million and was almost as large as total imports of food, raw materials and semi-manufactures.[17] Dalton sought substantial cuts. It was not surprising that he was unable to prevent expenditure on the development of a British atomic bomb.[18] Bevin was determined to have an atom bomb adorned with the union flag. He deceived himself with the notion that possession of an atomic weapon would give the UK status with the Americans. He did not like being bossed by those who had made fewer sacrifices for victory than 'his' people. He appears not to have appreciated that nothing was so important in giving the UK status with the Americans as an economy independent of American aid. The investment of financial and technological resources in an independent atom bomb would probably delay the re-emergence of an independent economy.

But even to conventional defence expenditure the Labour government would not take the scythe that the Treasury considered necessary. The government was fearful that Britain might once more have to stand alone, this time against a Communist Europe. It was suffused with the importance of its global role and its special relationship with the USA, and was therefore prepared to accept the foreign exchange costs and the absorption of labour that could have been producing goods for home consumption and export. The Cabinet ignored Dalton's justified message that 'We must think of our national defence, in these hard and heavy years of transition, not only against the more distant possibility of armed aggression, but also against the far more immediate risk of economic and financial overstrain and collapse.'[19] Correlli Barnett points out that 'In October 1946, fourteen months after VJ Day, the armed forces still totalled 1.76 million men and women while defence industries swallowed another 590,000, making a grand total of 2.35 million.' Barnett comments that this was equal to one and two-thirds the man-power engaged in export manufacturing.[20] It was Dalton's view early in 1947 that the British economy was short of nearly 650,000 workers.[21] It was not until the beginning of 1947 that Dalton made his great drive against defence expenditure and its costs in manpower which would have been better employed on the export drive. An Economic Planning Committee had been established consisting of Morrison, Cripps, Dalton and George Isaacs, the Minister of Labour. On 16 January 1947, the Cabinet rejected all the principal proposals of the Committee made in a Report on Economic Planning. Dalton was particularly furious at the refusal by the Cabinet of a substantial cut in services manpower. He drafted a paper which he called *Note of a Difference of Opinion*. In it he threatened to 'reconsider my position'.

The *Note of a Difference of Opinion* was replete with strong language but the general impression is of a weak plea from a Chancellor who could not get his way. Dalton, the note said, feared 'a first-class economic and political disaster'. He warned that 'we shall exhaust the American and Canadian credits, at the present rate of drawing, early in 1949. Unless we can build up exports much faster than at present and hold them at a new high level, we shall have no remedies two years from now, except to borrow more abroad – and where from, and on what terms? – or to cut imports much below even the present low level.' Adopting biblical language, Dalton demanded, 'What shall it profit Britain to have even 1,500,000 men in the Forces and Supply, and to be spending nearly £1000 millions a year on them, if we come an economic and financial cropper two years hence?' At this point, the cropper was, in fact, only six months off. Once more he threatened, 'I must warn my colleagues that I could not carry on indefinitely, if my views on such important matters were to continue to be brushed aside as of no account.' Although his message was already late and was insufficiently urgent, Dalton's language was eloquent. 'We are, I am afraid, drifting, in a state of semi-animation, towards the rapids.' One of the criticisms that Dalton met in Cabinet was that no one could be sure that labour released from the forces would move into the export industries. There was no direction of labour. Dalton's correct response was that that implied a need for the release of more rather than less people so that there could be some assurance that some would move into the export industries.[22]

This was January 1947. Two years hence, at which date Dalton was threatening retribution for the Cabinet's failure to take his advice, meant early 1949. Why should a Cabinet worry about a crisis that might hit it two years hence? In any case the warning only came from the Treasury. The Treasury is known to have its own agenda, which is to cut departmental expenditures. Treasury forecasts are distrusted by departmental Ministers as a matter of political virility. The forebodings of the Chancellor needed reinforcement from the Prime Minister. Dalton lacked the consistent support that a Chancellor looks for in his Prime Minister.

In his memoirs, Dalton reflects 'my stand was not wholly without effect. On January 27th in Cabinet we reverted to the Defence Estimates. I had demanded last time a cut of 10 per cent in Defence expenditure, other than terminals. This would have saved £80 millions next year. I had been met with a most obstinate response from Alexander [Minister of Defence], who now offered me a cut of 5 per cent, or £40 millions. I accepted this, as a payment on account, without further debate.'[23] He had asked little enough and now he accepted a compromise. The urgent tone he had sounded in his Note was silent. Economic pressure did compel a British withdrawal in 1947 from a commitment to the defence of Greece, a responsibility taken over by the USA through the Truman Doctrine. It was a signal that the Labour government was becoming aware of a limit to its ability to maintain global security responsibilities in alliance with the USA. The cost of its occupation zone in Germany helped to persuade the government to accept its unification with that of the USA which, after an interval, brought significant financial relief.[24] But all this was late and it was only a beginning.

AN OPPORTUNITY WASTED

Meanwhile what was, in 1945, an exceptional opportunity was being wasted. Before the war the British share of world trade in manufactures had been falling. It had already been surpassed by Germany and Japan's trade was expanding rapidly.[25] During the war and after, there was deep concern in Whitehall and in industry about the competitiveness of the British economy. Now, for the moment, Germany and Japan were absent from the market place. Competition was, in consequence, less to be feared than it would subsequently become. For the world as a whole, dollars were scarce. If a country had dollars, it preferred to conserve them for imports for which there really was no other than a dollar source. Taking this together with the absence of Germany and Japan from the market, Britain had an unequalled opportunity to win export orders and rebuild its industry. Officials at least were aware that the breathing space would be of finite, perhaps quite brief, duration. The story of the Dalton Chancellorship is of how this opportunity was neglected. Though exports increased substantially, it was not nearly enough, as Dalton knew, and too little was being exported to hard currency areas.[26] One test of performance is what happened to Britain's share of world trade in manufactures. In the absence of German and Japanese competition, Britain's share rose, by 1950, from 17.5% pre-war – but only to 20.7%. By 1957 Britain's share had dropped well below its pre-war proportion to 14.7% and Japan had still not recovered her pre-war level of exports.[27] While British exports easily outstripped imports up to 1950, that was no longer the case thereafter; and in 1947 and 1949, the years of crisis, imports either grew faster than exports or just as fast.[28] Britain had been condemned by false priorities to become the stumbling laggard in the international economic race.

ECONOMIC PLANNING

There was a great deal of talk about the benefits of economic planning, accompanied by little of effective substance. A Chancellor, with his wits about him, might retain a certain scepticism as to the effectiveness of attempts at economic planning, at least in the short term, and insist that there should be some evidence of a return before there was a dividend. It was not Dalton's privilege to make economic policy alone. Fiscal policy was Dalton's responsibility. Economic planning, on the other hand, was for the Lord President's Committee of which Dalton was a member.[29] It presided over 'planning' which, in Labour theology, was the efficient part of economic policy, the part that would strengthen the British economy. That there should be a division between fiscal policy, charged to the Treasury, and economic planning, charged to some other Ministry, was in accordance with the thinking of Morrison and Dalton before the war. Such a division of responsibility had been found useful during the war. As the government was inheriting the planning controls developed during the war, it appeared not inappropriate to continue the division into peacetime.

At the election, Labour had committed itself to 'plan from the ground up'.[30] Intellectually it seemed so obvious that the application of the human mind to the improvement of economic processes must be better than leaving them to the mindless market. 'A body of competent engineers' could do it, wrote Sir Stafford Cripps in 1934.[31] This conviction was particularly strong after the success of wartime planning. Britain had successfully mobilized its resources for war. Now they would be mobilized for peace. The unemployment of the 1930s had proved that capitalism was not merely unjust, it was inefficient.

With the Labour victory in July 1945, the opportunity came of actually applying the resources of the human mind to the improvement of economic processes. It then emerged that even the human mind can stumble before the complexities. It was found to be much more difficult than, in theory, it ought to have been. There was no plan of the kind Monnet was developing in France. The government's concept of planning related, in practice, mainly to the management of shortages and to the control of prices. In the years after 1945, the shortages were serious. There were problems of availability from non-dollar sources. There were limits on the government's ability to fund imports from the USA. At the level of the hunch, which is one of the principal suppliers of guidance to Chancellors, it made sense, in these circumstances, not to rely on the price mechanism but to control imports, to switch them as far as possible to non-dollar sources, to facilitate production in non-dollar areas, and to ration supplies to industry and domestic consumers according to a defensible system of priority.[32] For this purpose, the principal priority was the balance of payments and the encouragement of exports. Price controls were in place to limit increases stimulated by excess demand. There was a determination to avoid, by controls, a repetition of the inflation that had occurred after the First World War when inflation had led to slump. To control prices in the aftermath of war until supplies recovered perhaps made sense. Whether government bulk-buying on long-term contracts also made sense is less certain.

This was planning only in a very limited sense. Although an apparatus of control inherited from the war existed and was useful during the transition from war to recovery, there was, very sensibly, no commitment to continue the controls when shortages disappeared. Planning through physical controls for its own sake was more likely to become a bureaucratic hindrance than a positive stimulus. Indeed controls were dismantled, beginning in 1948 as supplies became more available. Controls might ensure that the funds available for imports were expended with the greatest benefit to the British economy and that existing productive capacity was fed with the necessary inputs of raw materials and equipment. It was not planning of a kind that would transform economic performance. Planning of this kind may have had a role at a time of postwar shortages. But, as shortages were relieved, the role would decline. It was in these circumstances that, a little later, Keynesianism would come to the rescue. If resources could not be planned in detail in an economy as complex as that of the UK, Keynesianism would provide an alternative through the management of demand. Yet, for the time being, Ministers persuaded themselves that because there were controls there was also in some sense a plan. The most important effect of 'planning' was Ministerial self-deception. Ministers might believe that something was being done to transform the performance of the British economy. If so, they were in for a shock. Perhaps, if Dalton's confidence in the success of the government's policies had been less, his resistance to the government's mounting public expenditure commitments would have come earlier and been more effective.

Morrison knew little of economic policy. Yet the real criticism of the Lord President's Committee was not that its chairman was no planner or, even less, that he was no economic theoretician. Few Ministers are, and those that are have not always made the best economic Ministers. The problems were different. The first was that its existence as a kind of economic overlord prompted within the government a gross overestimate of the effectiveness of policy on economic performance. The existence of such a high-powered Committee signalled that something effective was being done, but the signal was not accompanied by much substance. The second problem was that the Committee became an alibi for the failures of economic policy. In April 1947 Cripps was to complain to Dalton that Morrison was incapable of handling planning, even if his health was good enough.[33] The implication was that the failures of the previous two years were attributable to Morrison's Committee and that someone else, presumably Cripps, would be capable of economic planning and thus of ensuring that it made a significant difference to the performance of the British economy. On 27 March 1947, Sir Edwin Plowden, plucked from industry after a wartime career which included service in the Ministry of Aircraft Production where he met Stafford Cripps, had reluctantly accepted appointment as Chief Planning Officer. He was to be assisted by a small staff which became known as the Central Economic Planning Staff (CEPS). It was located in the Cabinet Office. In July, together with his other duties, Plowden became chairman of a new tripartite Economic Planning Board. In fact, despite the new machinery, the government had still no capacity to plan anything which would make much difference either in 1947 or subsequently. Plowden became one of the very few industrialists who, since the war, have made a significant and positive contribution to the formation of economic policy. But it was not as a socialist planner.

Thirdly, where responsibility for economic policy is divided, confusion is the inevitable result and so it happened. The division of authority between Morrison and Dalton led to clashes. It diluted the Chancellor's power. It conflicted with what should have been Dalton's clear responsibilities for the state of the economy as a whole. One identifiable person should be responsible for economic policy. That person can only be the Chancellor of the Exchequer who, in conducting it, must carry the confidence of the Prime Minister. Dalton, in his memoirs, showed that he was averse to any such ideas of personal Ministerial responsibility. He devoted a chapter to advice to Ministers. He says, 'A Minister is wise, if he foresees the possibility of serious trouble, to persuade his colleagues, in advance, to share his personal responsibility. "It was all discussed and agreed to by the Cabinet" is a comforting reply to critics.'[34] Such comfort is the device by which, under the British system of collective responsibility, Ministers defend themselves against criticism. But there is a significant cost to the public service. Where everyone is responsible, no one is responsible.

The most effective instruments for controlling the economy lay with the Treasury, not with the planners. The most effective instruments were fiscal policy and, though less regarded at this time, monetary policy. Although he had followed so many of Keynes's specific recommendations while Keynes was alive, Dalton was not a Keynesian. The economy, Dalton thought, should be managed not so much by fiscal policy which, in principle, should be neutral, but by physical controls and planning. Up to 1938, the accepted object of fiscal policy had been a balanced Budget.[35] Dalton had begun in 1945–6 with a Budget deficit of £2200 million. His intention, following tradition, was to achieve fiscal balance over a period of years. In fact he was compelled to do a great deal more. In the course of his four Budgets he transformed the large deficit with which he began, and which was the result of waging war, into a large surplus. This he achieved even though in his first two Budgets of October 1945 and April 1946 he reduced taxation by about £530 million. At the outset of his reign he would not have considered any such surplus appropriate. By November 1947 he had begun to understand that Budget surpluses can be an instrument of economic planning more effective than anything offered by the planners. The concentration of responsibility for economic policy in the hands of the Chancellor was implemented, entirely by accident, when Cripps succeeded Dalton.

NATIONALIZATION

There was a vast nationalization programme without much by way of preliminary thought as to how it could make a positive contribution to economic recovery rather than just satisfy a socialist ideology. With the rest of his colleagues Dalton shared the policy of nationalization. Nationalization was regarded as an essential instrument of the planned economy that Labour was supposed to be introducing. It was to give the government control of the commanding heights of the economy. But it was an experiment; a positive outcome could not be assured, though it might be assumed. Given the uncertainties, it would have been prudent to delay some of the government's expenditure commitments until the experiment of nationalization had justified itself and the nation was actually benefiting from the additional wealth the policy was assumed to create. Cairncross comments, 'It took a long time to learn that the "commanding heights" of the British economy lay not in the steel industry but in the balance of payments and energy supply.'[36] This government's interpretation of the phrase specified transport, the energy industries, coal, electricity and gas, as well as iron and steel. Apart from road transport, and iron and steel, there was little dramatic or intensely controversial about this on the assumption that a programme of nationalization was, at this time, an appropriate priority. The private coal owners were not popular in any part of the political spectrum. Electricity and gas were to a large extent in municipal hands in any case. Rationalization of these fragmented industries seemed sensible, and had much support among industrial consumers. But, beyond this, it was not at all clear, including to the government, how the control achieved by nationalization was to be used as part of economic planning.

The nationalizers, who included Dalton, had a battle to ensure that iron and steel were included in the programme. In Cabinet, on 12 April 1946:

> I said we weren't really beginning our Socialist programme, until we had gone past all the public utilities – such as transport and electricity – which were publicly owned in nearly every capitalist country in the world. Practical Socialism in Britain, I said, only really began with coal and with iron and steel, two cases where there was a specially strong political argument for breaking the power of a most reactionary body of capitalists.[37]

The fact that it was necessary to use arguments of this quality showed that the Cabinet was not over-confident of the economic benefits of nationalization, and it was certainly becoming increasingly aware that it was not widely popular. While arguing a possible exception for coal, Cairncross comments: 'Whatever the merits of public ownership in the longer run, an extensive programme of nationalization did not fit very well into a policy of postwar reconstruction.'[38]

Nationalization was another burden on the Exchequer which the Treasury had to accept. There was not just the problem of compensation to previous owners but the funding of future investment and of any future losses. This was the cost. At best the corresponding benefit could not be expected to accrue for years. It was not to be assumed that an industry would become more productive immediately it was nationalized. Miners might claim it. They would not be prepared to deliver it. The best that could be argued for coal nationalization was that if it had not taken place, the performance of the mines would have been even worse. As it was, output of coal expanded only slowly. Inadequate supplies of coal hampered the export drive. It was ironic that this great industrial nation should be so dependent for its exports on a raw material, coal, and one which it could not produce or deliver in the quantities required by the export drive. It was Bevin's frequent complaint that production left little for exports and therefore gave little support for his foreign policy.

NATIONALIZATION OF THE BANK OF ENGLAND

Dalton's particular contribution as Chancellor was the nationalization of the Bank of England. Despite occasional problems with Governors, the Bank had been the Treasury's poodle since Bonar Law as Chancellor brought Governor Philip Cunliffe to heel during the First World War. The idea that by nationalizing the Bank, Labour would secure the necessary control effectively to plan the British economy was the stuff of dreams or, more exactly, of politics. On Second Reading of the Nationalization Bill, Dalton did his best to turn it into a confrontational matter in order to hearten the 'Young Guard on the Back Benches' behind him.[39] In this, he had effective debating support on the back-benches from Hugh Gaitskell, making his mark in the House as a high-flyer. Dalton said that, through nationalization of the Bank, power in British central banking would pass from private financiers and the City establishment to the Chancellor of the Exchequer. In fact the power had already passed long before. Dalton's anachronism no doubt served to rouse the troops on the backbenches. He wanted to provoke the Tories into voting against the Bill and many took the bait. But nationalization of the Bank was so benign that Winston Churchill himself did not oppose it. He had blunted criticism in advance by arguing, in the debate on the King's Speech, that nationalization did not raise any question of principle. British credit would be resolutely upheld. Dalton attributes Churchill's attitude to the fact that he had had, when Chancellor of the Exchequer, his own difficulties with Montagu Norman, then Governor of the Bank.[40] The Bank's status as poodle was now official, but otherwise little had changed. Fforde comments, 'The Bank of England Act 1946 brought Norman's creation under public ownership while doing little to change it.'[41] Such appearance of independence as the Bank retained after nationalization would, in the years to come, prove useful when, confronted by serious funding problems, the Treasury turned to the Governor to solicit the support of other Central Banks.

The Nationalization Bill was debated and passed at a time when the American Loan was being negotiated and before the ratification by Congress. This fact alone was likely to force caution upon the government. Nor could nationalization of the Bank be anything other than benign in a country in which, although the 'mix' of the economy might have changed, the clearing banks remained in private ownership and the private sector would remain overwhelmingly dominant even after the completion of the government's nationalization programme. Those on the Left who were looking to the nationalization of the Bank as a decisive step in overthrowing the existing capitalist structure in Britain were to be disappointed. Some City figures, supposedly more knowledgeable, who had been advising Labour politicians, expected nationalization to enable the government, through the Bank, to exercise control over the City and hence over the planning of the British economy. Their ideas would require the government, on nationalization, to clear out the existing Court of merchant bankers and other City worthies and install obedient technocrats. This illustrates the fact that naive advice does not come only from those without experience. Labour governments have never learnt sufficiently to distrust the advice of such businessmen as, no doubt with the best intentions, offer Labour the benefit of their informed judgement.[42] One friendly City figure, Nicholas Davenport, had a scheme for linking the Bank to a National Investment Board.[43] Dalton did create a National Investment Council, but its functions were advisory. This, Dalton assured the Cabinet, would be enough because there was now a government that was ready itself to take positive action to plan the nation's economy.[44] It was ready if only it knew how.

The Nationalization Bill received the Royal Assent on 14 February 1946 and on 1 March ownership of the Bank was transferred to the Treasury. Lord Catto was reappointed Governor and Cameron Cobbold as Deputy Governor.[45] Apart from the four Executive Directors, it did not much matter who served on its Court except as an opportunity for patronage.[46] Monetary policy was for the Treasury, advised by the Governor, not for the Court; but then in recent decades decisions had always been taken in agreement with the Treasury. The Bank certainly had its views – but while the Bank had views, the Treasury made the decisions. This was the way the Bank itself wanted it. It rejected the idea of sharing responsibility for monetary policy, as was the position in Australia and Canada. To share the responsibility, it thought, was inconsistent with the climate of the times. The Bank took the view that while it should remain operationally and institutionally distinct from Government, regarding this as 'independence', it should accept Treasury control of 'policy'.[47] Fforde comments, 'The wisdom of this course remained to be demonstrated. After forty-five years of almost uninterrupted inflation, some may judge that it still remains to be demonstrated.'[48]

One major source of conflicts to come was left unresolved in the Nationalization Act. No consideration had been given to the fact that 'the country was about to adopt a new economic strategy, one that implied a persistent and prolonged inflationary undertow whose adequate constraint might in turn imply the need for a strong and specific monetary constitution.'[49] The Act did not give the Treasury the right to instruct the Bank to issue directives to the commercial banks, for example to limit their lending, though the Treasury could authorize the Bank to do so if the Bank itself was willing. This was an omission that greatly annoyed Treasury economists who saw, in bank lending, a source of inflationary pressure. It was to lead in 1957 to a major row between Chancellor Thorneycroft and Governor Cobbold.[50] The Bank seldom thought it appropriate to issue directives to the clearing banks about their lending. In the Bank's view the problem was that successive governments conducted inflationary policies. It was for governments to change policy, cut public expenditure, and thereby generate cash sur-pluses in the Budget. This, in the Bank's view, would be sufficient to limit the growth in bank deposits and hence of lending.[51] In the Bank's view, the government should carry its own responsibilities and not shovel them on to Threadneedle Street.

CHEAP MONEY

Dalton conducted a cheap money policy. Dow comments that Dalton 'converted a cheap money policy into a cheap money campaign'.[52] Although the policy is particularly associated with the name of Dalton, it was conducted with the initial support of the Opposition.[53] Dow says that 'By the end of the war, cheap money was an unquestioned, and bipartisan, orthodoxy.'[54] There was no question in Britain of using mon-etary policy against inflation as was being done, after the war, in many continental countries. Bank Rate, which had been at 2 per cent since 1932, was kept there.[55] This achievement was assisted by the American loan. Dalton was less successful in his attempts to reduce long-term interest rates. One immediate problem was that gilt-edged tended to droop whenever nationalization, and especially iron and steel nationaliz-ation, made the headlines. The slightly longer-term problem would be inflation. The convertibility crisis finally undermined City confidence in the government, in its economic policies and in its debt. Gilt-edged prices fell, thereby raising interest rates. Dalton's policies bequeathed to the City the undated 'Daltons' by which he is still remembered, because they left ill-advised investors with considerable losses. Dalton says that he acted on unanimous Treasury and Bank advice.[56] But the Bank clearly distrusted the cheap money policy. It did not press its views because it knew they were unacceptable to the Chancellor.[57]

Keynes encouraged Dalton in his low interest rate policy.[58] When the policy came under criticism Dalton regretted Keynes's absence. In his Budget speech of 15 April 1947, Dalton praised Keynes. 'Now that he is dead, I can say that his advice to me was to persevere with cheap money.'[59] Keynes could not change his advice. Death had denied him the flexibility in prescription that had characterized him in life. He had not merely recommended cheap money, he had also recommended a tough policy on the sterling balances and an end to government extravagance, including on overseas military expenditure. It was politically easy for the government to take his advice on cheap money. It rightly ignored his advice on the sterling balances and wrongly on government extravagance. It was disingenuous to claim Keynes's support for cheap money when the government's overall economic policies were so different from what he would have wished.

There was some discussion at the time whether the cheap money policy was inflationary. Dalton was advised by his Parliamentary Private Secretary, Evan Durbin, who was a professional economist, that it was. Dalton's memory was that, at the time, most other critical expert views seemed to be that, if inflationary, cheap money was not so to a major degree.[60] These days it might well be judged more harshly. Whatever its inflationary effect, the cheap money policy was inappropriate given the market's lack of confidence, which would be reflected when the commitment to convertibility on 15 July 1947 had to be implemented.

Low interest rates were intended to reduce the burden of interest charges on the Exchequer, particularly necessary in view of the programme of nationalization and the size of the sterling balances held in London in the form of Treasury bills.[61] 'A national debt of £24,000 million is only endurable if the average rate of interest is kept low.'[62] Low interest rates were not seen primarily as a means of encouraging investment though Dalton hoped that they might have that effect.[63] When the convertibility crisis struck, one of the government's measures to meet the emergency was to make cuts in capital projects. Attlee, in his speech of 6 August 1947, announced that the government would concentrate on capital projects that would give quick returns.[64] This suggests that there had not been sufficient attention to priorities in the public sector. This failure may well have been encouraged by the low interest rates available to the public sector. Any such failure *would* increase inflationary pressures.

THE CONVERTIBILITY CRISIS

At the beginning of July 1947, Dalton's reputation was at its highest. George Brown, his new Parliamentary Private Secretary, told him that he was thought of by some as a possible leader of the Party. He was one Minister who was generally believed to be on top of his job.[65] The reality was different. The market was about to intervene and destroy him. In his memoirs, Dalton describes 1947 as his *annus horrendus* in contrast to 1946 which was his *annus mirabilis*. His ease of mind during his *annus mirabilis* had always suffered from the dollar problem and from his inability to frighten his Cabinet colleagues with the mention of it. As things turned out, the American loan provided relief for a far shorter period than had been expected. The balance of payments turned seriously unfavourable during 1947. During 1946 the gold and dollar deficit had been steady at about $50 million a month. By February 1947 it was over $200 million a month. Dalton again warned his colleagues. He added, 'I will not have it said hereafter that I have left my colleagues unwarned until the eleventh hour.'[66] Early in May Dalton proposed a cut of £200 million in dollar imports. In June he was forced to settle for £100 million.[67]

It would have been possible to request US agreement to the deferment of convertibility. One excuse that could possibly have been advanced was the unexpectedly high dollar cost falling on Britain for feeding the Germans in the British Zone of Occupation.[68] No such application was made. The problem was that while Article 12 permitted modification of the Agreement, this was subject to the approval of Congress. Deferment would have involved a long and acrimonious debate in Congress. Dalton contemplated an approach to Washington in February 1947.[69] He was advised against, both by the Treasury and the Bank, primarily because there was no certainty that Congress would agree and raising the issue could itself be damaging.[70] Fforde considers that this advice was 'mistaken on a longer view'. Although neither the Finance Division under Eady in the Treasury, nor the Bank, thought it likely that the UK could sustain convertibility, and expected that eventually it would have to be suspended, neither seems to have anticipated the haemorrhage that would occur when sterling became convertible. Fforde suggests that, if they had, the advice to Dalton might have been different.[71] Postponement was discussed with William Clayton,

Under Secretary of State for Economic Affairs, when he visited London in June 1947. Clayton had come to talk about State Department business, the Marshall Plan. The Government's principal concern with the Marshall Plan at that time was to impress upon Clayton that, in Dalton's words, 'we are something more than a bit of Europe'.[72] By that time it was, in any case, too late to secure Congressional agreement to a delay in convertibility; Congress was about to go into recess.[73]

Sterling became convertible on the due date, 15 July 1947. The run on sterling developed slowly but then took off and became unsustainable. The market perceived an economy that could not pay its way, and leapt at the chance of dumping sterling for dollars. It still proved difficult to persuade Cabinet colleagues of the reality of the crisis. The decision to proceed with steel nationalization was taken in the midst of the crisis. It is not untypical that a Labour government should wish to show its virility particularly at those points when it feels itself to be under pressure from the market. Dalton himself was in favour of it. But he was resisted where he wished to conciliate the market, for example in his attempts to cut imports, particularly food imports. Dalton was at first unable to persuade his colleagues, even though he had on his desk a worrying report from Treasury officials. They had been considering the consequences for the British standard of life if the run on reserves continued, and Britain was unable to buy from the USA. Officials had developed ideas to meet such a contingency. The ideas would not be popular.[74] Dalton was considering resignation. If he had gone, Cripps might have gone with him. If they had resigned, Attlee would not have known where to turn, certainly not to himself or Morrison. Dalton and Cripps thought that the man to blame for the crisis was Attlee and attempted to persuade Bevin to step into Attlee's shoes. Attlee was to be the scapegoat for failures that they shared with him. For Dalton to blame Attlee, demonstrates how a Minister's mind can grow a carapace which protects it against consciousness of its own errors. It is, sometimes, the only way to keep sane. Attlee's responsibility was, no doubt, considerable, mitigated only by his total ignorance of economic policy. But Dalton was Chancellor. Here was a crisis which had developed on Dalton's watch and he had given the public little enough warning of it. In July the drain on the reserves rose to over $500 million, an annual rate of $6 billion. Dalton's arguments, combined with the continued outflow of dollars, at last prompted the Cabinet into some action and some promises of action.

ATTLEE ON THE STATE OF THE NATION

There was to be a debate in the House on 6–7 August 1947 on the State of the Nation. It was appropriate that the Prime Minister should lead on such an occasion. That he should lead was, however, made inevitable by the devaluation suffered already by the Chancellor's reputation. Dalton was to speak later in the debate. Advice flowed to Attlee from all the affected departments. The first question was how far the crisis could be blamed on others than the British government. How far could the government blame factors beyond its control? How far, for example, was the crisis attributable to the failure in Europe and the rest of the world to recover from the war as rapidly as had been hoped? If the world had lived up to expectations, there would now be alternative sources of supply. Dollars would be less important. It was the world that had failed Britain, not Britain that had failed. Leslie Rowan, Attlee's Principal Private Secretary, told Attlee in a minute dated 4 August 1947 that, bearing in mind the worldwide audience for his speech, 'I do not think it right psychologically to put it down to factors outside our control.'[75]

Yet, in a crisis, governments feel the need for excuses. What excuses were there? How far could the government excuse itself for previous inaction by claiming that there had been a recent increase in the outflow of dollars? In a minute of 5 August 1947, Leslie Rowan advised the Prime Minister, 'You *must* build up the story of the acceleration of the dollar drain ... You *cannot* leave the Chancellor to explain this; the Opposition charge is "you should have done this sooner". The responsibility for answering must lie with you.'[76]

But the best excuse was that the crisis would have occurred whatever Party was in power. In this speech Attlee insisted:

> Whether the Government of this country had been Conservative or Labour it would have been faced with this position. No doubt this Government like all Governments has made mistakes, but if we had made none we should not have escaped from these difficulties ... I am not disposed for a moment to accept the proposition that had we not fulfilled our election programme, had we followed a Conservative instead of a Labour policy, we should have been free from these anxieties. Nor do I admit for one moment the proposition that to unite the nation we must follow the Conservative policy, whatever that may be.

Officials debated how to find the right balance for the speech; bearing the reactions of the market in mind, it would be wrong to be too alarmist. Therefore Attlee drew attention to the remaining reserves of the sterling area. In addition to the £250 million still outstanding of the United States credit, there remained £125 million of the Canadian credit and the ultimate reserves of about £600 million. On the other hand, it had to be made clear to the British public that, little though they may have expected such a crisis, the situation was indeed serious. While providing the comfort that there were still some reserves, Attlee found it necessary to add: 'It must be remembered . . . that there is a point below which these ultimate reserves, which represent the reserves of the sterling area as a whole, cannot be allowed to fall.'

In his speech Attlee said:

> The problem of convertibility is . . . a problem of the world shortage of dollars more than a problem arising out of one particular loan agreement with America . . . But it is clear that in the world shortage of dollars the formal obligation under the loan agreement puts an increasing strain upon us. So far as non-discrimination is concerned, the provisions of the Loan Agreement have hardly been operative at all, because it is the low production in other countries that has driven us to buy so largely in the Western Hemisphere. The position is now however changing, and with the cuts in imports now proposed, the question of discriminating purchases becomes of much more importance, and will be a very real factor in our future food and raw material purchases . . . It is clear that unless the multilateral system can be made to work, and supported by adequate finance, it will become incumbent upon us to seek ways out of our present difficulties along other lines . . .

Therefore the government had asked for discussions with the USA, and Secretary of State Marshall had agreed. Without waiting for those discussions, the government had measures to announce. The measures would be directed to saving imports, to boosting output, and to expanding production in the Colonial Empire. The government was concerned to make available to the world the potential wealth of Britain's African colonies. These schemes would, however, take time to mature.

Attlee insisted that the government would not rely for salvation on Secretary Marshall's 'historic speech' which had led to the calling of the Marshall Aid conference in Paris which was about to convene. The outcome of that conference might help but the government would not rely on it. The government would act now. To increase coal production, the government would ask, as an emergency measure for a limited period, that the miners should work an extra half-day. There would be measures to increase production, particularly of steel, transport, and agriculture. The agricultural target would be 'nothing less than an extra one hundred million pounds worth of food by 1951–2, that is to say a 30% increase on present output.' Attlee referred to the 'Taunts on his addiction to austerity [which] have been hurled at the President of the Board of Trade.' This because of Cripps's wish to limit home consumption for the benefit of exports. But now: 'It is obvious that today we must lean still further to the side of export . . . Our target will be 140% of 1938 by the end of the first half of [of 1948] and 160% by the end of the year.' Controls would be reimposed over the engagement of labour. The government would also be proposing as an emergency measure, longer hours of work, for example, half an hour wherever it would contribute to increased production. When the present scheme ran out, there would be no more dollars for Germany. There would also be a cut in the foreign travel allowance: 'We are asking our Colonies to help us by restricting to essentials their claims on our foreign exchange resources which are of course also theirs.' He paid tribute to the Commonwealth. There was the credit from Canada, and, more recently, the action taken by Australia and New Zealand in, in effect, cancelling part of their sterling balances.

Then Attlee turned to the defence cuts which should have been made months before. 'We now expect to withdraw some 133,000 men from overseas by the end of December 1947 and to raise the total withdrawals from overseas stations to over 200,000 men by the end of March 1948.' The Defence White Paper had estimated that between 11 January 1947 and 31 March 1948 the numbers in the forces would be reduced from 1,427,000 to 1,087,000. The government had now decided to make a further reduction by 31 March 1948 to 1,007,000. Attlee added words that Dalton would have been happy to hear from him earlier. 'I do not pretend that the Government can contemplate with equanimity the retention in the Armed Services of so large a proportion of our manpower.' Therefore an 'exhaustive enquiry' had been instituted into the whole future of our Defence Policy and of the shape and size of the armed forces required to implement that policy.

There would be import cuts, especially of food and petrol. 'We must make an immediate and substantial reduction in our purchases of food from hard currency sources . . . of the order of £12 million a month.' But this, contrary to the Loan Agreement, would be discriminatory.

> In so far as these soft currency sources [for foodstuffs] are, all things considered, more favourable from the commercial point of view the question of discrimination under Article 9 of the Loan Agreement will not of course arise. Where, however, such purchases cannot be justified under the terms of the Loan Agreement, we shall be exploring the situation immediately with the United States Government to see what steps can be taken to enable us to obtain supplies from soft currency areas.

There was debate in Whitehall whether the Prime Minister should make reference to the need for counter-inflationary action. On the one hand he was told that

> A great deal of the criticism of the Government in recent weeks has taken the form of saying that their difficulties in getting exports are largely due to the inflationary pressures on home market. These are already considerable. The measures proposed in the speech will undoubtedly increase them. In very round figures we propose import cuts of £200 millions and an increase of exports of £100 millions. Possible cuts on investment outside housing cannot greatly exceed £200 millions. It is inescapable that some fiscal measures will be needed to prevent inflation.[77]

On the other hand, a minute from Dalton dated 5 August 1947 opposed any reference to physical controls and fiscal measures. It might be interpreted as committing the government to a Budget in the near future. Although in his Budget speech of 15 April 1947, he had referred to inflationary pressure and had therefore made some increase in taxation, Dalton was not now convinced that further action would be necessary.[78] Disregarding this advice from his Chancellor, Attlee warned that what the government was proposing would increase inflationary pressure. He appealed for wage restraint and to employers not to use wage increases to tempt workers away from other employers. He appealed for voluntary dividend restraint.

Among those who commented on early drafts of Attlee's speech was Clem Leslie, public relations adviser to Herbert Morrison, the Lord President. On 4 August 1947 he expressed concern that there might be an explosion of public opinion because the public had not been told the whole story sooner. But there would inevitably be an explosion if 'anything were held back *now*, or even if the Government managed to give the impression that something was being held back . . .' Leslie added, 'The general effect of the speech should be to make it perfectly clear that the Government really has grasped the nettle – "Out of this nettle danger we pluck this flower safety". The Prime Minister might do worse than quote Shakespeare on this occasion.'[79] The Prime Minister did not quote Shakespeare. But he did conclude his speech by evoking heroic days of the more recent past. 'Today we are engaged in another Battle of Britain.'

Attlee's speech incorporated much of the action recommended by the Chancellor at least a year before during his *annus mirabilis*. But Dalton had failed to win Attlee's support and his colleagues were recalcitrant. Such action would have drained the euphoria of the *annus mirabilis* but it would have been relevant to the needs of the economy. Even now it was uncertain whether the measures proposed would be enough. The appeal for longer hours would encounter strong resistance among trade unionists, particularly in the mining industry. Although action was to be taken on defence expenditure and manpower, more was needed but was subject to further review. The market wanted more action, particularly on public expenditure, and it wanted it at once, not after further consideration. The government had acted at last but, as was to become traditional with Labour governments, it had acted too little and too late.

Attlee had been assured that there was reason to believe that the very high drain in July was exceptional.[80] But in August it was over $600 million a month or an annual rate of about $7.5 billion. During the first six months of 1947, $1,890 million of the loan had been spent. The conversion of sterling into dollars was not limited to current transactions.[81] Dow calculates that the UK's current deficit could account for only three-fifths of the £1,250 million loss of gold and dollars in 1946 and 1947. The rest must have been due almost entirely to capital movements.[82] During 1947 the total drain on the sterling area's dollar pool was $4,100 million.[83] The loan had been intended to fund Britain's imports until 1951. At this rate it would be exhausted by the end of 1947.[84]

A delegation led by Sir Wilfrid Eady went to Washington on 17 August.[85] He requested the suspension of convertibility. The officials at the US Treasury took the view that it would not have been possible to agree at any earlier date or on any other facts beyond the figures about the 'run on the bank' which were then given to them.[86] On 20 August, it was announced that, with the agreement of the USA, convertibility was being suspended. All but $400 million of the American Loan had been drawn. Five days before, India had become independent. There was that great act of liberation and recognition to be placed in the balance. But for the economic policy of the government, it was a great and humiliating defeat.

One option considered within the Bank in the weeks before convertibility was a devaluation of sterling to, say, \$3.00.[87] Whether such a course of action would have made sense depends on whether the British economy, in the summer of 1947, while shortages still persisted, would have been capable of exploiting the competitiveness created by devaluation. If it could not, the devaluation would simply have worsened the balance of payments and have increased domestic prices of imports with its inflationary effect. Devaluing sterling at that point would necessarily have been accompanied by measures at least as stringent as those foreshadowed by Attlee on 6 August 1947. Those measures were based on the assumption that resources could be freed for exports both by restricting domestic consumption and by releasing manpower from the forces. The correct moment for a voluntary devaluation is always difficult to judge. It would have come earlier if the government had earlier been seriously engaged in encouraging manpower into the export industries instead of retaining them in the forces. Whether it would have been right in the summer of 1947 at least merited more sustained consideration. It is doubtful whether devaluation would have made convertibility viable.

DALTON'S FAILURE

The appearance of failure was the greater in that Dalton had appeared so confident. It did not help him that his confidence had been shared by journals such as *The Economist* and *The Times*. Nor did it help him that the ultimate responsibility for economic planning lay with Morrison, not with Dalton. Indeed Donoughue and Jones attribute the 'main blame' for the convertibility crisis to Morrison in his role as economic chief.[88] But that these two scholars can take this exotic view serves mainly to underline the dangers of splitting responsibility for economic management.

Three factors maximized the unfavourable public impact of the disaster. The first was that people had already that year suffered from the fuel crisis brought on by harsh weather and low coal stocks. Unemployment had risen temporarily to over 2 million. Production, including for export, was lost. 'Planning' had left the government unprepared. This experience had already made many even of its own supporters doubt the competence of the government. Whatever Minister is in fact responsible, and in this case it was primarily Emanuel Shinwell, Minister of Fuel and Power, economic problems of any kind seldom leave the Chancellor blameless in public opinion. Nor is this unreasonable. The Chancellor has eyes throughout Whitehall. If mistakes which can have a major impact on the economy are being made, the Treasury should know and should act.[89] Like Dalton over convertibility, Shinwell had shut his eyes to the risks of a disastrous coal shortage and the implications both for industry and for the public. He had preferred to make confident speeches. In their conduct as Ministers, Shinwell and Dalton appear to have had much in common. They also had it in common that Attlee, apparently, could not bear to be without them. Attlee's tendency was to keep his senior Ministers in office however old, sick or incompetent they proved.

The second factor was optimistic forecasting. Economic forecasting was, and has remained, a crude and unreliable craft. Any Chancellor who takes serious risks relying on an economic forecast is elevating optimism above experience. One excuse that Shinwell did not have was lack of warning – the figures available to him pointed the dangers. Dalton had an excuse. He was being advised before July that convertibility would create no special problem.[90] Fforde comments that there is little recorded evidence that the Bank gave clear warning to the Treasury or the Government that such a run was likely to happen. The Bank was the Government's source of market advice; the Treasury had little market expertise of its own on which to rely. The Bank, therefore, has to take the blame that Whitehall was taken by surprise.[91] On 8 July 1947, Dalton told the House, 'in large measure, 15th July has already been discounted and the additional burden of assuming these new obligations . . . will be noticeably less than many people may suppose'.[92] He says in his memoirs that he 'never gave this theory any credence' but his public statements reflected the 'theory'.[93] Perhaps he was merely displaying the brave face that Chancellors normally assume before disaster strikes. The predatory instincts of the market were not to be encouraged by Ministerial hesitations. But the advice Dalton was receiving was wrong.

The third factor was disappointment. It had been believed that the government could plan its way out of economic difficulties and was in the process of doing so. Labour, supposedly, was in the planning business. It knew, supposedly, how to manage an economy so that, by the time the convertibility commitment was to be implemented, the government would be ready for it. What had Dalton been doing for two years if by July 1947 he could not safeguard the economy against the convertibility of sterling? Should not exports, in accordance with such a plan, be soaring, particularly to North America whence came so much on which the British economy and its people were dependent? Should not investment have been managed, and manpower located, to ensure that the necessary export potential was available? His colleagues may have frustrated him particularly in the matter of defence cuts but it was disillusioning to find that, after two years in office, apparently successfully, the market had such little confidence in sterling and the British economy that it would seize so eagerly the opportunity to convert its sterling into dollars.

DIMINUENDO

Dalton remained in office for the time being. He was protected by the convenient fact that when convertibility was suspended, the House was in recess. Nevertheless, his reputation and his authority did not recover from the convertibility crisis. He and his colleagues had preferred to accept the American money rather than default on their election promises even though the Americans were demanding an impossible commitment. The decisive moment in Dalton's Chancellorship was not the convertibility crisis. It was his decision to recommend acceptance of the loan on American terms because he believed the government could not inflict further austerity on the British people. It was a decision made on behalf of the British people by a government that lacked sufficient courage to tell the truth because it feared defeat at a coming General Election, though it had an overwhelming majority in the House of Commons and the Parliament had four years to run.

Pimlott's ultimate excuse on behalf of Dalton and the Labour government is that the Loan Agreement was 'badly drafted'. Should the government have sacrificed its domestic expenditures, he asks, 'in order to fulfil the terms of a badly drafted Agreement'?[94] Dalton and the British government may not have liked the Agreement but it was clear enough and they had accepted it. It is disreputable to enter into an agreement if there is no serious intention of implementing it. This is even more the case if the government that lacks such a serious intention is the beneficiary of a considerable transfer of resources from its partner. However reluctant Dalton may privately have been about the convertibility commitment, he had no excuse – he had recommended it. The public perception of Dalton's performance was devastating. He had failed. The irony was that he had failed in public perception, and in the perception of his colleagues, because he had not achieved what he could not possibly have achieved. The Lord President's Committee also lost what reputation it had and, shortly afterwards, lost its responsibility for economic planning. Attlee remained under attack for lack of leadership. But he was protected by Bevin who would not have wished to serve under another Prime Minister and, evidently, did not want the job himself. Attlee's dependence on Bevin had implications for foreign policy. Bevin could be even more sure of victory in Cabinet. But although Bevin did not want to be Prime Minister, one gets the impression that perhaps he did not mind people trying to persuade him. Given that support, Attlee could exploit a Prime Minister's considerable power of manoeuvre among ambitious subordinates. A move here, a promotion there, can usually defuse even the most difficult situations. Attlee survived to mishandle other economic conjunctures.

Despite the experience of the dreadful weeks of convertibility, the Cabinet continued recalcitrant. Even with the support of Cripps, Dalton still had to compromise on his programme of import and defence cuts. All he could do was utilize the Chancellor's privilege to determine budgetary policy. Public expenditure decisions require collective consent. Budgets can be introduced with only the most minimal consultation with Cabinet colleagues other than the Prime Minister. It was the convertibility crisis that forced his hand. On 12 November 1947, Dalton introduced his fourth and last Budget. Its object was 'to strengthen still further, and without delay, our budgetary defences against inflation'.[95] This, he now recognized, must be the object of his emergency Budget. The Budget increased a range of consumer taxes. The official Treasury had pressed on Dalton the need drastically to reduce food subsidies. This he refused to do, as too risky politically. But he did freeze food subsidies at £329 million per annum.[96] Hall had originally been disappointed with the Budget because the surplus for which the Chancellor budgeted was too small to teach anything about the extent of inflation.[97] Dalton had estimated the Budget surplus 'above the line' at £318 million plus £48 million from additional taxes. In fact the surplus turned out at £635 million in 1947–8, larger than the Treasury's estimate and the largest in history. This was as compared with a deficit of £569 million in 1946–7. There is always a nice argument whether a Chancellor can claim to have done enough simply because it turns out that he has done more than he expected. He should have gone for a larger surplus earlier in view of the inflationary pressures in the economy. It is generally the case that action earlier has to be less deflationary than action later, but action later is better than no action at all. There was, however, one snag and it was not a small one. Although, at last, Dalton himself had been converted to the need for deflationary action, he had still not persuaded his Cabinet colleagues. Cripps would have to struggle to preserve the surplus which he inherited from Dalton.[98] His colleagues did not understand why, if the Treasury had money, they should not spend it.

Despite this final achievement, so great had been Dalton's fall from grace, so bitter the effect on his morale, that it was understandable that, experienced politician though he was, he should have overlooked the dangers of leaking his Budget secrets to a journalist he met on his way into the House to deliver his statement. No doubt he thought he was consolidating an old press friendship and that nothing could conceivably be made public before he had announced it in the Commons. This venial indiscretion led to his resignation whereas the convertibility humiliation had not. Dalton, clearly determined to present his offence as serious, at once offered his resignation and later pressed Attlee to accept it. He knew he had failed as Chancellor and his deflationary Budget had been a reversal of his longstanding policy. He probably felt that he could no longer do the job. A strong Chancellor with a record behind him of the successful conduct of economic policy would not resign for such a minor indiscretion, which probably had no effect at all on markets. It is easier to believe this straightforward account than the various conspiracy theories prompted by his resignation. There are those who argue that Attlee, perhaps, was not unwilling to see Dalton go.[99] He knew that Dalton had been trying to persuade Bevin to take over as Prime Minister.[100] He knew that Dalton had frequently spoken disparagingly of him. Dalton himself did not believe that Attlee wanted his resignation. According to his memoirs, the Prime Minister was deeply moved at their parting.[101] Attlee did bring Dalton back into the Cabinet as soon as he decently could. Even from the point of view of conspiracy theory, Attlee had more reason to maintain in office a devalued Chancellor who was no longer a threat than to appoint Cripps whose reputation was rising and who had been even more eager than Dalton to see Attlee replaced.[102] Moreover, by appointing Cripps to the Treasury as his only possible choice, Attlee united fiscal policy with economic planning, which he had not wanted to do. Other senior Ministers who had clashed with Dalton may have been happy to see him go, but there is no evidence that any of them pressed Attlee to seek Dalton's departure. The probability is that Attlee reluctantly accepted Dalton's resignation because he was determined to go.

The reputations of Chancellors are built on sand. They gain or lose reputation as a result of decisions taken under great pressure and for reasons well outside their own control. At their moments of difficulty, they do not find their Cabinet colleagues crowding in with offers of support. Thus was it with Dalton. Less sympathy is, however, necessary in his case than it might be with less complacent Chancellors. In retrospect, he became once more convinced that he had done well. He could find justification in the fact that, after he had left office, growth leapt forward. The deficit on the balance of payments was eliminated in 1948.[103] While this could be a source of satisfaction, it is also the kind of mortification that ex-Chancellors regularly suffer. The trouble is that better performance tends to be attributed to the man in office rather than to the man who prepared the ground. But faster growth under Cripps promised only to deceive. Dalton had left office before he could be personally blamed for the discovery that the convertibility crisis had been no more than a symptom of the fact that the UK economy was not performing as superbly as he had claimed. It was not his fault alone. His fault lay in believing the claim.

THREE

The Uncertain Austerity of Sir Stafford Cripps

The events of July–August 1947 led to a crisis of confidence in the government. Cripps had already come to the conclusion that Attlee was not strong enough, nor competent enough, as Prime Minister. He thought that Bevin should replace Attlee. Together with the office of Prime Minister, Bevin should hold that of Minister of Production. Cripps knew that Bevin would need an assistant actually to perform the duties of Minister of Production. He saw that role for himself. Once convertibility had been suspended, Cripps proposed to Dalton that, together with Morrison, the three of them should procure Bevin's succession. Various shapes were given to the intended reshuffle. In one, Dalton was to succeed Bevin as Foreign Secretary and Attlee was to succeed Dalton as Chancellor. What was most important to Cripps was that, as the only member of the government capable of organizing economic planning, he should be allocated what he saw as the principal economic responsibility within the government.

Political planning can be as difficult as economic planning and as uncertain in its results. Morrison, it turned out, was ready to see Attlee go but felt that he, not Bevin, should be the successor. Bevin did not want the succession for himself and would certainly not tolerate Morrison as Prime Minister. Like Franz-Josef Strauss, at a later date, he was quite happy as Foreign Secretary, to have Attlee, as Prime Minister, serving under him![1] Not merely did Bevin reject his proffered promotion, he turned on Dalton for his disloyalty. None of this deflected Cripps. On 9 September 1947, he went to see Attlee with the professed intention of resigning if he was unsuccessful in his objective of persuading Attlee to yield his position to Bevin. Their conversation took an unexpected turn. Attlee told Cripps that Bevin did not want to be Prime Minister and that he himself did not have the financial knowledge to be Chancellor of the Exchequer. However, he had a better idea that he wished to put to Cripps. Cripps emerged, not with Attlee's scalp, and not to draft a letter of resignation, but with the appointment he really wanted. Attlee had suggested that Cripps should be the Minister in charge of economic planning. At first the idea was that this appointment should be entitled Minister of Production. By the time the appointment was actually gazetted, on 30 September 1947, it had become Minister for Economic Affairs. Dalton noted the irony. Cripps had set out to replace Attlee by Bevin and had ended by himself taking over the most important part of Morrison's job.[2] Everyone, including Attlee, could now be happy except Morrison. Attlee had survived because of the support of Bevin. He had also bought off the most determined of his critics, the one who had actually been prepared to tell him to his face that he should go.

Attlee's offer to Cripps had not been the inspiration of the moment. He could hardly have been unaware of the threat to his position. As well as devising ways of deflecting his critics, he had been occupying his mind assessing the implications of the convertibility crisis for the structure of the government. He decided to establish an Economic Policy Committee (EPC), with himself in the chair, to deal with economic matters. This Committee would take over from the ad hoc meetings of senior Ministers which had been considering the balance of payments position as well as from the existing home and overseas economic committees. The members of the Committee would include the Lord President, Herbert Morrison, the Foreign Secretary, Ernest Bevin, the Chancellor, Hugh Dalton, the Minister for Economic Affairs, and the Minister of Labour, George Isaacs. It was obvious, Attlee wrote to Morrison on holiday in Guernsey, that the work of the Treasury had to be coordinated with that of the new Minister for Economic Affairs. It was for this reason that the Chancellor would be a member of the new Committee. But, continued Attlee, 'it would not be right to put the Chancellor of the Exchequer in charge of all economic affairs . . .'

Attlee then outlined the scope of the new Minister's work. He would oversee the whole production programme. With the Chancellor of the Exchequer, he would supervise and coordinate the import programme. He would preside over a Committee of Ministers with economic functions. The Economic Planning Group and the Economic Section of the Cabinet secretariat would work primarily to him. Finally Attlee listed his other proposed Ministerial changes. The list included Harold Wilson, who would become President of the Board of Trade and a member of the Cabinet.[3] That other rising star, Hugh Gaitskell, would succeed Shinwell as Minister of Fuel and Power but the post would no longer be in the Cabinet.[4]

Cripps became Minister for Economic Affairs. So he would have remained but for the accident of Dalton's resignation. Morrison, in his letters from Guernsey, had warned Attlee that although 'present circumstances require something more in the nature of a full-time executive Minister', nevertheless 'I think you will have to be careful about C's power to give directions to other Ministers if friction is to be avoided . . .' The press greeted the announcement of Cripps's appointment as that of an overlord over economic affairs, exactly the kind of interpretation that both Morrison and Attlee wished to avoid. There was even concern in the Private Office at No. 10 that Attlee himself was being shunted aside. On 13 October 1947, W. L. Gorell Barnes, an adviser to Attlee, wrote to Lawrence Helsby, Attlee's new Principal Private Secretary, 'I think we have got to be careful to ensure that the country is given the impression not that the Prime Minister has, so to speak, surrendered command, but rather that he has appointed a "Chief of Staff".'[5]

The reality of Cripps's position was different from the appearance. The probability is that a battle would have ensued between the Chancellor and the Minister for Economic Affairs for control over economic policy. Plowden comments that, in the brief period of six weeks after Cripps's appointment, 'there were already signs that confusion was developing between the Ministry for Economic Affairs and the Treasury.'[6] Cripps's star was rising. When a Minister is losing reputation, it is even more difficult for him to work in comfortable concert with a colleague who is gaining reputation. Nevertheless, if Dalton had survived, and recovered his spirits, it would have been found that the levers of power were still with the Treasury. Out of the confusion, Dalton would have emerged the victor. It was he, as Chancellor, who had at his disposal the effective levers of economic power. Cripps would rapidly have discovered that he was little more effective as a planner than Morrison had been. He did not have at his disposal what he would come to regard as the principal instrument of economic planning, the Budget. He did not even have a department of his own and lack of a department is always a disadvantage; particularly, perhaps, in any conflict with the Treasury. He had no executive powers. He could not give instructions to other Ministers who had their own responsibility to Parliament.

A coordinating role would hardly have satisfied Cripps; he would rapidly have found himself at war not just with the Treasury but with the Ministers responsible for the departments he was supposed to coordinate. He would have found himself merely a spectator of Dalton's economic management. Dalton's resignation rescued him from such a fate. Attlee, who had not wished to combine the Treasury and economic planning under one Minister, now found that he had no choice. Cripps became Chancellor while retaining economic planning. The newly created CEPS, of which Plowden was head, was transferred from the Cabinet Office to the Treasury. If there was fear of the concentration of power in Cripps's hands when he was simply Minister for Economic Affairs, that fear now certainly had a stronger basis. Owing to the increased responsibilities of the Treasury, a new Ministerial post was created, that of Economic Secretary. Douglas Jay was appointed to fill it. He had been an adviser to Attlee at No. 10 but had been returned to Parliament at a by-election. Later Jay was promoted to Financial Secretary. As time passed there would be frequent friction between the Chancellor and his economically literate Financial Secretary and, indeed, between Jay and Treasury officials.

A VARIED CAREER

Cripps had a volatile political career. He was the son of a peer, Lord Parmoor, also a distinguished lawyer who had been Lord President of the Council in Ramsay MacDonald's 1924 government after having started his political life as a Conservative MP. Like Attlee's other two Chancellors, Cripps attended a public school, but Winchester like Gaitskell rather than Eton like Dalton. He was educated as a scientist. When, as a barrister, he took silk, he was the youngest King's Counsel.[7] During the First World War he managed an ordnance factory, an experience which may have encouraged in him an illusion characteristic of many able industrialists. The illusion is that if only they were given charge of the economy they would know how to plan it. He had combined great success as a barrister with a commitment to socialism. But the practical commitment to socialism came late. He did not join the Labour Party until he was 39 years of age. He was a devout Anglican and eventually decided that socialism was the practical expression of his religious beliefs. Having at last joined the Labour Party, he was, almost immediately, appointed Solicitor General and entered the House of Commons at a by-election in the strongly Labour constituency of Bristol

East in January 1931. He was 42, relatively old for an aspiring politician. His sudden emergence was illustrative of the problems faced by the Labour Party in finding MPs competent to hold important offices. He made his maiden speech from the government front bench. Eight months later, economic crisis tore the Labour government apart.

Apparently after some hesitation, Cripps declined an invitation from MacDonald to continue as Solicitor General in the coalition government. Instead he stayed on the Labour front bench. He narrowly survived the 1931 General Election which reduced the Parliamentary Labour Party to only 46 members. In a Parliamentary Party of 46 members, he had every opportunity to make an impact, and his forensic skills ensured that he did. Later, he moved far to the left and advocated a united front of all left-wing forces including the Communist Party and, later still, a Popular Front of all opponents of fascism including 'bourgeois' opponents. His gyrations in policy led eventually to his expulsion from the Parliamentary Labour Party in January 1939. Despite this, Cripps served effectively in various positions in the wartime coalition government. He made a virtue of the fact that he was not a member of any political Party. Churchill appreciated his abilities, and in the early days of the Churchill coalition he served as Ambassador in Moscow, which brought him into contact with Stalin and Molotov. On his return from Moscow, he was, for a time, a member of the War Cabinet. In 1942 he became Minister of Aircraft Production, another appointment which might have deceived him into an exaggerated belief in the power of economic planning. Churchill also involved him in the question of India's future and, in the Attlee government, he would emerge as one of the strongest advocates of early Indian independence.[8] He rejoined the Labour Party only shortly before the 1945 General Election. This experience consolidated a relationship with Aneurin Bevan, who had also been expelled. It was a cement between them when Cripps became Chancellor. Cripps was always anxious to keep Bevan informed, sometimes using Plowden for that purpose.[9]

Perhaps Cripps's cast of mind, devout Anglican, scientist, lawyer, explains both his earlier extremism and his political gyrations. It was his nature to seek certainty. It was his frailty to find it too easily. There is, however, another factor which might explain, or help to explain, his difference from other politicians – he was an outstandingly successful man who had come into politics. Experience of other walks of life made Cripps impatient of the inadequacy of so many of his colleagues, whether in Opposition or in government. Cripps had this in common with Bevin.

They had both made their way, with outstanding success, outside politics. No one in any walk of life, even the most eminent, could say of them that they were 'just politicians'. Indeed they shared the impatience with mere politicians exhibited by so many captains of industry. Yet Bevin was to start with very wary of Cripps.

In July 1947 Bevin told Dalton that Cripps was more than halfway to Moscow. Cripps had recently invited Sir Roger Makins of the Foreign Office to lunch. According to Makins, Cripps had argued that the UK must be ready at any moment to switch its friendship from the United States to Moscow. Makins had been deeply shocked by the conversation and had reported it to Bevin.[10] There was, however, another explanation of Cripps's comment than the one Bevin conveyed to Dalton. Bevin was always too inclined to believe what his officials told him. Cripps had recently been at the receiving end of a battering from Will Clayton of the State Department and from Lewis Douglas, American Ambassador to London, about imperial preference. They had threatened him that unless Britain abandoned imperial preference, it would not be a beneficiary of Marshall Aid. When Cripps told them that he would recommend the Cabinet to reject their blackmail, the Americans moved on to Bevin where they hoped for a more receptive response but did not get it. Cripps was, no doubt, deeply offended both by the threat and by the appeal to Bevin over his head. He was unlikely at that moment to be in love with the USA.

Officials concerned with economic policy knew that in Cripps they had an exceptional Minister. Cripps was regarded as being different from other Ministers. He was known to be extremely able but also courteous.[11] He was prepared to listen to argument. Plowden writes that Cripps was 'a tremendously kind and generous man . . . His kindness, his generosity and his disciplined devotion to duty were inseparable from his strongly held religious beliefs . . . He had the clearest and most incisive mind that I have ever dealt with . . . He always tried to be scrupulously honest . . . He was a wonderful man to work for, and I had great affection for him.'[12]

ON INHERITING A WHIRLWIND

In the alternating drama of postwar economic management, Cripps appeared as an economic Chancellor who had inherited a whirlwind from a political Chancellor. In fact, his was a mixed inheritance that included advantages which his predecessor had not enjoyed. Most important, he was unquestionably pre-eminent over the whole economic field. He was following a Chancellor who was thought to have failed. The conclusion could hardly be escaped that Dalton's failure owed something to the insouciance of his colleagues. It could be an advantage that Attlee was now in the chair of the EPC. He had no excuse, therefore, for not being informed. The question that remained was whether the shock of the convertibility crisis was enough to persuade him to support his Chancellor. The government had survived the convertibility crisis – the whirlwind had, for the moment, passed – but it had been frightened enough to permit Dalton to introduce his deflationary Budget of November 1947. That Budget, as it turned out, had been a major step in the right direction. Cripps appeared to have inherited a whirlwind. In fact he inherited a substantial Budget surplus.

AN IRON CHANCELLOR?

Cripps had in the past given the impression that he was a brilliant man who had, nevertheless, no star by which to steer. Now he was Chancellor and the direction was only too clear. Could he lock on to a star and become an iron Chancellor? It was not difficult for Cripps to sustain the *appearance* of an iron Chancellor. The contrast with his predecessor would help with that. But could he manage the substance? Could Cripps, with all the advantages that Dalton had lacked, do the job at which Dalton had failed? During his two years in the Labour government Cripps had acquired a reputation for austerity. As President of the Board of Trade he had done what he could in an inflationary environment to encourage exports. For that purpose he had fought to reduce home consumption so that more resources could be transferred into the balance of payments. The question now was whether, as Chancellor, Cripps would be able to preserve his reputation for austerity in a more powerful and demanding role. He was not an economist. He had told Dalton that the Treasury 'was not his line of country'.[13] But he had learned on the job as President of the Board of Trade. Any residual ignorance could be compensated by singleness of purpose in a situation where singleness of purpose was emphatically what was required. The irony of Cripps's reputation as the iron Chancellor was that he himself was beset by doubts which never left him. Was he being too deflationary? He spoke of the 'narrow and difficult path between inflation ... and deflation.'[14] Then there were the political questions. Could he carry his colleagues with him? What would be the effect of what he was doing on Labour's electoral prospects? The trouble was that in economic policy there are no certainties, yet decisions have to be made and firmly implemented. Chancellors require a combination of humility and strength. Cripps's questioning was evidence of humility; it was the strength that was in the end lacking. He appeared strong and austere, but the reality was different. Gaitskell noticed the contrast between appearance and reality shortly after joining the Treasury in February 1950:

> One of the illusions about [Cripps] which I have discovered really is an illusion is that in bargaining either with his colleagues or with outsiders he is particularly tough. This is really not so at all. Indeed, we all of us are nervous when such discussions are going on lest he gives way too much. I find myself in the rather surprising position of having to stiffen him up on almost every occasion.[15]

RESTORING CREDIBILITY

In restoring credibility to the government, the first priority had to be the balance of payments. In 1948 the government embarked on a major expansion of agriculture. This had implications not merely for the Americans but also for those European suppliers who, pre-war, had relied on a surplus in agricultural trade with Britain to earn the convertible sterling which they could then use for their dollar purchases. By developing its agriculture, the UK was reducing the scope for a return to these pre-war trade patterns. On the other hand, any programme of agricultural expansion was bound to take time to make any impact. The effect of Britain's previous neglect of agriculture is illustrated by the fact that the UK was alone among European countries in allocating a large proportion of its Marshall Aid to American agricultural imports.[16] The fact that Britain did so may have encouraged the differentially favourable allocations which the UK received under Marshall Aid.[17] The need to save dollars would have a continuing influence on agricultural policies in the UK and in Europe in the years to come.

Other instruments employed were import control and export promotion. Import control implied coordination with other members of the sterling area. It would be of little use the UK depriving itself if other members of the sterling area dollar pool fed better because of UK sacrifices. Import control is inevitably a crude instrument; nevertheless, it may assist with the establishment of priorities, and it may therefore be defensible in situations of great difficulty. The controls did succeed in holding imports down well below pre-war levels. Rationing of food and petrol continued under Cripps in order to save dollars. Exports may have been encouraged by rationing the home market, for example for clothing, and by the planned allocation of resources.[18] As President of the Board of Trade, Cripps negotiated export targets with industry. In September 1947 he announced targets for 153 classes of exports. This made some political impact, but their economic value was questionable. In a world of inconvertible currencies, exports to soft currency areas did not translate into a capacity to pay for hard currency imports. The targets were not enforceable by the government. Exports grew during Cripps's three years but growth petered out in 1951.[19] Even before 1951, there was a tendency to exaggerate how well exports were growing. It was not that the figures were wrong; it was simply that the spectre of a German recovery was becoming a reality. In July 1950 Cripps told his ministerial colleagues that, taking the sterling area as a whole, 'If Marshall Aid was ignored, the year 1950–51 was expected to show a dollar deficit of over $200 million.'[20] Such success as was achieved by controls of this kind was attributable to the cooperation, while it lasted, of the Federation of British Industries and of the trade union movement, (where the principal advocate of cooperation was Arthur Deakin, General Secretary of the TGWU), to the sense of social cohesion which had so far outlasted the war, to fears of a return of pre-war levels of unemployment, and perhaps also to the fervent advocacy of Cripps himself.

Whether, in the circumstances of the time, controls were a better instrument than the price mechanism, is a subject still controversial. Politically they had the advantage, for a Labour government, of appearing fairer than the price mechanism. There were alternatives. One would have been to float the pound. This would leave it to the market to establish import priorities. It would promote exports if the capacity existed to supply them. If the capacity did not exist, export opportunities would help to create it. While the capacity did not exist, an overvalued currency had its benefits; imports were cheaper in terms of the domestic currency and additional inflationary pressures were avoided. But it could not be a policy for the long term to sustain an overvalued exchange rate. The market would be bound, eventually, to intervene. But in the environment of the time, that would suggest devaluation rather than floating. Floating, however attractive at first sight, would still present the problems already discussed. Above all, with Marshall Aid in prospect, there would have been little desire to add one more grievance to American discontent with Britain. While Marshall Aid was flowing, floating was unlikely to be a realistic option, but devaluation to another fixed rate against the dollar might become so. But Marshall Aid would certainly expire by 1952. As time passed, the attraction of floating would become increasingly apparent to many of those thinking about the British economic dilemma.

Cripps's second problem was inflationary pressure in the British economy. Inflationary pressure had implications for the balance of payments. It had many elements, none of them particularly new. There was still the pent-up demand from the days of war, and as a result the savings ratio was low. Though it was their government in power, the trade unions continued to demand a better standard of living for their members. Politicians believed that wage demands can cause inflation, a view controversial among many economists and in the trade union movement. The Labour government's policy with the trade unions contained many of the elements that became characteristic of postwar politics. There was exhortation to greater effort, and appeals for moderation in wage demands. Cripps was particularly eloquent in the cause. As he told his colleagues, it would be impossible to operate a planned economy if wages were free. On the other hand, in a free society, restraint must be voluntary, not by *diktat*. The government did achieve in February 1948, by agreement with the TUC, a voluntary freeze on most wage rates.[21] In the 1948 Budget the TUC was sweetened by Cripps's once-for-all capital levy. It has never seemed to the TUC that an incomes policy is of such advantage to its members as to be acceptable in its own right. The incomes policy always had to be accompanied by some action against the employers, however irrelevant to the inflationary situation or, indeed, damaging to the economy. In the five years that followed the end of the war the rise in wage rates was 4.4 per cent. This was only double the rise in the last five years before the war which had been 2.2 per cent.[22] Arguably this was a considerable achievement given the inflationary pressure, and the fall in unemployment from 2 million to 350,000.

The Labour government did have one other resource that future governments would lack. There was Ernest Bevin. Bevin could talk to his brothers with an authority that no other politician could match. But

Bevin was more influential with trade union leaders than with trade union members – with them he was a diminishing asset. The memories of trade union members were short. By the time Cripps became Chancellor, it was already seven years since Bevin had, in effect, ceased to be General Secretary of the Transport and General Workers' Union. Even he might prove an insufficient barrier against the rush for money in the pocket. The shock and the consequences of the 1949 devaluation did not help. When the 1949–50 wage freeze broke down and the 1951 rearmament programme added to the inflationary pressures in the economy, the first double-digit wage increases occurred.[23] Even if only as a support for planning and for incomes policy, inflationary pressures had to be 'disinflated'.[24] The fiscal balance in the economy had to be right so that resources could be freed for that high, if not always absolute, priority, the balance of payments. All this was leading to the use of the Budget as the principal instrument in directing the resources of the economy towards the priorities set by the government.

One problem for which there appeared to be no effective solution was that of the sterling balances. Robert Hall became Director of the Economic Section in the Cabinet Office almost simultaneously with Cripps's appointment as Minister for Economic Affairs. After six months in post, he had become worried without seeing any practical solution. 'I am beginning to wonder if we are not paying too high a price for the luxury of the sterling area: we are certainly paying too high a price for the luxury of not blocking the sterling balances . . .'[25] In 1947 the government had made arrangements with India and Egypt, the countries whose balances constituted the greatest potential danger. Rather over a third of the total balances were blocked and could only be drawn upon with UK agreement. However the government had completely failed to persuade India, Egypt or other countries that their wartime accumulations of sterling should be subject to cancellation or to any treatment more drastic than the system of agreed releases. The government had decided that it could not found its policy in this matter exclusively upon the economic interests of the UK. It could not disregard the urgent needs of some countries to spend sterling on rehabilitation after the war, or on essential development. In the summer of 1949 the government entered into an agreement with India which provided for agreed releases up to 30 June 1951.

An iron Chancellor will ensure that he controls public expenditure. The crisis had made it mandatory to consider seriously the question of public expenditure over the whole field of government activity. In principle, the battle to control public expenditure, while never easy, should, politically, now have been easier. From another point of view, the problem would be more difficult than ever before. Cripps would have to fight to preserve the surplus which he inherited from Dalton against the impatient demands of hungry colleagues. He would have to insist that his task was to restore the credibility of a badly damaged government and that there were now no options other than fiscal sanity. Over the years 1948–9 to 1950–1, the Budget surplus for the public sector as a whole averaged some £700 million per annum or about 7 per cent of GNP. These surpluses were sufficient to finance all, or nearly all, loan expenditure in the public sector.[26]

The difference between the estimate and the out-turn of Dalton's last Budget demonstrates that the problems here were not simply political problems. There were also the errors of forecasting upon which Ministerial colleagues will always be prepared to seize. They will use them as a weapon with which to defeat the Chancellor's demands. What right has he to press them when his own figures are so unreliable? Owing to the problems of forecasting, he may wish, particularly in the aftermath of a crisis, to err on the side of safety. He will be aware that just as the Treasury can overestimate a Budget surplus at Budget time, so it can underestimate it. He will wish to be risk-averse. Which risk is preferable? Is it the risk that may lead to a balance of payments crisis or the risk that leaves his colleagues short of money? From an economic point of view the second risk is clearly preferable.

But the politics will look very different. Colleagues may accept intellectually the argument that the government may have to do the saving if the population, by its spending, is creating inflationary pressures. But such an argument will not seem nearly as persuasive as the requirements of departmental expenditure and the fact that the government now has money in its purse. This is why Cripps, though in the advantageous position of succeeding to his post after a major crisis, would, in defending the surplus, have to fight very hard. As the last crisis recedes in memory, Ministers' inclination will be to take more risks with the national economy and less with the adequacy of their departmental budgets. Cripps said in January 1949 that Britain's consumption requirements were 'the last in the list of priorities. First [were] exports; second [was] capital investment in industry; and last [were] the needs, comforts and amenities of the family.'[27] This was a correct description of Britain's economic priorities. But, while such a statement reinforced the popular image of the iron Chancellor, it was not a statement of the government's real priorities. Those priorities began with the protection and even extension of the social services created during Dalton's Chancellorship. They made it virtually impossible to make policy sufficiently deflationary, certainly without very high levels of taxation. From the beginning, Cripps was riding for a fall.

MARSHALL AID

In a speech delivered on 6 June 1947 at Harvard, General George Marshall, US Secretary of State, had made his offer of economic supports for European recovery. Bevin had followed the offer up and the Committee for European Economic Cooperation (CEEC), consisting of representatives of the thirteen European nations willing and able to participate, sat in Paris from July to September 1947.[28] The Americans wanted a European plan, not just national plans. It would be the responsibility of the CEEC to provide it. In the chair of the CEEC was Sir Oliver Franks, Provost of The Queen's College, Oxford, philosopher and public servant. If the US Administration then felt able to recommend the plan to Congress and Congress was prepared to fund it, enormous resources would flow to Europe to implement a European Recovery Programme (ERP) administered by an American Economic Cooperation Administration (ECA). Thus there would be three stages, the European Plan, endorsement by the US Administration, and the approval of Congress. On the assumption that these three critical stages were successfully completed, Marshall Aid would contribute to solving the British balance of payments by providing a flow of unearned dollars. It would help with inflation by adding to the supply of goods for consumption or investment within the British economy. The only question was whether the Cabinet could bring themselves to accept it on the terms proposed by the Americans. Ministers were upset by the draft ERP agreement. It impinged too much on British sovereignty. Just as Ministers once contemplated refusing the American Loan, now they were contemplating refusal of Marshall Aid. There were seven meetings of EPC between 3 and 26 June 1948. Hall was contemptuous. 'I sometimes wish that Ministers *would* refuse the aid – it would be very popular and do the country a great deal of good, and people might actually work if they had the prospect of independence in front of them.'[29]

On 23 June 1948, Cripps put in a paper to the Cabinet entitled *Economic Consequences of receiving no ERP aid.*[30] It discussed the readjustments that would be necessary if the Cabinet decided not to accept Marshall Aid:

> These readjustments to the balance of payments would administer a number of violent shocks to the home economy at a number of separate points. The results to the structure of output, exports, investment, consumption and employment are extremely difficult to assess. We should be faced with an abrupt transition from a partially suppressed inflation to something not unlike a slump.

Compromise language was found, consistent with UK sovereignty. No doubt the US Administration realized the absurdity of handing a propaganda triumph to the Kremlin by insisting on terminology that the UK Government would not be able, honourably, to accept. Concessions on the terms were made. On 25 June 1948, the Cabinet consented to sign the Marshall Aid agreement.[31]

The Cabinet might well now have asked itself, do we need an iron Chancellor if we are to be the beneficiary of such largesse? Cripps, on the other hand, noted that Marshall Aid would be finite both in time and amount. How could he ensure that the British economy was self-sustaining without hardship for its citizens by 1952? Would the benefit of Marshall Aid go to investment or to consumption? One would build for the future. The other would merely cushion the present.

RELATIONS WITH EUROPE

With Marshall Aid, there emerged a further problem from which Cripps and the government could no longer avert their eyes. Bevin's principal concern had been European security. A series of treaties led up to the formation of the North Atlantic Treaty Organization (NATO), but there remained the problem of political and economic relationships with Europe. The Americans believed that European economic recovery required European political and economic integration. Europe was less enthusiastic for American political and economic remedies than it was for American money and American troops. The Americans therefore exerted pressure. They did not always do it with the diplomatic finesse that can safeguard the pride of the weaker partner. The pressure fell first on the UK. The UK had the most stable government in Europe, and was the obvious leader for European integration. The Americans were angered when the British government resisted the role which

Washington had allocated to it, that of leading the political and economic integration of Europe. When, in June 1947, Will Clayton of the State Department came to London to explain Marshall's ideas, Bevin told him that Britain was not just part of Europe. Clayton brushed aside any idea that there would be a programme of Marshall Aid for Britain separate from that for the rest of western Europe. Britain found that American ideas about European integration had to be taken seriously.

The British government could feel fairly confident in opposing any immediate idea of European political federation. It was not merely Britain that was not ready for such an adventure. Other European countries were not ready either. Britain insisted, against American opposition, on an intergovermental, rather than supranational, basis for the Organization for European Economic Cooperation (OEEC) which grew out of the CEEC. It rejected federalist sounding ideas for a European Parliament and ensured that the Council of Europe would also be intergovernmental. Economic integration was different and more plausible. If the Americans were to give aid, economic integration was the least they would expect. But what form should it take? The settled view in British government circles was that Europe was, for Britain, a diversion from the priority of pushing sales in hard currency markets. During these debates, British scepticism proved its value in puncturing dreams and in bringing down to earth far-reaching ideas with, at that stage, little real political support. But Britain's attitude was entirely negative and there was no attempt to elaborate practical ideas for forms of European integration acceptable to British public opinion and to that in the rest of Europe, particularly in France. Cripps made clear in discussions in OEEC that Britain would not accept any supranational control of Britain's economy. It was while these questions were under debate in Britain and in the rest of western Europe that the French came forward with an initiative of their own, the Schuman Plan for a European Coal and Steel Community, announced on 9 May 1950. The objective was more political than economic, reconciliation between France and Germany secured on the foundation of supranational control of Europe's coal and steel industries. Britain, though invited, refused to participate. The supranationalism implicit in the Schuman Plan was unacceptable. British policy makers, including Cripps, had in fact decided to exclude Britain from the construction of a new Europe.

ECONOMIC PLANNING

The agenda for Cripps's tenure of the Treasury could have exhausted a stronger man. But he had longstanding health problems that increasingly forced austerity upon him in his personal habits as well as in his public persona. He would require long periods of treatment and of convalescence. As was already clear with Bevin, and would too soon become clear with Cripps, neither had the health to cope even adequately with their responsibilities.

Cripps regarded himself as the Minister who alone understood economic planning. When still President of the Board of Trade, he had written the economic planning section of the first *Economic Survey*, that for 1947. The *Survey* conveyed his concept of planning. It was essentially *dirigiste* but it accepted that little could be achieved without voluntary cooperation. The *Survey* said:

> There is an essential difference between totalitarian and democratic planning. The former subordinates all individual desires and preferences to the demands of the State ... But in normal times the people of a democratic country will not give their freedom of choice to their Government. A democratic government must therefore conduct its economic planning in a manner which preserves the maximum possible freedom of choice to the individual citizens.

Priorities were required in the allocation of resources but controls had to be acceptable to public opinion. Voluntary cooperation and acceptability to public opinion had to be ensured by emphasizing the moral nature of the crusade on which he was engaged. Edwin Plowden has described Labour's concept of 'democratic planning'. He writes, 'It can best be described as a mixture of physical controls, nationalization and exhortation, laced with a dash of Keynesianism and a liberal dose of wishful thinking.'[32] Plowden, who was close to Cripps, had an idea of planning which was not that of the government. In his view, planning should work towards its own abolition. 'I was ... convinced that fiscal and monetary policy ... would become increasingly important in the management of the economy as time went on.'[33]

Civil servants and economists were particularly contemptuous of the government's approach to planning. Otto Clarke, who had the principal responsibility for drafting the *Economic Survey*, complained in early February 1947, after a Ministerial meeting with the Prime Minister in the chair: 'Not a single one of them with the shadowiest concept of what they meant by planning.'[34] But it was not just the Ministers who could not plan. Nor could the economists. They had arrived on the governmental scene with high pretensions but less understanding. Even if the methodology had been available, the information was lacking. A great deal of time and effort was devoted to preparing long-term economic surveys when the economy was subject to such uncertainty and, consequently, to such swings in policy, that the calculations and extrapolations were virtually valueless.[35] Any resemblance between forecast and out-turn was purely accidental. In 1948 Cripps visited France to find out how planning worked under Monnet's *Commissariat Général du Plan*, but no lessons were brought back and it is questionable whether there were any. The attempt to plan under the Attlee government was a diversion from serious thought about the economy. Ministers were to blame for entertaining the ideology without the least idea of how to implement it. The economists were to blame for holding out false hopes.

Cripps gradually learnt the inadequacy of controls as an instrument of planning. They were not sufficiently powerful and could not prevent the cycle of biennial crises which was becoming characteristic of the British economy. They stood in danger of declining public acceptability. In his April 1948 Budget, he said, 'the new task of the Chancellor is not merely to balance the Budget – it is a much wider one – to match our resources against our needs.' Plowden described it as the first 'planning' Budget.[36] How far, at that stage, Cripps accepted the primacy of the Budget over physical planning is less sure. It appears to have been the devaluation crisis and its outcome that finally influenced him. After it, he circulated to the Cabinet a memorandum prepared by the Treasury which set out the government's primary aim in economic policy. This was to manage demand and offset cyclical fluctuations in the economy through fiscal policy without producing either inflation or unemployment.[37] Plowden comments that this approach illustrated 'both that ministers and officials were at this time moving towards Keynesianism and that planning was increasingly being seen in terms of demand management'.[38] Sir Edward Bridges attributes to this time what he describes as the biggest change of all in Treasury business since the end of the First World War. This was 'the assumption by the Treasury of the duties of Economic Coordination which has enormously widened the scope of Treasury business and increased the weight of its responsibilities'.[39] It was not the case that the complete Keynesian philosophy had been accepted. There was as yet no suggestion that demand management might, at times, require a Budget *deficit*. Any such suggestion would still have been regarded as dangerous heresy. Given the existing inflationary pressures, it was better that it should be so.

By the time of his Budget speech on 15 April 1950, Cripps regarded the Budget as 'the most powerful instrument for influencing economic policy which is available to the Government'.[40]

He added, 'Excessive demand produces inflation and inadequate demand results in deflation. The fiscal policy of the Government is the most important single instrument for maintaining that balance.'[41] Thus the Budget was the most powerful instrument. It was not the *only* instrument. Cripps consolidated the Keynesian revolution in British economic policy. But controls and physical planning retained their validity in his concept of economic management. He would have been embarrassed to deny them any role. An example of Cripps's continued belief in controls was his refusal to increase short-term interest rates, despite advice from the Treasury and the Bank of England, and despite warnings that his disinflationary fiscal policy could be offset by an increase in bank credit. Dalton's return to the Cabinet as Chancellor of the Duchy of Lancaster in May 1948 increased the political difficulty of any change in the cheap money policy. Neither Cripps, nor his successor Gaitskell, could be persuaded to allow a rise in money rates. Fforde comments, 'There was a strong element of irrationality or even hysteria about this opposition to any use of the interest-rate weapon. High interest rates ... belonged to the restored Gold Standard, to depressive deflation, and to heavy unemployment.'[42] Plowden cites this as 'another example of [Ministers'] dislike of the price mechanism and preference for controls which they did not really know how to use'.[43]

Each Chancellor now had to make a 'Budget judgement'. The 'Budget judgement' was concerned with 'demand management'. That judgement balanced many factors, not always pointing in the same direction. There was the pressure of inflation in the economy and how far it could be disinflated without turning into deflation. There was the quantity of resources available in the economy, the demands on them, and how the Chancellor wished to influence the distribution of demand. Influence did not amount to control. It was impossible to be sure how the influence of a Budget would operate. The Budget judgement was truly a judgement. Though the Chancellor came down to the House of Commons to announce his Budget judgement as though his last consultation had been on Mount Sinai rather than at the Treasury, his judgement was not backed by anything in the nature of scientific accuracy either in the calculation of resources or as to the effect of any of his measures on inflation or exports. The judgement would almost certainly be to some degree wrong. Therefore, among the judgements, was a judgement of risk. Even with an iron Chancellor, it would take account of political pressures as well as of economic priorities. Yet this judgement, with all its uncertainties and risks, was now indicated as the most powerful instrument of economic management available to the government.

Among the elements that went into the Budget judgement was the level of public expenditure. Too high and it would eat unacceptably into resources available for exports. Too low and it would eat unacceptably into the support the Chancellor could expect from his own Party. Cripps laid down the principle that extensions to the social services must be limited by the country's ability to pay for them. That ability would increase only with national income.[44] In his 1949 Budget, Cripps enunciated the principle that there must be a ceiling on the social services until new wealth had been created. But, as with many Chancellors to come, Cripps's severity was directed more to the future than to the present. Politically that was easier. It did not deprive colleagues of their existing budgets. It merely warned them about the future. The problem about the future is that it is unknowable. The principle that extensions to the social services must be limited by the country's ability to pay for them is fine provided there is no extension until an increase in the country's ability to pay has been actually achieved. But spending Ministers will complain that such a principle, interpreted in this way, imposes an unreasonable restriction on their ability to plan the development of their services.

There were two massive, and increasing, elements in the public expenditure side of the Budget about which Cripps was bound to be concerned. These were food subsidies and the National Health Service. In his 1949 Budget he proposed to place a ceiling on food subsidies. In his 1948 Budget he had hoped to limit food subsidies to £400 million. In fact, to encourage wage restraint, they had been allowed to rise to £485 million. In the coming year they were likely to rise further to £570 million. Cripps proposed for the future a ceiling of £465 million.[45] The National Health Service was politically even more sensitive. The political sensitivity lay not just between Cripps and the Party or between Cripps and the electorate. It lay between Cripps and his old ally and friend Aneurin Bevan, Minister of Health. The NHS was the government's greatest domestic achievement. But its cost was rising fast. Here was a crisis, personal and political, waiting to break. It would be the ultimate test which would determine which came first, Cripps the iron Chancellor or Cripps the politician.

The emergence of demand management had unspoken implications for Labour Party philosophy. If the Budget rather than physical planning was the principal instrument for influencing economic policy, what had become of socialism? Socialism was about planning, not about influence. Had socialism been replaced by Keynesianism which also operated through the Budget? Or had Keynesianism become the road to socialism? Keynes's own objective had been to save capitalism, not to further socialism. Was it now necessary to redefine socialism as relating not to physical planning or even nationalization but to some other concepts such as public expenditure for the purposes of social and economic welfare or even, vaguely, 'equality'. Some of the best minds in the Labour Party would, in the next few years, exercise themselves attempting to find new definitions of socialism consistent with Cripps's discovery. It would cause a great deal of controversy within the Labour Party between those, considering themselves enlightened, who had adopted Keynesianism, public expenditure, and equality, and accordingly produced new definitions of socialism, and those considered blinkered who held fast to older definitions of socialism. In the end it would be found that both parties to this controversy were mistaken, the modernizers as well as the traditionalists, and that socialism had been sucked dry by its irrelevance.

STERLING DEVALUED

For the Labour government, the convertibility crisis was not the end of unpleasant surprises. Cripps had set himself his own litmus test, the exchange rate of sterling against the dollar. In 1945 it had been set, despite contrary indications, at $4.03 to the pound. Three years on, that exchange rate was under challenge. The scarcity of dollars, the problems of exporting to the USA, the severely adverse balance of trade with the USA, all these interconnected facts were bound to inspire the question whether European currencies as a whole, and not sterling alone, stood at a realistic exchange rate against the dollar. As there was a scarcity of dollars, the appreciation of the dollar against other currencies was the appropriate response. The question became particularly pressing when at the end of 1948 the USA entered a recession. While short by some subsequent standards, it lasted well into 1949. Exports to the USA fell, European recovery was damaged. But no country suffered as much as did the UK. For the UK, with its dollar problem seriously worsened by the American recession, the costs and benefits of devaluation were bound to return to the agenda. It was not simply a failure of *British* exports. Something like half the deterioration in sterling area dollar earnings in 1949 related to goods originating outside the UK.[46]

The utility of devaluation against the dollar to balance the UK's external account had been frequently discussed during the war. A serious analysis of the optimal sterling-dollar exchange rate would seem to have been an appropriate response to the dollar shortage at any time after the conclusion of the war. It was discussed by officials when the current account moved back into surplus in 1948. The surplus concealed a continuing deficit with the dollar area balanced by an inconvertible surplus of 'unrequited' exports.[47] It also concealed the fact that Britain's economic performance, although it appeared good in London, was already falling behind that of its continental neighbours, largely because of the beneficial effect on them of Germany's accelerating recovery. Cairncross has said, 'If you have hard currencies and soft currencies the natural thing to ask yourself is whether you shouldn't try and make the hard currencies softer and the soft currencies harder by changing their relative price.'[48] A possibility informally discussed between February and September 1948 between the Treasury and the Bank of England was to float the pound. The conclusion was that the case was not proven.[49] Dollar exports were in short supply and inflation in the USA might produce the same effect hoped for from devaluation.[50]

Devaluation was a subject that Cripps did not want discussed, particularly in public. To discuss it in public could make it unavoidable. In November 1948, Sweden wished to raise the question of devaluation in OEEC. It was firmly advised by the UK to forget the whole subject.[51] Yet it was proving impossible to keep the subject off the public agenda. On 16 February 1949, John W. Snyder, US Treasury Secretary, gave evidence in public to a Joint Congressional Committee:

> When we are contributing billions of dollars to build up the European economies, it becomes a matter of grave direct concern to us insofar as the exchange policies which a country may be pursuing tend to retard its exports or misdirect its trade and increase its Western Hemisphere deficit, and thus indirectly increase its calls upon the United States for assistance. Where an exchange rate adjustment is indicated, a member country will be expected to propose a new par value to the International Monetary Fund.[52]

Edwin Plowden describes Snyder as 'often overtly anti-British and diffi-cult to deal with'.[53] But, in the circumstances, it would have been odd if Snyder had not been addressing his mind to a possible realignment of European currencies against the dollar. However inconvenient such public statements were for the British government, and even though they would make the fight for the sterling parity even more difficult, Marshall Aid dollars gave Snyder a right to speak as he did.

Alec Cairncross, Economic Adviser to Harold Wilson at the Board of Trade, was advocating devaluation at the end of 1948.[54] By March 1949, Robert Hall and Edwin Plowden had both come to the conclusion that devaluation was inevitable.[55] Senior Treasury officials had not yet accepted the necessity of devaluation and the Bank of England remained opposed. The Bank was, reasonably enough, fearful that Ministers would refuse to accompany it by the necessary deflation.[56] Cripps was a deter-mined opponent. Though the balance of payments was deteriorating rapidly and reserves were being lost, Cripps remained persuaded that the problem was a temporary one due to the American recession and that, pending an American recovery, it could be handled by direct con-trols on imports from the USA. On Cripps's advice, the Cabinet cut dollar expenditures by 25 per cent over the coming year, fresh dollar commitments were suspended until the end of September, and a Conference of Commonwealth Finance Ministers was called for July.

Meanwhile the UK continued to discourage discussion of devaluation at international institutions such as the OEEC. Cripps sent a personal message objecting to the matter being raised by the USA in the IMF. Despite this plea, the IMF, on 6 April 1949, as a result of US pressure, voted to ask the Managing Director, Camille Gutt, to begin an enquiry into European exchange rates. Gutt himself was in favour of devaluation. By May 1949, both the US Treasury and the ECA believed a devalu-ation of the pound to be an urgent necessity. In the same month, a Report from the Economic Commission for Europe concluded that 'European currencies are overvalued in respect to the dollar'. The pros-pect of devaluation was discussed with varying degrees of openness in the British press.[57] In June, British officials were in Washington. There was a general assumption that the UK would devalue before long and that if it did not it certainly ought to. British officials challenged the US Executive Director of the IMF about the US action in raising the matter at the Fund. He replied that if devaluation could not be discussed by the IMF, what was the IMF for?[58]

Certainly by the spring of 1949 at latest, devaluation was the appropriate step for sterling, if floating was ruled out, and, given the recovery of output and investment on the continent, for Europe also. Cripps continued to fight against it. The Cabinet was not, in this case, an obstacle. They would do what they were told about the value of sterling, even if they would fight against consequential cuts in public expenditure. To put the most sympathetic interpretation on Cripps's view, there was in it something of the disposition that governed so many expensive British policies. Britain was a global power with global responsibilities, including responsibilities to the sterling area. Cripps would accept instructions neither from the USA nor from the market. Resentment against the USA was not a policy. Moreover, behind these elevated sentiments was a more political consideration. Devaluation would have to be accompanied by politically unpopular deflation. The government entertained the illusion that deflation could be avoided if the parity was maintained. The austere and sick Chancellor was, at that stage, no more ready for deflation, and the battles in Cabinet that such a policy would require, than were his Cabinet colleagues or his Party in Parliament. There was in Cripps's attitude much of pride – devaluation would be a defeat for his policies. There was in it much of conviction. He appears to have thought that it would represent the triumph of the market over socialist planning. But his convictions were not being challenged by adequate advice from the Treasury because the Treasury itself remained opposed. Cairncross complains that the problem was always put to Ministers as the devaluation of sterling rather than as the devaluation of sterling specifically against the dollar. He adds, 'I do not recall any paper which set out the case for and the case against devaluation for the benefit of ministers . . .'[59]

Robert Hall advised Cripps to devalue as early as 6 April. Hall later reflected on why devaluation had become necessary. 'It gets more and more of a bitter joke, that Ministers should believe so strongly in planning and be so anxious to do nothing about it that we have been gradually driven in despair to disinflation, to devaluation, and now are trying to get rid of controls to restore some semblance of competition.'[60] But although Hall, as Director of the Economic Section of the Cabinet Office, had direct access to Cripps, he was not part of the Treasury. This robbed him of influence. When faced with momentous decisions, Cripps was not himself knowledgeable enough to rely on Hall against the advice of his permanent Treasury officials. Edwin Plowden *was* in the Treasury as Head of the CEPS. But, able though he was, respected though he was, he was not part of the permanent establishment. He was in the Treasury as a planner, not as an expert on exchange rates. The probability was that Cripps would not move until the official Treasury moved. They, on the other hand, were likely to be slower in moving than they should have been due to the known views of their Chancellor and his extraordinary dominance in argument.

On 28 June 1949, Cripps told EPC, 'I do not think this is the right time to carry it out, whatever the ultimate decision may be.' He did advocate cuts in dollar imports, cuts in food subsidies, and action to preserve the wage freeze. A rise in Bank Rate should be deferred.[61] The Bank of England was still opposed to devaluation. Opinion in the Treasury was divided, though supporters of devaluation like Hall, Plowden and Leslie Rowan, now back in the Treasury, had been working hard. They pointed out that UK exports had become uncompetitive in the USA, that severe deflation was implausible, and that there was no time for improvements in productivity to reverse the payments trend. Those against devaluation, including the Bank of England, argued that it did not go to the root causes of Britain's problems which really were excessive public expenditure, nationalization, the burden of sterling liabilities and the US recession. Their conclusion was that, given the price elasticities of UK exports and imports, devaluation would have an adverse effect on the dollar balance. In any case the UK could not expect to devalue alone. Devaluation by others would deprive the UK of a good part of its expected added competitiveness. The Cabinet ruled out devaluation and also any attempt to tighten monetary policy by raising interest rates which the Bank of England and Robert Hall recommended.[62] Ministers continued to prefer controls to the price mechanism. Herbert Morrison alone supported devaluation.[63]

Morrison, the planner who had been rejected, now appears to have had a firmer grasp of the realities than either the Chancellor or his predecessor. He was prepared to argue in Cabinet that there was a relationship between high public expenditure and the country's dollar difficulties.[64] This view, unsurprisingly, was attacked by Dalton. Any idea that public expenditure was too high merely reflected reactionary views in the City as relayed by *The Economist*.[65] Cripps was wanting to cut food subsidies by £100 million. There was an obvious connection between food subsidies and the balance of payments. He found himself opposed by Dalton and, in respect of food subsidies, by Morrison.[66] It would cause grave political trouble. It would dishearten the Party's followers in the country. It was a conspiracy by Bridges, Plowden and the Bank. Cripps weakly abandoned the cuts which left him relying only on the controls on dollar imports.[67] Dalton's return to the Cabinet had not been welcomed among officials.[68] When Dalton had been Chancellor, Cripps had given him faithful support in his battles within the Cabinet. Dalton saw no reason to repay the debt.

When EPC met on 1 July, Cripps was still against devaluation. He could not forecast to what level it would be necessary to devalue or whether that level could be maintained. He was anxious not to devalue the sterling balances. The only circumstances in which he would be ready to consider devaluation were if the sterling balances were guaranteed.[69] The sterling balances were, for Cripps, a strong moral argument against devaluation, shared by Sir Edward Bridges. Bridges gave devaluation the code name CALIBAN in order to signal his detestation of the proposal. It does, however, appear that even Cripps was beginning to consider the circumstances under which he might agree to devaluation.[70] Only Morrison was prepared at that meeting to contemplate devaluation.

American pressure was building up. There was debate in Washington as to how the UK could be influenced to act in its own interest. But American views were not disinterested; the USA wanted a market solution to the problems of Britain and the sterling area. Controls and discrimination might now be a necessary feature of British policy, but they must not be allowed to become a permanent feature.[71] Devaluation of sterling was the *sine qua non* of convertibility and non-discrimination. On 7 July Snyder arrived in London. It was the day that Cripps emphasized to the House of Commons that devaluation was not on his agenda. The strength of his words would later cause him distress. Snyder stressed that his government was convinced that devaluation was an essential element in any long-term solution to Britain's dollar and general balance of payments problem. Cripps replied that devaluation would be acceptable only within the limits of a general settlement the nature of which he was, as yet, unprepared to elaborate. Cripps tried to persuade Snyder to agree to a communiqué saying that devaluation was not 'an appropriate measure'. It can hardly have been a surprise that Snyder refused. The communiqué only said that devaluation was not discussed. Snyder returned home talking of 'a fundamental difference' between the US and the UK in their approach to the problem of economic recovery and stability. The only positive outcome of the talks was an agreement to hold further official and ministerial meetings in Washington at the end of August and early September.[72]

At this point, with the run on the reserves continuing and Cripps in poor health, he became distrustful of his officials. It is typical of Ministers, when policy has gone awry, that they should blame their officials. Gaitskell had a private conversation with Cripps in early July. Cripps told him that 'One of my difficulties is that my official advisers are all "liberals" and I cannot really rely on them to carry through a "socialist" (sic) policy . . .'[73] Gaitskell himself was very suspicious of officials. It was his view also that they were too liberal. They did not understand a socialist policy. On 8 July, Cripps conveyed to Plowden the same fears he had expressed to Gaitskell. Plowden told Hall. Hall's enthusiasm for his Chancellor was fading.[74] Plowden, too, was now falling out with the Chancellor he had served so faithfully for two years. He was threatening to resign because he and Cripps were now out of sympathy.[75] A Ministerial meeting at Chequers criticized 'reactionary (*laissez-faire* or liberal) officials and economists'. Gaitskell was acutely worried by those Treasury officials for whom convertibility was the main long-term objective, with devaluation and heavy deflation at home as the immediate steps.[76] It had been decided at Chequers that Ministers would have to supervise the preparation of policy more closely, and that they ought to recruit a sympathetic economist to help.[77]

At this crucial moment, on 18 July, Cripps had to go to Switzerland for treatment and to convalesce. Attlee announced in the House that he was taking charge of the Treasury in Cripps's absence and that he was establishing a triumvirate of three to assist him. It consisted of Harold Wilson, President of the Board of Trade, Hugh Gaitskell, Minister of Fuel and Power, and Douglas Jay, Economic Secretary to the Treasury. These were the three economists in the Attlee government. Gaitskell and Wilson had been first elected to Parliament in 1945. Jay was an even more recent recruit. The younger generation were coming forward, but almost too late. Whether by coincidence or not, with Cripps due to leave for Switzerland, these three socialist economists were all now in the course of changing their minds and coming out in favour of devaluation. Did the dominant figure of Cripps restrain his subordinates from enunciating the conclusion that had become obvious? There is some conflict as to who changed first and who influenced whom. Jay told Cripps of his change of mind just before he left for Switzerland.[78] But the three economists all ended up in the same position, that sterling must be devalued. Others had been wiser earlier, and it was very late.

On Wednesday 20 July, Douglas Jay lunched with Gaitskell and, between them, they rehearsed the arguments that had won them both over, rather late in the day, to devaluation:

(a) Because exchange control had clearly not been able to prevent the continuation of the capital drain; devaluation on the other hand would not only check it, but bring the money back.

(b) The US Government were clearly not going to be able to do anything in the short term to help and might insist on very stiff terms for the long term.

(c) The Commonwealth countries were obviously influenced in their import policy by relative prices of sterling and dollar goods. Thus the control over dollar expenditure was clearly much looser than we had supposed.

(d) The prospect of expanding exports to dollar areas was probably greater than we had at first supposed – because of the great profitability of exporting to these areas as a result of devaluation.

(e) To delay devaluation might be exceedingly dangerous because as the reserves fell we should find it more and more difficult to carry out the operation without risk of a 'collapse of the currency': in consequence we would be completely dependent on the USA and be at their mercy.[79]

Harold Wilson, advised by Cairncross, had come to the same conclusion.[80] Gaitskell and Jay did not trust Wilson. Jay has commented, 'he changed sides three times within eight days and finished up facing both ways'.[81] No doubt there was some manoeuvring. With the Chancellor so sick, the minds of ambitious men might well turn to the succession.

Even now, with the reserves running out, and with key Ministers converted to the necessity and inevitability of devaluation, there was debate in London as to what conditions could be imposed on the USA in return for a devaluation of sterling. What would the USA pay to dissuade the UK from committing economic suicide? There was already Marshall Aid but there were, of course, many other ways in which the USA could help. They could certainly reduce their tariffs. They could, perhaps, take steps to increase US imports from Europe. They could, perhaps, find some way of providing extra US support for those sterling area countries whose dollar earnings were falling due to the recession. There could be an increase of US investment in Europe and European colonies.[82] The significance of all this was, in reality, to find some means of saving face. If there could be some kind of comprehensive settlement of the relationship between sterling and the dollar, devaluation would look more respectable.

By 21 July the gold and dollar reserves had fallen below £400 million. Gaitskell, Jay and Wilson met and decided to advise the Prime Minister to devalue sterling. Bevin and Dalton soon agreed. A few days later, Bridges sent a note to Attlee expressing the combined view of himself, his two Second Secretaries, and of Robert Hall and Edwin Plowden, supporting a 'substantial' devaluation. Perhaps the Treasury had been deterred from giving this advice earlier by loyalty to their Chancellor. Cripps's absence was certainly freeing minds to think afresh. Bridges added that it was 'essential' that other accompanying steps should be taken to reduce inflationary pressures operating in the economy which 'would soon cancel out any benefits to be obtained from devaluation'. Plowden tells us that they had in mind a 5 per cent reduction in public spending in the current and succeeding financial years and a 'moderate rise in money rates of interest'. Attlee at first cavilled at any idea of deflationary measures but was eventually persuaded that there was a connection between budgetary policy and the external account.[83]

The debate in London turned to the date of the devaluation. Treasury officials had come late to the conviction that sterling should be devalued. They now thought that the devaluation could wait until early September when Cripps would be in Washington to meet Snyder and for the regular meeting of the World Bank and IMF. It would, they argued, avoid international dislocation and resentment. In this they were backed by Harold Wilson. Morrison and Jay wished to act at once. There was always a danger that news of the government's intentions would break and there was an urgent need to reduce pressure on the pound. Attlee and Gaitskell took a more political view. They did not wish it to appear that the UK had simply submitted to American pressure. They wanted Cripps to have returned to England so that he could explain the decision to the country. In August 1947 it had been Morrison rather than Attlee who had explained to the country the suspension of convertibility.[84] Now, apparently, it was for Cripps, not for Attlee, to inform the country of this further setback in government policy. This calculation pointed to late August for the announcement. On 29 July, with Oliver Franks, Ambassador to Washington, present, the Cabinet agreed in principle to devaluation. The Prime Minister was given authority to take such steps as he felt necessary. He told the Cabinet that he would do whatever was needed during the holidays as it would look bad to summon Ministers.

All that was now required before final ratification of the decision was to secure the assent of the man who would have to announce his defeat to the country. Attlee, it was decided, would write to Cripps in Zurich. Wilson, who would be holidaying nearby, would deliver the letter to Cripps. The reasons advanced in the letter to persuade the reluctant Cripps were that the expectation that sterling would be devalued was causing an unwillingness to hold sterling or to buy British goods, that short-term financial assistance from North America was unlikely and that long-term help could not be expected until the reserves fell to crisis levels. The letter added that officials 'unanimously' believed that inflationary pressures must be tackled urgently. Attlee favoured a date for the devaluation before the Washington talks to avoid the impression that Britain was 'trading an offer of devaluation for concessions' from the Americans.[85] When he received the letter, Cripps insisted that a final decision should be delayed until his return to London but his preliminary view, to which he adhered after his return, was that devaluation should not be announced until 18 September 1949 after a return visit to Snyder in Washington to discuss the UK's July proposals.

Cripps returned to London on Thursday 18 August to be greeted by two elaborate memoranda prepared by Gaitskell. There were copies for Attlee as well as for Cripps. It seems doubtful whether Cripps, who was still very unwell, read them at the time.[86] One, a ten-page memorandum, argued the case for devaluation. The other, rather shorter, gave Attlee Gaitskell's advice on the date of the next General Election which could not be delayed beyond July 1950. It might appear impertinent for Gaitskell, not yet in the Cabinet, to advise Attlee on the date of the election. But he was writing about his own political future and those of other young and rising men in the Party – he might be robbed of it if Attlee got the date wrong. We do not know how grateful Attlee was for the advice. What we do know is that he did not act on it.[87] By the end of September, Gaitskell was satisfied that the conditions existed for an election in the autumn. Cripps and Bevan pressed Attlee to announce the dissolution of Parliament in his winding up speech at the conclusion of the devaluation debate on 29 September. Gaitskell agreed, but other advice prevailed.[88]

Gaitskell's long document on the economic situation began by emphasizing that '*the only major economic problem is the dollar problem.* Employment is high, production is high, the overall balance of payments is not bad, there is inflationary pressure, but no runaway inflation. If it were not for this dollar gap we should have little to worry about.' It then proceeded to deploy all the arguments in favour of devaluation that had now been debated for many months. He was obviously very unhappy with the UK's state of dependence on the USA. 'There is a raging press campaign in USA against the British people in general and the Labour Government in particular. Moreover official opinion seems to have hardened strongly against doing anything to help us, *unless we help ourselves . . . There is no way out of this dilemma except devaluation of sterling.*'

He accepted that there was a case for cutting public expenditure. 'The case for curbing public expenditure . . . is simply part of the general case for curbing inflation.' It was difficult to increase taxation much further. 'Hence one falls back on the necessity for cutting public expenditure – though this should certainly be combined with stricter control over investment and credit.' From the point of view of Cripps, this section of this long paper, if he ever read it, must have been unsatisfactory. It made no recommendation as to the extent of the necessary cuts in public expenditure. Cripps could therefore have no idea how far he would be able to rely on Gaitskell's support when he came to put his proposals to the Cabinet. The most interesting part of the paper came when Gaitskell discussed the size of the necessary devaluation. He favoured floating, possibly within declared bands.

> It seems to be agreed by all concerned that the minimum change is 25 per cent, i.e. to £1 = 3 dollars ratio and that it would probably be wiser to go rather further – to – say 2.75 or 2.80 dollars to the pound . . . There seem to me to be very powerful arguments in favour of not going to another fixed rate immediately. We want to create the impression that the pound may appreciate . . . If it is felt that we cannot risk leaving the market free (within the limits of exchange control), then I should still prefer that we announced that the pound would be held within a band of rates – say 2.60–2.80 dollars to the pound . . .

There had been some discussion between Robert Hall, Gaitskell and Plowden whether the pound should be allowed to float for an experimental period before a new fixed rate was decided. The Bank of England had also been considering whether the pound should float. It advised against. In any case, whatever the merits, there was no longer the time, in the few weeks before the devaluation, to set up the necessary planning for floating.[89]

Gaitskell then went on to press the urgency of the devaluation. 'I . . . most strongly urge that devaluation should be announced not later than

September 4th together with the statement on public expenditure . . .'
He then warned against any commitments.

> We should under no circumstances get committed to convertibility at
> any particular date – however distant or under any specific conditions.
> After all, convertibility with the dollar at fixed exchange rates does mean
> a return to the Gold Standard, to the 'automatic' system of achieving and
> maintaining equilibrium in international trade. It is almost certainly not
> compatible with the maintenance of our own full employment policy. It
> could be used to force deflation upon us and deprive us of certain instru-
> ments of economic planning, which even if they are not always to be
> used, should surely always be kept handy . . . We must be wary of definite
> commitments not only on convertibility but also on specific steps towards
> multilateralism and non-discrimination . . . It cannot be too strongly
> emphasized that anything like a system of complete multilateral trade
> with free convertibility of currencies is quite out of the question until
> *after* the fundamental problem of disequilibrium between the dollar and
> the non-dollar world has been solved.

Keynes should have lived to read this condemnation of his Loan Agreement and of the premature commitment to Bretton Woods and to
non-discrimination which he had urged upon the British government.
Britain's next Chancellor was saying that convertibility with a fixed
exchange rate against the dollar was in effect a return to the Gold
Standard and was not compatible with full employment.[90]

This memorandum, like the one on the date of the election, is suffused
with impatience and with the frustration of a young man confronted by
the obstruction of these old and sick survivors from a previous era,
hanging on to office without the ability to discharge the responsibilities
of office. These men could deprive him of his political future. In the
end, this is precisely what they did. In mitigation it can be said only
that Gaitskell himself had been tardy in coming to the conclusion that
he now so vigorously advocated.

On 19 August, Attlee, Bevin, Cripps, Gaitskell and Wilson met at
Chequers with Sir Edward Bridges. Cripps was still very unwell. At the
meeting Bevin promised to support devaluation. Cripps said that he was
not flatly against devaluation but was also very doubtful if it would do
any good. There was now, however, a further reason for a delay until
after Washington. Not until then would Cripps have the health and
strength to defend the decision publicly. On 26 August, Cameron Cobbold, Governor of the Bank, told Cripps that he was coming reluctantly
to the conclusion that it would be difficult to restore confidence in the

present rate now that the idea of devaluation was so deeply rooted all over the world. It should be made part of a general realignment against the dollar. He argued strongly against floating. The Bank was of the opinion that it represented 'the antithesis of the exchange rate stability in which the UK has rightly taken the lead in the past'; that it was 'inconsistent with IMF obligations'; that it would encourage 'uncertainty' and 'nervousness which would affect all other countries and every section of world trade'; and that the reserves were by then insufficient to enable them to manage a float effectively. Cobbold advocated devaluation to a new rate 'where the world will think we are a little undervalued'. He suggested that this might be in the region of $2.75.[91]

On 29 August, Cabinet confirmed the decision to devalue and the need to take the strong consequential measures against inflation. The UK delegation in Washington consisted of Bevin and Cripps, both very sick men, supported by officials. Among the matters which had not been decided before Bevin and Cripps left for Washington was the extent of the devaluation. This was left to them as though it was a matter of subsidiary importance. On floating, Cripps preferred the Bank's advice to Gaitskell's, in Plowden's view rightly.[92] That left the question of the rate. This was not discussed until the delegation reached the British Embassy in Washington. According to Plowden, Cripps had to be dissuaded from asking the Americans and Canadians for their opinion about the new rate. He was warned that it would create a dangerous precedent.[93] Officials thought it was better to go too low and risk upward pressure on the rate rather than too high and risk a further devaluation. Their recommendation to Bevin and Cripps was for a rate of $2.80. Bevin asked what the effect would be on the price of a loaf of bread. Plowden had the answer. It was acceptable and the official recommendation was accepted.[94]

George Kennan, Head of the State Department Planning Staff, tells us that before the arrival of the British delegation in Washington, 'For reasons which . . . escape me, Mr Snyder now seemed full of hostility and suspicion towards the British . . .'[95] At the Washington talks, the Americans, according to Plowden, were pleasantly surprised by the decision to devalue and to inform them of the extent and the timing. Bevin and Cripps had always wanted a deal with the USA as part of the decision to devalue. They hoped to secure from the Americans a more favourable administration of ERP, a resumption of stockpiling, loans from the Export-Import Bank, drawing rights from the IMF, reciprocal tariff reductions, help with the burden of the sterling balances, and an increase in the dollar price of gold. Bevin and Cripps agreed a) to make proposals for a gradual drawing down of the sterling balances, now larger than at the time of the 1947 crisis; b) to participate in the trade liberalization programme within the OEEC and also in the formation of a European Payments Union; c) to embark on a joint productivity programme with the USA; d) to study incentives for increasing exports to the USA; and e) to give higher priority to the negotiation of a commercial treaty with the USA which would include UK colonial territories. In return the US Administration agreed to help with the run-down of the sterling balances once the UK's proposals were received, to encourage more overseas investment, to embark on a programme for the relaxation and simplification of tariffs, to allow the UK to use ERP dollars to buy Canadian wheat, and also to take a stronger line with the domestic shipping lobby which had been able to get a high proportion of ERP goods shipped in US bottoms at high dollar freight rates. The US also agreed to look at stockpiling, especially of natural rubber, an idea rejected by Snyder during the July discussions in London.[96] How much these concessions were worth remained to be seen. Some were not within the power of the Administration to deliver. At any rate the Americans were friendly. With the help of the market, they had got their way.

On Cripps's return to London the Cabinet met secretly on Saturday 17 September. Next day, Sunday, the pound was devalued by 30 per cent to $2.80[97] Despite the almost two months delay between the decision to devalue and the actual devaluation, there had been no leaks. Most OEEC countries followed sterling all or part of the way, with only the Swiss franc and the Swedish Krona remaining at their old dollar parity. The trade-weighted devaluation of sterling was only 9 per cent.[98]

Should Cripps have resigned following the devaluation? The answer, perhaps cruel, must be yes. This was not because of any question mark against his integrity following the strength of his public rejection of devaluation in the previous July.[99] Cripps's policies had been insufficiently deflationary. Having opposed devaluation privately as well as publicly, he had been forced into it. Crises demand the appointment of effective Ministers. Cripps could no longer be as effective as the situation required. His sway over the Cabinet had been undermined by the failure of his policies. An adequate follow-up to devaluation would require of him efforts that he no longer had the spirits, the health, nor the authority to demand. Even if he had resigned, the probability is that Attlee would have considered himself compelled to refuse. Cripps was content to regard himself, like Bevin, as indispensable and considered that it was his duty to stay.

For the UK there remained the question of the complementary austerity package. The draft brief by officials for the Washington talks had recommended that there should be announcements about a reduction in government expenditure and about monetary policy before Bevin and Cripps left for Washington.[100] This had not happened, though officials in Washington had been allowed to talk about eliminating inessential expenditure. Robert Hall calculated that cuts of the order of £200 million were required merely to keep the pressure of demand to that originally deemed appropriate in the spring. Devaluation, according to Hall, necessitated at least a further £100 million of cuts. Otherwise there would be no resources available to reap the benefits of the devaluation. In Hall's view, his estimate was conservative. He was worried that the existing supplementary estimates submitted by departments were likely to underestimate the overshoot in government expenditure. No allowance had been made for an overshoot in investment programmes, he had not received estimates from all government departments of the increased costs resulting from devaluation, and in his original calculations he had assumed that wages would remain constant. The Cabinet, on the other hand, considered such recommendations too deflationary and that they would result in unemployment and broken promises. Cripps, in his devaluation broadcast, had also given the impression that devaluation was an alternative to deflation. It was not surprising therefore that other Ministers also took that view. Dalton characterized the deflationary proposals as 'another flank attack by officials'. Gaitskell thought that Dalton's view that public expenditure and the balance of payments were quite unrelated was a 'very rosy view'.[101] He also characterized Dalton's attack on expenditure cuts at a meeting of EPC as 'rather dishonest'.[102]

Cripps threatened to resign unless economies of at least £300 million were agreed. The EPC reduced the target for economies to £280 million divided equally between government expenditure and investment, including £35 million off housing.[103] Even this, however, brought threats of resignation from Bevan, Alexander and Bevin as these ministers sought to stop the axe falling on their own departments. Cripps probably fought less hard than he might have done because he was unwell and because he himself was always concerned that he might be taking too deflationary a fiscal stance. The expenditure cuts left the social services and the food subsidies virtually intact. The Ministry of Defence got away with a very small reduction in expenditure of some £30 million. The future was burdened with some of the proposed economies and it would be difficult to be certain that they had occurred even then. The cut in investment was largely on paper except for housing. The initial reaction of the City was that the cuts did not go far enough and threatened a further exchange crisis. The Americans took the same view, blaming the Government's timidity on the forthcoming General Election.[104] The implication is that some of the benefits of the devaluation were thrown away. It had become a government, incapable of learning, in which argument had been reduced to threats of resignation.

The Cabinet did accept official advice to strengthen the voluntary incomes policy agreed the previous year in the *Statement on Personal Incomes, Costs and Prices*. After meetings between the TUC and Cripps, Bevin, Bevan and Isaacs, Minister of Labour, a new and tighter wage policy received the endorsement of senior trade unionists. On 23 November 1949, the TUC General Council announced its recommendation of a one-year stabilization of wage rates, and the suspension of cost-of-living agreements, provided that the RPI did not increase by more than 5 per cent. Especially low-paid workers were exempted, despite Bevin's objection to the narrowing of differentials, and the package included an increase in profits tax. In practice this incomes policy only survived for six months. For a year beyond devaluation the RPI rose by only 2 per cent compared with 3.2 per cent for the year to September 1949. Domestic wage inflation averaged only 1.4 per cent per annum in the twelve months after devaluation, about half the pre-devaluation rate, while hourly earnings continued to rise at about 3 per cent per annum. Thus the effect of devaluation on costs and prices was remarkably small.

UK gold and dollar reserves, which had fallen to some £330 million on 18 September 1949, had, within nine months, increased by 70 per cent though they remained lower than before Marshall Aid and the suspension of convertibility.[105] The lion's share of the competitive advantage from devaluation remained after the Korean War. The UK enjoyed a current account surplus in every year between 1950 and 1954 except 1951, and a cumulative surplus of £500 million over this period. In 1950 there was an improvement in the UK's current account with the dollar area of £200 million, and a slightly greater improvement in the dollar balance of the rest of the sterling area. During the Korean War the UK's deficit with the dollar area increased but, after the end of hostilities, it started to improve again. So far as the rest of the sterling area was concerned, after 1950 a small and consistent surplus came to replace the habitual deficit. As the USA pulled out of recession, it increased its imports from the sterling area while the dollar curbs of the previous year meant that the sterling area was buying significantly less from the dollar area.

Plowden summarizes the outcome of the devaluation as follows:

> Although devaluation was delayed for too long, leading to an excessive loss to the reserves, and although the financial measures that accompanied it were by no means as wide-ranging as they should have been, its results were satisfactory in terms of both the short and the longer term, both from the point of view of Britain and the world as a whole. The rate of $2.80 to the pound was subsequently maintained for 18 years and this period of almost two decades witnessed unprecedented exchange rate stability, economic growth and employment levels throughout the world.[106]

Against the background of such a commentary, it may seem unappreciative to emphasize that if devaluation was not more frequent in the first 25 years after the war, it was only because of the fall in commodity prices following the Korean War, the buoyant state of the world economy, and the inflation of foreign incomes it promoted.[107] None of this could be foreseen and therefore it is necessary to underline Plowden's criticism of the inadequacy of the accompanying financial measures. Good government required firm action, not just the kind of action that might, or equally might not, turn out to be just sufficient. More important, the devaluation had given Britain another chance to ensure not just that its economy survived in an increasingly competitive world but that it flourished. Politics combined with Cripps's weakness wasted the opportunity. In making that judgement it matters little whether Cripps's weakness derived from ill-health or from irresolution.

EUROPE ALIENATED

The British government had informed the US Administration well in advance of its intention to devalue sterling by thirty per cent. Other governments were not granted this privilege. Most foreign governments were informed of the UK intention on the weekend it was announced. The IMF was given less than 24 hours notice.[108] There was some anger in Commonwealth countries. In July they had agreed to a 25 per cent reduction in dollar imports to help stave off a devaluation; now they were given little warning despite the fact that they would be almost bound to follow suit.[109] Even though a French Ministerial delegation including Robert Schuman, the Foreign Minister, and Maurice Petsche, the Finance Minister, was in Washington at the same time as Bevin and Cripps, it was thought impossible, for reasons of security, to give the French more warning. The lack of consultation badly damaged the UK's relations with France. Cripps himself later accepted that the UK should have consulted the Europeans.[110]

The offence was reinforced by Cripps's reaction to a speech made by Paul Hoffman, Administrator of the ERP, at OEEC on 31 October 1949. It had been feared that Hoffman intended to attempt to extract from European countries a commitment to the creation of a European currency unit against which national currencies would be stabilized. Bevin appealed to Dean Acheson, the American Secretary of State, and Acheson succeeded in persuading Hoffman to tone down his speech.[111] In late October 1949, just before Hoffman was due to deliver his speech, Bevin and Cripps put a joint paper to Cabinet. Their paper reaffirmed decisions already taken the previous January that the UK would not involve itself in any European association beyond the point at which it could withdraw. They argued that devaluation had proved Britain's need to rely on countries outside Europe. The paper declared that America and the Commonwealth 'take priority over our relations with Europe'. They insisted that the UK must not surrender its sole responsibility for its own budgetary policy and its own reserves, and that no commitment must be undertaken that would hinder the attainment of equilibrium between the dollar area and the sterling area: 'We cannot sacrifice opportunities for dollar-earning (or dollar-saving) in order to make it easier for other European countries to earn or save dollars.' Britain could not engage in any form of joint European planning which might imply the reduction in size of any dollar-earning industry. Imperial preferences must be retained. The paper still talked of doing everything possible to help European economic cooperation but a message was sent to Acheson so that he should be clear on the limits of Britain's European commitment.[112] Acheson had already taken the point and had turned to France to lead European integration. The speech that Hoffman actually made was not as bad from the British point of view as had at one point been feared. He only demanded specific pledges to liberalization. But in his official reply to Hoffman's speech, Cripps emphasized that it was British policy not to integrate the British economy into western Europe in any way that would prejudice British responsibilities elsewhere. His categorical statement on that matter was hardly softened by his declaration that Britain would encourage regional schemes. French newspapers were bitterly critical. Some said Cripps's speech represented the end of Franco-British collaboration in European reconstruction.[113]

Among other possible forms of European cooperation ruled out in London was a European customs union. Bevin himself had canvassed that idea before being persuaded by the Treasury and the Board of Trade to abandon it. They told him that it was against British interests because it would cut across imperial preference. His own perceptions of the state of Europe convinced him that Europe was no more ready for a customs union than for a federation. Another possibility was a European payments union of some kind. If European currencies were not yet ready for convertibility against the dollar, perhaps nevertheless they could be made ready for convertibility against each other. Europe could thus move on from bilateral clearings which inhibited trade. It would gain, at least within Europe, the benefits of enhanced trade and thus of enhanced prosperity. Here too there were problems. Even within a European payments union, surpluses and deficits would accumulate. How could they be cleared with the main European currencies still unconvertible against the dollar? How much credit would the clearing union extend to countries in deficit? What disciplines would operate to discourage countries that saw in the clearing union an opportunity to obtain cheap credit from their neighbours? There was also the opposite problem. Belgium was conducting a deflationary economic policy which won it a trade surplus with Britain. A payments union could become an instrument whereby Belgium sucked gold and dollars from Britain. Though desirable in principle, Cripps and the Treasury were convinced that much negotiation lay ahead before this halfway advance towards general convertibility would be acceptable to Britain and the sterling area. They also knew that there was no problem that an additional supply of free dollars could not resolve, provided only that the dollar remained a reliable store of value. On the other hand, was dollar backing for an EPU the best use that could be made of the dollars? Would they not be better used buying goods from the USA? On 17 November 1949, Cripps, at a press conference, explained that the ECA proposals for a European payments union, a central commercial authority, and integration, would be a danger to the sterling area and to full employment. In February 1950 Cripps rejected the principles upon which a European payments union was to be constituted. He wished to reserve to the government the right to restrict imports. That right was not in fact at risk. It was only in September 1950, when the British balance of payments had moved into surplus, that the government regained the confidence to agree to the constitution of an EPU incorporating sterling, with Gaitskell, not Cripps, negotiating on its behalf.

If the Americans could not get their European federation or even a customs union, trade liberalization was the least with which they would be satisfied. Cripps was prepared to support liberalization of private sector trade as an alternative to the more extravagant demands of the Americans. His willingness to do so went beyond what his Economic Secretary, Douglas Jay, found prudent. Jay drew attention to the effect on the UK of Belgian policies. He pointed out that whereas imports from the Commonwealth were normally essentials, those from Europe were often inessential. Treasury officials criticized the distinction that Jay was making and Cripps stuck to his policy.[114] Nevertheless, with the recession in the USA which commenced in late 1948, other European countries were becoming sceptical of unregulated trade liberalization. With the outbreak of the Korean War, and its effect on commodity prices and therefore on the balance of payments, the UK was compelled to reimpose import restrictions.[115]

The devaluation which had opened further Britain's breach with Europe did not even reconcile British policy with that of the USA. The US Administration was delighted with the devaluation but was not overpleased with other aspects of British policy. It had reconciled itself to the fact that Britain would not lead European integration. Now it saw that convertibility had been postponed and non-discrimination delayed indefinitely. The UK did not feel it was ready to try the experiment of convertibility again so soon. The main burden for making this possible lay, in the UK view, on the USA which should conduct a more expansionary policy. Meanwhile, it was insisted, the most the UK could do was to continue its policy of disinflation, try to resolve the problems of the sterling balances, and maintain an adequate payments surplus with the rest of the world. Nine months after the devaluation, the announcement of the Schuman Plan gave Britain an opportunity for a reconciliation with France. The opportunity was neglected. Cripps himself, after at first seeming attracted by the Plan, turned against it and, in the absence of Bevin sick, defended the government's position in the House of Commons.

AVOIDING A CLASH WITH BEVAN

A General Election was called for February 1950 largely because Cripps said he could not hold sterling beyond February.[116] Labour won with a small majority. Now, in his Budget statement of 18 April 1950, Cripps had to decide how to treat the growing expenditure on the NHS. A power to impose prescription charges had been taken in November 1949. But charges beyond those authorized by that Act, for example on dental and optical services, might now be needed in the interests of fiscal prudence. Cripps had to decide whether to clash with Bevan or to compromise with Bevan. Bevan was prepared under pressure to accept a ceiling for the NHS Budget. He bitterly opposed any idea of a Bill to authorize charges. Cripps in effect gave way and allowed, as a solution, the establishment of a high-powered monitoring committee chaired by Attlee which was to ensure that the agreed ceiling was not in fact raised. The committee included Gaitskell who, after the February election, had been appointed Minister of State for Economic Affairs at the Treasury. In effect Cripps was leaving the problem to his successor.

In a Personal and Confidential letter to Attlee dated 26 April 1950, written by hand, Cripps said: 'Now that the Budget is over and through I feel that the time has come to let you know that I cannot continue very much longer at my job, and that I shall have to relinquish it by the end of this summer at the latest.' He made a further attempt to resign in the summer but was dissuaded by Gaitskell and Plowden, particularly as the Korean War had just broken out. Instead he went away for a long holiday, leaving Gaitskell in possession of his room in the Treasury, and with the intention of not returning to the Treasury until October.[117] In fact he continued as Chancellor until 19 October 1950 and then resigned both his appointment and his seat in the House. He was never to return. He died in 1952.

Devaluations tend to be written from the point of view of the devaluationists. The fact that it occurred, and appeared to be successful, is taken as final proof that they were right and that those who opposed it were wrong. Yet there is always room for legitimate doubt. British exports after the devaluation were certainly assisted by the American recovery. The history of the UK's successive devaluations since the war would tend to establish that devaluation has not been a panacea or a remedy for the UK's economic ills. It may be foolish to allow an economy to continue in a state of fundamental disequilibrium, but devaluation as a cure for fundamental disequilibrium depends on the willingness of governments to take other parallel measures and on the willingness of the electorate to support them and not to fritter away the additional competitiveness in wage claims. In the course of international economic relations, countries do suffer defeats, not always through their own failures. This devaluation was perhaps the most excusable of all. It is a pity only that the follow-up was so inadequate. It was, nevertheless, a defeat. Hall and Plowden wanted Cripps to admit in his broadcast to the nation on 18 September that it was a defeat. He refused, saying that Bevin had told him never to apologize for his actions as a Minister.[118]

Cripps's reputation has remained high. But it is the reputation of a man who said the right things rather than did the right things. The tragedy is that Cripps reached the summit of his career when he was no longer capable of exercising effectively the powers of a Chancellor.

FOUR

Hugh Gaitskell: Rearmament and Civil War

THE APPOINTMENT

The General Election had taken place in February 1950, contrary to Gaitskell's advice. In his reshuffle of the government following his narrow, 6-seat victory, Attlee was mindful of the need to give Cripps some more assistance. He appointed Gaitskell Minister of State for Economic Affairs at the Treasury. Though there was no necessary implication, this might have indicated an intention that Gaitskell would inherit the Treasury when Cripps did eventually retire. But his name had little political resonance. He had played a leading and much praised role in the devaluation of 1949, and, although he was not in the Cabinet, he attended many of the most important meetings. That he was not in the Cabinet is evidence of Attlee's failures in man-management. He had done little to bring forward able MPs elected in 1945. It would have involved him in the disagreeable task of dispensing with the services of some of his old-timers. He preferred to wait until illness or accident opened gaps in the Cabinet ranks.

In October 1950, Stafford Cripps was at last allowed to go. Who was there who might be selected to succeed Cripps from among those whose Membership of Parliament preceded 1945 and who now had long Cabinet service? There was only one name that even appeared possible. The Cabinet consisted to an undesirable extent of politicians who could not expect to go further, who indeed would have been horrified to be invited to undertake the responsibilities of a Chancellor of the Exchequer. All the paramount leaders of 1945 could at once be ruled out. Bevin was ill. Dalton had failed once at the Treasury and was, indeed, promoting the candidature of Gaitskell.[1] Morrison had been one of the earliest Ministerial advocates of devaluation which now appeared to have resolved the problem with the balance of payments and the shortage of dollars. But he rightly did not consider himself qualified for the Treasury.[2] The only other possible name from among the members of Cabinet elected before 1945 was Bevan. Bevan was not a man to consider himself unqualified. To promote Bevan would have been a risk. It would have been disliked by Attlee's senior colleagues and by many trade union leaders, and might not have played well with the market. Bevan had not helped himself with his 'vermin' speech.[3]

From the small group of very senior Ministers closest to Attlee, the advice was unanimous. Though he was not yet in the Cabinet, though he had not even been a full member of EPC until he became Minister of State for Economic Affairs, the succession should go to Gaitskell. His appointment would be accepted by all those members of the Cabinet who may have thought themselves fortunate to have survived as long as they had in the posts they held. Gaitskell understood matters they did not understand, he was an economist by profession, he had taught at LSE. He had the details at his fingertips. indeed, he wore out his officials ensuring that he did have the details at his fingertips. Cripps's advice on the succession would have been particularly influential. There were two young economists in the senior ranks of the Government, Wilson and Gaitskell. Both would consider themselves in the running. Both had worked for Cripps. Cripps designated Gaitskell.[4]

With the effective choice lying between Bevan and Gaitskell, Attlee preferred, as he thought, to play safe. He did not attempt to recreate the situation which had existed for a few weeks before Dalton's resignation in 1947, with a fiscal chief and a planning chief. On 19 October 1950, Hugh Gaitskell became Chancellor of the Exchequer with all the powers that Cripps had held before him. A Chancellor in good health, however slight his political standing on appointment, could, even at the age of 44, *only* 44 as it must have seemed to the elderly members of the Cabinet, rapidly emerge as a rival even to one of Labour's historic leaders. Yet, for the moment, he was of little political substance. Cripps had insisted that Gaitskell be allocated his own position in the Cabinet list, immediately after Attlee, Bevin and Morrison. Gaitskell himself had insisted.[5] Neither authority nor influence is determined by position on the Cabinet list. The fact that there was so much agitation about the issue shows that Gaitskell's position in the Party and the Cabinet was weak. He behaved as though he believed it himself. A Chancellor who has to establish his authority as well as his competence will necessarily be under great strain. He would need powerful support from the Prime Minister. If that was given, it would be something new; Attlee, as Prime

Minister, had never shown a strong inclination to support his Chancellors in Cabinet. Gaitskell would be compared with and measured against Cripps. Senior Treasury officials were somewhat concerned to see Cripps replaced with a Chancellor with so little standing in his Party. Morrison's claims had been urged, by Sir Edward Bridges among others, because he was considered the only possible candidate with the necessary political weight. The Treasury needs a Chancellor who can get his way in Cabinet.

The need for strong Prime Ministerial support was underlined by the jealousies Gaitskell's appointment would undoubtedly provoke. It could hardly have escaped Attlee that it would be an appointment that would frustrate the ambitions of at least two colleagues, one with considerable standing in the Party. Bevan had expected Cripps to recommend him, and was deeply hurt when his old comrade proposed Gaitskell. Bevan was bound to see Gaitskell's appointment as a humiliation. He was certainly very angry and made his resentment clear to Attlee.[6] It was not just a personal matter; Bevan saw the Labour Party being wrenched away from working-class socialists such as himself and into the hands of *apparatchiks* such as Gaitskell. There had been months of bitter controversy between the two. Gaitskell had been arguing for the imposition of health service charges since the time he became Minister of State for Economic Affairs.[7] As a member of the Ministerial Committee set up after the 1950 Budget to monitor the cost of the health service, he had frequent conflicts with Bevan. The clash at one such meeting, probably on 28 June 1950, provoked Bevan into rising and walking towards the door of the Cabinet room. Attlee, in the chair, called him back and smoothed things down.[8] Gaitskell's persistence with the argument led Bevan to withdraw from Cripps's weekly Thursday night dinners for economic Ministers.[9]

There was one other Minister besides Bevan who could hardly welcome it. Wilson had now been a Cabinet Minister for three years. He could easily have accepted the appointment of Bevan, but would regard himself as having been passed over when Gaitskell won the nomination. Wilson may have thought his seniority over Gaitskell in Cabinet service, if not in age, indicated his name as Cripps's probable successor. But, although an effective President of the Board of Trade, he was alleged not to have played a heroic role in the devaluation, and some thought he tended to overestimate his own importance. He was regarded as a technician rather than as a politician – but the same, of course, was said about Gaitskell.

Bevan's story raises the question of whether a left-wing figure can be the Chancellor of the Exchequer in a Labour government. Labour is so burdened with market suspicions that the temptation must always be to appoint a safe figure if any can be found. Dalton was an irresponsible Chancellor but that is not necessarily the same thing as left-wing. Cripps had a left-wing past but by the time he became Chancellor he had established his reputation for austerity, and austerity in public expenditure is what the market likes. Gaitskell was thought of as being on the right of his Party. For the moment the conclusion to this question will be that it is probably easier for a left-wing figure to become a Labour Prime Minister than a Labour Chancellor.

GAITSKELL AS ECONOMIST

Gaitskell was a professional economist and therefore appeared well-qualified for the office of Chancellor. The economists now had, once again, one of their own as Chancellor.[10] Robert Hall, who earlier had had doubts about Gaitskell, had been won over by the devaluation crisis.[11] Plowden subsequently wrote: 'When he became Chancellor, Gaitskell was as well qualified for the job of running the economy as any holder of that office before or since.'[12]

His successor as Chancellor, R. A. Butler, wrote that Gaitskell 'could bring to the Exchequer the best professional qualifications of any Chancellor in this century'.[13] But Butler was hardly an authority.

Brittan, writing in 1971, underlines Gaitskell's qualifications: 'Hugh Gaitskell ... probably understood his job better than any Chancellor before or since ... His officials had great respect for him; but they complained that he insisted on doing himself a great deal of detailed work, for example in relation to economic forecasts, which he would have been better advised to delegate.'[14] One comment seems in order. Many Chancellors show an intense interest in economic forecasts. They suspect that pessimistic forecasts are used by officials to divert them from what are regarded as unsound policies. A Chancellor who insists on doing his own economic forecasts is either naive in investing in them too much confidence, or is suspicious of the loyalty of his officials to the implementation of his government's policies. Or he finds difficulty in seeing the wood for the trees.

Gaitskell had on many occasions before his appointment shown suspicion of Treasury officials. He had been warned by Cripps and he had learnt to share Cripps's doubts about how he was served. He was a socialist. Socialism had not yet been dissipated into a vague egalitarianism. He was a planner and was not content to rely on fiscal planning through the Budget alone. Whatever the merits of demand management, he saw a continuing, and probably permanent, need for direct controls such as on imports.[15] For Gaitskell, controls were not a temporary necessity but an instrument of policy. He was concerned really to redistribute wealth and, no doubt, had he been in office longer, would have brought forward proposals.

Whatever his officials' attitude might be to planning in the light of postwar experience, he was sure that they were not socialists. It soon became apparent, in his conduct of excessively long meetings, and his entry into unnecessary detail, that it would take time before mutual trust was established and a workable balance developed between Ministerial intervention and delegation to officials. Nevertheless, it is comforting for officials to have a Chancellor who can talk about economic policy on a basis of equality. Some Chancellors have to be protected from themselves and from their own ignorance. Treasury officials did not feel a need to be protective with this one; rather, the danger with Gaitskell was that he could refute the arguments of his professional advisers with a veneer of economics that concealed political calculation.

There is, however, a question mark against Gaitskell's level of preparation for the office of Chancellor. When he first went to the Treasury under Cripps in February 1950, he was allocated responsibility for overseas finance. His appointment gave him an opportunity to travel and to learn. His economics had always been insular – he displayed exaggerated confidence in the absolute validity of British perspectives. In order to defend the British economy and its full employment policies, he was as sceptical of liberalization as his friend and junior, Douglas Jay, who had been conducting 'a continual struggle inside the Treasury for Stafford's soul'.[16] One of the reasons for Gaitskell's late conversion to devaluation in 1949 was that it smacked of the price mechanism and he believed in planning and controls. At the time of the devaluation crisis, and before he himself had been converted to devaluation, he had been opposed to convertibility as an objective even in the long term and was critical of Treasury advisers who advocated a 'one-world economy' and consequently were in favour of devaluation and deflation as the only way of sustaining the British economy within the one-world system that was bound to come.[17] Gaitskell had then been converted to devaluation but that did not make him any more sympathetic to liberal policies.

In January 1950 he circulated a paper to the EPC entitled *Control and Liberalisation*. It said: 'On "liberalisation" we have gone about far enough. But we have done it for political reasons – US and Europe.'[18] To the dismay of 'liberal' Treasury officials, Gaitskell wanted to tell the Americans that they could expect no movement on their 'fundamentals', convertibility and non-discrimination, until it was clear that they could avoid a slump with disastrous consequences for the British economy.[19] There had, after all, been the American recession of 1948–9 from the effects of which Britain had escaped only by devaluation. Gaitskell felt, despite Keynes, that there was no international commitment to full employment. To some extent he changed his mind after becoming Minister of State for Economic Affairs as a result of contact with Americans, particularly in the course of negotiating the EPU. He found that Americans were divided and that many New Dealers had concerns similar to his own.[20] But they did not necessarily determine American policy.

He still feared strong deflationary pressures from abroad, and was critical of what he regarded as the deflationary policies of other countries. He criticized Belgium for its deflationary policies which he saw as responsible for the Belgian payments surplus with Britain. It was sucking gold and dollars out of the UK. At a meeting in Paris with Harriman and Katz on 25 March 1950 at which the future EPU was discussed, Gaitskell questioned the need for gold payments within the proposed system. This was intended as a means of exercising discipline on debtor countries. There must be a limit to the credit extended within the system. Gaitskell's view was that while it was the duty of a debtor to get his balance of payments right, this could be done by devaluation or import controls, not only by deflation. He could not accept any obligation to deflate. Gaitskell justified trade discrimination to avoid the loss of gold and dollars. He added that if there were a further US recession and the UK had to choose between a policy which threatened 'a high level of income and employment in the UK' and another dollar crisis, the British government would choose the dollar crisis which it would deal with by further restrictions on dollar supplies.[21]

At a meeting of the UN Economic and Social Council at Geneva, in the summer of 1950, he excoriated the economic policies of the creditor countries. They should plan, he held, for full employment by creating demand at home, and should run down their balance of payments surpluses rather than impose deflation on their neighbours.[22] It was a message that would be repeated by British Chancellors, equally unavailingly, through the decades to come. By the summer of 1950, Britain, following devaluation, had achieved its own precarious surplus. Preaching to the unconverted economic heathens can be more confident when one's own country can claim success, however tenuous. Nevertheless, the heathens were in charge. Gaitskell's speech was attacked by the US Treasury and by Camille Gutt, Managing Director of the IMF.[23] It should have been a warning that he was operating in a world hostile to the policies of the British Labour government, which were interpreted as inflationary. It never seems to have occurred to him that others had their reasons as well as he, were as concerned about the fate of their economies and the employment of their citizens as he and, just possibly, had insights from which he could learn. In due course it would be revealed by the evidence of economic performance that the countries he had criticized possessed more of the secrets of economic success than he did. By that time he had passed into an eternity of Opposition.

Gaitskell was particularly contemptuous of the views of bankers. In December 1950, he rejected advice from Cameron Cobbold, Governor of the Bank of England, that monetary policy should be changed and short-term interest rates raised. In this Cobbold had the support of Hall and of Treasury officials.[24] Gaitskell regarded the advice as 'completely antiquated'.[25] Anything that could be done by higher interest rates could be done by direct controls. Early in January 1951, Gaitskell told the Governor there would be great difficulty negotiating expenditure cuts with his colleagues if he were to put up short-term interest rates and as a result pay out more money to the banks. Why should he add that burden to his shoulders when he saw no positive advantage in a course of action whose effect was admitted to be mainly psychological.[26] In June and July 1951, when the idea of an increase in interest rates was once more being pressed upon him by the Bank of England, Gaitskell told Cobbold that to follow his advice would make his own position with the trade unions untenable.[27] Even as late as the end of August 1951, when there could be no further doubt that the country was faced once again with a major external crisis, Gaitskell rejected advice to increase interest rates.[28] The most he was prepared to do, following Cripps, was to call on the banks to restrict credit.[29] Apparently for this Chancellor with his firm economic opinions, it was impermissible even to experiment with an increase in interest rates in order to discover whether, at a time of great peril for the country, it would help. But there was more to Gaitskell's stance than a difference of economic judgement. In order to win the battle he had launched against the entrenched prejudices of the Bevanites, Gaitskell had to conciliate the entrenched prejudices of the trade unions. His attitude was at odds with the needs of a government in constant battle against inflation and repeatedly in search of some source from which to fund its frequent balance of payments deficits.[30]

THE EUROPEAN PAYMENTS UNION

Gaitskell's principal achievement while Minister for Economic Affairs was the negotiation of the European Payments Union (EPU). He had been deeply suspicious of the idea of such a union because he suspected that it would simply be a means by which gold and dollars were sucked out of the UK by continental deflationists. He reluctantly submitted, however, to the realities of political power. The Americans wanted an EPU in order to promote European economic integration. American views having been resisted on so many European fronts, some ground had to be given. Gaitskell negotiated credit arrangements with the other potential members which provided a level of protection for the UK with which he was prepared to feel satisfied. The Bank of England also disliked the EPU, seeing European integration as an opportunity for the restoration of sterling as an international trading currency. On 8 May 1950 Cobbold wrote to Cripps:

> I have always disliked the EPU proposals and I still do. I regard them mainly as an attempt by some Americans (with strong support from Belgium) to force Europe (under threat of loss of ECA dollars) prematurely back to a form of Gold Standard . . . If it were possible to drop the whole thing and proceed on our own lines of gradually extending transferability, I would be vastly relieved.

But Cobbold, too, saw the political realities. Definitive agreement on the EPU was achieved by the Ministerial Council of the OEEC on 18 August 1950. Despite the fears of Gaitskell and of the Bank, the EPU proved a great success and survived until sterling convertibility in 1958.[31]

A PROBLEM TOO FAR

However qualified a Chancellor is, he cannot perform the impossible and Gaitskell was faced by the impossible. Whether he managed his responsibilities in all cases with good judgement is a matter of legitimate controversy. But he faced a combination of political and economic problems which would have defeated better economists and more experienced politicians. He did well to emerge from the experience with so high a reputation. The evidence might seem to suggest that the Chancellors who emerge with the highest reputation are those who spend the least time in the office.[32]

The domestic difficulties were formidable enough. They were essentially political problems. Cripps, despite some tough words, had left unresolved the battle over health service funding. This problem should have been soluble, given a rational approach on both sides of the argument; but political problems have dimensions other than the rational. In this case, the solution was made more difficult by a mixture, on both sides, of pride and resentment. The inflation problem was of an altogether different magnitude. During the preceding five years too little had been done. Inflationary pressure persisted. It had not been lessened either by Budget surpluses or by incomes policies. Cripps had won two years of wage freeze from the trade unions. Two years is a long time for any incomes policy, whether voluntary or statutory, and they had expired. In September 1950, the TUC voted narrowly against a continuation of the wages freeze. It was unwilling to accept even a wages advisory council. There was no wages explosion, but there was an upward drift in wage demands. For Gaitskell wage pressure was therefore another problem awaiting a solution. It was not possible to make up lost time in the space allowed to Gaitskell as Chancellor. The narrow victory of February 1950 made a further, decisive, election probable in the near future, and the run-up to a decisive election is never the best time for strong anti-inflationary measures.

It was the outbreak of war in Korea the previous June that made Gaitskell's problems insoluble. The Korean crisis was developing in a manner which appeared to threaten general war. A Soviet offensive in Europe was feared. There was little respect in London or in Washington for the defensive capacity of continental Europe west of the iron curtain. Morale was low, and there were too few arms and too many communists. The British defence Budget was raised from £2.3 billion over three years to £3.6 billion. The American Chiefs of Staff regarded this as quite inadequate. They demanded that Britain, to deter Soviet aggression if possible, to help defeat it if not, should undertake an even more massive rearmament programme, £6 billion over three years. The demand had the support of the British Chiefs of Staff. It was pressed on Attlee during his visit to Washington in December 1950. He had flown there to persuade Truman not to drop the atomic bomb to force the withdrawal of the Chinese Army which had all but evicted General MacArthur's forces from Korea. Attlee returned with assurances on that score, but also with the conviction that Britain must do more. On 29 January 1951, he told the Commons that the Cabinet had decided on a further expansion in the defence Budget from the £3.6 billion to which it had been raised since the beginning of the Korean War to £4.7 billion. The expenditure of £4.7 billion would take place over the next three years. The planned defence expenditure over three years had, therefore, been doubled. This increase in the defence Budget implied multiplying the output of munitions by a factor of four.[33] The share of GNP going to defence would rise from 8 per cent before the crisis to 14 per cent after it, a proportion exceeded among the member states of the North Atlantic Treaty Organization (NATO) only by the USA.[34] At the peak, 2.5 million people, or 11 per cent of the active population, would be in the armed forces or engaged in defence work.[35] It would mean an *additional* defence expenditure of £500 million in the first year, £800 million in the second year, and £1 billion in the third. The economists had persuaded themselves that such a programme was practical.[36] It was to prove beyond the capacity of the British economy.

Just at this moment Marshall Aid to Britain was terminated, officially on 1 January 1951, six weeks earlier in practice. Marshall Aid had brought over $3.1 billion to the support of the British balance of payments in the previous three years.[37] The strength of the British balance of payments was held to make it no longer necessary. It should have been a proud moment, but the evidence was already accumulating that the Korean War was threatening a sharp reversal of Britain's economic fortunes. Gaitskell visited Washington, his first visit to the USA, in October 1950, just prior to his appointment as Chancellor. He warned the US Administration that the costs of rearmament and the movement in the terms of trade against Britain were already causing problems.[38] In August 1950, two months after the North invaded South Korea, when the defence Budget had first been increased under American pressure, it had appeared that the Americans would help to fund the British rearmament programme.[39] It was now clear that any assistance was doubtful and would be, at best, long delayed. Congress, with its typical attitude to feckless Europeans, and even to its faithful British ally, thought that Europe and Britain should do more to defend themselves and not rely so much on American help.

The British Minister of Defence, since the February election, was

Emanuel Shinwell. It was a ludicrous appointment. No failure was ever great enough to persuade Attlee to deny one of his old cohorts new opportunities to do damage. Shinwell was the man of the 1947 fuel crisis. In October 1947, Shinwell had been dismissed from his post as Minister of Fuel and Power, removed from the Cabinet, and downgraded to the non-Cabinet post of Minister for War. At Fuel and Power he had been replaced by Gaitskell. Shinwell never forgave Gaitskell whom he blamed for his disgrace. Now Gaitskell was Chancellor of the Exchequer. Gaitskell found that Shinwell, in Cabinet, 'never loses an opportunity of picking a quarrel with me, sometimes on the most ridiculous grounds'.[40] Shinwell, at Defence, had his opportunity for rehabilitation by pressing the demands of the British Chiefs of Staff. He could hardly be expected to question them or their costings. There could now be a tactical alliance between Shinwell and the Chancellor provided Gaitskell was prepared to support and to fund the rearmament programme.

For the time being, he was. Gaitskell did not realize how ill-prepared the UK economy was for the rearmament programme, though he did warn his Cabinet colleagues in January 1951 that it was bound to cause problems. In his view, which was the view of the great majority of the Cabinet, a major commitment to rearmament was inescapable. His visit to Washington in October 1950 had dissipated many of his earlier suspicions of the Americans.[41] He remained opposed to convertibility and non-discrimination, but in foreign and security policy, he now wished to prove himself a loyal ally. By February 1951 he had become very critical of anti-Americanism in the Cabinet.[42] Britain was, after all, America's principal and most reliable ally. The fact that Washington could not, for the time being, help fund its rearmament programme, the fact that Marshall Aid had come to an end, neither of these facts diminished Britain's responsibilities to the Alliance and to its own security. There was also a desire to prove Britain's qualifications for a seat at the top table at a time of crisis. That was not Gaitskell's policy alone but that of the Cabinet. Presumably, it was Bevan's policy – he had lived with it in Cabinet. Years later he was to identify a need for nuclear weapons under the union flag in order to conceal his nakedness in the conference chamber. Even if Gaitskell *had* been critical of the policy, he could hardly be expected to reverse it between his entry into the Cabinet on 19 October and the rearmament announcement of 29 January 1951. He was quite aware of the irony that he who, as Chancellor, would have to cope with the funding of the additional defence expenditure, and with its economic consequences, was often its principal advocate in Cabinet.[43]

There were Ministers who were sceptical about the scale of the rearmament programme. Gaitskell was warned by Harold Wilson that it was impractical – the raw materials for it and the manufacturing capacity were simply unavailable. George Strauss, Minister of Supply, took the same view. Gaitskell tended to discount their view, which was to prove entirely correct, on the ground that they were friends of Bevan.[44] Gaitskell was concerned about the practicality of the programme, and had warned the Cabinet about the difficulties it might cause, but thought it too soon to come to so firm a conclusion.

If there was to be a revolt against the rearmament programme, the leader would be not Wilson but Bevan. On 17 January 1951, disappointed at losing the Chancellorship to Gaitskell, Bevan was moved from the Ministry of Health to the Ministry of Labour. If it was intended as a consolation prize, it was not much.[45] If it was hoped to turn his consuming interest away from his NHS, it failed. Hilary Marquand replaced Bevan at Health, but outside the Cabinet.[46] Then, on 9 March, Bevin was removed from the Foreign Office and, by way of consolation, was made Lord Privy Seal. To his disgust, he was replaced by Morrison. Bevan had thus, in the course of six months, been passed over for the two most senior offices other than that of the Prime Minister himself. Bevan, more than any other Minister, was the link between the government and the Party in the country. He was the government's most brilliant orator. He was always being called upon to defend government policies in the House of Commons, far outside his departmental brief.[47] He made a superb speech in defence of the government's rearmament programme in the House of Commons on 15 February 1951. His speech was described by Gaitskell in his diary as 'one of the most brilliant performances I have ever heard him give . . .'[48] He was the creator of the NHS, demonstrating thereby that he had administrative skills as well as oratorical skills. Yet he was distrusted both as the spokesman of the left, and, as Gaitskell went on to say in the same diary entry, as 'such a difficult team worker, and some would say even worse – a thoroughly unreliable and disloyal colleague'.[49] As a result, real promotion appeared to be closed to him, and the man in command of the nation's finances was no longer his old friend Cripps, whom he greatly admired, but Gaitskell, who had come from nowhere to the greatest office in the land other than that of Prime Minister.

THE BUDGET

The immediate task facing Gaitskell on appointment was his 1951 Budget, to be introduced in April. He therefore had six months to prepare it. On his appointment as Chancellor, Gaitskell told William Armstrong, his Principal Private Secretary, that over the next few years the principal task of a socialist Chancellor would be the redistribution of wealth. As the recipient of that radical message, William Armstrong makes his first appearance in this chronicle. As so often in the history of political ideals, other matters had to take priority over the redistribution of wealth. A capital gains tax was left for the 1952 Budget.[50] So far as the 1951 Budget was concerned, his political problem was with Bevan and with health. The political problem was greater than the financial problem. This is not to say that the financial problem was slight but that Gaitskell did not propose to make a fundamental attack on it. In November 1949, under pressure from Cripps, Bevan had introduced an Act permitting prescription charges. The Act was now on the Statute Book; a charge of one shilling per prescription had been planned but then abandoned under pressure from Bevan. In the 1949–50 financial year, Cripps had allowed £90 million of health services supplementaries.[51] Gaitskell found this embarrassing. He did not want to do anything that looked like criticism of his predecessor, and therefore found it necessary to accept that the supplementaries had been justified. At the time of his 1950 Budget, Cripps had ducked further action on the mounting cost of the NHS. The Treasury view had been that £350 million a year was as much as should be spent on the health service. That expenditure would itself be much higher than was contemplated when the NHS was introduced. Cripps had, nevertheless, accepted that in practice the cost could not be reduced below £392 million in the 1950–51 financial year. He had insisted only that at least that ceiling should not be breached and that provision should be made by legislation for charges other than prescription charges if, in the end, it was breached. In fact, the ceiling was adhered to, but no legislative provision was made for the charges. Now the Ministry of Health was demanding £422 million for the 1951–2 financial year. Gaitskell, under political pressure, was prepared to concede £400 million. This figure allowed the prescription charge to be dropped, but it still required that charges be imposed on the dental and optical services. To keep within £400 million, the Budget, according to Gaitskell, would have to charge half the cost of false teeth and spectacles which would bring in £13 million in 1951–2 and £23 million in a full year.[52]

It would have been forgivable, and might have been wise, if, at this early stage in his Chancellorship, with higher priorities and with an election pending, Gaitskell had deferred action on this issue. The charges he was contemplating were insignificant in the context of his Budget. They did not represent a resolution of the problem of health service funding; at best, they would be a very small beginning. If, however, he was now to make a stand on an issue on which Cripps had capitulated, he would find himself in immediate confrontation with Bevan. Bevan was claiming that charges were unacceptable as a matter of principle. He saw as his greatest achievement a health service free at the point of delivery. It was unclear where such a confrontation would lead. On the one hand Bevan, already aggrieved at being passed over for promotion, appeared to be preparing his resignation. On the other hand, could these minor charges justify a resignation at such a time even if the question was raised to the level of principle? Resignation would divide the Party on the eve of a probable election.

With major decisions to be made, the government was absorbed not by the devastating consequences of the rearmament programme for the economy but by the political battle between Gaitskell and Bevan about health service charges. Various compromises were suggested. In the last month of his life, Bevin, who also did not much like the idea of health service charges, tried his hand at a compromise but without success.[53] An arrangement suggested by George Tomlinson, Minister of Education, was based on the formula which had been agreed between Cripps and Bevan for the 1950 Budget. There was to be a £400 million ceiling on the cost of the health service but without the imposition of charges. Morrison supported the Tomlinson formula but Gaitskell refused it as a dishonest dodge to avoid the charges. He knew that, without the charges, it would be impossible to keep the health service within the £400 million ceiling.[54] At the crucial moment in the search for a political compromise, on 21 March, Attlee went into hospital for an operation on a duodenal ulcer. From his hospital bed he wrote to the Cabinet what Kenneth Morgan describes as a 'remarkably vacuous letter' which 'dealt with none of the substantive points at issue'.[55] The search for a compromise was perhaps less intense partly because Attlee was in hospital, partly because it was suspected that Bevan intended to find some excuse for resignation whatever concessions Gaitskell made. If he insisted on resigning because of personal grievances, it remained important to deprive him of good ground for resignation. To some small degree, Gaitskell did move. Bevan's opposition to charges was now in the public arena. If it helped Bevan to save face, Gaitskell was prepared to drop his proposal for the charges to come into force at once. In that way, the Bill that would be required need not be retrospective to April 12, as had been intended, and could be delayed a little. One concession Gaitskell would not make – there must be legislation and there must be charges. Attlee in hospital urged Gaitskell to accept the Tomlinson formula. Gaitskell refused and offered to resign. He insisted that there should be health service charges.[56] If there were to be no charges, he himself would resign. Attlee, reluctantly, decided he had to support Gaitskell.

One element in the situation was the changed attitude to Gaitskell of Treasury officials. By his stand on the issue of health service charges, he had won their admiration. On the morning of his Budget, on 10 April 1951, after six months in office and in the midst of the clash with Bevan over health service charges, Sir Edward Bridges came to see him. 'I want you to know that not only all those in the Treasury who know about it tremendously admire the stand you have made, but that all the others who do not at present know but will know feel the same way. It is the best day we have had in the Treasury for ten years.' Gaitskell tells us that he was 'overcome with emotion' and could barely manage to murmur 'Thank you'. Gaitskell also records that 'the advice of Bridges and Plowden and Leslie [head of Information] and William Armstrong, my Private Secretary, never wavered. They did not ask the impossible from me but they made clear where they thought I should stand and why they thought I should stand.'[57] The admiration of officials can be an embarrassment to Ministers except the strongest, and an impediment to compromise with colleagues where compromise would otherwise be sensible.

Gaitskell presented his Budget on 10 April 1951. The additional cost of the health service was insignificant compared with the funding necessary for the new defence programme. The first question was how the inevitably deleterious effects on the British economy could be minimized. The second question, for a government probably facing an election in the not too far distant future, was how to manage what could well be the adverse political effects of a substantial increase in taxes. The Budget speech was widely praised for its lucidity. Gaitskell's own Party seemed pleased. His predecessor, Stafford Cripps, wrote to him that he should not be diverted from what he believed to be right 'by arguments of political expediency'.[58] He set himself, in his Budget, to fund the full rearmament commitment for the first year. He was helped by the substantial Budget surplus Cripps had left him. With the aid of higher taxes imposed mainly on the better off, and some helpful forecasts as to the growth of Gross Domestic Product, he not only made provision for the increase of £500 million to nearly £1,500 million in defence expenditure in 1951–2, he also increased old age pensions and safeguarded the health service, though at the cost of the charges that were to be implemented.[59]

Ten days after the Budget, Bevan resigned, followed by Wilson and John Freeman, Parliamentary Secretary at the Ministry of Supply, a junior Minister regarded as having a great future. Bevan saw that the health service charges were not a big enough issue to justify resignation, and therefore turned to an attack on the rearmament programme. This had been Wilson's theme from the beginning of the controversy, and also John Freeman's. It is unlikely, however, that Wilson and Freeman would have resigned without Bevan and it is unlikely that Bevan would have resigned had he not been provoked beyond his very limited endurance by the health service charges.

In his determination to fund the first year of the rearmament programme in full, Gaitskell was supported by his friend and future Chancellor, another graduate economist, Roy Jenkins.[60] Jenkins had taken throughout an optimistic view of the rearmament programme. In an article published in the left-wing weekly *Tribune* on 9 March, he had written that 'the impact of the rearmament programme upon our standard of living is likely to be less dramatic than many people at first believed, since much of the resources would come from increased production'.[61] This was optimism indeed. Perhaps Gaitskell had not informed his friend of his own doubts and of the warnings that he had been giving to the Cabinet and the EPC at least since January. Gaitskell was also supported by his other young friend, Tony Crosland, who later, when the Churchill government cut the rearmament programme back, went around complaining that his support for Gaitskell had made him look like a complete idiot.[62] This does not mean that on the big question, the rearmament programme, Gaitskell was wrong.

Budgets seldom look as brilliant in retrospect as they do on Budget day. On Budget day Chancellors have the advantage. As the days pass, the consequences flow, the critics acquire ammunition and can begin to shoot. Gaitskell had to contend not just with critics on the benches opposite but with powerful voices on his own backbenches, newly released from responsibility, only too anxious to proclaim that he was wrong and that they had told him so. Gaitskell was well aware of the risk that the programme could not be implemented in full. Both he and Attlee issued cautions in the House as to its practicality at a time when Bevan was telling the House that it would be implemented in full.[63] Gaitskell alerted the EPC to a grave shortage of machine tools on 3 April, seven days before the Budget. He thought it might be relieved by imports from the USA but, to the extent that such relief was available, it would add to the burden on the balance of payments.[64] In a speech to the Parliamentary Labour Party on 24 April 1951, Gaitskell denied Bevan's charge in his resignation speech that he knew the defence expenditure was already 'unrealizable'.[65] Gaitskell had always known that there were grave risks. He knew that the rearmament programme would provoke a serious reverse in national economic recovery, but he still believed that it was too early to be sure that the rearmament could not be implemented. The question would have been resolved by practical experience of the actual operation of the rearmament programme in a matter of months. It was certainly not a question warranting Cabinet resignations.

Whether or not Gaitskell was justified in his claim that it was premature at the time of his Budget to concede that the rearmament programme could not be implemented, he certainly had not realized how bad the consequences would be and how rapidly he would be facing a deficit on the balance of payments that would compel at least a partial reversal of policy. The responsibility lay with American rearmament much more than with British rearmament. The Americans, pressing Britain and Europe to rearm, were stockpiling and competing with their allies for the necessary raw materials. They demanded action from Europe and then acted in a way that made it economically impracticable. What ideally was needed was some way of organizing the exceptional demand that the West was placing on the world's raw materials. Gaitskell was able, through a visit to Washington in the autumn of 1951, to secure some prospect of help from the Americans even though US Treasury Secretary Snyder 'revealed himself as a pretty small-minded, small town, semi-isolationist'.[66] American officials inevitably appear ugly when they are refusing dole to mendicants. Nevertheless Gaitskell's visit did move opinion, and a committee of 'wise men' was set up under the chairmanship of Averell Harriman to investigate. Plowden was the British member. The concept of burden sharing re-emerged. It showed what a capable British Minister could achieve even in Washington if he was prepared to make the effort.

The British balance of payments went seriously into deficit. This was only partly due to the deterioration in the British terms of trade. It was also partly due to the diversion to rearmament of British export capacity. The Iranian oil crisis exacerbated the payments problem. It had been hoped in London that sales of commodities at inflated prices by the rest of the sterling area would add to the sterling area dollar pool and thereby help to fund the British payments deficit. Unfortunately, from the middle of 1951, prices for wool, tin and rubber began to fall and the rest of the sterling area decided to spend their dollars for their own benefit rather than to fund Britain's deficit. In the second half of 1951, the overseas sterling area was importing from North America at double the 1950 rate.[67] It was no doubt selfish but understandable. Dow says: 'The swing in the United Kingdom balance was the most sudden on record – from £300 million surplus in 1950 to over £400 million deficit in 1951, mostly concentrated in the second half of the year, and all of it with the non-sterling world. The overseas sterling area's position with the non-sterling world also worsened, and by about as much.'[68] By August 1951, Gaitskell was telling his diary that 'the balance of payments has gone wrong, chiefly because of a more rapid rise in import prices than we had allowed for, while at the same time the export drive has been very slow in getting under way'.[69] He was also writing in his diary that the increase in the cost of living, though not unexpected, was worrying politically.[70] But he was also being accused, for example in the *Financial Times* and *The Economist*, of deliberately using the increase in prices to force the consumer out of the market to an extent sufficient to release resources for the rearmament programme.[71] In a situation of this kind, appeals to the TUC for restraint, however well received, were likely to be ineffectual.

ON BLAMING GAITSKELL

Two fears led to the British rearmament programme. One was the fear that if Europe did nothing for itself, the USA would do nothing for it. The other was the fear of a Soviet invasion. If those fears can be discounted, the criticisms by Bevan and Wilson of the Gaitskell Budget of 1951 can be justified. In that case it would be right to argue that economic calculation was submerged by questionable anxieties about a

Soviet invasion and by an exaggerated ambition to be helpful to the USA. If there was no significant security risk, then Gaitskell and the Cabinet had indeed failed to limit the UK's commitments to what could sensibly be performed.

Whatever assessment is made in retrospect of the actual dangers in 1951, or in the following years, of a Soviet invasion of western Europe, they seemed real enough at the time. Stalin had established his defensive perimeter around eastern Europe, finally crushing Czechoslovak democracy in 1948. The war in the Far East was a further warning that communist expansionism had not been halted. British security depended on an American commitment to Europe. NATO had been established in 1949 to the great relief of the British government. Would the American commitment to Europe survive a British failure to respond to American pressure for rearmament? It was a secondary question whether the British government wholly accepted what, in retrospect, appears an unnecessarily alarmist interpretation of Soviet intentions. Despite his own private doubts, Gaitskell thought it important to avoid any danger of the State Department and Congress reacting badly to signs of hesitancy on the other side of the Atlantic. The State Department, if not Congress, was prepared to regard Britain as a serious, if often misguided, ally. Britain had continued to carry an excessive burden of defence expenditure since the end of the war. If that was to be changed, the occasion was not now. The judgement made by Gaitskell and the majority of the Cabinet was entirely defensible even if experience was to confirm that the programme could not be implemented in full either at the cost or in the time originally estimated. For the British government the essential point was to ensure American commitment to the security of Europe. It is arguable that as the Americans had come to regard Europe as a front line in the confrontation with the other super-power, it would have remained committed to Europe whatever Britain did. This is to underestimate the recalcitrance of Congress. At best it would have been to take a serious risk. There are considerations more important than economics and security is one of them.

Much is made in criticism of Gaitskell of the fact that the Churchill government, immediately on election, and in the subsequent years, pared down the rearmament programme to more practical limits.[72] So, no doubt, would a Labour government had it continued in office. But by the time of the election there was already less danger of the Korean War spreading into a general war. Shinwell, as was to be expected, was putty in the hands of the defence chiefs. He wanted yet further increases in the defence Budget and Gaitskell had to restrain him.[73] By the end of 1951 the Treasury had had a better opportunity to assess the defence estimates, and was exercising its talent for experienced scepticism.[74] However, when it was launched, it was a three-year programme with phased increases in expenditure each year. It was known that there would be time to learn from experience how the programme itself actually developed and, indeed, how the Soviet threat developed. The total programme over the three years ended up about 20 per cent lower than had been originally estimated. The important point in early 1951 was to send signals, westwards to the Americans, eastwards to the Soviet Union.

The principal criticism of the Gaitskell Budget is that it was not sufficiently anti-inflationary. The additional government expenditure wiped out the previous huge Budget surplus, so slashing the government's large contribution to savings. But that surplus, if not more, was required to contain the inflationary pressures within the economy. Though Gaitskell had done what he politically could to close the inflationary gap opened up by his Budget, his tax proposals were quite insufficient for the purpose. By August he was confessing to his dairy that 'it is clear that we under-estimated the extent of the inflationary pressure at home; this was partly due to dis-saving by the public in anticipation of price increases, partly because the impact of the defence programme, through contracts placed, has been rather greater than we allowed for. At any rate, the level of unemployment has fallen sharply to the 1945 figure.'[75] Another legitimate criticism is that Gaitskell did not act strongly enough against imports. His successor, Butler, took drastic action, cutting external expenditure by £550 million in his first months of office. With the assistance of these cuts, there was actually a surplus in the balance of payments in 1952. Gaitskell was probably constrained from such action by the imminence of an election and by his desire, during his September visit to Washington, to get help from the Americans, not further to offend them by a discriminatory policy. His failure in this respect entitled his successor, Butler, to characterize him as being 'a political mouse who, confronted with a gigantic deterioration in the balance of payments, responded by cutting a sliver off the cheese ration'.[76]

ASSESSMENT

The resignations of Aneurin Bevan and Harold Wilson divided the Labour Party at a sensitive moment, facing a probable early General Election. Their motivation in resigning may have included jealousy and resentment. On the other hand, it is fair to Bevan to say that he had been fighting against health service charges for at least a year before the final clash with Gaitskell in April 1951 and, therefore, well before he had any reason for *personal* resentment about Gaitskell's elevation. It may have been a bad principle but he had left no doubt, over a long period, that it was *his* principle.

Equally in question is Gaitskell's judgement in providing an excuse for their resignation. As his diary of the time shows, Gaitskell was obsessed by Bevan and by the need to establish his authority over him. His tragedy is not that he failed to contend with the impossible fiscal demands he had imposed on himself but that he split the government by insisting on the dental and optical charges which, financially, were neither here nor there. In an important sense he was right; the NHS *was* costing too much and charges were a reasonable requirement. Chancellors are always fighting for what seem insignificant cuts in departmental budgets. If they give way to one department, they will be pressed to give way to others. The whole concept of universal access to treatment free at the point of delivery was highly questionable. However, the charges Gaitskell imposed came nowhere near dealing with the problem. He himself, in his Budget speech, suggested that the ceiling on the cost of the NHS was not necessarily permanent. Later he was prepared to make a statement that the health service charges were not necessarily permanent.[77] When the legislation was before the House, it was agreed to limit the charges to three years unless an affirmative resolution was passed. If there was a question as to their permanence, there was a question also whether they were intended to be part of a permanent answer to the problem of health service costs. Gaitskell was prepared to make a costly concession to the Trade Union Group of the Parliamentary Labour Party on pensions.[78] He was forced to make a number of other concessions he did not like in order 'not to lose control of the Party to Bevan'.[79] Reading between the lines of his diary, he was not very happy at being forced, in the summer of 1951, to propose dividend limitation.[80]

So Gaitskell was quite capable of making concessions to win political support. But, apparently, to introduce £13 million of health service charges at that time had, for Gaitskell, an absolute priority which overrode all political considerations. On other matters he could compromise – not on this. The Cabinet, while supporting Gaitskell if there really was no alternative, was looking for a compromise. The necessary concession to Bevan would have been understood even though he was impatient and arrogant and noisy and apparently intent on exhausting the tolerance of his Cabinet colleagues. The political cost of the resignation to Labour and to Gaitskell was very great. Labour narrowly lost the election and Gaitskell never held office again.

To their critics within the Labour Party, neither Gaitskell nor Bevan ended up on strong ground. Gaitskell was accused of defending the marginal arithmetic of an impossible Budget. Bevan was accused of defending an impossible principle, that there should be no charges for NHS services. There was truth in both criticisms. This was not, of course, how the protagonists saw the dispute. Gaitskell saw himself as rallying the forces of the nation to its own defence and to the support of its great ally and, in the course of it, establishing the principle that a health service as expensive as the NHS had proved to be could not, in all circumstances, remain immune from charges at the point of delivery. Bevan, with Wilson's support, saw himself as defending the principles upon which his creation, the NHS, had been founded as part of a battle to defend the British economy against the poor economic judgement of the economist now in control at the Treasury. Out of this supposedly titanic battle, myths inevitably emerged. These myths were to dominate the history of the Labour Party for years to come.

A less weary Prime Minister might have told Gaitskell not to be silly, not to resign, not to get on his high horse, and to wait to impose adequate charges once Labour had regained office with a significant majority, after the coming General Election. A more self-confident and politically experienced Chancellor might not have needed such prodding from his Prime Minister. He would not have felt the need to establish his authority over his principal rival in so much of a hurry. He did not have to emulate Cripps in every facet of his predecessor's austere personality; indeed, he could have remembered that Cripps himself had made many compromises at a time when the political environment was much easier. Philip Williams argues that 'Gaitskell's whole case was that Labour had to prove itself a responsible Party of government . . .'[81] If it had not proved, after six years in office, that it was a responsible

Party of government, it was the fault of the Cabinet, and of Attlee, Dalton and Cripps specifically, not of Bevan personally. The split in the Cabinet, and the deeply personal way in which the disagreement was trawled before the public, was far more damaging to Labour's prospects than any earlier perception among the electorate of irresponsibility. In fact, Labour *was* regarded as a responsible Party of government because the ill consequences of its inflationary economic policies were not perceived. Nor was it yet perceived that the anti-inflationary action taken by Gaitskell in his Budget, and in his appeals to the TUC, was quite inadequate. Gaitskell was aware of the fact that his action on inflation had been insufficient and that the Budget was too soft, not too harsh. Things might have been different if a weary Attlee had not chosen October 1951 to face the electorate. The King was due to make a six-month Commonwealth tour in the new year and was concerned that a government with a mandate should be in office before he left so that no political crisis should occur while he was away. Attlee was persuaded by this argument despite the opposition of Morrison and Gaitskell both of whom were in North America when they heard of Attlee's decision, announced on 19 September 1951, and were deeply shocked.[82] It would probably have been better for the Labour Party if Attlee had hung on for another six or nine months, by which time the economic outlook appeared more favourable and the majority of the electorate would have had time to forget the resignations. Yet Gaitskell cannot escape all responsibility for the defeat.

The episode does credit to the judgement neither of Gaitskell nor Bevan. It is not possible, on the basis of this storm in a teacup, to claim great moral credit for Gaitskell. Rather is the truth of the matter revealed in a comment made nine years later by Gaitskell to George Brown. 'It was a battle between us for power – he knew it and so did I.'[83] His comment to Dalton at the time was that ' "It is really a fight for the soul of the Labour Party" . . . I am afraid that if Bevan [wins] we shall be out of power for years and years.'[84] The judgement on this paltry and ill-timed squabble lies in the record. With Bevan for this purpose his ardent collaborator, and with his other Cabinet colleagues looking helplessly on, Gaitskell brought down the temple of Labour and did not live to see it reconstructed by his more flexible successor as leader of the Party, Harold Wilson.

THE END OF A GOVERNMENT

When Labour left power in October 1951, it had done much for social improvement in the short term, nothing for the standard of living, nothing for the redistribution of wealth, nothing for the economy. Its failure on the economy was due primarily to its political commitments at the 1945 election but also to its fantasies about economic planning. By 1951 supposedly inconvertible sterling was being traded on foreign markets at $2.40 when the official rate was $2.80 and there was no way within existing policies of stopping such deals, despite the cost to the reserves. A foreign exchange crisis was brewing. It struck very suddenly. As late as July 1951, neither the Treasury nor the Bank seem to have been aware of the external crisis that was to hit sterling two months later. Early in September, the Treasury prepared a paper which declared the onset of the worst external crisis yet experienced. The Attlee government handed a serious sterling crisis to its successors and did nothing about it for the understandable, if not immaculate, reason that an election was pending. The Attlee government thus established one postwar tradition which other governments would happily follow.

For governments of any colour, it has always been easier to spend the national product than to stimulate its increase. Dalton committed the government to levels of public expenditure which it was then impossible politically to reverse. Cripps's reputation shone by contrast but he did little to justify it. Gaitskell, faced by a worrying security situation, had in his one Budget no chance to correct the errors of the past, but there is no evidence that he would have wanted to. It is in its way symptomatic that the final crisis of the Labour government should have been about £13 million of health service charges at a time when, in so many respects, Britain had been left unprepared for the competitive world that was emerging.

FIVE

Butler and the Liberation of Sterling

THE FIRST CHANCELLOR OF A NEW GOVERNMENT

Butler was not a compelling choice as Chancellor. Rather he was Chancellor *faute de mieux*. He lacked both the professional qualifications and the political base necessary for the job. As the only professional qualification is experience of economic management, it went without saying that he was lacking in that department. The absence of a strong political base was quite as important. He lacked the standing in his Party that a Chancellor needs and he was not sufficiently close to his Prime Minister to compensate for this lack. Churchill was unlikely to forget that in the 1930s Butler had been the Foreign Office's spokesman for appeasement in the House of Commons. Due to his withered arm, he could not fight in the war. The Butler Education Act might, in some eyes, be a glorious testimonial but, during the war, it was only for the Ministry of Education that Churchill had considered him fit.

Butler describes his appointment as Chancellor. Churchill received him in bed. He had prepared some comfort for his new Chancellor. 'It is no matter that you are not an economist. I wasn't either. And in any case I am going to appoint the best economist since Jesus Christ to help you.'[1] Churchill's tenure of the Treasury is not normally considered his period of greatest achievement, but he was confident that, if things had gone wrong on his watch, it had not been his fault. He had acted on the advice of the technicians and what else was a Chancellor supposed to do? Was he really supposed to have his own economic policy? Now a new era had arrived, the era of Keynes; Chancellors had to manage the economy. Did that imply that they must *understand* something about the economy? Or was it expected that officials would provide a new Chancellor with the necessary economics?

Butler was certainly no economist. It was not necessarily a disadvantage, though he was very dependent on advice. The postwar Chancellor whose prestige Butler hoped to emulate was Cripps, no economist himself. Dow says of him: 'Mr Butler never sought to rival his predecessor's display of economic erudition; and was averse neither to the broad statements acceptable to the plain man, nor to the metaphorical language frequently employed for the discussion of monetary policy.'[2] So far as economic management was concerned, Butler was a plain man. He fell back on broad statements and metaphorical language because it was in such language that he himself perceived economic problems. Butler was also no Keynesian. For many economists it was a matter for despair that so many politicians, not to mention Treasury officials, remained impervious to their increasingly influential science. Contrary to the views of his economic advisers, Butler was instinctively disinclined to Budget for a deficit. So indeed, was the Prime Minister. Despite the inroads being made by Keynesianism into British economic thought, it was an instinct that was widely shared, including in the Treasury. It was clear that, as between the old-time Treasury music and the enticements of modern economic pop, Butler knew which he would instinctively prefer.[3]

ALTERNATIVE ADVICE

The best economist since Jesus Christ turned out to be Sir Arthur Salter, a former international civil servant, then aged 70, who had served in the junior ranks of government during the war, mainly in shipping and transport. Salter describes his own initiation into the Treasury in 1951:

> When Churchill had invited me to join his Government . . . he gave me the choice of creating a new Economic Department, with myself as its Minister, or of joining the Treasury as second Minister. I chose the latter, being convinced that a new department would have no chance of winning any conflict with the powerful Treasury. But I did so with the proviso . . . that I should when I found it necessary, have full access to the Cabinet.[4]

Salter took the title of Minister of State for Economic Affairs. There must be some suspicion that he was appointed as a watchdog on Butler. He was rapidly to find an occupation in opposing the ideas of his master, the Chancellor. He may not have been the greatest economist since Jesus Christ but neither was he the figure of fun superciliously portrayed by Butler in his memoirs. Butler would have done well to take his views more seriously.

Churchill was keen on the concept of Ministerial overlords for groups of departments, and his government was constructed on that basis. He invited Sir John Anderson, who had served as Chancellor of the Exchequer during the war, to act as overlord of the Treasury, the Board of Trade and the Ministry of Supply, but Anderson refused as he regarded the system as inappropriate in peacetime.[5] As a substitute, Churchill constituted a Treasury Advisory Committee consisting of other close wartime colleagues such as Woolton, who was no friend of Butler's, and the Earl of Swinton who, as Air Minister before the war, had shared Churchill's doubts about the adequacy of the Chamberlain government's defence preparations. At the same time, Churchill's old friend and adviser, the scientist Lord Cherwell, was appointed to the freelance office of Paymaster General and brought the Oxford economist Donald MacDougall back into government service as his adviser. Cherwell's role was to provide the Prime Minister with yet one more source of economic advice alternative to the Treasury.

A NARROW VICTORY

The Conservative government had won the 1951 election with a narrow majority and, indeed, Labour had actually received more votes. The General Elections of 1950 and 1951 had both given narrow results. The electorate was clearly reserving judgement on both Parties. The Tories were determined not to be once again the Party of unemployment or to lay themselves open to the charge that they were undermining the welfare state. Polls suggested that as much as one-third of the working class had voted Tory. The Tories were also resolved not to antagonize the trade unions again, and were unwilling to confront them with the problem of wage inflation although, in the fourth quarter of 1951, wages were rising at an annual rate of 11 per cent.[6] Walter Monckton, the new Minister of Labour, was not allowed to attend Conservative Party conferences for three years after the election of Churchill's 1951 government. He had to be a non-partisan arbitrator and to be above suspicion.[7] Butler recounts how, against his wishes, Churchill and Monckton settled a railway pay dispute which seemed destined to disturb the 1953 Christmas holiday. Churchill phoned Butler about midnight to announce the settlement. Butler asked on what terms Churchill had settled. 'Theirs, old cock,' responded the Prime Minster.[8] Having regained power, it was the prime Tory objective not to lose it; it left little room for radical change or for radical disturbance of existing policy.

On the other hand, the Treasury and the Bank of England, misunderstanding the politics, saw in the election of a Conservative government the opportunity for change for which they had long been waiting. Many in the Treasury, including Bridges, thought the economy overloaded. The overload could be reduced if the rearmament programme was reduced. Perhaps a reduction would be easier to justify to the Americans with the hero Churchill in the chair at No. 10. But there would still be a larger rearmament programme than before the Korean War, and even then there had been many in the Treasury who complained that the economy was overloaded. The performance of the economy also left a great deal to be desired. Only a real willingness to start afresh and to overturn the heritage of the six postwar years would make possible a new departure in economic management. But it was not in the mind of the Prime Minister or of his Cabinet to implement such a change and Butler found he lacked the political standing to force change upon them.

So far from reducing inflationary pressure in the economy, the Tories appeared determined to increase it. At its Conference in October 1950 the Conservative Party Chairman, Lord Woolton, accepted as the policy of the Party a target of 300,000 houses. Butler considered the target unwise and inflationary, but he lacked the political muscle to overturn it.[9] It was the virtually unanimous advice of economists that the housing target should be abandoned. Macmillan, who had been appointed to implement the housing programme and whose career depended on his success, tells us of the battle he was compelled, during the first months and even years of the new government, to wage against the Treasury. He accepts that he won rather more than his fair share of the resources which the experts said would be available. Macmillan attributed his victory in these battles to Butler's 'warm expansionist heart'.[10] Butler had little choice; though he might have preferred a different course, his policy preferences were never strong enough to lead him seriously to contemplate resignation. He saw it as his task to manage policy agreed by the Cabinet rather than to insist on his own view.

INHERITING A CRISIS

Gaitskell assumed that Butler would be a leader in the struggle within the Conservative Party to improve its popular image.[11] This would have accurately defined Butler's sentiments in any situation other than that which he found on arrival at the Treasury. What he found, or was told, persuaded him that the government must break free of the political constraints, and he sought to stray from the consensual path. His colleagues would not permit it. They insisted that he should be a political Chancellor sensitive to their demands, not a revolutionary Chancellor striving to overturn the postwar economic settlement at home and abroad. Exhausted, he sank back into consensus, scared, in hindsight, at what he had, so adventurously but also so untypically, attempted. At first, and somewhat to his surprise, the policies which the Cabinet did allow him to implement were blessed with success and his reputation among the public soared. His success did not have the same effect on his political colleagues. They knew how narrow had been their escape.

Butler arrived at the Treasury to be greeted by dire foreboding about economic prospects. On leaving Churchill's bedroom, he had been given a deeply worrying introduction to his new responsibilities. He met Sir Edward Bridges, his Permanent Secretary, and William Armstrong, his Principal Private Secretary, at the Athenaeum. 'Their story was of blood draining from the system and a collapse greater than had been foretold in 1931.'[12] Blood was a euphemism for the gold and dollar reserves which were draining away because of the need to fund a large balance of payments deficit and maintain the exchange value of sterling. Because of uncertainty about the real value of sterling, the crisis was being compounded by leads and lags. As was already clear from the Labour government's negotiations with Washington, whatever help was to be expected from that quarter was not imminent and would be less than had been expected. Churchill, who had been briefed immediately on his return to office, conveyed his alarm to Oliver Lyttelton, who might have been Chancellor had he been a better performer in the House. Churchill had summoned him to discuss another appointment in the new government.[13] Perhaps by way of consolation that he would not be Chancellor, Churchill confided to Lyttelton: 'I have seen a Treasury Minute and already I know that the financial position is almost irretrievable: the country has lost its way. In the worst of the war I could always see how to do it. Today's problems are elusive and intangible, and it would be a bold man who could look forward to certain success.'[14]

Most of the measures taken by Butler to meet the crisis, and the more effective part, were those his predecessor Gaitskell would have taken once the election was out of the way. On 7 November, during the debate on the Address, he announced a savage cut in imports designed to save £360 million on the import bill.[15] Britain itself thus reversed the liberalization policy which had recently been adopted by OEEC under British leadership. The rearmament programme was re-phased over a longer period. In the circumstances, Gaitskell would probably have done that too. Butler also raised Bank Rate from 2 to 2.5 per cent. This his three Labour predecessors would not have done. The Bank of England had advised that, if an increase in interest rates was to have any real effect, it should be to 4 per cent but that a first small gesture, to show the market that interest rate policy was back on the agenda, would be useful. It also advised that no increase in interest rates could be expected to have much effect unless the government drastically reduced its expenditure.[16]

Butler's actions had implications for relations with the USA. The import cuts were clearly discriminatory and therefore contrary to the Anglo-American Financial Agreement. The US Administration had, in practice, accepted the deferment of convertibility and of non-discrimination and was prepared to be understanding of the practical economic realities of the moment. At a meeting in November in London, John W. Snyder, the US Treasury Secretary, pressed Butler to write him a letter reaffirming Britain's commitment to convertibility and multilateralism. Butler refused to arm the US Administration with a weapon that could, in due course, be used against him. He told Snyder that convertibility and non-discrimination were unlikely for some time to come.[17] Butler was not greatly in love with the USA and had no motive for being more cooperative – Snyder had confirmed that expectations of help from Washington must be kept modest, and the same message was conveyed during the visit of Churchill and Eden to Washington in January 1952.[18] This was an election year in the USA, not the most propitious time for countries with begging bowls. In an Emergency Action Paper dated 8 February 1952, prepared by the Overseas Finance Division of the Treasury (OF) in consultation with Robert Hall and Sir George Bolton of the Bank of England, American policy was bitterly attacked. It said: 'Our whole experience since their first approaches on rearmament in July 1950 has been most unfortunate. Indeed, the results of the United States' actions . . . would be more readily understandable if their purpose was to weaken the UK economy, rather than to strengthen it.'[19]

Hardly had Butler absorbed one set of horrifying figures and forecasts about the balance of payments and the loss of reserves than an even worse set was presented to him. On 27 November 1951, there was the usual meeting of Treasury Second Secretaries under the chairmanship of Sir Edward Bridges. Among those present were Sir Leslie Rowan, in charge of OF, Sir Norman Brook, Secretary of the Cabinet, and Robert Hall. The Bank of England was emphasizing that, once more, overseas opinion was losing confidence in sterling.[20] There was no good news. The reserves were still running out. Bridges said that in his view the economy was heavily overloaded. In summing up, he concluded that 'the Chancellor should be told as soon as possible that the position had deteriorated rapidly since the beginning of the month, and additional action was necessary in order to save the country from early bankruptcy . . .'[21]

The remedial measures in mind, necessary to restore confidence in sterling, were severe cuts in public expenditure, especially in food subsidies. This could be politically embarrassing – Woolton had given an assurance during the election that food subsidies would not be cut. At the meeting Hall demurred; he thought the alarm was exaggerated. No one could yet know what had been the effect of the November import cuts. Any action taken should be directed to the problem, and that was the balance of payments. If necessary there could be more import cuts. Hall, the most politically sensitive of economic advisers, considered that cutting food subsidies was not directed to the problem and would simply stir up trouble with the trade unions. But Bridges 'seemed determined to railroad it through . . .'[22] Hall considered that the whole incident was very disturbing and showed how silly senior Treasury officials could be. 'If they are not careful it will be 1931 and another Bankers' ramp.'[23]

The prospect of 'early bankruptcy' was one to stir Ministers, even the Prime Minister. On 28 November, the Cabinet set up a small group of Ministers to start considering a plan for the economy.[24] In January 1952, the government introduced hire purchase terms control on cars and on most other durable consumer goods, thereby inaugurating a form of discrimination against specific industries that was certainly damaging to them. Butler made a further cut of £150 million in imports. These early measures had the support of the Commonwealth. At a meeting of Commonwealth Finance Ministers between 8 and 21

January, the other sterling countries agreed to make cuts in their own imports with the object of restoring the sterling area to balance by the second half of the year.[25] There was, however, unease at the meeting that the sterling area was continually running into crisis and a demand that, although there could be no immediate prospect of it, a long-term plan should be elaborated which would lead to the convertibility of sterling. At the penultimate session, Arthur Salter spelt out the preconditions for sterling convertibility and added, unexpectedly, that it would be necessary to decide whether convertibility should be at a fixed or floating rate.[26] This was the only mention at the conference of the possibility of convertibility at a floating rate. From the point of view of the UK the immediate question raised by the conference was whether the other sterling area countries would, whatever their promises, make deep enough import cuts to safeguard sterling. Many of Butler's advisers were sceptical. They were equally sceptical whether the UK itself had yet done enough. Preparation began for what was to be a drastic deflationary Budget to be opened on 4 March 1952.

ROBOT

It was in these circumstances of panic and despair that Robot was proposed to Butler by the Treasury and the Bank. What was Robot or the External Sterling Policy (ESP), as it was sometimes called, or, as Butler described it, 'the Plan for External Action to Save Sterling'?

The name Robot has at least two possible derivations. The first is that it signified an intention to allow the price mechanism to regulate the economy, including in principle the value of sterling which was to be allowed to float. Thus the economy was to be put on automatic pilot. An alternative derivation is from the names of its three principal advocates, Sir Leslie **RO**wan, (Head of OF), Sir George **B**olton (an executive director of the Bank of England) and **OT**to Clarke, Under Secretary at OF.[27] OF was the section of the Treasury normally most influenced by overseas opinion. By the nature of its work, it had close relations with the Bank of England. Sir Leslie Rowan, formerly Principal Private Secretary to Attlee, was brilliant, difficult, and impatient.[28] Sir George Bolton was the brilliant but erratic director of the Bank principally concerned with overseas financial relations. Then there was Otto Clarke, the brilliant, erratic, overbearing and volatile brains of OF. He was an example of the truth that someone who can draft well and quickly can acquire enormous influence. The influence thus acquired is not always benign.

Robot was presented to Butler on 14 February by the Governor, Cameron Cobbold, together with a supporting paper from Bolton. Their recommendations carried the general support of the Treasury. Cobbold told Butler that nobody could predict the outcome of Robot but that the alternative was a 'wasting disease'.[29] The policy Butler was being invited by his Treasury and Bank of England advisers to adopt represented a revolution. It was proposed to introduce non-resident sterling convertibility as required by the Bretton Woods settlement but at the cost of reversing one key element in that settlement. The UK would abandon the 1 per cent margin mandatory under Bretton Woods and operate a floating rate for sterling, not a fixed rate. Convertibility at a floating rate was a simple principle. It was also a revolutionary principle. Fixed rates enforced discipline on governments and were the cornerstone of the new world economic order. They were to be adjusted only with the consent of the IMF under conditions of fundamental disequilibrium. The system of fixed rates was designed to prevent the competitive devaluations which, some believed, had been an important cause of the 1930s depression. Since the devaluation of September 1949, the fixed rate had been $2.80 to the £. The British government, issuer of the major international trading currency, was being invited by the advocates of Robot to undermine the postwar economic settlement crafted, in part, by Keynes.

A floating rate system for sterling did, however, impose its own disciplines. The advocates of Robot who, henceforth, we will call the roboteers, were well aware of the dangers and they concluded that the simple principle of convertibility at a floating rate would have to be surrounded by a variety of limitations and safeguards. An effect of the limitations and safeguards proposed was to turn simplicity into complexity. It became very difficult for most Ministers, and even for the Chancellor, to understand either the total project or its implications. One prerequisite was to be strong deflationary action at home to strengthen sterling. This would include a significant rise in interest rates and cuts in public expenditure, especially food subsidies, defence and housing. Housing had an important dollar cost as well as its domestic costs. A further prerequisite was that there must not be an excess of sterling in the market. In the view of the roboteers, that implied that the sterling balances had to be blocked with a view to funding them in long bonds at low rates of interest.[30] This was thought necessary because it was feared that with the world greedy for dollars and awash both with current sterling and the sterling balances, a convertible pound would be sold for dollars and its exchange rate would drop like a stone.

There was to be some discrimination in favour of sterling area sterling balances and sterling area developing country balances. The sterling area sterling balances were to be blocked to the extent of 80 per cent, the non-sterling area sterling balances to the extent of 90 per cent. There were already agreements with India, Pakistan and Ceylon, major holders of sterling balances, controlling their release. In order to avoid the accusation that the interests of Britain, a much richer country, were being put ahead of those of these three very poor countries, they would be told that if they really needed to use their sterling they would be permitted to do so.[31] On the other hand it would be made clear to Australia and New Zealand that if they could not accept these proposals they would have to leave the sterling area and receive treatment analogous to that accorded to non-sterling countries, but perhaps somewhat more favourable.[32]

The unblocked proportions of the balances were to be part of a new category of 'overseas sterling'. It was overseas sterling alone that would be freely convertible. Overseas sterling would also include sterling earned from current transactions except where it was held by residents of the sterling area. By the time that the roboteers had finished modifying the simplicity of the original concept, what was being proposed was a very limited form of convertibility. In practice the sterling that would be convertible would be the sterling held in the dollar area, or earned in current transactions by other foreigners, or held by sterling area central banks. Residents of the sterling area would, as before, be subject to exchange control. It was of the essence of the scheme that convertibility would apply only to so-called 'non-resident' sterling. It was hoped that the convertibility of a part of their sterling balances would reconcile holders to the blocking of the remainder. It was a view that required great optimism in those who held it.

There was unanimity about Robot neither within the Bank nor the Treasury. Intelligent and patriotic men took violently different positions, and relations within the Treasury suffered. According to E. G. Copleston, colleague of Clarke's in OF, the probable result of Robot would be the utter disruption of UK trade, the disintegration of the sterling area, the probable disintegration of the Commonwealth, the disintegration and economic collapse of Europe, and the possible emergence of a three-world economic system. He added that 'If we haven't got the resolution to get ourselves out of our present difficulties, why suppose that we should have more resolution when convertible? Surely we would simply choose the slippery slope of depreciation.'[33] Plowden, Head of the Central Economic Planning Staff, who had been close to Cripps but had been invited by Butler to stay on in the Treasury, also opposed Robot. Plowden looked to Robert Hall for economic advice. Hall, who had not been consulted before the plan was presented to the Chancellor, and whose relations with Clarke had never been entirely harmonious, was ready to do everything he reasonably could to prevent the implementation of Robot. In his opposition he was supported by the generality of government economists.

AN INVITATION TO REVOLUTION BUT NOT WITHOUT ITS PARADOXES

That the Treasury and the Bank of England should be attempting to frighten a new and inexperienced Chancellor into dramatic action will not surprise sophisticates. But such advice from such sources had its paradoxical aspects. Edward Bridges had opposed devaluation until the last possible moment in 1949 because it implied default; only when devaluation became inescapable did Bridges switch to support it. Now he was supporting Robot even though it clearly implied the depreciation of sterling. Clarke was a longstanding opponent of sterling convertibility – it had been his view that there could be no question of it until there was a reasonable balance with the dollar area. He was an equally long-standing upholder of discrimination against dollar supplies, but an impli-cation of convertibility could be that such discrimination would end. In 1945, Clarke's plea for delay had been ignored. Now, in February 1952, it was Clarke who was in a hurry, who forecast economic disaster, who demanded action by Ministers this day.

By the time of Churchill's return to government, six years had passed since the end of the war. From Clarke's point of view they were dis-appointing years. He could hardly conceal from himself that, despite inconvertibility and discrimination against dollar supplies, the British economy had staggered from one crisis to another. Now it was facing yet one more crisis. He was ready to take the opportunity of a new government to rethink policy. Previously, the advice Clarke had been giving was to a Labour government opposed, as he had been, to con-vertibility and non-discrimination. Now he was serving a Conservative government, which believed in 'freedom'. Its leader, Winston Churchill, was an advocate of a 'free pound'. Perhaps Clarke thought that he was advising within the context of the new government's political philosophy as well as in reaction to a manifest crisis. The temptation to try to persuade the incoming government to cut loose from the expedients and devices which, apparently, had failed must have been very great. Instead of a multiplicity of controls, there would be a dash for freedom. Instead of complexity, there would be the simplicity of convertibility and a floating pound. As with all simple ideas in economic management, when he and Bolton came to elaborate this apparently simple policy, it became more and more complex. But the fundamental concept had the virtue of simplicity, and the protective devices would be necessary only, he would hope, to cover the transition to freedom. Nevertheless, despite everything that can be said by way of explanation, it was an extraordinary reversal of attitude.

The Bank of England's advice was also not entirely consistent with its previous positions. As recently as January 1952, Cobbold had argued that, while convertibility was the objective, it could not be introduced until the sterling area was in equilibrium on its balance of payments, the reserves were substantially larger, and the USA was prepared to play the role of a good creditor.[34] That the Bank of England should want the earliest possible convertibility of sterling was not a surprise. The fact that Britain was bound by its adherence to the Bretton Woods articles to maintain its fixed rate had become welcome to the Bank. Every time, during the previous postwar years, when adventurous minds in or out of the Treasury had thought aloud about floating, the Bank had squashed them by reference to the UK's commitments to the IMF. Central Bankers always suspect that, if the currency floats, domestic fiscal and monetary policy will be too lax, and political convenience will have priority over economic discipline. A fixed rate acts as a constraint on the irresponsibility of governments, a proposition for which there is considerable evidence. So far as Britain's balance of payments problems were concerned, it had been Bank policy that they should be dealt with by deflation, not by floating. It was also something new that the Bank should propose in peacetime to block foreign holdings of sterling.

BUT WHAT IS FLOATING?

There was one significant difference in emphasis between the Treasury and the Bank. It lay in the interpretation to be placed on the word 'floating'. Was the pound to be allowed to float entirely free or was there still to be a fixed parity but with wider, possibly unpublicized, margins? The Bank's attitude on this question restores some consistency to its thinking. To the Treasury, a great part of the attraction of Robot was that, with sterling floating, there would be no requirement to spend the reserves to sustain a particular exchange rate. Clarke had always conceded that, although the rate would be 'flexible', it should nevertheless be supported within limits.[35] But the Treasury wished to be left free to judge, at the time, the scale and purpose of any intervention, depending, among other considerations, on the state of the reserves. On the other hand, Bolton had written to Salter on 25 January: 'There is . . . one price that must not be brought under the general principle of free market movements: that is the sterling-dollar rate.'[36] The Governor, in his note of 14 February to the Chancellor, insisted that the existing parity of $2.80 should not be abandoned, that the intention must be stability. He argued only that there should be wider spreads, say of 15 per cent.[37] This could imply a rate as low as $2.40.

So far as this could be called floating at all, it was 'dirty floating', that is floating subject to intervention by the reserves to ensure stability. Oliver Lyttelton, Secretary of State for the Colonies, probably the most knowledgeable supporter of Robot in the Cabinet, minuted the Prime Minister on 26 February: 'It is nonsense to determine in advance at what rate the pound is to be supported. There is not a great (though some) difference between saying "I will devalue the pound to a new fixed rate of $2.40" and saying "I will have a floating rate but I will support the pound at $2.40".'[38] The Governor noted on 22 February on a copy of a Clarke paper, 'I told the Chancellor that I thought the argumentation good, but that there was much too much "floating". We must have a high degree of stability.'[39] The rate could not be allowed to take the whole of the strain. The Bank's consistent view was founded in its belief, first that it would be impossible to maintain sterling as an international currency if no one would know what its value would be tomorrow or even later today; and, secondly, that politicians cannot be trusted with a freely floating rate.

The Treasury was gradually forced to abandon the position that the rate, not the reserves, should take the whole of the strain. Clarke's paper of 26 February says 'The present intention is to hold the rate within a range of 15% either side of $2.80 *provided that this is possible without dangerous loss of reserves.*'[40] In his paper for the series of Cabinet meetings on Robot on 28 and 29 February, Butler wrote: 'The official parity of $2.80 remains but the existing margins ($2.78-$2.82) are abandoned and the Exchange Equalisation Account is used to secure the maximum stability of the international value of sterling . . .' He added that the intention would be to seek initially to keep the rate within say 15 per cent of the official parity, that is about $2.40 to $3.20, *'as long as this does not dangerously weaken the reserves'.*[41]

The trouble with the Bank view, as Arthur Salter clearly perceived, was that what was now being proposed did not necessarily take the strain off the reserves and might amount to no more than a further devaluation of the pound. He wrote:

> The Plan, as now modified by support of the £ at $2.40, does not in net result improve, indeed it worsens, the balance of payments position . . .
> I consider the conclusion inescapable that the £ will be worth less than $2.40 in the market. If that is so, and on the assumption that the £ is supported resolutely at this point, the Plan would not achieve either of its primary objectives of making sterling a good and acceptable currency and saving the reserves. In effect the £ would be devalued to $2.40 and the reserves used in trying to support that rate.[42]

Salter's suspicion that sterling would fall below $2.40, unless supported, was probably justified. Non-residents of the sterling area already enjoyed *de facto* convertibility at $2.40. It was the phenomenon known as 'cheap sterling' which demonstrated that, at a significant discount to the official rate, foreigners could evade exchange control. Cheap sterling trans-actions reduced the dollar income of the sterling area. They damaged confidence in the official rate, the status of the pound as a reserve currency, and retarded the recovery of London as an international financial centre.[43] Convertibility within wider margins, combined with tough deflation, was the Bank's answer to this problem. In other words, the answer was the Bank's version of Robot.

By mid-March, the Treasury abandoned any qualification on its com-mitment to stability. In a Bank/Treasury paper of 19 March, the Treas-ury accepted Bank arguments so far as to agree to keeping the official parity of $2.80 but with a 10 per cent margin each way, say between $2.50-$3.10. Thus what had started out in the Treasury as convertibility at a floating rate in order to take the strain off the reserves had become, by mid-March, convertibility at a fixed rate but with wider margins.

THERE IS NO ALTERNATIVE

Butler was assured by the Treasury and the Bank that there really was no alternative to Robot. The loss of reserves in the first quarter of 1952 was expected to be not much less than $800 million.[44] On existing policies, the reserves were forecast to run down so fast that the government might soon find it had no choice but to float sterling simply because it did not have the reserves to sustain the fixed $2.80 rate. Over $2 billion had been lost from the reserves since June 1951 and they now stood at $1.8 billion.[45] It was better to take the plunge now, to deflate and to float voluntarily while the reserves were still sufficient to exercise some control over the rate. The intention was that after the Chancellor had taken the proposed action, the Bank should then strengthen the reserves by borrowing, pledging the UK's dollar securities in the New York market, and negotiating new loans from Canada, and from the IMF. It might seem optimistic to think that, in the circumstances, there could be help from the IMF, but the calculation was that it would be the end of IMF unless it acted cooperatively in this crisis, and that therefore help from that source might be available.

Clarke concluded his paper of 26 February by saying, 'ESP has not many attractions; it is forced action which no-one would take if there were a sound and prospectful alternative; but it at any rate has some possibilities of success, and if the accompanying internal action is strong enough, it should certainly ward off disaster and offer some prospects for recovery.' In other words Robot was an act of desperation.

The economist Professor Lionel Robbins had been a participant in many Anglo-American negotiations, during and after the war, including on the commercial aspects of the American Loan. He was now back at the London School of Economics, and the Treasury and Robert Hall saw him as a source of confidential advice. In his view, there were alternatives to Robot. When consulted informally on 27 February, he offered a prescription very different from Robot. First, he would raise Bank Rate to 4 per cent 'tomorrow' and would enjoin a very stiff credit policy on the Bank. If necessary he would be ready to see Bank Rate go to 5 per cent, a very high level by the standards of those days. He would then introduce a really stiff Budget with a big reduction in food subsidies and big increases in petrol tax and other indirect taxes. 'On subsidies, he thought the Government's policy was absolutely wrong and that it needed complete recasting. Indeed he would like to see the housing subsidy abolished altogether.' He saw no reason why the UK government should not approach the sterling area countries and ask them to agree voluntarily to fund a considerable proportion of the balances. He would not attempt to freeze foreign sterling balances at the present time. Finally, he added, 'The real essential' was 'to stop inflation and from the economist's point of view this could be done without the slightest difficulty, provided Ministers were prepared to take resolute action.'[46] In March, Robbins submitted his views in writing. He commented, 'one of the most perplexing features of the whole situation is the apparent prevalence of the view that no other course is conceivable, that human ingenuity is exhausted, and that the only choice is between sitting still and doing nothing, and taking a deep breath, shutting one's eyes and plunging into the abyss'.[47]

BUTLER ACCEPTS THE ADVICE

Butler accepted the Bank/Treasury advice even though it represented a revolution and had clearly been cobbled together in great haste. For a new Chancellor in a new government, there is always attraction in doing something radically different. Butler had no ideas of his own. He was the more ready to accept ideas from others as they appeared to chime in with Conservative propaganda. Conservatives stood for freedom, not for restriction, and here was the path of freedom. Butler was being offered a dramatic opportunity to change policy radically and to become the saviour of his country. Without the necessary understanding of the political and economic realities, without adequate analysis and discussion, he succumbed to the temptation, and decided to take the advice of the Treasury and the Bank of England.

On 19 February, the Governor dined with Churchill, Butler, and the Leader of the House, Harry Crookshank. The meeting concluded that if any drastic changes were decided on, it would be wrong to introduce a Budget in which the Government gave the impression that it had no intention to take further, radical, action. The deduction drawn from this was that if the new plan were to be put in force it would have to be announced on Budget day, 4 March.[48] It is, after all, the first principle of democracy that if a new government has to implement unpleasant action, it should do it quickly and get it over with. Butler agreed that action must be taken in the Budget. One of the fears was that the publication early in April of the reserve figures, which would show a large loss, would cause a panic in the exchanges and sterling would come under pressure that could not be resisted. This was taken to underline need for action in the Budget. Hall was horrified at the rush. The Treasury also saw that the decision to incorporate Robot, if approved, in the Budget made a Budget on 4 March impracticable. For example, time was needed to draft the necessary messages to Commonwealth governments, not a small matter given what was proposed. Commonwealth governments were to be kindly allowed a few days' notice of the blow they were about to suffer. Budget day was, therefore, deferred for one week to 11 March. It was still impracticable in the time for the Treasury or the Bank, or the Cabinet, to give proper consideration to what was a revolutionary proposal. The Treasury and the Bank had barely a fortnight to develop in precise detail a major reversal in British economic policy, of which they themselves had only just thought, and which they knew would have widespread international consequences, not just economic but political. During the next few days, two processes were in train simultaneously. The Treasury and the Bank were refining the plan in so far as the time permitted. Butler was trying to persuade his Cabinet colleagues that the plan should go forward in the Budget even though they were not to be allowed time to think. In that effort Butler was not at all assisted by the noise of controversy emanating ever louder from among his embattled official advisers.

ADVISERS DEBATE

The arguments about Robot among officials mainly took place *after* Butler had committed himself to it rather than before. There were four main issues. First, the compulsory blocking or funding of the sterling balances was bound to cause a major row with the whole of the non-dollar world including the sterling area. Commonwealth Finance Ministers, at their conference in London, had looked forward to the day when sterling would be convertible. But now they were to be forced, as the price of convertibility of a new category of 'overseas sterling', to accept the funding or blocking of by far the greater part of their sterling balances. This might be attractive to a British government which felt, as Churchill did, that Britain had inherited an unfair burden from the war. But this was different from the blocking proposed in the discussions leading to the Anglo-American Financial Agreement. That referred to the balances accumulated during the war, to which Churchill's grievance had some relevance. The balances now included sterling earnings accumulated during six years of postwar trade.[49] To block them would be a major breach of faith with serious effects on Britain's international relations. Robbins, when privately consulted on 27 February, was outraged that a British government should consider such a proposal.[50] Subsequently he wrote, 'I must confess myself amazed by the picture that has been revealed to me. After the war, some of us were very keen to see some operation of this sort on the abnormal accumulation of wartime. We got very little attention for our pains. We were told that such a policy was unthinkably dishonourable, etc. etc. But now in circumstances when it is much less easy to justify on moral grounds and when the internal situation is entirely different, just this policy is proposed . . .'[51] In a later paper, after he had once more been consulted informally, Robbins wrote, 'In the end, I believe what worries me most about all this is the question of honour . . . what is proposed, although proposed by men of the highest integrity and with the best possible intentions, is not in fact strictly honourable.'[52]

Secondly, Robot would damage Europe and Britain's relations with Europe. It would destroy the European Payments Union (EPU), the principal instrument of multilateral trade in western Europe of which sterling was part. The EPU brought partial convertibility to inconvertible European currencies. Its destruction would therefore set back the process of European integration on which both the US Administration and most Europeans set great store. In his paper of 26 February prepared for the Cabinet, Butler wrote that the UK would have to withdraw from the EPU. It could not withdraw without the obvious consequence. 'Both the EPU and the liberalisation of intra-European trade are in any case very near collapse, but our becoming convertible would kill them altogether.'[53] There were certainly difficulties in EPU including a vast German deficit. Thus, in the view of the roboteers, the EPU was doomed whatever Britain did. They did not much mind that. Rowan was hostile to the European movement and Clarke wrote, 'I think that the economic future is with the United States and Canada rather than with the sterling area and Europe.'[54] But it was one thing for the EPU to collapse, another for Britain to destroy it. If Britain destroyed the EPU, the US Administration was unlikely to feel sympathy, nor would Britain's European trading partners. The roboteers' forecast of the demise of the EPU proved wildly exaggerated. It was not their only forecast that went astray. The EPU survived with great success until 1958.

Thirdly, the opponents of Robot claimed that if current sterling was convertible into dollars it would harm British exports. Those who earned sterling would at once convert it into dollars because there was more that they wanted to buy from the USA than from the UK. This risk was admitted by the roboteers. But they drew comfort from the fact that sterling would be floating, would presumably float down if there were any such trend, and that therefore British exports would become more competitive and imports less attractive because more expensive in sterling terms. This should help the UK balance of payments. But, as was argued by the critics and accepted by the advocates, this would be so only on two conditions. The first condition was that imports, which were already heavily restricted, could be reduced further without damage to economic activity. The second was that British exporters could supply. Even those opponents of Robot who were not opposed to floating in principle were confident that, due in large measure to the defence programme, there were serious supply shortages in the UK and that therefore it was the worst time to allow sterling to float down. The trouble with this kind of calculation is that it is static. It is always uncertain how rapidly an economy will respond to greater competitiveness and increased demand. Similar arguments had been adduced against the 1949 devaluation, but the economy had in fact responded quite rapidly. In any case, insisted the Treasury roboteers, sustaining sterling at an unrealistic exchange rate involved the expenditure of dollars from the reserves which could be better used for other purposes.

A Conservative government with a small majority was unlikely to ignore the domestic political implications of Robot. This was the fourth, and probably decisive, area of controversy, the effect of Robot on inflation and on unemployment. There was a strong difference of opinion on how far floating would raise prices. Lionel Robbins believed that it could cause runaway inflation.[55] Clarke, on the other hand, estimated that if the depreciation against all non-sterling currencies was 10 per cent, the rise in the cost of living would be 1.25 per cent. If the depreciation was against the dollar alone, the rise would be less than 0.5 per cent.[56] But who knew how far sterling would depreciate and how many other currencies would float with sterling? Even the Bank had allowed for 15 per cent depreciation. Salter was prudent to argue that one of the costs of Robot might be an increase in unemployment.

If resources were to be diverted into exports on a scale necessary to correct the external deficit, it would require major deflation. Hall estimated that unemployment might rise by from 300,000 to 500,000 above the existing level of about 400,000.[57] Clarke considered that a rise in unemployment was in any case desirable. It was a question of redefining full employment. He wrote, 'My own impression is that you need about 3% unemployment . . . but if you get up to 1,000,000 or more it is self-destroying, as it was in the '20's and '30's.' Thus a rise in unemployment was one of the inevitable necessities of Robot, but not just of Robot. He added 'There is nothing in ESP which avoids the need for most drastic internal action. The Budget, credit policy, defence, housing – all the most vigorous policies possible to release resources for exports are most urgently needed.'[58] Although Beveridge had thought 3 per cent unemployment acceptable, neither Labour nor the Tories in government, did so. It was a powerful weapon in the hands of the opponents of Robot that its first effect could be a rise in unemployment.

Here there was a straight difference of economic judgement. Treasury officials, and Bridges specifically, thought that the economy was overloaded and that deflation was essential whether or not Robot was implemented. Robot might add to the need for deflation because, with the pound floating down, a greater diversion of resources into exports would be necessary. But, whatever the truth, it was, in the Treasury judgement, a matter of degree. The economists, and certainly Robert Hall as demonstrated at the meeting on 27 November, appeared to take a more relaxed view of the overloading. They did not deny it, but it was something to be managed in a politically sensitive way. Hall considered deflation economically undesirable. Consumer demand had already fallen. In any case, he believed, deflation would not be politically acceptable. As an adviser he was always concerned with what would be politically acceptable. It was not the right political climate to encourage dangerous experiments. Plowden was deeply concerned by the political consequences of Robot. He believed that it would have terrible consequences for the government and for the political Party of which the government was formed. Nevertheless he conceded that if the government was not prepared to adopt his ideas, which had much in common with those of Robbins and Salter, there was no alternative but Robot.[59]

In face of all these controversies, there was, for the roboteers, the argument of last resort. Obviously Robot involved great risks. So far from denying them, they emphasized them. The Treasury was so confident that there was no alternative that it had no hesitation in making the risks absolutely clear in the advice it presented to Butler. Indeed they were made so clear that when the proposals, with Butler's support, became the subject of controversy in Cabinet, his principal opponent, Lord Cherwell, was able to make a major part of his case simply by quoting Butler. Normally, the roboteers confessed, one would hesitate a long time before taking such risks. Yet, they argued, the government could not afford to hesitate. The forecasts provided by OF and the Bank of England of the consequences for the reserves if Robot was not activated were dire in the extreme.

OF STRONG MEN AND DITHERERS

Butler was no doubt influenced by the fact that most of the opponents of Robot, such as Salter, Hall and Plowden, did not say that it should not be done, indeed they thought that probably it would in the end need to be done, but that implementation should wait, at least until the government could assess the effects of the Budget and of the import cuts. In other words, the opponents of Robot appeared, to Butler, as ditherers compared with the strong, desperate, but determined roboteers. Much of the roboteers' argument was conceded. Hall's early alternative to Robot included the blocking of non-sterling area sterling balances, one of the features of Robot that might have given Butler pause.[60] Many of the opponents were not against floating but against floating now. Hall and Plowden both saw merit in a floating rate provided sterling was strong enough. Even Robbins, who was sceptical about the merits of a floating rate, thought that it might perhaps be done, provided it was from a position of strength and there was strict control of credit to prevent inflation.[61] The report of the meeting with him on 27 February concludes as follows:

> Having said all this Professor Robbins said it was subject to the overriding condition that matters might so develop that we should have to take action on the lines proposed in two or three months time. But he thought that if we did so, after we had made a resolute attempt to cure our troubles by determined action at home, we should be able to act without the risk of offending all our friends throughout the world, inside and outside the Commonwealth.

Thus those, other than Cherwell, who emerged as the strongest opponents, and who later took credit for their opposition, were ambivalent in their attitude. This ambivalence affected Butler, who had no standards of judgement of his own. For example, on the record of the discussion with Robbins on 27 February, he minuted, 'I note that the Professor thinks we shall need this B-plan in the end. He shows wisdom in his approach but does not have to run the risk.'[62] Butler was not prepared to take the risk of dithering. He would follow the strong men.

DEFEAT

Butler then found that whatever the economic merits of the policy he had adopted as his own, in the view of his colleagues the political risks were too great. A paper was presented to a Committee of Ministers on 22 February which they were expected to read and absorb there and then and leave on the table at the end of the meeting. Cherwell refused to leave the paper behind. He wished to study it with the help of MacDougall, his economic adviser. There and then the scheme began to unravel and in the worst possible atmosphere. There were too many political doubts. At a Ministerial meeting on 27 February, Butler argued that he had no doubt that sterling was overvalued and that no alternative policy could be put forward which would save the currency. He was opposed by Cherwell and Salter. Cherwell said that 'If the Chancellor's scheme is proceeded with, it would lead to an appalling disaster.' Only Lyttelton, the one experienced industrialist in the Cabinet, strongly supported Butler. Once Ministers were given time to think, the instinct of self-preservation took charge.

In the course of three Cabinet meetings on 28 and 29 February, action in the Budget was rejected by the Cabinet. Robot itself was not rejected – it was simply deferred. The Cabinet was unwilling, without further evidence, to take the risks with the future of the Commonwealth and the sterling area, with the UK's other international relations, with its international trade, with inflation, and with unemployment. There was the memory of the disaster over convertibility in 1947. The danger of saddling the Conservative Party once more with the reputation as the Party of unemployment was too great. There was considerable doubt whether, with the Government's small majority, it could get Robot through the House. Salter argued that twenty Tory abstentions would bring the government down and Labour would win the subsequent election. As an alternative, the opponents suggested 'a severe Budget', cuts in imports equal to what was expected from Robot, increases in coal exports and the Bank Rate.[63] It was argued that the measures already taken had not yet had time to take effect and that, supported by a strong Budget and an increase in Bank Rate, they might prove to be enough. It was better to wait and see whether the Bank's dire forecasts were justified by events. In an emergency, there could be recourse to the IMF.

The Cabinet minutes of 28–29 February record the following fascinating argument against Robot:

> Under democratic government with universal suffrage such violent reversals of policy were hardly practicable. Even if the case for this change were abundantly clear on the merits, there would be very great difficulty in persuading the public to accept it. Moreover, the adoption of this policy would create an unbridgeable gap between the Government and the Opposition; and, if it were thought possible that an even more grave economic crisis might develop later in the year, it would be unjustifiable to take as this stage a step which might exclude all possibility of forming a National Government to handle that situation.[64]

It is not possible at this stage to be certain what arguments most influenced the Cabinet. It may be that the political arguments against Robot were felt to be so strong that they carried the economic arguments, which were more debatable.

Butler was exceedingly distressed by the Cabinet's refusal to allow him to save the country. He called a meeting and upbraided Salter and Plowden.[65] In the heat of battle, Butler resented Plowden's attitude. Plowden had been at a NATO meeting in Lisbon with Anthony Eden, the Foreign Secretary, when he was warned by Hall of the advice being given to the Chancellor by the Treasury and Bank of England. Plowden was placed in a quandary. He owed loyalty to the Chancellor but he was horrified at the advice the Chancellor, in his absence, was receiving. He decided to alert Eden to the international implications of Robot and advised him to signal London that no decision should be taken in his absence.[66] Bridges, apparently, was 'very cross' and thought Plowden 'had behaved badly in intriguing against the Chancellor'.[67] William Armstrong told Plowden that Butler had lost confidence in him.[68] Butler, who only months before had persuaded Plowden to stay, now appeared to be trying to get rid of him.[69] Plowden, who had expected to leave the Treasury when the Conservatives won the election, was now refusing to move while his reputation was under a cloud. Relations within the Treasury, and between the Treasury and the Economic Section, particularly between Hall and Rowan, became, and for some years remained, very bad.[70]

BUDGET

On 11 March, Butler introduced a Budget in which there was no mention of Robot. He reduced income tax, announced that Bank Rate was being raised to 4 per cent, and made further cuts in imports, and in expenditure. Food subsidies were cut by £160 million though they remained substantial, protecting both the cost of living and the interests of small farmers. It was considered quite a mild Budget. Dow comments that the mildness of the Budget appeared to have taken opinion by surprise.[71] But Hall expected the increase in Bank Rate to have 'a severely deflationary effect'.[72] Not fully appreciated at the time was that there was already a recession in demand exacerbated by the decision of the Australian government to include British goods in their import cuts. Overseas opinion was, perhaps, convinced by the increase in Bank Rate. Sterling strengthened. The outflow of reserves slowed and then reversed. The inevitable crisis did not occur. The Bank's forecasts proved wrong. 1952 produced a balance of payments surplus of £300 million, a turnaround of almost £700 million from the previous year, despite a 10 per cent fall in export volume.[73] The British economy had been saved for the moment. Not until the autumn of 1954 was sterling to come under pressure again. It was six more years before non-resident sterling became finally convertible though a significant step towards it was taken in January 1955. Temporary salvation had come not just from actions of the government but from the end of the 1951 stock-building boom, and from the reversal in the trends of overseas prices, specifically the improvement in Britain's terms of trade. Now began that period of declining commodity prices that so much enriched the British economy as well as the economies of other developed countries at the expense of the developing world.[74] The roboteers never really recovered their credibility. If one bases revolutionary proposals on a forecast, at least the forecast should be right.

Robot was re-examined in summer 1952. Cobbold, betrayed by the facts, tried to make the best of it by continuing to threaten woe. He warned that the remission following the Budget was not a reprieve but a temporary stay of execution. The debate continued within the government. The Bank and the Treasury prepared massive papers examining every aspect of Robot. Much more study was given to Robot after the Budget than had ever been given before. On 21 June, Cobbold wrote to Butler that 'the risks and dangers [of implementation] must be accepted as greater than they would have been if the plan had been adopted in March.' Nevertheless, 'It is our earnest hope that Her Majesty's Government will give this problem their most urgent attention with a view to comprehensive action at a very early date.'[75] The Treasury remained committed to Robot and, indeed, convinced that its time would soon come. Butler resumed the battle. He still thought 'that a Currency slide and crisis is very likely unless some further move is made, while yet there is time . . .' Robbins was consulted again but had not changed his mind. Hall and Salter wrote minutes that they admitted to be repetitive.[76] Butler presented a paper to a group of Ministers, repeating the arguments for Robot that had persuaded him in February.[77] But it is much easier to inspire enthusiasm for revolutions in economic policy when bankruptcy threatens than when life appears to have returned to normal, even if, as the Bank argued, it is a precarious normality. If Butler could not carry the Cabinet in February, he certainly would not carry it in June. Butler's own enthusiasm was diminishing. The experience of Robot was teaching him to forgo enthusiasm. He would never be enthusiastic again. He had warned of disaster unless he acted in his Budget, he had been refused the necessary clearance by his Cabinet colleagues, and now lacked even the satisfaction of the disaster he had foretold with which to reproach them. Churchill's enthusiasm for dramatic action on the economic front had also waned. Chancellors look to their Prime Ministers for support. Like Attlee's Chancellors before him, Butler looked in vain. He thought he had Churchill's sympathy. It was more difficult to command his attention. It was long past the era in which Churchill could direct his mind to such complex issues; he now had other ways of making decisions than by a study of the merits. The opposition to Robot was still led by Cherwell and Salter. They had, in the past, been rivals. Salter had defeated Cherwell in 1937 when they contested a by-election for one of the Oxford University seats. They were not fond of one another. Now, unusually, they were united. At the end of much discussion, Churchill, in June, is reported to have said: 'I don't know much about these technical financial matters myself, but I can't help feeling that when Cherwell and Salter agree there must be something in what they say.'[78] Robot in effect died, though it had a slow and miserable demise through something known as the collective approach.

Butler's regret about his defeat on Robot is clearly recorded, many years later, in *The Art of the Possible*. 'In the long-term . . . I believe that the decision not to free the pound was a fundamental mistake. The absence of a floating exchange rate robbed successive Chancellors of an external regulator for the balance of payments corresponding to the internal regulator provided principally by Bank Rate.'[79] Nevertheless he did not push his view to the point of resignation; he fought, but then allowed Robot to die. He saw his role as managing the policies adopted by his colleagues rather than as insisting on his own policies. Butler lamented the word 'Butskell' which *The Economist* had compounded out of his name and that of his predecessor. Politically, it had done him harm. 'If the pound had been set free in 1952 the word "Butskellism" might never have been invented.'[80] The term 'Butskell' was justified by Butler's inability, and subsequently unwillingness, to implement a radical change in policy. Eventually he abandoned the cause of floating. The day came, in 1953, when Butler confessed to Hall that he had been wrong about Robot.[81] He also seems to have told Bridges that Hall had been right all along.[82] When Salter retired from the government in 1953, Churchill said to him, 'You did a great public service in that affair about sterling last year – and Rab now knows you are right.'[83] The regrets that Butler expressed in *The Art of the Possible* do not seem to have been present in 1953 or after. They made their reappearance just in time for his autobiography. The story of Butler as Chancellor is of a transition from alarming crisis, with Treasury officials almost hysterical as they contemplated collapse and disaster for the British economy, to the more normal state of amiable drift.

THE COLLECTIVE APPROACH TO CONVERTIBILITY

The difference in the collective approach was that what it had been intended to explode on an astonished world by unilateral British action, was now to be accomplished by international agreement and with the help of American dollars. There had by late 1952 been so much consultation, particularly with the French, that the Robot idea was no longer a precious secret in the bosom of the British government. It began to be hoped that, although Robot might be inadvisable as a unilateral action by the British government, it might be possible to achieve the same objectives by a 'collective approach' involving the Commonwealth and Europe with American support. Sterling convertibility was thought to require an IMF standby of $2.5 billion. Only $1.3 billion was available from the UK quota and the IMF would have to borrow dollars from the USA if it was to supply the balance.[84] Through the intermediary of the IMF, the British begging bowl was once more to be extended in the direction of Washington. The ensuing negotiations tended to weaken sterling in the market owing to the rumours generated that it might be made convertible and float. They did not lead to any positive outcome.

The trouble with the collective approach was that the collectivity was notable only by its absence. Collective approaches come up against differences of national interest. There was no reliable support from other countries and the rest of western Europe was positively against it. Also notable by its absence was any intention by the USA to subscribe any dollars. In November 1952, Churchill's old friend Eisenhower was elected to succeed Truman as President of the USA. In March 1953, without proper previous consultation with its EPU associates, the views of the new US Administration were tested by Eden and Butler. They informed the US Administration that it should help towards convertibility both by large scale financial assistance through the IMF and by lowering US tariffs. But the Administration saw no reason for further generosity towards the UK. It felt that the UK was not yet ready for convertibility, and, in any case, it did not favour floating.[85] In the American scale of priorities, non-discrimination now came ahead of convertibility.[86] The collective approach was in fact as dead as Robot. However, it refused to lie down, adopting various disguises over the next few years without deceiving either the Americans or the Europeans into giving it any support.

WHO WAS RIGHT?

Since the defeat of Robot, those on the winning side of the argument have proudly displayed their campaign medals – bravery in the service of the British economy – even though not all of them were quite as certain they were right before the decision against as they have found it convenient to claim since the decision. The principal victors were Cherwell and Salter among ministers, and Plowden, Hall and MacDougall among officials.

The economists generally were against Robot, both at the time and in retrospect. MacDougall writes that, if Robot had been implemented, 'I am at least certain that the twenty years [from 1952] would have got off to a very bad start, with high unemployment and inflation, intensified

controls, chaos in the international monetary system, and highly unfavourable reactions from our trading partners.'[87] Cairncross writes, 'Robot
would have been disastrous, politically and economically . . .'[88] Plowden
writes: 'I believe that the introduction of "Robot" in 1952 would have
been an economic and political disaster for this country and the world.'[89]
On the other hand the economic journalist, Samuel Brittan, has found
merit in Robot. He is worth quoting at some length because he rep-
resents the alternative point of view:

> It is questionable if the fierce hostility of the progressives to Robot was
> well judged even in 1952. The operation might well have led to a realign-
> ment of currencies which would have put an end to the dollar shortage.
> Although British living standards would temporarily have fallen, the auth-
> orities would have been left with an automatic balance-of-payments
> adjustment mechanism, and many of the 'stops' of the next decade and
> a half might have been avoided. But even if the case against Robot is
> conceded for 1952 . . . in the following years the dollar shortage eased
> and defence spending was no longer pre-empting the resources that could
> have supported an export drive. If the economic planners in the Treasury
> had come out wholeheartedly in favour of convertibility at a floating rate
> in, say, 1954, the whole course of subsequent British economic history
> might have been changed immeasurably for the better.[90]

More recently Lord Roll has written: 'I would now say that the decision
to turn down ROBOT was an error.'[91]

The view of this author, sadly, is that the Cabinet was right to turn
Robot down. I say that, although I believe in floating rates and I believe
that sterling should have been floated, or at least devalued, in 1945 –
accompanied by appropriate domestic policies. But in 1952, or even in
1954, Robot was impossible politically. It was politically impossible in
1952 to block the sterling balances except *in extremis* and it was not yet
in extremis – an alternative policy was available and, in a sense, it worked.
It would have been difficult enough to block the sterling balances in
1945 but now it was impossible. Robot would have caused a major row
with the USA and with Europe. With the USA, not so much because
of floating, but because of the effect of Robot on the integration of
Europe. Britain had refused to join the ECSC. It could not also force
Europe back to bilateralism in trade. In any event, the Cabinet were
not prepared to accept the expenditure cuts that would have been needed
with Robot. Would Macmillan, for example, have been prepared to
abandon the housing programme which he had been appointed specifically to implement?

In this sense then, the anti-roboteers were right. But for all that, I have great sympathy with the roboteers. The battle essentially was between, on the one hand, those who thought that, except for a crisis attributable mainly to the bad behaviour of the USA, the UK was really doing rather well;[92] and those, on the other hand, who saw that the UK economy was doing rather badly and thought some stiff competition would force better performance. The roboteers were the discontented men. They were discontented with the performance of the British economy and indeed with that of British governments, and demanded urgent action to improve economic performance. Their mistake was to attempt to bluster their ideas through a new British government without the necessary preparation.

Hall recognized that the UK had a problem and that, even though Robot might not be the answer, an answer was necessary. But his own answer was at least as unrealistic as Robot. Hall was asked to prepare a paper saying what he would do in what even he admitted were grave difficulties. He attempted to revive earlier ideas from the days of the Attlee government. Hall's mind was continually reverting to the policies of the Attlee government. With the help of their economic advisers, the Attlee government had in the end, in his view, got it more or less right, not absolutely right but certainly enough to make unnecessary any such radical change in policy as was represented by Robot. He prepared a paper in which the crisis was blamed almost entirely on the USA including on American protectionism. 'It is from . . . the violent swings in US buying, rather than from any special weakness in the United Kingdom, that our difficulties arise.' Hall suggested that the way forward was to divide the world in two, a first world that was the dollar world and a second world based on sterling. Europe was to be recruited to the sterling area. Trade within this second world would be conducted without recourse to gold or dollars and on the basis of large credit extended by participating countries to each other. The USA would thus be isolated, apart from buying absolute essentials from it, until it learnt to behave better. Hall also wrote that 'it was recognized by both parties to the 1949 talks that the bridge between the dollar and non-dollar world could only be built from both ends. Our experience since then has not been encouraging. No system which puts all the strain of adjustment on the weaker Party is likely to be permanent.'[93] It is one of the lessons of the postwar world that the strain of adjustment will always be placed on the weaker Party.

It was an absurd paper to which Clarke wrote a devastating response.

If Robot had its problems, Hall's ideas had even greater problems. Assuming their practicality, they would have created an isolated and uncompetitive trading group built round sterling. Plowden reports that when, many years later, he reminded Hall of his paper, 'he could hardly believe he had drafted it, and said that he felt ashamed of himself'.[94] He deserved to be. Nevertheless, Hall's two-world paper represented the view not just of Hall but of the Economic Section in general.[95] That Hall and his supporters could be as misguided as the roboteers is forgotten because Hall fought Robot and Robot in the end seemed to have been proved unnecessary.

The roboteers, on the other hand, accepted that Britain must learn to live in a one-world economy. Their proposals were designed to manage Britain's difficult transition to a one-world economy. They questioned Hall's denial of 'any special weakness in the United Kingdom'. On this the roboteers were right. They said, yes, the Americans are protectionist and must share the responsibility. But the roboteers added, how can you blame the Americans as the cause of our problems after all the dollars the USA has poured out. The fault lies in us. 'In the three years from the beginning of the Marshall Plan to March 1951, US extended Government assistance (loans and grants) to a total of $14.3 billion. This actually *exceeded* their $13.4 billion balance of payments surplus. So their gold reserve fell by $1.3 billion – *ours* rose by $1.5 billion, all from the US taxpayer's pockets.'[96] The problem had been inflationary growth of demand outside the USA and failure of non-US countries to supply. Clarke, in his response to Hall's paper, wrote that the 'dollar shortage' is now fundamentally the inadequacy of British (and other non-dollar) competitive power. 'It is our weakness, rather than the vagaries of US policy, which creates our crisis. The Americans help, and usually they don't. But that does not avoid our basic responsibility.'[97]

The economists who opposed Robot point out that, contrary to the Bank's fears, Britain remained in current account surplus throughout the 1950s. But that is not the whole of the story. Cairncross puts it this way: 'The United Kingdom moved back into surplus on current account in 1952 and remained in current surplus throughout the 1950s except in 1955, losing ground steadily to her competitors but not at a rate incompatible with external balance and full employment.'[98] But is that gentle decline in competitiveness, that loss of ground to her competitors, to be allowed no part in the judgement on Robot? At the same time Germany was building up the spectacular surpluses in its balance of payments which led to consistent speculation as to when the DM would be revalued while the equally consistent speculation about sterling was about when it would be devalued. It is true that sterling was not actually devalued until November 1967, but that was after an extended period during which sterling was increasingly overvalued. The decision had been made to navigate an overloaded British economy as near to a crisis of confidence as successive governments would dare. But as the instruments of navigation were poor, and the economic charts plotted neither the rocks nor the whirlpools, governments would repeatedly find themselves faced unexpectedly by a crisis of confidence and compelled by means of emergency measures to scuttle back to safety. This was Stop-Go. It was wearing to the nerves of successive Chancellors and successive Cabinets. It was undignified and often humiliating. But it was the option chosen.

A DAMAGED BUTLER SURVIVES ROBOT

Almost the only question about Robot that has been debated is the question: Who was right? But there are other questions. In retrospect, Butler has emerged as one of the more sweet-smelling postwar Ministers and Chancellors. Perhaps it is sympathy with his many disappointments. Perhaps it is appreciation of his humour. Perhaps it is his long and faithful service, at the time unrivalled in the twentieth century other than by Lloyd George and Churchill, both of whom, however, did reach the top. Perhaps it is his face. There is that old man, First Secretary of State and Deputy Prime Minister, heavy with years and with wisdom, with that extraordinary melancholy mask looking like Father Time himself, dropping his unintentional *doubles entendres* all over the place, twice deprived of the premiership by allegedly lesser men, but the essential No. 2 in every Conservative government. But what was he in 1951 when, at the age of 48, he became Chancellor?

Butler was a Chancellor of three months' standing when the Robot controversies were brought before him. He was totally without experience of economic management and lacked any feel for it. For an inexperienced Chancellor, confronting a financial crisis, there is comfort in taking the experienced advice of the Treasury and the Bank of England, particularly when he has no standards of his own by which to make his judgements. While the conduct of his advisers was highly questionable, that of Butler in accepting such advice almost as soon as it was offered,

and then trying to impose it on the government without proper discussion and enquiry, is also extraordinary. It can be explained only by
Butler's total dependence on official advice.[99]

Butler did not even manage the politics well. He enraged Eden by
trying to bulldoze through, in Eden's absence in Lisbon at a NATO
Council, a plan which obviously had major implications for international
relations. He was thought to have tried to exploit the procedures of
Budget secrecy so as to prevent or stifle opposition. He recklessly committed himself in Cabinet to a forecast of disaster which turned out to
be far from accurate. When out-argued in Cabinet, he became sulky
and told his colleagues that they would like the deflationary alternative
quite as little; but the truth was that sensible economic management
would need the deflationary alternative whether or not Robot.

Yet Butler not merely survived but prospered; the improving condition of the British economy was raising his public reputation. The
country, after his 1952 Budget, was moving into more prosperous
times.[100] Nothing so enhances the reputation of a captain with his pas-
sengers than to take the helm in the midst of a storm and then successfully steer the ship of state into calm waters. It may be simply that
the winds have dropped rather than any change of course, but only the
most sophisticated and churlish will attempt to deny the captain the
praise of the multitude by emphasizing that the prevailing calm reflects
his luck rather than his judgement. In giving credit to Butler, the public
was unaware of the Cabinet's rejection of his policy prescription
although, on 8 August 1952, A. J. Cummings of the *News Chronicle* did
report, without grasping the whole truth of the matter, that Butler had
lost all his battles in Cabinet to Cherwell and had not even been allowed
to introduce the Budget he had wanted.[101]

While the public was not in the secret, the Cabinet was. What view
would be taken of Butler by colleagues who had supported him and
then found that they had been led up the garden path? What view
would be taken of him by colleagues who had opposed him despite
repeated warnings of disaster when it was discovered that further import
cuts, a cut in expenditure including food subsidies, and an increase in
Bank Rate, had avoided much of the nastiness of Robot? Butler was not
greatly liked in some parts of the Cabinet. He was, after all, a man of
Munich. Now he had been shown not merely to be fallible on a major
matter of departmental responsibility but to have placed the government
in grave danger without adequate reason. In that most esteemed of
political qualities, judgement, Butler had been found wanting. If Chur-

chill had been capable of exercising the role of Prime Minister, it could well have been the end of Butler as Chancellor. Of all this, the Cabinet was aware. When Churchill and Eden were sick, everything was done to ensure that Butler did not succeed. When Eden at last became Prime Minister, he got rid of Butler as Chancellor as soon as he could even though Butler wanted to stay. Butler suffered the ignominy of being the first postwar Chancellor to be removed from the Treasury against his will.

THE ROLE OF THE TREASURY

Even though the risks in Robot were carefully presented to Butler, the handling of the question by the official Treasury was certainly remarkable. The conduct of the Permanent Secretary, Sir Edward Bridges, as well as of Rowan, the Second Secretary in charge of OF, do not pass muster. As though there would not have been enough reason for Commonwealth resentment, there had not been the least suggestion, at the Commonwealth Finance Ministers' meeting in January, of any such dramatic change in UK policy. There had been vague talk of sterling convertibility, but there had been no suggestion from British Ministers that convertibility might be imminent, let alone that it would be just a matter of five or six weeks, and would be accompanied by forced funding of their sterling balances. Suddenly, in mid-February, a fortnight before the original date of the Budget, an inexperienced Chancellor was being rushed into policies the implications of which he did not understand, on a timescale which prohibited proper examination of what was proposed.

High on the official Treasury's agenda is that it should stand well with the Chancellor of the Exchequer and that the Chancellor of the Exchequer should stand well with his Cabinet colleagues. Like all great institutions, the Treasury has its own agenda. Building its own reputation is high on that agenda. That is not an attitude to be despised. The Treasury's reputation will, in the end, depend on the success of the British economy. The nation has every reason for satisfaction if the Treasury's reputation is high. Ultimately the Treasury stands well in Whitehall if the Chancellor stands well in Cabinet. The last thing the official Treasury wants is a Chancellor who has lost his reputation. It knows that the Chancellor cannot be expected always to win. But a Chancellor must not be left helpless in face of the arguments. A

Chancellor defeated in argument has nothing further to offer the Treasury or indeed the government. The position of the Chancellor must, therefore, be most carefully preserved and protected. The official Treasury will not normally send its Chancellor into battle with his Cabinet colleagues on an issue likely to be highly controversial without the most careful preparation of its case. Here was a project admitted to involve the greatest risks both politically and in international relationships. Yet, as the Treasury's changes in position during the argument clearly showed, it sent its Chancellor into battle without proper preparation.

Many questions had received only the most cursory examination. For example, was it really necessary to force-fund the sterling balances? By the summer of 1952, the Bank had decided that it was unnecessary in respect of the sterling area sterling balances. The Bank had now come to the conclusion that 'there can be no question of further drastic measures of funding or blocking sterling area balances. Politically this is impossible to contemplate.' It was a pity that the Bank had not come to that conclusion earlier. It would have removed a major obstacle to their plan. All the Bank wanted now was an analysis of the sterling balance position designed to show the market that the true sight liabilities were £1000 million or less out of the total balances amounting to £3430 million as at 30th May 1952. They still, however, wanted to freeze the non-sterling area balances of £872 million in order to reduce the overseas sterling element to perhaps £100-£125 million.[102] At the time Robot was presented to Butler and for weeks thereafter, nothing had been worked out regarding the future of the EPU, although it was everywhere understood that it would be damaging for the UK to make itself responsible for its collapse.

Bridges allowed his inexperienced Chancellor to be frog-marched into an ill-digested scheme, for announcement in a Budget barely three weeks hence, without any of the details having been adequately thought through. Of course, Ministers are not supposed to be inexperienced. But Treasury officials know well enough not to rely on such an absurd constitutional theory. Instead of protecting his Chancellor, Bridges allowed himself to be seduced by the radicalism and argumentation of his subordinates. The official Treasury can be politically sensitive. But the men now in the lead in the Treasury had had enough of political sensitivity. Political sensitivity has frequently been the death of economic policy. The Treasury could hardly be happy with its record of economic management in the years since the war. It is very difficult to make revolutionary changes in economic policy other than under great pressure, in other words when there is no choice but to make revolutionary changes in policy. In the midst of what was claimed to be a final crisis, there would be a temptation to ignore Hall and his economists, with their politically sensitive noses, and to seek from Ministers more radical action than could normally be expected from governments. Bridges and Rowan persuaded themselves that the crisis was so intense, the complexity of the subject so great, that once the Chancellor was convinced there would be no argument with colleagues. They already knew that they had a Prime Minister who was sympathetic even if uncomprehending. They may therefore have thought that the ground was sufficiently prepared for their *coup d'état*. After all, what great thing is done if the experts pore over it for months in advance? Conscience makes cowards of us all. They felt justified in telling the Chancellor that he had no choice but to take their advice. Bridges and Rowan made a profound mistake, Bridges more than Rowan because it was Bridges' duty to supply the cool head even if Rowan had lost his. Even if they had succeeded in slipping so radical a change in policy through Cabinet without it being noticed, the immediate repercussions would have caused a crisis in the government. The greater the risks, the more essential that the government as a whole should understand and accept them. If the justification was urgency, it remains true that the case was insufficiently prepared. The only excuse can be panic.

One of the most damaging costs of Robot, and it was entirely their own fault, was that the official Treasury, and men like Rowan and Clarke and Bolton, lost influence in favour of safe men with less understanding. Butler was a Chancellor who depended on advice and who needed to feel confidence in his advisers. In retrospect Butler knew that he had been sent into battle insufficiently armed.[103] Those who gained were Plowden and Hall. Hall was not in the Treasury at this stage and Plowden, while in it, was not of it. In retrospect, Butler forgot his angry reaction to their dissidence. When he saw things come right without Robot, Hall acquired greater and greater influence. The fact that his own alternative to Robot had been nonsense was forgotten. Butler writes: 'Robert Hall, the chief economic adviser, was our strong silent man who came to have more and more influence.'[104] In due course Hall was even able to persuade Butler, against his strong inclinations, that, in certain circumstances, a Budget deficit could be acceptable.[105] During 1953, on Butler's specific instructions, the Economic Section under Hall was moved from the Cabinet Office into the Treasury so that Hall could be close at hand. This reinforced the complacency about British economic performance characteristic of the 1950s. Butler's tribute to Plowden is lavish. 'Plowden was to become my faithful watchdog-in-chief, and his departure for industry in 1953 undoubtedly weakened my position and that of the British economy.'[106]

Although Robot itself was really dead, within the Treasury the argument continued about the merits of convertibility and floating throughout 1953, and was not resolved by firm leadership. Lacking any impetus and direction from the top, officials could only debate. During 1953, the debate incorporated the question what should Britain do if there was another American recession, but that debate too lacked urgency because there was no crisis. Butler had no policy – he could only ask for one. As officials still disagreed, they could not even do what officials often do for a Minister who has no policy, that is give him one. The upshot was a divided Treasury under a weak Chancellor, disguised by an economic upturn which did much for Butler's public reputation but nothing for the UK's long-term economic performance.

BRITAIN'S ECONOMIC SUEZ

At Suez Britain discovered how little it could do in foreign and security policy without American support. At the time of Robot, Britain discovered how constrained were its options in economic management. In future when there were major changes in macro-economic policy, as for example when sterling did float in 1972, they would take place under external pressure imposing itself on British policy. Never again would a British government contemplate the possibility of imposing its policy on its external economic environment. In 1952, for the last time, the thought was there that it might be attempted. That is not to say that there were no options; there were in fact two. One was to accept the Robot analysis if not, at that time, its specific measures. The Robot analysis was that Britain was doing badly, that public expenditure must be cut and resources released to strengthen the balance of payments. Robot represented a strategy. It was designed to force the British economy to become what successive governments said they wanted it to become but never achieved, that is an export-oriented economy. The alternative option was that first selected by Attlee, followed by Butler and the 1950s Conservative governments, and endorsed by subsequent Labour and Conservative governments; the option of slithering from economic crisis to economic crisis, and eventually from devaluation to devaluation. Instead of a strategy, governments were left with the tactic of maintaining full employment not through overseas demand but by manipulating home demand. The policy was pursued although no answer had been found, or at first was even sought, to the inflationary consequences of full employment. Hall describes 'the problem of our times' as being 'to maintain inflationary impetus while avoiding inflationary prices'.[107] It was a very good description of the policy characteristic of British governments from this time and for which the opponents of Robot should take their share of the responsibility because, while rejecting Robot, they either denied the urgency of finding some alternative to existing policy or failed to provide one. All that was left to successive governments was a policy of drift filled out by rhetorical devices such as national economic planning, dashes for growth, and departments of economic affairs, which may have brought temporary comfort to the masses, and employment for economists, but were found, in the end, to provide no relief. British economic policy, buffeted by external events, turned into the management of relative decline which it remained throughout our period. As successive governments refused to take politically difficult domestic decisions, Britain's economic future was left in the hands of a world that could never be persuaded to regard it as a question of prime concern. In the 1950s, the world was being kind to Britain. Should it ever turn nasty, Britain would find itself ill-prepared.

THE LAST YEAR AS CHANCELLOR

Butler's last year as Chancellor was the most eventful of his four and certainly the unhappiest. It showed him as still lacking in feel for economic management and as dependent on advice, which he failed fully to understand, as when he first entered the Treasury in October 1951. In December 1954, he suffered a severe personal blow in the death of his wife. Those who knew him felt that the loss might have affected his judgement and certainly his willingness to fight, but it is not too unkind to say that that had not been too obvious in earlier years. In the autumn of 1954, sterling once more came under pressure. Inflationary pressure continued but nothing was done about it for fear of creating unemployment. Even the Keynesian economists saw the need for a higher level of unemployment; but to take action which would increase unemployment in the autumn of 1954 was even more unappetizing politically than at other times. It was quite clear that in 1955 there would be an election following the long-delayed retirement of Churchill.

Sterling became more exposed as a result of Butler's decision, in February 1955, that the Bank of England should support the transferable rate for sterling. For this, he had the backing of his Cabinet colleagues. In effect it created a general right for non-residents to convert sterling into dollars at a rate very near to the official parity. It was quite a long step towards convertibility. It was understood, however, that the final move to convertibility had to be coordinated with Britain's partners in the EPU and they were not yet ready. This decision to support the transferable rate was taken on the recommendation of the Bank of England but against the advice of OF and the Economic Section, now at one in their opposition to the Bank's recommendation but not for the same reason.[108] As the Bank of England had now achieved virtual convertibility, it was no more in favour of free floating than it had ever been. The step to convertibility was to be with the official rate still fixed at $2.80 within the normal 1 per cent margin. The Bank still wished to widen the margin but that too would have to be coordinated with Britain's EPU partners. Contrariwise, when the Treasury found that the European veto, and the importance of Anglo-American relations, were prohibiting a move to floating, it became anxious to defer convertibility and began to distance itself from the Bank. The Economic Section, while emphasizing the risks of a move unless there were some slack in the system, was now in favour of early convertibility at a floating rate, because, in any case, non-residents could convert sterling so easily.[109] As was normal with such controversies, it was to be resolved not by a decision of the Chancellor or the Cabinet but by external pressure.

The decision to support the transferable rate was followed by sterling crises later in 1955, in 1956, and again in 1957. Among the reasons was the inadequacy of the reserves. For most of the 1950s, the reserves varied between 2 and 3 billion dollars and never exceeded 4 billion dollars. On the other hand liquid liabilities, the sterling balances, never fell below 4 billion dollars. The reserves were also inadequate measured against the level of imports. Reserves averaging about 2.5 billion dollars were not much more than enough to pay for three months' imports in the first half of the decade and even less in the second half. The only hope of building the reserves and thereby providing more adequate defence for sterling, was for the UK to achieve a much larger surplus in its balance of payments. For this reason, OF in the Treasury pressed for policies which would achieve much larger surpluses. In 1953, it had demanded a balance of payments surplus of £350 million. But the policies necessary to achieve such surpluses would involve strenuous efforts to restrain domestic demand, and such policies were inconsistent with the government's political priorities. Only in the recessionary year of 1958, when the surplus reached £455 million, was the Treasury's target met. In four out of the six years 1951–6, the reserves fell and although imports roughly doubled between 1950 and 1960, the reserves were lower at the end of 1960 than they had been at the end of 1950.[110]

AN ELECTION BUDGET

While Butler had taken the Bank's advice on supporting the transferable rate, he failed to take the accompanying advice from the Bank to tighten the fiscal position. Certainly it was very difficult for Butler as the government entered an election year. The Treasury was in one of its understanding moods, typical before elections. Officials were quite aware that it was likely to be an election year following the resignation of Churchill; they were, therefore, less resistant to tax cuts in their advice to the Chancellor than they should have been. They were, however, insistent that monetary policy should be tightened.[111] Butler raised Bank Rate to 3.5 per cent in January, and to 4.5 per cent in February, thus taking in advance the action recommended to him by officials to balance his election Budget, and believing supposedly that this would restrain any boom consequent on the tax cuts he was planning for his Budget. As it turned out, this was a gross overestimate of the power of monetary policy in such circumstances.[112] Butler claims to have derived the impression from Treasury advice that an increase in interest rates would countervail the inflationary effects of a reduction in taxes. It was a politically convenient impression to have gained. Butler was perfectly well aware that tax cuts make a greater political impact than increases in Bank Rate. Butler would announce his tax cuts amidst the full glory of a Budget statement in the House of Commons. The Bank of England announced changes in Bank Rate, though on the authority of the Chancellor.

Butler's advisers in the Treasury and the Bank of England were none of them equipped to judge the exact relative force of monetary and fiscal policy. Since 1952 there had been much debate in the Treasury, the Bank, and the Economic Section as to the effectiveness of monetary policy, but there was little agreement. There was disagreement also within the Economic Section.[113] The Bank of England itself blew hot and cold on the effectiveness of monetary policy and the Governor, not for the first or last time, showed himself unwilling to bring pressure on the clearing banks to limit advances.[114] This long debate about monetary policy led eventually to the appointment, three years later, of the Radcliffe Committee. Precisely because of its uncertainty, the Bank was always insisting on cuts in public expenditure. It never thought that the full weight of anti-inflationary policy should be placed on interest rate movements. Thus the advisers upon whom Butler was dependent were either ignorant, uncertain, or unwilling.

The Governor of the Bank had, however, given Butler a warning, adopting what Fforde describes as 'the very rare course' of sending a formal letter to the Chancellor on behalf of the Bank Court. On 24 February, after the 4.5% Bank Rate had been announced, Cobbold wrote that the Court wished to emphasize

> their view, to which I have given expression from time to time, that the possible contribution of credit policy to a balanced economy should not be overestimated. The earlier rise in Bank Rate to 3.5% had a considerable warning effect ... It is to be hoped that this new move will materially assist in strengthening the 'disinflationary' climate. But the inflationary pressures which have threatened to develop in recent months have their origins much less in the monetary than in the cost and wages structure. Whilst monetary policy can be of assistance, it is the Court's view that the battle against inflationary tendencies must mainly be fought in the wider fields of economic policy.

The letter went on to express the hope 'that the results of the general economic policy of HM Government will make possible some relaxation in credit policy at a fairly early date'.[115] The Bank, in other words, was refusing to take responsibility for an election Budget.

A KEYNESIAN VICTORY

Eden succeeded Churchill as Prime Minister on 5 April. On 19 April, Butler introduced what was widely regarded as an election Budget. In the midst of a boom, he handed out £150 million of tax reliefs.[116] This included a cut of 6d in income tax. An election followed in May which the Tories won with a greatly increased majority of 58 over all other parties.

The Conservative triumph in the General Election of 1955 may perhaps be regarded as the first Keynesian election victory. It has long been alleged that those who possess the power to manipulate the economy can always, using Keynesian methods, engineer a boom and hence success at the polls. Experience shows that, from the point of view of their own Parties, Prime Ministers are singularly poor at selecting the date of a General Election. Attlee chose two very bad dates, February 1950 and October 1951. If he had held the 1950 election earlier and the 1951 election later, he might well have won both by a comfortable margin. Douglas-Home left himself no choice in 1964 by postponing the election date to the end of that Parliament's life. Wilson chose well in 1966 but very poorly in 1970. Heath, like Douglas-Home, had only one chance to get the election date right and he got it wrong. Callaghan condemned his Party to at least 17 years in the wilderness by allowing himself, in the autumn of 1978, to be persuaded that the economy would be looking up in the spring of 1979. Thatcher, on the other hand, could do no wrong; on the two occasions when she had a choice, 1984 and 1987, the Opposition was hopelessly divided. She was bound to win. So the Thatcher decade is not appropriate material for the study of this phenomenon. Even with the assistance of Keynesian techniques, the Prime Minister's responsibility is not easy and mistakes are frequent. The myth that Prime Ministers have the world at their feet because they can always select the date of the election, and can manipulate the economy accordingly, depends on the two occasions only when it did, apparently, work, 1955 and 1959. But in both cases, the inappropriate election Budgets that preceded them were almost certainly unnecessary for victory.

AFTERMATH

Butler, up to this point, had appeared as a highly successful Chancellor. In this country, nothing is more brittle than a reputation for successful economic management. The reason lies in the problems of managing an exposed economy with over-full employment. 1955 proved a bad year for the British economy. Suddenly the economy which Butler had managed for four years seemed weak. The confidence of the previous year, when he had spoken of doubling the standard of living in 20 or 25 years, had evaporated. Sterling was under pressure even before the election, partly because of an adverse turn in the country's current account and partly because of rumours that the Government was still contemplating floating the pound. The day of disaster long foretold by the roboteers seemed at last to have arrived. On that ground alone an election Budget was inappropriate. After the Conservative victory in the election, pressure continued.

For the precipitous fall in his reputation after the election, Butler has no one but himself to blame. The 19 April Budget was totally inappropriate to the economic circumstances, and the setback drained Butler's already low morale. He felt entitled to criticize his advisers for his error, a defence which ex-Chancellors are happy to employ, though they are more reluctant to attribute their successes to those same advisers. He may, before his April Budget, have received questionable advice from both the Treasury and the Bank, and it is true that his advisers in the Treasury were too accommodating. Officials are supposed to give firm advice whatever the political preoccupations of their Minister. At official level, everyone was unloading responsibility upon someone else.[117] But Butler was responsible – a Chancellor of four years' standing should have had a better appreciation of what he was doing in his April Budget. The theory that Ministers can be excused if their only fault is to accept bad advice had not yet achieved the acceptance that it was to receive in a later decade.

Butler attempted, in July, to secure Cabinet agreement to cuts in the milk and bread subsidies but Eden was opposed. After four years as Chancellor, the undoubted Number 2 in the government who took the chair of the Cabinet in the absence of the Prime Minister, he was still unable to command the Cabinet or rely on the succour of his Prime Minister. Even with a Prime Minister innocent of the least economic sophistication, Eden's support was the indispensable lever for ensuring Cabinet approval of difficult measures, and it was not available. Butler's measures of 25 July were therefore limited to making hire purchase more expensive, calling on the banks to cut advances, restricting the investment programmes of the nationalized industries and raising coal and steel prices to absorb purchasing power. The programme for cutting public investment was insufficiently specific to command the confidence Butler was trying to induce in the market.[118] Calling on the banks to cut advances was of uncertain effect. The half-measures to which Butler had been constrained by the opposition of the Prime Minister, failed to produce the impact required.

Firm action in July would have saved Butler his subsequent distress. His officials became seriously alarmed about the inadequacy of the July measures. On 27 July, Bridges warned the Chancellor that it might be necessary to recall Parliament. Hall, on 2 September, advocated 'a decisive measure of deflation' and cautioned about the unwisdom of relying on credit policy alone. Butler attempted to secure the recall of Parliament before the Party Conference, a clear sign of panic, but was overruled.

With sterling under pressure, Butler was obliged to give the world his firm assurances that the government was committed to the fixed rate for sterling. On 26 July 1955 he told the House that 'there is no doubt about the policy of the Government in relation to the exchange value of the pound sterling ... It has been, and will continue to be the maintenance of exchange parity of 2.80 dollars to the pound, either in existing circumstances or when sterling is convertible.'[119] In September, he repeated the assurance at the annual conference of the Bretton Woods institutions in Istanbul.[120] The irony was complete. 'With Sir George Bolton beside me, excitedly whispering into my ears, I repeated to the domes and minarets several times the incantation that the pound was not to float but would remain within fixed margins and be steadily defended by our resources combined with stiff anti-inflationary measures.'[121] Butler saw the irony but 'I felt that in the exigencies of the moment the Robot vision ... was clearly inappropriate.'[122] Rowan also was beside Butler in Istanbul, accepting now the inevitability of the fixed rate, praising Butler's presentational skills at the conference, but anxiously pressing on him the need to reinforce his words with tough domestic measures for which, he feared, Butler saw no necessity.[123] A Chancellor who had begun by advocating the floating of sterling, was now doing as much as Ministerial words could do to imprison Britain and his successors in a fixed rate against the dollar.

Sterling, for the moment, stabilized following Butler's statement to the IMF.[124] In October he was compelled to reverse his pre-election Budget concessions virtually entirely, apart from the 6d cut in income tax.[125] He had, once more, been defeated in Cabinet when he made a further attempt to get agreement on the abolition of the bread subsidy. His failures in Cabinet enabled his successor, Macmillan, to accuse him of drift. But there were other and better justifications for the criticism. It was not surprising that these events damaged his reputation and that he had little recourse when Eden removed him as Chancellor in December 1955. He would have preferred to stay, as do all Ministers when they have misjudgements to outlive. He was warned by a colleague who was not normally to be regarded as his friend that to leave the

Treasury at that time was to commit political suicide. But he did not fight seriously.[126]

In his memoirs, Butler suggested that 'If I had been less scrupulous about the economy I would have retired in May.'[127] But it is difficult to see, in view of what happened after the election, that that would have saved his reputation and he would still have suffered the loss of authority in the government that a move from the Treasury, other than to No. 10, is likely to cause. Sir Edward Bridges, loyally protecting the Minister who had been undermined by his department's advice, tried to delay the change so that Butler could recover his reputation.[128] It was not a consideration to which Eden felt it necessary to give priority. Eden had lost confidence in the Treasury; it appears that, even before Butler's error of judgement on the 1955 Budget, he was intending to move him from the Treasury. There was certainly enough evidence of lack of grip. If that is the way a Prime Minister feels, he is entitled to act, but it will not improve the reputation of the Minister who is sacrificed. In this case, Eden seems to have had another motive. Macmillan was Foreign Secretary. He and Eden did not always see eye to eye, notably on relations with Europe and their assessment of what was happening in Egypt.[129] By moving Macmillan to the Treasury, Eden killed two birds with one stone. He regained total control of foreign policy, and he had a new, and perhaps more effective, Chancellor.[130] A third, perhaps unintended, effect was the damage to the reputation of the man hitherto considered the most successful Chancellor since the war and who might have become a rival.

ASSESSMENT

What then is one to make of Butler as Chancellor? The key is Robot. The choice seems stark. If one believes the critics of Robot, this was a Chancellor who would have led his country and his Party, and possibly even the world, into political and economic disaster. If the more friendly judgement of Brittan is accepted, here is a Chancellor who lost a battle for which he was insufficiently prepared, then abandoned the cause instead of persisting in what he had said he believed and, even when a better opportunity occurred two years later, missed it through lack of drive and conviction, with great cost to the British economy. Butler was to acquire an exceptional reputation as an expert in the business of government. He was, or was supposed to be, the ultimate safe pair of hands. But there was no evidence of it during his tenure of the Treasury. His career, he claimed, exemplified the art of the possible. It exemplified at least as much the art of survival.

Many, in commenting on Butler's failure, twice, to gain the Tory leadership, have divined a lack of steel in his character. Butler was ambivalent on great issues. His indecisiveness, his dismissive wit, all those characteristics that made him so attractive to the intelligentsia, they all showed that he was no leader. Because he was no leader, he was condemned simply to be useful, to oversee the reform of Tory policy in Opposition in the role of Chairman of the Research Department, to accept the burden of the Treasury in difficult times but under careful political oversight, to act as the effective deputy to Churchill when Churchill and Eden were ill, and then to undertake one great office of state after another, but for ever to be denied the leadership.[131] He could even be an unquestioned No. 2. But, though he could always be useful, he was unfit for the highest office. He might be admired by some few Tory colleagues who respected his intelligence and enjoyed his irony. These were the colleagues who, by Tory standards, were, like Butler himself, too clever by half. But they were always easily outnumbered by the sound men. The undoubted fascination of Butler's character has been allowed to obscure the fact that he was a poor Chancellor and would probably have made a poor Prime Minister. Owing to the system of selecting Tory leaders that then existed, Butler's name was never submitted for election by his colleagues in the House of Commons, though in 1963, if not in 1957, they were at least consulted. But his Cabinet colleagues knew him well and looked elsewhere, even when the alternatives were Macmillan and Alec Douglas-Home. It was an unkind, but probably an accurate, judgement.

PART II

DOWNHILL
ALL THE WAY
1955–70

SIX

Harold Macmillan: Promise Unperformed

A REFORMING CHANCELLOR

We know in considerable detail what Macmillan thought of his own
record as Chancellor of the Exchequer and, indeed, as Prime Minister,
because we have his memoirs in six volumes and over 3000 pages. Such
self-indulgence would hardly be possible for a politician, not of the
highest significance, if he were not also his own publisher. But even a
publisher would hardly go to such lengths if he were not largely satisfied
with almost everything in his own record. The principal exception to
this self-satisfaction is Suez. His performance over Suez defeated even
Macmillan's vainglory.

Macmillan did not want to leave the Foreign Office for the Treasury.
To be Foreign Secretary, he claims, had been the height of his
ambitions. He was happy with the Foreign Office and he was confident
that the Office was happy with him. If, however, he had to leave the
Foreign Office, he would demand a price as well as ensuring in his
memoirs that the world would be aware of his sacrifice. In a letter to
Prime Minister Eden dated 24 October 1955 he stated his conditions.
He must have the 'firm' support of the Prime Minister through the
early troubles. He must also have a position in the government not
inferior to that of Butler. Specifically Butler must not be made Deputy
Prime Minister, a position which, he added, did not in any case exist
constitutionally. As Chancellor he must be the undisputed head of the
Home Front under Eden.[1]

Macmillan admits in his memoirs that anyone reading this letter with
the knowledge of subsequent events would not unnaturally assume that
he was actuated by some degree of personal rivalry with Butler. But, he
adds, this was not the case.[2] How could it be the case when he had no
reason to suppose that Eden would be struck down by illness and that,
in a year's time, a choice would have to be made between himself and

Butler for the succession to No. 10? If a memorialist wishes to disarm his critics, he should find better weapons. Eden was a sick man. His health had kept him away from the Foreign Office for months at a time while Churchill was still Prime Minister. He was subject to repeated bouts of ill-health during his early months at No. 10. If to this was added his habit of alienating his closest friends, there was every reason to consider the possibility that Eden might not last the Parliament. Macmillan, in fact, told Woolton, before writing his letter to Eden, that 'he saw no reason why if he was going to take over all the troubles of the Treasury, he should be ruled out of the succession for the Premiership in order to ease in Butler'.[3] Politicians who wish to deny their baser thoughts should not leave such traces behind them.

Macmillan had served in Cabinet for five years by the time he was invited to go to the Treasury. He had been involved in the discussions on Robot. As Minister of Housing, he had found himself in constant conflict with the Treasury. He had been, briefly, Minister of Defence. Defence was an area of government expenditure which the Treasury was always wishing to attack. While Minister, Macmillan appears to have formed the view that, with the atomic bomb now in the hands of the British, there was no point in spending huge sums of money on conventional arms.[4] He had been, again briefly, Foreign Secretary. In so far, therefore, as a Minister, with no obvious qualifications for the job, can prepare himself for the Treasury, Macmillan had had every opportunity to become prepared. Though reluctant to go to the Treasury, Macmillan thought that he did have something new and valuable to offer to the art of economic management.

In his letter to Eden, Macmillan set out the course he would intend to follow if he became Chancellor: 'there is no point in my leaving the Foreign Office to be an orthodox Chancellor of the Exchequer. I must be, if not a revolutionary, something of a reformer'.[5] He might want, he says, to make considerable changes in the set-up, to bring in outside advisers, and to reorganize the Bank of England. It was because he intended to be a reforming Chancellor, he said, that he so much needed the support of the Prime Minister and assurance that Butler would not have a higher status. Whatever safeguard it was to this new, reforming, Chancellor, Butler did not become Deputy Prime Minister. He became Lord Privy Seal and Leader of the House. He continued to take the chair of the Cabinet in the absence of Eden. Of that degree of pre-eminence, Eden felt unable to deprive him.

The tragic story of Britain's postwar economic management should not deny the reader such pleasure as can be derived from sensitivity to the rhythm. When, on 21 December 1955, Macmillan became Chancellor, his Permanent Secretary, Sir Edward Bridges, still had a few months to serve. In July 1945, Bridges had been the newly appointed Permanent Secretary to the Treasury when Dalton was confronted with the poor state of the reserves. In November 1951, it had been Bridges' solemn duty to warn Butler, the incoming Chancellor in the new Conservative government, that the reserves were running out. Now, in December 1955, Bridges had the melancholy task of warning Macmillan that the reserves were again running out. The problem in 1955 was attributable to the performance of the UK economy, not to that of the sterling area as a whole.[6]

Macmillan noted in his diary on 22 December 1955 that whereas everyone agreed that the situation was precarious, nobody agreed on the diagnosis or the treatment.[7] It was an opportunity to show what a reforming Chancellor could do to close this era of mercurial reserves. The evident need for yet further measures, to supplement those taken by Butler in July and October, would also demonstrate that there really had been need of a new Chancellor. Macmillan clearly believed it. He thought that Butler had had little idea of the state of affairs or the financial dangers and had allowed things to drift.[8] It does a new Chancellor no harm to be seen rectifying the omissions of his predecessor. The initial impression made by Macmillan on Treasury officials was good – unlike Butler he was decisive. He was also effective. He was even orthodox.

Macmillan at once clashed with his colleagues on milk and bread subsidies. He demanded that he be allowed to abolish them or he would resign. Eden was opposed but appeared unwilling to discuss the issue face to face with his new Chancellor. Eden had been making speeches calling for a reduction in prices and taxes.[9] Instead of a face to face meeting, Eden sent a delegation to Macmillan. It was led by Butler, who now found himself the messenger of a Prime Minister who had defeated him the previous October when he had himself wanted to abolish the bread subsidy. Butler was accompanied by Derick Heathcoat Amory and Peter Thorneycroft, both Chancellors-to-be.[10] The delegation informed Macmillan of what he already knew, that the Prime Minister was opposed to abolition. Macmillan told them that, in that case, Eden must find a new Chancellor. Eden must have been aware of the risks of losing a Chancellor two months after his appointment, for in the end there was a compromise. Macmillan says he obtained 80 per cent of what he wanted and that he was prepared to regard it as enough.[11] Hall's calculation was 40 per cent but at least Macmillan got something on these subsidies whereas Butler had got nothing.[12] With the help of an increase in Bank Rate from 4.5 to 5.5 per cent, restrictions on credit for consumption, and cuts in public expenditure, the immediate crisis was resolved.

THE BUDGET AND BRADSHAW

Macmillan was fully aware how embarrassing the financial situation must be to Butler who could only watch and wait as his successor, with his eye on market reaction, played with the different elements that might make up his April Budget. One possibility would have been to raise income tax by 6d in the £. He suggested it in his initial paper to Treasury officials.[13] It was advocated by the Economic Secretary, Edward Boyle.[14] It would have brought in £100 million, but it would have reversed the last important surviving constituent of Butler's April 1955 Budget. He discussed the question with Butler, and comforted him with the thought that nothing could take away from the outstanding success of his four years at the Treasury. Nevertheless, he said, this question had to be decided on its merits.[15] Macmillan evidently enjoyed the discussion more than did Butler. Butler, in fact, threatened to resign.[16] Despite Boyle's advocacy, it is difficult to believe that Macmillan seriously considered any such measure, which would have required exceptional political courage. In the end Macmillan generously decided to leave income tax alone. Foreigners, he concluded, would not be impressed by the stability and strength of a government which reversed its own policy in so notorious a fashion.[17] Nor is it likely that his Party would easily have forgiven Macmillan if he had raised income tax by 6d. Instead, he says, he demanded from his Cabinet colleagues a further £100 million in public expenditure cuts. Butler enthusiastically supported this solution.[18] The Cabinet promised, and he was prepared to rely on the promise although, according to Hall, it caused alarm and despondency in the Treasury which wrongly considered the cut impossible.[19]

Macmillan's Budget statement acquired a reputation as the funniest Budget speech since the war. It is, however, remembered more for his statement that 'We are always, as it were, looking up a train in last year's Bradshaw' than for its economic content.[20] He tells us that he stimulated steps to improve the equipment for the economic forecaster. The result, he claims, was to have added greatly to the accuracy with which economic weather can be predicted.[21] Moves were, in fact, set on foot which made possible quarterly, instead of just annual, economic forecasts.[22]

The complaints about the forecasts were a reflection of the nature of the economic policy being conducted. Information about the state of the economy is of particular importance when there is no margin of safety and the economy is always being driven along the edge of a precipice. In other words information is particularly vital to the conduct of a Keynesian economic policy in which full employment emerges from the manipulation of home demand with the balance of payments a worrying residual to be managed, if necessary, by an application for funds from the IMF or, in the last resort, by a devaluation to another fixed rate. The trouble is that the information required is complex, is always out of date, and the most recent information is likely to be the most unreliable. This is not surprising given the many elements that entered into the making of the forecasts. The accuracy of forecasts depended on getting all these elements reasonably right, or if not right, at least the errors should not be all in the same direction. The task was well beyond the skill of the statisticians, despite the improvements on which Macmillan complimented himself. Chancellors have never ceased to complain. Many a Chancellor was to feel let down by the inaccuracy of information, statistical and otherwise, fed to him by his advisers and by the unreliability of the forecasts derived from it.

The uncertainties extend not just to the information and the forecasts but to the actual effect of the budgetary and monetary measures a Chancellor may take. He is condemned to sitting in the driving seat, often without very much experience of this kind of driving, turning the wheel this way and that in accordance with his latest guess as to where he is at any particular moment, and in the hope that his actions are in some way positively linked to the direction of his vehicle. He can never be certain that he will not be confronted by a sudden crisis which will require a more than usually violent twist of the wheel to be sure that the vehicle actually reacts to his steering. The postwar economic history of this country, as written by Keynesian economists, describes in detail this precarious navigation to which Chancellors were condemned by the precepts of their only too fallible Master. Dow's judgement of economic management during this period is worth quoting: 'As far as internal conditions are concerned . . . budgetary and monetary policy failed to be stabilizing and must on the contrary be regarded as having been positively destabilizing.'[23]

Budgets that are not proof against the inaccuracy of economic forecasts lack, by definition, the margin of prudence required in managing an economy as exposed to international pressures as is that of the UK. No one could object to the search for more accurate information. But the emphasis on it reveals something about the conduct of economic policy under the influence of economists and of domestic politics.

BUT WHAT HAD HAPPENED TO THE REFORMING CHANCELLOR?

As a reforming Chancellor, Macmillan was a disappointment. There was no evidence of reforming zeal, unless one regards the introduction of Premium Bonds in his April 1956 Budget as such evidence. Before his appointment, Macmillan had, at the request of Eden, written a paper on how he saw the economic problem. His paper was called *Dizzy with Success* and its theme was that the country was trying to do too much with the resources available. There was over-full employment. Growth must be kept going, but not at so headlong a pace. Credit should be squeezed by the use of Bank Rate; government subsidies on housing, milk and bread should be reduced or abolished; incentives should be increased by reducing direct taxation and saving should be encouraged.[24] There was much in the analysis that was splendid and, in respect of what was said about housing subsidies, ironic. But the fundamental theme of *Dizzy with Success*, that the country was trying to do too much and that there was over-full employment, was neglected by Macmillan both as Chancellor and Prime Minister.

The problem of wages in a full-employment society had become increasingly dominant in the ten years since the war. It was not, no doubt, the only reason for Britain's loss of competitiveness, but it was one reason and a reforming Conservative Chancellor, who had written so excellent a prospectus, would presumably know what to do. The 1956 White Paper on the *Economic Implications of Full Employment* stated the problem.

> The Government is pledged to foster conditions in which the nation can, if it so wills, realize its full potentialities for growth . . . But the Government must no less seek to ensure that the pressure of domestic demand does not reach a level which threatens price stability and endangers the

balance of payments. To maintain full employment without inflation necessarily involves continual adjustments.[25]

The question remained whether the government was in fact prepared, other than in conditions of crisis, to restrain domestic demand to achieve price stability. On inflation and over-full employment, Macmillan had, while Chancellor, much to say but could find little to do. In his speech to the House on 20 February 1956, Macmillan indicated that he would not even allow unemployment to rise as high as the 3 per cent laid down by Beveridge as a fair average.[26] In his Budget speech of April 1956 Macmillan rejected wage control as inconsistent with a free society.[27] He took the politically easy path of proclaiming that 'The problem of inflation cannot be dealt with by cutting down demand; the other side of the picture is the need for increasing production.'[28] Cutting down demand was, at least in principle, within his power. He could certainly stimulate production but only by taking even greater risks with inflation and the balance of payments.

All he was left with was the usual combination of exhortation and lamentation. Just before the 1956 TUC Congress, Macmillan held a press conference. He pointed out that since 1953 wages and output had risen *pari passu* in Germany and America while in Britain wages had risen twice as fast as output per head.[29] On 6 September 1956, Macmillan noted in his diary that the TUC Congress had gone very badly so far as wages and prices were concerned.[30] The Congress, after a strong speech by Frank Cousins, General Secretary of the Transport and General Workers Union (TGWU), had rejected wage restraint. Exhortation had failed, but Macmillan would continue to rely on it for some years yet.

The recommendation in Macmillan's paper *Dizzy with Success* which would have attracted most attention was on the exchange rate of sterling. Sterling was already virtually convertible for those who knew how to do it. Macmillan raised the possibility, if the more orthodox methods did not succeed, and the government was forced into another devaluation, that sterling should instead float.

> The rate may fall violently at first. But, if so, a lot of people will get their fingers burned. In any case, in present conditions, it may be safer to take the strain this way than any other way. In the second half of the twentieth century sound government in our country is more likely to be endangered by either a collapse of the reserves or a million on the dole than by occasional fluctuations in the value of sterling in relation to the dollar.[31]

On 2 January 1956, Macmillan circulated a paper in the Treasury containing his latest thoughts as the reserves continued to run down despite the action taken by his predecessor before he left the Treasury. Once more the idea of floating was mentioned but it still appeared that priority would be given to orthodox methods of restoring confidence. Revolutionary policies such as floating were to be considered only if all else failed.[32] He was even prepared to contemplate use, once again, of import controls, and gave instructions that a scheme should be prepared against an emergency.[33] It must rapidly have appeared to his officials that Macmillan, like his predecessor, would do just enough to pull the economy back from the edge of catastrophe but not enough to change the whole direction of policy. His officials would certainly have told him that floating was not a panacea and certainly not a substitute for deflation.

Macmillan spoke, as did so many Chancellors, of the 'excess of home demand which threatens our exports'.[34] Nothing adequate was ever done about it although, as early as 1956, German exports were threatening to overtake British exports. It was imagined that, with the help of accurate information, a careful calculation could be made of how much home demand should be reduced to secure the necessary additional exports. It was known as 'fine tuning'. It was a hopeless task. Even if the information was available, which it was not and was never likely to be, the crudity of the instruments of economic management available to a Chancellor prohibited such fine adjustments.

Macmillan's reforming zeal had come to nothing. The economy would continue to be managed just this side of a collapse of confidence in sterling. Nothing had been done about floating and nothing either about over-full employment. Macmillan's educated complacency in confronting the economic problems of the country did not rule out the use of heroic language: 'The trouble is that we are acting as if we were just a bit better off than we really are. Therefore, although I regard the situation as serious, and as one which easily might become dangerous if it were not dealt with firmly, I do not regard it as a situation which it is beyond our power to master if we but have the will.'[35] But the deeds did not measure up to the language. Macmillan had an image, borrowed from the *Financial Times*, to describe his conception of economic management – it was like driving a car. There were the accelerator and the brake, each to be used as appropriate. Sensible people did not use them both at once.[36] The objective of economic management was expansion. For the moment that was impossible because the reserves were running out, but once the reserves were stabilized, there would come the time for the accelerator. This was the Tory conception of economic management mid-century. It was a Keynesian conception, neither revolutionary nor reforming. More important, it was not successful.

Macmillan himself subsequently wrote:

> To maintain the British economy at the right level, between inflation and deflation, balancing correctly between too much and too little growth, was a delicate exercise. All the clever young economists and journalists and all the armchair experts could not resolve it. There were so many imponderables, and so many uncertainties. It was not a subject to be solved by mathematical formulae, or exact calculation. It was like bicycling along a tightrope.[37]

Macmillan attributes this lesson to his year in the Treasury and to 'the rest of my active life in politics'. The tragedies of British economic management can, perhaps, be ascribed to the fact that such an obvious lesson is learnt by Chancellors and Prime Ministers, if at all, only in retrospect. It is a lesson which a Chancellor should bring with him into office, not just take away as he leaves it. It should be passed on from Chancellor to Chancellor. Yet there is little evidence that Macmillan had really learnt it after a further six years as Prime Minister. He was a typical Chancellor and a typical Prime Minister. He had neither the wisdom nor the political courage to permit the lesson to be learnt or acted on during the years when he was the supreme manager of his country's affairs. Consequently, under Macmillan as Chancellor and Prime Minister, the economy staggered from crisis to crisis.

Ministers in foreign governments were not reticent in giving their view of British economic management. The German Economics Minister, Ludwig Erhard, annoyed Macmillan by stating publicly that sterling would have to be devalued. Macmillan found this 'irritating' and agreed to the issue of a Treasury denial. If one cannot laugh at such statements as Erhard's, it is pointless, if human, to be irritated by them. Macmillan found Erhard's intervention particularly irritating because of the amount of foreign exchange Britain was spending on the defence of Germany, to which Germany was refusing, despite pressure, to make any contribution. If British economic management had come near corresponding to the recommendations in Macmillan's *Dizzy with Success*, it would have been less of a burden.

A NEW PERMANENT SECRETARY TO THE TREASURY

Macmillan hardly improved the quality of economic advice that would be given to him or his successors by arranging for a Foreign Office official to succeed Bridges at the Treasury. During the life of the Attlee government, Macmillan had been hostile to the Foreign Office policy on Europe. When back in government in early 1952, he criticized the Foreign Office for showing 'a degree of myopia which a mole might envy'.[38] A principal author of Foreign Office policy on Europe was Sir Roger Makins, now Ambassador in Washington. The moles now attracted Macmillan's warmest admiration. When Bridges retired, leaving succession problems at the Treasury, Macmillan arranged that Makins should become Joint Permanent Secretary to the Treasury.[39] The appointment of a Foreign Office official to head the Treasury was, as Macmillan says, 'a startling breach of tradition'.[40] It was not obvious that it made any other contribution to economic management. Rowan told Macmillan that the appointment of Makins was the biggest blow the Civil Service had ever received.[41] The Parliamentary system makes it inevitable that, frequently, the Chancellor will have no experience of economic management.[42] There is no requirement that his chief adviser should suffer under the same disability.

SUEZ

Macmillan shared with Eden, almost equally, the responsibility for the Suez fiasco. In one sense, as he admits, his responsibility was greater. He knew President Eisenhower and Secretary of State John Foster Dulles better than did Eden and his relations with them were warmer. He had worked for Eisenhower during the war and he thought he had succeeded, as Foreign Secretary, in the difficult task of understanding Dulles. Dulles had gone so far as to express regret when Macmillan was moved from the Foreign Office to the Treasury. Eden relied excessively on Macmillan as an interpreter of the American response to Nasser's action in nationalizing the Suez Canal. Though Eisenhower had declared himself consistently in favour of a peaceful solution to the crisis, and Dulles always seemed to be proposing devices which could only delay action, Macmillan assured Eden that the President would not react adversely to the use of force against Egypt. He was regarded as speaking authoritatively on the issue because, on 24 September 1956, during a visit to Washington, he was given 35 minutes of Eisenhower's time. In this case, on Eisenhower's side, the chat with Macmillan seemed to be for old time's sake rather than to discuss serious matters, though Eisenhower may have been waiting for Macmillan to say something substantial about British policy on Suez and may have been comforted when he did not.

Makins, who was present, and took a note of the meeting, was astonished at Macmillan's handling of it. The exchange of courtesies and inconsequential reminiscences ended with Eisenhower showing Macmillan the street lamp at which he aimed when practising his golf strokes. Years later, in an interview with Alistair Horne, Makins recalled: '. . . I was expecting Harold to make a statement, say something important on Suez – but in fact he said nothing. I was very much surprised. Nor did Ike say anything. I was amazed . . .'[43] Macmillan managed to interpret this conversation as an expression of support, and so informed Eden. Makins comments that he could see 'no basis at all for Harold's optimism'. Certainly 'the Americans were willing to see Nasser put down, *but* what they could not contemplate were military operations – especially ahead of the 1956 Presidential election.'[44] Macmillan in his memoirs fully accepts his heavy responsibility in misleading Eden and the Cabinet. He had altogether failed to appreciate the force of the resentment which would be directed against the UK. He had believed that the Americans would issue a protest, even a violent protest in public; but that they would in their hearts be glad to see the matter brought to a conclusion.[45]

Such success as the Suez adventure was likely to achieve was dependent, and known to be dependent, on American forbearance. It was, in the circumstances, more than ordinarily insouciant to assume American forbearance on the basis that, whatever the Administration was actually saying, Macmillan had a deeper insight into what was really meant. On the British side, there was too much sentimentality in relations with the USA, too much reliance on personal links. Prominent among the personal links was that the mothers of both Churchill and Macmillan were American by birth. Before arriving in Washington, Macmillan made a well-publicized visit to the town in the Middle West where his mother was born. It was as though he considered his sentimental journey an act of policy. It may have been in terms of UK domestic politics, but not so far as concerned British relations with the USA.

Macmillan's responsibilities as Chancellor of the Exchequer became submerged by the preparations for Suez. But the Treasury was doing its duty and keeping him informed of the pressure on sterling arising from the tension in the Middle East and of the fact that the reserves were, once more, running out. On 8 August 1956, Bridges warned Macmillan of the cost of 'going it alone' without American support and that measures to protect sterling might be necessary in the autumn even if there were no hostilities.[46] On 3 September, the loss of $120 million from the reserves was made public. On 7 September 1956, Bridges, in a minute to Macmillan, wrote that if there were war with Egypt without overt US support, the strain on sterling might be so great that it would not be possible to maintain the exchange rate.[47] While still in the USA, Macmillan noted that the state of the reserves and the pressure on sterling must prompt considerable anxiety. Rowan warned him that, even if Nasser was overthrown, confidence in sterling might not return without some joint US-UK action. After the outbreak of hostilities Treasury officials warned their Chancellor that that whatever rights the British had under the IMF statutes might not be exercisable if a UK application did not have the support of the US Administration.[48]

Macmillan's choice as Joint Permanent Secretary to the Treasury, Sir Roger Makins, left Washington in September and took several weeks holiday before taking up his new post in London on 11 October 1956.[49] Until 8 November 1956, Britain was not represented in Washington at ambassadorial level. On Suez, Makins was a dove.[50] At a crucial moment in the unfolding of the Suez crisis, he was removed from Washington and the high-level link with the US Administration was broken. It probably made no difference but it is just possible that, had he been able to brief Eden and Macmillan, he might, even at this late stage, have been able to disabuse them of their conviction that the USA would remain at worst neutral in face of an Anglo-French invasion of Egypt. If he had remained in Washington, he would, it appears, have felt it necessary to resign when the Suez adventure went ahead. He would not have felt able to defend Britain's deception in its relations with Washington.[51] On arrival in London, he found that none of the leading Ministers, neither Eden, nor Macmillan, nor Foreign Secretary Selwyn Lloyd, wanted to see him.[52] They did not appear interested in his interpretation of American attitudes. On 28 October, Macmillan summoned Makins to tell him that the invasion fleet had sailed and that he, the new Permanent Secretary to the Treasury, could at last be told the whole truth. Makins recalled that Macmillan 'simply hadn't thought about the Americans . . . I think I did give him a jolt by telling him what

Suez would do to Anglo-American relations . . .' Makins was amazed that the Anglo-French alliance had not even waited until after the Presidential election, a delay of only a few more days.[53]

Makins' forecast of the American reaction to the invasion of Egypt proved accurate. It was violent and uncompromising, including action in the Security Council calling for a withdrawal of the Anglo-French forces which Britain and France vetoed. What Britain could not veto was action against sterling. In one respect Britain was doing its supposed international duty. Instead of meeting the pressure on sterling by floating, it was, as required under Bretton Woods, spending its reserves to maintain the value of its currency even when Macmillan's friend US Treasury Secretary George Humphrey was placing obstacles in the way of a British drawing from the IMF to which Macmillan was sure he was entitled. On 30 October, Macmillan informed his Cabinet colleagues that the reserves of gold and dollars were 'still falling at a dangerously rapid rate; and in view of the extent to which we might have to rely on American economic assistance we could not afford to alienate the US Government more than was absolutely necessary . . .'[54] It was a nice thought that, if Britain had actually tried, it could have found ways of alienating the Americans even more. There was, perhaps, such a way. Britain could have allowed sterling to float. Hall's view was that sterling should float.[55] Cobbold, however, was now calling floating a 'catastrophe course'.[56] It was not done. The rate of loss of reserves multiplied. Eisenhower seemed determined not just to force a reversal of British policy but to humiliate his old ally. Oil sanctions were threatened. Only when British forces were withdrawn from Egypt would there be any assistance. Macmillan panicked. Having, along with Eden, marched the troops into Egypt, he now insisted on marching them out of Egypt. The historian of Suez, Keith Kyle, describes Macmillan's somersault as 'a sensational loss of nerve'.[57]

Macmillan, as Chancellor, had protested against the enormous burden of the defence Budget on the British economy. Britain was devoting 9 per cent of its gross national product to defence. The average for the other countries of the OEEC was 5 per cent. Military expenditure overseas was running at the rate of £160 million. This was equal to the exports of the whole of the UK tractor industry, its agricultural machinery industry, its aircraft, to which could be added the total exports of whisky and cocoa preparations, 'all gone down the drain, as it were, to pay for our military expenditure abroad', he told the Foreign Press Association in May 1956.[58] Like other Chancellors before, and after, he had striven for Draconian cuts in defence.[59] Now it was shown that, despite the vast cost, and despite British strategic interests in the Middle East, British forces lacked the capacity for a rapid invasion of Egypt. As a result the Israeli forces had pushed to the Canal before British forces had landed at Port Said. The one service to the Israeli aggression that British forces had provided was the destruction of the Egyptian air force.

The Duke of Plaza Toro is famous for having led his regiment from behind. Macmillan was a prime mover in the Suez affair, but it was Eden and then, when Eden was away sick, Butler, who had to carry the burden in the House of Commons. The Duke of Plaza Toro is equally famous in that, when away his regiment ran, 'his place was in the fore-o'. Macmillan's switch from belligerence against Nasser to ingratiation with Eisenhower puts his record as a military strategist on a par with that of the Duke. What was it that persuaded Macmillan that the time had come to grovel to the Americans? He denies that his change of mind was due to the state of the reserves. He argues that the losses in September and October were 'tolerable'.[60] The reserves fell $50 million in the third quarter of 1956 but would have fallen by $230 million but for the fortuitous receipt of $180 million from the sale of Trinidad Leaseholds Ltd to Texaco.[61]

Even when, with the actual invasion, losses increased substantially, they were, according to Macmillan, sustainable. He claims that he would not have been unduly concerned had the UK been able to obtain either the money to which it was entitled from the IMF, or, better still, some aid by way of temporary loan from the United States.[62] However, asserts Macmillan, even if such support was not available, 'our resources were not so depleted as to make us yield to this new pressure. Our gold and dollar reserves were still over $2000 million.'[63] In fact, among the lessons of Suez was that Britain's reserves were still inadequate to defend sterling against a strong attack without the support of the Americans. Macmillan was to find that it was expedient to forgive Washington even if it was not easy considering the humiliations almost vindictively inflicted upon the UK by the US government.[64] The withdrawal from Egypt was completed by 22 December. Once completed, the American Government was ready to assist. 'It was, of course, a little wounding to feel that we were to be given a "reward" for our submission to American pressure. Nevertheless I was not foolish enough to refuse, even though the conditions were somewhat distasteful.' In December 1956, the UK drew £200 million from its quota with the IMF and further credits were arranged with the IMF and the US Export-Import Bank amounting to about £440 million. These credits could be drawn as required.[65] It was an American interest to help sustain the pound at $2.80 once the prime interest of forcing the British out of Egypt had been accomplished. Macmillan's obsequious use of the word 'generous' to describe the assistance that the US Administration now extended is yet further evidence of the way economic policy since the war had made Britain dependent on American good will.[66]

Macmillan's explanation of his change of position was that the objectives of British intervention had been achieved.[67] He quoted Eden: 'We had intervened to divide and, above all, to contain the conflict. The occasion for our intervention was over, the fire was out.'[68] This explanation cannot be taken seriously. The objective of British intervention had not been achieved. Nasser was still there and, having survived, had become a greater danger to British interests in the Middle East even than before.

Britain abstracted its forces from Egypt under instruction from the United States and in face of world hostility. The run on sterling was one way in which American disapproval could be brought to bear rapidly. It made the British capitulation more urgent if the government was not prepared to float sterling. Eden and Macmillan had brought the maximum humiliation on Britain. Its economic dependence on the USA had been underlined. Macmillan, the European, had helped to alienate France. France refused to accept that American pressure justified an ignominious scuttle. The offence was multiplied by the subsequent British scramble to restore relations with Washington. The French realized, once and for all, that no reliance was to be placed on Britain, a factor not without its influence on French policy when, in due course, a belated application was made for membership of the European Economic Community.[69]

To critics of the British action who wrote to him, Macmillan replied along the lines that 'I am sure history will prove that we have taken the right course' and that 'I am fortified in this view by the support for what we have done given by the man whose experience, character and knowledge I have more respect for than anyone else, Sir Winston Churchill.'[70] For Macmillan to take Churchill's great reputation hostage and turn it into a shield was not the least distasteful aspect of his role in the Suez affair.

WAB OR HAWOLD?

Within three weeks of the last British soldier leaving Egypt, Macmillan was Prime Minister. Eden, thoroughly discredited, resigned on 9 January 1957. His ill-health was genuine enough but his resignation made possible a new start. Each Cabinet Minister was invited separately into the Lord President's room in the Cabinet Office where they found the Marquis of Salisbury together with Lord Kilmuir, the Lord Chancellor, both ruled out of the succession by their membership of the House of Lords. Salisbury asked the question, 'Well, which is it, WAB or Hawold?' Hawold got it by a landslide. It has to be regarded as a judgement on Butler that, in the circumstances prevailing, the Cabinet opted for Macmillan. On the evidence before the Cabinet they could hardly have made any other choice. Macmillan had built 300,000 houses. He may have attracted criticism as Foreign Secretary but as Chancellor he appeared to have pulled the country back from the brink on which Butler had left it. He had supported Suez, totally misinterpreted American attitudes, and then led the scuttle, but his crimes in that respect were being carried away on the shoulders of Eden. Indeed, his relationship with Eisenhower might now prove valuable. Butler, on the other hand, had ended his period as Chancellor in some disgrace. He had twice been found guilty of lack of judgement, over Robot and over his 1955 Budget. He had not been able to make up his mind whether he was for or against the Suez adventure. It was no help to Butler that he had indicated doubts about the wisdom of the Suez adventure and that his rival Macmillan had joined in the war cries before suddenly switching and sounding the retreat. Butler's ambivalence did him greater harm than if he had steadfastly followed Eden's lead to disaster. The choice lay between one man who had made terrible errors of judgement and another who had shown himself reluctant, not for the first time, to make any judgement at all. It was a poor choice for the Conservative Party, but, more importantly, for the country.

SEVEN

Peter Thorneycroft: a Chancellor Betrayed

HENRY VIII HAD SIX WIVES. With one, Jane Seymour, he appears to have been in love, but she died very young. Macmillan had four Chancellors. With one, Derick Heathcoat Amory, he appears to have been in love but, in July 1960, Amory insisted on resigning after only two and a half years in the office. Henry VIII reigned for almost 38 years, Macmillan only for 7. Thus Macmillan got through Chancellors faster than Henry got through wives and, it would appear, with even less satisfaction. He was a Prime Minister who had spent a year at the Treasury but refused to learn the lesson that a successful Chancellor needs the backing of a strong Prime Minister. Rather it was his view that a successful Prime Minister needs the backing of an obedient Chancellor. This was despite Macmillan's own plea to Eden, when he himself became Chancellor, that he should have the Prime Minister's full support in managing the difficult conjuncture that he had inherited. Macmillan, when he became Prime Minister, saw it as his first duty to restore the unity of his Party and the tattered popularity of his government. Restoring the popularity of a government can be at odds with restoring its authority and effectiveness in economic management.

Macmillan also understood that Prime Ministers need myths. Macmillan's myth was that the key to his economics was to be found in his experience as MP for Stockton-on-Tees between the wars. Stockton-on-Tees was a depressed area with much poverty and high unemployment. Macmillan had been defeated there in the 1945 General Election. He was fortunate to have been able to return to the House through an early by-election in the more forgiving constituency of Bromley in Kent. Stockton-on-Tees was now a strong Labour constituency, but he found his link to Stockton-on-Tees politically valuable. It characterized him as a 'One Nation' Tory, a Tory in the Disraeli tradition, a Tory who cared. To that end, Macmillan portrayed himself as an enemy of

Treasury orthodoxy and as a dedicated expansionist. It was a convenient creed politically. While himself Chancellor, he had, no doubt, been compelled to take orthodox measures, but these had been dictated by the economic conjuncture he had inherited from Butler's listless management. As soon as the sun shone again, and burnt up the clouds, expansion would resume. Indeed, on further consideration, free of Treasury briefs, it might be that expansion was the way to make the sun shine again. The economics of Stockton-on-Tees would bring Macmillan into conflict with his first three Chancellors.

PETER THORNEYCROFT

Peter Thorneycroft was an obvious choice as Chancellor of the Exchequer. He was an effective debater in the House of Commons, and at the time he was appointed Chancellor, he had served successfully for five years as President of the Board of Trade, the longest stint in that post in modern times. He had therefore been well situated to witness the uncertain trajectory of British economic policy under Tory government. If there was anything to be learnt about economic management outside the chair of the Chancellor, he should have learnt it. There was one item in Thorneycroft's political record which indicated that he might be prepared to think radically about the British economy. In December 1945, he had voted against ratification of the Anglo-American Financial Agreement when his Party whip told him to abstain. Thorneycroft felt sufficiently strongly to reject his leaders' attempt at appeasing their backbenches. Macmillan, on the other hand, had obeyed the whip and had found himself in 'the disagreeable and inglorious position of abstaining'.[1]

Thorneycroft's appointment would appeal to Macmillan on political grounds. In Opposition they had both been on the reforming wing of the Conservative Party.[2] In government, their names would figure in any list of 'Europeans' in the Cabinet. This did not mean that they were contemplating British entry into the European Economic Community. But Thorneycroft, at the Board of Trade, together with Foreign Secretary Macmillan, had helped to devise the idea of a European free trade area of which the common market, together with other western European countries including Britain, would be members. It would liberate trade between Britain and the common market without seriously prejudicing Britain's political and economic relationships with the

Commonwealth. Britain would be able to maintain its own external tariff and therefore continue its preferential arrangements with the Commonwealth. It was an ingenious idea. It would maintain the unity of western Europe that might otherwise be disrupted by the Treaty of Rome. It was thought to be attractive to Germany. From the point of view of acceptability to France, the idea had however one major disadvantage. French manufacturing industry would be confronted not just by German competition but by British as well. It was an additional problem that the proposed Free Trade Area would not cover agriculture and therefore would deny French agricultural produce any advantages in the British market. The negotiations eventually ran into the sand when General de Gaulle, in the middle of 1958, reassumed the government of France. De Gaulle would have none of this bright British idea. He issued the first of several vetoes on 14 November 1958. The European Free Trade Area, when it did come into existence, did not include the common market and therefore the main object of the exercise was defeated. The British attempt to secure the economic advantages of free trade in Europe without participating in the European Economic Community had failed.

To assist him as Chancellor, Thorneycroft had Enoch Powell as his Financial Secretary and Nigel Birch as his Economic Secretary. They were both men of high intelligence, at least as capable as Thorneycroft of forming a judgement on the country's economic dilemmas. It can be a mixed blessing for a Chancellor to have, as his subordinates, men as intelligent, if not more so, than himself. They do not sit in Cabinet with him, they do not see the problems he has to negotiate with his colleagues, and they perhaps expect him to win more of the arguments than political realities make possible. The blessing of able subordinates will be particularly mixed if, as in the case of Powell, their approach to economic problems is dogmatic. In the battle that was to come, it was of some comfort to Thorneycroft's opponents in Cabinet to be able to claim that he was being mesmerized by a fanatic but for whose pressure he would have been prepared to compromise.

A CHEERFUL START DESPITE OMINOUS WARNINGS

As he ended his year's tenure at the Treasury, Macmillan was still an orthodox Chancellor. The Governor warned him in December 1956 that 'a radical attack on the fundamentals' was necessary including 'dramatic, far-reaching and convincing measures' to be implemented in the first three months of 1957. The Governor repeated the warning at a meeting with Eden and Macmillan early in January when Eden was on the point of resignation.[3] Macmillan was getting the same advice from OF. He adopted the advice as his own. On 4 January 1957, six days before becoming Prime Minister, he circulated a paper to his Cabinet colleagues arguing the need for a balance of payments surplus of £300–350 million instead of the £50 million which was the most that could be expected in 1956. He considered such a surplus necessary to build up the reserves which, during the troubles of 1955 and 1956, had been found insufficient to protect sterling without damaging restrictions on the domestic economy. To that end, Macmillan proposed cuts in expenditure. He specified £200 million in defence and £80–100 million in the social services, mainly from the National Health Service. He wanted action to ensure that public investment was concentrated on the most productive projects.[4]

The same strongly deflationary advice was given to Thorneycroft as soon as he had passed the Treasury's threshold. OF recalled the repeated crises that the economy had faced and the need to repay the IMF drawing. It therefore advocated a target surplus on current account of £350–400 million. This surplus was calculated as necessary to fund the government's own overseas expenditure and the regular capital outflow by way of overseas investment. But the forecast surplus was only about half that amount.[5] Thus Thorneycroft was not spared the miserable messages that had greeted all his postwar predecessors on their arrival in Treasury Chambers. On 19 February 1957, he announced to the House a series of government economies. They included increases in the cost of welfare milk and school meals as well as an increase in the Health Service stamp from 10d to 20d.[6] This would save £57 million in a full year.

At first, in the aftermath of Suez, with the help of his February measures and the friendly noises and the reinforcement to the reserves emanating from Washington, life at the Treasury seemed to be going as well as could be expected.[7] By the time of his April Budget, Thorneycroft felt able to encourage the troops on the backbenches behind him: 'I see some grounds for cheerfulness. As I see it, the temperature of the economy has been brought down to a more normal level . . . Resources appear to be at least adequate to the demand on them. It is reasonable to hope for further substantial export gains. All this seems to be a basis not for standing still, but for going forward. Expansion must be the theme . . .'[8] Thorneycroft reduced taxes by £100 million, or £140 million in a full year. He left an overall deficit of £125 million. Macmillan had appointed Duncan Sandys as Minister of Defence and he had found significant savings in the defence Budget. Thorneycroft's tax cuts could be justified as more or less equivalent to the cuts in the defence Budget, though they cancelled the deflationary effect of the defence cuts. The Opposition was infuriated by the fact that one quarter of the reduction was in the form of a cut in surtax.[9]

Thorneycroft's Budget moved in a direction directly opposite to that advocated by Macmillan just before he left the Treasury. It was unlikely to achieve the balance of payments surplus that Macmillan had argued was so necessary to build up the reserves. It certainly did not satisfy the Bank of England.[10] Yet the Prime Minister was not offended that Thorneycroft had ignored his final deflationary exhortations to the Cabinet before becoming its leader. Despite the stern, unbending view he had taken in January, it could not but be a relief, in the political predicament he now faced as Prime Minister and leader of his Party, to find that his Chancellor was dedicated to expansion and cheerfulness, and had found room to cut taxes.

The cheerfulness was of short duration. Already by May, Thorneycroft was expressing alarm.[11] At the end of May, Cobbold wrote to the Chancellor in gloomy terms about growing anxiety over the long-term future of sterling, and growing doubts about whether any government would be able to reverse the inflationary drift.[12] Despite everything the Treasury could do to influence the clearing banks, advances were too high and the Governor said he was unable to help.[13] Thorneycroft wrote to the Prime Minister that unless the claims of departments for additional expenditure were resisted, cuts in taxation would be out of the question, prices would rise and there was 'a good chance that we may have an economic crash'.[14]

As the summer wore on, the reserves ran down. There was a small loss in July. In August there was a loss of £80 million and a deficit of nearly £65 million in the EPU. The drain continued at an accelerated rate in the first half of September.[15] A debate arose as to the cause of the trouble. Though nowhere near the Macmillan target of 4 January, the country was still in supportable balance of payments surplus, though fears were growing of a recession in the USA and the fall in commodity prices would in due course affect the overseas sterling area. Was not the market being premature in reacting against sterling, thereby forcing the government to use the reserves to sustain its value against the dollar?

Rowan believed that the problem was evidence of the need to implement domestic policies that would ensure a surplus in the balance of payments of the required size, year in, year out.[16] The economists in the Treasury were less exigent. They regarded it, in the words of Dow, as entirely a crisis of confidence initiated by movements and anticipations in the foreign exchange market.[17] The Deutschmark was the favoured currency of resort, an attitude reinforced when, in August, the French franc was, in effect, devalued.[18] British governments are inclined to seek the source of their distresses in the policies of other governments rather than their own. Germany's large and chronic current account surplus suggested to the British government and to the Bank of England that the DM should be revalued. The Germans, on the other hand, denied that the DM was undervalued against the dollar. They claimed that other European currencies were overvalued and argued that the 'collective approach', originally urged by the British in the time of Butler, should be put into effect and that European currencies should float within appreciable margins.[19] The invitation, in effect to devalue, was refused. On 22 August, the Governor told Thorneycroft, 'We have a difficult time ahead. The Germans are going to behave like Germans.'[20]

The problems caused by the German current account surplus were being exacerbated by the temporary return of an American surplus. As a result, the USA was no longer adding dollars to world liquidity. The clamour that the Americans should not be allowed to pay for the import of goods with paper greenbacks had not yet reached the decibels it would achieve during the later stages of the Vietnam war and General de Gaulle's Presidency. The flow of dollars resulting from the normal American balance of payments deficit was still welcomed as a support for international prosperity. The unusual American surplus in 1957 raised questions in London about the sufficiency of international liquidity. It gave rise to the theory that the annual increment to the world's reserves of gold and dollars was inadequate to sustain an ever-growing volume of international trade. This suggested a need for an increase in IMF resources upon which countries in temporary balance of payments difficulties could draw for relief. But expanding the resources of the IMF would only be possible with the support of the USA. Those who had grown wary of seeking help from the USA feared that a proposal for an increase in IMF quotas would be regarded in Washington as a thinly disguised request for an interest-free American loan. However, at the end of the IMF/IBRD meeting in September 1957, it was agreed that the IMF would undertake a study of international liquidity.[21]

FLOATING?

Once more floating was being considered within both the Treasury and the Bank. Robert Hall was, once again, of the view that government should 'consider' floating, though combined with the necessary deflationary measures.[22] Robbins, to whom Thorneycroft had turned for advice, recommended against floating.[23] He held that, whatever its theoretical merits, it was not sensible to float at a time of extreme weakness.[24] In fact, the balance of payments in 1957 was relatively strong, if not as strong as Macmillan, while still at the Treasury, had planned for it to be. If British governments were to wait until the economy was strong before floating they would in the end find that they had waited until it was so weak that there was no alternative to floating. From a purely economic point of view, it was an ideal time to combine the rise in the Bank Rate, and the assault on public expenditure, with the floating of the pound. There were, however, the usual political objections. It would open up further controversy with the USA. To float sterling could damage the dollar. To the government, as well as one more offence to the USA, it would have appeared yet one further humiliation after Suez if the pound fell in value. There was also still the European veto in the sense that the member countries of the EPU as a whole were not yet quite ready to wind it up. The veto could be ignored but not easily by a government which was trying to build a new relationship with Europe.

WAGE PRESSURE

An element in the market's lack of confidence in sterling was the government's attitude to wage claims. But Thorneycroft could expect no help from the Prime Minister. Macmillan believed in peace with the unions, not war.[25] For example, while he was in Bermuda in March 1957 making peace with Eisenhower, Macmillan decided that it was inadvisable to make war on the railway workers' union when battle could be avoided at the price of paying 5 per cent instead of 3 per cent. The economy, he thought, was too weak to justify a fight.[26] On 26 June, Macmillan acknowledged the problem in a letter to Harold Nicholson. 'The country simply did not realize that we were living beyond our income,

and would have to pay for it sooner or later . . .'[27] But however justified
the diagnosis, Macmillan showed no sign of any intention to do anything
about it. Politics had to come first and he was clearly determined that
the day of payment, when the country would have to face up to the fact
that it was living beyond its means, should be postponed beyond the
date of the next election.

Inflation was an anxiety for the government on political grounds as well
as because of its effect on competitiveness. The government was conscious
of the support it had won among trade unionists. On the other hand,
inflation alienated middle-class opinion, particularly among those whose
incomes did not rise to the extent necessary to compensate, or thought
that was the case. Such people saw themselves losing out in a society in
which the trade unions were using their industrial muscle and achieving
for their members substantially more than compensation for price rises.
Therefore Macmillan was bound to talk about the problem, to show
understanding of the anxieties of many of his supporters even if no significant action followed. In Bradford, on 20 July, he asserted:

> Let us be frank about it; most of our people have never had it so good
> . . . What is beginning to worry some of us is 'Is it too good to be true?'
> or perhaps I should say 'Is it too good to last?' For amidst all this pros-
> perity, there is one problem that has troubled us – in one way or another
> – ever since the war. It's the problem of rising prices. Our constant
> concern today is – can prices be steadied while at the same time we
> maintain full employment in an expanding economy? Can we control
> inflation? This is the problem of our time.[28]

His words may have been intended to convey a warning to his
countrymen but sounded instead like a cry of triumph. It was natural
that the cry that 'most of our people have never had it so good' should
drown the warning which was at best *sotto voce*. The speech at Bradford
was typical. No one could say after this speech that Macmillan had not
warned about inflation and the dangers it brought with it. On the other
hand, the speech sounded more like an attempt to win political capital
than a challenge to the trade unions. As it was not a challenge, Macmillan
was disingenuous in complaining that he was misinterpreted.[29] The
political fact with which Thorneycroft had to contend was that Macmillan's response to the problem of inflation was to talk about it but
without unnecessary exertions which could have large political costs to
balance against any possible political gains.

In July 1957, a Council on Prices, Productivity and Incomes (CPPI)
was established. It consisted of three independent members whose remit

was to keep under review changes in prices, productivity, and the level of incomes, and to report from time to time.[30] As there were three members, it was inevitable that they should be regarded as wise. Samuel Brittan describes it as 'the vestigial remnant' of an attempt by Thorneycroft, rejected by the Cabinet, to develop an incomes policy. The wise men were to provide what Macmillan, in his memoirs, was to call 'restraint without tears', tears not being a political desideratum at that time.[31] It was hardly a persuasive answer to the increasing suspicion that the government was not prepared to resist wage claims from major public service unions. Thorneycroft himself did not, at this stage, help matters by announcing in the House on 25 July that 'There is clearly no simple act of policy which is a remedy for inflation. If there had been, it would have been discovered a very long time ago.' Everything depended on the cooperation of the government, public and private sector employers, and the unions.[32] It appeared therefore that, if the unions were not prepared to oblige with their cooperation, there was nothing the government could do. But events were pushing Thorneycroft away from this consensual approach towards less helpless conclusions about inflation.

THORNEYCROFT AND INFLATION

The lesson that Thorneycroft derived from his experience of battling against the market was that the lack of confidence in sterling was the result of inflationary pressure at home. The inflationary pressure derived from the fact that the economy was overloaded. Thorneycroft had found himself criticized by some City Editors for not using monetary policy more vigorously.[33] To start with he was unsure whether he had effective monetary instruments at his disposal. Early in 1957, he had been worried about the increase in bank advances. In February he had written to Cobbold: 'It is not so much that I think we ought to apply the brake any harder at the moment; but I do want to know that we have a brake that works.'[34] He began to believe that inflation could be controlled by controlling the money supply. He had sought the advice of Lionel Robbins and he, without committing himself to a mechanical version of the quantity theory of money, certainly believed that strong action on the money supply would help.[35] The advice implied that, if there was no restraint in wage settlements, unemployment should be allowed to rise.

Thorneycroft was now intent on dealing both with the immediate pressure on the reserves, and with what he saw as the underlying crisis of the British economy, by a combination of monetary and fiscal measures. His fiscal approach required that the estimates for the following financial year, 1958–9, should not exceed expenditure for the current fiscal year, 1957–8. By August, he had persuaded the Prime Minister to issue a directive to that effect.[36]

His monetary approach included an appeal to the banks that the average level of bank advances for the next twelve months should be held at the average level for the previous twelve months.[37] Thorneycroft hoped to persuade the clearing banks to accept a fixed limit on their lending. They refused, though indicating a willingness to use their best endeavours to meet the Chancellor's requirements. Thorneycroft then wished to instruct the Bank of England to issue a directive to the banks to make a 5 per cent cut in advances. The Governor, Cameron Cobbold, refused to issue any such directive and Thorneycroft found that, under the 1946 Bank Act, he had the power neither to instruct the Governor to issue the directive nor to sack him. Makins was in any case horrified at the idea that the Governor should be sacked as he believed that it would complete the debacle over the pound.[38] The appeal to the banks, which was the best alternative, had no effect on bank advances.

The monetary measures also included, on the recommendation of the Governor, an almost unprecedented increase of 2 per cent in Bank Rate from 5 per cent to 7 per cent, the highest level since 1921. Macmillan at first resisted the increase in Bank Rate. He argued that, as the intention was also to use quantitative controls, there was no need to use the indirect method of a large increase in Bank Rate. Thorneycroft and the Governor were preoccupied not just with the present lack of confidence in sterling but also with the likely additional effect on confidence when the September reserves figures, which would show a serious fall, were published. After a night's sleep, the Prime Minister, with reluctance, acquiesced though he notes that 'I stored up this incident in my mind and was determined not to yield indefinitely to pressure.'[39] Macmillan, in a memorandum to the Cabinet, told his colleagues that so far as the exchange rate of sterling was concerned, the government had 'nailed our colours to the mast'.[40] Macmillan had suddenly discovered that the defence of sterling had a moral side because one should not default on one's debts, as well as a practical side because to default would bring ruin and unemployment.[41] This was hardly consistent with earlier positions taken by Macmillan.

The monetary measures were announced on 19 September together with a firm statement by the Chancellor that 'The Government are determined to maintain the internal and external value of the pound.' Quite as significant, the statement also said: 'There can be no remedy for inflation and the steadily rising prices that go with it which does not include, and indeed is not founded upon, a control of the money supply. So long as it is generally believed that the Government are prepared to see the necessary finance produced to match the upward spiral of costs, inflation will continue and prices will go up.'[42] Treasury Ministers appear to have had an even greater influence on the drafting of this statement than is normal. In any case, it horrified Treasury economists.

With the statement of 19 September, the run on the reserves stopped. It was not just that the government had committed itself once again to the exchange rate but that it was seen to be taking firm, if unpopular, action against inflation. Politically the situation was eased by the agreement of the shadow Chancellor, Harold Wilson, though naturally he was of the opinion that nothing comparable would have been necessary had Labour been in power.[43] Labour, like the government, was determined to maintain the value of sterling. If 7 per cent Bank Rate was necessary to repel the speculators against sterling, 7 per cent it must be. Anything was better than underlining in the public mind that Labour was the Party of devaluation. Nothing could have been more insistent than the demands of Labour leaders to be assured that the exchange rate of sterling would be held.[44]

A BREAKDOWN IN TRUST

Thorneycroft was beginning to distrust his officials and, according to Hall, 'especially me'.[45] It was for this reason that Thorneycroft had turned to Lionel Robbins. Hall and the other economists in the Treasury were pleased to believe that the Chancellor did not really understand the economics of what he was doing.[46] He was not considered in the Treasury to be an intellectual giant. The money supply is a difficult subject – was he not grossly oversimplifying? Did he even understand what the money supply was? Would his policies work even if they were implemented? Could they be implemented? The statement of 19 September, Hall thought, did not make much sense as economics.[47] Did Thorneycroft appreciate how much additional unemployment might be caused by an attempt to implement his policies? It is quite normal for a Minister to be outranked intellectually by his officials. It is a regular requirement on officials to put the incoherent impulses of their political masters into an intellectually respectable form. But, precisely because economic management is an art not a science, the possibility should never be forgotten that a Minister's instincts may have more of the essence in them than the sophistications of economic advisers. Thorneycroft's instincts told him that there must be something wrong with a country's economic management when it led to one crisis after another.

An ideological debate now arose within the government. There was no recent experience of the use of the money supply to control inflation, but the way it was supposed to work implied a readiness to accept higher levels of unemployment. How much higher would be discovered only by experience. Thorneycroft was advocating a policy apparently inconsistent with the message of the 1944 White Paper on Employment. Did Thorneycroft's intended breach of promise reflect the kind of Party the Conservatives had set out to be after 1945? Monetary policy was now being implemented in a way far more aggressive than was contemplated when Butler raised Bank Rate first to 2.5 per cent and then to 4 per cent. It could be argued that if the defence of sterling now required a readiness to employ exceptional levels of Bank Rate then, whatever the effect on the money supply, a sacrifice in economic activity, and hence employment, must follow. When Thorneycroft was asked in the House whether his measures would lead to unemployment, he replied that it would 'not on our expectations or our intentions, provided moderation is exercised all round'. He added more threateningly, 'By that I do not mean that we must stick at any cost to an unemployment figure of 1–2 per cent, nor does any thoughtful person of any political persuasion mean it either.'[48]

Part of the problem, at least so far as Hall was concerned, was that he suspected that Thorneycroft was taking what he believed to be the politically easy way of dealing with inflation. It was easier for the Chancellor to talk about the money supply or to increase the level of unemployment a bit than to stand up to the unions. But the priority at the time, in Hall's view, was to stand up to the unions, especially on the railways.[49] That was the way to make full employment consistent with low inflation. The irony was that a Chancellor who was trying to find a way of being tough with inflation was being despised by his Chief Economic Adviser for being soft on inflation and for abandoning the cause of full employment. Thorneycroft's inadequacy as an economic theorist was, no doubt, distressing. It should have been compensated, even for Hall's sensitive mind, by the fact that Thorneycroft was demonstrating a praiseworthy determination untypical of previous Tory Chancellors. It was Macmillan who was Prime Minister and it was Macmillan who was dictating policy on wage claims. At least Thorneycroft was trying to do what he could by way of fiscal and monetary policy. It is the function of civil servants to advise and, having advised, to help their Ministers win their battles. One would expect that to be particularly true in the case of the Treasury when it has a Chancellor prepared to fight for policies that were in most respects what it wanted, however faulty his technical economic analyses. There was not even, in practice, all that much divergence between the Chancellor and his Chief Economic Adviser. Hall was prepared to accept some rise in unemployment and to use monetary measures. He would want to present policy as restricting demand rather than the money supply. But, whatever the convergence at the level of practical action, the two men could not get on terms with one another. Cairncross tells us that Hall was twice driven to offer his resignation, not primarily by any objection to the measures decided but because of the theoretical dressing in which they were presented.[50] The effect of what was done and what was said on 19 September had been to strengthen the pound. Hall found this result welcome, however inadequate the theoretical justification offered for the action taken.[51] Talking to Maurice Allen of the Bank early in January 1958, he placed considerable weight on the effectiveness of the 7 per cent Bank Rate and argued that there should be no early relaxation, 'no green light anywhere'.[52] On 3 January 1958, just before Thorneycroft's resignation, sterling was standing at its best dollar rate since 1954.[53]

THE FINAL BATTLE – PUBLIC EXPENDITURE

The final struggle came over public expenditure. The run on sterling had ceased after the statement of 19 September, and in October the reserves had flooded back. Thorneycroft, nevertheless, was still determined to restrain the following year's estimates within the previous year's level. It was a major step in his battle to eliminate overload, that over-full employment about which Macmillan had complained in 1955 before failing to do anything very much about it. Given the level of inflation, Thorneycroft's challenge to his Cabinet colleagues, which had been endorsed in Macmillan's August directive, implied a cut in public expenditure estimates for 1958–9 which could not be satisfied by the defence cuts that had been agreed earlier in 1957.[54] Into Thorneycroft's demands could be read a blow to the welfare state to which the Conservative Party was now as firmly committed as its Labour opponents. Macmillan had 'a useful talk' with Thorneycroft on the evening of Sunday, 22 December. He found that his Chancellor was wanting some swingeing cuts in welfare state expenditure, more than was feasible politically.[55] Thorneycroft was challenging the whole ethos of postwar conservatism.

The Chancellor's dilemma was acute. The government was intensely unpopular; Eden as Prime Minister had not done well in popular estimation even before Suez. Suez represented the final blow to the credibility of his government. Macmillan's succession had, as yet, made no difference. Throughout 1957, the government continued to do badly in by-elections and in the opinion polls.[56] Labour was behaving as though it would be forming the next government, two or three years hence, and it appeared to have reason on its side. It was hardly the time to make a drastic change in economic policy which would certainly be unpopular. On the other hand, no time is ever perfectly ripe. Interest rates had been forced to crisis level by the weakness of sterling. If a Chancellor does not seize such an opportunity, what further opportunity can he expect? This was not Thorneycroft's only timing problem. He was launching a battle of such importance that if there was to be any chance of winning it, it needed to be well prepared. Here he was at a severe disadvantage. He was demanding urgent decisions which his colleagues found distasteful. He sat in Cabinet with his two predecessors, Butler and Macmillan. Neither of them was offering him any help. If Macmillan is to be believed, Butler had an excuse that reads oddly in the light of his own attempt to rush Robot through the Cabinet. According to Macmillan, Butler was shocked at the irresponsibility by which Cabinet was being asked to make great changes of policy at a few days' notice, without study or preparation.[57] If Butler wanted an excuse for prevarication, this was as good as any.

Thorneycroft did not even have the official Treasury on his side, apart from Sir Leslie Rowan at OF. The government economists had not been given furiously to think by this latest crisis. They attributed it to external events rather than to the state of the British economy. They were not entirely happy with the state of the British economy. On the other hand, they did not see a crisis of confidence attributable to external events as a compelling reason for action on the domestic front. Was Britain to deflate each time foreign speculators attacked sterling?[58] While Thorneycroft had become active and demanding, they were relaxed. The politically sensitive Hall agreed that the economy should be run under less pressure, but he did not think it politically practical to change the whole emphasis of policy so quickly.[59] In any case, unemployment was already rising following earlier deflationary action.[60] For some years the money supply had been falling as a percentage of GNP.[61] A recession appeared to be already on its way. The market, influenced by the TUC's decision in September to reject wage restraint, might believe that the unions were out of control. For that reason it would be sensible if the government was seen to take a firm stand against wage claims. By the autumn, the government *was* taking a firmer stand against wage claims in the public sector. The pace of wage inflation was already declining.[62] As a further disincentive to taking his Chancellor seriously, Hall had heard that, in August, Roy Harrod, Keynes's principal representative on earth, had written to the Prime Minister suggesting that the economy needed a powerful stimulus.[63] This, Hall knew, was far more in line with Macmillan's approach to economic management, and more consistent with the political compulsions of the time, than Thorneycroft's rush to salvation by deflation.

In the end what mattered was that Robert Hall did not share his Chancellor's urgency, his insistence that this was the time to reduce overload in the economy. What Thorneycroft was proposing was not just politically impossible. It was economically undesirable. What was the urgency? At the end of 1957, the economy seemed strong. Hall's assessment was that the British people had never had so high a standard of living nor the British economy been so productive, nor had the balance of payments forecast ever been so good. Even the over-full employment was moderating.[64] Why provoke a crisis when everything was going so well? Of course, this optimism was sadly premature, as Hall would later have to admit. Thorneycroft's instincts about the real state of the economy had more validity than Hall's economic analyses. Hall, however, was not lacking in justifications for betraying his political master. Another consideration dragged in was that it was essential to maintain economic activity in the West not just for its own sake but to help the underdeveloped world. The Chancellor was guilty of bad errors of judgement based on a kind of *laissez-faire* morality.[65]

Thorneycroft had also lost the support of his Permanent Secretary. Makins' sympathies did not run with those of his Chancellor. He regarded his main responsibility as being to the Prime Minister who had secured his appointment, and was, after all, First Lord of the Treasury. If Thorneycroft had been allowed his way, it could well have led to resignations by other members of the Cabinet and the overthrow of the Prime Minister. It is not surprising that Thorneycroft lost confidence in a Treasury represented by Hall and Makins. Thirty years later Makins told Alistair Horne that he had found Thorneycroft's actions incomprehensible, adding: 'It is hardly a point in any Permanent Under-Secretary's favour when he loses all his ministers overnight.' At the time, it was Hall's opinion that Makins was quite happy to see the back of Birch and Powell and on the whole relieved about the departure of Thorneycroft.[66] Perhaps, if Makins' sympathies had run with Thorneycroft, he could have used his diplomatic skills to persuade the Chancellor that such a drastic change of direction required preparation and planning and could not be imposed by the ultimatum of resignation. As it was, he tried 'to prevent my ministers throwing themselves and the Government overboard' but failed.[67]

At a time when the Treasury, for once, had a Chancellor who was prepared to fight against the laxity that had characterized British economic policy since the war, it decided to abandon him. The Treasury does not like losing battles. This battle, it knew, would be lost. Because it would be lost, it should not be joined. It was because he had come to distrust his officials that Thorneycroft had turned to Robbins. But, though Robbins could advise, he could not, certainly not in the time, plan a strategy that might get through Cabinet. The consequence was that Thorneycroft was outmanoeuvred tactically. He took his stand on a second increase in the Health Service Stamp in one year and on a major cut in the allowance for the second child which was, as Macleod pointed out, the only element in the Welfare State that the Conservatives had themselves introduced. Thorneycroft's demands could be presented as likely to add to wage pressure and hence to inflation.

Thorneycroft was also outmanoeuvred in that he could be accused of refusing a compromise which, it was claimed, went a long way to meet his point. His demand that there be no increase in the estimates implied a cut in the estimates of about £150 million. The Cabinet laboured and offered him about £100 million. He was told that more was impossible. In summing up the Cabinet Conclusions of its meetings on 3, 5 and 6 January, Macmillan said that 'Disinflation, if enforced to the point at which it created a stagnant economy or provoked a new outbreak of industrial unrest, would defeat its own ends.' Abolishing the family allowance for the second child 'was neither politically nor socially desirable. It would be contrary to the traditions of the Conservative Party.' Other cuts in welfare services would create disaffection and provoke a concrete basis for fresh wage claims.[68] Thorneycroft was warned that it was absurd that he should threaten resignation because of a difference with his Cabinet colleagues amounting to only 1 per cent of total government expenditure. But this was not a fair representation of the truth. Thorneycroft was separated from his colleagues not just by £50 million of public expenditure cuts which could certainly have been found without incurring significant political costs if only Departments and the Treasury had been serious about it, but by a different, and more determined, approach to economic management.

One of the troubles in British Cabinet government is that spending Ministers are expected not just to *administer* their Departmental Budgets but to *agree* them. With various Ministers round the table refusing to agree and threatening to resign, Thorneycroft remained adamant. Most Chancellors would, in similar circumstances, forget the economy and reconcile themselves to a policy of drift and hope. That had been Butler's choice. Thorneycroft, after a long battle in Cabinet during which his manner as well as his matter excited Macmillan's keen disapproval, decided to resign and his two junior Ministers resigned with him.[69] Only two Chancellors of the Exchequer had resigned in the previous 100 years.[70]

What does a Chancellor do when his Prime Minister is intent on popularity and he is intent on the economy? Should he accept the compromise offered and work towards a better opportunity to secure the change in thinking that he believed necessary? In retrospect, that was exactly what Thorneycroft thought he should have done.[71] He should have fought on, not abandoned the war because he had only drawn the first battle. But, if he could not win in the aftermath of a crisis, when could he hope to win? His Prime Minister's eyes would remain firmly fixed on the next General Election, his advisers would remain complacent, and the economic experience of the remainder of his Chancellorship would simply be of continued inflationary drift. What compromises would he be expected to make in the future?

Macmillan appointed Derick Heathcoat Amory as Thorneycroft's successor, a move of some subtlety as Amory was probably the member of the Cabinet with most sympathy with Thorneycroft's views.[72] In his replies to the letters of resignation from the three Treasury Ministers, Macmillan emphasized that 'This Government has already proved that they are not afraid of unpopularity'.[73] He then demonstrated his unflappability by proceeding with his Commonwealth tour and telling the reporters at the airport that the resignations were just 'a little local difficulty'. Almost the whole Cabinet appeared at the airport to see him off in an act of collective loyalty. The public and the Party were instructed that the Chancellor, having failed to persuade the Cabinet by argument, had demanded from them an act of faith under threat of resignation. His refusal to accept the £50 million compromise showed fanatical rigidity.[74] The main issue had become psychological. The Chancellor had been 'over-rigid and even pedantic'.[75] The ideologues, Birch and Powell, were the men really responsible for Thorneycroft's unyielding attitude.[76] Macmillan comfortably won the battle with public opinion.

Peter Thorneycroft's explanation of his resignation awaited the economic debate on 23 January 1958. He then told the House of Commons:

> For twelve years we have been attempting to do more than our resources could manage, and in the process we have been gravely weakening ourselves. We have . . . been trying to do two things at the same time. First, we have sought to be a nuclear power . . . At the same time, we have sought to maintain a Welfare State at as high a level – sometimes at an even higher level than – that of the United States of America. We have been trying to do these things against the background of having to repay debt abroad during the next eight years of a total equal to the whole of our existing reserves . . . It has meant that over twelve years we have slithered from one crisis to another. Sometimes it has been a balance of payments crisis and sometimes it has been an exchange crisis . . . It is a picture of a nation in full retreat from its responsibilities . . . It is the road to ruin . . . I do not believe that the problem is technical at all. I do not believe it lies in an answer to the question whether we should use Bank Rate or physical controls. To tell the truth, neither of them works very well . . . The simple truth is that we have been spending more money than we should.[77]

Thorneycroft's speech to the House was considered very powerful. It was a declaration of principle that criticized six years of Conservative government equally with the preceding six years of Labour government. But so deeply entrenched was the policy that he criticized that it was hardly surprising that Ministers preferred to live from day to day, from crisis to crisis, rather than follow the path that Thorneycroft attempted to lay out for them with which, at least in words, many of them agreed. Indeed, they would feel uncomfortable with a colleague who was at once so right and so unreasonable.

Few Ministers have prospered in their careers as a result of resigning on a point of principle. It seems to make little difference whether the point of principle is right or wrong. In any case, if it is a point of economic principle, it is always highly debatable. Although Thorneycroft returned to the Cabinet in 1960 as Minister of Aviation and then of Defence, it was as a much diminished figure. He had to wait until the accession of Margaret Thatcher for his real apotheosis, as Chairman of the Conservative Party. However, after 1979, he appeared to become increasingly troubled by the social effects of Mrs Thatcher's economic policies. At a time when to be wet was to be wrong, he caused her distress by confessing publicly that he was a victim of 'rising damp'. Shortly thereafter, he retired from the Chairmanship, and disappeared finally from political life.[78]

With Macmillan out of the country, Butler was left in charge. Macmillan was very pleased by how well Butler handled the government in his absence. He told his diary: 'Butler, Chief Whip and all the others seem to have kept things going very well.'[79] But he feared that Thorneycroft was engaged in a deep conspiracy, and was disturbed by his powerful speech in the economic debate. A sterling crisis later in the year would enable him to seize the leadership of the Party.[80] Prime Ministers with a guilty conscience appear remarkably prone to fears of successful conspiracy, however well entrenched their own position in fact is.

EIGHT

Derick Heathcoat Amory:
His Master's Voice

VOICE OR ECHO

In his memoirs, Macmillan reflects on Cabinet government in his time. He found that on external affairs his Cabinet was ready to follow the advice of the Prime Minister and the Ministers immediately responsible. But on internal affairs all Ministers felt both the right and the duty to express their opinions, sometimes at considerable length.[1] There was nothing new in these reflections. The Cabinet as a whole would certainly insist on its collective responsibility on questions of public expenditure or where a perilous economic situation was endangering the future of the government. Nevertheless, even in an economic crisis, if the Prime Minister and the Chancellor were agreed, they would probably have their way. There were major aspects of economic policy which the Cabinet as a whole would normally pass over with the same tolerant neglect with which they normally regarded external policy. On monetary policy, and on the Budget, decisions would be made by the Chancellor in consultation with the Prime Minister without significant challenge from the Cabinet. Where there was a Minister as experienced as Butler, he might be brought into the consultation. But the Cabinet as a whole would not be involved. Bank Rate was a matter for the Prime Minister, the Chancellor and the Governor, with Butler probably available to add his advice. Budgets, then as now, were presented to the Cabinet too late for any amendment except in abnormal circumstances. In the practice of Cabinet government, economic management will lie almost as much in the hands of the Prime Minister and Chancellor, if they are agreed, as foreign policy normally is in the hands of the Prime Minister and Foreign Secretary, if they are agreed. Whether this duopoly works satisfactorily must depend in great measure on the Chancellor. If the Chancellor's input simply parrots that of the Prime Minister, economic management is reduced to the more or less informed whims of the Prime Minister. There is no way of avoiding this danger except in the wisdom of a Prime Minister who insists that his Chancellor shall be a voice and not an echo. Amory made feeble efforts to be a voice but was never more than an echo. Macmillan did not have the wisdom to perceive that this was not the way to run a government.

A strong Chancellor who succeeds a comrade fallen in battle against Cabinet colleagues is in a particularly powerful position politically. The Prime Minister cannot afford to see him go. In January 1958, when Amory succeeded Thorneycroft, Macmillan feared a further sterling crisis later that year. For this reason also, it was not a good time for a Prime Minister who had just lost one Chancellor to do combat with his successor. When Eden moved Butler from the Treasury in December 1955, Macmillan was able, as Chancellor, to insist on the very cuts in bread and milk subsidies that Butler had failed to secure against Eden's opposition. Now Amory was in a position to insist on getting his way if there was a way that he wanted to get. But, as Macmillan well knew, he had neither the character nor the experience nor the intellect to put himself in opposition to his Prime Minister. A Chancellor needs to be *papabile*, capable of succession to the highest post. Macmillan knew that whatever qualities Amory brought to the job of Chancellor, they were not those of a potential rival.

Macmillan now had both a Foreign Secretary, Selwyn Lloyd, and a Chancellor, Amory, neither of whom had regarded themselves as serious contenders for the high positions they now held and both of whom were prepared to defer to their maker. Butler was out of the way at the Home Office, a department whose affairs did not greatly interest Macmillan. In any case Butler, having lost the race to No. 10, was now a compulsive loyalist except when he was led into indulging his wit. In 1958 and 1959, the Prime Minister was preoccupied with the imminence of a General Election, and he was in the best possible position to have his way.

Macmillan ruthlessly exploited Amory's reputation for honesty and his lack of ambition. It was not Amory's view in retrospect that he had been exploited. But then even the most modest of men do not like being remembered as the reluctant instrument of someone else's policies. Amory told Alistair Horne that Macmillan never 'bullied me, as I think he did bully Selwyn ... He was terrified of one thing, a slump ... he did ring me up occasionally. "Don't you think there might be a slump in a month?" – that was the influence of Roy Harrod. He was always pleased by anything that was expansionary, almost a wild inflationist at that time . . .'[2] Amory told one of his successors, James Callaghan, that 'after he had pored over all the figures he would come to the conclusion that the only thing to do was to "fly by the seat of my pants".'[3] The evidence creates a very different impression from the one that Amory tried to convey to Horne and Callaghan. During Amory's reign at the Treasury, it was Macmillan who was, in fact, the recidivist Chancellor. Amory was not a Chancellor flying by the seat of his own pants. This was a Chancellor who *was* bullied by his Prime Minister, and was coerced into actions of which he did not approve.

What is true is that Amory increasingly resented the position in which he found himself. It is not easy for a Chancellor when it is widely known that policy is determined at No. 10, leaving No. 11 a laggard, and ever more reluctant, follower. Not having the strength to resist Macmillan, it was not long before Amory was pressing for permission to resign. But he was too valuable to Macmillan to be allowed to return too soon to the West Country despite his claims that his textile company in Devon demanded his attention.

MORE ENGLISH THAN THE ENGLISH

Amory is now little remembered, as with so many politicians who were great men in their day. In his day, he was greatly liked and respected in the House of Commons. Reginald Maudling who, as Paymaster General, had been asked to help Amory writes of 'Derick's delightful personality. Modest, unassuming, shy, he nevertheless has a mind of clarity and a great strength of character . . . He often seemed the original of the "downy old bird".'[4] His biographer comments that, by the time of his appointment, Amory 'had come to be regarded as almost above the Party struggle'.[5] Though he had Scottish connections, his biographer describes him as '*more* English than the English'.[6] He once suggested that a Union Jack should be flown over every factory and farm throughout the country.[7] For Butler, Amory was 'closer to the Liberal school of thought than any of us'.[8] His grandfather was elected Liberal MP for Tiverton in Devon in the 1860s, loyally supported Gladstone for twenty years, but then broke with him on Home Rule. The Heathcoat family had established a textile company in Devon which was still in existence and gave Amory his political base.

This was not the first time that Amory had taken over from a Minister who had resigned. He had become Minister of Agriculture as a result of the resignation of Sir Thomas Dugdale over the Crichel Down affair. Unlike his predecessors as Chancellor since the war, Amory did not regard himself as a professional politician. In 1958 he visited India and, during an interview with the *Bombay Sunday Standard*, he said, 'I began as a businessman and it took me almost twenty years to get over my initial distrust of politicians, whom I had heard defined as people who always looked for trouble and found it, generally made the wrong diagnoses and consequently applied the wrong remedies.'[9] As Minister of Agriculture, Amory was reported to have been only a very reluctant supporter of Suez.[10] But he did support it.

AMORY'S FIRST BUDGET

Macmillan knew that a Conservative victory in the next General Election had lower priority in the Treasury's calculations than in his own. He had no reason to blame the Treasury for the resignations of Thorney-croft and his team but, to avoid any repetition and to ensure that Amory's mind did not become infested with deflationary conceits, he himself undertook Amory's education, a task in which he had the welcome assistance of the inflationist, Roy Harrod.

1958 was a year of recession. At the beginning of the year sterling stood at its highest level since 1954. This is the compliment that the market frequently pays Britain in recession because it sometimes means a stronger balance of payments and lower inflation. Industrial production was falling and unemployment was rising. There had been a series of measures which had had a depressing effect on the economy. They had started with those taken by Butler in the summer and autumn of 1955, they had continued with Macmillan's display of economic orthodoxy during his own brief tenure as Chancellor and with the measures that Thorneycroft had been allowed to take in the autumn of 1957 before his resignation. The American economy was moving deeper into recession; because of this, commodity prices were falling. This had its inevitable effect on economic activity in Britain and the sterling area. The political fall-out was reflected in the Rochdale by-election of February 1958. Rochdale had been held by the Conservatives in the elections of 1951 and 1955. In the by-election, Labour won, the Liberals came a good second, and the Conservatives were a poor third. In March

1958, the Tory constituency of Torrington fell to the Liberal, Mark Bonham Carter.

Yet caution seemed appropriate for Amory's first Budget. He introduced a standstill Budget incorporating only minor changes. Macmillan agreed to a standstill Budget. There was no political or economic sense in risking a further sterling crisis and thereby justifying Thorneycroft in his resignation. Moreover, a standstill Budget might help to win the wages battle, particularly in the bus and railway industries. Expansion could be resumed when these battles were won.[11] The tax changes were all in a downward direction but the total to be 'given away', £50 million, left the overall balance of the economy deflationary. It was not, at this stage, thought sensible to attempt to compensate for a fall in exports by increasing home demand. In his Budget speech on 7 April 1958, Amory pointed to the two risks which compelled him to hold his hand. The first was the danger of provoking wage inflation where we seemed to 'have only just emerged from a dangerously strained position'.[12] The second was fear of another foreign exchange crisis.[13] At least Macmillan had the satisfaction that Bank Rate was being reduced from 7 per cent to 6 per cent.

INTERNATIONAL LIQUIDITY – EXPLANATION OR EXCUSE?

Amory's cautionary words were a reflection of the perennial problems of the British economy, always facing one crisis after another. World trade was expanding rapidly but the UK's share was in fast decline. In 1948, over 29 per cent of world trade in manufactures was supplied by Britain. By 1950 it was 25.4 per cent. By 1960 it had fallen to 16.3 per cent.[14] The economies of Britain's continental neighbours were growing at about double the rate of the UK. Explanations could be found in the fact that unemployment and underemployment had been higher on the continent than in Britain and that, therefore, the continental countries had more unused or under-used resources to bring into action. Such explanations did not console an increasingly critical public opinion. Advice emerged from the 'Three Wise Men' in February 1958 in their first report. They regarded the deflationary measures of September 1957 as 'justified and indeed overdue'. They argued that 'a free and flexible economic system [cannot] work efficiently without a perceptible ... margin of unemployment.'[15] The theory that Britain required a greater margin of unemployment flew in the face of the postwar political consensus. Gaitskell condemned the report as a political tract. Hall had come to regard the Committee as 'nothing but an embarrassment'.[16] Although Macmillan himself was pleased enough at the support given to his government's measures of the previous autumn, what was being suggested was fundamentally unacceptable to him too.

One reason for Britain's problems perceived by the government was a shortage of international liquidity. More liquidity would mean fewer balance of payments crises, more trade, and would help to raise the reserves of the sterling area, which always seemed insufficient to resist pressure against sterling. Rowan and the Treasury had concluded after analysing all the options and possibilities and all the objections to various courses that: 'In spite of these difficulties it does seem that in the longer-term an all-round increase in [IMF] quotas would be the most satisfactory way of increasing liquidity.'[17] In the Bank of England, however, there were those who considered that all this British talk about international liquidity was merely a diversion from the main task of eliminating 'excessive liquidity in terms of domestic money'.[18] British governments, the Bank thought, would find any excuse to avoid addressing the real problems of the British economy.

Undeterred by the Bank, the government and the Chancellor continued the long British campaign for an increase in international liquidity. There had been much questioning by economists of the value to Britain of the sterling area. Such questioning led Amory to defend it in his 1958 Budget speech. He argued that the sterling area was an essential contributor to world liquidity. Sterling, he pointed out, financed a large part of the world's trade. 'There is no other currency in a position to take its place; nor could one be quickly developed . . . In a world where liquid reserves in other forms are all too scarce, sterling and the sterling area are indispensable to the smooth functioning of a large part of the world's trade . . .' To point to the contribution of the sterling area to international liquidity still left the fundamental question unanswered. Was there a shortage of international liquidity, and, if so, how should it be remedied? Amory accepted the Treasury's advice that there was a problem of world liquidity. He told the Commons that 'the problem of world liquidity . . . is a matter of increasing importance and urgency'. Any sound plan would have the support of HMG.[19] Britain's battle for increased international liquidity would extend far beyond Amory's tenure of the Treasury. It would be a constant theme in the statements of Chancellors. The trouble with such arguments, however meritorious, is that action depended on the cooperation of other governments, especially that of the USA. Those who were not sharing in the difficulties repeatedly experienced by the British government might deny the existence of any shortage, might regard British ideas as typically inflationary, and might, therefore, reject whatever remedies emerged from Whitehall.

During a visit to Washington in June 1958, Macmillan tried to persuade the Administration to take steps to counter the recession in the USA. That the American Administration should act was an opinion widely held in the UK and on both sides of the House. Speaking in the House of Commons in January 1958, Roy Jenkins called upon the USA to do better. 'In these circumstances, we . . . ought to be urging the rest of the world to re-inflate. We ought to be urging the United States to set her economy going up again as quickly as possible . . .'[20] Macmillan failed to disguise from the Americans that the British were, once more, up to their old inflationary tricks. Because Britain was seemingly less and less able to compete, the USA was expected to provide uncompetitive British goods with a market by inflating. It was neither the first nor the last occasion on which a British Prime Minister would find that the condition of the British economy was of rather less concern to others than to the British government. Macmillan had to tell the Cabinet on his return to London that the US Administration was not prepared to abandon the most orthodox financial policies.[21]

CONVERTIBILITY BUT AT A FIXED RATE

As, in 1958, sterling was strong, the idea of floating it from a position of strength was discussed within the Bank and the Treasury. Macmillan attributes the discussion to his insistence. On 21 March, he asked Heathcoat Amory to prepare a paper on the constitutional and technical processes needed for a move to a floating rate. 'I do not want an argument as to whether we ought to do it. I want a presentation of how to do it if we decide to do it.'[22] The Treasury and the Bank recommended against floating. The Bank had resumed its ancient theme that a fully floating rate for sterling was contrary to IMF rules and would bring the 'whole world structure of exchange rates into question'.[23] Hall was now once more against it and so was Leslie Rowan and OF. There was a strong feeling in the Treasury, shared with the Bank, that to allow a Macmillan government the soft option of freedom from the discipline of a fixed exchange rate would be a recipe for exchange rate depreciation, inflation and economic irresponsibility of every kind. Despite some dissent within its portals, the Bank even abandoned its argument for a wider dealing spread than provided under Bretton Woods. Fforde attributes this to the wish in the Bank to make common cause with the Treasury against floating.[24] There were, apparently, subtle distinctions beyond the comprehension of Ministers. To suggest a fixed rate but with wider margins could only bring their minds back to the soft option of floating.[25]

By August, after hesitations earlier in the year, both Rowan who would shortly leave the public service, disappointed at his failure to make Permanent Secretary at the Treasury, and Hall were prepared to support convertibility.[26] 1958 saw the balance of payments in very substantial surplus and, despite the American recession, the reserves increased by $840 million to over $3 billion.[27] Inflation was down to 2 per cent, it had been possible to bring Bank Rate down by stages until on 27 June it had been reduced to 5 per cent, and, as the year wore on, the American economy was recovering from recession. The opportunity was not one to be missed. On 27 December 1958, discussion was at last brought to an end and it was announced that sterling held by non-residents would at last be made freely convertible on 29 December. The decision was provoked by Germany and France, both of which wished to move to convertibility, in the case of France combining it with a devaluation.[28] Throughout western Europe, the EPU was seen to have served its purpose and could now pass peacefully into history. The European veto on sterling convertibility had thus been removed. Residents of the sterling area remained subject to exchange control. Exchange control was almost the only example of a wartime control that survived into the 1960s.

It had been widely expected that when sterling was made convertible, it would float. Once more the opportunity was missed. Convertibility was at the fixed rate of $2.80 set by Bevin and Cripps in September 1949. Thus, with the winding-up of the EPU, ended the battle for convertibility that had been launched by Butler in 1952. The irony was that convertibility arrived with the 1 per cent margin either side of parity to which Britain had committed itself in December 1945. The Bank, once the advocate of floating as a means to convertibility, was now pressing for convertibility for non-residents without floating and without even wider margins.[29] The Bank had always insisted on the importance of stability and what it had wanted was, not floating, but wider margins to assist it in the management of its international currency, supported precariously as it was by scarce reserves and over-hung by large sterling balances. By July 1955, acceptance of a 6 per cent spread for sterling, to be implemented when the EPU was wound up, had been secured from the Europeans.[30] Thus when, at the end of 1958, the EPU was liquidated, and non-resident sterling became convertible, there would have been an opportunity to widen the sterling margins of fluctuation. But neither the Bank nor the Treasury dared recommend it. One argument was that the fixed rate would be a useful weapon of persuasion in the battle on the wages front. Unions could be threatened that if they did not keep their wage claims moderate, Britain would become even more uncompetitive and jobs would be lost. It was an illusion that the unions would find the argument from the fixed rate compelling. Moreover, the existence of the fixed rate weapon did not dissuade the government from continuing to accommodate wage claims that, if economic policy had been the criterion, would have been resisted. The Cabinet avoided publicizing its 'guiding light' for pay claims and decided against the Chancellor's idea of a pay pause.[31] For the government to nail its colours to a 'guiding light' or to attempt to enforce a pay pause could have been politically embarrassing. Under Macmillan's benevolent gaze, the history of concessions, notably to the railwaymen, continued. Another argument was the one which had influenced the Bank and the Treasury against floating earlier in the year. Macmillan was Prime Minister. What responsible person would voluntarily free a government led by Macmillan from the constraints of a fixed exchange rate within the narrowest possible margins? Cobbold was thus a collaborator in the decision to neglect the opportunity, created by the dissolution of EPU, to introduce wider margins. He thereby helped to entrench the outcome for sterling that he had long feared. He had warned Butler in June 1955, that when convertibility did come Britain would allow itself to be 'tied up to something very like the Gold Standard practice at fixed rates and narrow margins'.[32]

REFLATING INTO AN ELECTION

By the summer of 1958, the opinion polls began to turn in favour of the Conservative government. Public opinion was perhaps encouraged by the reduction in the rate of inflation and by the government's success-ful, and untypical, resistance to the bus strike in London launched by Frank Cousins and the TGWU. The government's worry was that, as

1958 grew older, unemployment rose. Macmillan as Chancellor had refused to contemplate 3 per cent unemployment. With an election approaching ever nearer, it was enough for the unemployment rate to pass 2 per cent to provoke him and his Cabinet to demand action. It was feared that unemployment might reach 750,000, or about 3 per cent, by spring 1959. Treasury officials were willing to relax the deflationary stance of policy but were fearful that this might lead the Cabinet to inflationary excesses. The Treasury therefore began to devise regional policies for areas of especially high unemployment which might be acceptable to the government as an alternative to general reflation.[33] However welcome the regional policies, they would not dissuade Macmillan from pressing for a general reflation.

Amory had a target for 1958 of a £450 million surplus in the balance of payments. He did not wish to prejudice his target but he was persuaded, during the summer and early autumn of 1958, to take some reflationary action. In July the ceiling on bank advances was removed. Hire purchase restrictions were reduced in September and removed altogether in October. It was sufficiently late in the year not to influence the balance of payments out-turn and, for once, the balance of payments target was achieved. Macmillan was certainly not prepared to trust the future of his government to popular appreciation of his government's success with the balance of payments. As unemployment continued to rise, he became increasingly exigent. He was being advised by Harrod and Harrod was, as ever, in favour of stimulating the economy.[34]

On 24 October, the Cabinet discussed the economic situation. Macmillan put the Chancellor under pressure to reflate and the Chancellor appeared willing.[35] Macmillan could have done without explicit Cabinet support but it was psychologically helpful that the Chancellor should feel totally isolated in Cabinet. On 27 October Macmillan issued a directive calling for prompt corrective action to expand demand so long as it involved no future commitments. On 20 November, Bank Rate was reduced to 4 per cent. After Christmas, Macmillan called a further meeting of Ministers with the clear intention of putting Amory under even greater pressure. Amory was anxious about inflation while Macmillan feared that existing policies were leading to a slump.[36] By January 1959 unemployment was still rising and had reached 2.8 per cent. It was the highest figure since the fuel crisis in 1947. With support from Butler, Macmillan continued to exert pressure on Amory. Amory was still uncertain. He thought a recovery might actually have begun.[37]

Macmillan was sure that the Treasury was giving Amory bad advice as, in his view, it had to every Chancellor. He had a greater belief in Roy Harrod.[38] It was a belief not shared by Hall, who regarded Harrod as completely incompetent and irresponsible.[39]

In February, unemployment showed a further rise of 60,000. But, to Macmillan's intense relief, Amory was now in a definitely expansionist mood. Amory's justification for the extraordinary stimulus which he gave the economy in his 1959 Budget on 7 April combined classical Keynesianism with emphasis on Britain's duty to the world economy.

> The prospect for home production ... does not represent a full enough use of the capital resources which have been created in recent years. Nor can we be content with the possibility that unemployment might continue at around the present levels ... [Moreover] we must not forget ... that we in the United Kingdom have our own contribution to make to the re-expansion of the world economy after the mild recession of last year. If each nation were to pursue too cautious a policy in regard to its balance of payments, international trade would stagnate.

Nevertheless, he warned, 'We must at all costs make it our business not to return to an overload on the economy, which would make a resumption of inflation inevitable.' He concluded with his judgement that 'it would be right for me to seek, through the Budget, to give a further limited but effective impetus to the expansion of economic activity'.[40] The conviction that the UK has a special responsibility to keep international trade expanding, even against the trend of policy in the larger economies, and even at the cost of a balance of payments deficit, is a form of hubris that has been politically convenient to other British governments looking for a reason to reflate.

The Budget certainly gave an 'effective' impetus to expansion but it was not 'limited'. During the 1950s, as Cairncross puts it, the Tories were 'reluctant Keynesians'.[41] Now caution was thrown to the winds. The overall Budget deficit projected, £730 million, was larger than any since the war. The Budget made very considerable tax reductions. They were calculated to increase consumers' spendable incomes by £300 million in a full year. Income tax was reduced from 8s 6d by no less than ninepence.[42] Purchase tax was reduced by about one-sixth. There was a cut in the duty on beer. A start was made in the more rapid repayment of postwar credits which added a further £70 million to spendable income. Investment allowances, introduced in 1954, abandoned in 1956, were reinstated.

Yet it was already known that in March there had been a substantial fall in unemployment, from 2.8 per cent to 2.5 per cent.[43] As Iain Macleod, the Minister of Labour, boasted in the House of Commons on 18 March, unemployment in Britain was already the lowest in western Europe.[44] The stimulus was given in full knowledge of the decline in unemployment in March and clearly for political reasons. In the Treasury the figures were interpreted as not having much meaning as they simply reversed very bad figures in January and total employment was down.[45] In fact the fall in unemployment continued at a rate to satisfy even Macmillan's political requirements.[46] Hall's view at the time was that the economy could easily stand Amory's reflation, though he would have preferred to go more slowly so as to see how the economy reacted.[47] With hindsight, the economist and former civil servant Christopher Dow comments: 'In the light of its full effects, the stimulus provided by the 1959 Budget – another pre-election Budget – was excessive.'[48] By May, Amory was already worried that he had gone too far.[49] He had launched not a recovery but a boom.

THE RADCLIFFE COMMITTEE

The Radcliffe Report, *The Report of the Committee on the Working of the Monetary System* was published in August 1959.[50] It was another contribution to discussion of the art or science of economic management. The Committee had been appointed by Thorneycroft. The Report allocated no great role for monetary policy and for that reason was criticized by many commentators. 'Monetary measures are . . . part of one general economic policy which includes among its instruments fiscal and monetary measures and direct physical controls.' The policies conducted by the Bank of England should be 'from first to last in harmony with those avowed and defended by Ministers of the Crown responsible to Parliament'.[51] Such banalities are the inevitable product of the appointment of such a committee, with such a remit, headed by a judge learned in the law but ill-equipped to resolve the ardent differences of view among economists and among practitioners in the money markets. When the Report was debated in the House of Commons, Amory, who had been assured by the Committee that the control of monetary policy should continue to reside in his hands, was constrained to comment that 'Members may well doubt my personal qualifications for pronouncing on these formidable issues, on which eminent economists hold passionately such divergent views.' But, 'as has been well said, if only those who were qualified spoke, the world would be filled with a profound silence . . .'[52] Amory did feel courageous enough to say that he thought that the Committee might have underestimated the importance of monetary measures.

AFTERMATH

The General Election took place on 8 October 1959. It gave the Conservatives an increased overall majority of 100. On 10 October, Amory visited Macmillan and asked to be relieved of his post in the near future. Macmillan, however, did not wish to lose his pliable Chancellor and persuaded him to stay on until at least the middle of 1960. This left Amory to face the consequences of his 1959 Budget. The balance of payments surplus fell by £200 million between 1958 and 1959. Unemployment had fallen fast. By April 1960 it had reached 1.6 per cent. Prices, after two years of stability, showed signs of rising again. The reserves had fallen. This *could* be attributed to convertibility and to the removal of controls on imports from the dollar area and western Europe in October and November 1959, but prudence would have suggested fiscal caution precisely because such changes were taking place. Amory was deeply concerned at the economic aftermath of his 1959 Budget. On 21 January 1960, Macmillan, during his visit to South Africa, agreed to an increase in Bank Rate from 4 to 5 per cent. Political comfort was, as ever, available. There had been an increase in American and German discount rates which Britain had to match.[53] Yet if interest rates in Britain had become the plaything of international forces, it might, in other circumstances, have been considered another reason for fiscal caution.

The fruit of the 1959 Budget could be seen more clearly when it came to formulating the 1960 Budget. Macmillan, as was to be expected with a great election victory behind him, was philosophical; Amory was far less so. On 31 December 1959, Makins had retired. From 1 January 1960, Amory's Permanent Secretary was Sir Frank Lee, who had been for seven years Permanent Secretary at the Board of Trade. Samuel Brittan describes Lee as 'the first postwar Permanent Secretary to be familiar with economic issues'.[54] He had his own ideas on economic policy, he believed strongly in competition, distrusted planning and incomes policies, and considered that there needed to be a margin of spare capacity in the economy. Lee was also aware from his tenure at the Board of Trade how damaging to British industry was the continual chopping and changing with hire purchase controls and investment incentives that had become characteristic of British economic management. It was the inevitable price of the rapid swings between crisis and precarious stability which was characteristic of British economic management. It is odd that Macmillan should have sent to the Treasury a Permanent Secretary whose instincts were so antithetical to his own. Lee was unlikely to wish to dissuade his Chancellor from the deflationary course he, too, appeared now to have chosen.

On 26 February 1960, Amory and Cobbold were united in thinking in terms of a deflationary Budget and made their judgement known to Macmillan. The Chancellor and the Governor were not alone in this view. Even the Keynesian National Institute saw the case for a restrictive Budget.[55] The following day, Macmillan, in his role of candid friend and, no doubt, remembering what had happened to Butler's reputation after the 1955 Budget, wrote to Amory that following the Budget of last year, a deflationary Budget would either be very foolish or very dishonest. He recommended a *standstill* Budget.[56] In this political judgement, Macmillan, despite Lee, seems to have had the support of some Treasury officials who no doubt also remembered Butler's fate. Once more Amory struggled and then succumbed.[57] He was not the man to resist the Prime Minister, especially as he was getting similar advice from Treasury economists. A standstill Budget it was to be. Macmillan was pleased but had one remaining anxiety; he knew that Amory genuinely felt lugubrious about the economy and he feared that his real feelings would emerge in Amory's Budget statement.[58] Could Amory be persuaded to exhibit a cheer that he did not feel?

Macmillan need not have worried. The Budget, upon which Amory had decided under Macmillan's coaxing, increased taxes by £72 million in a full year. This would do little political harm because it was the result, almost entirely, of an increase in profits tax. In his Budget statement on 4 April 1960, Amory was optimistic about progress on employment and exports. His main concern, despite the increase in exports, was the balance of payments: it was deteriorating and this could be the first sign of incipient overstrain. It was to moderate this tendency that the Bank Rate had been raised on 21 January from 4 per cent to 5 per cent.[59] Amory also warned, 'We no longer have the reserves of labour and capacity on which we could count a year ago.' Demand was likely 'at least fully to absorb' and perhaps even to be in 'danger of outrunning' the capacity of the economy.[60] In his 1959 Budget, Amory had insisted on the need to avoid overload. Now he had to recognize that overload had returned and was his responsibility.

Macmillan foresaw that the Opposition would contrast the Budget of 1960 with that of 1959. But the government had the protection of the Chancellor's high reputation. Macmillan tells us that Amory, as Chancellor, had soon established an almost unique position in the House of Commons, by his combination of wit and good humour with common sense.[61] Macmillan was quite prepared to exploit that unique position to the full. In fact the Opposition was stymied also by their eloquence, the previous year, in arguing that Amory had not gone far enough in reflation. For the Opposition too, the 1959 Budget had been a pre-election Budget, and politics determined that it should claim that, what the government could do, it could do better.[62] Any satisfaction Macmillan could derive from the Budget speech and its delivery was soon to be disappointed. By the end of April, he had been forced to agree that the economy needed 'a touch of the "brake"'.[63] Hire purchase restrictions were reimposed and, for the first time, use was made of the power to call on the banks for 'special deposits', a system of control of bank advances endorsed by the Radcliffe Committee.[64] At the end of June, Bank Rate was raised further to 6 per cent and there was a further increase in special deposit requirements. While these measures checked the rise in consumption, exports fell and imports flourished. The balance of payments fell into deficit. But by that time, Amory had at last won his merciful release from servitude. On 27 July, having fulfilled every promise to his master, he resigned. When resigning he warned Macmillan that, if he had stayed on, he would have insisted on running the economy at a much higher level of unemployment, or, preferably, on the government accepting an incomes policy.[65] Many years later he told Alistair Horne, 'I was much more cautious than [Macmillan] was. I foresaw our paths would have diverged in one or two years' time.'[66] His final warning to Macmillan, and this retrospective judgement, no doubt helped his peace of mind. He forgave himself for not diverging from Macmillan when he held responsibility.

Amory was rewarded for his loyalty by his appointment as High Commissioner in Canada. He died full of honours, a Viscount, a Knight of the Garter, a holder of the Grand Cross of the Order of St Michael and St George, highly regarded, popular, and the recipient of invitations to deliver wise words to suitable audiences on suitable occasions. In 1975 he was invited to lecture on 'The Service of Youth'. He commented that 'some of the problems which we are apt to think unique to our generation have a respectable history'.[67] The problems he had confronted as Chancellor had a long, if not respectable, history. Despite their long history, and his reputed wisdom, he had been willing to follow his Prime Minister in an expansionary and politically convenient policy in which he himself did not believe. Chancellors should be made of sterner stuff.

NINE

Selwyn Lloyd: Scapegoat

As a man with limited intellectual horizons, Selwyn Lloyd was fortunate to occupy two of the highest offices in the state. He was less fortunate in his timing. He became Foreign Secretary just in time for Suez. He became Chancellor of the Exchequer just when the veil was being lifted on Britain's poor economic performance relative to its continental competitors. Lloyd was ill-equipped to participate in the consequent public debate. There was no evidence that he understood economic arguments or the nature of economic constraints. He was a man tied to his brief, lacking the conviction or understanding to make an independent contribution to the discussion of economic policy.

Macmillan was always deluding himself that he would like to be relieved of the economic problem. As have so many other Prime Ministers, he preferred foreign travel and summitry to the more demanding problems of the British economy. It was an understandable human weakness. His ideal Chancellor would free himself of the orthodoxy of the despised Treasury and the equally misguided Bank of England, would find a way of rescuing the British economy from its perennial problems, and would deliver a durable boom. Macmillan told Lloyd that he wanted as Chancellor someone with original ideas. Lloyd warned Macmillan that he was not an original thinker about economic policy or anything else. Macmillan was not deterred. He had made his arrangements for the succession to Amory and he did not intend to be deflected from them. He was unwilling to appoint any of the three men in his Cabinet who had the character and capacity for the job and might have had original ideas. They were David Eccles, Iain Macleod, and Reginald Maudling. All three of them were critics of the Treasury and in favour of faster expansion. On the face of it, therefore, all three of them should have been much to Macmillan's taste as economic managers. But Macmillan, in reality, wished to remain in charge of economic policy. It was too important politically to be delegated to men like Eccles and Macleod who might show too much independence. He knew perfectly well that Lloyd was a staff officer, not a man of ideas. If necessary, he himself could provide the ideas and the faithful Lloyd would implement them without forcing him to fight too hard to get his way. Lloyd would be another Amory. He might wriggle – it was impossible to tell what would happen to a man when exposed to those seductive Treasury civil servants – but, in the end, like Amory, he would obey.[1]

Lloyd's prospects of giving satisfaction were never great. Years later, he reflected on his acceptance of the responsibilities of Chancellor of the Exchequer.

> With hindsight, I realize that I was foolish not to go into the state of the economy more thoroughly before accepting ... The result was that in July when I became Chancellor it took quite a time for me to bring myself up to date. I was described as being very much on the defensive with the financial correspondents and experts. This was not surprising because frequently I did not know how qualified they were to offer advice which they gave in no uncertain fashion and moment.[2]

Failure to go into the state of the economy was not Lloyd's real mistake; he knew that the economy was once more in trouble. One of his first questions to Robert Hall when they met for the first time at the Treasury on 29 July 1960 was about 'how soon we were going bust'.[3] Whether he knew enough about economic management was a question which all prospective Chancellors are entitled to ask themselves. It was true that, because of the deterioration in the underlying balance of payments, and the perception that Britain was lagging behind its continental neighbours, Lloyd's problems would be greater than those with which his Tory predecessors had had to cope. But for anyone afraid that ignorance renders him ineligible for responsibility, politics is not the right profession.

The first real question Lloyd needed to consider was whether he was prepared to fill the role that Macmillan, only too obviously, had designed for him. He had little reason to expect that Macmillan would concede to him the lead in economic management, that he would be allowed to be Chancellor of the Exchequer in anything more than name. One of his trials as Chancellor would be the stories in the press that Macmillan, not he, was running the Treasury. On 16 March 1961 he wrote to Macmillan protesting that the public relations people at No. 10 seemed to be conveying to the press the impression that the Prime Minister was 'controlling and directing in minute detail every aspect of Government effort'. He could at least be sure that if policy went wrong No. 10 would be quite happy to allow him to take the responsibility.

The second question that should have been in Lloyd's mind related to his prospects of survival. It was a question for any prudent intimate of Macmillan, especially for one occupying so exposed a role. If he failed to satisfy his Prime Minister, or in the course of duty became a political liability, it would not help him to plead that he had made no pretence about his lack of most of the specified qualifications. Accepting appointment as Chancellor under Macmillan was a high risk for anyone with further ambitions in politics. Lloyd was aware of the risks. He would, after all, be Macmillan's third Chancellor. Lloyd, understandably, wanted guarantees as to his security of tenure. He received the guarantee he wanted. Macmillan promised that if he agreed to go to Treasury, he could stay until the General Election.[4]

As a bait, Macmillan held out to Lloyd the prospect of his leading the Party. To be in the running for the leadership, he was told, he must broaden his experience.[5] There were other baits. Accommodation is important to senior Tory Ministers. As Macmillan had his own country home at Birch Grove in Sussex and his wife, Dorothy, did not like Chequers, its use had been allocated to Lloyd.[6] As Foreign Secretary, he had also occupied 1, Carlton Gardens. The Chancellor's traditional London home at 11 Downing Street was, like the rest of Downing Street, being reconstructed. The Prime Minister himself had been forced to move to Admiralty House. Lloyd made it a condition of acceptance that he be allowed to stay on in Carlton Gardens, and that too was granted. In due course he would learn the sadness of losing, at the whim of a discontented Prime Minister, both his job and his homes.

THE CONJUNCTURE

After a decade during which the balance of payments was usually in surplus, it was now running into deficit. As Hall, author of much complacent advice to Chancellors, had become ready to accept, it was the surpluses in the balance of payments enjoyed during the 1950s that were 'the cause of our long complacency and why we took so long to start to deflate'.[7] There were the repeated foreign exchange crises. Britain's share of world manufactured exports was falling sharply. Despite repeated exhortation to producers of all kinds, Britain had not developed an export-oriented economy. Despite Keynesian manoeuvres with domestic demand, economic growth was slower in Britain than on the continent. Lloyd inherited the calamitous consequences of Amory's pliable acceptance of Macmillan's guidance. The British economy in 1960 suffered the worst balance of payments crisis since 1950. The crisis was at first disguised by an inflow of funds to London. Such inflows were not to be relied upon, especially when the 5 per cent revaluation of the DM in March 1961 reminded the market that exchange rates were not fixed for all time. The DM's revaluation was enough to raise questions about sterling but not enough to reassure the market of the stability of the new currency values. Even Harrod had become a prophet of woe and feared that the pound would crash in the summer [of 1961].[8] It was not surprising in the circumstances that questions began to be asked and criticisms to be heard about the quality of British economic management. The criticisms were heard even in government circles among those who had been responsible during the previous decade.

Obviously, if British economic management had performed poorly, the Treasury was to blame. It could not escape blame simply by claiming that its views had been repeatedly disregarded by Ministers and, in particular, by the present Prime Minister. That was partly true but it was also true that the Treasury had repeatedly connived in policies designed to achieve short-run political objectives. Thus Lloyd, confronted by major problems, found himself the political head of a department whose reputation was low. The problem with which Lloyd and the Treasury were confronted was insoluble. They had to find a way of resisting Macmillan's continual pressure for expansion, which would only lead to a further run on the reserves, and yet offer him the prospect of faster economic growth. This insoluble dilemma stimulated a rush of measures under Lloyd which were intended to improve Britain's economic performance. Unfortunately the measures were self-defeating. They served to divert attention and action from the principal sources of poor economic performance open to remedy by government, over-full employment and a currency at a fixed rate which was increasingly overvalued.

THE FIRST BUDGET

When Lloyd opened his first Budget on 17 April 1961 he began by informing the House that during the fiscal year 1960–1 there had been an overall fiscal deficit of £394 million or £76 million more than Amory had forecast in his 1960 Budget[9]. He declared himself determined to cut the borrowing requirement. 'I am sure that the broad effect of the Budget must be counter-inflationary; there must be a larger surplus above-the-line than last year and a smaller overall deficit.'[10] He informed the House that the effect of his Budget measures would be a much reduced borrowing requirement of £69 million.[11] Nevertheless, he did less than the Treasury recommended in extra taxation and did not in fact achieve even what he set out to achieve.[12] The overall deficit for 1961–2 turned out to be £211 million.[13]

He expressed his concerns on many issues. There was the inexorable growth of public expenditure.[14] There was the problem of inflation: 'At the end of 1960, the index of retail prices was two points higher than it had been a year before. The underlying trend of costs has begun to rise appreciably.'[15] His conclusion was that 'The first and most obvious need is a marked improvement in our balance of payments.'[16] On this topic he had a point of view to express: 'It is wrong to think of more exports and growth and a healthy balance of payments as being, in the last resort, competing objectives ... The question, to my mind, is whether our economy is sufficiently resilient and flexible to cope with the demand of the home market and the need for increased exports.'[17]

Much of the Budget was concerned with devices and incentives. Thinking up devices which might improve the management of the British economy was becoming a principal preoccupation at the Treasury. Macmillan's analogy for the running of an economy was driving a car with the alternate use of brake and accelerator. But Budgets are normally annual and therefore opportunities to change speed were far apart. Lloyd introduced the 'regulator'. The idea was that both a brake and an accelerator were to be available for use by a Chancellor without having to wait for the annual Budget or having to introduce an emergency Budget. There were, in fact, two regulators. The first gave the Chancellor power to adjust the amount of most indirect taxes up or down by up to 10% between Budgets without the prior consent of Parliament, though Parliament was required to approve the move within three weeks.[18] The second regulator permitted an impost of up to 4s (20p) per week on employers' National Insurance contributions. The second regulator was criticized because it would raise costs and as inimical to full employment because it would discriminate against labour-intensive companies. Boyd Carpenter, the Minister of Pensions, objected strongly, claiming that its use would remove a constraint on irresponsible claims for increased National Insurance benefits.[19] At the time of the July measures, three months later, Treasury officials advised its use but Lloyd refused.[20] It was, he said, a 'dead rat'. Cairncross, who by July had succeeded Robert Hall as Economic Adviser, thought that Lloyd had given a private assurance of some kind not to use it.[21] It was the indirect tax regulator that was available to desperate Chancellors wishing to ensure the prompt application of the appropriate degree of braking or acceleration according to the latest reading of the economy. But as an additional tool for the Treasury, it could not but be damaging to British industry that tax rates should be subject to frequent change at a moment's notice. It did nothing, moreover, to steer the economy, driven so near the precipice, permanently towards firmer ground.

The invention of the regulator did not exhaust Treasury imagination. Lloyd also raised the surtax threshold from £2000, where it had stood since 1909, to £5000. Though bitterly criticized by the Opposition this was an act of distributional justice. Whether it had any effect as an incentive was much more debatable. Could the tax system be used to improve the balance of payments? How could exports be increased without deflation or devaluation, which Macmillan thought appropriate only to Labour governments?[22] The decline in the UK share of world manufactured exports suggested another device. This was to slant the tax system so as to encourage businessmen to spend more time abroad. That was the easy part. More difficult was it to ensure that, while abroad, they actually sold British products. Such devices could have only a minimal effect on the volume of British exports.

ROBERT HALL

A few days after Lloyd's first Budget, Robert Hall retired. He had been in effect, if not in title, the chief economic adviser to the Chancellor since 1947. He was a man of left-wing inclinations who believed nevertheless that a Tory government was better for Britain though he seldom held a very high opinion of those he served and was inclined to judge Chancellors by their susceptibility to his advice. He sought to guide governments in accordance with his Keynesian convictions. He was somewhat contemptuous of old-fashioned economic views which he encountered among Chancellors mainly in the form of a belief that the Budget must never do worse than balance above the line. He repeatedly expressed his concern about 'over-full' employment in the UK and about its inflationary effects. He was highly sensitive politically and though in his diary he occasionally expressed the wish that governments would show greater heroism he never really expected it and moulded his advice on the assumption that it was not to be expected. He wanted an effective incomes policy, though none was ever achieved in his time, and whenever unemployment began to rise, he would spring forward with ideas for reflation. In the days of Robot he had opposed floating the currency. With the gradual disappearance of the dollar shortage he returned frequently to the idea of floating. But he did so without conviction and without force.

It is often said that all lives in politics end in disappointment. The same may be true of economic advisers. The approach of retirement provoked Hall into reflections on Britain's economic performance. He concluded that unemployment should have been allowed to rise higher and that the British working man and the British manager did not, on average, work hard enough.[23] Further reflection was provoked by a revision in the balance of payments figures which wrote down rather substantially what he had believed to be the out-turn in recent years.

> The new balance of payments figures . . . were very discouraging to me since I felt that all my judgements in recent years had been based on somewhat false views of the actual situation . . . I feel that we ought to have had a more austere policy basically . . . we have really run the economy too full ever since I came to this job . . . I feel now that we ought to have put more weight than we did on the need for deflation from the beginning . . .[24]

In fact all those whom Hall had criticized because they did not accept easily enough the new economics were right after all. But, for him, at the point of retirement, it was a little late to come to that conclusion. Hall was the economist of the new British consensus and shares responsibility for the poor management of the British economy.

THE AFTERMATH OF THE 1961 BUDGET

Macmillan had been enthusiastic about Lloyd's first Budget. The change in the surtax threshold had been his idea and he was proud of it. But life was unkind; continuing bad trade figures stimulated a run on the reserves, and the inflow of 'hot money' that had sustained sterling in 1960 was now reversed.[25] The market evidently did not have confidence in the management of the British economy or in the Budget. Towards the end of June, the Continental central banks which had given their assistance by buying sterling indicated that with a stockpile of £300 million they had enough.[26] Treasury economists advised the Chancellor to make a cut of £300 million in demand. They would have preferred more but their advice, as Cairncross noted, was 'watered down to what might be acceptable politically'. Treasury economists would also have liked Lloyd to withdraw the surtax concessions but that was certainly politically impossible.[27]

The Cabinet debated the options. Some Ministers advocated floating, but that was not an alternative to deflation. Only three months after the Budget, the Chancellor was back at the old business of 'steering' the economy away from the precipice by selection from the customary list of deflationary measures reinforced now by the new regulators. Ironically, as would be later revealed, the balance of payments was already back in surplus.[28] Last year's Bradshaw was still the best information available. The measures, announced by Lloyd on 25 July 1961, included cuts in public expenditure, and an increase in Bank Rate to a high point of 7 per cent. In addition the UK was forced to make a large conditional borrowing of $1.5 billion from the IMF. The toughest conditions which the IMF wished to impose were resisted. But the IMF had to be satisfied that enough had been done. It was the kind of humiliation to which Britain would become increasingly accustomed. On 28 July, Macmillan wrote to his Cabinet colleagues impressing upon them the imperative need for the strictest possible economy in public spending.[29]

Lloyd also announced a 'pay pause' destined to last until 31 March 1962. The government had found itself confronted with exaggerated wage settlements which, if continued, could only lead to devaluation.[30] The pay pause was discriminatory in that it could only be imposed in the public sector. Even if private sector employers had been willing to cooperate with the government at a time of labour shortage, in some private sector industries there were arrangements for automatic adjustments to compensate for price increases, in others agreements providing for compulsory arbitration. The pay pause was profoundly unpopular. The Gallup poll showed Labour with a five per cent lead.[31] This was the first time for three years that Labour had been shown ahead. In the period of the pay pause, there was for the government a series of bad by-election results of which the worst was the loss of the safe Tory seat of Orpington to the Liberals in March 1962 on a swing of almost 27 per cent. There had been a fall in real wages since the pay pause. Iain Macleod, Chairman of the Conservative Party, attributed Tory unpopularity to the pay pause.[32] It was becoming customary for governments to become intensely unpopular mid-term, so customary that commentators began to write of such defeats as though they did not matter. But they did matter because of their effect on the behaviour of the government of the day. Could a Conservative government govern effectively if it could not hold Orpington, especially with a Prime Minister as given to panic as the unflappable Macmillan? In due course, Lloyd would become the scapegoat for the unpopularity of the pay pause.

It would have been possible to float the pound. That option was repeatedly considered at Macmillan's urging, but nothing ever came of it. In his diary on 23 July 1961, Macmillan questioned whether it mattered if sterling was devalued.[33] But the symbolic character of the $2.80 rate for sterling had become a determinant of policy, helping to frustrate not merely a devaluation of sterling to another fixed rate but also the alternative of floating. To float sterling would not merely have had symbolic costs. It would have been offensive to the USA and Britain did not want to offend the USA. Quite as important, to float would not have been enough. It would have had to be accompanied by deflation and that, for Macmillan, was beyond the limits of policy as he understood it.

THE NATIONAL ECONOMIC DEVELOPMENT COUNCIL

Lloyd, having been asked by the Prime Minister to produce new ideas, contributed an old idea in new guise. The idea was to establish a new body which would bring together at one table the government, management, and the trade unions. There was a history of such bodies. In 1930, an Economic Advisory Council (EAC) was appointed to advise the government on economic matters. The Prime Minister was in the chair, the Chancellor of the Exchequer was a member, and the economists Stamp and Keynes were among the outside members. In 1941 a National Production Advisory Council on Industry (NPAC) was established, chaired by the Chancellor of the Exchequer. In 1947 there arrived the Economic Planning Board (EPB) established under the chairmanship of the Chief Economic Planner, Sir Edwin Plowden. It contained industrialists and trade unionists as well as civil servants and, when Plowden retired from the Treasury in 1953, the chairmanship had been taken over by a Treasury Permanent Secretary. The EPB held numerous, and no doubt interesting, discussions. Its members took seriously their function to give advice and did so by correspondence as well as in person. One thing it did not do was plan. Plowden acknowledges that the EPB had little influence.[34] In 1957 arrived the CPPI, the so-called Three Wise Men, who pronounced on many matters relating to the state of the economy. But, once more, all they could do was to give advice, possibly good advice – decisions remained for the government. None of these bodies added greatly to the sum of human welfare or to the performance of the economy.

In addition to the British precedents, there were influential foreign models. The principal of these was the French *Commissariat Générale du Plan*. For this, Jean Monnet was a propagandist. He had been its first Director-General and was now Chairman of the Action Committee for a United States of Europe. Its actual responsibility for French economic success is highly debatable but it was attractive for Britain to clutch at such straws when its own economic performance was so much inferior. France would not provide the only model. In due course there would be those who would look to Japan for lessons and find them in the activities of the Ministry of International Trade and Industry. It was necessary to go so far afield because the other major European performer, Germany, appeared to reject any type of government planning, and Italy, also making strong economic progress, barely had any government at all, let alone a Plan.

On 25 July 1961, Lloyd proposed a national economic council as part of the group of measures intended to deal with the balance of payments crisis. He wanted to prove that he had a long-term vision, not just a series of emergency measures. He said, 'The controversial matter of planning at once arises. I am not frightened of the word. One of the first things I did when appointed Chancellor was to ask for a plan of the programme for development and expenditure in the public sector for five years ahead.'[35] On 26 July, there followed a debate on the emergency measures announced the previous day. Lloyd explained himself further:

> Let me be quite clear as to my objective. At the moment, we have these various bodies whose function is to take stock of the present situation, to comment on what is happening, or what happened, and to advise . . . I say frankly to the House that I want something more purposeful than that. I envisage a joint examination of the economic prospects of the country stretching five or more years into the future . . . Above all, it would try to establish what are the essential conditions for realising potential growth. That covers, first, the supply of labour and capital, secondly,

the balance of payments conditions and the development of imports and exports, and, thirdly, the growth of incomes. In other words, I want both sides of industry to share with the Government the task of relating plans to the resources likely to be available.[36]

All this was in tune with much that was being advocated outside the government. It was felt that government in Britain lacked a long-term view. Plowden had chaired a committee, the report of which argued for long-term planning of public expenditure. The CPPI argued at the end of July the need for a long-term view as the basis of economic policy. The idea of planning had gained ground in the Treasury. In attempting to understand the reasons for the failure of economic management, some Treasury officials thought it desirable to establish whether the plans and forecasts of different industries were coherent. They visited Paris to discover what the French were doing in this regard.[37] It was an autarkic approach to the economy, ignoring the contribution which international trade is supposed to make to economic development. Then there were two phenomena which appeared to discredit a market approach to the management of the economy. The first was that, even though restricting demand stopped production rising, it did not necessarily cause sufficient unemployment or even stop the labour force increasing. The second was that the restriction of home demand failed to boost exports even though there was buoyant export demand.[38] A combination of these concerns led to the experiment in 'planning', the inauguration of which was the principal characteristic of the Lloyd era.

In reality, the trouble lay not in the expectations from more deflationary economic management. The trouble was first that an increasingly overvalued fixed exchange rate is not conducive to a rapid growth in exports even if there is spare capacity and, secondly, that the time allowed for results was too short. The economy will take its own time depending on circumstances, not all of which can be foreseen or understood. Politically, uncertainty as to the time of reaction is unacceptable. The economy is expected to react in a politically convenient timescale. There are numerous postwar examples where British governments of both parties have expected the economy to react to their policies more rapidly than circumstances seemed to allow. It is one of the factors that leads to such mistakes as adding to reflationary pressure in an economy that has already turned. The trouble for the Treasury is that it is subject to political masters who demand rapid returns to policy even when the right prescription is not to act but to wait. Politicians, and the Treasury under the guidance of politicians, were looking for a hypothesis of economic management more politically attractive than deflation and more consistent with the political timetable. They found it in the hypothesis that rapid growth, by reducing unit costs and discouraging inflationary wage claims, was the path to a strong balance of payments and hence to the avoidance of devaluation. This hypothesis was adopted on both sides of the House and by the most sophisticated economic thinkers on both sides of the House. It was a hypothesis shared by the most distinguished economic journalists.[39]

After the emergency measures of 25 July, there followed a period of consultation between the Chancellor and employers' organizations on the one hand and the TUC on the other. On 25 September 1961, Lloyd sent a letter to the representative bodies of industry and trade unionism. In it he said, 'I believe that the time has come to establish new and more effective machinery for the consideration of plans and forecasts for the main sectors of our economy.' He made two key proposals. The first was for the creation of the National Economic Development Council (NEDC). Unofficially, it was known as Neddy. NEDC, with the Chancellor of the Exchequer in the chair, would comprise one or two other Ministers such as the President of the Board of Trade and the Minister of Labour, together with outside members appointed by the Chancellor after appropriate consultation. The intention was that the outside members should be industrialists and trade unionists in a representative capacity together with some independent personalities. The second proposal was for the establishment of a National Economic Development Office (NEDO) with full-time staff of the right calibre which would service the Council. The Director was to be appointed from outside the civil service.

The first meeting of NEDC took place on 7 March 1962. At it, Lloyd delivered one of those rather pompous warnings which, to some politicians, sound statesmanlike. Given the distinction of his audience, one would have thought it unnecessary. But perhaps it was intended for a wider audience which might otherwise have been deceived into believing that the government had done something significant in establishing NEDC. 'This Council is not the panacea, the cure-all, for our economic troubles and diseases. We cannot perform economic conjuring tricks. It is important that people should not fall into the national fault of complacency, and of thinking that the establishment of this Council is the end of their troubles.' But if NEDC was not a panacea, if it could not perform economic conjuring tricks, if it was not a justification for complacency, what was it?

One function it certainly did not have. Lloyd had great difficulty with the TUC owing to their objection to the pay pause and to what Cairncross describes as Lloyd's inability 'to enter into the psychology of trade union leaders ... or to communicate to them his own ideas.'[40] The Economic Committee of the TUC eventually agreed to join NEDC only on the express understanding that their representatives were not expected to preach wage-restraint.

In his Budget speech of 9 April 1962, Lloyd referred to the setting up of NEDC as 'a step of major importance'. He defined for it two specific tasks. The first was 'to examine the economic performance of the nation'. The second was 'to consider ... what are the obstacles to quicker growth'.[41] About economic growth he explained, 'What the Council must do is to set an ambitious but realistic target figure.'[42] In fact, under pressure from Lloyd, it set a figure of 4 per cent as what it described as 'a reasonably ambitious figure likely to bring out problems that have to be solved if faster growth is to be achieved and as a help in focusing thinking on the problems of faster growth.' But the 4 per cent was rapidly understood to be a target rather than a tool of analysis and, as a target, it was certainly ambitious but equally certainly not realistic.[43] To extract the 4 per cent target from NEDC was regarded as Lloyd's great achievement. But he was not really happy with 4 per cent though he had to be satisfied for the time being. He was aiming for 5 per cent.[44]

It was an extraordinary misunderstanding to suppose that a group of leaders from industry and the trade unions, together with Government ministers and a few independent personalities, were in a position to determine the nation's potential growth rate. In offering their 'reasonably ambitious figure', they were the victims of advice. They listened to their advisers from NEDO and the Treasury, principally economists with an exaggerated belief in their own ability to foresee the future. They added a point or so to the historical record to demonstrate that they were not wasting everyone's time, including their own. They then issued their pontifical message to the British public and anyone else who cared to take notice. By current European standards, 4 per cent did not seem unduly sanguine. Within the Treasury there was, nevertheless, considerable scepticism. Treasury officials knew the record, which showed a growth rate under 3 per cent, and saw no reason to think that Britain could escape the record by so wide a margin. Moreover the NEDC target raised the question what rate of growth was to be assumed in planning public expenditure? Would there not be a danger that it would be planned on exactly the same optimistic basis as had been adopted by NEDC? As a result would it not demand an ever-increasing proportion of national resources unless the NEDC rate of growth was actually achieved over the planning period which, to sober judgements, seemed unlikely? Would this not make the perennial problems of the economy worse rather than better? The ideal of programmes and plans extending over a much longer period than twelve months was unexceptional except in the matter of practicality within a politically driven economy.

If the members of NEDC had been as wise as they allowed themselves to be presented, they would have refused to indulge in so absurd an exercise. The blessing which, despite the convoluted language, NEDC was understood to have given to the 4 per cent target was seriously damaging. Such a target was beyond the foreseeable capacity of the economy. Attempts to achieve it ran rapidly into the balance of payments constraint, and the idea that it was practical delayed consideration of the sterling exchange rate. An increasingly overvalued currency was a constraint on sustainable economic growth, but NEDC was lending its prestige to the illusion that the constraint could be relaxed by tripartite consultations and 'planning'.

In its attempt to facilitate the identification and removal of obstacles to growth, NEDC was assisted by a number of Economic Development Committees ((EDCs). As NEDC was popularly known as 'Neddy', the EDCs won the description of Little Neddies. The Little Neddies considered obstacles to growth as they manifested themselves in separate industries. Unfortunately the combined work of NEDC and of the EDCs was to make little if any perceptible difference to the country's rate of growth. However wise their recommendations, they made no impact on the factory floor. The subject of obstacles to growth may appear to be susceptible of scientific analysis, and the obstacles identified may appear to be removable given sufficient good will, but it is in fact a highly political subject. Trade unions will complain about lack of investment. Industrialists will insist that they would invest more if they had a cooperative workforce, if the government was not so frequently forced into deflation by the inflationary consequences of its own policies, and if the exchange rate was competitive. As for the Chancellor, all he could do in answer to complaints about deflation and twists and turns in budgetary policy damaging to industry, was to assert that if cooperation round the table could secure a higher growth rate, such problems would fade into the past. As the identification of obstacles to growth puts the industrialists and the trade unionists in contention, they are likely to find agreement only on one subject, an attack on the government, perhaps because its policies are insufficiently expansionist for their liking, perhaps also because they are not sufficiently protection-ist. When jointly these members of NEDC set a growth target, they were not actually helping the government. They were setting a standard by which, in due time, the government would stand to be criticized and they would be in the forefront of the critics.

There was a particular problem with trade unions. They expected to be paid for their pains. If they were called upon by government to assist in the solution of some national problem, they would demand political concessions. Normally the concessions demanded are of a kind more attractive to the leaders of trade unions than to their followers. The principal concession is influence over policy or, at least, the appearance of influence over policy. But influence will not be the only reward they will attempt to extract in return for cooperation. Knowing that, in addition to the other objects of policy, it has now become necessary to coax the trade unions into cooperation, the government will consider what it can do to conciliate the trade unions which will cause the mini-mum of damage. In his 1962 Budget, Lloyd introduced a speculative gains tax. Those who gained from short-term dealings in the market were to be subject to tax at the rate appropriate to their income. Lloyd did not think it right 'that those who supplement their incomes by speculative gains should escape tax on those gains.'[45] It was a kind of capital gains tax, though Lloyd refused that description because he believed that a capital gains tax would militate against saving and econ-omic growth. It was a rather half-hearted gesture. In attempting to protect saving and economic growth, Lloyd made the tax so easy to avoid that the revenue produced by it was negligible. Another gesture was an increase of 2.5 per cent in profits tax. Whatever it achieved politically, economically it was counter-productive.

It would have been splendid if, by dint of planning, the economy could have kept to a path of steady 4 per cent growth extending over a period of years. But how was planning to be reconciled with annual or biennial crises in the balance of payments brought about by over-full employment and resolved inevitably by deflationary measures which would include not merely cuts in private consumption but in capital expenditure in the nationalized industries?

Once NEDC had been created, it was difficult to abolish it. Membership conferred prestige. To abolish NEDC would imply that the government did not want the cooperation of industry and the trade unions. NEDC was the most visible evidence of a desire to cooperate and economic policy was never so successful that a government could claim that it could do perfectly well without this particular kind of assistance. Certainly it was impossible for Labour governments to abolish NEDC first because of their relations with the TUC and secondly because they believed that they needed this avenue of contact with industrial management and this forum for tripartite discussion. Industrialists, quite as naive as governments, had come to believe that planning held advantages for them too. NEDC became a burden and a bore for the next thirty years but no Chancellor had the courage to say so publicly. Under Mrs Thatcher, who was playing the anti-corporatist card, meetings were after some years scaled down from monthly to quarterly. After her days in government, NEDC and NEDO were abolished. But it took even the crusading Conservatives of the Thatcher/Major era many years to use this surgical knife.

THE SEARCH FOR AN INCOMES POLICY BEGINS

Macmillan did not come from the *laissez-faire* wing of his Party and he pays lavish tribute to Lloyd and his Treasury advisers for the creation of NEDC.[46] However, from his point of view, there were two troubles with it. NEDC would not bring rapid results. Its activities could not be made to synchronize with the political timetable. Macmillan had an election to fight not more than two and a half years after its first meeting. Secondly, NEDC was not in the business of wage restraint; the most that could be hoped for from NEDC was that it might agree the general level of wage increases that could be afforded. It was in no position to deal with the phenomenon which Macmillan regarded as the source of all the other troubles, the irresponsibility of the workforce.[47] Influencing him towards this critical appraisal of the people he had been elected to lead were the numerous wage claims and wage settlements far in excess of any productivity improvements. There had been, in November 1961, in the electricity industry, a particularly unwelcome breach in the pay pause due both to the negotiating strength of the power workers and the weakness of the Minister responsible, Richard Wood. In the private sector excessive claims were not being discouraged by the pause in the public sector. There were strikes and threats of strikes. The straw that broke the camel's back was a threat to strike by all the 120 workers employed in the manufacture of cricket balls.[48] Macmillan was now determined to win the battle against inflation but was still equally determined to win it without deflation and in a politically sensitive manner.[49] What was necessary was an effective, but politically sensitive, incomes policy. The pay pause of 1961–2 was an amateurish beginning.[50] Like subsequent incomes policies, the pay pause had been productive of short-term benefits to the economy associated with a series of anomalies that added to its unpopularity. On 29 January 1962, John Hare, the Minister of Labour, announced that the end of the pay pause proper would come on 31 March 1962. Thereafter a new and slightly more flexible system would begin to operate.[51]

Lloyd was at one with the Prime Minister on the need for continued wage restraint after the end of the pay pause. His February 1962 White Paper on Incomes Policy set out the national interest criteria in accordance with which the government intended to judge, and intended others including arbitration tribunals to judge, wage demands.[52] The idea of a 'guiding light', long advocated by the Treasury but long resisted by the Cabinet, at last emerged as government policy. The 'guiding light' would be 2.5 per cent. The White Paper condemned the principle of comparability on the grounds that it meant that one inflationary increase would be matched by another. It denied that increases in the cost of living justified wage rises because that simply validated the inflationary spiral. Productivity improvements would also provide no justification unless the result of more exacting work or the renunciation of restrictive practices.[53] These were strong and commendable principles which had never yet informed the practice of postwar Conservative governments. Despite these high principles, Macmillan invited the railway unions, which were threatening a strike, to come to see him at No. 10 on 14 February 1962. There, with the assistance of much whisky, agreement was achieved and the strike was called off. Macmillan appreciated the, by then, unusual approbation he received from the press for his successful appeasement. 'Mac's triumph', it was called.[54]

THE 1962 BUDGET

Since July 1961, the deflationary measures then imposed had been gradually reversed. In planning his 1962 Budget, Lloyd clearly believed that the relaxations had already gone to the limit of safety and possibly beyond. Macmillan appears to have agreed that it could not be a popular Budget. But when Lloyd presented his Budget to the Cabinet, there was a revolt which he lacked the resources of eloquence and argument to quell. Budgets are usually presented to the Cabinet too late for it to make any significant changes but, in this case, the Cabinet, anxious about the political situation, was not deterred. This was a grave embarrassment not just to the Chancellor but to the Prime Minister, who had been fully consulted about the Budget and had assented to what Lloyd proposed. The fact that he had assented would not, however, diminish his mounting irritation with Lloyd's inadequacies. To meet the Cabinet's criticism, Lloyd introduced into his Budget statement the promise that Schedule A tax on residential property would be ended the following year. It would involve a loss of £50 million to the Exchequer. The tax was levied on valuations for rating. These were to be revised the following year and, Lloyd argued, it would not be possible to levy the tax on the revised valuations.[55] Lloyd was now giving a year's notice of an intention to abolish the tax. He had intended to abolish it but had not yet prepared the necessary legislation. But, for political reasons, the Cabinet forced his hand into a premature announcement which he would have preferred to avoid. The abolition of this tax on residential property was a great boon to the property-owning classes.

Lloyd's 1962 Budget was neutral in the sense that tax reductions were balanced by tax increases. Its principal public impact was made by the introduction of purchase tax on confectionery which would yield £30 million in the current financial year and £50 million in a full year.[56] But in his Budget statement of 9 April 1962, he revealed the extent of his worries. He referred to the measures he had taken on 25 July 1961 and to the drawing from the IMF of $1.5 billion. He asserted that as a result confidence had been restored. 'In the light of all these developments it had proved possible to make successive reductions in Bank Rate and to repay £225 million to the International Monetary Fund.' In addition the balance of payments was improving.[57] 'I would sum up the experience of the last financial year as follows. The pound was in danger last summer. That danger has been averted. But we still have a considerable way to go to achieve a satisfactory surplus on our balance of payments having regard to our heavy and continuing obligations for defence, aid and investment overseas.'[58]

So much for the positive outcome of policy. A cautionary word was necessary. 'In total ... the increase in home demand over the next twelve months looks like being substantial. Since it is so necessary to keep the way clear for the growth of exports, this must be carefully watched. By the end of 1962 . . . the cumulative effect of all the factors I have mentioned could result in too great a call on our resources . . .'[59] Behind these cautionary words lay the conviction that further expansionary measures would be unwise. In fact the forecasting apparatus had got it wrong once again due in part, in this case, to an overestimate by the Board of Trade of the likely increase in exports.[60] The pressure of demand was not rising. It was falling. It was the kind of error that not merely undermined Ministers' confidence in the Treasury; it also undermined the Treasury's confidence in itself. Lloyd rapidly became convinced that he had been unduly cautious – it was time to use the accelerator. Despite the cautionary words in his Budget statement, Bank Rate was cut to 4.5 per cent on 26 April. On 31 May £70 million of special deposits were released. Lloyd informed Macmillan that he was ready to do more if it should prove necessary.

SACKING LLOYD

The Prime Minister thought that, provided there was an incomes policy, the constraints on growth could be removed and expansion encouraged. His view was politically convenient, and for that reason he was not alone in it. The Opposition could hardly be less expansionist than the government. Expansion was popular. Restriction was not. Gaitskell and Roy Jenkins, a past Chancellor and a future Chancellor, both took the Macmillan view. Indeed Gaitskell thought that one could overdo the concern with pay. It was a line of argument that Labour normally took while in Opposition, however much it might be regretted if Labour ever came back into office. It was a line popular with trade union leaders. In his reply as Leader of the Opposition to Lloyd's 1962 Budget statement, Gaitskell said, 'the Chancellor seemed to me to have overweighted the dangers of the situation last July . . .' This was a view for which there was now, with the benefit of hindsight, much support. But if the July measures had been too deflationary, it merely illustrated the difficulty of making precise judgements about an economy rocking to and fro between crisis and crisis. Gaitskell continued:

> it is a great mistake to concentrate on the wages and to forget about the productivity. The plain fact is that what we should be doing is to concentrate on labour costs, and the trouble is that when there is a fall in production, even if there is no rise in wages, the wage costs go up . . . I

believe that this Budget errs on the side of being too little expansionist at a moment when the crucial thing is to increase production and, with it, to increase exports too.[61]

Many industrialists, those who partook of the illusions surrounding NEDC, shared the same view. A faster rate of growth, stimulated by the government, might be the best way of achieving both stable prices and a stronger balance of payments.[62] Roy Jenkins, in his speech in the Budget debate, quoted the *Financial Times* to the effect that industry felt that the Chancellor had done nothing for exports, nothing for investment, and nothing to reduce costs.[63] He then emphasized that 'we have never accepted the view, and rightly never accepted it, that the most likely way of dealing with balance of payments difficulties is by restriction rather than expansion'.[64]

Macmillan explained his thoughts about Britain's economic problems to his Cabinet on 28 May 1962. The dilemma, he told the Cabinet, was the incompatibility of the government's economic objectives under current conditions.

> We have four objectives – to retain full employment, to secure if we can stable prices, to have a strong pound which means a favourable balance of payments both on current and capital accounts; and to gain growth and expansion in the economy. So far as I know these four objectives have never been sustained for any length of time by any nation. Nor have they been so clearly the purpose of political economic policy at any period in the history of nations . . .[65]

Nor could Macmillan forget that in addition to the task of achieving these four objectives at the same time, the UK faced the special complication that sterling was not merely a means of exchange but formed part of the world's currency reserves.[66]

To the conundrum of how to achieve simultaneously these four great economic objectives, Macmillan explained that he had at last found the clue. The country's difficulties were not due to an attempt to run the economy at too high a rate or to the strains of government expenditure. They were primarily due to the simple fact that rising personal demand was not being met by rising productivity.[67] His conclusion was that either one of the objectives must be abandoned, which was unacceptable, or there must be some permanent form of incomes policy applying both to the private and the public sector. The incomes policy would relate incomes to productivity. It would have to be accompanied by more stimulation of demand as all the growth could not go into exports.[68] An effective incomes policy in an expansionary climate was, therefore, the answer and would make possible the achievement of his four objectives.

There was no difference between Macmillan and Lloyd on the need for faster growth. The problem with which Macmillan's analysis left the government and the Chancellor was how to design a politically sensitive incomes policy that would be effective in the economic environment that they both wanted to create. The Treasury was bound to be sceptical about how effective any incomes policy could be in restraining inflation under conditions of high economic growth. Quite apart from the problems of design, there was a question about the government's political will. Its record in appeasing public sector unions would hardly create much confidence in the Treasury, even if it was assumed that an incomes policy could hold under conditions of fast growth and over-full employment. Macmillan had posed an insoluble problem and it was no surprise that the Treasury was slow in solving it. If the Treasury was unable to provide Lloyd with the solution for which Macmillan was looking, it was unlikely that Lloyd would be able to find the answer by himself.

Whether or not Lloyd realized it, Macmillan's discontent with his Chancellor was reaching a pitch at which he might actually be prepared to contemplate the unpleasantness of sacking him. The reality was that Lloyd had become a political liability and was, therefore, dispensable. The excuse, lavishly detailed in Macmillan's memoirs, was that although an effective incomes policy was clearly urgent, the Treasury, under Lloyd, was listless and uncreative. As a result the burden of elaborating the effective incomes policy was falling on the Prime Minister. He tells us that he got no help from his Chancellor. He was resentful of the apparent readiness of the Chancellor to place the chief burden upon him.[69] On 19 June Macmillan presented his ideas on incomes policy to three or four colleagues at Chequers. Lloyd, he found, was rather chilly; the others seemed strongly in favour.[70] Macmillan's plan had four elements: a 'guiding light' such as had been introduced at the beginning of the year; a Standing Commission on Pay to give advice, but not to make binding decisions; the abolition of resale price maintenance; and the creation of a Consumers' Council.[71] Such ideas could, no doubt, have emerged from the Treasury, from Lloyd, or from many other sources. It was easy to see why the Treasury would be sceptical of the effectiveness of such an incomes policy. Macmillan himself was perfectly aware that an entirely voluntary system, such as he was proposing, would probably fail, because it could easily be ignored. But he appeared to believe that publicity was a way of achieving effectiveness without compulsion. He was falling back on the 'open-air cure', publicity, which he considered effective in treating other ailments.[72] But if Macmillan's own incomes policy was expansion plus the 'open-air cure', it is difficult to see of what value it would have been for Lloyd to advance any alternative. Anything stronger would have been politically unacceptable. It would equally have been useless if the environment in which it was expected to work was one of the headlong expansion on which Macmillan and the Cabinet were now ready to insist.

On 21 June, Macmillan had lunch with Butler. Butler was in favour of drastic action to repair the political situation. Drastic action could only mean replacing Lloyd.[73] Five and a half years had passed since Butler had been ejected from the Treasury by Eden. There had been four Chancellors since then. In Butler's critical perspective, none of them had proved to be the best Chancellor we have had, though he did not himself want the job back. Macleod, Home, and the Chief Whip, Martin Redmayne, were also pressing for a change at the Treasury. So, evidently, was Sir Norman Brook, who combined the functions of Cabinet Secretary with Joint Permanent Secretary to the Treasury, though he dealt with civil service management rather than the economic side.[74] On 22 June there was a further Ministerial discussion of Macmillan's incomes policy paper.[75] A further meeting on incomes policy took place on 6 July. The meeting, Macmillan alleges, showed that the Treasury was still the great problem.[76] But the real problem was Macmillan's highly questionable analysis of the economic situation. All depended on an effective incomes policy, but neither Macmillan nor anyone else had the least idea of how to design or implement an incomes policy which would carry the weight of his expansionary intentions. Even if the problem had been soluble intellectually, there remained the lack of the necessary political will. The government was not prepared to take coercive action against exaggerated pay claims. But, for Macmillan's failure, it was easier to blame Lloyd, who also did not know how to mount an effective incomes policy in an inflationary situation.

Macmillan was given to panic, as Suez had clearly illustrated. He knew he was unpopular, and his mind had become permeated with suspicions of conspiracy against him. The unlikely conspirators were sometimes Lloyd, sometimes Butler, sometimes Eccles.[77] Panic is, in any case, encouraged by the British electoral system under which quite a small swing in votes can lead to the overthrow of a government and, by June 1962, Labour, in a National Opinion Poll, had a lead of 11 per cent. On 13 July, Macmillan sacked not merely his Chancellor but a third of his Cabinet. Unless one considers Butler's removal in December 1955 to fall under the same heading, Lloyd was the only Chancellor of the period to have been actually sacked. No other Chancellor would be sacked until Norman Lamont thirty years later. It was the 'night of the long knives'. It gave the impression to the public that Macmillan had panicked because of the unpopularity of his government. Macmillan denies that he panicked; it was merely a misjudgement. He had intended to reshuffle his Cabinet in order to introduce some younger spirits. His mistake, he thought, was to combine the reshuffle with the removal of his Chancellor. He should have delayed the reshuffle until the autumn.[78] In support of the misjudgement thesis is that Macmillan's hand was undoubtedly forced by a leak of his intentions clearly attributable to Butler, who had never excelled in keeping secrets.[79] It is difficult, nevertheless, to accept the argument that the night of the long knives was all merely a misjudgement, and not panic. The scale of the reshuffle, if not the exact timing, had clearly been decided in advance and discussed with Butler.[80] Dismissing the Chancellor had repercussions within the Cabinet which could hardly be regarded as minor. It would have looked odd to have one major reshuffle in July and another in September. If, therefore, it was Macmillan's intention to rid himself of a third of his Cabinet at some time during the summer months, it was better done quickly and not serially.[81]

But if it *was* merely a misjudgement, and not panic, then there were at least two miscalculations. The first was to sack a third of his Cabinet. The second was to believe that an incomes policy such as he now introduced could contain inflation if the economy was to be expanded faster. One might add that there was a third misjudgement and that was to sack Lloyd. Lloyd may not have been the most inspiring, articulate or incisive of Chancellors but he had won a higher reputation than, perhaps, he deserved. Anthony Eden, now Earl of Avon, who, over the years following his own resignation as Prime Minister, had shown himself reserved about his successor, let it be known that he considered that Lloyd had been 'harshly treated'.[82] Politically, Lloyd carried the cross of having introduced the pay pause; but if the government, having designed an effective incomes policy, intended to introduce it, it would have to accept the associated unpopularity and persuade the electorate at the polls that it had been right in what it had done. Lloyd was the wrong man to persuade an electorate with words but it could perhaps be persuaded by steadfastness. It was less likely to be persuaded by the ritual sacrifice of the author of the pay pause.

NATIONAL INCOMES COMMISSION

Certainly the National Incomes Commission (Nicky) announced on 26 July 1962 was a poor thing.[83] There was nothing in Nicky to justify much hope. The TUC, which considered itself inadequately consulted, decided to boycott Nicky. Nicky had only one remedy for inflation, the 'open-air cure'. Any idea of compulsory reference of wage claims was abandoned. The only recourse was that, where a settlement which appeared to conflict with the national interest had been reached without reference to the Commission, the Government would ask the Commission to conduct an *ex post facto* review and it would be given power to send for papers and persons, and to make constructive as well as negative criticisms in its report. Only three cases were ever submitted to it.

THE STORY CONTINUES

Macmillan had long lost patience with Treasury caution. Without being at all sure what he was doing, he appointed as Chancellor one of the three more qualified men he had passed over when he selected Selwyn Lloyd in 1960. There was now a fourth qualified candidate. Since 1960, Edward Heath had made a great reputation by his conduct of the negotiations for entry into the EEC. There were those who thought that Heath or Macleod had a better claim than Maudling. But Heath was still needed in the Brussels negotiations and Macleod had the key task, as Chairman of the Party, of preparing for the next election. Eccles resigned from the government voluntarily during the night of the long knives because he was refused appointment as Chancellor. Though Macmillan had had his own doubts about Maudling, he did have one advantage over possible rivals – he was the candidate expected to be most amenable to his Prime Minister's advice. The agenda was to be expansion but the effective incomes policy which Macmillan regarded as an essential concomitant was still missing.

Unusually for a dismissed Minister, Lloyd returned to office in 1963, as Leader of the House of Commons, under Alec Douglas-Home. His restoration to favour did not save him from blame for the Tory defeat in the General Election of October 1964. Whatever his faults as

Chancellor, in the office of Leader of the House he was so popular that, in 1971, he became Speaker of the House of Commons. This too was unusual. Former Cabinet Ministers normally do not qualify as it is a post demanding the abandonment of Party loyalties. So, in the end, fate rewarded Lloyd, which shows that there is a place among the stars even for Chancellors of the Exchequer who are not up to the job.

·TEN

Reginald Maudling and
the Dash for Growth

THERE COULD NOT been a greater contrast than that between Maudling and his predecessor. Maudling was articulate and he could grasp ideas. He could repulse criticism from Cabinet colleagues without painful recourse to a brief. He was probably more confident in his own economic judgement than any of his postwar Tory predecessors. He was at ease with City Editors. There were few others in the House of Commons who could speak lucidly about economic problems with barely a note, often with no more notes than would fit on the back of an envelope. He was quite capable of making a front-bench speech in the House of Commons from which Party points were absent. Jay describes him as 'far the best economic mind, together with Gaitskell, in the House of Commons in the thirty years I was a Member'.[1] That he was one of the more attractive characters to have held the office of Chancellor since the war is an accolade bestowed by many observers.[2] There were other views, such as that of Frank Lee, who had been his Permanent Secretary at the Board of Trade. Lee thought that Maudling lacked principle and was simply a kind of rich man's Harold Wilson.[3] Lee had perhaps detected what the Treasury in its turn would also discover, that Maudling did not display that devotion to duty, in all its senses, that the ideal civil servant expects of the ideal Minister. Whether Maudling's facility with words and ideas implied a powerful intellect was never quite clear. He did not particularly distinguish himself as a student at Oxford compared, for example, with one contemporary, William Armstrong, who became Permanent Secretary at the Treasury two weeks after Maudling's own appointment when Frank Lee retired on grounds of health.[4]

After Oxford and war service, Maudling read for the bar and then, under Butler, became a member of that forcing-house of future Tory Cabinet Ministers, the Conservative Research Department. He entered

Parliament in 1950. Because things came easily to him, he gained a reputation for laziness. Whatever his Ministerial duties, he always seemed to be left with plenty of time for enjoyment. In his youth he had been a great traveller, and as a Minister he was never slow in exploiting his opportunities. He travelled and he enjoyed himself. Maudling came from a middle-class background.[5] He records his pleasure at working for Harold Macmillan. Macmillan was not always so complimentary; he penned a private assessment of the rising young politician that, perhaps, tells us as much about Macmillan as about Maudling. 'No background.'[6] Before he made him Chancellor, Macmillan was often critical for other reasons than his lack of background.[7] Nevertheless, despite the question marks he put against Maudling's name in his assessments of his Ministers, and despite the lack of background, Macmillan piled responsibilities upon him. They had included the Ministry of Supply and nuclear energy. Maudling had also played a key role in negotiating Britain's alternative to membership of the European Economic Community (EEC), a European Free Trade Area (EFTA) which was to include the EEC. When invited to become Chancellor, he had been a Minister for ten years, mainly on the economic side of government. From 1959–61 he was President of the Board of Trade. The Treasury was not strange to Maudling. He had been Economic Secretary under Butler and, in the office of Paymaster General, he had been asked to assist Amory. After all this experience, he may well have thought that he was quite as equipped to advise himself, and make his own judgements, as any official. He was 45 years of age.

THE INTERNATIONAL ECONOMIC ENVIRONMENT – AN ASKING BRITAIN

In one striking respect, the world since 1951 had become more friendly to Britain. Falling commodity prices had helped to contain inflation and support the balance of payments. Cairncross calculates that in the 1950s there was a favourable shift of 10 per cent in the terms of trade which represented a windfall of about £300 million a year in foreign exchange. In other respects the world had become more hostile while at the same time Britain's economy had become more exposed. Trade was being liberalized. Since Butler's long step towards the convertibility of sterling at a fixed rate in January 1955, Britain had suffered repeated exchange crises. Full convertibility of sterling held by non-residents, conceded in

December 1958, was followed by a deteriorating balance of payments and Selwyn Lloyd's politically unwelcome measures of July 1961. British Chancellors were finding that a balance of payments constraint limited their ability to stimulate the economy to faster growth. The economic signals were alternating between Stop and Go. The fact that, thus far, Tory governments had been able to arrange that in the months before an election the signals should be at Go was convenient, but the suspense could be nerve-racking.

No. 10 Downing Street and the Treasury were increasingly preoccupied with the discrimination against British supplies implicit in the creation of the EEC, with the burden represented by the sterling balances, and with the problem of persuading the other major industrial countries that there was a damaging shortage of international liquidity. In the view of the government, British prosperity depended on resolving these problems. The EEC was certainly an anxiety. As national tariffs fell towards zero within the common market, the discrimination against British goods would increase because the common external tariff of the EEC would have to be paid on imports from Britain. Macmillan's belated application for membership of the EEC would, if successful, remove this handicap. But success in the application depended on negotiations and on avoiding a French veto now in the jaundiced hands of President de Gaulle.

The problem of international liquidity had been under debate for many years both within Whitehall and within the world financial community. In London, it was assumed, prematurely, that the interests of Britain and of the international community were the same. It was an unwise hypothesis – there were manifest conflicts of interest and of perception. The thinking behind the British initiatives on international liquidity was simple enough. It was now supported by the Bank as well as the Treasury. If only there was more money in the world, there would be greater demand for British goods and the British economy could grow with less danger of running into problems with the balance of payments. It would also help the developing world. With more resources at their disposal, poor countries could buy more and some of the orders would come to Britain in aid of its balance of payments. Adding to international liquidity and, thereby, mitigating Britain's woes, would mitigate also those of the world's poor. If true, it would be a politically convenient conjunction of interests.[8]

The British government claimed that, if the open trading system was to survive and the world economy to prosper, countries must cooperate.

If they did not cooperate, if they acted without regard for the interests of their trading partners, their failure would be damaging to international trade, damaging therefore to the world economy, damaging to the cold war against communism, damaging finally to the British economy and hence to the political prospects of the Conservative Party. Maudling tells us that Macmillan had a happy way of describing the problem of international liquidity. It was a matter of increasing the supply of internationally acceptable cowrie shells.[9] If a group of people were playing a game of cards, and using cowrie shells as money, the game could continue as long as all the participants had some shells to spend. If any of them ran out of shells because the total supply was won by a small number of participants, the game would come to an end.

Macmillan was determined that Britain should not become the victim of the economic misbehaviour of others. Unfortunately, in the view of the other major countries, it was Britain that was misbehaving. They appeared to believe that Britain's problems were Britain's fault and that British solutions were designed to be in the interests of Britain rather than of the world as a whole. They did not accept that what might be good for Britain was necessarily good either for their own countries or for the world. In Washington eyes, the UK's domestic policies were inflationary. Balance of payments problems were the inevitable consequence of government extravagance. If British domestic policy changed, the British perception of world economic problems would change.[10] In February 1961, Macmillan told Chancellor Adenauer of Germany that it was in the interests of surplus countries to avoid the imposition by countries in deficit of restrictions on trade.[11] Germany had accumulated a large surplus in its balance of payments. Thereby it was sucking up everyone else's stock of cowrie shells. In Macmillan's view, its large surplus placed upon Germany an obligation to help its trading partners. It must inflate its economy and thus reduce its surplus. It must revalue its currency, which would make life easier for its competitors in international trade, and it must invest abroad. Adenauer was not impressed. He seemed more interested in what would benefit Germany. An appreciation in the DM would raise the standard of living of the German people and help Germany's battle against inflation. In March 1961, shortly after this exchange between the two leaders, Germany did revalue its currency but, from Britain's point of view, to a quite inadequate extent. Germany rapidly returned to surplus in its balance of payments.

Macmillan had become critical of the operations of the Bretton

Woods system. Fixed exchange rates tied to the American dollar combined with the shortage of international liquidity had become, in his view, an obstacle to economic expansion in Britain and to the expansion of world trade.[12] He reminded whoever would listen that Keynes, one of the two progenitors of the Bretton Woods settlement, had advocated the creation of an international currency, bancor, to prevent deficit countries being forced into deflationary and protectionist policies and as a lubricant for world trade. Macmillan thought he should have the support of the IMF. The IMF had been invented to encourage expansion, not to frustrate it. Unfortunately Per Jacobsson, Managing Director of the IMF, was critical of British views on international liquidity. Jacobsson had support where it mattered, from the Americans. The Americans had always taken a far more conservative view than Keynes of the management of the world economy. The Americans had made the world in which Britain was finding it so difficult to live. Increasing the price of gold was one of Macmillan's favourite schemes for increasing international liquidity.[13] This was not, however, an idea that the USA found attractive. On the contrary it insisted, and guaranteed, that the price of gold would remain at $35 an ounce. Without American support or at least acquiescence, nothing could be done.

One aspect of the problem of international liquidity was the sterling balances. International liquidity was largely comprised, apart from gold, of the two reserve currencies, the dollar and sterling. To issue a reserve currency was to some extent beneficial to British trade. Countries with sterling had an incentive to buy in Britain though a lesser incentive once sterling had become convertible. A strong reserve currency which would be accepted unhesitatingly by suppliers in payment for goods because it was a reliable store of value was certainly an advantage. But sterling had long ceased to be a strong currency. France complained of the privilege possessed by the USA and the UK in issuing reserve currencies. France was right; it was a privilege, provided the country issuing the reserve currency was not conducting inflationary policies. Maudling, like his successor James Callaghan did not regard it as a privilege but as a burden.[14] But then Maudling and Callaghan both did conduct inflationary policies. In Maudling's view, whatever the advantages of issuing a reserve currency, the sterling balances had become an excessive load on the relatively small British economy. Sterling held by other countries represented a claim on British resources. Sterling holdings might be reasonably stable where they were held as reserves. Other large holdings were more volatile. This was particularly the case when

British government policy or the performance of the economy threatened market confidence. As British economic policy was always managed on the edge of danger, the overhang of sterling held internationally was always a threat to Britain's economic stability. It followed that the required increase in international liquidity must be in currencies other than sterling.

In September 1962, at the annual Bank/Fund meeting in Washington, Maudling proposed a Mutual Currency Account scheme which became known as the Maudling Plan though it was being elaborated in the Bank of England and the Treasury in Selwyn Lloyd's time.[15] The Plan was advanced in very general terms, leaving many details to be worked out by experts. It was not the kind of thing most Finance Ministers would understand, but the purpose was clear enough, even to them. Britain, in its wish to be relieved of the hazards associated with managing a reserve currency, was asking the rest of the world for the privilege of being able to conduct inflationary policies more safely. Maudling makes it transparent in his memoirs. 'The basic idea of the scheme . . . was to stamp . . . a lot of the internationally held sterling and dollars with the imprint of the International Monetary Fund, in other words, to transfer part of the international reserve liability to the main international institution.'[16]

It was a proposition born out of weakness. Because it implied weakness, it was not acceptable to the Americans, who felt that their economy could meet the demands upon it despite the American balance of payments deficit. Liquidity was being provided by the outflow of dollars from the USA consequent on its balance of payments deficit. The Americans did not like any suggestion of an affinity between the state of sterling and that of the dollar. They wanted there to be confidence in the dollar, they wanted the world to go on accepting the dollar as a reliable store of value in payment for goods, and as a constituent in national reserves, whatever happened to sterling. Robert Roosa, the Under Secretary for monetary affairs at the US Treasury, declared that Maudling's proposal was at best for the far distant future and added that for the next five years the world need not worry about liquidity. The problem for the US Administration was that questions were being asked about the reliability of the dollar also, particularly by France. The Administration did not wish to do anything that might encourage those who were asking such questions. The American rejection of Maudling's plan put sterling momentarily under pressure. Four years later, after the July 1966 crisis in Britain, President Johnson would say to Prime

Minister Harold Wilson that 'the dollar and sterling should link arms'.[17] Nine anxious years would elapse before President Nixon found it necessary on 15 August 1971 to suspend the convertibility of the dollar.

Opposition to the Maudling Plan came not just from the USA. The Germans were particularly sensitive about the dangers of importing inflation as a result of an expansion of international liquidity. Giscard d'Estaing, the French Finance Minister, denied that economic expansion was hindered by insufficient liquidity. The general feeling seemed to be that international economic problems were not to be solved by technical tricks but by better domestic economic management.[18] The problem for an increasingly uncompetitive Britain was not that nothing was being done. The DM *had* been revalued. Britain *had* received substantial help from the IMF. The resources of the IMF *had* been increased. The IMF was therefore in a stronger position to support countries that ran into balance of payments difficulties, though the conditions on which the support was supplied might be politically inconvenient. Under swap arrangements negotiated through the Bank of International Settlements, Britain in 1961 was able to draw £325 million from foreign central banks in exchange for sterling. In December 1961, ten major countries entered into the General Arrangements to Borrow. If the ten contributors agreed, yet further resources could be deployed by the IMF in support of countries that ran into trouble. The problem was not that nothing was being done but that the sterling balances remained outstanding and that the supply of cowrie shells remained inadequate to remove Britain's balance of payments constraint. But that was Britain's problem.

British governments should have been learning that in an increasingly open and 'interdependent' world, Keynesianism in one country was not viable. They should also have been learning that successful countries saw their success as the reflection of their own merits and that what they owed to the international community would be measured out cautiously on the basis of their perception of their own interests. British governments developed a grievance against the world. Here, they thought, were we British, good economic citizens of the world, conducting policies which ensured full employment in Britain, but the other major industrial countries were doing their best to make it impossible for us to continue on our meritorious path. Successive Chancellors would make their eloquent pleas at international financial gatherings. The schemes that they advanced demonstrated high intelligence in all but one crucial respect; a failure to recognize that national interests differed, at least in the perception of the separate governments, and that few recognized in Britain a persuasive champion of international economic reform when its own economic performance was so poor. So far as the major industrial countries were concerned there would be no dash for growth if the price was an inflationary injection of demand. After all, their economies were growing very fast without exceptional stimuli. It was Britain that was lagging. That too was Britain's problem.

THE DASH FOR GROWTH

In domestic policy, Maudling's start was circumspect. Selwyn Lloyd had earned a reputation for prudence and his removal was likely to worry the market. A statement was issued, on Macmillan's instructions, assuring the world that a new Chancellor did not imply a new policy. Yet Selwyn Lloyd, as he had told Macmillan, feared that his 1962 Budget had erred on the side of caution. As a result he had been preparing a reflationary package on a contingency basis; for example, he was planning a reduction in purchase tax in October when Parliament reassembled. Maudling waited before acting, and irritated some commentators by not acting earlier and more drastically. He was urged on by Nigel Lawson, then a financial journalist, who had been a severe critic of Selwyn Lloyd. The message in the popular press was that Maudling should stop dawdling. Alec Cairncross, his Economic Adviser, urged him to take expansionary action but found him reluctant to change policy so soon after taking office in case it reflected on his predecessor.[19] He wished to be sure of the ground before moving forward. Another factor causing delay in the autumn of 1962 was the sterling scare that had followed the rejection of the Maudling Plan at the Bank/Fund meeting. Lloyd had been contemplating a reduction in Bank Rate to 4 per cent in early August. It was first postponed by Maudling's arrival at the Treasury and the uncertainty that caused. It was further postponed when, in October, both Maudling and the Governor, Lord Cromer, advised against it in the prevailing circumstances.

Unemployment was rising. Maudling found himself under considerable pressure, not just from the Prime Minister but from the Treasury, the press, and from the community of economists. Yet it was not until his Mansion House speech on 4 October, nearly three months after his appointment, that Maudling at last displayed his reflationary mettle. He announced the partial release of special deposits, the withdrawal of the request to the banks to exercise special restraint on lending, the release of another instalment of £42 million of postwar credits, and an increase in public investment of £70 million over the following eighteen months. In early November, he added a full £100 million or more a year through investment incentives and a reduction of purchase tax on motor cars from 45 per cent to 25 per cent, thus bringing the tax on cars into line with most other consumer durables.[20] Motor car production was everywhere else the engine of economic growth. Why should Britain be the exception? *The Economist* described these measures as 'the third largest sudden injection of tax reliefs in British fiscal history'.[21] It was equivalent to a shilling (5p) off income tax. Nevertheless, Maudling had not satisfied his activist critics. Many commentators still felt that the total reflationary effect of these measures was insufficient. If the regulator had been used much more could have been done. Unemployment was continuing to rise and industrial production to fall. The unemployment count on 10 December reached 566,196. In Scotland the unemployment rate was 4.7 per cent. Other reflationary steps were taken in January 1963, including the delayed reduction in Bank Rate to 4 per cent, further reductions in purchase tax, and increases in unemployment pay and pensions.

In his Mansion House speech on 4 October, Maudling warned his audience that inflation was not the only danger. Another danger was 'a general contraction of world trade or a tendency towards world deflation'.[22] His failure to convince at the IMF gathering had not deterred him. He was now proposing that, at the OECD Ministerial meeting in Paris at the end of November, he should persuade the world's industrial powers to undertake a coordinated expansion of their economics. If he was to persuade other countries, he could hardly allow the UK to sink into a recession. That Britain was leading by example became a justification for its inflationary policies. There was also NEDC's 4 per cent growth target to be respected.

When Maudling was appointed Chancellor, the next election could not be more than two and a quarter years away. By the time of his 3 April 1963 Budget the election could not be more than eighteen months away. The reputation of the government continued low. In February 1963, unemployment reached 873,000, or 3.5 per cent, a very high figure by postwar standards though it was partly due to a severe winter.[23] There was no more time to waste. Maudling was still under pressure to do more, not just from the Prime Minister but from the Treasury and independent sources of advice. The downturn had been beyond the

Treasury's expectations and therefore, in the view of the Treasury, the time had come to stimulate an upturn. Although the 1963 Budget went somewhat beyond the recommendations of the official Treasury Budget Committee, it was not by much. Maudling and the Treasury were still more cautious than Macmillan and, indeed, than many economists and economic commentators. By Macmillan's standards it would be a measured reflation but it would still be substantial. A streak of caution in Maudling's make-up prevented his going too far beyond his official advice.

There remained the balance of payments constraint. All expansionary ambitions courted nemesis in the form of a sterling crisis. Here came Maudling's peculiar contribution to British economic policy, to endorse as Chancellor the idea of the dash for growth. The method of untying the knots which were strangling the British economy would be faster growth. According to the theory predominant among politicians of all parties, faster growth was the answer to inflation and, by reducing unit costs, it was the key to successful exporting and hence to solving the balance of payments constraint. Maudling now proposed to act on this politically convenient, but highly improbable, theory. He made the general point in his 1963 Budget statement. 'Not only is it untrue that expansion and a strong pound need conflict: in fact the two depend upon one another.'[24] There would be a virtuous circle. The British economy in spate would, perhaps after an anxious interval, contain inflation by satisfying the desire for an enhanced standard of living, and balance the nation's payments through surging exports. This would be achieved despite an expectation that in 1963 world trade would increase at a slower pace than in recent years.[25] This approach presented a strong contrast with Selwyn Lloyd's July 1961 measures which had suggested that exports would be encouraged by the restriction of home demand. Thus was launched the so-called 'Maudling Experiment'. It was not, of course, an experiment. The best that could be said of it was that it was a hallucination. Maudling's 1963 Budget is the ultimate example of the effect of a combination of politics, ignorance, and hubris on economic management.

The 1963 Budget, introduced on 3 April, was, as Maudling claims, 'designed on an ambitious scale'.[26] In his Budget statement Maudling said, 'The theme of this Budget is expansion: expansion without inflation, expansion that can be sustained.'[27] There was a very large increase in public expenditure. There was a substantial reduction in income tax.[28] There was a range of other measures to encourage investment and industrial training. Total reliefs plus some additional government expenditures amounted to about £300 million. There would be a very large borrowing requirement which would approach £700 million, though Maudling could claim that both absolutely and in relation to national income this was less than budgeted for in 1959.[29] Observers would recall that 1959 was an election year and that the 1959 Budget had led to the July 1961 measures. Tax reliefs announced in a Budget take some time before they fructify in the pockets of the taxpayer. Cairncross believed that what had been needed was a stimulus in 1963 that would fade somewhat in 1964. Maudling's first Budget worked rather differently. The full effect would not be felt until the following year, the election year of 1964. The Budget was so successful with Conservative backbenchers that Maudling briefly emerged as favourite to succeed Macmillan as Prime Minister. Macmillan had found in Maudling a worthy collaborator, flexible and ingenious.[30]

At the Board of Trade, Maudling had not been a great enthusiast for NEDC.[31] NEDC's targets should have reinforced his scepticism. Instead, the 4 per cent growth target was to be adopted by the Conservatives in their election manifesto as well as by Labour. Maudling's Budget pointed the way. He specifically linked what he was doing to the NEDC target. As he listened on the radio to the details of the Budget speech, Donald MacDougall, Economic Director of NEDO, was 'amazed – and sometimes amused – how closely [Maudling] was following Neddy's recommendations' as set out in its contemporary publication, *Conditions for Faster Growth*.[32] In his Budget speech, Maudling also announced a revised 'guiding light' of 3–3.5 per cent. He justified raising the guiding light by reference to NEDC's target of 4 per cent growth in national production.[33] If that was to be achieved, annual productivity per head could be expected to rise by between 3 and 3.5 per cent. The new guiding light was, according to Maudling's version of economic theory, the logical consequence of NEDC's targeting. But NEDC should not take all the blame. It was the government's responsibility if it was prepared, clearly for political reasons, to validate a new higher guiding light even before the necessary growth rate had been achieved.

The Labour Party could hardly criticize Maudling's economic motivation. Labour's leading spokesmen on economic policy had fervently preached sermons on the text that expansion was good for inflation and for exports. Harold Wilson, responding to a Budget statement for the first time as leader of the Labour Party, could hardly have been more fulsome. His single complaint was that the Tories seemed to wait for election years before introducing expansionary Budgets. The only question for the Labour Party was whether Maudling had done enough. Callaghan, the shadow Chancellor, feared that he had not. 'In my view, the Chancellor has been too cautious . . . I think that there would be a case for arguing economically that we should have a relatively sudden spurt for a period of twelve months before we settle down to a steady rate of growth . . . of 4 per cent . . .'[34] He warned that Maudling's Budget might imply a need for import controls.[35]

In the view that Maudling had not yet done enough, Callaghan was supported by Labour's two most prominent backbench economists, Tony Crosland and Roy Jenkins. Crosland, after condemning as an 'imbecile' anyone who was too dogmatic on such matters as whether the Chancellor had done too little or too much, concluded that 'Nevertheless there is something to be said for [the view] that the Chancellor has acted on the cautious side.'[36] Roy Jenkins spoke of Maudling's 'half-hearted approach to expansion this year'.[37] Butler appeared to agree with them. On 14 May he spoke at a lunch and said that steps might have to be taken to expand demand. Maudling was furious.[38] NEDC had, at the end of February, insisted on demonstrating that it was as naive as any politician. It was concerned that the 4 per cent growth target had been missed in 1961 and 1962. The arithmetic suggested that if an average of 4 per cent was to be achieved over the period 1961–6, a 5 per cent growth rate would now be necessary. NEDC thought it possible. Callaghan, Crosland, Jenkins and, apparently, Butler had been seduced by NEDC's calculations into believing that it was now appropriate to dash to 5 per cent in order to catch up with the 4 per cent growth target.[39]

In his Budget statement, Maudling tended to discount the dangers in what he was doing, but he was too intelligent not to be aware of them. One was that he might have injected too much additional spending power into the economy at a time when it was already on the turn. This is precisely what he had done. He was unaware, as he embarked on his economic pilgrimage, from where exactly, in the economic cycle, he started. Bradshaw was not telling. Maudling was aware that the economy was recovering; he did not know how rapidly it was recovering.[40] By May, unemployment was down to 2.4 per cent and by June to 2.1 per cent, well before the Budget could have had any effect.[41] It was fortunate that, at least by some standards, he had been moderate. Macmillan had wanted an injection of £400 million.[42] The National Institute had also argued for £400 million, thus demonstrating once again the fallibility of Keynesian calculations.

The second danger which Maudling must have perceived was of adding to inflation in an economy working at more than capacity. He did not even have an incomes policy worthy of the name. Maudling had designed his income tax reductions in order to attract TUC support. 'The effect of my proposals as a whole is to give relief to all existing Income Tax payers on a scale that proportionately gives greatest benefit at the lower levels.'[43] The reliefs were the equivalent for many workers of a wage increase of 2 per cent.[44] Wilson and Callaghan approved of the distribution of the income tax reductions.[45] The Budget was praised by the TUC Economic Committee.[46] But there was no understanding between the government and the TUC that unions would moderate their claims in return for the bounty the government had extended to their members.

Eighteen months before an election which Labour was quite likely to win was not the best time for a Conservative government to negotiate an incomes policy with the TUC. Even if there had been such an understanding, its implementation must have been doubtful in the inflationary atmosphere created by the Budget. After the Budget, wage settlements, notably in the public sector, continued to exceed the new guiding light, some by a large margin. Maudling tended to take rather a relaxed view, despite the concerns of his advisers, defending excessive settlements on grounds of productivity.[47] Macmillan and Maudling had embarked on what turned out to be a wild reflation without even the institutional structure or the social consensus necessary to restrain wage demands.

Maudling's third problem was the balance of payments. It was becoming a habit for Chancellors to add up what they supposed to be the nation's overseas assets and borrowing capacity and then comfort themselves with the thought that they could safely take risks with the balance of payments. The market was less easily persuaded of the wisdom of such risks. In his Budget statement, Maudling said that '*in so far as there is a stocking up movement related to expansion*. . . then I think that it is perfectly reasonable and sensible to finance such a movement out of our reserves or out of our borrowing facilities in the International Monetary Fund and elsewhere'.[48] In fact he had no control over how the borrowing capacity of the nation was used, whether for investment or for consumption. Years later, Maudling was to confess that he had underestimated the power of the speculators against sterling in such situations.[49]

The probability of success was far from sufficient to justify such a leap in the dark. There could be no guarantee that the short-term difficulties would be followed by a stronger long-term balance. There was not even a probability. Yet Maudling was given the comfort of Treasury forecasts. In July 1963, the Treasury forecast that in 1963 there would be no big deficit and that there would be a surplus on current account in 1964.[50] He therefore has the justification of official advice when he tells us that, 'the whole policy was deliberate, calculated and coherent. No one could guarantee success, but the chances were high, and the alternatives were drab and depressing.'[51]

Samuel Brittan argues that the only recent year in which there had been serious balance of payments problems was 1960 and that, 'Given the political inhibition on tampering with the exchange rate, a case could be made for taking a calculated risk and attempting a home-based expansion, *provided that there was an ultimate willingness to devalue should this prove necessary to sustain expansion*.'[52] Yet, as the commentators who were pressing Maudling even further than he went would have noticed, the balance of payments had not recently seemed particularly healthy. In 1962 the surplus had been only £67 million.[53] It already seemed probable before the Budget that there would be a deficit in 1963. Even without such concerns about the balance of payments, the *calculation* of risks would necessarily be hazardous. The objective of economic management should be to reduce risk, not to enhance it. A politician facing an election should not be allowed the justification that he was taking a *calculated* risk.

Professor Nicholas Kaldor argued at the time that the stimulus to the economy should have been given not through the home market but by devaluing in order to promote an export-led boom. NEDC published *Conditions for Faster Growth* in April 1963. NEDC devoted six full days to it before agreeing on publication, an indication of the importance its members attached to their labours. It contained no discussion of exchange rate policy. There had been a section on the subject but it had been omitted at the request of the Treasury.[54] Although he denied advocating devaluation, Crosland's speech in the 1963 Budget debate can only be understood on the basis that he believed devaluation necessary. By 1963 the UK was probably in a condition of fundamental disequilibrium and, under Bretton Woods, was entitled to devalue. Maudling claims to have been an advocate of flexible exchange rates. Maudling's name must therefore be added to the extensive list of leading Conservative Ministers of the period who favoured floating but never seemed able to bring it about. The government had repeatedly considered floating and had repeatedly rejected it, in part because Bank and Treasury advice was against it, in part because of its inconsistency with Bretton Woods, in part because of excessive respect for American opinion. In the circumstances the alternative of a devaluation to another fixed rate was an option on economic grounds if not, eighteen months before the last possible date for an election, on political grounds.

Maudling denies that he ever considered devaluation. It is difficult to see how an intention to devalue if necessary could have been any part of the 'Maudling Experiment' launched in the 1963 Budget. However moderate that Budget might be considered to be, it was a reflationary Budget and devaluation and domestic expansion are inconsistent policies, politically as well as economically. There is a vast political difference between reflation, which makes the electorate happy, and devaluation, which may make exporters happy but makes the electorate poorer. To gain economic benefit from devaluation, spare resources must be available, otherwise the balance of payments deficit will simply increase. Deflation was the last policy in the minds of the Prime Minister and Chancellor in the spring of 1963. The only debate was how far and how rapidly domestic demand should be expanded.

During the course of 1963 there were exchanges between Macmillan and Maudling about the role of import controls and of floating as methods of staving off a balance of payments crisis if it should threaten. The problems with such devices were the same as they had always been. Import controls would not be particularly effective and would evoke strong international pressure on the government to reverse them.[55] Floating was not a short-term device to solve an imminent crisis. Its immediate effect would be to worsen the balance of payments, and it would have to be accompanied by deflation, which was no part of the strategy of either Macmillan or Maudling shortly before an election. In 1964, floating may have appeared to Maudling as an option to which he might be compelled to turn in order to deal with the increasingly adverse balance of payments.[56] But that would be after the election.

Macmillan was taken ill just before the 1963 Conservative Party Conference and resigned on 18 October. At least one prominent Labour MP regarded Maudling as the most dangerous among potential successors.[57] Maudling demonstrated the attractive, or perhaps just the lazy, side of his character by failing to convert his Conference speech into a bid for the leadership. Thereafter he was no longer a serious candidate and then, together with other men of no background like Macleod and Powell, threw his support behind Butler. Alec Douglas-Home, however, emerged from the mysterious processes of Tory selection and, when Butler agreed to serve, so did Maudling. Douglas-Home made no claim to expertise in economic policy. It was probably a disadvantage electorally, but it left Maudling greater freedom. Maudling tells us that he and Alec had one major disagreement, the date of the election. Maudling wanted an early election so that the political uncertainties surrounding economic management could be removed. Douglas-Home, advised by Butler and Party professionals, preferred to wait until the last possible moment in order to give the Maudling Experiment the maximum time to yield its full political benefit.[58] As a result the period of political uncertainty was extended, but the Tories did come near winning.

COOLING

After the emergence of Douglas-Home, tensions grew between Maudling and his Treasury advisers. The evidence that was accumulating suggested that he had done enough for his Party. He did not want to do more. On the other hand he did not want to take back anything that he had done. He employed his characteristic nonchalance to protect himself from unwelcome pressure. There were also disagreements between Maudling and Cromer. Cromer distrusted Maudling's strategy. There was a meeting between Cromer and Sir Alec Douglas-Home which Maudling discovered only by accident.[59] But Douglas-Home showed no more desire than Maudling to stop the politically convenient boom which the country was beginning to enjoy.

By the end of 1963, output was growing faster than could possibly be sustained for long without trouble with the balance of payments. The current account had moved into deficit in the middle of 1963 and the deficit was increasing. There was talk of large deficits well into the future.[60] There had been a great deal of anxious debate in the Treasury and the Bank about how to deal with the threatening balance of payments. On 27 February 1964 Bank Rate was raised by 1 per cent to 5 per cent. Maudling delivered his 1964 Budget statement on 14 April. He said, 'The economy has developed in the last 12 months much as I then anticipated.'[61] It is more likely that Maudling was surprised at the speed with which the economy had reacted and at the emerging current account deficit. He commented wryly that 'Although last year's Budget was described as timid and cautious, it has been followed by an expansion at the annual rate of at least 5 per cent . . .'[62] The current account of the balance of payments was in 1963 still in surplus to the extent of £120 million. He confessed that 'the combination of an increased capital outflow with a deterioration in the current account will mean a worsening of the overall balance of payments this year. Provided that it is temporary, this should give rise neither to alarm nor dismay ...' He nevertheless considered it right to refer once again to the availability of 'very large first and second line reserves and other borrowing facilities'.[63] He said this although claiming that the forecast of the balance of payments at the time of the 1964 Budget did not predict any deficit at all. Lord Cromer took a directly opposed view of what was wise in the stockbuilding phase of the cycle.

> There are some who argue that it is right and proper for a great industrial country to borrow abroad in order to finance the stockbuilding phase of the economic cycle. I do not subscribe to this view. As a matter of hard fact, we have no automatic access to the resources or savings of other countries. More important still, the tacit acceptance of dependence on overseas creditors must undermine the political influence that we could exercise in world affairs.[64]

Maudling defined the purpose of his 1964 Budget as being 'to achieve a smooth transition from the recent exceptionally rapid rate of growth to the long-term growth rate of 4 per cent'.[65] He increased taxation, mainly on alcohol and tobacco, by £100 million which, he notes, was, by the standards of 1964, 'considerable'. The figure of £100 million was proposed to him by Cairncross because he felt that Maudling was unlikely to agree to more.[66] While in 1963 Maudling had been more cautious than the National Institute, now, with an election inescapable in a matter of months, he was prepared to accept greater risks. In February 1964, the National Institute, turning the steering wheel desperately to avoid the precipice towards which its advice the year before had helped to direct the economy, had suggested a tax increase of £200 million in 1964 with another £200 million to follow in 1965. Maudling's comment was:

> Just as, last year, it was not necessary to provide a stimulus to the economy of the order of £400 million ... so, this year, I do not believe it to be necessary to increase taxation by the figures that have, in many quarters, been put forward. The best judgement I can make is that if taxation is increased in this Budget by about £100 million ... I should be doing enough to steady the economy without going so far as to give a definite shock to expansion.[67]

Neither Harold Wilson, Leader of the Opposition, nor James Callaghan, Shadow Chancellor, challenged Maudling's judgement of what was necessary to steady the booming economy. To suggest higher taxation just before an election was no part of the Opposition's strategy. Although they knew that the balance of payments was worrying, all they were prepared to say was that Maudling's Budget had been 'irrelevant' to the nation's economic problems.[68] They would have different ways of approaching those problems. As Wilson put it, 'we shall deal with this not by monetary methods, not in the main by budgetary methods, but by industrial policy . . .'[69] The illusion that these problems could be solved by industrial policy dominated the first half of Wilson's 1964 government.

By July the balance of payments deficit was being estimated at £600 million at an annual rate. Trade figures published on 17 July showed that the second quarter had been worse than the first with exports down and imports up. There could be a change of market sentiment at any time. Prudence dictated action to steady the economy. Maudling's budgetary contribution to economic stability had been too little and too late. As the situation deteriorated, he remained calm and, apparently, confident. The Opposition later claimed, with justice, that Maudling had been irresponsible and that he was not prepared to allow financial prudence to stand in the way of the Tories' last desperate attempt to win the coming election on the back of a boom.

In the Treasury there were those who thought that something ought to be done, for example a further increase in Bank Rate. But insufficient pressure was exerted on the Chancellor. One can only speculate why Treasury officials were content to wait and watch as the figures grew worse. Experience of Treasury behaviour on other occasions suggests the following explanations. First, there was, as usual, too much under-standing among senior Treasury officials of the political dilemma facing Maudling with an election coming in the autumn. Secondly, Treasury officials felt too little confidence in their own fears. They had repeatedly got their forecasts wrong. How could they be sure now that the Chancellor was not right in claiming that everything would turn out right in the end even if they thought they were going over the cliff? Were Treasury officials justified in pressing action too hard on the Chancellor when his nonchalance might turn out to be better founded than their anxieties and there was no sign of the market reacting against his policies? Then, quite apart from the election, there was the NEDC growth target to protect. Restrictive action would suggest doubts about the feasibility of the 4 per cent target. To appear to question the feasibility of 4 per cent, and just before an election, was beyond the courage of Treasury officials whatever their private thoughts. There was no démarche from the Permanent Secretary to the Chancellor or to the Prime Minister, such as the Treasury might have thought necessary in the national interest. In any case, no one in the Treasury was suggesting the degree of deflation that would have been necessary to prevent the exchange crisis later that year.[70] Years later, in 1970, when Chancellor Jenkins was preparing his pre-election Budget, Sir Douglas Allen let him know that he felt William Armstrong had behaved weakly in not restraining Maudling during the spring and summer of 1964.[71] The worst trade figures coincided with the election itself. Maudling himself did not see them until the night of the election.[72] Thereby he was saved the embarrassment of deciding whether to tell the electorate the truth about his economic management while they were still settling how to vote.

In his memoirs, Maudling is totally unapologetic. It was not in his character to be prolific with the *meas culpas*. Why should he show bad conscience when he had acted so moderately and when, in the event, the denouement had been taken out of his management by an ungrateful electorate? He could hardly advance the defence, either at the time or in his memoirs, that, having only last year's Bradshaw available, he had not had the least idea what he *was* doing. But this was, in reality, the most respectable defence open to him. Instead he defends himself by taking the easy target of his successors. He insists quite fairly that, in assessing his performance as Chancellor in the light of subsequent events, allowance must be made for the many and grave errors of the Labour government. Of the incoming Labour government he writes, 'I believe all the evidence is that they made a profoundly wrong decision. They immediately declared that the situation was disastrous, and that they had to take action. Thereby they magnified Britain's difficulties dramatically, and virtually ruined the prospects of the policy of expansion without inflation on which we were set. Foreign opinion naturally took them at their word.'[73] He claims that the trade position was already dramatically on the mend.[74] He concludes that 'A great opportunity for Britain which the Conservative Government had created had been destroyed by Labour's loss of nerve.'[75] It is true that by the end of 1965, the current account was in surplus before plunging into deficit again in 1967.

This, however, is not the point. The problem at the time lay with the overall balance of payments, not just with the current account. The Treasury repeatedly, and Macmillan himself as Chancellor, had proclaimed the need for an overall balance of payments surplus of £350–450 million. Only once, in 1958, had it been achieved, but no other Chancellor had presented his successor with an £800 million overall *deficit* in the balance of payments. Whatever allowance is made for Labour's errors, and they were many, the record of Britain's economic performance after October 1964 does not suggest that, had the Tories been re-elected, and Maudling had continued as Chancellor, he could have escaped the difficult choices that confronted Labour after its narrow victory. The policy behind the 1963 Budget was a gamble fashioned by politics. Maudling writes: 'we went for expansion, quite deliberately, with our eyes open, recognizing the dangers', though the dangers had not figured prominently in his 1963 Budget statement.[76] After the election, Maudling tried to rescue his reputation by claiming that he had, at all times, acted with the support of official advice. This was questioned in the Treasury. Cairncross comments that Maudling

> took risks with the balance of payments in the hope of a breakthrough in economic growth in which we had little faith; and delayed – in the end abandoned – action of any kind to check an obvious boom in 1964, comforting himself with the thought that, if necessary, the pound could be allowed to float, and ensuring that the alternatives of import quotas and an import surcharge were given careful study.[77]

This is the crux of the charge against Maudling. Although he had the general support of the Treasury on his 1963 Budget, the thinking behind the Treasury's advice was different from that which Maudling claims to have motivated him. He was going for the great breakthrough which would banish the balance of payments constraint once and for all. The Treasury, on the contrary, was, in the traditional Keynesian way, trying to absorb unutilized capacity in the economy and knew that whatever was done would have to be monitored, managed and, quite possibly, reversed if inadvertently they had gone too far. Maudling persisted with his breakthrough policy in 1964, despite the evidence that it was going wrong, because he had an election to win and was not averse to the cynical exploitation of the opportunity he found in the Treasury's earlier support and in the feeling, by no means confined to politicians, that *something* had to be done about the performance of the British economy. It is no defence that his Opposition critics had advanced the same argument, and would continue to do so in the future whenever it seemed convenient. Edward Heath would, in his turn, find the idea politically useful. The idea of breakthrough by precipitate expansion was one that only businessmen, politicians in a hole, and their friends in the economics profession, could possibly claim to believe. There was also, in Maudling's attitude, an element of carefree, romantic, cavalier defiance. If the world insisted on confining the British economy within a strait-jacket entitled the balance of payments, he would show that, like Houdini, he could break free.[78]

It was Maudling rather than Alec Douglas-Home who had almost won his Party the 1964 General Election. But, to his dismay, Maudling found that the judgement of his own Party was against him. As it turned out, he had laid down his reputation for his Party, but his Party saw no reason to thank him for it. To have gambled and won was one thing. To have gambled and lost, and to leave behind the reputation of a gambler, was quite another. When Alec Douglas-Home retired in 1965, Maudling lost the succession to Edward Heath. In the early months of Opposition he had lazily released the position of shadow Chancellor to Edward Heath in favour of foreign affairs. He thereby deprived himself of the opportunity of becoming acquainted with the new young Tories who first entered the House in October 1964 and of fighting with them against Callaghan's 1965 Finance Bill. His personal responsibility for what the Tories themselves came to regard as a debacle was, nevertheless, probably the main factor which cost him the leadership. The preference of Lord Cromer, Governor of the Bank of England, for Heath was made known to Tory MPs.[79] Maudling had presented himself as moderate and statesmanlike only to find that he was regarded as rash and, in the eyes of many even in his own Party, irresponsible. His subsequent career was dismal enough. In Opposition under Heath he was shadow Foreign Secretary. In 1970 he returned to government as Home Secretary but was compelled to resign two years later by his involvement, however innocent, in the Poulson affair. Briefly he was Mrs Thatcher's shadow Foreign Secretary. He died still quite young, a sad ending to a life so full of promise which somehow went wrong.

ELEVEN

James Callaghan: Devaluation Defied

ONE OF THE HAZARDS of democracy is that it may, in the midst of a major crisis, bring to power a totally unprepared government. The probability will be that, at the preceding General Election, shadow Ministers will have spoken persuasively about their plans. Their plans will seldom have been drawn in dark colours. They will have been intended to instil hope under new management, not despair, and may well have been drawn in ignorance of the full depth of the crisis. As it is of the character of British political Parties to encourage exaggerated expectations, the only protection is the scepticism of the electorate. The probability will, nevertheless, remain that the incoming Ministers will arrive in their offices committed to policies unaffordable even in better times and inconsistent with the obligations their new duties will impose upon them.

By 1964, Labour had been out of power for thirteen years. In the new Cabinet only two Ministers, Harold Wilson himself and Douglas Jay, now President of the Board of Trade, could claim any serious experience of economic management. In reality, only Douglas Jay had any claim. He alone had served in the Treasury. But though Jay was often a source of good sense, he was out of the decision-making loop. Wilson remembered that he himself had been a Cabinet Minister when the senior officials advising him were still quite junior. What would they have to teach him? He did not seem to realize that the world had changed dramatically since 1951. Nor did he get much help – Treasury civil servants proved better equipped to describe the problems than to suggest the remedies.

Wilson's skilled leadership of the Opposition after the death of Gaitskell had seemingly left the electorate still uncertain as to how much confidence it should repose in the Labour Party. In the election, the Labour vote had not significantly increased; Tory voters had given Labour victory by simply staying away from the polls. The new Labour

Hugh Dalton. He enjoyed an *annus mirabilis* on borrowed money and paid for it politically in the following year.

Sir Stafford Cripps. He was not as austere as he looked.

▲ **Reginald Maudling**. He followed the fashionable economic prescription of the time, a dash for growth, and was briefly a hero until the country found that his legacy was a vast balance of payments deficit. His career never recovered.

► **Hugh Gaitskell**. He epitomized the insularity of postwar British economic policy. Promoted into the Cabinet as Chancellor, he lacked the guidance and restraint of a strong Prime Minister.

▲ **R. A. Butler**. His high public reputation, later tarnished by his 1955 election budget, derived from the fortunate timing of his tenure of the Exchequer. The slave of advice, he was too easily rushed into decisions he had not thought through.

◄ **Harold Macmillan**. He asserted a need to reform the Treasury, but had no ideas on reform other than to import into the Treasury the least-equipped Permanent Secretary of the period.

► **Peter Thorneycroft**. With little understanding of economic management, he nevertheless wanted to do the right thing, but was abandoned by his Prime Minister and the Treasury.

► **Derick Heathcoat Amory**. For two and a half years the obedient servant of a frivolous Prime Minister, he resigned when he was no longer prepared to act contrary to his own convictions.

◄ **Selwyn Lloyd**.
Lacking any qualifications
for appointment as
Chancellor, he became an
easy scapegoat for
Macmillan's failures.

▼ **James Callaghan**. At
sea in the Treasury, he
was the second Labour
Chancellor to be forced
unwillingly into devalua-
tion. He neither forgot
nor forgave those he
blamed for his downfall.

▶ **Roy Jenkins**. His measures were too little and too late but were invariably presented with style.

▼ **Iain Macleod**. The lost Chancellor.

▶ **Anthony Barber**. Chancellor in little more than name, he bequeathed to his successor a total breakdown in economic management.

▲ **Denis Healey**. He
at first mishandled
the major crisis he
inherited. But he
rescued the govern-
ment and redeemed
his own reputation
by his courage in the
autumn of 1976.

◄ **Sir Geoffrey
Howe**. Learned in
the law, he hoped
economic manage-
ment could be made
as certain.

▶ **Nigel Lawson**. In some ways the most qualified Chancellor of this era, he is, alas, best remembered for the unsustainable Lawson boom.

▶ **John Major**. He thought that entry into the ERM could be decided on grounds of party advantage and was fortunate to become Prime Minister before his party had realized the cost.

government had been returned with a minuscule overall majority of four. It would, therefore, be looking for a favourable moment and excuse for a further General Election. The assumption would probably be that the electorate dislikes crises and will rapidly take against a government that talks too much about one even if it can be blamed, initially, on the departed. The temptation will be to exploit to the full the guilt and follies of the predecessor while doing nothing by way of cure that will hurt electoral prospects.

The paramount leaders of the Labour government were Harold Wilson, George Brown and James Callaghan. Of the three, Callaghan, the new Chancellor, was the least influential. In the election to succeed Gaitskell as leader of the Party, Callaghan had polled the lowest vote, thought it was a select vote of MPs who, for one set of reasons, did not trust Wilson and, for a different set of reasons, felt they could not rely on Brown. For the first two years of the government, economic policy was in commission to these three with the Prime Minister, in effect, in absolute charge even though this did not appear in public. So far as the public was concerned, it was Brown rather than Wilson who was in charge of transforming the performance of the British economy.

For Callaghan, as for Gaitskell, the Chancellorship was his first Cabinet appointment. As shadow Chancellor, he had had a multiplicity of economic advisers, among whom the most eminent was Nicholas Kaldor. He had sought enlightenment, as a Visiting Fellow at Nuffield College, Oxford, on the heavy responsibilities that might fall upon him. But, inevitably, he was totally without experience of economic management. He lacked even the pretensions to understanding of economic management that an academic qualification in economics would have provided; he was not a University graduate of any kind. One advantage he had. First elected in 1945, he was a supreme House of Commons man. He had made his reputation in the House. The House knew him and rather liked him. His self-deprecating modesty, added to an easy manner and an assured understanding of his audience, made him a master of the House of Commons where many pretend to be expert on economic policy but few in fact are so. He was aware that he himself was no expert, and with his customary, and attractive, candour, he was prepared to admit it openly. A less self-confident man would have demurred at such confessions of ignorance, but they were far from being false modesty. It was not surprising in the circumstances that he frequently, in the early days, turned to Wilson for comfort and advice, wrongly believing the Prime Minister to have deeper insights into the economic conjuncture than he had himself.[1]

The time had now come in which Labour's pretensions would be tested. As shadow Chancellor Callaghan had attempted to lower the expectations of his Party. He had argued that the Conservative government's enlarged public expenditure programme was as big as an incoming Labour government could sustain. In his memoirs, he comments that, so far as his colleagues were concerned, he might as well have saved his breath. Explaining to them the problems of the British economy was 'as difficult as convincing a dipsomaniac of the virtues of barley water'.[2] Callaghan found himself not so much holding the purse strings as holding them open for his colleagues to dip into. While the circumstances surrounding Labour's return to power in 1964 were certainly difficult, and in some ways exceptional, the prime responsibility must lie with Harold Wilson for the fact that the next three years are among the unhappiest in the history of British economic management. Wilson was Prime Minister. It was Wilson who had asked the electorate to contrast his own economic expertise with the innumeracy of Alec Douglas-Home. It was Wilson who had raised expectations by his advocacy of the new technologies as the way to lift Britain's relatively poor economic performance. It was he that presided over the crucial initial decisions that would determine the world's view of his government. It is with Wilson rather than with Callaghan, or even Brown, that the main responsibility must lie for the two initial errors that would dog the government for the next three years. The first error was the divided responsibility for economic policy. The second was the failure to devalue or float. Ironically, the period would end with the resignation of Callaghan as Chancellor, not with that of Wilson as Prime Minister. By that time Brown had long ago escaped from the economic stage.

THE DEPARTMENT OF ECONOMIC AFFAIRS

Labour's claim for the confidence of the electorate was as the Party of economic growth. Experience over the previous 'wasted' thirteen years of Tory rule had demonstrated to the satisfaction of many, including the Labour leaders, that the Treasury could not be trusted with economic growth. It had stultified Britain's economic prospects with its Stop-Go pendulum. Therefore there must be a new 'growth' department which would guarantee results despite the Treasury. There were in fact to be two growth departments, the Department of Economic Affairs (DEA) under George Brown, Deputy Leader of the Labour Party, and the Ministry of Technology (Mintech) under Frank Cousins, seconded from his position as General Secretary of the Transport and General Workers Union (TGWU). The DEA would be the Ministry of growth through planning. Mintech would be the Ministry of growth through technology. There were thus numerous opportunities for turf battles between these two new departments as well as between them and the older departments of state. Wilson's cultivation of technology had a double purpose. So far as the electorate was concerned, it offered a vision of a new and more prosperous Britain constructed with the aid of science. So far as the Labour Party was concerned, it was intended to wean it from mass nationalization, though there remained the commitment to nationalize iron and steel.

Wilson's only previous Cabinet post had been as President of the Board of Trade in the Attlee government. He appeared to be attempting to reinvent the Attlee government as it existed when he himself became President of the Board of Trade. At that time, in October 1947, Stafford Cripps was appointed to the new post of Minister for Economic Affairs in charge of planning while Dalton remained Chancellor of the Exchequer in charge of fiscal policy. Fortunately, Dalton resigned six weeks later and Cripps inherited the Treasury, and therefore fiscal policy, as well as economic planning. Concentrating both aspects of economic policy in one hand had avoided the conflict between Cripps and the Treasury that would otherwise have been inevitable. Now the very same imbroglio from which the Attlee government had been rescued by the accident of Dalton's indiscretion and resignation, was to be deliberately resuscitated in the new Labour government. From Callaghan's point of view, the division had a major political disadvantage. Chancellors in Labour governments are always suspect. Behind their backs, but not always behind their backs, they are accused of selling out to the Treasury, aping Tory economic policies, and even of following the discreditable path of Macdonald and Snowden. Callaghan's fate would not merely be to suffer all this but to have alongside him, and even above him, a 'growth' Minister, George Brown, who would be winning all the glory while Callaghan was trying to balance the books.[3]

Cripps, as Minister for Economic Affairs, was an overlord, without his own department but supervising all the economic departments other than the Treasury. George Brown, under the pretentious title of First Secretary of State and Secretary of State for Economic Affairs, was to have his own department, newly created for him by surgery on the living body of the Treasury. The decision to create the DEA had been preceded by a great deal of discussion. It included discussion between Labour Party parliamentarians and Treasury officials. Brown had a conversation with Eric Roll, his future Permanent Secretary, in the early summer of 1963. Roll was then a Treasury official. He told Brown that the Treasury was so powerful by status and tradition that any new department would have an almost impossible task in trying to assert itself, and that departmental machinery was seldom as important as the relative power of Ministers.[4] Cairncross gave similar advice to Crosland on 23 October 1963. It would be necessary to get Ministerial jurisdiction clear and there was bound to be some conflict with the Treasury and the Board of Trade.[5] Douglas Jay who, alone among Ministers, had experience of the Treasury, strongly advised against the creation of the new Department.[6] But Jay's views and experience were ignored. Wilson had not merely his memories. He also had George Brown.

Despite the discussions and advice, there was no blueprint for the DEA. Brown attributes the lack of a blueprint to the inadequacy of the Labour Party's secretarial services, but the lack is attributable in reality to the difficulty of drawing it. George Brown had wanted the DEA to be superior to the Treasury in determining economic priorities.[7] That would have been unacceptable to Callaghan. It would have made Brown the effective Chancellor of the Exchequer. If neither department was superior to the other, how would decisions be made in those cases where the two departments had different priorities? A concordat dictating who should do what was painfully worked out between the Treasury and the DEA.[8] Since 1951, monetary policy had been reluctantly accepted into the armoury of a Labour government. Under the concordat, fiscal and monetary policy would remain with the Treasury. Planning, whatever that turned out to mean, would lie with the DEA together with prices and incomes policy. But the concordat was of little use. No concordat could anticipate all the chances of economic life. Lacking the direct responsibility for fiscal and monetary policy, the DEA would be watching the Treasury hawk-eyed because its own reputation and that of its Ministers would depend on the rate of growth. The DEA would want the Treasury's fiscal and monetary policies to validate, not obstruct, its growth policies.

Who was to arbitrate? The answer could only be the Prime Minister. Even if he had not shared Brown's belief in planning, and his distrust of the Treasury, politics would, in the early days, have led him to favour

Brown rather than Callaghan. However, having once established the new machinery of government, he did not want to be too much bothered with it. Except on the great issues of economic management on which his word was law, he was inclined to allow his mind to wander off in the direction of Washington, and other capitals west and east, where he could display his talent for international statesmanship. In the end, decisions would be made. But delay was inevitable at a time when the market was waiting, alert and distrustful, to assess the mettle of this new government. In direct confrontations between Brown and Callaghan, Brown usually got his way by the sheer force of his irrationality. It was not long before Callaghan was appealing to the Prime Minister to find a way out of the impasse. There was no response.[9]

Brown never understood why the DEA failed and why, in the end, despite his fearsome energy, the Treasury defeated him. He writes that the DEA 'envisaged a wholly novel form of national social accountancy to replace the orthodox financial accountancy by which the Treasury has always dominated British life'.[10] This 'wholly novel form of national social accountancy' had no existence outside Brown's imagination and those of his supporters. There was no escaping the pressures on the British economy that arose from the fact that the Treasury had never been allowed by its political masters to implement orthodox financial accountancy even when it had wanted to. Those pressures continued because financial irresponsibility had continued. Under conditions of crisis and panic, Wilson would be compelled to throw his weight against the DEA and in favour of the Treasury. Brown's other delusion was that if only he had persuaded William Armstrong, Permanent Secretary to the Treasury, to move as Permanent Secretary to the DEA, victory in his battle with the Treasury would have lain with the DEA.[11] First, such a personnel change would have made no difference to the balance of power between the Treasury and the DEA. The DEA did not fail for lack of people of the highest ability. Nor did it fail for lack of the trappings of power. Brown became Chairman of the Economic Committee of the Cabinet and replaced the Chancellor as Chairman of NEDC. Secondly, Armstrong with his deliberate, uncommitted approach to problems was not the man to work comfortably with George Brown though he did, apparently, see a role for a planning department.[12] If Armstrong had wanted the job, he would have found a way of offering himself for it.

DEVALUATION?

Callaghan records how, having received from Wilson in No. 10 Downing Street confirmation that he was to be Chancellor, his Principal Private Secretary, Ian Bancroft, introduced himself and then ushered him through the connecting door to No. 11 where William Armstrong was waiting to receive him. Armstrong, as Principal Private Secretary, had opened the Treasury's books for Butler at the commencement of a new period of Tory government. Now, as Permanent Secretary, he would open them for Callaghan at the commencement of a new period of Labour government. Armstrong had been commended to Callaghan by Maudling as the best civil servant he knew. But his time as Permanent Secretary was a period of crisis, not of achievement. Perhaps he was unfortunate in his Chancellors.

Labour had always expected speculation against sterling when it came to office. It knew it was distrusted as both inexperienced and profligate.[13] During the election campaign Wilson had warned of a possible deficit on the 1964 balance of payments of about £400 million. When the books were opened, they revealed to Labour Ministers contents far worse than they had anticipated. It was now estimated that Britain would, during 1964, accumulate an £800 million deficit on its balance of payments, the worst in British history. The estimated £800 million *deficit* had to be compared with the £400 million *surplus* which was regarded in Whitehall, and on the Labour backbenches when in Opposition, as necessary to cover the UK's overseas defence expenditure and its overseas investment.[14] It was now not just the fact of a Labour government that might upset the markets and provoke a run on the reserves. There would have been a run on the reserves even under a Tory government, when such figures became public, unless rapid steps were taken to calm the market.

It was now revealed that Labour Ministers had no plans of their own with which to meet the contingency of a run on the reserves that they had themselves forecast. What they found, awaiting their consideration, were the expedients Maudling had asked the Treasury to prepare against the possibility that the balance of payments out-turn from his Experiment would be worse than had been forecast. Those expedients were to limit imports by means of import quotas or an import surcharge and to encourage exports by means of a small export incentive.[15]

Saturday, 17 October, two days after the election, was a busy, a worrying, and also a decisive day. In the morning, the three paramount Ministers met at No. 10 Downing Street with officials. The same evening, Callaghan and Brown discussed the economic situation at No. 11 Downing Street with their two Permanent Secretaries, William Armstrong and Eric Roll. Donald MacDougall, who had been brought in from NEDO to be Director General at the DEA, was also present. MacDougall recommended devaluation. He was alone in doing so.[16] He was also the only official present who was not a permanent civil servant.[17] Callaghan and Brown then joined Wilson once more in No. 10. Wilson, Brown and Callaghan, men who had held no government responsibility for thirteen years, men who had no experience of economic management, certainly not since sterling had become convertible, now met without officials to make decisions that would shape the future of the country and of their government. The first question was whether they should make public the balance of payments estimates with which they had been supplied. The £800 million was as yet only an estimate.[18] Douglas Allen, Deputy Secretary at the DEA, had persuaded Callaghan and Brown that the figure should be held close to the chest for the time being. The Prime Minister decided that the world must know the new government's inheritance. That left the crucial second question; with what policy decisions would they accompany the announcement of the estimated deficit.

It did not take Wilson and his two colleagues long to decide against devaluation.[19] They had spent the previous thirteen years trying to discard the reputation that Labour was the Party of devaluation, widely regarded as a 'soft option'.[20] Callaghan had made promises in Washington before the election which he did not wish to dishonour even though the situation he now faced was far worse than he had expected. He had even suggested privately to Maudling that, during the election, they should jointly denounce devaluation as an option but Maudling had seen difficulties in such a statement.[21] Callaghan is still convinced that the decision not to devalue was right. He writes, 'The Conservatives would have crucified us.' They would have 'hammered home' that devaluation was always Labour's 'soft option'.[22] Wilson made the same political judgement.[23] It was typical of the Wilson government that it should have been deterred by debating points. The balance of payments deficit provided a sufficient reply to such charges.

Actually, devaluation, properly implemented, was not a soft option at all. A devaluation, to be successful, had to be accompanied by deflation. The problem was not that devaluation was a soft option but that a Labour government was only too likely to treat it as such. It was understandable that a government facing another election did not want to deflate. But it was the government and it did have an overall majority. However, given the politics, the three Ministers were not likely to spend much time assessing the two essential questions, whether Britain was in a state of fundamental disequilibrium and whether, with all their commitment to planning, they had a realistic chance of restoring balance without a devaluation. Douglas Jay, who had not been present at any of these initial meetings at No. 10, agreed with the decision not to devalue. 'If I had been asked, I would have ruled out devaluation on moral grounds.' Labour had denied an intention to devalue at the election and there were obligations to foreign holders of sterling. Jay would have introduced import quotas, stronger exchange controls and, if after a time these measures proved ineffective, he would have floated the pound.[24] After the decision had been taken, there was a gathering, still that same evening, at Brown's flat. Tony Crosland, who was to be Minister of State at the DEA, tried to persuade Brown that the government should devalue. Roy Jenkins, newly appointed Minister of Aviation, arriving later, expressed the same view 'but not as strongly as I should have done'.[25] By that time it was too late and Brown was committed.

Callaghan explains that 'I held the view that the amount of sterling's overvaluation could be corrected and its value maintained' on two conditions. His first condition was that industry must improve its productivity and efficiency. His second was that employers and trade unions must ensure prudence in wage increases and labour costs.[26] Over the first condition, the government, if it rejected devaluation and deflation, had no control whatever. At best it could provide incentives. They would take time to be enacted and even more time to have any effect. The effect was unlikely to be large. To be able to base any hope on the second of Callaghan's conditions, there needed to be at once a statutory incomes policy. The government had no such intention. It did begin discussions with the TUC on an incomes policy, and George Brown did secure from the unions and the employers a joint statement of intent to keep money incomes in line with increases in national output, and he did establish in March 1965 a board, the National Board for Prices and Incomes (NBPI), with the former Tory Minister, Aubrey Jones, as chairman, to keep prices and incomes under review on a voluntary basis. But the credibility of the statement of intent, inevitably low, was further undermined by the fact that it was opposed by the TGWU although its seconded General Secretary, Frank Cousins, was in the Cabinet. TUC support for an incomes policy was also dependent on the government not deflating. But if the government did not deflate, there was certainly no hope for a voluntary incomes policy with unemployment down to 1.2 per cent. Even if there had been a statutory policy in 1964, it could not have been expected to have more than a marginal effect on incomes unless there was deflation and a freeze.

Wilson supports the case against devaluation with a further argument. He argues that, if Labour had devalued in 1964, there would have been speculation against sterling in anticipation of a further devaluation each time Britain 'ran into even minor economic difficulties – or even without them'.[27] That consequence, however, would have depended on the austerity of Labour's economic policies. It was certainly true if Labour continued the policies characteristic of economic management ever since 1945 which left Britain constantly on the edge of a breakdown in market confidence. But, in that case, the market would continuously fear devaluation whether or not a Labour government devalued immediately on achieving office. The market had feared devaluation or floating for most of the Tory years. Confidence could only be permanently established on the basis of a transformation in Britain's economic performance that Labour, whether or not it knew how to bring it about, had been elected to accomplish. The transformation could only begin with a harsh deflation supported by floating or a devaluation. It was inconceivable that 'planning' could be enough.

Much fun was had at the time by the Tory press and by Tory MPs, and perhaps some political capital was accumulated, alleging that the government's economic decisions were made by the two economists of Hungarian origin, Thomas Balogh and Nicholas Kaldor, Britain's B and K.[28] Wilson was persuaded by Balogh, his economic adviser, that 'socialist' policies would soon resolve the balance of payments problem without devaluation.[29] It was a position that Balogh, having contributed to the damage, rapidly abandoned though he retained an exaggerated faith in industrial policy.[30] Kaldor, on the other hand, advised Callaghan that the government should devalue. Wilson told him that devaluation 'would water the weeds as well as the flowers'.[31] The remark was illustrative of the Labour government's great illusion, that it knew how to discriminate between flowers and weeds. The great merit of devaluation would have been that its influence would have been diffused throughout the economy without bureaucratic interventions in selected industries, in other words precisely that it would have watered both those industries Wilson considered weeds and those he considered flowers.

Meanwhile, Balogh's initial advice was what Ministers wanted to hear. Not merely would they fight a heroic battle for sterling, they would be able to demonstrate conclusively the superiority of their policies by winning that battle. Callaghan admits, 'I am not certain that we in government fully understood how big were the changes that would be required if Britain's industrial decline was to be reversed.'[32] Even if the government *had* understood, and had known how to contribute to the transformation, the changes needed to reverse industrial decline would require far more time than would divide this government from the eventual forced devaluation of November 1967. In retrospect Brown came to the conclusion that Labour should have devalued in 1964 but he never seems to have realized that devaluation was not an alternative to deflation, simply a way of ensuring that the deflation was given the best opportunity to balance Britain's overseas accounts, after which growth could have been resumed on a more secure basis.[33]

Once the decision had been taken, new obstacles to devaluation had been raised. One was that the prestige of the government now depended on a successful defence of the parity. A second was that Wilson, at least, considered that there had been only one occasion on which devaluation was an option and that was in October 1964. Once the decision had been made not to devalue, it was irrevocable. On 9 November 1964, Wilson told Walter Heller, Chairman of President Johnson's Council of Economic Advisers, that 'It was the first day or never ... now it's never.'[34] Wilson wrote to Johnson himself that devaluation had been rejected 'for all time'.[35] The fact that the US Administration, in the interests of its own policies, found it useful to appear impressed did not mean that they had lost their powers of judgement. Whatever the Labour government pretended to itself, devaluation remained an option which foreign governments and the market knew could never be ruled out, one that in the end the British government might be compelled to adopt.

Callaghan's and Wilson's retrospective self-justification is evidence that they considered that, in rejecting devaluation, they were making the right decision on economic grounds. The decisive argument against devaluation was, nevertheless, the political argument; but for the political argument, they would have given themselves time to think and consult. There was, after all, a difference of opinion among their advisers. The rushed decision was eventually taken, at the end of a long day, at one brief discussion among three Ministers, naive in everything except the politics of Party advantage. By allowing questionable political calculations to rush them into a decision they were, right at the commencement of the Labour government, committing it to endless difficulties and possibly destruction. They had thereby made Callaghan's task as Chancellor impossible and his future as Chancellor doubtful. Pimlott argues that Wilson's priority in 1964 was, and had to be, survival.[36] The inescapable paradox was that survival in the short term, if that was taken to rule out devaluation, would certainly threaten survival in the longer term.

THE TREASURY AND DEVALUATION

We have seen that Armstrong did not advocate devaluation at the meeting at No. 11 with Brown and Callaghan. Even these Ministers, committed as they were against devaluation, would have given more consideration to it if the Treasury had itself recommended it. It was not one of the options Maudling had asked Treasury officials to consider on a contingency basis. It was, nevertheless, their duty to consider it and they did. There might be a new government and, in any case, they knew the situation to be far worse than anything of which they had forewarned Maudling. Wilson tells us that a contingency plan for the devaluation of sterling had been in the Treasury files *'when we took office'*.[37] The Treasury did present devaluation and floating to Ministers as options but it recommended rejection.[38] In the discussion that follows, the word 'devaluation' is used to cover both floating the currency, the better option, as well as devaluation to another fixed rate. Floating removed the need to decide the extent of any devaluation. If accompanied by adequate deflationary measures, the rate might indeed move relatively little.

A different Permanent Secretary might have made a different recommendation, developing the argument for devaluation, not neglecting the arguments against nor the political difficulties it might cause the new government. There was here a personal problem as well as a constitutional dilemma. The personal problem was the character of William Armstrong. In July 1962, as a Third Treasury Secretary, he had, on the retirement of Frank Lee, been promoted above his superiors, the Second Secretaries, to become Permanent Secretary of the Treasury. There had, however, been another Third Secretary, whose nose was put out of joint by Armstrong's promotion. That was Otto Clarke. The two men, equally able, were very different. It is not surprising that, between the two, Armstrong was chosen. His was a safe pair of hands. If Otto Clarke had been chosen, the probability must be that there would have been, right or wrong, firmer guidance to Ministers. That guidance might well have been for devaluation.

The most powerful argument against devaluation was that regularly presented by the Bank of England, both to this government and to its predecessors. This was that the competitiveness restored by devaluation would be rapidly squandered by inflation and by inflationary policies. The best defence Wilson could have advanced for his refusal to contemplate devaluation in 1964 was that an unaltered parity would assist him to tug the coat tails of his inflationary followers. But his enthusiastic support for the fulfilment of Labour's election promises proves that that defence was not open to him. The Bank's fears were certainly cogent and they may have influenced the attitude of the Treasury. Devaluation without deflation, implemented by a government with strong links to the trade unions, and with a programme that it was determined to enact, could well have resulted in hyperinflation. Unreasonable expectations for the standard of living of their members are always aroused in the trade unions by a Labour victory. If Maudling could authorize a 3.5 per cent guiding light, surely far more was to be expected from a Labour government. These were legitimate fears. But the fears hardly justify the Treasury's failure to recommend to the government a viable economic policy. The dilemma would have to be faced now or in the near future. The Treasury's recommendation should have been that the new government should float the currency or devalue *provided, but only provided, it was prepared to associate the floating or the devaluation with a harsh deflation*.

The Treasury's advice to Ministers should have begun by considering whether, as required before a devaluation under Bretton Woods, Britain was in truth in a state of fundamental disequilibrium. Given the balance of payments out-turn for 1964 and the Treasury forecast for 1965 which was not much better,[39] there was a strong presumption that that was the situation. Within a month of becoming Chancellor, Callaghan was advised by Emile van Lennep, Chairman of the EEC's Monetary Committee, and later Secretary General of the Organization for Economic Co-operation and Development, that sterling was in fundamental disequilibrium and ought to be devalued by between 10 and 15 per cent. Van Lennep thought that such a step could coincide with an agreed realignment with other countries.[40] The Treasury could hardly have been less aware than van Lennep of the facts that led him to that conclusion. It could hardly weigh such a conjuncture at less than a presumption of fundamental disequilibrium. Even though it might only be a presumption, it was a presumption strong enough to suggest an immediate move in the rate while it could be voluntary, rather than risking a delay at the end of which there might be no choice. No long-term reliance could be placed on import controls. They would necessarily be temporary.

The Treasury's advice would continue by discussing what steps other than devaluation could return the country to a condition of equilibrium. There would be the short term and the long term. In the short term the speculators would have to be warned off in order to give any alternative measures time to work. In the longer term, there would have to be a realistic chance that the alternative policies would achieve the objective of equilibrium. The short-term measures would need to be tough, deflationary, and exceedingly unpleasant for a new government with a majority in single figures facing another General Election. But the Treasury would warn Ministers that by rejecting devaluation they would not escape the need for measures that were tough, deflationary and unpopular. Regarding the longer term the Treasury should have brought its sceptical mind to bear on Labour's growth policies and on the history of planning in this country, its record of success and its record of failure. Assessing Labour's growth policies at their highest possible potential, they would take time to have any effect, probably a long time. It would have to say that the overall record of planning in this country was not persuasive. If Ministers intended to reject devaluation, what measures did they have to suggest that would justify confidence that devaluation could be avoided?

The Treasury would have reviewed the likely reaction of other countries. The USA was known to be strongly against a sterling devaluation because it would expose the dollar, already under attack from President de Gaulle who was preparing to demand gold in return for his dollars. Once the British navy had sailed sentinel in the Atlantic, guarantor not just of British security but of American security as well. Now an increasingly suspect pound was the guarantor of an increasingly questionable dollar. The government would have to show itself ready, thus early in its term of office, to risk a breach with Washington.[41] But Ministers would have to take that risk at some stage in any case unless they were convinced that they had alternative solutions to the disequilibrium. If the government was seen not just to devalue but to deflate, it would demonstrate to foreign opinion that it was serious in its efforts to restore the British economy.

Devaluation would deprive countries with sterling in their reserves of part of their value. Such countries might regard devaluation as a form of theft. It might damage relations internationally, particularly within the Commonwealth.[42] Sterling would never be trusted as a store of value again. But then the continuing crisis of sterling, long predating the £800 million deficit, was a reflection of the fact that it was not trusted now. This argument, the Treasury could have suggested, had far less force in 1964 than it had in 1945 or 1949. The sterling balances were no longer the product of the exercise of imperial power during the Second World War. They were now largely the product of an infinity of financial and commercial transactions in the intervening years during which the holders of the balances had made their choices in the light of sterling's continued weakness.

The Treasury paper would reflect on the even more questionable argument, one that yet had influence as is shown by Callaghan's memoirs, that the devaluation of sterling might set off a series of competitive devaluations as had, supposedly, happened in the 1930s.[43] According to this argument, the competitiveness of the UK economy might end up little better relatively than it now was. It was true that in 1949 other countries had followed sterling down so that in the end the trade weighted devaluation had been only 9 per cent. But the 1949 devaluation had, in reality, been an overdue realignment of all currencies against the dollar, in the light of postwar experience. Governments, the Treasury might have suggested, do not lightly devalue their currencies even if they see a trading partner stealing a competitive edge. The view of Emile van Lennep would suggest that a devaluation of sterling would be understood in Europe and could become part of an agreed realignment. Even if a realignment could not be agreed, no country would devalue by more than it considered its own necessities required. No country would devalue out of spite. In fact, when sterling was devalued in November 1967, few other countries followed, of which the most important were Denmark and New Zealand.

A stronger argument against an immediate devaluation was that it might require a support operation by foreign central banks. They would have to be prepared to buy sterling at its new exchange rate, or to lend the UK resources for the purchase of sterling, in order to ensure that the devaluation did not turn into a rout, that the new exchange rate could be sustained against market scepticism. The sum needed might be massive and, as the US Administration clearly did not wish to see sterling devalued, and would be expected to be in the lead of any such support operation, there could be problems. But the last outcome that the US authorities would want would be sterling floating down uncontrollably. They would, almost certainly, have helped to sustain the new parity, whether fixed or floating, provided the move was accompanied by other domestic measures considered adequate.

This is an outline of the advice that the Treasury might have presented to incoming Ministers. To have left Ministers to consider devaluation without the benefit of a strong Treasury position in favour was a grave failure even if Ministers were intent on taking a contrary decision. There were, for the official Treasury, three policy options. The best was to recommend devaluation plus deflation. It was the policy with the greatest prospect of success provided that the government was not allowed to regard it as a soft option. There was time to prepare a devaluation before the balance of payments figures had to be revealed. The second option was to recommend the maintenance of the parity provided that it was underlined that this would require from the government a real battle to which its growth policies had virtually nothing to contribute and in which its election promises would present a major problem. With a new, untrustworthy, government, dedicated to its election promises, this did have the advantage that it would provide a learning period during which the government might appreciate the constraints on its economic freedom. The Treasury's third option was the one it in fact adopted. This was to demonstrate its typical professional deformation, its tendency to treat Ministers too seriously. This third option involved sitting quietly watching Ministers commit themselves to the parity without providing any real evidence of the necessary associated determination to defend it. It involved allowing Ministers, without benefit of critical comment, to make a hash of everything they touched.

The attitude of the Treasury at the time was so passive that it is reasonable to speculate on the cause. There is a constitutional dilemma as to how far civil servants should guide Ministers, especially perhaps Ministers newly in office with an electoral mandate. Whereas Armstrong could be confident that a recommendation against devaluation would be acceptable to Ministers, he would be equally confident that a recommendation to devalue would not, even though he might accept the high probability that, in the end, the government would be forced into devaluation. He was giving the advice Ministers would want to hear and therefore could not be accused of bringing pressure to bear upon them contrary to the constitutional role of civil servants. But there was not merely a constitutional dilemma. The record of Treasury advice since the war had not been impeccable. What right had Treasury officials to bring pressure on Ministers when their own record had been so questionable? They might be diverted from making radical recommendations not just by constitutional convention but by all the uncertainties of economic management. A Permanent Secretary such as Armstrong might well feel that the only secure basis for the relationship between officials and Ministers is for officials to present options and for Ministers to make policy and decisions on policy. He might think that economic management is so difficult and its product so uncertain that decisions must be freely made by politicians who will, in due course, meet their makers, the electorate, and not under pressure from unelected officials. On this view, everything conspired against a Treasury recommendation of devaluation even though many in the Treasury must have known that the government was unlikely to be able to escape it. Armstrong, personally, could well have been influenced by the damage done to Butler when Robot was pressed upon him by the Treasury without sufficient preparation. The Treasury should, by this time, have outlived any modesty induced by the experience with Robot. Treasury officials should have known that the education of Ministers, particularly Ministers who have been out of office for thirteen years, but nevertheless think they are wise beyond their years, is part of their function. Wilson writes that 'Whitehall is always well prepared for a change of government.'[44] On the evidence of 1945, 1951, 1964 and 1974, it would be truer to say that Whitehall is never prepared for a change in government.

Callaghan had appointed as his personal economic adviser Professor Robert Neild of Cambridge.[45] Over the next two and a half years, Neild and Kaldor were to be the most pertinacious advocates of action on the exchange rate. Neild together with MacDougall and Balogh prepared a paper arguing that devaluation was inevitable sooner or later. For Neild the open question was whether it was better to float or to move to a new fixed rate.[46] It is ironic that the two most senior economic advisers brought into the Treasury by Callaghan both opposed his policies.

MEASURES GALORE

The government had rejected devaluation and floating. The need remained to act firmly. We now enter a period of heroic words unmatched by heroic deeds. Typically, Wilson let it be known from time to time to his private circle that he was the real hero and that Callaghan lacked his particular quality of backbone.[47] What in fact was being revealed in the early weeks of Wilson's government was not lack of backbone but unfitness for office. In these first days of his government, there was nothing that was not being mishandled, whether it was the question of devaluation, or import controls, or the aborted cancellation of the Anglo-French Concorde project, or anything else to which the government set its hand.[48] One result, paradoxically given the lack of strong advice from the Treasury, was that Treasury officials came rapidly to hold Ministers in contempt. The contempt was felt not just by permanent officials but even by advisers, brought in by Ministers, who saw the opportunity created by Labour's victory being frittered away in one incoherent meeting after another.

On 26 October 1964, ten days after taking office, the government announced in its White Paper, *The Economic Situation*, that the estimated deficit on the balance of payments for 1964 was now £800 million and that, of the contingency plans prepared under Maudling's direction, it had selected a 'temporary' import surcharge of 15 per cent on all imports except food, tobacco and raw materials, and the small rebate of indirect taxes on exports amounting to something under 2 per cent.[49] At that stage no indication was given of what 'temporary' actually meant. There seems to have been no advance consultation with any capital, even Washington.[50] If import controls were to be imposed, the Treasury view was that the economic rationale was in favour of an import surcharge because it was less discriminatory and less bureaucratic. It was also argued that an import surcharge would do some of the work of deflation necessitated by the conjuncture, whereas import quotas would not have any such effect. Douglas Jay would have preferred import quotas because they were authorized under international rules as a legitimate reaction to balance of payments difficulties, whereas an import surcharge was not. He found himself unsupported in his arguments both at a mixed Ministerial/official meeting and at Cabinet.[51] It was for the surcharge that Callaghan and Brown argued and they had their way.[52] Even if the government had stuck to the rules and imposed quotas there would certainly have been a row with Britain's foreign critics. The use of an 'illegal' device provided the critics with additional inflammatory material.[53] That, however, would not have been important had the government realized the storm that its actions would raise and had shown determination to stick to its guns. In fact it was taken by surprise by the outcry, particularly from its EFTA partners, who had not been consulted and for whom access to the UK market, about half of the total EFTA market, presented their main gain from the establishment of the European Free Trade Area.[54] Consultation about a realignment of parities could hardly have caused more international tension than did the imposition of the import surcharge without consultation.

The White Paper also made a gratuitous present to the government's Conservative critics by asserting that, with some few exceptions, there was 'no undue pressure on resources calling for action'.[55] The assertion was made though unemployment was down to 1.2 per cent.[56] It would be a long time before Labour MPs would be allowed to forget the phrase. It was endlessly repeated. It made it easier for Labour's political opponents to claim that all subsequent disasters, including the inflationary pressures, were the fruit of Labour's profligate policies and were in no way attributable to the Maudling Experiment. It may be that Callaghan and his colleagues genuinely believed that, with the aid of socialist measures, the economy could be run at such a level of unemployment without inflation and without problems on the balance of payments. It may be that the object of the assertion was to reassure the market that if, despite the crisis, the government rejected deflation and proceeded to implement its social programme, there was no reason to worry that it would be overstretching resources. It must have been a fine calculation which enabled Callaghan to reconcile the assertion in the White Paper with his own convictions about the level of public expenditure. By 7 December, he was saying that 'during the summer months, for electoral reasons, the economy [had been allowed] to become overheated'.[57]

When introduced, the import surcharge was deflationary to the extent that it increased the price of foreign goods in the British market, inflationary in that it thereby might provoke compensating wage claims. It is ever thus in economic management; clouds have their silver linings, but silver linings have their clouds. After the announcement of the import surcharge came Callaghan's first Budget, opened on 11 November. The government was pledged to increase old age pensions and abolish health service charges. Bevan was influencing policy from beyond the grave. In Cabinet, Callaghan, greatly daring, proposed a pension increase of 10 shillings (50p). The Cabinet, with Wilson assenting, overruled him and insisted on 12s. 6d (62.5p). The market would have been disturbed by either figure. Callaghan raised in increased taxation and higher National Insurance contributions more than was necessary to compensate for the increased cost of the pensions, the health service and other benefits. The standard rate of income tax was raised by 6d (2.5p). Petrol duty was increased. The sophisticated computations that go to the making of such economic judgements led economists to conclude that, taking the import surcharge into account, the Budget was roughly neutral in its effect on demand.

The Budget confirmed the market's suspicions about the character of this new Labour government. There was nothing here that spoke of determination to defend the parity. The market was not persuaded by the arithmetic. Pensioners would spend. Higher rate taxpayers would probably pay out of savings. The Budget would increase consumer demand in what the market, if not the White Paper, regarded as an already overloaded economy. In the market's eyes a government that could increase social expenditure when it had just announced such a balance of payments deficit was profligate, and a profligate government could not, in the end, defend the parity. Moreover Callaghan had given notice of his intention to introduce in his next Budget in April 1965 a Corporation Tax and a Capital Gains Tax. Details were left obscure. Neither was necessarily a 'socialist' measure. Indeed, as Jay argues, the substitution of Corporation Tax for Profits Tax was not even a necessary measure.[58] But, in the absence of information, it was assumed that such an announcement coming from a Labour government could not be good for sterling. The implication for any accountable market operator was to sell pounds for other more reliable currencies. There arose a flood of selling. The Budget provoked the speculation against sterling which Callaghan had always anticipated as the market's likely reaction to the election of a Labour government. Despite the bad news about the balance of payments and the provocation of the import surcharge, the market appeared previously to have suspended judgement. Now Callaghan saw his fears justified in full measure and his Budget had provoked it.

Despite strong words from the Prime Minister about the government's continuing determination to maintain the sterling parity, the impression given by the government was of total disarray. The advice of Lord Cromer, the Governor of the Bank, that Bank Rate should be raised by 1 per cent on Thursday 19 November was ignored. Thursday was the normal day for moving Bank Rate. Though this was clearly a necessary step if the adverse impressions created by the Budget were to be reversed, Callaghan could not get agreement.[59] George Brown considered that an increase in Bank Rate was inconsistent with his responsibilities for growth and President Johnson cabled to say that any increase in Bank Rate should be coordinated with the USA.[60] At the meeting of the EFTA Ministerial Council on 19 and 20 November, it was demonstrated that the backbone on which Wilson congratulated himself when it was a matter of the sterling exchange rate, rapidly bent under the attacks on the surcharge by the UK's outraged trading partners. The Foreign Secretary, Patrick Gordon Walker, and Douglas Jay capitulated before a threat of retaliation and secured from Wilson permission to agree a communiqué conceding that a beginning would be made in reducing the import surcharge 'in a matter of months'.[61] The promise was honoured by a reduction in the surcharge to 10 per cent in April 1965.[62] After a weekend meeting at Chequers, Bank Rate was raised by 2 per cent on Monday 23 November, from 5 to 7 per cent. It had been decided that the outflow from the reserves was too serious to wait for the following Thursday and that a 1 per cent increase would no longer suffice. This series of events gave all the appearance of a government in panic and the flight from sterling accelerated despite the increase in Bank Rate.

LORD CROMER'S UNPALATABLE LESSONS

The dilemma facing the government was discussed in a confrontation between Wilson and Lord Cromer on Tuesday 24 November after the 2 per cent increase in Bank Rate had failed to steady sterling. It ranks as one of the key confrontations in modern British political history. We are fortunate to have both Wilson's and Callaghan's account. In his account, Wilson presents himself as the democratic hero in battle against dark forces. Cromer warned him of the need for a deflationary package in addition to the increase in Bank Rate made the day before. Wilson treated Cromer as an enemy rather than as an adviser. He demanded whether the implication of Cromer's advice was that a Labour government could not carry out its election promises without the permission of the money-lenders. Cromer admitted that that was the implication of what he was saying. Wilson responded that he was not prepared to accept the doctrine that an election in Britain was simply a farce. He threatened a General election and told Cromer he would win by a landslide.[63] The election would be on the issue of who governs Britain, the elected government or the Gnomes of Zurich. Among the minor faults of this Labour government was its inclination to insult money-lenders by describing them as 'Gnomes of Zurich' and then expect to be able to borrow from them on favourable terms. Cromer himself was regularly abused by Labour Ministers behind his back and, occasionally, by George Brown, to his face. Cromer and the Bank of England were convenient whipping boys for a government that thought it could combine its election promises with the maintenance of the parity if only the Bank did its democratic duty and summoned the international financial community to assist. Presumably, Wilson expected Cromer to believe that an election would reinforce the government's mandate.[64] It was an extraordinary threat. Another General Election, however much it might confirm Labour in office, would not have affected its need to borrow. Cromer responded that during the four weeks that Wilson would require to obtain his new mandate, the reserves would have disappeared.

Wilson's tough stance impressed Callaghan and his other Cabinet colleagues. Callaghan told Barbara Castle that 'he's tough, much tougher than you and I. You should see him handling the Governor of the Bank.'[65] Michael Stewart was similarly admiring. 'The wily York-shireman spreadeagled Cromer's stumps with a googly.'[66] There is no doubt that, politically, Cromer was no friend of the Labour government. But he was trying to educate the innocents of that government, with whom he was compelled to work, with some of the facts of life, including the implications of Wilson's own decision not to devalue.

The encounter between Wilson and Cromer illustrates a genuine dilemma of democratic government. Even if it is assumed that governments have a disposition to be honest, if they have to borrow to fund their election promises, if, when they come into office, circumstances have deprived their promises of any kind of priority, and if the financiers withhold trust, implementation may not be possible. If a government with a deficit to fund persists in actions which dismay potential lenders, it should not be surprised if lending becomes highly conditional. The conditions may include a change in government policy. Lenders are not to be blamed for limiting their lending by consideration of the probability of repayment. The traumas of office were creating within the Labour Party a class of people, not all of them on the left, who believed that the Gnomes had a duty to lend to their government whatever its policies. Wilson's attitude was part of the problem. He had much to learn and he was a slow learner. He attributed his problems to 'a great deal of political malice' in the City of London rather than to the incoherence of his own policies.[67] He writes bitterly, 'We were soon to learn that decisions on pensions and taxation were no longer to be regarded, as in the past, as decisions for Parliament alone.' They had also to be approved by speculators in sterling.[68] It is remarkable that a Prime Minister should have been surprised at this speculators' veto. Such decisions were for Parliament alone only if Parliament alone could fund them. Wilson was attempting to borrow large sums of money. That politics would be playing a part was to be expected. Callaghan had expected the election of a Labour government to provoke speculation against sterling. But there would have been less speculation if the policies of the government had attracted more confidence. That meant getting the priorities right and that the election promises would have to wait. After all, there was what Wilson would have considered impeccable authority for the proposition that there was an economic crisis. He himself had said so and the market had believed him.

There was an exchange rate option other than devaluation. It was the option repeatedly considered and rejected during the Tory years, an option inconsistent with Bretton Woods, the option of floating the currency. The idea commended itself to Wilson momentarily during his confrontation with Cromer on 24 November. He threatened that he would float sterling. Cromer warned that to float sterling would cause a world financial crisis. This was true, but only in the sense that it might have forced a general reappraisal of world imbalances and, as a minimum, a realignment of parities. Though inconvenient to Washington, by whose self-interested advice British governments were too prone to be guided, it would, for the UK, have been a beneficent crisis. A combination of floating with a large but temporary rise in Bank Rate and a major deflation would probably have been successful and would have given Ministers that opportunity to display their heroism in a practical cause which they appeared so much to want. Wilson often spoke of Labour as the Party of government. This was the action that might have accomplished that honourable ambition. But Wilson was not serious. He was simply trying out a debating point.

Despite the spirit in which it was made, Wilson's threat to float was probably more influential with Cromer than his threat to call a General Election. Callaghan believes that Cromer was sufficiently frightened to approach his friends in the other central banks for support for sterling.

On 25 November, the Bank of England announced that it had secured from eleven central banks, the Bank of International Settlements, and the US Export-Import Bank, a short term credit of $3 billion. At a meeting under Wilson's chairmanship on 25 November, Brown made 'a passionate speech against even thinking of devaluation and said there must be no further talk of it'.[69] On 2 December, the government drew $1 billion from the IMF. The drain on the reserves continued despite this massive support, but sterling was for the moment saved. By this time a majority of the leading economists in Whitehall favoured devaluation though with different assessments of the two key issues, the extent of the devaluation and of the associated deflation. It was Ministers who were still opposed. At a meeting of economic Ministers and officials on 23 December at No. 10, Wilson tried to lay the devaluation idea finally to rest. He told the gathering that he was passionately against devaluation. It was unthinkable. Those present who were thinking it should make some effort to ensure that the government's determination was widely understood.[70] Prime Ministerial ukases were, however, insufficient to ban discussion of devaluation in Whitehall. The word might be kept from the eyes of the Prime Minister but officials could not be kept from discussing it. They could not even be restrained from mentioning it in the presence of the Chancellor, when they saw no policy emerging from Ministers that persuaded them that, in the end, it could be avoided.

STUMBLING ON

Short-term credits, such as had been negotiated by Cromer in November, contain an implicit threat demanding deflationary action without too much delay. Enough was done to persuade reluctant central banks to give the government more time but never enough to persuade the market. In December 1964, steps were taken to restrict bank lending. Then, in January 1965, the loss of the Leyton by-election by the Foreign Secretary, Patrick Gordon Walker, made the government even less willing to deflate. Even defence expenditure appeared to be escaping the 'stern review' that had been promised the previous autumn. Callaghan defined the objective of his 1965 Budget, opened on 6 April, as being 'to achieve a state of balance on our combined current and long-term capital account . . . I aim to get most of the way towards closing the gap this year and to complete the process in the course of 1966.' He also aimed to reduce the net outflow of long-term capital from the UK by at least £100 million a year.[71] The Budget was somewhat deflationary. Callaghan said, 'I intend to decrease the pressure on resources through lower public expenditure and higher taxation, by £250 million.'[72] This was judged to be the minimum necessary to secure renewal of the $3 billion credits. Though the credits were renewed, market opinion had been looking for more. Moreover it seemed improbable that Callaghan would achieve the deflationary effect for which he was hoping. Already public expenditure and wage rates were rising far faster than anything that could be justified by any probable increase in GNP. The inadequacy of the Budget left sterling at the mercy of speculative flurries whenever there was any bad news.[73] May 1965 produced poor trade figures. Against an average deficit on visible trade of £17 millions in the first four months of 1965, the May figure slumped to £57 million.

Experience was opening a breach between the three Ministers who had, the previous October, so confidently rejected devaluation. George Brown's problem was that the commitment to the sterling parity had become far more visible and demanding than the commitment to growth. The result was that while he had become a convert to devaluation, Wilson and Callaghan were moving to accept the need for more resolute deflationary action to save the parity. The case for devaluation was still being argued by the economists within the Treasury and even, by Robert Neild, at No. 10 in the presence of the Prime Minister. On 30 May, Armstrong told Callaghan that the government would be lucky to avoid devaluation. But Callaghan remained firm and was beginning to see his own reputation as Chancellor bound up with the parity.[74] That provided him with a strong incentive to fight even at the cost of a degree of deflation that he had ruled out earlier in the year and had refused for his Budget. In any case, the decisive voice was that of Wilson and he had used the word 'never'.

On 27 July 1965 Callaghan, continuing an already well-established tradition of July measures to save sterling, announced a series of restrictions indistinguishable from those characteristic of Tory governments faced with market anxiety about sterling.[75] Shortly before he spoke the government's economic advisers had once more recommended devaluation to accompany the deflation but neither Callaghan nor Wilson was moved.[76] The measures included cuts in what Callaghan described as the 'swollen' public expenditure programmes left behind by the Tories, limits on local authority lending, postponement of public sector construction projects, and a hardening of hire purchase terms. For the market, perhaps the most persuasive words in Callaghan's statement were,

> We shall also have to defer some of the desirable social reforms we had hoped to do in the immediate future. While priority must go to wage-related unemployment and sickness benefits, the Government have decided that it will not be possible to introduce an income guarantee scheme or remove the remaining National Health Service charges in the next Session.[77]

But these words were not persuasive enough. Callaghan had begun his statement by drawing attention to a marked improvement in the balance of payments, but confidence once dissipated is not easily regained, particularly by Labour governments. Wilson busily underlined to President Johnson the 'determination' exemplified by these July measures 'to put the strength of sterling before politics' despite criticism from the left and the TUC. But Johnson's advisers warned him that Callaghan's measures did not deserve even a pass mark.[78] Pressure on sterling continued during August. During this period the British government sought support for sterling in the USA and Europe. It became clear that the French saw support for sterling as a way of helping the dollar, and therefore would not participate, and that the Germans thought that sterling should be devalued.[79] Pressure was at last relieved by the beginnings of a statutory incomes policy negotiated by George Brown with employers and unions, announced by him on 2 September, and endorsed by the TUC Conference on 6 September.[80] The NBPI would become a statutory institution and there would be a compulsory 'early warning' system for wage and price increases. Four days later, the US Federal Reserve entered the market and bought massive quantities of sterling.[81] European central banks other than the French, whose participation was vetoed by de Gaulle, helped in other ways. But for the self-interested actions of the Americans in supporting sterling on this and other occasions, sterling would certainly have been devalued sooner and deflation would have been forced on the British government. At least, for all the stress he was suffering in his thankless job, Callaghan now had one compensation. Nothing gives a Labour Chancellor under pressure greater satisfaction than when speculators against sterling are caught out and lose large sums of money. The activities of speculators are clearly reprehensible except when they are buying sterling. The fact that it may be overvalued, and that they may lose money, should not deter them. This time the speculators had lost due to a political decision, taken by the Federal Reserve, to support sterling.[82] But George Brown, at least, had at last listened to his officials and had concluded that the price paid by Britain for such political support had become too high.

'SOCIALISM' TO THE RESCUE OF STERLING

When Wilson and his two colleagues decided against devaluation they were determined not to rely for the defence of the parity on deflation but on better ways, socialist ways. Under the stimulating direction of George Brown, the preparation of a National Plan began. It was endorsed by NEDC on 5 August 1965 and unveiled on 16 September 1965.[83] It set a target of 25 per cent growth between 1964 and 1970, or 3.8 per cent per annum. George Brown had wanted a higher rate of growth so that he could offer the trade unions a higher norm, but MacDougall had by now persuaded him that a higher growth rate would be impossible without devaluation and there was insufficient support within the Cabinet to force devaluation.[84] The Plan listed 39 actions necessary to achieve its target. The Plan was not a particularly 'socialist' instrument. It was a by-product of the conviction that the way of dealing with the balance of payments was by a dramatic expansion of the domestic market. As we have seen, this conviction was held as much by politicians of an economic bent within the Labour Party as within the later Conservative governments of the thirteen 'wasted years'. In particular it was held by George Brown. It was absurd, but it was not socialist. Both Parties had also come to accept that an incomes policy of some kind was necessary to deal with the inflation which was pushing up costs and thereby threatening the sterling parity. Expansion was expected to improve the chances for an incomes policy.

The Plan was widely praised and welcomed in all parts of the political and industrial spectrum but was, in fact, stillborn. By the time it was published the government had found that, if it really wished to defend the parity, some degree of deflation was inescapable. The belief held by Labour over many years that expansion was the way to overcome the balance of payments constraint, and thereby preserve the parity, was effectively abandoned in the July measures. The July measures were irreconcilable with the Plan's targets. Those who had prepared the Plan had assumed that the pound would if necessary be devalued.[85] But, after the July measures, that was, even more clearly than before, not the government's intention.

It is customarily argued that the National Plan was killed by the devotion of Wilson and Callaghan to the sterling parity. It is true that the Plan could hardly have been launched at a less propitious moment. The battle for the sterling parity imposed restrictive measures which were inconsistent with the ambitions of the National Plan and, in the end, would go far beyond those of July 1965. The death of the Plan is also attributed to Wilson's lack of commitment and to the scepticism, and even defeatism, of Callaghan and of the Treasury, which believed that the numbers in the Plan did not add up.[86] It is certainly true that the Treasury was concerned that Ministers were committing themselves to levels of public expenditure which not merely assumed the achievement of the Plan's growth targets before that had actually occurred but exceeded them. In the Plan the government decided to 'limit' the growth of public expenditure between 1964–5 and 1969–70 to an average of 4.5 per cent at constant prices.[87] Callaghan, with his views about public expenditure, must have been under considerable pressure to permit such a commitment. In this sense the Plan was bound to self-destruct. It would itself add to inflationary pressure in the economy and help to force deflation on the government.

The National Plan, however, was damned not by its over-optimism but by its lack of any useful role. It was otiose without devaluation but would have been no less otiose with it. It was a political gesture, supported equally by naive politicians, naive businessmen and naive civil servants in the DEA. It was intended to suggest that Labour had something special to offer in the field of economic management. In fact Labour had nothing special to offer in the field of economic management.

In its attempt to avoid devaluation, the Labour government was prepared to exploit a variety of ideas either of its own creation or put to it by its advisers. It may have lacked economic successes but it never lacked ideas. None of them were particularly 'socialist' but they came to define a new kind of 'socialism' of which nationalization was no longer the shibboleth. The Industrial Reorganization Corporation (IRC) was established as a marriage broker between companies. The greatest achievement of the IRC was Arnold Weinstock's GEC, its greatest failure was the British motor car industry whose demise was probably hastened by its intervention.[88] Wilson was delighted at the distinguished list of senior industrialists recruited to the board of the IRC.[89] Later, Mintech, now under Tony Benn, was permitted to enact an Industrial Expansion Act which gave the government considerable powers of intervention in the interests of British industrial success. Although these measures were criticized by the Tory opposition at the time, the Heath government would, in due course, turn to similar, and perhaps even more expensive and vain, devices, in its attempt to stimulate the British economy.

As an incentive to investment, investment allowances, administered by the Inland Revenue, were replaced by investment grants administered by the Board of Trade. Labour's idea was that investment would be encouraged by grants because they would make it easier to earn a profit because the cost of capital would be lower. The grants were at the level of 20 per cent of eligible capital expenditure except in development areas where they were 40 per cent. The ever-creative Nicholas Kaldor persuaded Callaghan in his 1966 Budget to introduce a Selective Employment Tax (SET). Cheated of his devaluation, Kaldor was looking for ways of achieving some of the effects of devaluation. Kaldor believed that a reason for Britain's slow growth was that too much labour was employed in services and too little in manufacturing. Moreover manufacturing, the major source of the country's exports, was highly taxed and services were little taxed. SET was thus seen as a way of remedying a counter-productive anomaly in Britain's system of taxation. The tax, introduced in a great hurry, in circumstances which we will discuss later, was an administrative nightmare. Later, the existence of the tax made possible a Regional Employment Premium (REP) intended to give greater support to manufacturing industry in the development areas, and to supply the effect of a localized devaluation.

These devices had several characteristics in common. Whatever their positive contribution, which was always debatable, their effect was insufficient both in time and quality to rectify the fundamental disequilibrium. Moreover, these devices involved bureaucracy on such a scale that even the British administrative machine could not cope without gross anomalies and, therefore, the creation of great grievances and injustices. It was being discovered that the advantage of the market and of the price mechanism lay not just in their influence on parts of the economy the bureaucrats could not reach but in the avoidance of bureaucracy. In so far as these devices were direct substitutes for devaluation, they gave rise to international controversy, especially as the import surcharge had already alerted Britain's trading partners to the Wilson government's readiness to act illegally. The fact that all this was done with the beneficent intention of avoiding a devaluation which would give a much greater boost to British competitiveness than any of these devices, did not seem to soften adverse foreign reaction.

DOWNHILL MOST OF THE WAY

The TUC's acceptance in September 1965 of a statutory element in the prices and incomes policy, assisted by the July 1965 measures and perhaps by the widespread welcome and euphoria that greeted the National Plan, won a breathing space for the government. With some skill, Wilson used it to call a General Election on 31 March 1966. He won it with an overall majority approaching 100. The electorate seemed to rejoice in a government that had fought with apparent success against the adverse circumstances that had surrounded its birth and had won through. In fact the incomes policy was not working and the government was benefiting politically from the fact that wages were rising faster than prices.[90] A voluntary prices and incomes policy is always likely to have more effect on prices than on incomes and its effect can therefore be self-defeating. On 7 February 1966, Douglas Jay announced a tightening of hire purchase controls.[91] It was the act of responsibility that typically precedes the irresponsibility of election claims and promises. On 8 February Callaghan felt able to assure the House that the government was on target to clear the payments deficit by the end of 1966.[92] In a confident speech on the economic situation on 1 March, Callaghan proclaimed the successes of Labour's policies thus far. He was able to speak of the prospect, now before the nation, of repaying the IMF and other lenders the large debts which had been incurred during the period of deficit. Referring to the steps he had taken during 1965 to reduce domestic consumption he offered the hope that 'A modest sacrifice in consumption in 1966 will make possible greater consumption in the years ahead.'[93] Turning to a description of the Budget he would intend to introduce if Labour won the coming election, he gave his considered reassurance that 'The economy is ... reasonably well-poised ... The best guidance I can give ... is that I do not foresee the need for severe increases in taxation.'[94] Callaghan tells us that he gave that reassurance after consulting his advisers.[95]

Callaghan's advisers did not behave as though they shared his euphoria about the economy. Led by Robert Neild, the government's economic advisers, including Balogh, Cairncross, Kaldor and MacDougall, produced during the election a paper recommending floating or devaluation. Other than MacDougall, they all accepted that the move on the exchange rate would have to be accompanied by deflation. Kaldor said explicitly that unemployment, then barely over 1 per cent, must be higher. William Armstrong associated himself with the work but not with the recommendation.[96] It had become almost impossible for Armstrong to give Callaghan the advice which, by now, he must have thought appropriate. Callaghan had committed his reputation to the parity. If his Permanent Secretary advised devaluation, it would appear that he was trying to force the resignation of his Chancellor. On his return to Downing Street after the election, Wilson was told what had been going on and was extremely angry. He made clear that he was not prepared to receive advice based on the assumption of devaluation.[97]

The election was called only just in time. When Callaghan returned to the Treasury after the election, he found 'longer faces . . . the forecasts had changed for the worse. I was naturally put out for I knew I would be accused of having misled Parliament . . .'[98] Chancellors should not, of course, believe forecasts. But it is rather difficult to disbelieve a favourable forecast just before an election. Callaghan was not the man to forget such *contretemps*. By the time he had to make his 1966 Budget statement, on 3 May, there was no concealing that the tone of his 1 March speech had been over-confident. Despite the new forecasts, Callaghan announced the abolition of the import surcharge as from November 1966.[99] The burden to be carried by other policies was thereby enhanced. It was clear that a measure of deflation would once more be required. It was also clear that, after the old-fashioned traditional Treasury deflation of July 1965, and after an election victory based on supposed achievements, old-fashioned Treasury deflation would no longer be acceptable to the Cabinet or the Party. To increase income tax would be singularly unattractive so soon after the election. To raise duties on spirits and tobacco would adversely affect the retail price index and consequently Brown's battle for an effective incomes policy. It was in this context that SET became the principal feature of Callaghan's 1966 Budget. Unfortunately, whereas the traditional Treasury methods could have an immediate deflationary effect, SET would have only a delayed effect. Whatever the arguments for or against it as a piece of economic engineering, in the context of the deflationary requirements of May 1966, it was a source of confusion and mystification rather than deflation. Once more the market turned against a Callaghan Budget and there were the first stirrings of another sterling crisis. The electorate found that it had given its trust prematurely.

Sterling was further undermined by the onset of a seven-week seamen's strike. The strike was fought by the government in order to protect the incomes policy. In that it had some success. Unfortunately, the strike was bound to damage Britain's trade. So precarious was the condition of the economy in the eyes of the market, that even praise-worthy courage in resisting inflationary claims reinforced scepticism whether the parity of sterling could survive. The strike ended on 1 July and Callaghan, with renewed optimism, assured the Prime Minister that he now hoped to get through the summer without further measures. The economy, he said, was not over-heated. Clearly he did not realize the fragility of the situation. He returned to the Treasury to find that serious selling of sterling had begun.[100] 'Such,' he comments, 'is the frailty of a Chancellor's hopes and forecasts.'[101] Two days later, after the publication of a new Prices and Incomes Bill, Frank Cousins resigned as Minister of Technology and returned to the TGWU as General Secretary, employing his remaining time as an MP to oppose the statu-tory incomes policy and to raise the left of the Parliamentary Labour Party against it. The support of the TUC for the incomes policy could no longer be relied upon. Publication of the reserves showed a large fall due to the seamen's strike. The French Prime Minister Pompidou, returning to Paris after a visit to London during which he believed he had been discourteously treated by Wilson, let it be known that he had recommended devaluation of sterling if the British economy was to be fitted for membership of the EEC.[102] A new forecast of the balance of payments out-turn for 1966 showed a deficit of £350 million. At Wilson's request this forecast was concealed from the Cabinet which was simply told that the balance of payments was not improving fast enough.[103]

Devaluation was again an option, not as an alternative to deflation but as the key supplement that carried the greatest hopes of emerging from the deflation in a condition of resumed growth and reliable balance. With a secure majority behind it and five years to go before the next election, the domestic political difficulties in devaluation were far less daunting than in October 1964. But, of the economic triumvirate, only Brown was fighting for it and he was fighting for it in the misguided belief that it *was* a soft option. Callaghan feared that if there was a forced devaluation, he would not get the support of the Cabinet for the necessary accompanying measures.[104] It was hardly a good enough reason for continuing a battle that was every day more hopeless. During his visit, Pompidou's arguments had, momentarily, influenced Calla-ghan. He even told Jenkins that he now favoured devaluation. Though he rapidly returned to his previous stance on the parity it was not before his wavering had excited Wilson's distrust.[105] There was a brief period during which Brown and Callaghan might have agreed on devaluation plus deflation and might then have attempted to force the Prime Minister's hand. Callaghan would still have been a reluctant devaluer and Brown a reluctant deflater but, if they had conscripted Wilson's agreement, there would at last have been a realistic economic policy.[106] Both Brown and Callaghan soon reverted to their traditional stances, Brown on deflation and Callaghan on devaluation. As Wilson knew his own mind and remained firm for the parity throughout, it was his view that prevailed.[107] Callaghan's flirtation with devaluation certainly ended when he found that he would have Wilson's support for the strong deflationary measures required to save the parity.

A major deflation of a traditional Treasury variety was now inescapable despite continued rumblings from Brown. But measures were dribbled out instead of being presented in one package. On 14 July Bank Rate was raised from 6 to 7 per cent and the Bank doubled its call for special deposits from the clearing banks. The impact of the increase in the discount rate was lessened by the fact that interest rates were rising internationally. So far as fiscal measures were concerned, there was nothing more than a holding statement by Wilson in the House. The parity would be held by unspecified action to be detailed in due course.[108] The Cabinet met for five hours on 19 July; it discussed the exchange rate, though without the benefit of any paper on so sensitive a topic, but rejected any move. Wilson says, 'A small number put the case for floating the pound, though almost all agreed that it would be impossible to float at a moment of extreme crisis. Once the crisis was over we should examine the idea in a calmer atmosphere. There was virtually no pressure for devaluation to a fixed, lower parity.'[109] There is here some discrepancy between Wilson and Callaghan. Callaghan certainly believed that devaluation was advocated by a substantial body of opinion in the Cabinet and he lists the names.[110]

Instead of floating, the Cabinet adopted a traditional deflationary Treasury package. Wilson announced it in the House on 20 July. Wilson's was a long statement as well as a massive package. Callaghan had wanted to make it.[111] The fact that it was made by the Prime Minister could not conceal the implication that if this package did not work, the credibility of the Chancellor would be fatally undermined. Wilson claimed that the government had been 'blown off course by the seven-week seamen's strike'.[112] But, he suggested, there were more fundamental problems. There was an acute shortage of dollars in world trade which had caused a worldwide increase in interest rates to which the Bank had already reacted. But there was need also for a 'shake-out' which would release the nation's manpower for the purpose of increasing exports. 'This redeployment can be achieved only by cuts in the present inflated level of demand . . .'[113] Wilson did not explain why, thus far, the government had permitted this 'inflated' level of demand. Nevertheless, what he said was true and had been for many years. Redeployment could not, of course mean that everyone who was 'redeployed' would move straight from one job into another. A successful redeployment would have to tolerate a higher level of unemployment. As, moreover, economies need to adjust continuously, the higher level of unemployment would need to become a constant feature of the economy. It was not likely that, whatever might be acceptable in a manifest crisis, the Labour movement was yet ready to adopt a higher level of unemployment as an objective of policy.

Wilson then listed the package. It included hire purchase restrictions, the activation of Selwyn Lloyd's regulator on indirect taxation, cuts in public investment programmes, cuts in the government's overseas expenditures and on private expenditure on foreign travel. It included also a one-year surcharge of 10 per cent on surtax, intended no doubt more to entice cooperation from the trade unions than because of any economic impact. Wilson estimated that the measures would reduce the demand on the domestic economy by more than £500 million. This, he said, was in addition to the earlier budgetary measures reducing the pressure of demand in the private sector by over £700 million. It was a massive deflationary package. But there was more to come. Wilson turned to prices and incomes policy. 'The Government are now calling for a six-month standstill on wages, salaries and other types of income, followed by a further six months of severe restraint, and for a similar standstill on prices . . . it is our intention to strengthen the provisions of the Prices and Incomes Bill, to speed its passage through Parliament and to redefine the role of the National Board for Prices and Incomes.'[114] It was deflation without devaluation. The question remained, how much deflation and how tight a statutory incomes policy were needed to ward off devaluation for a country in fundamental disequilibrium. No one knew, and what was done was not enough.

Brown, having withdrawn his most recent resignation from the government under the impression that Wilson would welcome his departure, stayed at the DEA only long enough to pilot the Prices and Incomes Act, of which he claims not to have approved, through the

House. The Bill established the NBPI formally. A Bill had been introduced in the autumn of 1965 but it had lapsed at the General Election. The new Bill contained powers, absent from the previous Bill, to be held in reserve for use if the voluntary policy failed. Under these powers it would be possible to employ punitive measures to enforce a wage freeze.[115]

There was then a competition between Brown and Callaghan as to which of them would be allowed to drop his economic responsibilities. Callaghan's morale was low. He would like to have been released from the rigours, and the uncertainties, of the Treasury and of economic management. Two years, he thought, was enough. Unwisely, he allowed a journalist to know that the Foreign Office would have suited him.[116] Wilson reacted angrily against this public bid for the Foreign Office, and it was Brown who won the reprieve. He exchanged jobs with Michael Stewart, becoming Foreign Secretary. Callaghan must have been jealous. There was George Brown, the cross Callaghan had had to bear, escaping from real responsibilities to the marbled corridors of the Foreign Office. Yet, so far as the public was concerned, Callaghan was the strong man who had got his way on the economy while George Brown had gone down to defeat. The public was unaware of Callaghan's equivocations in the midst of the crisis. Callaghan, on the other hand, felt cheated, not victorious. There was only one compensation – Callaghan's position in economic management was strengthened. A major obstacle to the rational conduct of economic policy had been removed.[117] Brown, for his part, was able to devote himself to his other cause, British membership of the EEC. But was British membership consistent with the present sterling parity? At a meeting at Chequers in October 1966 which decided on a new attempt to join the EEC, William Armstrong had warned that membership implied devaluation.[118] At the end of April 1967, he again warned Wilson that he would have to choose between incompatible objectives, the sterling parity and membership of the EEC.[119]

In his memoirs, Brown lists the DEA innovations that survived; the IRC, the Regional Planning Councils, the prices and incomes machinery.[120] But his real pride had been the National Plan. In the debate in the House on 27 July 1966, he even tried to pretend that it was still extant. Rhetorically he asked, 'How does this affect the National Plan? . . . It means that the rate of growth we intended to get, and were set to get, and on the basis of which we predicated all other things for 1970, is no longer available.'[121] He added, 'We go on with the Plan. In the light of this, we rewrite the figures and the timescale, but the check list of action of things to be done by industry, management, the unions and Government becomes more important than ever, not less important.'[122] In fact the National Plan and the DEA were both dead even though both were allowed to linger on, the DEA with decreasing influence on events, the National Plan forgotten and despised. The saddest moment in the career of a man who had brought to his work great energy and dedication, if not great wisdom, was when Brown tried to justify to the House nearly two years of failure. With great emphasis he cried, 'For almost two years now we have tried to manage the economy in a way that no economy has been managed before.'[123] The whole House dissolved in laughter.

DESCENT TO DEVALUATION

During the Labour Party Conference at the end of September 1966, it became necessary to activate the statutory provisions of the prices and incomes policy to deal with attempts by the trade union, ASSET, to undermine it. [124] Thereafter the wage freeze worked well though there was continual pressure from some trade unions for the government to reverse the effect of the deflationary July measures. Unemployment in the range of 450–500,000, or about 2 per cent, was considered much too high.[125] The government responded with a temporary increase in investment grants to 25 and 45 per cent, applicable only in 1967 and 1968, by a cut in Bank Rate by 1 per cent and by the announcement of an REP to assist employment in development areas.[126] However unemployment continued to rise and in the second half of 1967 reached 570,000 or about 2.3 per cent. The government, under pressure, started moving away from redeployment within months of announcing it as its policy. On 30 November 1966, the import surcharge was finally abolished. It had had some effect on the balance of payments but less probably than expected. As it was manifestly temporary, it gave industry no encouragement to invest to meet its increased opportunities in the British market. Importers had been prepared to absorb it, or some part of it, in order to maintain their share of the market. Once a date had been set for its disappearance, imports were delayed which helped to secure a deceptive surplus on visible trade in the last quarter of 1966.[127]

Thus, by the end of November 1966, Britain had not devalued and there was no import surcharge which had been adopted as an alternative.

The deficit for the year on current account was £61 million as compared with £393 million in 1965.[128] The balance of payments out-turn induced in the Cabinet, and even in the Chancellor, a certain complacency. Policy, evidently, was succeeding. Callaghan became, at least in his own mind, the skipper who had weathered the storm.[129] Apparently the government's view was that, by November 1966, nothing more was needed to restore equilibrium to the British economy other than the 'socialist' measures it had by then adopted and the harsh deflation of July 1966. There was discussion in Cabinet about relaxing the prices and incomes policy and increasing public expenditure. On 26 January Bank Rate was reduced from 7 to 6.5 per cent following a reduction in American interest rates. There was a further half per cent cut in March. By the end of March 1967, practically all central bank indebtedness had been repaid.[130] The Treasury was giving Callaghan cautiously optimistic forecasts of the balance of payments for 1967. The Bank shared the optimism. In his Budget speech on 11 April, Callaghan said, 'Taking everything together, the overall balance of payments should improve again substantially between 1966 and 1967. We should move from last year's deficit of £189 million to a surplus in 1967 as a whole, with an even bigger one in 1968.'[131] This was to be achieved together with a growth in total output of 'close to 3 per cent' in 1967 and in the medium term.[132] His Budget judgement was that he did not need to 'take any substantial action to influence demand just now'.[133] He concluded, 'We are back on course. The ship is picking up speed. The economy is moving. Every seaman knows the command at such a moment. "Steady as she goes".'[134] Callaghan and Wilson still believed in 'our sustained work in improving Britain's industrial structure'.[135]

On 17 April, Michael Stewart announced that the powers taken in the 1966 Prices and Incomes Act in support of the standstill and the six months of severe restraint, would not be renewed when they expired on 11 August 1967, but replaced by more limited powers providing for advance notification and temporary standstills where authorized by the National Board for Prices and Incomes (NBPI).[136] So, despite this major step back to a purely voluntary prices and incomes policy, and despite the deflationary measures of July 1966, the economy was to combine balance of payments surplus at the existing exchange rate with a reasonable rate of growth in both the short and medium term. The economic establishment did not regard this outlook as impossibly sanguine. Like the official Treasury, the Bank of England and their political masters, the economic establishment had made its forecasts and found that they were good. Bank Rate, already down to 6 per cent, was reduced to 5.5 per cent on 4 May. As late as June and July 1967, distress at the level of unemployment prompted reflationary actions of various kinds.[137] Why should a Chancellor repine when surrounded by so much expert optimism? They were the experts. He was just a politician reliant on experts.

In fact, whether or not Callaghan realized it, the Treasury was simply supplying him with an assessment of the balance of risks. It was a forecast with all the unreliability of economic forecasts. The debate before the Budget among officials and economic advisers within the Treasury illustrates the supreme difficulty of managing policy so close to the margin of safety. On the one hand the danger of a balance of payments crisis still existed and the possibility of devaluation was still being discussed. Public expenditure was increasing very rapidly, both absolutely and as a proportion of GDP. It had increased by one-sixth in real terms between 1963–4 and 1966–7. For this reason Kaldor advocated an increase in taxes. He believed the balance of payments to be a mirror-image of the borrowing requirement and that the prospective borrowing requirement was far too high.[138] On the other hand, the outlook appeared bright and it would be politically difficult both to show optimism and take measures that would increase unemployment.[139] In the Treasury there was talk of allowing the pound to float to a new level. It could now apparently be done from strength. But, with the prospect of a surplus in the balance of payments in 1967 and 1968, the idea was discarded.[140]

There was still too much emphasis on other countries' 'understanding' of British problems. In his Budget speech on 11 April, Callaghan, then Chairman of the Group of Ten major industrial countries, said: 'There is an increasing understanding of the responsibility of creditors, as well as debtors, to help in correcting imbalances in international trade and in financing them.'[141] In fact the creditor countries were becoming increasingly contemptuous of Britain's apparent inability to manage its own affairs. Under Callaghan's chairmanship, they agreed, in August 1967, to the creation, for the first time, of Special Drawing Rights (SDRs). It was, at best, a meagre contribution to the principle of creditors sharing responsibility for correcting imbalances.[142] In the view of the creditors, the principal responsibility for correcting imbalances lay with the debtors. But at least the government rejected an American idea that Britain should become an American mercenary and continue its role east of Suez in return for a large loan to fund the sterling balances.[143]

Britain was persisting at great cost in sustaining a parity that could not withstand any major shock. Despite favourable forecasts, the balance of payments and the exchange rate of sterling remained at the mercy of events. 1967 was a year of many events and sterling was a victim. Exports paused and imports recovered. In June there was the Six-Day War between Israel and Egypt which closed the Suez Canal for a time and put up British import costs. It was estimated that the balance of payments cost was £20 millions a month apart from the additional cost of oil with Middle East supplies cut off.[144] Even before this, visible trade had again fallen into deficit. With prospects for the balance of payments poor, with much advocacy of devaluation in the newspapers, and calls for Callaghan's replacement as Chancellor, Wilson, on 28 August 1967, suddenly announced that he was taking charge of economic policy. The electorate might have thought that he had been in charge throughout. If so, it would have been right. What the announcement meant in practice was that Wilson took nominal control of the DEA and the chairmanship of the Economic Committee of the Cabinet that went with it. Peter Shore, a close supporter of Wilson, entered the Cabinet as Secretary of State for Economic Affairs. Michael Stewart was left shorn with the title of First Secretary of State and responsibility, but not departmental responsibility, for social affairs. Wilson also took the opportunity to replace Douglas Jay as President of the Board of Trade by Tony Crosland. Jay had annoyed Wilson by preparing a paper estimating the balance of payments cost of joining the EEC at £500–750 million.[145] Wilson said that Ministers should retire at 60.

Such a shuffle could not have any influence on events even if Wilson had been inspired by new ideas which had previously escaped him. In fact his private lunchtime seminars with DEA Ministers were concerned more with the conspiracies which he believed his colleagues were devising against him than with economic policy.[146] The first fruit was a relaxation of hire purchase restrictions which ran directly contrary to economic rationality and the redeployment philosophy of July 1966.[147] The relaxation was opposed by both the Bank of England and, less wholeheartedly because of its 'understanding' of political realities, by the Treasury. The Bank and the Treasury feared the probable effect on sterling. But Ministers were scared at the level of unemployment and were demanding reflation. The will to avoid devaluation was evaporating. In September 1967, Commonwealth Finance Ministers were told, against all the evidence, that there would be an overall surplus of £100 million between mid-1967 and mid-1968.[148] For 1967 as a whole the overall balance of payments deficit would come in at £417 million. In the autumn there were dock strikes in Liverpool and London. At the beginning of October the European Commission, in a report on Britain's application for membership, implied a need to devalue sterling. On 19 October, Bank Rate was moved back up by half of one per cent to 6 per cent, but the market found the increase inadequate and reacted against sterling in the usual way, by selling it. On 25 October, the French Foreign Minister, Couve de Murville, indicated in a speech that he agreed with the Commission.[149] This French view was by no means outrageous. It appears to have been held by both Callaghan and Wilson as well as by the Governor of the Bank.[150] To those still wishing to maintain the exchange parity of sterling, and that still included both Callaghan and Wilson, it was unhelpful, however, that such views, with the authority of the French government, should become public. On the other hand, the Cabinet's newly acquired urge to enter the EEC could be interpreted by the market as an acceptance of the need for devaluation.[151]

A further rise in Bank Rate on 9 November, to 6.5 per cent, evoked from the market the same perverse reaction as had the earlier increase. Meanwhile minds were changing within government. It was one crisis too many. Callaghan could not but observe the continuing run on the reserves. On 2 November, Sir Alec Cairncross, the Head of the Government's Economic Service, let Callaghan know that, in his view, devaluation was inescapable. He had seen the latest forecasts for the balance of payments in 1967 and 1968 and knew that there was now no alternative. The forecasts showed deficits of the order of £500 million in both years. Callaghan says he was strongly influenced by this message. When he informed Wilson that the parity could no longer be held, he met no resistance. Wilson told him that if he thought all the alternatives to devaluation were unacceptable, he would accept his advice. Callaghan had concluded that the devaluation must be accompanied by a major deflation. On 13 November 1967, he told Crossman, 'the only point of devaluing would be the package we could lay down ... it will be a chance to teach the people of this country what a fool's paradise they've been living in'.[152] The people evidently deserved to be taught a lesson. Perhaps Callaghan thought they had let him down. But Wilson rejected any such Treasury doctrine. 'I warned [Callaghan] ... that, apart from certain inevitable measures to restrain home consumption, I should be opposed to a major lurch into deflation.' Wilson added that 'I favoured floating, rather than a cut to a lower fixed parity.'[153] The question now was whether a foreign loan could be obtained which would make possible a dignified exit from the $2.80 parity at a time of the government's own choosing.[154] But all that was available on acceptable conditions was a standby with which to defend a new parity.[155]

Such resistance as there was to a sterling devaluation came from France and the USA. When it came to the point, France opposed the devaluation but could not prevent it. The French franc did not, however, follow sterling down. The French government did devalue but some months later, one devaluation among many. Meanwhile de Gaulle's resentment at Britain's support during the war was further assuaged by his second veto, a week after the devaluation, of British membership of the EEC. Britain's loyalty to the USA could not withstand the pressure from the market or the depressing force of the balance of payments forecasts. The US Administration had to accept that sterling would go down and that the dollar would be even more exposed. The devaluation was supported by $3 billion of standby credits, $1.4 billion from the IMF and the rest from central banks. There was considerable complaint from developing countries that the IMF had not been tough enough in imposing conditions on the UK before granting its standby.

The Cabinet approved the decision to devalue to $2.40 on 16 November.[156] The decision had already in effect been taken by Wilson and Callaghan. Callaghan spoke of his anguish, but there was no alternative. Despite all postwar experience, and Wilson's declared preference, it was to be another fixed rate. Some members of the Cabinet expressed a preference for floating. In his memoirs, Jenkins expresses the view that it might have been better to float in November 1967.[157] But the Cabinet accepted, as Wilson had already done, 'our inability to float'.[158]

Immediately after the devaluation decision had been taken by the Cabinet, Callaghan had to cope with a Private Notice Question from Robert Sheldon who was Chairman of the Parliamentary Labour Party's backbench Economic Committee. Sheldon, a strong advocate of devaluation, had been worried by press reports that the parity would be held with the help of further international credits. Callaghan answered that MPs should not believe all they read. He expressed the hope that 'some of the speculators would get their fingers burned'.[159] Callaghan could not, without directly lying to the House, have avoided the impression that devaluation was imminent. The reserves flooded away while large profits were made by selling sterling at the $2.80 parity. The loss to the reserves between Callaghan's replies in the House on 16 November and the announcement of devaluation on 18 November has been calculated at about $1.5 billion.[160] It was not the speculators whose fingers were burned; they were betting on a virtual certainty. Sheldon could have been asked privately to withdraw the PNQ and would have been willing to do so.[161] Instead, the Cabinet sent the Chief Whip, John Silkin, to ask the Speaker, Horace King, not to allow the Question but the reports were certainly a matter of major public interest and the Speaker upheld the rights of the backbencher against the government. Both Sheldon and Callaghan did their duty as they saw it and the outcome was costly to the British economy.

Three years of fruitless struggle were over. Wilson in retrospect commented that 'The Middle East crisis of June 1967 was the biggest contributing factor to the devaluation which came five months later.'[162] Callaghan in retrospect reflected that while the unhelpful events of the summer and autumn of 1967 'were important in precipitating devaluation on Saturday 18 November 1967, they were not the basic cause of devaluation. The fundamental reason was that the world was not convinced that Britain could establish a long-term equilibrium in its balance of payments.'[163]

Having at last accepted the need to devalue, the Cabinet resisted the further deflationary package that devaluation had made essential, despite strong Treasury and Bank of England advocacy. Something was done, but it was quite inadequate to the purpose of exploiting to the full, and with the greatest rapidity, the opportunity created by devaluation. There was some increase in HP restrictions on motor cars, a ceiling was imposed on bank advances and Bank Rate was raised from 6.5 to 8 per cent. The best that could be done on public expenditure was to announce a cut of £400 million in the expected rate of growth and to remove, outside the development areas, the minor devaluation devices such as the export rebate and the SET premium to manufacturers that had provoked so much foreign hostility. There were to be cuts in nationalized industry capital expenditure. Corporation Tax was increased from 40 to 42.5 per cent so that companies should not make too much profit from devaluation.[164] No account was taken of the fact that by the same token some of the incentive to export was removed. This moment of economic opportunity was thus clouded over by political compromises.

It was also clouded over by a self-justifying broadcast by Wilson who ventured to comfort the electorate with the thought that the pound in its pocket had not been devalued to the same extent as the devaluation in the sterling rate. The sentence was adapted from a Treasury draft.[165]

But politicians, and especially politicians as experienced as Prime Ministers, are expected to foresee the pitfalls in the words they use. Wilson can legitimately claim that his words were misunderstood, that they were deliberately misinterpreted by the Opposition and by a hostile press. But even he admits that the tone of his broadcast was wrong, insufficiently apologetic for the defeat his government had undoubtedly suffered. He should not therefore have been too surprised at the misrepresentation by his enemies of his little attempt to be helpful to the folks back home who might have thought that 3 shillings in the £ had been knocked off their savings. For the Opposition it was a successful ploy, political capital was accumulated, and Wilson, unable to catch up with the misrepresentation, suffered seriously in his reputation. None of this was compensated for by what Wilson calls his 'hard-hitting attacks on those who had been selling Britain short'.[166] The foreign exchange dealers had been doing their job. The trouble was that Wilson had not been doing his.

Callaghan insisted on resigning as Chancellor as a matter of honour, exchanged jobs with Roy Jenkins, and went to the Home Office. Thereafter he opposed Barbara Castle's *In Place of Strife*, in Opposition he opposed entry into the EEC on the terms negotiated by Edward Heath, he returned to office as Foreign Secretary in 1974, re-negotiated in a minor degree the terms of entry and helped to carry the referendum of June 1975 in favour of remaining a member. In April 1976, on Wilson's resignation, he became Prime Minister. In terms of the offices he had held, he was the most experienced Prime Minister of the century. Even Churchill had never been Foreign Secretary. Callaghan had not, however, brought away with him happy memories of the Treasury. He was unlikely to accept Treasury forecasts as reliable nor would Treasury judgements carry his wholehearted confidence. The question was whether his unhappiness with the Treasury would deprive his Chancellor of the Exchequer of the support which only a Prime Minister can give and, without which, the tasks of a Chancellor become impossible.

TWELVE

Roy Jenkins: Mastery in Retrospect

OPPORTUNITY AND CHOICE

To take over the management of a business or an economy at a time of crisis is a great challenge. It can also be a great opportunity. It is an opportunity the more valuable when the path ahead is clear and all that is needed is the will to act swiftly and ruthlessly and to persist until the clouds lift. After the devaluation of November 1967, the road ahead for Britain was for once relatively uncontroversial. The situation demanded a combination of deflation and incomes control. The deflation was necessary to dampen domestic demand and release capacity for exports. The incomes control was necessary to ensure that the competitiveness acquired by devaluation was not squandered in inflation. Of course, such policies would not be uncontroversial in a Labour Cabinet where devaluation would be regarded as the soft option too long neglected. But the new Chancellor would have great power. He could not be removed. He could insist on having his way. His strongest incentive would be that, for him, it would be make or break. If he failed, he would destroy the government and the Party as well as his own reputation. But if he succeeded, if, despite the catastrophe of November 1967, he could win Labour another term of office, he would be heir presumptive, the saviour of his Party and his government. Indeed Wilson might well fear that a new and successful Chancellor could become the candidate of a *coup d'état* against the much weakened Prime Minister who had appointed him.

One buttress to Wilson's position was that he had a choice. There was no one Minister to whom the succession as Chancellor had unquestionably to go. The individual he selected might feel less secure and therefore more compliant because there had been other possibilities. He might even feel some gratitude to his Prime Minister for having given him the chance rather than some other qualified colleague. There were in the Cabinet at the time three youngish crown princes. None of them would, in the end, succeed to the crown which would, nine years later, pass to a man older than his predecessor, and from him would move preposterously on. But the three crown princes were all ambitious and all appeared to themselves and to others as *papabile*. The three were Healey, Crosland, and Jenkins. From these three, Wilson could make his choice. No one else in the Cabinet would be credible at such a moment. Healey's story was, in its way, the most remarkable. He had been accounted a most successful International Secretary to the Labour Party, a task to which he had come bearing the most lavish academic laurels as well as the reputation of having had a good war. He had been elected to Parliament in a by-election in 1952, some years after Jenkins and Crosland had first made it to the green benches of the House of Commons. He had been elected to the Shadow Cabinet while they were still delivering their learned sermons from the back-benches. As a member of the Shadow Cabinet he had been appointed to the real Cabinet as Secretary of State for Defence on the formation of the Labour government. The other two had had to wait for appropriate vacancies. At Defence he had discovered his ability as an administrator. He was expert in military strategy, which in the postwar world was too important to be left to the generals. He proved capable of debating on at least equal terms with the specialist strategic think tanks in the USA. As Secretary for Defence, Healey had one major problem. Britain was no longer a great power. He was forced to cut rather than to build Britain's military strength. As a potential Chancellor, he had other problems. Though a brilliant speaker outside the House of Commons, he was much less successful in the House. He had never built up a following in the Party, and he could not claim to be an economist. In other words he did not possess the particular academic qualification which fingered Crosland and Jenkins as the more likely aspirants. The relevance of the academic qualification to the tasks now ahead was debatable, but this was not considered an appropriate time to debate it.

Crosland and Jenkins both possessed the relevant qualification in economics, though it came from Oxford, a university whose reputation in this field fell well below that of Cambridge. Both Crosland and Jenkins could claim to have been right about devaluation, though this is not always the most persuasive argument for preferment among the majority who have been wrong. As an economist Crosland had a much greater claim than Jenkins. He had succeeded Robert Hall as Fellow in Economics at Trinity College, Oxford, when Hall left to be Director of the Economic Section. He was a real economist, not just a dilettante with an economics degree. If qualification in economics was to be the decisive criterion, Crosland had it. He also had the recommendation of Callaghan. His writings, particularly *The Future of Socialism*, had pointed the way for the younger generation of Labour intellectuals searching for a rationale for socialism in a world in which socialism appeared increasingly irrelevant. For the previous three months, he had been, as President of the Board of Trade, an economics Minister, one sufficiently expert or arrogant to make it clear to his Permanent Secretaries that he would not need advice on economic policy. As President of the Board of Trade, he had been a member of Wilson's Steering Committee on Economic Policy which Jenkins, as Home Secretary, had not. He had been called upon to open the debate on devaluation on 21 November 1967.

However, in political reputation, much to his own dismay, he had fallen well behind Jenkins. Almost anyone who might think of Crosland as leader would prefer Jenkins. Crosland had suffered from losing his seat at the 1955 General Election, not returning until 1959. Like Healey, Crosland was not good in the House. Unlike Healey, he was not even good in Cabinet. He might be right but he was not, in his manner, persuasive. As a departmental minister he suffered from an inability to measure his decision-making processes to the urgency of events. From Wilson's point of view, Crosland was also the candidate who would feel least grateful for his promotion because he would be confident that there really was no other sensible choice. Moreover while Wilson, in good Christian spirit, was prepared to forgive those who during the Gaitskellite years had been his critics, Crosland, who had been one of the severest critics, was a man who did not invite forgiveness and was acutely difficult to forgive. Though he would be deeply resentful at evident merit scandalously neglected, Crosland could hardly have a lower opinion of Wilson after being denied the Treasury than he had had before. After Gaitskell's death, Crosland had the status neither in the Party, the House, nor the Cabinet, to overcome the antipathy of Gaitskell's successor. To have argued for devaluation from the beginning was not enough.

Jenkins had been a highly successful Home Secretary in the eyes of social reformers. He was assured and authoritative in Cabinet. In the House, he was the most stylish, though not the most eloquent, Minister of his time. With the aid of well prepared speeches, he had won debating victories without number and had, when most needed, raised the morale of the troops on the backbenches. In Wilson's eyes he carried other strengths. Despite a lifestyle in which Wilson had no share, and would have desired no share, Jenkins did have his origins deep in the Labour movement. Jenkins's father, a miners' MP from Wales, had been Attlee's Parliamentary Private Secretary. Attlee had been Wilson's Prime Minister. Jenkins, biographer of Attlee, was in the apostolic succession. If, at this dire moment in the government's history, peace was to be made with the Gaitskellites, it would be through Jenkins rather than through Crosland. In moving from the Home Office, Jenkins would leave vacant a position sufficiently prestigious for Callaghan to fill without unacceptable loss of status. There would be no need for a general reshuffle so short a time after that of August 1967. Wilson's choice descended on Jenkins. When the deed was done, it seemed both obvious and right.

ON DIGGING HOLES

When Jenkins exchanged departments with Callaghan on 29 November 1967, three years had been wasted. Three years remained in the life of the Parliament and there was a Labour majority that could withstand the cost of many lost by-elections in the meantime. There was, therefore, time to recover from the defeat of devaluation. But there was not a great deal of time. No one could be sure how rapidly the economy would respond to the incentives created by devaluation and it was known that, due to the J curve phenomenon, the first effects would be adverse. Moreover it was a difficult world. The drive for the exports with which to reverse the balance of payments deficit could be blunted, and the move into surplus delayed, not just by lack of capacity in British industry but by the activity of foreign competitors, above all by the Germans who, despite their large payments surplus and their highly competitive exports, showed no sign of revaluing their currency further, at least until after their next General Election in September 1969. If the government was to survive the defeat of devaluation, and win the next General Election, the critical path to recovery allocated no room for delay.

The two years after devaluation demonstrate little of the mastery over economic management attributed to Jenkins in retrospect. They show him very dependent on advice, as dependent as any of his postwar predecessors. His memoirs are full of elegant apologies, none more self-critical than the failures justify. They also include a full ration of excuses. 'Whatever the reason, the one time in my ministerial career when I consider I was badly advised on major questions was in my first two or three months as Chancellor ... I arrived with a considerable respect for the smooth-working Treasury machine.'[1] He was not the only Chancellor whose expectations of Treasury expertise were to be disappointed. But although not a professional economist in the way Dalton, Gaitskell and Crosland could claim to be, he did possess an academic qualification in economics and he had, for many years in Opposition, been one of the leading Labour spokesmen on economic policy. Indeed, from time to time, the Tory government benches had found his arrogant assumption of superiority in economic debates more than they could bear. It was his reputation as an economist that had indicated him as Callaghan's successor. Treasury officials may have believed the encomia about their new Chancellor that they had read in the press and that he needed no advice. He may even, at the time, have believed them himself.

Some of Jenkins's excuses are surprising. The most surprising reads as follows:

> The Treasury's initial omission was that it never forcefully presented me with an urgent package of measures which would promote the diversion of resources into exports. Callaghan, it subsequently emerged, had been urged to put through such a programme immediately after devaluation, but had said (not unreasonably) that he was too much the used-up man for such an initiative. It ought manifestly to have been re-presented to me on almost my first day in my new office. It was not.[2]

We have already observed that the Armstrong Treasury was remarkably reticent in advising new Chancellors and, indeed, in restraining old Chancellors at election time. But did Jenkins really need to be advised by the Treasury that action was needed and urgent? He had been an advocate of devaluation at least since October 1964. He presumably knew the measures that must accompany devaluation if it was to yield its full benefits to the British economy. There was a political requirement for urgent action as well as an economic. The sense of crisis should have been used to revive popular readiness to accept painful measures. But the sense of crisis would rapidly dissipate if the government itself showed no urgency. Jenkins was still relatively little known outside political and literary circles. Immediate action was needed if he was to assert his authority in Cabinet and in the House of Commons. The fact that the reserves had been sadly depleted, following Callaghan's response to Sheldon's PNQ just before the devaluation, was another factor that would have been expected to push Jenkins into urgent action. Inadequate reserves added to the dangers of a further attack on sterling which might even lead to a further devaluation. In any case, as Shakespeare had put it in a rather different context, there is a tide in the affairs of man which, taken at the flood, leads on to fortune. It would be absurd, at a moment of such high drama, to permit the flood to recede. Many in the Parliamentary Labour Party felt this in their bones and some of them made representations to Jenkins in that sense.

Michael Foot raised a debate in the House on 5 December because he disliked the Letter of Intent despatched by Callaghan on 23 November to the IMF. Jenkins, in an exercise in open government, published Callaghan's Letter, thereby revealing the commitments into which the government had been forced to enter. It was the right step to take even though publication gave a handle to the government's left-wing critics. Foot thought that the Letter implied constraints on the government which were humiliating and which would force it into deflation. It was, he said, 'an ignominious letter which should never have been signed by a member of a British Cabinet, and should never have been despatched by a British Labour Government'.[3] Foot would live to be a member of a Cabinet which despatched an equally ignominious letter of intent to the IMF. Nevertheless, he was right so far as the ignominy is concerned. But such is the fate of governments that are forced to borrow from the IMF because they have failed to exercise their own sovereignty with prudence. British governments repeatedly argued unavailingly for terms which respected their sovereignty and importance in the world community. But the only way of avoiding such humiliations was to conduct economic policies that kept the country clear of IMF conditionality.

Jenkins responded to Foot in a way which may have been politically sensitive but was certainly economically flawed:

> As the export demand builds up, we have to make room for it in the economy. Some room has been made already, but almost certainly not enough, and this is intentional. We do not want to dig a hole and leave it empty. We want it to be there only when the export demand is ready to fill it, and we think that the Budget is likely to be about the right time for this further excavation.[4]

Jenkins now writes: 'This was nonsense, and rather dangerous nonsense. It implied that you could control the allocation of resources in an economy with the precision of air-traffic controllers allowing planes on to a glide path . . . I ought to have been shovelling earth out like mad from the moment of my appointment.' He says that his speech was seen by Treasury officials but that, so far as he can recall, they made no remonstrance.[5] But perhaps Treasury officials were looking to him, as Chancellor, to lay down policy.

DIGGING SHALLOW HOLES

There followed a long battle to secure Cabinet agreement to the cuts in public expenditure necessary in addition to those agreed at the time of the devaluation when Callaghan was still Chancellor. The battle illustrated once more how inappropriate a Cabinet consisting largely of spending Ministers is to the management of an economy, particularly an economy in crisis. Among Jenkins's problems was that, in seeking cuts in public expenditure, he lacked the support of his predecessor and of his friend and rival, Crosland.

In his memoirs, Callaghan says he had recommended Crosland for the succession not just because of his support for his candidature in the 1963 leadership election but because, in his view, Crosland understood what was required following the devaluation and how rapidly it was required. Crosland knew that devaluation was not a soft option. He believed that it must be followed by measures that the Party and the public would find unpleasant. He believed that they should be implemented within a week or two of the devaluation. That was also Callaghan's view but Wilson, Callaghan says, wanted to defer the cuts until the April Budget. 'This,' Callaghan says, 'was too late.'[6] In this retrospective judgement Callaghan is right. Crossman's diaries, supported by those of Castle and Benn, provide some evidence that this was not Callaghan's view once he had left the Treasury. On the contrary, instead of supporting the package of public expenditure cuts that he had advocated in his last days as Chancellor, and which Jenkins had, after an interval, brought forward, he had reverted to other priorities such as rebuilding his status in the Party by opposing his successor. Moreover, the same sources suggest that Crosland was a great deal less helpful than he should have been. Reasonably, perhaps, he demanded a general Treasury appreciation of why public expenditure cuts were necessary. When he got it, and this was already mid-January, his recommendation was for half the cuts that Jenkins was demanding. For Crosland to set his judgement against that of the Chancellor at such a moment of crisis, instead of giving him full backing, was typical of the man. Jenkins won that battle but there is no suggestion here of the kind of support a new Chancellor might have expected from his predecessor and from the most professional economist in the Cabinet.[7]

The public expenditure cuts were announced by Wilson on 16 January 1968 when the House reassembled after the Christmas recess. Nothing was done about public expenditure in 1967–8, which was allowed to increase by 12.8 per cent. No doubt it was considered too late to take action but the increase throws a sad light on the supposed attempts previously made to avoid devaluation. The 1968–9 Estimates were reduced by £300 million and those for 1969–70 by £416 million.[8] The largest reductions were in defence, including in Britain's commitments east of Suez. Britain's frontiers were no longer to be, as Wilson had once claimed, on the Himalayas. The saddest casualty was the intended rise in the school leaving age to 16, deferred from 1971 to 1973. The decision most controversial within the Parliamentary Labour Party was the reintroduction of prescription charges. The PLP enjoyed its emotional spasm and then submitted. It was already two months after the devaluation.

In addition to cuts in public expenditure, there was the need to cut domestic consumption. William Armstrong and Sir Leslie O'Brien, Governor of the Bank, recommended that Jenkins should use Selwyn Lloyd's regulator for that purpose. But, according to Jenkins, they made their recommendation 'not at all strongly' and nothing was done. How strongly would Armstrong and O'Brien have needed to make their recommendation to extract action from their Chancellor? Jenkins then had the idea of bringing forward the Budget to February so that the public expenditure cuts and the increases in taxation intended to reduce consumption could be announced at the same time. Armstrong advised strongly against this. It would mean making the Budget statement without benefit of the short-term economic forecast due at the end of February. 'Such a course would be irresponsible.' This was strong language in contrast to the recommendation about the regulator. The short-term forecast, Jenkins says, proved totally useless. Presumably, as an economist, he knew what value can be placed on short-term, or any, economic forecasts, more particularly when the currency has just been devalued. He also knew that he was being advised by a Permanent Secretary who had signally failed his predecessor. But Jenkins accepted this advice which, thirty years later, he condemns as being 'as wrong as it was well intentioned'.[9] The government would now take two bites at the cherry; one, in January, the cuts in public expenditure, and the other, in March, the tax increases. The Budget statement was not made until 19 March, four months after the devaluation. The separation of the two statements, and the further delay before the Budget, was damaging to the credibility of the government's economic management. The market was left for months ignorant of the government's total post-devaluation posture. Its hostile reaction should have been foreseen but was not.

GEORGE BROWN DEPARTS IN ANGER

In the first few months after devaluation, the government drifted. Wilson had been devalued along with sterling and Jenkins had not exerted his own authority. It was because he did not take immediate strong control over economic policy that Jenkins, in the early hours of Friday 15 March 1968, shortly before his first Budget, found himself embroiled with George Brown, and other members of the Cabinet, including Tony Crosland, in an episode extraordinary even by the standards of the Wilson governments. Sterling had remained under pressure since devaluation while an exasperated market awaited the appropriate measures which it had been promised. There was considerable danger of a further forced devaluation. Nor, at this time, was sterling the lone target of the speculators. With the USA's Vietnam war being funded by borrowing, and France threatening to convert its dollars into gold, there was foreboding that even the dollar might be forced to devalue against gold. As ever, the fortunes of sterling became a by-product of those of the dollar. Both sterling and the dollar were in peril, sterling doubly so as a reflection of the dollar's problems as well as its own. The sterling area foreign currency reserves, already depleted by the events preceding devaluation, were suffering further huge losses in the attempt to keep sterling at the new level of $2.40.

It was in these circumstances that, late on Thursday 14 March, President Johnson requested that the London gold market, the principal market in which gold was traded, should be temporarily closed. With sterling on the brink, Jenkins decided, on advice, to exploit the opportunity given by Johnson's request to close the foreign exchange market also. Wilson agreed. An attempt had been made to find the Foreign Secretary, George Brown, so that he could be associated with the decision but he could not be located and perhaps the attempt was too perfunctory. Brown could not be relied upon to be helpful, particularly as the Thursday evening wore on. To close the foreign exchange market needed an Order in Council. An emergency meeting of the Privy Council was held at Buckingham Palace just after midnight on Friday March 15. It was attended by Wilson and Jenkins, with Peter Shore conscripted at the last minute to make up the numbers.

It so happened that the House of Commons was sitting late. Cabinet Ministers were lingering around the Palace of Westminster against the possibility of a vote, no doubt too tired to attend to their own departmental problems and therefore open to suggestions of alternative sources of excitement. Brown had now been discovered and was told about the late-night meeting of the Privy Council by Wilson's Principal Private Secretary. In what he was told Brown found one more piece of evidence of Wilson's dictatorial style of government. But the main problem with Wilson's style of government was not the way he took decisions but the decisions he took. In this case he had taken the only possible decision. Brown was particularly affronted by the presence at the Privy Council of Peter Shore whom he regarded simply as a Wilson stooge.

Brown gathered around him in his room at the Commons a bevy of Cabinet ministers, all of them very ready to feel themselves affronted by the lack of consultation. He then phoned Wilson to demand his attendance. So enfeebled was Wilson in spirit and reputation that he almost obeyed the summons from his deputy. After further consideration of the proprieties, Wilson told Brown that he would receive the claque of Ministers in the Cabinet room at No. 10. They arrived. Jenkins explained the night's events but was not able to prevent a shouting match between Wilson and Brown with a 'glowering' Crosland lending Brown his support. The shouting match ended with Brown announcing his resignation which, for once, proved to be final. A Prime Minister with any authority would have given his colleagues some instruction in the facts of life. Economic management requires that, in an emergency, the Prime Minister and the Chancellor should take decisions, and Wilson should have made that clear instead of trembling incoherently under the impact of Brown's abuse. The idea that the whole Cabinet must be involved is nonsense. Fortunately for the government, the temporary closing of the foreign exchange market allowed time to secure a standby credit from the USA which, though as usual less than requested, did help to preserve the sterling parity. And authority over economic policy was at long last about to be reasserted through Jenkins's first Budget.

The lack of urgency in Jenkins's conduct of affairs was made possible by the decision in November 1967 to devalue to a fixed rate rather than to float. Jenkins himself now suggests that it might have been better in November 1967 to float.[10] The Bretton Woods system was dying, undermined by American policy, but Britain's continued loyalty to it, expressed by the devaluation to a fixed rate, may have helped the government to secure standby credits from the IMF and the US government. The standby credits funded the delays. If sterling had been allowed to float, there could have been no delay in taking the necessary associated measures. The announcement of major cuts in public expenditure and major increases in taxation would have had to be simultaneous with the decision to float. Such drastic action would have been essential if the market and the holders of the sterling balances were to be given any confidence in the floating currency. Credits would still have been necessary and would have been available provided the necessary domestic measures were urgently taken. Thus a decision to float would not just have been the better option. It would have enforced urgency.

When Jenkins did at last introduce his Budget, he added £923 million to taxation in a full year, double the imposts ever before imposed in a single Budget, even in wartime. That such an amount of additional taxation had to be imposed in order to deflect resources into exports was a reflection of the increase in public expenditure under the Wilson government. Despite the cuts in public expenditure estimates that were being made, public expenditure as a proportion of gross domestic product would rise from 44 per cent in 1964 to about 50 per cent in 1970. The Budget speech itself was a masterpiece. Never has pain been inflicted with greater elegance. There has been no finer Budget speech since the war. Politically, it was a triumph, and to achieve a triumph in such circumstances demanded all the literary capacity that Jenkins had displayed as a biographer. Unfortunately the Budget was too late – the delay carried with it a huge political and economic cost.

AN ANXIOUS YEAR

The 1968 Budget was not simply too late; it also proved to be too little. The size of the tax increase, and of the previous cuts in public expenditure estimates, were evidence of the previous incoherence of economic management. Yet Jenkins's action to date, though massive by previous standards, proved insufficient to achieve the necessary diversion of resources into exports. There was further delay in bringing domestic credit, in which there was a large expansion in 1967 and 1968, under control.[11] That expansion too was fuelling domestic consumption and inhibiting the transfer of resources into exports. 1968 continued as a miserable year for the Chancellor. During 1968, over £1400 million had to be found to hold the parity.[12] The hoped-for movement into surplus on the balance of payments had been delayed by the various delays in the government's measures. The Chancellor could never be sure when the next burst of speculation against sterling would occur or what would trigger it. The international economic environment was an important element in his problems; but then the international economic environment was an inescapable element in any Chancellor's panorama. With help from central banks, the enduring problem of the sterling balances was mishandled through the so-called Basle Agreement of July 1968. Holders of the sterling balances were guaranteed the dollar value of their holdings while still earning the interest rates necessitated by the continuing vulnerability of sterling. It was an expensive agreement, initially for three years, extendable to five. It led to a substantial increase in the size of the sterling balances, and had an effect directly opposite to that intended by those, including Jenkins, who believed that the balances should in some way be phased out.

Speculation against sterling was now more likely to derive from rumours about prospects for other currencies than from movements in the sterling balances. In November 1968, the strength of the Deutsch-mark (DM), resulting from the large German trade surplus, led the German government to summon a conference of Finance Ministers in Bonn to consider how to mitigate the effect on other currencies. Sterling was once more under pressure. In addition, there was speculation against the French franc caused by an expectation that it would be devalued. If the French franc went, could sterling be far behind? Yet the German government, in summoning the conference, denied any intention of revaluing its currency, regarded in Britain as the natural, cooperative, curative, action. The German government still had an election to fight. Winning it was its first priority, the effect of its policies on other currencies an entirely secondary anxiety. Before the Bonn conference, Wilson and Jenkins summoned the German Ambassador and conveyed to him the British government's demand that the DM should be revalued. Wilson used undiplomatic language. The behaviour of the German government was 'irresponsible' and 'intolerable'. Jenkins, in support, told the Ambassador that 'If your refusal to revalue forces us to let the pound float down, as it may well do, we could not in these circumstances afford anything like the present level of military expenditure in Germany.'[13] Under the distressing impact of yet one more sterling crisis it was perhaps forgotten among Ministers in Whitehall that British troops were in Germany to defend the UK and not just the host country, and that the Germans might believe that the strength of their currency, far from being an offence against humanity, was a reflection of solid German merit and that there was no reason to accept instructions from the feckless British or their profligate government.

There being little expectation that threats or advice would exert any influence on the self-confident Germans, Wilson and Jenkins took decisions, pending the Bonn conference, to use Selwyn Lloyd's regulator and to introduce import deposits.[14] The conference in Bonn brought no effective action by the German government to repel the flow of reserves and other funds into DMs other than a border tax adjustment which was claimed to give other countries a 4 per cent competitive advantage as against Germany. On his return from the conference on 22 November, the Chancellor, admitting that 'the speed of our movement into balance of payments surplus has been insufficient', announced the package of measures. It comprised the use of the regulator at a level of 10 per cent, thereby adding about £250 million to revenue in a full year, and, at last, a tightening in domestic credit through the imposition of a ceiling on bank lending. The tightening in domestic credit was assisted by the introduction of the scheme of import deposits covering about one-third of UK imports which was to last no longer than one year but the cost of which to importers was meanwhile to be accommodated within the new bank ceilings.[15] Following these measures, domestic credit contracted by about £200 million in 1969 compared with an expansion of about £1,900 million in 1968.[16] On 22 February 1969, Bank Rate had to be raised to 8 per cent where it stood until reduced to 7 per cent in the 1970 Budget. To make assurance doubly sure, Jenkins, in his 1969 Budget, added a further £340 million to taxation in a full year. As a result, the government accounts as well as the balance of payments moved into substantial surplus.[17] There were still flurries against sterling, some of them serious, as in May and August 1969. But Britain was at last firmly on the road to balance of payments surplus. British competitiveness temporarily owed something to President de Gaulle who surprised the currency markets by refusing to devalue the franc. With the aid of an international support operation, it retained its parity until August 1969, by which time de Gaulle had resigned. Of more permanent benefit to British competitiveness was that the Germans, when there could no longer be political embarrassment after the Federal Elections of September 1969, allowed the DM to float upwards.

The DM exchange rate was eventually fixed at a level representing an appreciation of 8.5 per cent. In 1969 Britain achieved a balance of payments surplus of about £400 million. The statistics, though not the reality, were improved by a discovery by Board of Trade statisticians that, for some years, there had been a significant under-recording of exports.

THE END OF THE DEA

One achievement of the Jenkins era was the abolition in 1969 of the DEA. Created by Wilson, it was abolished by Wilson, but it had not been Wilson's first thought to abolish it. In the spring of 1968 he thought rather of refreshing it with Barbara Castle as First Secretary and Secretary of State for Economic Affairs. Perhaps he saw the move to the DEA of such an effective and loyal Minister as Barbara Castle as one way of controlling the power of his new Chancellor, whose reputation had just been enhanced by his highly successful Budget statement. Wilson may also have seen the need for an effective Minister in charge of prices and incomes policy which remained within the remit of the DEA. Roy Jenkins objected strongly. He was right to do so. He writes that 'there could be no question of my allowing such a strong minister to reactivate the Department of Economic Affairs. A large part of the troubles of the first three years of the Government had arisen from the split of economic responsibility between Callaghan and Brown . . .'[18] Instead, in April 1968, Barbara Castle was moved to the newly baptized Department of Employment and Productivity, formerly known as the Ministry of Labour, taking with her prices and incomes policy from the DEA, which was thereby further diminished in influence pending its final dissolution in 1969. To emphasize her role she was not merely Secretary of State but was also gifted with the great title of First Secretary, which George Brown had sported. With her responsibility for prices and incomes policy, Barbara Castle was bound to exert great influence over economic policy because inflation had become the greatest danger to the government's success. But while she had influence, and a cooperative relationship between Jenkins and Castle was necessarily of the first importance, she did not have the roving brief that George Brown had allocated to himself. She could not scrutinize and interfere with every aspect of Treasury policy, except of course in so far as the practice of Cabinet government gave such rights to all its members.

Wilson's original wish to appoint Barbara Castle to the DEA, and Jenkins's objection to her taking up residence there, does suggest one idle speculation. Castle was a strong Minister, and a brave one. When she saw what was right she fought for it, as Jenkins says, obsessively.[19] She and Denis Healey were probably the most effective Cabinet Ministers in Wilson's 1960s governments. The idle speculation is whether the country and the government would not have been better off with Castle, not at the DEA but at the Treasury. When King George II was warned that General James Wolfe was 'mad', he replied that he wished Wolfe would bite some of his other generals. This country in 1967 needed an 'obsessive' Chancellor. It would have been necessary for the Treasury to ensure that she was obsessed with the need not to waste the devaluation but, once obsessed, there would have been no dallying. The market might not, at first, have liked the appointment of a Minister, however effective, who was accounted so left-wing. It would soon have learnt that Barbara Castle was not a Minister who allowed her label to influence her dedication to what she became persuaded was right. Politics more than the market would have prevented such an appointment. Callaghan would not have been the only colleague to be outraged. Wilson had had a choice as to who should be Chancellor but the choice almost certainly did not include Barbara Castle.

'IN PLACE OF STRIFE'

There is always a risk that the additional competitiveness achieved by devaluation will be squandered in higher inflation. In May 1968, a new Prices and Incomes Bill was introduced which continued, and to some degree extended, existing powers over prices and incomes. The powers in Part IV of the 1966 Act which had imposed the six months' freeze had expired in August 1967. The Bill met the anticipated opposition from the Labour Party's left wing, and from many trade unionists, but was enacted. The question remained whether this was enough. During 1968 there was a deterioration in the country's already poor strike record provoked by the effect of devaluation on standards of living. But then devaluation works, if at all, because it reduces standards of living. In the previous five years, days lost in strikes had never reached 3 million. In the first 8 months of 1968, 3.5 million days were lost.[20] Trade union independence of legal regulation had become a scandal, and there was no protection against unofficial strikes and inter-union disputes.

Britain's poor economic performance was attributed to the irresponsible conduct of trade unions or of their members. A Royal Commission under Lord Donovan had been asked to report and, in June 1968, made recommendations widely felt to come nowhere near addressing the problem. Wilson decided to confront the issue of trade union reform. With Barbara Castle now at Employment, he could have confidence that she would not be deflected by the traditional obeisances of the Ministry of Labour to the trade union movement. At the end of 1968, Castle produced a draft White Paper which she called *In Place of Strife*. It included proposals for pre-strike ballots, for a 28-day conciliation pause before strikes could begin, and for penalties if the rules were broken.

On 15 December 1968, Wilson, Castle and Jenkins, and a small group of trade union leaders including Frank Cousins of the TGWU, Jack Cooper of the General and Municipal Workers, and Alf Allen of the shopworkers, spent the night at Chequers.[21] There was an informal gathering after dinner around the library fire to discuss the government's ideas about which rumours were already circulating. Advocacy was left to Wilson and Castle. Jenkins soon went to sleep and then departed to bed leaving Wilson and Castle to continue the argument. All the trade union leaders present, except for Cooper, strongly opposed the proposals. It was therefore well known, before battle commenced in public, that strong trade union opposition was inevitable and Jenkins had been awake long enough to sense the strength of the opposition the proposals would arouse. Indeed, that would have been apparent even without the meeting at Chequers. The Cabinet reluctantly agreed to the publication of *In Place of Strife* on 17 January 1969 and then the storm broke. The trade unions bitterly opposed the penal powers proposed in the White Paper, the Cabinet was split, Labour MPs, many of them sponsored by trade unions, indicated that they would refuse to support penal legislation based on the White Paper.

It could be argued that the blame so widely attached to the trade unions for Britain's economic decline was unjustified, that trade unions were irrelevant to the problem of inflation, which was the inevitable result principally of over-full employment. There could be a suspicion that the subject was being appropriated by Wilson not for any good reason of economic management but in order to trump the ideas for trade union reform of the Opposition leader, Edward Heath, and because it would provide a good cry in the coming General Election if Labour were seen as sufficiently independent of the trade unions to undertake their reform against their will. It could also be argued persuasively that penal sanctions provided no answer to unofficial strikes, would be unenforceable against workers and trade union officials, and, indeed, could make matters worse rather than better. Such arguments had convinced the majority of the Donovan Commission. That was not, however, the view taken by Roy Jenkins, the Chancellor of the Exchequer. Wilson and Castle knew that in promoting *In Place of Strife* they had the strong support of the Chancellor. Given the high reputation of the Chancellor with public opinion and his unassailable position within the Cabinet, Jenkins's support was a very strong card in their hands provided, of course, that it could be played. They had no reason to think that his devotion to the cause of trade union reform was any weaker than theirs.

It was Jenkins who suggested that, in order to deny the opposition to *In Place of Strife* time to rally its troops, a short Bill should be rushed through the House of Commons without delay, even though such a Bill would be bound to emphasize the penal elements in Castle's proposals. In his Budget statement of 15 April 1969, Jenkins announced, with the assent of the whole Cabinet, that the statutory powers over incomes taken in the 1968 Act, which had been scarcely used, would be abandoned when they expired at the end of 1969 but that legislation based on *In Place of Strife* would be introduced in the current session of Parliament.[22] 'I thought,' he writes, 'that this was a good bargain.'[23] It was naive to expect any return from the trade union movement from concessions made to it unilaterally by the government. At the 1968 Labour Party conference, Frank Cousins had called for the repeal of all incomes legislation. His motion had been passed by a majority of 5 to 1. Jenkins's concession was not seen by the trade unions as part of a bargain but as a payment of what was due. However, the fact that Jenkins regarded it as part of a bargain, and included it in his Budget statement, confirms the importance he, as well as Wilson, attached to the Bill. Wilson defined its significance in a speech to the Parliamentary Labour Party on 17 April 1969. It was, he said:

> an essential Bill. Essential to our economic recovery. Essential to the balance of payments. Essential to full employment. It is an essential component of ensuring the economic success of the Government. It is on that economic success that the recovery of the nation, led by the Labour Government, depends. That is why I have to tell you that the passage of this Bill is essential to its continuance in office.[24]

There could hardly be stronger language or a clearer statement of the Bill's key role in economic recovery and the survival of the government as perceived by all its advocates. But strong words from Wilson had, by 1969, lost much of their force. Opposition from the trade union movement, opposition within the Parliamentary Labour Party, and defections within the Cabinet sapped his determination. It began to appear that Tory support or abstention would be necessary to enact the legislation and, in the British two-Party system, dependence on the Opposition is regarded as extremely reprehensible by zealots. The critical defection was that of Roy Jenkins. It was Jenkins's failure to give strong support to Wilson and Castle in Cabinet when the situation became critical, and his eventual defection from their side, that propelled Wilson into capitulation. In his memoirs Jenkins says, 'Wilson behaved with a touch of King Lear-like nobility. He sounded fairly unhinged at times and there was a wild outpouring of words. But he did not hedge and he did not whine . . . It was a sad story from which he and Barbara Castle emerged with more credit than the rest of us.'[25] Ziegler describes this apologia as exhibiting 'characteristic generosity'.[26] The question for the historian is whether it was also characteristic in other ways. There is a method of making an apology that incorporates its own excuses. This is a splendid example of the genre. Wilson was 'King Lear-like', 'fairly unhinged at times', pouring out 'wild words'. Of course such a man must be deserted when the battle grows hot. No one after this episode should underestimate the political flexibility of Roy Jenkins. He may not have fought very hard for the cause he had embraced but, if he deserted, at least he was the last man to desert. Perhaps the memory of the incident made him fight harder later for other causes.

In the end Wilson submitted to a humiliating compromise with the TUC. By way of excuse, he recalled his repeated pleas to the TUC to produce adequate alternative proposals. At last, he claimed, adequate alternative proposals were being advanced. The TUC gave a 'solemn and binding' undertaking intended to limit unofficial strikes. Thereby was created a new and ludicrous public personality known as Mr Solomon Binding whose fame, fanned by the media, vied with that of the Prime Minister himself. His activities, however, such as they were, did not appear to redound to the credit of the government of the day. Friendly voices claim that the TUC honoured its undertaking. But, in the view of one splendidly equipped to judge, adequate alternative proposals were never in fact produced. Callaghan had been one of the leading opponents of *In Place of Strife* within the Cabinet. It is Callaghan who, in his memoirs, blames the trade unions for failing, despite the warning they had been given by Barbara Castle's *In Place of Strife*, 'to make their own programme of reforms effective'.[27]

More important than Callaghan's retrospective judgement was the contemporary influence of these events on the electorate. So far as the electorate was concerned, the main impact of the abandonment of *In Place of Strife* lay in the confirmation that a Labour government could not take a view of the public interest on any matter relating to the trade unions if it was opposed by the trade unions. Whatever benefit could have been expected from the enactment of the White Paper proposals, their withdrawal was seriously damaging, certainly politically, probably economically. The economic problem lay in the green light the government's capitulation flashed to the trade union movement. Some of the less responsible elements in the trade unions now knew that in the run-up to the election, anything would go by way of wage claims. There had been little acceleration in inflation in 1968–9 following the devaluation; after the capitulation to the TUC, the situation worsened dramatically.

Both Callaghan and Jenkins appear to have speculated whether this was not a good time to get rid of the Prime Minister and then to have concluded that, even if there was success in deposing Wilson, it might well be the other who emerged as the beneficiary. In any case it was not open to Jenkins to conspire against the Prime Minister when allied with him on the issue on which the intended victim was supposed to be fighting for his political life. It does not appear, however, that all the Jenkinsites were prepared to deny themselves any opportunity to enthrone their hero. The threat to the Prime Minister seemed real in the frenetic atmosphere of Westminster. The trade union leaders, whatever their disagreements about *In Place of Strife*, certainly did not want to dispossess Wilson in favour of Jenkins or, quite as bad, Edward Heath. In truth, Wilson had the job as long as he wanted it, and there was a Labour majority in the House of Commons.

THE 1970 BUDGET

In his Budget statement of 14 April 1970, Jenkins summarized the achievements of his two and a half years at the Treasury. The accounts of the public sector had been transformed. A borrowing requirement of £1,956 million in 1967–8 had been transformed into a surplus of about £600 million in 1969–70. This was a turnaround in the public sector accounts of about £2,550 million.[28] Considering how little damage had been done by this transformation, the implication must be that if only earlier Chancellors, under less compulsion, had done as much the damage would have been even less and the effect on the British economy wholly salutary, especially if their action had been accompanied by the floating of sterling.

Comparing the middle two quarters of 1967 (selected to avoid the distorting effects of the dock strikes later in that year) with the last two quarters of 1969, the national product had grown by about 6.25 per cent, but exports of goods and services in volume terms, assisted by an abnormally rapid growth in world trade, by 24 per cent. This was twice the growth of manufacturing production which rose by 11 per cent and nearly two and a half times the growth in imports of goods and services which rose in real terms by about 10 per cent.[29]

Personal consumption, on the other hand, had increased during the period by less than 4 per cent, a fact that would have unfortunate electoral consequences for the government.[30] Personal consumption had suffered from the transfer of resources into exports. But the result was that, as Jenkins was speaking, 'the British balance of payments . . . is one of the strongest in the world'. Final figures for 1969–70 were not yet available but 'it is unlikely that the surplus [in the balance of payments] was less than £550 million, and it may have been considerably larger'.[31] The current account in 1969 had been in surplus to the extent of £366 million.[32]

Short- and medium-term debt, in other words the assistance received from the IMF, from central banks, and from some other institutions such as the Bank for International Settlements, had reached a peak at the end of 1968. The total then had been $8,071 million, or £3,363 million, while the reserves at the same date had been only £1,009 million. In the subsequent 15 months the debt had been reduced by £1,829 million which included an allocation of £171 million of SDRs. Thus the short- and medium-term debt had been reduced from over $8 billion to under $4 billion. 'What is left is clearly manageable . . . but we shall continue to need a strong balance of payments . . . and . . . we shall continue to need, over the years ahead, to build up our reserves, which are still low by comparison with other major industrial countries.'[33] What was left of debt may have been manageable, but it was also very large.

Jenkins then gave a very relevant warning. 'If serious inflation gets a grip it will be very difficult to shake it off ... Everyone concerned with wage settlements should understand that if we are to achieve the reasonable stability of prices which is necessary for a sound economy and a healthy social framework, incomes cannot for long continue to rise at their recent rate.'[34] Wage settlements had averaged 12 per cent by the late winter of 1969–70 as the result of a policy described by Brittan as 'all-round appeasement'.[35] The margin of competitiveness won by the devaluation was making it easier for employers to concede the demands. Jenkins was severely criticized by the shadow Chancellor, Iain Macleod, for insufficient emphasis on the problem of inflation in a speech devoted largely to self-congratulation.

Jenkins's Budget judgement led to fiscal changes which would cost the revenue only about £200 million in a full year.[36] In retrospect Jenkins comments that his 1970 Budget 'was more restrictive than perfect economic foresight would have made it'.[37] This is a judgement with which his Chief Economic Adviser, Sir Donald MacDougall, agrees. 'Jenkins settled for a mildly reflationary Budget whereas we should have had a more expansionary one.'[38] In a speech in the House in 1972, Jenkins went even further, arguing that 'with the benefit of perfect foresight ... it would have been right to start reflation in the autumn of 1969'.[39] But, given that earnings were increasing at 10–15 per cent per annum and prices at 7–8 per cent per annum, it would have been folly, whatever Jenkins and MacDougall now say, to have given a greater fiscal stimulus.[40] Wage settlements were already providing too great a stimulus. The fault in Jenkins's 1970 Budget is not that it gave too little away but that it gave too much.

Jenkins has been awarded both great credit and great blame for not introducing an electioneering Budget. His cautious 1970 Budget led to accusations that he lost Labour the General Election that followed two months later. Jenkins's worldly reputation has certainly not suffered from such criticism. A Chancellor who could ignore political pressures is regarded as a rare and precious being, to be admired not crucified. Any justification in the accusation that Jenkins lost Labour the 1970 General Election lies not in the relative austerity of his pre-election Budget but in his delays in taking action after the devaluation, and in his defection over *In Place of Strife*, so that Labour faced the election at a time of rapidly rising prices when even the widely acclaimed balance of payments surplus had only recently been acquired and still appeared precarious.

The achievement of a surplus in the balance of payments in 1970 was accounted a great triumph. The triumph was magnified by the anxiety that had preceded it. Labour's publicity raised Jenkins to heroic status. An attempt was made to milk the credit prematurely by calling a General Election in June 1970. Wilson could certainly have delayed the election until October, rather nearer the legal limit to the Parliament's life, and the fact that he did not may have aroused suspicion in a sceptical electorate. Cromer, long gone from the Bank of England, won his revenge for his earlier confrontations with Wilson, and ensured for himself employment under the new government, by proclaiming on television that there was 'no question that any government that comes into power is going to find a very much more difficult financial situation than the new government found in 1964'. During the last week of the election campaign, the triumph with the balance of payments was tarnished by one month's bad trade figures attributable to the import of some large aircraft. In any event, the electorate at the 1970 election was less impressed by the balance of payments surplus than by rising prices. Triumph turned to disaster and Edward Heath was returned as Prime Minister with a majority of about 30.

Jenkins was Chancellor for a relatively short period. His training in economics does not appear to have furnished him with insights or with options additional to those which any Chancellor, however trained, would have had in his place. He was heavily dependent on Treasury and Bank of England advice, which was not always as good as it could have been. His delay in taking action after the devaluation cost his Party, and even his country, dear. In the end, rather late, he found the right direction, but any Chancellor would have had to do what he did, though probably no other Chancellor would have done it with such élan. His achievement with the balance of payments became the foundation of Labour's claim for a further period of office. Yet the political and economic damage done by the abandonment of *In Place of Strife* more than cancelled out the political benefits of the balance of payments surplus. He was fortunate in the timing of his Chancellorship and fortunate also in being deprived of the responsibility for handling the subsequent inflation. We cannot know whether in that he would have had greater success than the Heath government had he remained at the Treasury. He had not had any success in that respect by the time he left office. It is to Jenkins's credit that, as Chancellor, he conducted himself with style, thus boosting morale in his Party at a time when, inevitably, it had sunk very low. The result was that he left the Treasury with an unsullied reputation, an experience rare enough for Chancellors in the postwar era. But he left the Treasury not, as he had hoped, for the relaxing *longueurs* of Foreign Office briefs, but for Opposition, and he certainly shared the blame.

After his defeat in the 1970 election Wilson claimed that 'No incoming Prime Minister . . . in living memory has taken over a stronger economic situation.'[41] It was not a very great claim. No postwar Prime Minister has had the good fortune to take over a strong economic situation. Edward Heath certainly did not have that good fortune. As the mishandling of economic management is to some degree inevitable due to lack both of information and of understanding of economic processes, one of the tests of a nation's economic strength is how much mishandling its economy will take without disaster. Despite the achievements of the years after the 1967 devaluation, it would not have taken much mishandling by the Heath government to generate a crisis worse even than that inherited by Wilson in 1964. But the Heath government was not to be content with minor mishandling of the British economy.

SUMMARY OF AN EPOCH

Those seeking to defend economic policy during the decade and a half since Butler can point to successes. There was growth, slightly higher in the 1960s than in the 1950s but certainly in both decades higher than pre-war and in the succeeding decade. The standard of living rose markedly. The level of unemployment, though a continual anxiety, was low, indeed very low as compared with pre-war and the succeeding decades. Inflation, though too high and gradually depriving the UK economy of competitiveness, was very low as compared with the 1970s and 1980s. It remains true that the UK's economic performance was poor by the standard of its major industrial competitors, whether in Europe or the Far East; that Britain was being surpassed in standard of living by European countries that had lagged behind it for at least two centuries; that it was losing market share; and that its continual troubles with the balance of payments and the exchange rate were humiliating, depriving it of influence in international economic affairs, attracting the despair of friends and the *Schadenfreude* of critics. All this was happening at a time when government involvement in the economy was deeper than ever before. Economic processes are little understood and it is impossible to say what would have happened if there had been more concern with inflation, if governments had not run scared whenever

unemployment threatened to pass 2 per cent, if, in other words, governments had been prepared to draw back from the precipice along the
edge of which they attempted to navigate the economy. It is at any rate
possible, if not probable, that if there had been the leadership to sur-
mount the short-term political problems which such an approach would
have created, Britain would have been a much more prosperous society
by 1970, able to punch its weight within the international economic
community.

As a minimum, Britain would have been saved from such frequent
use of the begging bowl.

PART III

FLOATING –
AND SINKING
1970–90

THIRTEEN

Anthony Barber: Chancellor in Office but Not in Power

IAIN MACLEOD

Iain Macleod died five weeks after he had been appointed Chancellor of the Exchequer in the Heath government. His death was a tragedy for the Conservative Party and possibly for the country. He was a man of considerable intellectual brilliance and one of the finest debaters in the House of Commons. How he would have fared as Chancellor of the Exchequer, no one can of course know. He was the first professional gambler to become Chancellor, but as he had made, rather than lost, money from his gambling, it shows a certain competence in risk assessment. Butler, who would have made Macleod Chancellor in 1963 if he had won the premiership, comments, 'I cannot help feeling that a man who always held all the bridge scores in his head, who seemed to know all the numbers, and played *vingt-et-un* so successfully would have been useful.'[1] Macleod had been brought forward under Macmillan, not a good teacher, and he had recommended the sacrifice of Selwyn Lloyd. He had shown principle by refusing to serve under Douglas-Home but the principles in question had nothing to do with economic management. He had not shown, as shadow Chancellor, any exceptional insights into economic management. He looked for briefing to Peter Walker who describes Macleod as not 'at ease on economics'.[2] Once again, there could have been better tutors. The economic ideas which Macleod brought with him into office seem, indeed, to have been fairly crude. He thought, for example, that he could break the wage-price spiral by holding down nationalized industry prices. He wanted to be a great tax-reforming Chancellor, not actually a high priority at the time.[3]

Yet, whatever Macleod knew or might have learned about economic management, he was politically strong enough to have been master in his own Ministerial bailiwick. He would have brought to his consultations with his Prime Minister a voice, not an echo. He had time as Chancellor to deliver only one speech in the House, which he made in great pain. In it he truly said that, 'There is no doubt that by far the most serious problem that we face, not just as a Government but as a country, is inflation.' There was the highest rate of wage increase for twenty years. Prices were following on behind.[4] He acknowledged the positive factor of the balance of payments surplus but observed that it was counterbalanced by the outstanding debt. He concluded that 'I do not see how anybody, looking at the level of unemployment – the worst since 1940; I do not see, above all, how anybody, studying the costs from which we are suffering, could conceivably claim that it is a happy heritage that we have taken over.'[5] It was a partisan, but not unfair, assessment. It was certainly not the worst inheritance of any Chancellor since the war, but it would require considerable partisanship on the other side to claim that it was a particularly happy inheritance. There was some disappointment at Macleod's speech. He did not take the expansionary stance expected of him, and there were those who felt that already the Treasury had entered into possession of Macleod's mind. It was understandable if he was not yet ready to make policy decisions. Jenkins's 1970 Budget measures had only just come into effect, providing an additional annual purchasing power of £200 million. It was understandable also if Macleod was deterred by the inflation from the further stimulus to the economy which Jenkins regrets he did not give in his last Budget.

CASTRATING THE TREASURY

Heath took the opportunity created by Macleod's death to follow the Macmillan tradition under which he was in fact his own Chancellor of the Exchequer. There is a strange tendency in Prime Ministers to believe that their mere arrival at No. 10, rather than any achievement while they are in residence there, justifies their adoption of heroic stature. Postwar history had demonstrated conclusively that becoming Prime Minister was not evidence of any understanding of economic management.[6] The appointment of Anthony Barber demonstrated Heath's intentions. Barber was not a negligible figure. He had gained a first-class degree in law during his time in a German prisoner-of-war camp, a qualification that probably helped him when he introduced Value Added Tax (VAT) and came to make reforms in the Corporation Tax system.

He had spent four years at the Treasury as a junior Minister before entering the Cabinet as Minister of Health in 1963. Junior Ministerial positions at the Treasury can be more influential, and certainly more interesting, than many Cabinet posts. Barber was a protégé of Heath although not one of Heath's personal friends. Between 1967 and 1970 he had been Heath's choice as Chairman of the Conservative Party and could therefore claim some credit for the election victory in 1970. But he lacked the political base, and perhaps also the will, to contradict the Prime Minister. There is evidence that he did not want to go to the Treasury.[7] Whatever his own wishes, he was told that he was now to be Chancellor of the Exchequer. When the Cabinet was formed, he had been nominated, as Chancellor of the Duchy of Lancaster, to conduct the negotiations for entry into the EEC, negotiations in which Heath would understandably take a close interest, as a dedicated enthusiast for British membership. Barber would not be less willing to take instructions from Heath as Chancellor of the Exchequer than he would have been as Chancellor of the Duchy.

Heath was another Prime Minister who distrusted the Treasury. In Heath's case, the distrust was reinforced by the Treasury's lack of enthusiasm for Europe. Like Wilson, he had been President of the Board of Trade, a role in which it is easy to become jealous of the Treasury. The Board of Trade has much closer relations with industry than has the Treasury. The President of the Board of Trade listens to industrialists and to their complaints about the damage the Treasury is doing through its Stop-Go and through its taxation policies, particularly its varying tax levels on consumer durables. How can a supplier of consumer durables assess his market when it may be dislocated at a moment's notice by some new, reduced or increased tax impost? There is some justification in what industrialists say but they overlook the fact that the responsibility lies rather in the decision of successive governments to implement inflationary economic policies than in the Treasury's desperate, and often unsuccessful, attempts to manage those policies without harming economic activity. Nevertheless a President of the Board of Trade may well believe that his jealousy of the Treasury's power is justified by the Treasury's failures in economic management.

Heath, again like Wilson, is an example of a Prime Minister who believed that problems can be solved by changes in the machinery of government. In fact the machinery of government is not that important. Heath had only three devices open to him to control the Treasury. He found employment for all three. The first was to appoint a Chancellor who would do his bidding rather than that of Treasury officials. The second was to establish a powerful Department of Trade and Industry, incorporating Wilson's Ministry of Technology, the residue that Wilson had left of the Board of Trade, and the Ministry of Fuel and Power. John Davies, formerly Director-General of the CBI, became Secretary of State. It was an unfortunate choice from Heath's point of view, not just because of Davies's lack of experience in the Commons, but because he did not carry the necessary intellectual weight to compete with the Treasury. Davies became associated with the idea that public money would no longer be employed to rescue industrial 'lame ducks'. His reputation was therefore at the mercy of the first lame duck which the government found it imperative to rescue.

Heath's third device was to create the Central Policy Review Staff (CPRS). The CPRS, which outlasted the Heath government for almost twenty years, was headed by a civil servant, temporary or otherwise, not by a Minister. Its first head was Lord (Victor) Rothschild who was thought to be rather brilliant. The head of the CPRS or his deputy sat in on meetings of Cabinet committees. They could comment orally and in writing on Treasury papers. The reputation of the CPRS has been largely oversold on the basis of a charming story that, in the summer of 1973, Lord Rothschild gave a meeting of Ministers an oral report that a substantial increase in the price of oil was in prospect. This was just a few months before the oil price hike in the autumn of 1973. According to Blackstone and Plowden, 'Many Ministers simply refused to accept the validity' of the forecast.[8] The story is odd. The previous winter, the Public Accounts Committee (PAC) had been investigating the government's management of North Sea oil. DTI officials had informed the PAC confidentially of their expectations of a substantial increase in the price of oil. It is difficult to believe that they would have done so without also warning their own Ministers. It would be extraordinary, if true, that Ministers collectively should have required the CPRS to tell them of a major concern that their own officials had already conveyed to the PAC.[9]

The CPRS was often a useful stimulant and sometimes a useful critic but its insights were not magical. It issued the usual proportion of banalities and, from time to time, gave very bad advice, especially in the field of industrial policy. Banalities can, of course, have their uses. One such occasion was Rothschild's claim in a speech on 24 September 1973 that Britain faced inexorable decline unless it improved its economic performance. The speech contradicted the claims for economic achievement being advanced by Ministers. Heath was outraged at such a speech coming from a public servant and Rothschild's relationship with his Prime Minister suffered.

By the autumn of 1971 Heath had found that none of his devices had served his purpose, and he remained dissatisfied. He summoned Sir William Armstrong who had moved, three years before, from Permanent Secretary of the Treasury to be Permanent Secretary of the Civil Service Department and Head of the Civil Service. While Armstrong continued in his official functions, Heath made of him a personal economic adviser. The time came when he was spoken of as Deputy Prime Minister. The promotion of Armstrong out of the Treasury early in 1968 and his replacement by Sir Douglas Allen had been of great advantage to Roy Jenkins. Bringing Armstrong back into economic management was a decision of consummate unwisdom. Treasury influence cannot survive without a strong Chancellor backed by a supportive Prime Minister. There was now a weak Chancellor propelled by a Prime Minister who had his own, supposedly experienced, source of official economic advice. To a greater extent than under any other postwar Prime Minister, the Treasury lost influence over economic management. It was a moment when the international economic environment had turned particularly hostile and when Treasury caution should have been at a premium.

UNPREPARED

Even without Macleod, Heath brought into government with him an experienced group of Ministers. Many of his Cabinet had served as Cabinet Ministers in the 1950s and 1960s. Yet, after six years out of office, the government was out of touch with the realities of economic management. It was, perhaps, less than surprising that Tory Ministers preferred to forget the pragmatism that they had learned during their thirteen years in office, for the record of pragmatic management had not been distinguished. It had ended with the Maudling boom. Now, as a substitute for pragmatism, they had discovered, or rediscovered, a right-wing economic ideology. The ideology emphasized 'disengagement' from government intervention in the economy. It was at a conference of the Conservative shadow cabinet at Selsdon Park in January 1970 that the Conservative leadership allowed itself to become ideologically fixated. Harold Wilson at once exploited the opportunity. He attempted to terrify the electorate with threats that the election of a Conservative government would unleash a right-wing monster entitled 'Selsdon Man'. Selsdon Man became the Labour answer to Solomon Binding. The Tory manifesto for the June 1970 election went even further to implant the right-wing economic ideology of the new government in the wider political consciousness.

'Disengagement' would, in the first instance, extract the government from industrial policy and incomes policy. Eventually it would extract it from exchange rate policy and monetary policy. As an early expression of disengagement, Barber, on 27 October 1970, announced cuts in public expenditure programmes. They would save about £330 million in 1970–1 and nearly £1,100 million by 1974–5. Much of the saving was in subsidy to industry. In addition he announced that in the April 1971 Budget, income tax would be reduced by 6d (2.5p). Barber explained that the object of the government was to limit the activities of government and of public authorities. 'Our object is to concentrate their activities and their expenditure on those tasks that they alone can perform; and to enable the individual citizen to keep more of the money he earns, have greater incentive to increase his earnings, and to have greater freedom in how he spends or saves his income.' So far as industry was concerned, 'Our object is to lessen Government interference and reduce Government subsidies; to extend the opportunities for profitable enterprise; to widen the area within which industry rather than Government will take decisions.'[10]

This was all very well in its way. It was difficult to pretend that industrial policy or incomes policy as conducted by previous governments had made much beneficial impact, except perhaps in encouraging industry to development areas, a process not without its costs to the economy as a whole. But the failures of the past were not necessarily convincing evidence in support of the new policies. The Selsdon ideology possessed coherence only on two assumptions. The first was that there should be some measure by which the government could guide its own economic management. There could, for example, be the exchange rate, the money supply, or the level of inflation. There had, in other words, to be some measure of the success of economic management from which the government would not disengage. If everything was left to the market to determine, the economy would soon run out of control. The second necessary assumption was that the new government really believed in the Selsdon ideology and would accept its implications without demur and without back-tracking. But, in the first year of the new government, there was no indication that the government was aware that its ideology made sense only on such terms. The two immediate problems were inflation and rising unemployment. The trend in both cases was strongly upwards and in both cases the trend had been visible long before the election. The two problems were in one sense connected. If unemployment was allowed to rise enough, inflation might come down. But did disengagement really mean that the government would remain carefree as unemployment rose and as major industrial companies collapsed? Was the government really prepared to contemplate the level of unemployment that might act as an effective substitute for incomes policies that had in the past been found ineffective? No one knew what the necessary level of unemployment would prove to be, except that it would probably be high, and there was no evidence that Heath intended political masochism of that order.

The new government was at once challenged by the dockers, and their strike, settled by arbitration, resulted in a grossly inflationary award. On 2 November 1970, it was announced that the NBPI would be phased out and replaced by a number of Review Bodies responsible for recommending pay in different parts of the public sector.[11] Thus there would be an incomes policy for the public sector if not for the economy as a whole. The implication was that the government would exercise its counter-inflationary responsibilities as the employer of the public sector. Anything more was condemned by the principle of disengagement. In December there began a work-to-rule by the power workers in pursuit of a 25 per cent claim. The government was thus at once confronted by that public sector workforce which could cause it the greatest difficulties and the public the greatest distress. The work-to-rule was settled by a Court of Enquiry, headed by Lord Wilberforce, at 15 per cent or more. If incomes policy was out of the policy frame in the private sector, what other methods did the government contemplate for avoiding hyperinflation in face of such settlements in the public sector?

Heath appeared at first to imagine that it would suffice, as a policy for the control of inflation, to make appeals for a reduction in the level of wage settlements and to bring industrial relations within the law. The Industrial Relations Bill, published on 1 December 1970, provided for a cooling-off period before strikes, for secret ballots before strikes, for a National Industrial Relations Court with which unions would be expected to register if they wanted immunity from civil action for damage caused by strike action and, to cap the package, it made collective agreements, once negotiated, legally binding unless agreed otherwise by both parties. Thus exhortation and legislation werc to be the weapons in the battle against the inflationary pressures that the Heath government had inherited. At least Heath carried through the legislation enabling this approach to the control of inflation to be tested to destruction. The Industrial Relations Act was found to create more problems than it solved. Bitterly resisted by the trade unions, it was in the end also condemned by the employers. Barbara Castle's legislation might well have proved equally unworkable.

The control of inflation was not the only area of policy in which the Heath government's ideology and its nerve were being tested to destruction. Within nine months of entering office, in January 1971, the government met a challenge to its intention to disengage from industrial policy. Rolls-Royce, the private sector company which was the British national champion in the aero-engine industry, faced bankruptcy. On 4 February 1971, the government announced that Rolls-Royce would be nationalized. Heroic words about disengagement and lame ducks were replaced by pragmatic action in defence of what the government was pleased to regard as a national asset. Disengagement had always appeared a curious philosophy for a Prime Minister of Heath's interventionist temperament. But if he was not really committed to Selsdon, did he have any alternative, other than muddle, and make-do and mend, as he and the electorate watched the crisis of the British economy deepening?

PRIORITIES

Governments have to determine their economic policy priorities and they have to be sure that their priorities do not conflict with one another. In his first Budget statement of 30 March 1971, Anthony Barber indicated a priority common to all governments. This was to improve the economic performance of the country.

> It will be agreed throughout the House that for many years ... the economic performance of our country has been poor. Over these years we have become accustomed to unfavourable comparisons with other countries – slow growth, recurring balance of payments weakness, faster-than-average inflation, a low rate of investment, a falling share in world exports, and increasingly bad industrial relations.[12]

But now, with the confidence of a new government, recently elected, equipped with a new philosophy, with not too much as yet for which to apologize, this long and disappointing record of decline was evidently to be transformed. It was odd, perhaps, that a Budget with such important objectives had been delayed for nine months before its introduction.

Regrettably there were, as Barber went on to recognize, some 'immediate economic problems'. At least they did not include the balance of payments, which remained strong, or the burden of debt, more of which had been repaid. The debt had been more than halved since the new government took office. Barber informed the House that 'Two problems, above all, command attention at the present time, inflation and unemployment, a new and ... baffling combination of evils.'[13] It was baffling because the combination of higher unemployment with inflation was 'paradoxical'.[14] It was a combination that would continue to baffle him throughout the government's period of office. Nevertheless, he insisted that 'it lies within our own power, as a nation, to deal with inflation' and that, if we did so, 'we shall break out into a new period of faster growth, higher investment, rising living standards and a renewed confidence in our future'.[15]

Thus there was no external impediment to success and the incentive to succeed was very great. Indeed, here was a Chancellor who knew, at least for the moment, where his priority among these two problems lay. 'Throughout these past few months my colleagues and I have recognised that the first priority must be to defeat cost inflation.' He felt he could claim some success, which he attributed to the government's policy of ensuring 'a progressive and substantial reduction in the level of pay settlements' in the public sector, the so-called N-1 policy under which each settlement was to be at a rate lower than the previous.[16] The language of the Budget speech was a little odd and suggests careful Treasury drafting. Clearly the defeat of cost inflation was not the *only* priority. Although the defeat of cost inflation was his *first* priority, Barber was concerned also at the continued rise in unemployment and by the fact that 'the pace of monetary expansion over the year as a whole was substantially faster than was foreseen last April'.[17] He did not attribute any part of his still modest success with inflation to the rise in unemployment. He did point to the danger that a lax monetary policy could 'compound the pressures of cost inflation'.[18] Nevertheless he found no reason 'to restrict the growth of money supply so as to reduce demand below the level needed to achieve a growth of output in line with the growth of productive potential'.[19]

Here we find this new Chancellor grappling, as many of his predecessors had done, with a series of inconsistent objectives. He wanted growth to be in line with something called 'productive potential', an inexact concept at best. He did not, in his Budget speech, quantify his Budget judgement. The Budget speech as a whole was cautiously sparse in quantified objectives. He would attempt to regulate the level of demand, making changes during the year as necessary, in order that the economy should achieve its productive potential.[20] He wanted thereby to get unemployment down. He refused to give 'a firm objective for money supply'.[21] He hoped that the necessary relaxation in the money supply would not be at odds with the reduction in cost inflation. But it was a hope, and nothing but words was now left of his 'first priority' to cut cost inflation. It is exceedingly difficult for any Chancellor, especially perhaps a new Chancellor, to pick his way through the thicket of considerations that he ought to bear in mind in making his Budget judgement. That is why it is helpful actually to have and to pursue a 'first priority' rather than to seek to balance all the imponderables. In so far as anything was made clear in Barber's first Budget, it was that the 'first priority' was not the reduction of cost inflation but the reduction of unemployment. It was in this first Budget speech that Barber also announced the intention to vary the character of Corporation Tax in the following year's Finance Bill and to abolish SET and purchase tax in the 1973 Finance Bill, replacing them by VAT.

The history of economic management shows frequent examples of Chancellors who have, in words, shown awareness of dangers, while at the same time walking straight towards them. In a debate on 28 June 1971, Barber once more ruled out both a wages and prices freeze and statutory control of incomes. He was seeking a lasting solution. 'So often in the past ... we have found a degree of success in solving one problem, only to find that, by our very solution, we have created other equally serious difficulties.' An example was the previous government's drive to balance of payments surplus which 'set back economic growth and sowed the seeds of the present inflation and unemployment'.[22] It was true that violent oscillation between contrary policies or inconsistent priorities had been a predominant characteristic of British postwar economic management. No doubt it is easier to walk on a stationary tightrope than on one swinging frantically from side to side.

The wisdom displayed in Barber's words, perhaps inserted by some worldly-wise Treasury official, proved insufficient to deter him, or his master the Prime Minister, from falling into the identical trap. By 19

July, a Treasury review of the economic situation had been completed. It had been found that the level of output in the first half of 1971 would probably be more than 1 per cent lower than assumed at the time of the Budget. In the absence of policy changes, unemployment would be higher in the first half of 1972 than expected at the time of the Budget and industrial investment would continue on its downward path. There was therefore, Barber claimed, a need for policy changes. They could be further excused by a CBI initiative intended to limit price increases by member firms to 5 per cent. Price control by the CBI was evidently acceptable even if inconsistent with disengagement if imposed by the government. 'From the Government's point of view, the more favourable outlook for prices which has been created by that initiative has important implications for economic policy.' Therefore 'the conclusion that I have reached is that it is now right to take action to provide some further stimulus to demand'. He employed the regulator to reduce indirect taxation. The effect of his measures was to increase the cuts in taxation announced at the time of the Budget to £1,100 million and in 1972–3 to £1,400 million.[23] It was a massive leap from the tax reductions of £546 million and £680 million in a full year that he had proposed in his Budget.[24] But unemployment continued to rise. By October it had passed 900,000. By the time of the Queen's Speech on 2 November, the 'Government's first care will be to increase employment'.[25] The first priority had given way to the first care. But still unemployment rose. In January 1972, it passed the one million mark.

In May 1971, a Bank of England consultative document entitled *Competition and Credit Control* was published. Its recommendations were implemented as from November 1971. MacDougall, at the time Chief Economic Adviser to the Treasury, describes the scheme as 'inherently inflationary'.[26] It was followed by a very rapid increase in the money supply.[27] Evidently Treasury Ministers were warned in advance that if quantitative controls on bank advances were removed, there would have to be more vigorous use of interest rates. They acknowledged the warning but claimed to be content as they believed so strongly in the price mechanism. MacDougall, however, tells us that when it became necessary to make very substantial increases in interest rates, Ministers were not amused. He suspects that politically-inspired delays in implementing the necessary increases in interest rates contributed to the explosion in the money supply.[28]

The government had always accepted its responsibility for incomes in the public sector. N-1 was now challenged by the National Union of Miners (NUM) and the government suffered a humiliating defeat by the miners following a six-week strike during January and February 1972. The NUM, which had not called a strike for nearly fifty years, had demanded a pay rise intended to restore its members to their leading position in the earnings league. Their claim showed no respect for N-1. Through lack of preparation, lack of intelligence about the determination of the miners in pursuit of their claim, and feebleness in response to flying pickets deployed to inhibit the movement of coal stocks to power stations, the government allowed itself to be defeated. It remained only to find the appropriate means of capitulation. The open-handed Lord Wilberforce was called in once again to cover the government's surrender.

The government was finally about to abandon a highly visible aspect of disengagement, its disengagement from industrial interventionism. MacDougall records how, in November 1971, when he had already for some months been forecasting that unemployment would pass one million, he went one weekend to a meeting at Chequers attended among others by William Armstrong, Victor Rothschild and Douglas Allen. Heath invited Armstrong to speak. Armstrong responded that 'we should think big, and try to build up our industry onto a Japanese scale. This would mean more public spending. We should ask companies what they needed in the way of financial and other help, and give it to them. To my surprise Ted warmed to this and said "fine, and of course we must give it only to the good firms, not the bad ones".'[29] Disengagement from industry was over. On 28 February 1972, John Davies announced that Upper Clyde Shipbuilders (UCS), a consortium put together by the Wilson government which earlier had been allowed to go into liquidation, would be saved with a vast outpouring of public money. Its salvation helped to avoid increased unemployment in Glasgow and also, according to the Chief Constable, was necessary to safeguard public order. The government admitted that its decision had been influenced by social considerations but claimed an expectation that UCS could now survive in a competitive world.

It was being shown once again how rapidly governments can lose credibility, and consequently authority, when they depart so visibly from the policies on which they have been elected. It did not help that Heath had recently won a great victory in securing Parliamentary endorsement for the terms he had negotiated for entry into the EEC. It did not help that the rising unemployment could fairly be attributed to the economic measures forced on the Wilson government by the need to secure a balance of payments surplus and to its complacency in 1969–70 about the level of wage settlements. It certainly did not help that Heath himself had never been a committed supporter of the Selsdon philosophy. By the early months of 1972, his was a government on the run. In Whitehall, the civil service, which had initially been impressed by Heath's determination, now found itself working for a government motivated by panic. Nothing is more infectious than panic, and of all the varieties of panic none is more infectious than Prime Ministerial panic. Senior civil servants began to fear that the country was becoming ungovernable and that therefore the conciliation of popular sentiment must be substituted for the confrontation of longstanding problems. The government's capitulation to the miners was soon to be followed by Barber's total capitulation on economic policy. In the interest of bringing unemployment down below the one million mark, caution would be thrown to the winds. He would even be prepared to imperil the remnant of British competitiveness earned by the devaluation and thereby thrust the country back into balance of payments deficit.

BRITAIN IN A WORLD WITHOUT RULES

While Britain was suffering its domestic traumas, the world was changing dramatically. On 15 August 1971, President Nixon declared the dollar inconvertible into gold and imposed a 10 per cent surcharge on imports into the USA. He thereby indicated that the USA had reached the limit of its commitment to an interdependent world. In its economic policies, the USA would in future be even less liberal, even less outward-looking. The world's currencies had been compelled to float. There followed a flurry of activity to find some way of reintroducing fixed exchange rates in a way that enabled the USA, long in deficit, to restore balance to its external payments. Exchange rates were eventually re-fixed at the Smithsonian Conference in December 1971 after a major realignment, the largest for nearly quarter of a century, had been agreed. The Smithsonian agreement widened the margins of fluctuation of any currency against its parity or central rate, expressed as a cross rate against the dollar, to 4.5 per cent. The central rate for the pound was fixed at $2.60, an increase of about 8.5 per cent against the devalued dollar, though the Chief Secretary, Maurice Macmillan, assured the House that, due to the revaluation of certain other currencies, 'this settlement will not impair Britain's overall competitive strength in the world'.[30] There was, in the House, considerable unease that Britain's overall competitiveness had already been impaired by the inflation of the previous three years, and therefore some questioning whether the Chancellor had not negotiated for Britain too high an exchange rate for the new, post-Smithsonian, era.

REFLATION

It was against the background of these external events that the government addressed itself to its new priority, the problem of unemployment. Its bewilderment was illustrated by the plaint of Robert Carr, Secretary of State for Employment, in a debate in the House of Commons, on 23 November 1971. 'The sort of measures of demand management which appeared to work, and indeed did work, to control the overall level of unemployment in the past seem now to have lost at least some of their previous effectiveness.'[31] If the reflationary steps so far taken had proved insufficient, clearly more must be done, whatever the inflationary risks and the risks to the hard-won balance of payments surplus. The Treasury was conscripted into the production of a Budget by which the government would seek its own rescue. It would be a Maudling-type dash for growth, except that what Maudling had launched by miscalculation, the Heath government would commit itself to deliberately. It was now the Tory view once again that it was the election of an incompetent Labour government in October 1964 that had undermined the Maudling Experiment. The government even had the inestimable benefit of the advice of Sir William Armstrong, Permanent Secretary to the Treasury at the time of the Maudling Experiment. Life could be lived all over again. There are only rare opportunities in public affairs to conduct repeat experiments – the surrounding circumstances change so much. Now, apparently, was one of those rare opportunities. Yet the international economic environment was even less favourable than that in which Maudling had acted, in that the dollar had been devalued. The domestic environment was even worse in that inflation was higher and the government had just suffered humiliating defeat by the miners.

Nevertheless Heath and Armstrong sought to prove what Maudling and Armstrong had not been able, or had not been given time, to prove, that a massive reflation could bring the era of Stop-Go to an end. There were, they thought, favourable as well as unfavourable factors in the

British position. The UK was just about to join the EEC which, they believed, would act as a spur to faster growth. The Common Market was known to possess the secret of economic growth for all its members. There were, as Barber was to put it in his Budget speech, 'more unused resources than there were at the beginning of any previous period of rapid expansion since the war'.[32] The balance of payments and reserve positions were stronger than at the beginning of previous periods of expansion. That there was truth in these elements of strength underlines the unwisdom of the 1972 Budget. Instead of waiting for a balanced expansion in which a high proportion of the unused resources would be absorbed in exports, the successful German policy after the war, the unused resources were to be consumed in a massive domestic reflation on the dubious theory that rapid expansion at home would make the economy more competitive internationally. After twenty-five years of over-full employment, the real target which the Heath government felt bound to adopt was not expansion into Europe, but an urgent return to over-full employment, whatever the consequences, even if the opportunity of Europe was itself wasted.

Barber opened his, or more strictly his Prime Minister's, Budget on 21 March 1972. He put his statement squarely within the context of the decision to join the EEC as from 1 January 1973 and of the 'level of unemployment which has persisted despite the unprecedented action to counter it which has been taken over the past year'. His Budget would be designed 'to help British industry to modernise, to re-equip and to reorganise to meet the challenge of greater international competition'.[33] On inflation he was now complacent. The CBI's initiative aided by his own action in reducing SET and purchase tax had halved the rate of increase in prices since the previous summer. Nevertheless there was still a considerable gap to be closed between the rate of increase in money incomes and of productivity.[34] Present policies would produce some recovery both in manufacturing industry and in the service sectors. His Budget judgement was, however, based on the expectation that 'On present policies . . . I do not believe that this recovery would be of the magnitude required either to meet the challenge of Europe or to provide an adequate basis for a return to full employment.'[35]

He concluded that he needed to take action which would have the effect of raising output in the first half of 1973 by about 2 per cent. 'The measures I shall put to the House are intended to ensure a growth of output at an annual rate of 5 per cent between the second half of last year and the first half of next.' This would mean that output would have risen by 10 per cent over the two-year period from the first half of 1971 to the first half of 1973.

He then added the comforting thought, disregarding all past experience and basing himself on the self-interested hunches of the business community, that 'I do not believe that stimulus to demand of the order I propose will be inimical to the fight against inflation. On the contrary, the business community had repeatedly said that the increase in productivity and profitability resulting from a faster growth of output is one of the most effective means of restraining price increases.'[36] In his efforts to be helpful, Barber introduced free depreciation on all investment in plant and machinery other than passenger cars.[37] He even reintroduced investment grants in development areas.[38] They had been abolished with contumely as recently as October 1970 on the ground that grants were distributed irrespective of the profitability of the enterprise. Altogether Barber reduced taxation in his Budget by £1,200 million in 1972–3, which included £1,000 million off income tax. He added that 'since this Government came to office, the burden of taxation in this coming year will have been reduced by over £3,000 million'.[39] Alongside the fiscal changes was the monetary explosion. There would be a very large public sector borrowing requirement, estimated at £3,358 million.[40] Barber was not at all anxious about the increase in money supply encouraged by *Competition and Credit Control*. He acknowledged that 'this Budget will entail a growth of money supply that is . . . high by the standards of past years, in order to ensure that adequate finance is available for the extra output. To proceed otherwise would reduce the growth of real output itself. This reasoning is now, I think, generally accepted.'[41]

The economy was now launched. British industry would be revitalized. The rate of growth would be double that in the preceding decade. Growth would be secure into the foreseeable future.[42] When Barber was giving the unions so much of what they wanted by way of economic expansion, how could they bring themselves to threaten success by demanding excessive wage settlements? 'I believe that the British people will now have no patience with any group whose actions endanger our hopes for prices and employment.'[43] Barber sat down to enthusiastic applause from his backbenches. In a prescient comment the following day, Roy Jenkins, leading for the Opposition as shadow Chancellor, said, 'My fear is that the Budget will in due course lead to the need either for swingeing and unacceptable public expenditure cuts or for substantial taxation increases.'[44] But *The Times* feared that Barber had not yet done enough.

Alongside the Budget came the revival of industrial policy on a scale more lavish than anything Labour had dared to attempt. It was announced the day after the Budget in a speech by John Davies which accompanied a White Paper, *Industry and Regional Development*. The White Paper became the basis of the 1972 Industry Act. Heath had the help of Sir William Armstrong in planning this reversion to the days before 'disengagement'. Here, too, Heath was the victim of an illusion – that industry could be prepared for the Common Market by methods of such crudity. Armstrong's advice to Heath combined the worst elements of Maudling's policy of 1963 – 4 with some of the most wasteful elements in Labour's policies, 1964 – 70. The government was now spinning like a top. The IRC, one of Labour's industrial policy instruments, had been abolished. The new objective would be to recreate a capacity for intervention within the DTI, to be called the Industrial Development ment Executive, sufficiently different from the IRC to deny Labour the opportunity to mock. It was a forlorn hope. Everyone would recognize that there had been another U-turn in government policy.[45]

FLOATING

In the course of his Budget speech, Barber made the most important statement about exchange rate policy uttered by any Conservative Chancellor since the war. He said that 'the lesson of the international balance of payments upsets of the last few years is that it is neither necessary nor desirable to distort domestic economies to an unacceptable extent in order to maintain unrealistic exchange rates, whether they are too high or too low'.[46] Barber accompanied this statement with the necessary assertion that 'There can be no soft options if we fail to get a grip on ever-rising costs.'[47] Unfortunately it was precisely as a soft option that the government would, in practice, use the new flexibility which, after a brief and humiliating episode, they decided to allow themselves. Despite their new philosophy on the subject of exchange rates, the government, in May 1972, joined the newly established 'German snake'. The snake had come into existence on 24 April 1972 with the six founder states of the EEC as its original members. The EEC wanted to constitute a zone of monetary stability. The snake established a maximum permitted margin of fluctuation between any two participant currencies of 2.25 per cent. At its centre was the DM. In an excess of European enthusiasm, the UK joined the snake. Six weeks later, on 23 June, sterling was driven out of the snake in a surge of market scepticism about Barber's economic policies. Barber came down to the House to explain. Due to market pressure, sterling would float 'as a temporary measure'. Exchange control would be applied to transactions with the sterling area. His growth targets, however, would remain. 'We have set our national economy on the path of a 5 per cent rate of expansion – more than twice as fast as the rate we have achieved over the past decade . . . we are well on course.'[48] The market did not believe him and, for a British government, there is no more serious test of economic policy than the market test. The pound floated down.

Barber's announcement that sterling was floating brought to the government and to the House of Commons a sense of combined relief and exaltation. Suddenly, it seemed, the walls of the prison in which the British economy had been confined had fallen away. The end of exchange parities would ensure balance in the country's overseas accounts. Unemployment could be brought down to acceptable levels without worrying about the reserves or the pound sterling. The economy could grow, free of any constraints including the exchange rate constraint. It could indeed be allowed to rip. Barber repeated in his statement on 23 June his Budget warning about soft options. But it was not believed that the government had rejected soft options and he, on the evidence of his actions, did not appear to have rejected them either. The responsible conduct of economic policy was not one of the Heath government's distinguishing characteristics. A floating rate of exchange should not have been regarded as a soft option providing the opportunity for absurdly expansionist policies. It did not guarantee a balance of payments that could never be out of balance. A floating rate demands as much responsibility and caution from a Chancellor as a fixed rate – unless he is prepared to see his exchange rate drop out of sight. The euphoric expectations of the House of Commons were to be disappointed. But at last sterling was floating – floating from weakness but, at last, floating. What was announced as temporary endured until sterling joined the Exchange Rate Mechanism (ERM) of the European Monetary System (EMS) in October 1990. Floating was not a soft option but, given the responsible conduct of fiscal and monetary policy, it could be a better option. Very soon all the world's major currencies were floating, those within the snake as a group. The Bretton Woods system was not merely dead but buried.

During the era of fixed exchange rates, some had yearned for the freedom of floating rates. Now, in the era of floating rates, some memories tended to exaggerate the benefits of an economic system with rules, dominated by the dollar. Arguably a return to such a system would ensure a more stable life, less fraught with unpleasant surprises, than a world of floating rates. Within British government, but not there alone, there remained among some a craving for a return to the certainties of the Bretton Woods years. As American economic hegemony had gone, there were to be attempts at international economic management by a group of leading industrial powers.

ROUT BY INFLATION

Inflation soared. The fundamental problem of the Heath government was that it had no effective way of dealing with inflation other than to allow unemployment to rise. That is the way to which Jenkins's policies, unintentionally, pointed. Jenkins had left an inheritance of rising inflation but he had also left rising unemployment. He had provided both the problem and the answer. The rise in unemployment required to dampen the inflation might be transitional, necessary only until inflation had fallen to an acceptable level. But the government could not be sure how high unemployment might need to go and whether it would in fact prove to be transitional. It was not prepared to take that path or that risk. In the first two years of Heath's government, inflation, while still far too high, did seem to be submitting to treatment by unemployment. But imbued with the Keynesian traditions of the post-war world, fearful that the Conservative Party would once more be labelled as the Party of unemployment, Heath was not prepared to use unemployment as a weapon against inflation. It was a crime of which the Labour Party accused the government, but never was a partisan accusation more unjustly levelled. The Heath government faced an unpalatable choice – whether to risk being destroyed by unemployment or by inflation. Whatever choice it made would be by inadvertence because it clearly did not understand the nature of the alternatives with which it was confronted. It chose to take the risk of being destroyed by inflation. No one can ever know whether if it had chosen the other course, to risk destruction by unemployment, which might need only to have been transitional, it might in fact have survived.

The story of the Heath government tells how a government can be destroyed almost as much by humiliation as by inflation. To its defeat by the miners, its U-turn on industrial policy and its retreat on industrial relations legislation, the Heath government was now to add a U-turn on incomes policy. Heath, searching desperately for an effective incomes policy, decided to sacrifice the Industrial Relations Act in the interests of cooperation with the trade unions. The Industrial Relations Act introduced as an alternative to an incomes policy was thus destroyed by the inflation it had failed to prevent.

To achieve agreement with the unions, Heath was ready to offer them a role in the management of the economy. It was a case of the blind leading the blind. It is not true that incomes policies are necessarily useless; they can have some beneficial effect. But for this to happen, the surrounding economic circumstances must be conducive to restraint in wage claims and settlements. The unions were only likely to agree an incomes policy of any kind if they were assured that economic policy would be moved into an even higher gear. But if it was moved into a higher gear, that fact would explode the incomes policy. It was only if the unions were prepared to accept that economic management had for the nonce to be in counter-inflationary mode, that incomes policy could have a positive role to play. The unions were still more likely to accept that need from a government of their own, a Labour government, than from a Conservative government. There was, therefore, always a danger that if Heath made the concessions necessary to secure the support of the unions, the outcome would be counter-productive. He might have his agreement with the union leaders but the result would be to move the economy on from inflation to hyperinflation.

More was demanded of the government by the unions than that economic management should be moved into an even more expansionary mode. Union leaders are professionally sceptical about the responsibility of wage settlements for inflation. In this they are at one with the monetarists. If, despite their scepticism, they are asked to make their contribution to a voluntary incomes policy then they will demand compensation. In the negotiations with Heath that ensued in the autumn of 1972, their first demand was statutory control of prices. A Labour government might concede *in extremis* a demand that incomes control be voluntary but price control statutory. It was much more difficult for a Conservative government. Alternatively the unions wanted an unqualified guarantee that the retail price index in general, and food prices in particular, would not rise by more than 5 per cent in the year ahead. It was unrealistic to demand an unqualified guarantee. The government had no control over the price of imports and commodity prices were rising. But the government and the CBI did offer to use their influence to ensure that the rise in domestic costs should not exceed 5 per cent over the 12 months. The government also made proposals to ensure that those on the lowest incomes enjoyed an increase in their standard of living and the CBI was willing that dividends should be controlled.

On 2 November 1972, it became quite clear that despite every effort by the government it would not be able to win the cooperation of the TUC. Union leaders cherish their own survival as much as any politician. Thinking of the likely attitude of activists and their annual conferences, they preferred to have the incomes policy imposed on them by statute than to be accused of betrayal by compromise.

Having received on 6 November confirmation that the General Council of the TUC would not accept the government's offer, Heath made a statement to the House. An interim Bill would be introduced at once to provide for a standstill on increases in pay, prices, rents and dividends. The standstill would last for 90 days with provision for an extension of up to 60 days. The standstill would give time to work out the 'statutory measures' required 'to secure the agreed objectives of economic management'. Heath then added: 'Let me remind the House . . . of the objectives: the maintenance of a high rate of growth and an improvement in real incomes; an improvement in the position of the lower paid and the pensioners; and moderation in the rate of cost and price inflation.'[49] The fact that the incomes policy had to be imposed by statute made the government eager to go as far as it could to meet union demands. The first of these had always been economic expansion.

Enoch Powell, still a Conservative MP, asked, 'Does [the Prime Minister] not know that it is fatal for any Government or Party to seek to govern in direct opposition to the principles on which they were entrusted to govern? In introducing a compulsory control of wages and prices, in contravention of the deepest commitments of this Party, has [the Prime Minister] taken leave of his senses?' The language of the intervention indicated no ordinary level of hostility to his Party's leader but its point was certainly germane. Heath could only reply that the government had been elected to take action in the national interest.[50] He could hardly pretend that the credibility, and therefore the authority, of government does not suffer when it is forced into courses of action which it has previously denounced as a matter of principle.

BREAKTHROUGH OR BREAKDOWN

The country was once more to pay the costs of having a Chancellor without a political base or strong convictions of his own, blown hither and thither by a dominant Prime Minister with an apocalyptic vision, and bound to his office by a sense of 'loyalty' to his colleagues and his Party rather than to the nation he is employed to serve. Barber clearly had doubts about what he was being asked to do. But doubts pay no bills. It cannot have helped any resolution to resist Heath's pressure that may from time to time have stirred in Barber's blood that, among the great majority of opinion leaders, there were few or no doubters. The Opposition was not going to damn itself by condemning another dash for growth. The Establishment press might have been expected to ask questions, especially after Maudling's equivalent escapade. Instead it gave the government its encouragement, including even the independent *Economist*. Here, at last, they argued, was a government under a dedicated leader, determined to fight inflation and achieve economic breakthrough. If their science had had any virtue, one might have expected Keynesian economists to query the possibility of miraculous transformations in economic performance. Instead the Keynesian *National Institute Economic Review (NIER)* gave the government every encouragement to persist before turning against it when life began to teach the inevitable lessons.

Whatever might be thought of the equivalences perceived by monetarists between the growth of the money supply and inflation, it was a situation in which their message should have had resonance. The idea that the objective should be stability and that therefore heroics had no place in economic management should have penetrated more deeply into public debate and into the decision-making processes of government. But, as reflected in the House of Commons through the passionate eloquence of Enoch Powell, monetarism failed to carry conviction. First he appeared to Conservatives as motivated more by hatred of Heath than by love of country. Secondly, his judgement in other respects was known to be deeply flawed. His condemnation of prices and incomes policy appeared purely negative. Even if he was right about the money supply, it did not seem to follow that there was no role for a prices and incomes policy in a critical situation. His belief that a floating rate ensured balance in the country's payments provided, if it provided anything, premature comfort that there was one constraint on economic performance that had finally been removed.

So far as the government was concerned, there was nothing in the intellectual debate, or in the political environment, to deter it. On the contrary, the political environment encouraged it to take risks to restore its electoral fortunes. In December 1972, it lost Sutton and Cheam, a safe Conservative constituency, to the Liberals in a by-election. As 1973 progressed, it would lose other by-elections. Its only comfort was that the Labour Party did not seem too popular either. Governments were now chosen *faute de mieux*. But Heath knew that he could change all that and that everything was now in place, even if inadvertently in some cases, that would enable him to do so. The Heath-Armstrong team looked at what they had done and found that it was good. First, the UK was at last, from 1 January 1973, in the Common Market. Secondly, sterling was floating. That was one constraint out of the way. If the exchange rate was 'unrealistic', the market would change it. One civil servant is reported as saying, 'Oh well, if the unions will insist on excessive wage claims, it won't effect expansion. We'll just let the exchange rate go.'[51] It was clearly the soft option approach to floating rates that possessed the soul of this government. Thirdly, there was now a statutory prices and incomes policy. But as it derived from an attempt to mobilize the voluntary support of the unions, it could itself only be inflationary. All the costs of buying union support were paid without even such benefit as union support might have provided. Fourthly a raging expansion had been launched through Barber's 1972 Budget reinforced by major increases in the level of public expenditure, largely in the Budgets of Sir Keith Joseph at the Department of Health and Social Security and Margaret Thatcher at Education. Fifthly, there was now an industrial policy such as, it was believed, had helped to restore the economies of France and Japan. The problem, unperceived by Heath and Armstrong, was to determine whether the success of the French and Japanese economies was due to the industrial policy or the success of the industrial policy was due to the success of their economies. Thus, while everything was now in place for the Heath-Armstrong miracle, it was highly questionable, though little questioned, where it would all lead. Barber followed on miserably behind. Whatever his doubts, he had the consolation that if it all worked, he, as Chancellor, would share in the credit.

The single benefit of Jenkins's struggles was now being squandered. The balance of payments had deteriorated seriously despite the fact that sterling was floating. In 1972 there was just about balance. In 1973 it was clear that there would be once more a deficit. The February 1973 trade deficit was already £77 million, that in March had risen to £197 million. The 1972 Budget left behind a large borrowing requirement. To fund it, interest rates had to remain high. Keynesian commentators remained complacent. In February 1973, the *NIER* did not see any necessary inconsistency between an improvement in the balance of payments and continued growth in domestic expenditure designed to moderate unemployment, which was still about 700,000. There was no imminent 'resource clash'. Immediate and severe deflation was to be ruled out.[52] *NIER*, and other commentators, grossly overstated the amount of spare capacity implied by unemployment at 700,000. On 6 March 1973 Barber introduced a Budget which he described as 'broadly neutral', adding, 'I believe that on this basis the economy will continue to grow at an annual rate of around 5 per cent over the 18 months from the second half of 1972 to the first half of 1974.'[53] The public sector borrowing requirement would be £4,423 million, an enormous figure by the standards of the time.[54] In the light of that figure, the description 'broadly neutral' hardly seemed appropriate. The press noticed that he was engaged in a gamble, but given the great prize to be won, encouraged him in it. The use of the word 'gamble' implies, however, a prospect of success, even if remote. There was no such prospect. Only two months later, on 21 May 1973, Barber announced public expenditure cuts in 1974–5 of about £500 million, estimated to reduce total output in 1974 by 0.5–0.75 per cent.[55] Difficult as is economic fine-tuning, it is particularly difficult to apply to an economy in headlong gallop. The only question was how long it would be before it met the hurdle at which it would fall. Some commentators began to speak of over-heating. They were rebuked by *NIER* which commented sardonically, 'Overheating is an expression which has gate-crashed the literature, thereby avoiding payment of the entrance fee of a definition, and escaping any critical scrutiny at the door.'[56] The inexactness of the term was not in fact greater than that of more sophisticated economic judgements.

No one should have been more conscious than Edward Heath of the impact of external events on the UK economy. He was after all a strong European and a former President of the Board of Trade. On 13 February 1973 the dollar was devalued to the extent of 10 per cent, carrying sterling part of the way down with it.[57] Commodity prices were rising strongly due to the buoyant world economy. 1972 had proved to be the most buoyant year for the world economy since 1966, and 1973 was expected to be even better.[58] All the elements were being put in place for the OPEC oil shock. A rise in the price of oil had been forecast by DTI officials during the winter of 1972–73. The buoyant world economy and the vast American imports of oil enlarged an increase that would have been imposed in any case. OPEC knew that its raw material was the basis of everyone else's prosperity, and decided to extract its share by taxing the rest of the world, rich and poor alike. Stimulated also by the Middle East War in the autumn of 1973, OPEC struck. The oil price was quadrupled. The effect was to worsen the balance of payments of the oil-consuming countries by something like $50 billion. In 1974 Britain would be paying £2.5 billion more for 5 per cent less oil than had been imported in 1973.

None of these events seriously dented the complacency of *NIER*. In November it was still claiming that the panic about over-heating had been overdone and that the reflationary policy 'appears . . . to have had almost complete success'. Nevertheless it did now inform its readers that its current price forecast for the balance of payments deficit for 1974 had worsened from £350 million, its August 1973 figure, to £2,100 million. It was no longer expecting the balance to return to zero by the end of 1974, rather a further worsening in the first quarter of 1974 followed by a 'sharp recovery' thereafter. This forecast took account of the oil price shock and of the increase in other commodity prices.[59] The November trade figures showed a deficit of £270 million. The Governor of the Bank of England, Gordon Richardson, did not share the complacency of *NIER*. On 15 January 1974 he said:

> Last year the current account showed a large deficit which, this year, will be further greatly increased by the rise in the oil price . . . But even before that factor became important, our balance of payments deficit on current account in the last quarter of the year was running at a rate equivalent to 4 per cent of our national product.[60]

Three days before the February 1974 General Election, the January trade figures showed a £383 million deficit, described by *The Times* as 'the largest monthly trade deficit that Britain has known'.[61] The trade figures would help Wilson to win his revenge for June 1970.

Meanwhile the government was developing its statutory prices and incomes policy through a series of 'Phases'. Phase 1 was the freeze which was extended to 31 March 1973. Phase 2, introduced in a White Paper on 17 January 1973, restricted pay increases to £1 plus 4 per cent with strict control on prices until the autumn. Again the government had Keynesian support. *NIER* was confident that the policy would hold. In May 1973 it wrote, 'It is already plain that both Phase 1 and Phase 2 of the present prices and incomes policy have had considerable success on the wages side . . . There is no reason to assume that any additional pressure from further falls in unemployment will be sufficient to break down what appears to be a robust structure.' It concluded that 'there is no reason why the present boom should either bust or have to be busted so long as the additional instruments of incomes policy and the floating exchanges are retained'.[62] Phase 3 of the incomes policy was announced on 8 October 1973, effective from 7 November. Phase 3 embodied flexibility. But flexibility, though probably inevitable after a year of strict unalterable rules under Phases 1 and 2, is the death of incomes policies. As an element of flexibility, it incorporated a cost-of-living safeguard if prices rose above a 'threshold' of 7 per cent. The idea was supported by the Labour Opposition. OPEC's strategy was perfectly clear by 7 November. It had announced its intention to raise the price of oil on 16 October.[63] With the sharp increase in import prices, the threshold formula became a built-in inflation accelerator.

Ministers are more readily exhausted by the collapse of their policies than by the burden of their duties. An exhausted Barber was allowed to take further deflationary measures. In 1964 it had been left to Labour to confront the consequences of the Maudling Experiment. On this occasion, it was the Chancellor who launched the boom who was forced to accept the responsibility for killing it. This time there could be no complaint that an incoming Labour government had blocked a Tory economic breakthrough. Barber's statement on 17 December 1973 amounted to a mini-Budget. Severe hire purchase controls were reintroduced, public expenditure programmes for 1974–5 were cut by some £1,200 million, there was to be a surcharge on surtax, and, to control the money supply, the supplementary special deposits scheme was introduced.[64] It penalized the banks by not paying interest on the special deposits they were required to make at the Bank of England. By January 1974, industry's investment intentions, which had at last reached a more respectable level, had collapsed. There had been much criticism by Heath of industry's failure to invest. There were suggestions even of lack of patriotism. But it showed extraordinary naiveté in a Prime Minister to imagine that industry, given earlier experience, would rush to invest on the basis of a 'dash for growth'. The experience of 1972–4 would add to industry's disinclination to invest in the UK.

Meanwhile the miners, finding in the oil price hike and the Arabs' oil boycott justification for a higher assessment of their own worth, decided once again to test the government's resolve by means of an overtime ban in support of a 35 per cent claim. Stubborn refusal to be seen to be defeated by the miners a second time denied Heath the insight that the miners might have a case. He felt unable to make further exceptions beyond the flexibility allowed in Phase 3 for fear that to do so would destroy the policy. He proved sufficiently resolute to put Britain on a three-day week from 1 January 1974. At a meeting of NEDC on 9 January, the TUC offered the government a way out. Other unions, it promised, would not use a special settlement with the miners as a precedent for their own claims. Barber, in the chair of NEDC as Chancellor of the Exchequer, rejected the offer instead of probing it. He had had no notice of it and, when consulted, Heath took the same attitude. There could be no certainty that, even if the trade union leaders were sincere, they could enforce their policy on their members. It would have sounded too much like the reincarnation of Solomon Binding.[65]

On 23 January 1974, the NUM Executive decided on a pithead ballot on 31 January to provide authority for a complete stoppage. In a prepared peroration to his speech on 6 February, his last as Chancellor, Barber told the House that 'the issue at stake is whether our affairs are to be governed by the rule of reason, by the rule of Parliament and by the rule of democracy'. The alternative could only be 'chaos, anarchy and a totalitarian or Communist regime'.[66] The next morning, Heath reluctantly called a General Election for 28 February 1974. Two days before the election, on 26 February, *NIER* published its latest appraisal. 'It is not often that a government finds itself confronted with a possibility of simultaneous failure to achieve all four main policy objectives – of adequate economic growth, full employment, a satisfactory balance of payments and reasonably stable prices.' These were the four policy objectives outlined by Macmillan to his Cabinet on 28 May 1962. *NIER* did not add that it felt any apology was needed on its own part for the encouragement it had given in the past to the policies that had led to this disaster. Nor did it consider the possibility that it was no longer feasible to achieve all four objectives simultaneously and that, in its ambitious attempt to do so, the Heath government, and its Chancellor Anthony Barber, had ensured failure on all four.

FOURTEEN

The Three Healeys

THE HEIR TO THE TREASURY

Labour unexpectedly became the largest Party in the General Election of 28 February 1974. Wilson proudly claimed when he returned to No. 10 Downing Street, a few days later, that the Cabinet was 'richer in experience than perhaps any incoming Government this century. Fourteen members had sat in the outgoing 1970 Cabinet.'[1] It was certainly true that as Labour Ministers moved back into their government offices after less than four years in the wilderness, it felt more like a reshuffle than a second coming. But the experience of 1964–70 was barely relevant to the problems of 1974. Some Ministers seemed unconscious of the economic crisis that had struck the country. Their attitude resembled that of the characters in Jane Austen's novels who carried on their lives undisturbed by the Napoleonic Wars. Before the election they had seen no reason why Labour should revise its electoral commitments. Now they saw no reason, other than the irksome lack of an overall majority, why the reborn Labour government should not at once begin to implement its electoral commitments. For the new Chancellor, Denis Healey, such insouciance was impossible. But he was a new Chancellor, he had no previous experience of economic management, and it would prove a major burden that he had to educate not merely himself but his Cabinet colleagues.

In 1972, Labour had committed itself to a referendum on continued membership of the European Community. Roy Jenkins resigned from the Labour front bench in protest and was succeeded as shadow Chancellor by Denis Healey. Tony Crosland had wanted the succession to Jenkins as he had that to Callaghan in 1967. But Wilson was still leader of the Party and Crosland was once more passed over. When Wilson accepted the call to form a government, Jenkins might have seemed an outstanding candidate for a second stint at the Treasury. Healey, for his part, had no experience even of economic departments. But by that time Healey had served as shadow for two years, and the appointment of Jenkins to so visible and influential a post would have offended a large section of the Labour Party which was still, by a majority, hostile to membership of the EEC. The Left was planning a revolution in economic policy. It was a scenario into which Jenkins did not fit. The Left could not be sure that Healey would fit either. But there was an ambiguity about Healey. In a sense he was entering into his inheritance because it had been quite likely that if Labour had won in 1970, Jenkins would have moved to the Foreign Office and Healey to the Treasury.

Healey was to serve as Chancellor throughout the entire period of the Wilson/Callaghan governments, at the time the longest tenure of the Treasury since the war. But a casual observer, intrigued by the differences in policy during the period, might have concluded that the Treasury had been occupied not by one Ministerial chief but by three. First there would be the 'political' Chancellor of the first year in office, Socratic with his official advisers and accommodating to his Cabinet colleagues. This first year embraces both the run-up to the General Election of October 1974 and its aftermath. It was the period during which Healey would subsequently claim to have been learning his job.[2] During the following three years the same casual observer would find the Treasury led by an orthodox Chancellor who dominated by force of intellect and personality the heroic struggles in 1975 for an incomes policy and in 1976 for an acceptable agreement with the IMF. In 1977, this same orthodox Chancellor would allow a newly buoyant sterling to rise against the dollar at the insistence of the market, whatever the consequences for the competitiveness of British exports. Finally, there would be a third Healey, who had come through the fire and emerged bronzed and resilient at the other side, resurrected as a political Chancellor, with his eye on another election victory and on the succession to No. 10. In this final episode the observer would note this 'political' Chancellor handling with experienced skill the major question of whether Britain should join as a founder member the Exchange Rate Mechanism (ERM) of the European Monetary System (EMS). For once the interests of the political Chancellor would coincide with the clear interests of the country, and membership of the ERM would be rejected. Perhaps, however, this observer, on deeper investigation, would conclude that it had been one man all the time, the aspiring politician accommodating his words and his music to the pressures as he found them.

The art of John Dryden would be required to encompass the complex personality of the ambitious and many-sided politician who, in 1974, became Chancellor of the Exchequer.[3] The most cultured of Chancellors, he could also be the greatest bully. Perhaps the most brilliant of Chancellors intellectually, he was possessed also of a common touch which attracted a wider public even when it most disliked his actions. His various disguises could confuse. A friendly commentator might attribute to him a deep seriousness worn lightly, sometime perhaps flippantly. The flippancy could have been diagnosed as a defence mechanism for a man whose outward ebullience concealed inner doubts. Or it could have been interpreted as an expression of total self-confidence. The friendly commentator would have detected great courage, normally kept in reserve, as though courage was only for the decisive moments and it would be tedious to fight too hard when the issues appeared not of the first importance. A less friendly commentator might have criticised the flippancy, encountered not just in words but in deeds, as indicative of irresponsibility. Certainly it was not always to the taste of those who worked for him. By civil servants in the Treasury, he came to be admired for the excitement he generated and feared for his penetration of official work less than first class. But by those, Ministers and officials, who could not take his dismissive rudeness, he might even be hated. He came to dominate the international community of Finance Ministers by his intellectual brilliance and his committee skills, even when the others round the table most strongly disagreed with him. Yet it took him a long time to win the ear of the House and he never achieved the command over it of a Callaghan or a Jenkins. His time as shadow Chancellor was not happy, partly because of his lack, not so much of economics, but of economic sophistication. He had advisers, but one of the fates of Labour shadow Chancellors is to fall into the hands of economists seeking influence.

THE INHERITANCE

Healey had the most difficult inheritance of any Chancellor since the war. More difficult than 1945 because Dalton had dollars on offer even if on unreasonable terms. More difficult than 1951 because, though Butler was at first frightened into Robot, the economic situation made a rapid turn in his favour without the exertion on his part of the least strength of character. More difficult than 1964 because in 1964 there was still time for a choice to be made, or avoided, before retribution struck. 1974 would have been the nadir of Britain's economic fortunes had it not been for 1976. First there was the political situation. The electorate had inadvertently left Britain at a moment of deep crisis without an effective government since no Party had an overall majority. The new government could be defeated at any time the other Parties thought it to their combined advantage to force a General Election. Wilson's objective was to hold on until the political environment seemed more favourable for a new election. Meanwhile he would buy votes where he could by concessions to pressure groups paid for out of the public purse. But he could not wait too long, because survival was at risk every day. Healey would not be thanked if he imperilled a Labour victory at the election to come by politically inept handling of the economic conjuncture.

Next, the Labour Party was probably more divided ideologically than at any other point in its history thus far. During the Bevanite struggles, at least the contenders were all recognizably socialist. Now, though the word 'socialist' was still a banner to be hoisted by any faction demanding consideration for its views, there were those on the right of the Party who had ceased to be socialist by any recognizable definition. It was a defection that some disguised by speaking of 'equality'. Some few others were sufficiently shameless to adopt no disguise for their abandonment of anything that could reasonably be called socialist. On the other side of the ideological fissure was the Left. The Left was aggrieved by the defeat of June 1970 and by the failures of 1964–70. It considered that it had been tranquillized rather than led by its supposedly left-of-centre Prime Minister Harold Wilson, and was now demanding that the Party abandon all new and revisionist doctrine and revert to its ancient superstitions. It was time to return to nationalization. Hence had arisen the proposal for a National Enterprise Board under which would be nationalized 25 unidentified large companies together with other major companies, such as Rolls-Royce and British Petroleum, in which the government held significant stakes. Electorally, the idea was an albatross but it was nevertheless popular among the activist rank and file. It was abominated by the Right and never accepted by Wilson as an election commitment. Yet, given the balance of power within the Party, and Wilson's notorious tendency to compromise in order, as he claimed, to keep his followers united, who could be sure that some elements in this policy might not be implemented? To all this dissension could now be added Europe. Europe had further divided Left from Right but had also divided the Right within itself.

Healey's economic inheritance comprised the four failures listed by *NIER* just before the February election. It compounded a vast current account deficit with high and rising inflation and the breakdown of Bretton Woods. At least the Bretton Woods system had provided economic policy with an anchor. the exchange rate. If the anchor was dragged, the signals of policy failure were at once apparent, and governments could react with their armoury of fiscal and monetary weapons. Now there was no anchor. Barber had not found one. On the contrary, he had exploited the lack of an anchor to indulge in a grossly inflationary orgy reversed belatedly in December 1973. With the oil price hike and rising commodity prices, the 7 per cent threshold of Phase 3 of Heath's incomes policy had loosed an inflationary balloon. It could not be hauled back to earth without dramatic policy changes, both fiscal and monetary, that appeared politically impossible to the new government in the months leading up to a new General Election.

A statutory incomes policy, which could have given assistance to fiscal and monetary measures, was ruled out by Labour's so-called Social Contract with the unions. The Social Contract had been negotiated with the TUC during the years of Opposition. It required a Labour government to consult with the unions on economic policy. The new government would be committed to keep down prices by food subsidies, by controls on rents and other costs, to redistribute income and wealth, and to encourage investment. There was no suggestion that there could be circumstances, such as a dramatic change in Britain's terms of trade, in which trade unionists would have to accept a reduced standard of living. A direct consequence of the Social Contract was that the new government had to accept Heath's 7 per cent threshold arrangement though, in truth, this was a commitment that would hardly have been escaped in any case. The Social Contract was based on the assumption that good behaviour by trade union members on the wages front could be secured by concessions to the political aims and ambitions of trade union leaders. But, although there were reforms that trade union leaders and their members wanted, for example the repeal of Heath's Industrial Relations Act, and direct action on prices always seemed to be welcome to the TUC, these actions by government were unlikely to bring sufficient material benefit to deter trade unionists from exploiting their industrial power. So far as a statutory incomes policy was concerned, Labour's hands were tied both by its election commitments and its weak position in Parliament. In July 1974, Heath's statutory incomes policy was abolished, though it left the 7 per cent threshold behind it. Wilson made it clear that in no circumstances would his new government break its pledge against the reintroduction of a statutory incomes policy. The senior civil service had thought that the one possible merit to be detected in the election of a Labour government lay in its relations with the trade unions which now, after their success in toppling Heath, seemed more powerful than Parliament and the government itself. Perhaps a Labour government could exact responsible behaviour from the unions where Heath had so miserably failed. Senior civil servants were doomed to disappointment even on this irreducible minimum of expectation.

THE KEYNESIAN APPROACH TO THE OIL PRICE HIKE

As though all this was not enough, Healey was being naively advised by the Treasury – but not only by the Treasury. The oil price hike was inflationary so far as the overall price level was concerned but it exercised a strong contractionary effect on output and employment. Keynesian economists, still dominant in the Treasury and elsewhere in centres of influence, wished to meet the contractionary impact by expansionary measures. They feared, legitimately, a rise in unemployment following Barber's measures of December 1973. Even where expansionary measures were not specifically advocated, they saw little urgency in a reduction of the balance of payments deficit. Further deflationary action was to be avoided because it would make bad worse and lead to even higher levels of unemployment. Any attack on the balance of payments deficit should be limited to the underlying deficit before the oil price hike and even that attack should not be too strenuous. The remaining deficit should be funded by borrowing. If the required improvement in the deficit proved impossible without further deflation, that would not be a matter primarily for the UK government but for the agenda of international discussions. The world would be brought back into the picture, but only for the purpose of instructing it how to behave, thereby rescuing British economic policy and enabling it to continue on the Keynesian path. Certainly the government should on no account deflate.

Towards the end of 1973, Sir Donald MacDougall left the Treasury where he had been Chief Economic Adviser, and joined the CBI with the same title. He tells us that at the CBI Council just before Christmas 1973, after the Barber measures of that month, he argued that it would be a wrong response to the oil producers' action if the UK and other industrial countries took further deflationary measures; these would do little to reduce their enormous external deficits on current account resulting from the jump in oil prices and would result in a pointless, beggar-my-neighbour cutting of imports from each other.[4]

This reasoning was reflected in the advice given to Healey both before he reached the Treasury and within the Treasury when he became Chancellor. On this question of the appropriate reaction to the oil price hike, there appeared, indeed, to be agreement between the front benches because similar advice had been given to Barber. In his final speech in the House as Chancellor on 6 February, Barber gave voice to this received wisdom:

> It is generally agreed – certainly on the two Front Benches – that we should borrow to cover the cost of the higher oil prices. Inevitably we shall run some balance-of-payments deficit apart from oil; and we shall also, as [Healey] agrees, need to borrow to cover part of that ... Our ability to borrow abroad the money that we need will depend crucially on confidence, and for that we should be seen to be making strong efforts to reduce our non-oil deficit. On the other hand, action which might increase the risk of a world recession must be avoided.[5]

Thus, according to Barber, there were two deficits, an oil deficit and a non-oil deficit. Only the latter was to be reduced but not in a way or to an extent that would prejudice the world economy.

Meanwhile the stage army of international economic cooperation had been at work. The IMF had established a Committee of Twenty to consider the reform of the international monetary system. At a meeting on 18 January 1974, at which Johannes Witteveen, Managing Director of the IMF, was present, the Committee decided to issue a statement. The statement concluded:

> In these difficult circumstances the Committee agreed that in managing their international payments, countries must not adopt policies which would merely aggravate the problems of other countries. Accordingly, they stressed the importance of avoiding competitive depreciation and the escalation of restrictions on trade and payments. They further resolved to pursue policies that would sustain appropriate levels of economic activity and employment, while minimizing inflation.[6]

To be instructed by the IMF not to deflate was manna to the new Labour government whose prime objective at the time was not to manage an economic crisis but to ensure that no elector was distressed nor vote lost. Though the IMF was no stranger to high-sounding declarations, this one could not possibly have been directed to Britain, a country with very limited reserves, with a vast balance of payments deficit, and with inflation rising without resistance to a peak of nearly 30 per cent. Or if it *was* directed to Britain, it should have been ignored as passing beyond the bounds of common sense. Some other countries were in a much stronger position. Germany never went into current account deficit during the oil price crisis and Japan rapidly emerged from the deficit caused by it. It could be hoped that countries such as Germany or Japan would have regard to the IMF's advice, though the hope would probably be in vain. Such advice could not be sensibly followed by Britain. In Britain, it had to be the first object of policy to cut the balance of payments deficit, oil and non-oil alike. It was nonsense to speak as though there were two separate deficits, the oil and the non-oil. There was one deficit and it had to be funded by borrowing.[7] To condemn vigorous action to reduce the deficit as in any way harming any other country was absurd. When, in the autumn of 1976, Britain was forced once again to turn for help to the IMF, it would then be found that the IMF had no patience with the claim that it had been providing an alibi for British economic management.

Healey later observed that only Britain and Italy obeyed these high-level injunctions. The USA, Germany and Japan, he wrote, 'deflated their economies so as to reduce their deficits at our expense . . .'[8] In other words, the governments of the USA, Germany and Japan saw it as their first responsibility in meeting the oil price hike to retain national control over inflation and the balance of payments. Only when they were satisfied that they had regained control, did they turn to other priorities such as the level of unemployment.

Healey may not, at this early stage in his career at the Treasury when he was receiving such advice, have had much experience of economic management. But it would be unfair to him to suggest that he was unaware of the domestic political benefits at that moment of proving himself a good world citizen by avoiding deflation. He proved himself a good world citizen, in the first place inadvertently, with perhaps some advantage to Labour's immediate electoral prospects. He did not deflate. Instead, he initiated the process which led inexorably to the autumn crisis of 1976 which almost ruined him.

THE FIRST BUDGET

If Healey needed evidence that the advice he was receiving from the Treasury should be tested before it was accepted, he would have found it in the out-turn of his first Budget. He discovered, too late, that he had been given faulty technical advice in the planning of his first Budget and, as a result, had been led seriously astray. As Healey believed that it was necessary to make an attack on the so-called non-oil deficit, he at first planned a Budget that would be deflationary to the extent of £500 million. He was seeking to achieve a difficult balance. An irresponsible Budget might lead the market to rebel and the government might be ejected from office. On the other hand, there was an election coming and there were recent electoral commitments which the electorate was quite likely to remember. Healey found that if he was to make the Budget deflationary to the extent he had initially thought necessary, and at the same time meet the new government's extensive expenditure commitments, there would have to be larger increases in taxation than he considered politically acceptable. He decided to be content with £200 million and told the House that 'My judgement is that this Budget should be broadly neutral on demand, with a bias, if any, on the side of caution.'[9] Even to achieve this reduced deflationary target, he had to raise income tax to 33p in the pound as against the 32p that he had originally intended, and raise Corporation Tax to 52p as against the 50p earlier expected.

The Treasury informed him that the out-turn of his Budget would be to reduce the PSBR to £2.7 billion, that is £1.5 billion less than 1973–4's £4.25 billion or £700 million less than the forecast PSBR for 1974–5 on unchanged policies. Healey made much of Barber's profligacy in bequeathing so large a PSBR, and of the discipline that, by implication, he was now introducing into fiscal policy. Unhappily, a year later in April 1975, he was compelled to announce that the PSBR out-turn for 1974–5 was £7.6 billion. The gap of nearly £5 billion between the forecast of March 1974 and the out-turn announced in April 1975 was due mainly to bad forecasting, though partly also to new decisions and inadequate control of public expenditure by a government intent on winning votes. Another error attributable to advice was the Treasury's overestimate of the liquidity of British companies. This led Healey, in the interest of a reduced PSBR, to impose a surcharge on

Advance Corporation Tax (ACT). This made such a deleterious impact on companies that its effect had to be urgently reversed soon after the October General Election. These errors did not enhance Healey's confidence in Treasury advice or Treasury forecasting. Nevertheless, the forecasting error on the PSBR was convenient politically. He could claim fiscal responsibility by planning a reduced PSBR without having to inflict too much embarrassing pain on the public. Despite the increases in expenditure and taxes, here was a Labour Chancellor who could claim a fiscal rectitude his Tory predecessor could not match. He could win merit with the market while escaping the political cost of actually deserving it.

For the actual PSBR out-turn, Healey had to carry public responsibility. To admit error was not his way. He had promised a PSBR lower than Barber's bequest but found himself saddled with one far larger. He had intended a slightly deflationary Budget but found that his Budget was reflationary. So be it. That would be the policy he would defend. It was after all in tune with the ideas of the Keynesian reflationists, even if it rejected the few cautious deflationists who also had access to his ear, for example his deputy and those Treasury officials concerned with overseas finance.[10] Healey, in his first year, could become attached to policies that had first emerged out of a bad forecast or had begun as debating points. For example, he attacked the 27 per cent increase in the money supply during Barber's last year. It was debating ammunition when he wanted to deflect criticism of rising inflation on to his predecessor. He did not have to be a monetarist to argue that an increase in money supply of that order must be inflationary but, having made the point, it became an incentive to ensure that such an increase never recurred on his watch.

THE ECONOMIC DEBATE – IN AND OUT OF THE TREASURY

The Treasury at official level had made its forecasting errors but, having launched the government unintentionally on a reflationary course, it now had the responsibility of advising the Chancellor where he should take his stand in the debate raging between the reflationists who feared rising unemployment and the deflationists who feared rising inflation and unsustainable balance of payments deficits. It was an important question but the Treasury was having difficulty making up its collective mind. It contained partisans of all schools of thought and of none.

Healey had indicated his preference for options and arguments rather than monolithic advice. He had a great love of enormous meetings at which he could listen, challenge and debate. His decisions were made more privately. While Healey's approach to policy formation added to the excitement of life in the Treasury, it also gave Treasury officials an excuse for not forming a Treasury view. The Treasury obeyed its political master and presented options, none of them too demanding.

The Treasury is a politically sensitive animal and it understands the role of Chancellors in winning elections. While there was an election to come, deflationary discipline could not be expected from any Chancellor who valued his occupancy of No. 11. Healey was perfectly happy, in the spirit of his revised reflationary philosophy, to offer the electorate in July a few titbits of concessions intended to influence votes in the coming General Election, even though he was by that time perfectly aware of the gross imperfections of the PSBR forecast. The July measures included a reduction in VAT which had a short-term effect on the RPI. There was some Treasury grumbling, but even more understanding. Healey presented his July measures as an attack on inflation whereas in fact they were designed as an attack on the Conservative Party's electoral prospects.[11]

The General Election of 10 October 1974 left Labour with an overall majority of three. By the time the election was out of the way, and the government was slightly more securely in office, the Treasury was running after Healey rather than guiding him. On 12 November 1974, the Chancellor opened his next Budget. It had three principal objects. The first was to make some redistribution in the burden of taxes so that the better-off paid more and the less well-off paid less. The second objective was to reduce by stages the subsidization of nationalized industry prices, thus reversing a policy employed by the Heath government in its attempt to control inflation. This was entirely sensible, especially as among the prices subsidized were energy prices. The third was to correct the error made in the March Budget in imposing a surcharge on ACT. This had imperilled the survival of some companies and made it more difficult for all companies to invest. The overall effect of the Budget was to add £800 million to the PSBR. Healey announced that the PSBR would now be £6.3 billion. It was not entirely a surprise either to the House or the market. The new estimate for the PSBR was, Healey added,

> a disturbingly large figure which one would never accept in normal circumstances. But in present circumstances, if I made an attempt to [reduce

it] ... the result could only have been a large fall in our national output and a massive increase in unemployment. This is because ... a large balance of payments deficit is inevitable in the present circumstances, and a large public sector deficit is the inevitable counterpart of this, given that the private sector as a whole cannot be in substantial deficit without grave consequences.[12]

So there was an inevitable PSBR counterpart to an inevitable balance of payments deficit. Yet, oddly, in March, Healey had aimed for a PSBR of £2.7 billion, less than half the figure he was now justifying to the House. He did not say that the theory of inevitable equivalences was due to his special adviser, Nicholas Kaldor, that Kaldor was deeply worried at an equivalence at such a high level and believed that far more strenuous efforts should be made to get both deficits down.[13] Some Keynesian economists were still explaining away the high PSBR. It simply compensated, they argued, for the high level of savings paradoxically provoked by the high level of inflation. Thus there were still economists who could find comfort for the Chancellor.

That the market was permitting Healey to take so complacent a view of his responsibilities was primarily due to two factors. The first was inertia. The oil producers were making large gains out of their sales of oil, needed somewhere to invest them, had traditionally invested a significant portion in London, and continued to do so. The effect was to support the exchange rate of sterling. The danger was that the oil producers would become more sophisticated in their investment planning, and would begin to diversify away from sterling. It could happen very suddenly. The other helpful factor was that oil had been discovered in the North Sea and that, sometime in the course of the next few years, Britain would become self-sufficient in oil, even a net exporter. British politicians who have long battled with the refractory British economy have a tendency to premature euphoria. The floating of sterling in 1972 had generated one such bout. The prospect of North Sea oil generated another. Here at last was the solution to Britain's balance of payments problems, an end to Stop-Go. Many in the market were initially influenced to take a more favourable view of sterling because of the prospect. Healey was inclined to share in the euphoria; it justified his softly-softly approach to the balance of payments problem. Why should he take a more energetic view of the balance of payments, with all the political and social disruption serious deflation might cause, when, within the lifetime of the present Parliament, Britain might be self-sufficient in oil? Yet the two economies of the developed world that were navigating most skilfully through the shoals, Germany and Japan, had neither indigenous oil in any quantity nor the prospect of it. It seemed possible to live in this new world without indigenous oil. It was far from clear that Britain's indigenous oil guaranteed balance in its overseas payments. If sterling reacted as might be expected to Britain's self-sufficiency in high-price oil, if public expenditure expanded at anything like the rate of Healey's first year, there could still be a balance of payments deficit. Any time gained for tough decision-making by the prospect of oil did not remove the need for tough decisions. Whatever the future held, there was still the present.

DÉMARCHE

By the end of 1974 the official Treasury had at last concluded that existing policies were not sustainable. This new concern was prompted by the fear that it might not be possible to fund the 1975 balance of payments deficit. The Co-ordinating Committee of Treasury Permanent Secretaries met and, early in January 1975, presented the Chancellor with a *démarche*. They told him that, while they were sorry about any political difficulties their advice might cause him, there was no longer support for his policies within the Treasury. Healey responded that he would like to see specific proposals but they must not constitute a typical Treasury deflationary package. That would be politically unacceptable. He said that he might be prepared to contemplate a tough, deflationary Budget in the spring of 1975 but any proposals must include measures with a direct effect in deflecting resources into the balance of payments. Such measures would enable him to persuade his colleagues that he had not become a prisoner of the Treasury.

Kaldor, one of the most brilliant economists of his time, had become a dominating influence within the Treasury. He was indifferent to incomes policies, voluntary or statutory, as a way of dealing with inflation. Their effect would be slight at best. He had long believed that the British economy needed a wider margin of spare capacity. He was quite prepared to accept a higher level of unemployment. In the 1960s and before, he had been one of the leading influences for devaluation or floating. The experience of 1967 had alerted him to the dangers of inflation after devaluation. He now wished to combine a strong deflationary package which would cut the PSBR, with an import surcharge/export subsidy scheme. Together these measures would reduce the current account deficit to manageable proportions without a politically disturbing rise in unemployment. A reduction in the PSBR would also gradually bring down the rate of inflation. That the import surcharge/export subsidy scheme was contrary to numerous international agreements into which the UK had entered, including the rules of the EEC, was not a matter that greatly disturbed Kaldor.

It was the Kaldor package, combining deflation with direct action on the balance of payments, that Treasury officials presented to Healey in response to his request for a package that was not just old-fashioned Treasury deflation. Their single point of difference from Kaldor was to put more emphasis on incomes policy. By this time, inflation in Britain was forecast to accelerate to the 20–25 per cent range. During 1974 wages nationally had risen 8–9 per cent faster than prices in the shops. Retail prices were rising at a rate of more than 20 per cent per annum.[14] There had been nothing like it in the previous 300 years. There was talk of wage settlements in the 40–45 per cent bracket. During 1974, Heath's thresholds could be allocated the blame. But rising oil and raw material prices were no longer the cause; indeed, commodity prices had fallen due to the contractionary effect internationally of the oil price hike. The prime cause now of accelerating inflation was wage settlements. Settlements of 20 per cent or more were being justified as consistent with the Social Contract. The Social Contract had not just failed – it had become counter-productive.

Already the UK rate of inflation was double that of almost all the UK's main competitors. Britain would be one of the few major countries in which inflation continued to accelerate during 1975. Barbara Castle, Secretary of State for the Social Services, begged trade unionists to take into account in their claims the benefits provided by government. She called it 'the social wage'. Trade unionists ignored her. They evidently wanted money in their pockets. They took the social wage for granted. It was not surprising in the circumstances that Treasury officials were not prepared to rely on deflation alone to deal with an inflation which was threatening to reach Latin American levels.

Healey had now received from Treasury officials the advice for which he had asked. They proposed an effective but 'voluntary' incomes policy, the import surcharge/export subsidy scheme, together with measures estimated to cut £2 billion from the 1975–6 PSBR, forecast on present policies to reach £10 billion. The package now had to withstand the exercise of Healey's Socratic skills. At a succession of long and large meetings, the advice was tested and the Treasury crumbled. It was easy enough for Treasury officials to remain united on incomes policy. At the prevailing level of inflation the only harm an incomes policy could do would be if the search for it deflected the government from the necessary deflation. But it was not the prospect of an incomes policy that was moving Healey's mind away from deflation. As time passed and no crisis erupted, he became less and less persuaded that it was necessary on the scale proposed by Kaldor and the Treasury. During 1974, the UK had suffered a record current account deficit of about £3.8 billion, or more than 5 per cent of GNP. During the first quarter of 1975, the deficit was running at an annual rate of £1.25 billion. It was arguable that the deflationary impact of the oil price hike was itself proving sufficient and that nothing more was required. The Keynesian influence remained strong in the Treasury. Sir Bryan Hopkin, the Chief Economic Adviser, wanted a neutral Budget. He, and other Treasury officials, soon showed themselves opposed to, or at least doubtful about, the import-export scheme although it had been part of the Treasury package. International agreements were not the only objection. It was highly uncertain whether it could get through the House of Commons, particularly with the referendum on continued British membership of the EEC looming up. Healey was from the beginning sceptical about it. Even Kaldor appeared to lose enthusiasm for it, though he remained staunch for serious cuts in the PSBR. Yet the import-export scheme was the only element in the package that would enable Healey to claim that he had not simply retreated into Treasury deflation. As the import-export scheme faded, the prospect of deflation to the extent recommended by Treasury officials faded with it. Treasury officials, to meet Healey's policy specifications, had put forward a package which included direct action on the balance of payments in which they did not really believe. They had been routed in debate by a Chancellor whose nose for nonsense was far more sensitive than it had been a year before, and had virtually abandoned the battlefield.

THE 1975 BUDGET AND A TOUCH ON THE TILLER

Yet, though the bodies of Treasury officials lay scattered around the field, the Chancellor himself remained alive, witty, well, and increasingly in command. He still had his Cabinet colleagues to deal with on the level of public expenditure but, in preparing his Budget, he had a much freer hand. The 15 April 1975 Budget, though it did not go nearly far

enough, provides the first indication of a change in Healey's approach
to the problems of economic management. He had decided that there
must be more rapid progress on the balance of payments and that the
battle against inflation had to take precedence over the battle against
unemployment. He was at last following the example of other countries
which always gave the control of inflation priority. For a Labour Chancellor, this change of approach could not be explicit, and implementing
it required great caution. It did not mean that he could give absolute
priority to inflation while unemployment remained on an upward trend.
But the change, fundamental in postwar British economic history, was
occurring.

In his Budget statement, Healey estimated the PSBR for 1974–5 at
£7.6 billion, a further large increase from the November 1974 estimate.
This represented 10 per cent of GNP. Pre-Budget PSBR estimates
for 1975–6 showed it reaching more than £10 billion. This would
represent 11 per cent of GNP. Healey therefore planned to reduce the
PSBR by well over £1 billion to £9 billion or to 10 per cent of the
previous year's GNP.[15] This was still £1 billion more than Treasury
officials had recommended but Healey felt that, judged on a full employment basis, it could be contemplated 'without alarm'.[16] He estimated
that, in 1976–7, there would be a further reduction of about £3 billion.
To achieve the reduction in the PSBR, Healey decided in 1975–6 to
rely on increases in indirect taxation and the basic rate of income tax
which would rise to 35 per cent. In the following year he promised to
achieve cuts in public expenditure. He assured the House that 'I have
aimed to keep the rate of monetary expansion firmly under control and
to avoid a repetition of the experience of 1972 and 1973 when excessive
monetary growth contributed substantially to inflationary pressures . . .
It is my intention that the growth of money supply should continue to
be contained at a level which does not fuel inflation.'[17] This statement
resulted in Healey's being accused of monetarism. The statement was
not necessarily monetarist. It is relatively uncontroversial, even among
economists, that a Budget deficit may increase the money supply and
that the increase may be inflationary. The Left, however, was not concerned by such niceties. For them, to speak of the money supply fuelling
inflation implied monetarism. Monetarism was associated with the
extreme right. It was therefore politically damaging to Healey to be
accused of monetarism. But, in April 1975, he felt he had to conciliate
the market even at some cost to his own political standing in the Labour
Party.

In emphasizing the necessity of swifter progress on the balance of payments, Healey, in his Budget statement, insisted that this was of political, not just economic, importance. 'We in Britain must keep control of our own policy . . . By relying unduly on borrowing we would run the risk of being forced to accept political and economic conditions imposed by the will of others. This would represent an absolute and unequivocal loss of sovereignty.'[18] Sovereignty was much in discussion as the referendum on Europe approached. Healey, never an enthusiastic 'European', had accepted the Cabinet's recommendation that the British people should vote in the referendum in favour of membership. It was in no way inconsistent that he was appealing for support to all those who valued Britain's continued ability to influence its own destiny. The loss of sovereignty that was now exercising him was to the money-lenders, not to Europe. The question that remained open after the Budget was whether he had yet done enough to avoid the loss of sovereignty that he feared.

Nevertheless, despite falling output and rising unemployment, Healey had introduced a somewhat deflationary Budget at the cost of heavy increases in taxation. It was a clear break with the Keynesian tradition. Subsequently he was to write:

> I abandoned Keynesianism in 1975 . . . his theories had two important weaknesses when applied in postwar Britain. They ignored the economic impact of social institutions, particularly the trade unions; in fact Keynesian policies were unlikely to work in Britain without strict control of incomes, a point of which the Treasury was already well aware. And they ignored the outside world.[19]

A 'VOLUNTARY' INCOMES POLICY

Healey was afraid that rising inflation could cause a massive, and sudden, withdrawal of foreign money from London. As he depended on foreign money to fund his deficits, it was a risk which he no longer felt able to ignore. With the Budget out of the way, he turned his attention to negotiating, with his Cabinet colleagues and with the trade unions, an incomes policy that would work. The negotiation had to be with his Cabinet colleagues as well as with the trade unions because not all of his colleagues had yet accepted that wage settlements were now the moving force behind inflation. Even if they did accept it, they were thinking in terms of an agreement with the trade unions which, like the Social Contract, would itself be grossly inflationary. Thus Michael Foot, Secretary of State for Employment, had adopted a proposal emanating from Jack Jones, General Secretary of the TGWU, the largest trade union of all, that pay increases should be governed by a flat-rate £9 per week norm equivalent to about 15 per cent. The adoption of such a norm would have been gravely inflationary. Foot was the principal representative of the trade unions in the Cabinet. Yet he was no Bevin, blood of their blood, flesh of their flesh. Day by day he had to convince them that he was their man. There came a time when even he found living with the trade unions physically and spiritually draining, but nothing could exhaust his loyalty to them. He had the power, by resignation, to bring the government down if it moved beyond limits that he was prepared to tolerate. It became a major object of policy to ensure that whatever was done on the incomes front did not provoke Foot's resignation. To achieve that object might require a considerable feat of legerdemain. If there was to be a statutory incomes policy, or if there were to be serious statutory elements to back up the policy, Foot would have to be persuaded that it could be presented as a voluntary policy.

Persuading the trade unions that wage settlements were now the source of inflation represented a challenge as great as reconciling Foot to the necessity of effective action. The trade unions believed that the Social Contract meant economic expansion and that the wage explosion had nothing to do with the inflation in prices. The TUC thought that the Budget should have been reflationary. If a Labour Chancellor deflated, it was he who was breaking the Contract. The TUC did not appear to understand that it was precisely the government's decision not to respond to rising unemployment by reflation that demonstrated how serious the inflationary situation had become. Evidence of the need for action piled up day by day and claim by claim. The National Union of Railwaymen had rejected an arbitration award which gave them 27 per cent and were demanding increases of up to 35 per cent which they claimed to be consistent with the Social Contract.

Only the most heroic efforts by Healey brought the unions to recognize the dangers of hyperinflation and to accept their responsibility in the matter. Even then he was only able to win barely sufficient cooperation when the inflation threatened the survival of the government. Fortunately he found an ally. Jack Jones had come to the conclusion that the TUC had to help the government to bring down inflation. Although he had at first set his target norm too high, he was prepared to negotiate both with the government and the CBI. He had his reasons. They included suspicions about the intentions of some Ministers whom he suspected of wishing to form a coalition. Jack Jones had great influence both with the TUC and with Foot. Once he had become an ally, it became possible to negotiate an agreement which met the different criteria of the key parties to it. To satisfy Jack Jones the policy had to be sufficiently socialist. This meant that the limit on wage increases, the norm, had to be flat-rate so that the lower paid would do proportionately better, and the increase had to be denied to those whose pay exceeded an agreed limit which would be the lowest he could negotiate with the rest of the TUC and with the government. To satisfy Foot, the policy had to be voluntary and any statutory back-up elements had to be sufficiently far in the background not to intrude too violently on his sensitivities. To satisfy Healey the flat rate norm could not be higher than £6 per week, though he would have preferred £5, and there had to be a statutory back-up somewhere in the wings to persuade a sceptical market that the incomes policy would actually have some effect. As a matter of political tact and judicial practicality, any sanctions held in reserve had to be against employers who yielded increases higher than the norm rather than against employees who demanded them. Fortunately, so serious was the situation that such discrimination against employers was acceptable to the CBI. With Harold Wilson, Healey and Foot leading for the government, and Jones for the TUC, everyone's criteria were sufficiently met. A flat-rate policy of £6 per week for those earning less than £8,000 per annum was agreed, and the government was saved. The success was announced to the House by Wilson on 11 July 1975.

Healey had now fought and won his battle for an incomes policy that would help rather than hinder the struggle against inflation. He hoped that his success would assist in bringing inflation down to 10 per cent by September 1976.[20] But, for his efforts, he had to pay a political price. At the annual conference of the Labour Party the following September, the Left organized to defeat him in the election for membership of the National Executive Committee of the Labour Party of which he had been a member. Not unexpectedly, they succeeded. It was a signal of the widening gap between the government and the activist members of the Labour Party.

THE CONTROL OF PUBLIC EXPENDITURE

Healey now turned to the control of public expenditure. It was not before time. In 1974 public expenditure increased in real terms by 8 per cent. The ratio of public expenditure to GDP in current market prices rose from 39.9 per cent in 1973–4 to 45.0 per cent in 1974–5.[21] In May 1975, Healey proposed a £3 billion package of cuts and higher charges. Discussion was deferred to July. The Chancellor found himself with scant support from the Prime Minister, and opposed not just by the Left, and by Barbara Castle, Secretary of State for the Social Services, but also by Tony Crosland, Secretary of State for the Environment, the real economist in the Cabinet, the Chancellor *manqué* who had been twice so cruelly overlooked. Crosland's view was that socialism was about public expenditure. It was the beginning of a battle that would last until Crosland's death in February 1977.

The market had been slow in realizing the risks to its money. It had continued depositing its money in London more by inertia than in the exercise of a considered judgement. It began to appreciate its risks at about the same time that Healey began to realize the risks in the policies he had conducted during his first year in office. Once the market was alerted, it proved very difficult to persuade. The market could be excused its doubts because it was exceedingly difficult for it, or anyone else, to believe anything it was told about the British economy or the public finances. It was soon to emerge that a Treasury forecast was once more undergoing serious revision. By the autumn of 1975, the Treasury was forecasting a PSBR not of £9 billion, as estimated at the time of the Budget, but of £12 billion. At a meeting of senior Ministers to consider the discrepancy, Callaghan, Foreign Secretary and former Chancellor, urged, 'Let us do the tough things now and get them out of the way.'[22] Recurrent public expenditure crises seemed to dog Labour governments. They were disruptive politically and damaging to the morale of the government. It became the continuing cry of those Ministers who thought something should be done that *enough* should be done to put the issue to sleep and thus avoid future crises. Unfortunately, the Cabinet's judgement of 'enough' was repeatedly faulted by a market that had good reasons to be distrustful both of the information it was given and of the willingness of the government to take any necessary corrective action.

Healey's battle for expenditure cuts was inhibited by a deformation

characteristic of Labour Chancellors. He had his own favourite beneficiary of public expenditure. It was industrial policy. When he
announced cuts in public expenditure, he liked to announce an increase
in expenditure on industrial policy, perhaps of as much as £200 million.
There were two reasons. The first was that he believed in it as an
instrument for regenerating the British economy. He wanted the Treasury to have a role in industrial policy. Lack of experience of industry
left him open to fantasies about the prospective value of industrial policy.
The second reason for Healey's devotion to industrial policy was that
the TUC also was devoted to it. He was so dependent on the TUC
for the success of his incomes policy that he felt a political compulsion
to give them something that they wanted. Industrial policy was not the
only tribute Healey had to pay to the trade union movement. Even
though the existing £6 flat-rate policy seemed to be holding, there would
be other rounds of incomes policy to come. The TUC claimed to be
very worried about the level of unemployment, and insisted that it be
brought down. From time to time Healey would produce a small nugget
of reflation and bid it up for more than it was worth. The whole time
he was manoeuvring on the brink; if he went too far, he would lose the
market. If he did not go far enough, he would lose the TUC.

Healey was now asking for cuts in public expenditure in future years
of more than £4 billion. At Cabinet meetings in December 1975, he
was given essentially what he had asked. It would make his task more
difficult when later he came back for more. Wilson counted the votes
in Cabinet and declared a majority for Healey; others present counted
the votes also and concluded that the majority went the other way. But
the Prime Minister's arithmetic was not challenged, which shows the
importance for Chancellors in having not merely the support of the
Prime Minister but of a Prime Minister with a reputation as a statis-
tician.[23] The Public Expenditure White Paper published in February
1976[24] showed cuts as compared with the previous year's White Paper[25]
of £1.6 billion in 1977–8 and £3 billion in 1978–9. Beyond that year,
the level of public expenditure was to be frozen. On the other hand,
comparisons with the previous year also showed increases of £1 billion
in 1975–6 and nearly £500 million in 1976–7. It was easier to extract
from Cabinet cuts in the longer term if demands for increases in the
short term were accommodated. Moreover an application had been
made to the IMF for a stand-by facility. Above certain limits, IMF
loans or standbys become conditional. This application was large enough
to subject the UK to IMF conditionality. By conceding cuts in public

expenditure, even if only in the longer term, the Cabinet was doing in advance what its lender of last resort might be considering asking it to do in any case. The British Executive Director, William Ryrie, excused the British application by telling the Executive Board of the IMF that British policy had been guided in part 'in line with the request of Mr Witteveen and the Committee of Twenty in January 1974 for countries to avoid excessive deflation'.[26]

THE KING IS DEAD, LONG LIVE THE KING

On the subject of public expenditure, the House of Commons also had to be reckoned with. The Left in the Parliamentary Labour Party believed that the IMF should be prepared to lend to the UK unconditionally and that, in any case, cuts in public expenditure were inappropriate for a socialist government. On 10 March 1976, the Public Expenditure White Paper which set out the revised public expenditure programme was defeated in a vote in the House of Commons due to a rebellion by the Left. The defeat did nothing for the credibility of the government internationally. The following day the government won a vote of confidence in a debate at the end of which Healey berated the Left. He knew they could not vote against the government on a vote of confidence and bring it down, whatever he said. He gave full vent to his feelings. He did not realize that the Left would have their petty revenge, if they wanted it, soon enough. Five days after the confidence debate, Wilson indicated his intention to resign as Prime Minister as soon as the PLP elected a successor. Healey was a candidate for the succession. He never had much hope. Unlike Callaghan, Jenkins, and Foot, there was no organized grouping within the PLP to support him. He had always disdained claques, or at least had always acted as though he disdained them. To organize his campaign, he had to rely on the small band of admirers who had found him to be the ablest and most attractive figure in the Cabinet. Whatever chance there was, the speech in the confidence debate killed it. Callaghan emerged as victor, the right coalescing behind him as Crosland, Healey and Jenkins fell at the successive ballots. Wilson had given way to an older man but, as it proved, a better Prime Minister. Foot was now Deputy Leader. Healey remained at the Treasury.

Three of the Prime Ministers in our period had been themselves Chancellor of the Exchequer. All appear to have acquired a distrust of the Treasury. Callaghan had not been comfortable at the Treasury and had emerged from it without great credit. He could hardly avoid feeling bruised, but the experience had taught him lessons. One was the uncertainty of economic prediction. Another was that the experts in the Treasury were not necessarily expert. Callaghan kept his Chancellor but gave him a hard time.

A DISCONTINUITY

A few days before Wilson's resignation a run on the pound began. The Treasury had been forecasting no improvement in the balance of payments in 1976 as compared with 1975 and deterioration beyond that. There had been renewed discussion within the Treasury and the Bank of England during the latter months of 1975 of such alternatives as import controls and depreciation, perhaps to a fixed rate in the German snake. But general import controls were no more an option than previously, and Healey intensely disliked policies which involved the depreciation of sterling. He was always fearful that sterling would fall out of control. His only decision had been to defer a decision.[27] During the first two months of 1976, sterling, supported by interest rates high by international standards, remained reasonably stable at about $2.05. OPEC money was still being attracted. The situation was difficult to read, so difficult that in its February 1976 issue, *NIER* succeeded, in the one edition, in recommending depreciation, forecasting greater stability in the exchange rate, and warning of 'a sharp discontinuity . . . precipitated by some unexpected development which shakes the confidence of creditors'.[28]

The sharp discontinuity occurred in the first days of March 1976. Minimum lending rate (MLR) had been coming down gradually since November 1975, when it stood at 12 per cent, to 9.25 per cent where it stood at the beginning of March.[29] The descent had not disturbed the exchange rate. On 4 March, the Bank of England sold sterling to meet a market demand. On 5 March, MLR was reduced by 0.25 per cent to 9 per cent. Neither action signalled an intention to devalue the currency. There was no such intention because there had been no such decision. Such a decision could not have been taken without Wilson's consent and he would not have consented just before his intended resignation. Healey would not have recommended it because he disliked deliberate depreciation. Both actions by the Bank were normal interventions in the market. According to its own account, the Bank was selling sterling to prevent a *rise* in the exchange rate and to strengthen the reserves.[30] The slight reduction in interest rates was the outcome of a perfectly normal market judgement. It was what happened next that, in combination with the Bank's actions, alerted the market. On 9 March, the Nigerians announced that their foreign exchange holdings had been diversified from their previous predominantly sterling content. Anyone who had been reading the tea leaves, and was long in sterling, could have decided to diversify out of sterling. Then, on 10 March, the government was defeated in the Commons on its Public Expenditure White Paper. This combination of events appears to have awakened the market to the overvaluation of sterling, to the prospects for the UK current account, to the government's lack of will and authority, and to the continued high inflation, exceeding the hopes of the previous July. Sterling began to weaken. Once it began to weaken, 'leads and lags' added to the downward pressure.[31] Despite expensive intervention by the Bank to support the rate, nothing seemed able to prevent its decline. The attack on sterling affected other of the weaker European currencies. In the middle of March, the French franc withdrew from the snake.

The run on sterling made it even more necessary to negotiate a second year of incomes policy. The first year had had some success but clearly was not going to achieve the objective of inflation down to 10 per cent by September 1976. Healey's new objective was inflation at international levels by the end of 1977. In an attempt to encourage the trade unions to accept a deal that would help to achieve that objective, Healey in his Budget of 6 April offered his tax-pay proposal. He offered to increase income tax reliefs in two stages, the first £370 million unconditionally, the second £1,000 million conditional on union agreement to limit wage increases in the following year to an average of 3 per cent. To make income tax changes conditional on union agreement to an incomes policy represented a further increment of trade union influence. But it was politically realistic. There were many respects in which the Budget was unattractive to the market. Healey argued that the Budget 'must not on balance add much to demand . . .'[32] He described it as 'an almost neutral Budget'.[33] Yet he had had to announce that the PSBR in 1975–76 had exceeded his target of a year earlier, and would be about £10.75 billion, and that his estimate for 1976–7 was £12 billion.[34] While £12 billion was lower as a percentage of GNP than in 1975–6, it could have been less but for the tax cuts provided for in the tax-pay proposal and if there had been further cuts in public expenditure.[35] The tax-pay proposal was not of a kind immediately appetizing to market opinion, while it would certainly have regarded cuts in current public expenditure as a sign of serious intention. In fact public expenditure was being cut by the operation of the system of cash limits developed in the Treasury during 1975 but neither the market nor even the Treasury were aware how effective they were being in cutting departmental expenditures. On 5 May, Healey announced to the House trade union agreement to limit wage increases to 5 per cent with a minimum of £2.50 and a top figure of £4 plus the income tax concessions that had been offered. To secure agreement Healey had moved from 3 per cent to 5 per cent. The 3 per cent had always been a negotiating position but the change hurt credibility.

THE JUNE STAND-BY

The agreement for a further year of incomes policy did not persuade the market, always sceptical about the efficacy of such arrangements. By 3 June, sterling had declined to a new low of $1.70. On Friday 4 June, Dr Jelle Zijlstra, President of the Netherlands Central Bank and also of the Bank of International Settlements, intervened. He had come to the conclusion that sterling was now undervalued and should be supported. He proposed, with the help of friendly central banks, to put together a stand-by credit which could be used to support the pound.[36] On 7 June, Healey was able to inform the House that the Bank of England had negotiated a short-term stand-by credit of $5.3 billion. Of this $2 billion was being provided by the US Federal Reserve. This gave the Federal Reserve and the US Administration a lever. Normally the stand-by would have been for three months, renewable once for a further three months. Sometimes, however, stand-bys have been permitted to linger beyond one renewal. Dr Zijlstra himself does not seem to have regarded it as necessary to fix a date for final repayment in advance and it was certainly hoped by the British government that there would be no predetermined repayment date. The US Administration, however, had a different idea. It wanted a fixed date for repayment. The US Treasury Secretary was William Simon. Simon was a rich man. He was sometimes referred to disparagingly in British government circles as a 'bond salesman'. The suggestion seemed to be that someone who actually had experience of markets should not be US Treasury Secretary and determining policy opposite the UK. The hostility to Simon arose from the fact that, unburdened by certain types of economic wisdom still prevalent in some parts of Whitehall, he did not accept that he had any duty, as a good creditor, to lend his country's money to support policies which the British government might consider enlightened but he did not. Healey regarded him as being 'far to the right of Genghis Khan'.[37] Unfortunately, debtors cannot always choose their creditors and it was with Simon that the British government had to deal. The Americans insisted that a condition of the stand-by was that it could only be renewed once, making the final date for repayment 9 December 1976. Callaghan and Healey were forced to agree that if, by that date, the British government could not repay any use it had made of the stand-by, it would go to the IMF for a longer-term stand-by. The question now was whether the UK would be able to repay the stand-by by 9 December out of its own reserves and thus avoid further recourse to the IMF. If it could not, British economic sovereignty would be in question.

The availability of the stand-by could have bolstered market confidence in sterling. The market seems, however, to have been less impressed by the availability of the stand-by than by the fact that such help had once more proved necessary. There were now favourable factors in the British economic panorama. Inflation was down, even if not nearly enough. The additional competitiveness deriving from the 10 per cent depreciation of sterling since March would have its eventual effect on the current account. There was, however, another less satisfactory side of the equation. The first effect of the depreciation was to increase the current account deficit. Inflation was still high and Healey had compromised on 5 per cent instead of 3 per cent for his incomes policy. Public expenditure and the PSBR were regarded as being excessive. The government could not be sure of the House of Commons and was overtly subject to trade union pressure. Finally, the stand-by would have to be repaid on December 9.

Put on notice by what was virtually an ultimatum by the Americans, Callaghan reluctantly accepted that he would have to agree to one more tiresome, morale-sapping round of public expenditure cuts. This conviction led him to clash with his old friend, Tony Crosland, whom he had elevated to the high office of Foreign Secretary. Healey was arguing that resources needed to be freed so that Britain could take advantage of the expansion expected in the world economy. The cuts for which he was asking, amounting to about £2 billion, were not, in his view, to be regarded as deflation but as making room for exports.

Crosland demanded how resources could be under any strain when unemployment was so high. The required resources, he argued, were already available. Tony Benn wanted to borrow from the IMF under the mistaken impression that it would uncomplainingly endorse British policies and that it was some kind of cash cow that spewed forth financial assistance unconditionally to willing but thirsty borrowers.[38] Between 6 and 21 July there were seven Cabinet meetings, climaxing with two on 21 July. Eventually cuts of just under £1 billion were agreed but, as it was expected that the market would not be satisfied, the package was topped up by higher taxation. A further £1 billion was to be extracted in the form of a 2 per cent addition to the employers' national insurance contribution. The effect was to be a PSBR in 1977–8 of no more than £9 billion. Healey hoped that at last enough had been done to convince the most critical observer of the seriousness of the government's intentions. In his statement of 22 July Healey gave what he hoped would be further comfort to the market. He asserted once more that he did not intend to allow the growth of the money supply to fuel inflation. He announced as an expectation, rather than as a target, that during the financial year, money supply growth would be about 12 per cent.[39] Healey was prepared for the purposes of policy to take it as an axiom that if the growth in the money supply was allowed to exceed the growth in the real economy, inflation would follow.[40] He also knew the importance of market prejudices to a government in trouble. For the moment it was as important to carry the market with him as it was the trade unions. It was the failure of the public expenditure exercise that let him down.

During August sterling held steady at about $1.77. But the outlook was sensitive to the least bad news. It is possible that if the government had, in July, made a £2 billion cut in public expenditure instead of supplementing a £1 billion cut with £1 billion of added taxation, the market might have been satisfied that enough had indeed been done. As it was, the July public expenditure exercise seems simply to have provided conclusive evidence that there just was no way of persuading this government to come to its senses. It soon became apparent that, so far as the market was concerned, the moving target of 'enough' had not yet been done. There were still too many worrying signals: inflation was still 14 per cent, the current account was deteriorating, the money supply figures were poor, it was difficult to sell gilts. As Healey knew, the PSBR estimate had risen since the July measures. The same forecast never seemed to hold for more than a few weeks. On 1 September, the

Federal Reserve in New York confirmed that up to 30 June, Britain had withdrawn $1.1 billion from the $5.3 billion stand-by. The conviction was growing that the government would have no choice but to make an application to the IMF to fund its repayment obligations on the June stand-by. On 10 September, MLR was raised by 1.5 per cent to 13 per cent. On 16 September the Bank of England called on the banks and finance houses for £350 million special deposits in order to slow the monetary expansion.

CALLAGHAN EDUCATES LABOUR

In the week before the Labour Party conference at the end of September, Healey warned the Economic Strategy Committee of the Cabinet that another sterling crisis was pending and that an application must be made to the IMF for another loan. However, no announcement was to be made before Healey had attended the annual IMF/IBRD Conference to be held that year in Manila. On 27 September, the first day of the Labour Party conference, sterling dropped 3 cents and fell below $1.70. On 28 September, as Healey, together with Gordon Richardson, Governor of the Bank, were at Heathrow about to leave for Manila, they learnt that there was panic on the exchanges. Sterling had fallen a further 4.5 cents to $1.64. Healey returned to London from the airport.

On the same Tuesday on which Healey retreated from Heathrow, Callaghan made a speech to the Labour Party conference, drafted in part by his son-in-law Peter Jay, which signalled that the government was at last coming to terms with the constraints imposed by the world economic crisis.

> For too long . . . we postponed facing up to fundamental choices and fundamental changes in our society and in our economy . . . The cosy world we were told would go on for ever, where full employment would be guaranteed by a stroke of the Chancellor's pen . . . We used to think that you could just spend your way out of a recession . . . I tell you in all candour that that option no longer exists, and that in so far as it ever did exist, it only worked . . . by injecting a bigger dose of inflation into the economy, followed by a higher level of unemployment . . . That is the history of the last twenty years.[41]

The speech was not popular with the Labour conference. It questioned truths that Labour Party members were satisfied had been long established. It implied that the world did not, as they had hoped, intend to arrange its affairs to ensure Britain a living. It was a reluctant admission that Britain was not an island, that its government had to retain the confidence of those upon whom the success of its economic policy depended. Successive British governments had proved rather bad at it and had exhausted the patience of their allies. Foreign governments had long accepted that a prime object of policy must be confidence and that, therefore, whatever the IMF or economists might say about the requirements of international cooperation, they should not threaten confidence in their national policies by increasing exposure to the market or to international lending institutions beyond what their national reputation would stand. Why could not Britain behave likewise? Those were the weary thoughts behind Callaghan's sermon. Among Callaghan's audience was the US Administration. He received gratifying confirmation from President Ford that it had been a good speech. But it was only a speech – whether Callaghan himself had really yet accepted the full implications of his own words was yet to be discovered. It was too much to expect that the Labour Party as a whole, or even the Cabinet as a whole, should understand its full implications.

On 29 September, with the agreement of Callaghan, Healey announced that an application was being made to the IMF for support amounting to $3.9 billion, the largest sum ever sought from it. The sum was so large that it would force the IMF to seek supplementary resources. Among the countries that would be invited to contribute were the USA and Germany. They would have to be satisfied that the British government accepted the full implications of Callaghan's words. They would have to be satisfied with the conditions imposed in any agreement between the IMF and the UK government. On 30 September, Healey made a speech at the Labour conference that demonstrated that, at last, he was in fighting mode. He was fighting for the country, for the government, and indeed for his own career. But he still felt able to claim that the economic fundamentals were in place, and that therefore all that was now needed was an IMF certificate of good housekeeping which would confirm that the fundamentals were in place and that therefore the market could be satisfied. He told the conference that he would negotiate with the IMF 'on existing policies'. 'I mean things we do not like as well as things we do like. It means sticking to the very painful cuts in public expenditure . . . It means sticking to the pay policy.' Healey was to discover very soon that existing policies were not enough, that 'enough' was still some way off. How far off would now be a matter for the IMF.

HEALEY SURVIVES

Healey was entering the most difficult period of a tenure at the Treasury which, thus far, could have brought him little satisfaction. One of his problems was that Callaghan, having evoked Peter Jay at the Labour Party conference, appeared to be regressing to Keynesian orthodoxy as expounded by his old friend and supporter Tony Crosland. Callaghan was being counselled by Crosland to turn against Healey. An incident in October made it apparent that Healey could not rely on the Prime Minister's support. Between the spring and autumn of 1976, the money supply was expanding too rapidly. Gilts were difficult to sell because of the market's expectation of higher interest rates. On 10 September MLR had been raised to 13 per cent but even that was not enough. On 6 October, Healey was advised by the Governor of the Bank to raise MLR to 15 per cent. Callaghan at first refused to agree. He warned Healey that if he raised the matter in Cabinet, he would not have the Prime Minister's support. Healey decided that he would have to raise the matter in Cabinet. In his memoirs he tells how he discussed the matter with this author 'as the only member of the Cabinet on whom I could count'. Fortunately, before the matter came to Cabinet, the Prime Minister conceded. The increase in MLR went ahead, accompanied by a further call for special deposits, this time for £700 million. These measures produced a sharp slowdown in monetary growth.

On 24 October the *Sunday Times* reported that the US Treasury and the IMF had agreed conditions for the UK drawing which included sterling at $1.50. Though vigorously denied both by the IMF and the US Treasury, sterling reacted sharply, falling 7 cents on Monday 25 October. Healey came under severe criticism, not just from the Conservative Party but in the *Financial Times*. Samuel Brittan wrote of Healey's loss of credibility. It was argued that sterling would not have fallen by 7 cents in response to a newspaper article but for the parlous condition of the UK economy under Healey's stewardship. It could have been the nadir of his fortunes. Callaghan, however, remained loyal. There is no evidence that he ever seriously contemplated replacing Healey though there were leaks to the press that he was fed up with his Chancellor.[42] Who should he appoint if he moved Healey? Jenkins had left the Cabinet to become President of the European Commission.

In any case it must be questionable whether, whatever Callaghan may have said to Jenkins at one time or another, he could really have brought himself to appoint as Chancellor the man who had taken the credit for *his* devaluation.[43] To give Jenkins the opportunity of saving the country twice was more than could be expected from Prime Ministerial flesh and blood. Crosland *might* be right but it was perfectly clear that the market did not like what it knew of his ideas. There was one member of the Cabinet whose views had long been liked by the market but that very fact ruled him out as too right-wing and too risky given that a Labour Cabinet had to be kept together.[44] Moreover, Healey wounded would be a dangerous animal whereas Healey as a weakened Chancellor might be more amenable to advice from his Prime Minister. Healey it had to be. What could have been the nadir of Healey's career became the apogee. During the next two months he displayed to the full all his considerable courage, and moral and intellectual strength. He fought back to achieve total command. He won not just the vote in Cabinet when, after some delay, Callaghan came to the conclusion that there was no alternative to Healey's policy of forging with the IMF the best agreement he could get. He also won the argument.

NEGOTIATING WITH THE IMF

The view of Callaghan, of many in the Treasury, of Crosland and, to start with, of Healey, was that the UK had already done enough to justify the IMF issuing its certificate of good housekeeping and making its money available. However, as Healey rapidly realized, whatever the economic arguments, something more would have to be given to the IMF. The IMF had to achieve an agreement with the UK that satisfied its own paymasters, primarily the USA and Germany, and that safe-guarded its own reputation. If it made an agreement with the British government that then failed to persuade the market, its reputation would be severely damaged. Even if it was true that the UK had done enough, it remained equally inevitable that it would now have to do more. It was the penalty for past misbehaviour. Callaghan at first did not seem to realize that the constraints on the IMF ensured that it must demand something more. Yet, though the Cabinet was far from accepting this, it was desirable to go for overkill from the point of view of the British government itself. It had tried to satisfy the market so many times and each time it had failed; if it failed again, the government might well collapse. There was thus a certain mutual interest between the IMF and the UK government. It had to be an agreement that would survive the practised scepticism of the market about anything the UK government did or said.

Callaghan seems to have feared the collapse of his government. In this he was not alone. There were many, including Tony Benn and even some senior officials in the Treasury, whose minds went back to 1931 when a Labour government had collapsed under the impact of economic crisis.[45] If it happened again, there would be a serious political reaction on the Left and among the trade unions, and Britain might indeed prove ungovernable. Callaghan therefore hoped that he could persuade his friends, Gerald Ford, President of the USA, and Helmut Schmidt, Chancellor of Germany, to understand his predicament and prevail upon the IMF to be understanding too. In the one case it would be some return for services rendered over the years, often against British national interests. In the other it would be the solidarity which one social democrat expects from another.

Both Ford and Schmidt may have wanted to help their old friend. But Ford was a lame duck President who, on 2 November, had lost his election to Jimmy Carter. Though the US Administration had considerable influence within the IMF, it was not the kind of influence that could persuade the IMF to prejudice its own credibility. Nor was the US Administration united in the belief that it had any duty to the UK, which was repeatedly returning to the IMF trough for more. Neither the US Treasury of Bill Simon, nor the Federal Reserve of Arthur Burns, saw any reason to bail Britain out from its misguided economic policies. In the context of the Anglo-American relationship, such as it was, the IMF could provide a useful service. It could enforce discipline on a country whose misbehaviour in the conduct of its economic affairs might seriously damage the international economy, while relieving the USA of the need to become too directly involved. Harold Lever, the Chancellor of the Duchy of Lancaster and personal economic adviser to both Wilson and Callaghan, was sent on an expedition to Washington. He was to get the IMF terms softened and he was to get agreement on funding the sterling balances to be announced at the same time as agreement with the IMF. He had conversations with the President and with other members of the Administration but not with the IMF which showed no wish to see him. But Lever's friendships in Washington proved no more helpful than Callaghan's. It was clearly Washington's view that the USA should leave the actual negotiations to the IMF.

Whatever was done about the sterling balances, the Administration did not want that question entangled with the negotiations between the British government and the IMF. There must be agreement with the IMF first. Then there could be a look at the question of the sterling balances.[46] The British government was back with the problem of negotiating agreement with the IMF.

A serious negotiation with the IMF implied for Callaghan two problems. The first was how to keep his Cabinet together without repeating the experience of 1931, without resignations, in particular without the resignation of Michael Foot. This was a problem that Callaghan probably exaggerated. There was no inclination on the part of members of his Cabinet to resign and, in the background, Jack Jones was being helpful, persuading left-wing Ministers to make the best of it and on no account to let the Tories in. However, Callaghan decided that to keep his Cabinet together, he would allow them to talk themselves out. They would then feel that they had been consulted and it would also give him time to make up his own mind. Early in November he said to Healey that Crosland had told him it was all a bankers' ramp and that he was inclined to believe it. The conversation was not good for Healey's morale. It did not suggest that much assistance would be available from the Prime Minister.[47]

Callaghan's decision to allow the Cabinet to talk itself out gave plenty of time for discussion of the options in Cabinet. It was a Cabinet in which Healey had few friends. The social democrats under the leadership of Crosland saw no reason for cuts in public expenditure to meet what they regarded as the IMF's unconscionable demands. The Left was adamantly opposed to any concessions to the IMF. The IMF appeared to them as a ferocious deflater threatening everything for which Labour stood. Callaghan's second problem was the question of substance. Was it right to make further cuts in public expenditure? The IMF team which arrived in London on 1 November had mentioned a figure of £3 billion as the appropriate cut in public expenditure for 1977–8 and £4 billion for 1978–9.[48] The team admitted, however, that they were open to persuasion. The members of the team were awaiting discussions with the Treasury at official level. Callaghan, however, pending the outcome of his probes in Washington and Bonn, had ordered Treasury officials to refrain from discussions of substance with the IMF. In any case, the official Treasury, divided on the merits and fearful that IMF pressure would bring about the fall of the government, was not in the best condition to give guidance to the IMF team. It was, however, clear to Treasury officials that the IMF's opening ideas were far beyond the bounds of political acceptability. It was clear also to the IMF team that this would be a tough negotiation and that it had better start with a tough negotiating position.

Healey's first task was to persuade Callaghan that the right course was to seek the best possible agreement with the IMF. He therefore had to show that Crosland, the intellectual leader of the opposition, was being unrealistic. He had to do this despite his own sympathy with the *merits* of Crosland's arguments. He himself thought that enough had already been done but he knew that he had a debt to discharge in December, that he could not discharge it without IMF assistance, and that therefore he would have to concede something, as far as he was concerned as little as possible, to the IMF. Crosland's arguments, extensively leaked in the press at the time, and often taken there as representing the intellectual high ground, are summarized by Susan Crosland:

> There was no economic case for the cuts, [Crosland] said. He dealt with the arguments one by one. With 1.25 million unemployed, nobody could say that there was not enough spare capacity to increase exports. Far from reducing the PSBR, the spending cuts would mean higher unemployment, which would in turn mean higher social security payments and lower tax revenue, thus actually increasing the PSBR. In any case, Treasury forecasts of the PSBR were unreliable; other experts' forecasts were much lower than the Treasury's ... So far as the trade unions were concerned, Jack Jones might agree, but the public sector would not. Without the public sector unions the Social Contract ... would collapse. The only serious argument for cuts was one in terms of international confidence. But what would happen to confidence if the Government bowed down and accepted the package, and as a result the Social Contract broke, and the smouldering resentment of the PLP meant that the Government could not deliver the cuts in the House of Commons[49]

As some of the Cabinet's social democrats were coming to appreciate, this was the kind of argument that might impress in the Senior Common Room of an Oxbridge College but which was hardly relevant to the political and economic realities of the moment. The Treasury might have its forecasts wrong but who was going to advance money on the basis of any forecast, whether from a government whose forecasts had been repeatedly faulted by the out-turn or from independent forecasters whose record was no better? Crosland himself could not know whether what he was saying was true or not. Inflation was still high, the trade figures were still worrying, there was a bill due for payment in December. Even if, as Crosland was wont to say, everything was now in place for the long-looked-for economic recovery, it could all be undermined by market disbelief. If the market had believed that everything was now in place, money would have flowed into London once again. In fact during the period early March to early December 1976, approximately the period of Callaghan's occupation of No. 10, the value of sterling as compared with a range of other currencies had fallen by 20 per cent, a depreciation greater than the devaluations of 1949 and 1967. When faced by such a riposte, Crosland further undermined his own credibility by taking refuge in threats. The government, he thought, should threaten to introduce import deposits. It should threaten to remove its troops from Germany.

Callaghan himself, at one point, seemed to be attracted by the use of threats, such as the withdrawal of British troops from Germany, to influence his foreign friends into a more helpful frame of mind.[50] It was becoming a British theme that the UK was especially deserving of help in consideration of its contribution to the defence of the West. As we have seen, Wilson and Jenkins tried the same line of argument in November 1968. It was a humiliating consequence of Britain's economic weakness that British Prime Ministers thought it appropriate to use threats of this kind when its allies showed themselves insufficiently considerate. Callaghan seemed particularly attracted by his discovery that import controls were permissible under the GATT. When Witteveen, at the request of President Ford, paid him and Healey a secret visit in London on 1 December, Callaghan had a copy of the GATT charter on the table. It was an idle gesture which was unlikely to influence Witteveen. It was made more idle by the fact that Callaghan had at last decided to support Healey. At a European Summit on 29 and 30 November it had become quite apparent that there was nothing to expect from Schmidt. If the government was to negotiate with the IMF, there was no question of import controls, whatever the GATT charter said.

Throughout the long debate in Cabinet and, before that, in the Economic Strategy Committee of the Cabinet, Healey had remained determined, eloquent and persuasive. He allowed no argument to pass unanswered. There was no nonsense uttered, no web of wish-fulfilment spun (and there was plenty of each) that was not immediately dismissed for what it was. It was the supreme achievement of a Chancellor who, having been for months under intolerable strain, was now drawing on what were, perhaps, his last resources of courage and intellectual power. On 2 December, he opened the discussion in Cabinet. There was a $1.6 billion drawing on the stand-by that had to be repaid. If it was repaid without an IMF drawing, it would leave less than $2 billion of usable reserves, not nearly enough to resist the onslaught on sterling that would follow a breakdown in negotiation with the IMF. Unless the PSBR was cut from the present forecast of £10.2 billion to £8.7 billion, the IMF would not lend and the government would be unable to borrow abroad. No one believed this would be deflationary. Helmut Schmidt might be to the right of Milton Friedman but the world agreed with him. Anything less than Healey was proposing would not restore confidence even if the IMF did accept it. On the other hand, if an agreement was made with the IMF, the government would be able to borrow again and there would be a safety-net for the sterling balances. He dangled the possibility of import deposits but recognized that they would be unacceptable to the IMF and therefore not negotiable.[51]

Callaghan then announced his support for Healey. He had previously gone as far as to accept that the Cabinet should be willing to make cuts that would reduce the swelling PSBR to the £9 billion figure agreed the previous July. Now he was prepared to support Healey and a rather lower PSBR. He suggested an approach on the analogy of a three-legged stool. The three legs were a cut in the PSBR of $1–1.5 billion, a safety net for the sterling balances, and import deposits. It was particularly odd that Callaghan should still have been proposing import deposits when he had such good reason to know from his conversations with his friends, and with Witteveen, how any such move would be regarded internationally. It is made even more remarkable by his desire for a solution to the problem of the sterling balances which could only be found, if at all, with the help of those friends who would be most outraged if he did introduce import deposits.

In a well-prepared pantomime, Crosland, who had been given notice of the Prime Minister's intentions, then conceded defeat. He said that Callaghan's statement had changed the situation. He would no longer press the issue. If it became known that the anti-deflationists had had a majority in the Cabinet or even a significant minority, it would ruin confidence in the market and smash the Party.[52] Crosland was letting himself down as gently as he could. He had, by this time, lost many of his social democrat followers. His threats about import deposits and troops in Germany had persuaded many of them that it would be too dangerous to follow him further. It was the decision that now mattered and that prevailed after a final skirmish with Michael Foot, who at first did not appear to realize that the battle was lost and that, if he wanted the government to survive, he too must rally to the Prime Minister's side.

All that remained now was for Healey to settle with the IMF, to divide the public expenditure cuts between departments, and to drop the idea of import deposits with everyone pretending not to notice that the Prime Minister's three-legged stool was miraculously standing on only two legs. In all, it took nine Cabinet meetings to come to a conclusion. Callaghan may have considered the long debate necessary if the government was to survive and resignations were to be avoided. But in days when media attention is greater even than it was in 1976, it would have been impossible to delay a decision so long, with the market waiting and apprehensive, and sterling on the brink. Today the decision would have had to be taken by a small group of senior Cabinet Ministers, as it was when, in September 1992, sterling left the ERM. The rest of the Cabinet would have had to accept it or resign. They would have accepted it.

The final agreement was embodied in a Letter of Intent approved by the Cabinet and despatched by Healey to the IMF as a statement of the government's commitments. In his statement to the House on 15 December, there emerged the full picture of the agreement the government had been forced to make. He announced that the latest forecasts for the PSBR had estimated it at the 'unacceptably high' level of £10.5 billion in 1977–8 and £11.5 billion in 1978–9. As a result of the measures the government was now to take, the PSBR would be reduced to £8.7 billion in 1977–8 and somewhat less, he expected £8.6 billion, in 1978–9. The PSBR would fall from 9 per cent of GDP in the current year to about 6 per cent in 1977–8 and 5 per cent in 1978–9.[53] Thus, in terms of the reduction in the PSBR, the IMF had achieved the greater part of its demand. Healey referred to the public expenditure adjustments of £1.5 billion in 1977–8 and £2 billion in 1978–9. This was in addition to the cuts already announced, including the £1 billion agreed the previous July. There were also to be formal targets for money supply and domestic credit expansion. Agreement was helped by the sale for approximately £500 million of BP shares acquired in the course of a Government rescue of Burmah Oil in the winter of 1974–5. Healey met less hostility from Labour backbenchers than had been expected. The Left wing was not going to besmirch its reputation by voting the government out. It appeared to be accepted that what had been done was what had to be done and that recrimination could wait for a time when it was safer. By March 1977, the Left was rampant again. The government, which had lost its overall majority as a result of by-election defeats, entered into the pact with the Liberal Party, the Lib-Lab pact, which helped to sustain it in power for a further two years during which the benefits of the agreement with the IMF could accrue. It thereby ensured that there would be no accident with the public expenditure cuts and that it could carry its business through the House.[54]

Subsequently, the PSBR in 1976–7 turned out to be £8.5 billion rather than the £10.5 billion Treasury forecast on which the Cabinet had acted. It was true, as Crosland had argued, that other forecasts had been lower than the Treasury's. What was not known at the time either to Crosland or to the Treasury was the effect the introduction of cash limits in 1975–6 was having on departmental expenditures.[55] But, even if the government had suspected what was happening, it could no longer, in the autumn of 1976, afford to thrust forecasts, whether optimistic or pessimistic, in the face of those it was asking for funds. It had to persuade the IMF and, from the point of view of its own survival, it could not afford to make another mistake. It turned out that nothing was lost other than the time spent in Cabinet meetings. In the two subsequent years, again due to the operation of cash limits, it proved that the Cabinet could quietly have accepted the IMF's first bid without comment and not a penny less would have been spent than was in fact spent. Public spending in 1976–7 was about 3.5 per cent less than in the previous year. Between 1975–6 and 1977–8, there was an unprecedented 8 per cent fall in public expenditure in real terms.[56] It appeared that the IMF, with its back-of-the-envelope initial bid, had more understanding of what was needed to provide public services than the government departments equipped with all the elaborate machinery of the Public Expenditure Survey.

THE STERLING BALANCES

Callaghan had remembered the nightmares he had suffered as Chancellor from uncertainty arising from the overhang of sterling balances. He somewhat overestimated the importance of the issue as a contribution to his government's problems in 1976. Those problems had their origin not in the sterling balances but in the government's conduct of economic policy. Callaghan now hoped that his friends who had done so little to help him with the IMF would at least help with the sterling balances. In January 1977, a safety-net for the sterling balances was negotiated. It covered only the official balances held as reserves by governments and central banks, but these were at the time the greater part of the sterling balances and the most volatile. It was an agreement for two years with a possible extension to a third, and was subject to the same conditions as the IMF stand-by. If there was another run on the pound, there were to be medium-term swap facilities which would permit the Bank of England to exchange sterling for foreign currencies from other central banks. The swaps would have to be reversed after an agreed period.

An agreement of this kind was totally unnecessary once the government was seen to be conducting a responsible economic policy. Although Callaghan wanted it, from an economic point of view this agreement shared this with the 1968 Basle Agreement, that it would probably have been better for the British economy if it had not been made. These matters are too specialized for the comprehension of most politicians. Callaghan could, therefore, hope that the agreement would escape serious criticism. From his point of view, it was important that there should be an agreement on the sterling balances and that it should be politically presentable to an ill-informed audience. That was achieved.[57] He describes the agreement as 'eminently satisfactory – just what I had hoped for'.[58] The agreement was not eminently satisfactory. The British search for an agreement derived from the typically naive assumption that because heads of government in Washington and Bonn were prepared to make friendly noises to a British Prime Minister about matters that they did not properly understand, their Treasuries and Central Banks would be similarly forgiving and would actually provide more in benefits than they withdrew in costs.

LIFE TRANSFORMED

After the agreement with the IMF, Healey's life changed beyond recognition. Suddenly all the economic indices were moving in the right direction. Between October 1976 and October 1977, MLR fell from 15 per cent to 5 per cent, an unprecedented rate of reduction determined by the need to discourage capital inflows. The pound recovered dramatically. By early 1977 it had risen above $1.70. The Bank of England was selling sterling for dollars, confident that it would not cause a run on the pound. Sterling was being sold in great quantities for dollars because there was concern about competitiveness. In the end it proved imposs-ible to resist the upward pressure on sterling. On 31 October 1977, a Treasury announcement stated that sterling would be allowed to find its own level. By the end of the year it had risen to more than $1.90. Less encouraging was that sterling continued to depreciate against the strong currencies.

In 1977, for the first time in five years, the UK was running a rough balance on current account; partly because of North Sea oil, though partly also because of the depressed level of real activity. Inflation, nearly 25 per cent in 1975, fell to 15 per cent in 1976 and 10 per cent in 1977. Unemployment, which had risen by 500,000 in 1975 and 170,000 in 1976, rose by about 100,000 in 1977. In 1978, unemployment fell. Industrial production increased. By 1978, growth of GDP was just over 3 per cent. At the end of 1977, the UK agreed not to draw on its full entitlement with the IMF. The IMF was released from its commitment to the UK and could deploy its resources where they were more needed. Healey's triumph did him little good on the Left of the Party. The safer they felt, the more critical they could be. The resentments were piling up against the man who had sold socialism to the IMF and, in due course, his critics would combine with others to deny him the succession to Callaghan as leader of the Party. Crosland died in February 1977 and therefore did not see the full extent of the recovery. But Roy Hattersley, who alone had stood with Crosland to the end, conceded a year after the IMF crisis that Healey had been right.

THE EUROPEAN MONETARY SYSTEM EMS

Britain had been forced by mounting indebtedness to respect the limita-tions imposed upon it by its own economic performance and by the difficult world economic environment. By respecting those limits, the British economy was enabled to begin repaying its debts and even to acquire a façade of strength, though the settlement with the IMF had done nothing to improve its economic performance in any fundamental respect. It was simply that sterling was now stronger, the reserves were high, the current account had been transformed, and inflation was coming down. To Helmut Schmidt, Federal Chancellor, it appeared that Britain could now make a respectable partner in a project which had been maturing in his mind, and for which he had won the support of Valéry Giscard d'Estaing, President of the French Republic. The project was for a European zone of monetary stability with membership extending beyond the snake.[59] It was to be a kind of European Bretton Woods equipped with fixed but adjustable exchange rates and a European Monetary Fund (EMF) subscribed from the reserves of member states. Experience had taught that the margins of fluctuation within the EMS should be wider than those of Bretton Woods. Exchange rates would be permitted to vary within a band 2.25 per cent either side of the central rate, not the 1 per cent mandated under Bretton Woods. It was later decided to add a wider band of 6 per cent to accommodate weaker brethren such as Italy. As one of the original Six, Italy did not want to be left out of this further development of European integration but could not contemplate confining the lira within the narrow 2.25 per cent band. The EMF was proclaimed both by Schmidt and Giscard to be a key element in the EMS, an element which made it fundamentally different from the snake which had existed with varying membership since 1972. Giscard needed a system fundamentally different from the snake from which France had twice been expelled. He did not wish the humiliation to be repeated. There was, from the beginning, some scepticism whether the EMF would ever come into existence. Here, apparently, was Helmut Schmidt disposing of German reserves over which he had, in fact, no power. Even as launched, the EMF was for the future, two years in the future according to the prospectus which the British government had to consider. In fact the EMF never did come into existence. The EMS itself was proclaimed as a precursor of monetary union within Europe.

On this issue the British Cabinet divided into various groupings, some of them eminently forecastable. There were those for whom the EMS was simply an expansion of European commitment. They had opposed British membership of the EEC and certainly did not want to deepen Britain's relationship with it through membership of the EMS. This group had, in effect, a power of veto over the decision at least until the General Election. Callaghan, whatever he himself thought of the Schmidt project, would not want to provoke controversy within the Cabinet on a European issue before a General Election. There was another grouping within the Cabinet which consisted of dedicated 'Europeans' who wished Britain to participate in any European development, the more so as the Schmidt project had the enthusiastic support of their departed hero, Roy Jenkins, now President of the European Commission. Even they realized that membership was not an option at least until after a General Election.

Callaghan was ambivalent. He understood perfectly well the veto possessed by the anti-Europeans. He had his own questions about Schmidt's motivations in launching his scheme. He had been gravely disappointed with Schmidt's response to his appeals in 1976 and was not ready to jump aboard Schmidt's bus without carefully ensuring that it was roadworthy. On the other hand, the difficulties of the years since sterling had floated had painted the memory of the Bretton Woods system with a roseate hue. He attempted to persuade the anti-Europeans that this was not a European issue of the old kind. The question at stake was not Europe but stable currency relationships. He was in favour of stable currency relationships. The EMS was a route to stable currency relationships within Europe. He was probably more in favour of it than politically he could afford to be. Moreover, as head of government of a major European state he did not wish to be left out of a major European development. The Left and the anti-Europeans did not trust Callaghan. They feared that in the heady atmosphere of European summits, he might be drawn into the EMS and take them with him against their will. They watched him like hawks.

Then there was a small group who, whether or not they were listed as 'Europeans', wished to consider the EMS on what they judged to be its merits. They were not *a priori* for or against. They could turn either way depending on the argument as it developed. Healey was the leader of this group. He appears to have been influenced by a conversation with Manfred Lahnstein, state secretary of the German Ministry of Economics: 'Manfred Lahnstein supported [the EMS] on grounds of Germany's national interest.' The weaker countries would have to intervene on the currency markets to keep the stronger currencies down.[60] The associated currencies, in other words, would act as lead in the DM's balloon. Healey writes, 'I was fairly agnostic until I realized, from long discussions with Lahnstein and others, how [the EMS] was likely to work in practice; then I turned against it.'[61]

As background to the discussion there was frequent mention both by Callaghan and Healey of the risk of market speculation against sterling. If it was decided that sterling should not join, the market might read such a decision as an expression by the British government of lack of confidence in its own currency. It was an argument for playing the issue long and not coming to a premature adverse conclusion. Callaghan very properly decided that the EMS should be thoroughly considered from the point of view of the national interest and not just ignored because it would cause difficulties for the Party. Healey was appointed chairman of a Cabinet Committee established to consider the merits of joining the EMS. The Cabinet would then make its political decision, taking account of the Committee's recommendation. All this would take time and the government was playing for time. The Committee did its job thoroughly and concluded by a majority against membership. That this was not just a Party decision is perhaps confirmed by the fact that it was another 11 years before a Conservative government took a contrary decision and joined.

The EMS was intended to be a system of fixed but adjustable exchange rates. One problem was whether, as in the era of Bretton Woods, it would be a political embarrassment if a currency was compelled to devalue against the DM, whether therefore governments would resist necessary adjustments to exchange rates, and whether as a result the EMS would become in effect a network of fixed exchange rates. Healey's Committee considered the old problem that exists in any system of fixed exchange rates, the problem of ensuring a 'symmetry of obligations'. The theory was that obligations and benefits should be shared symmetrically between strong and weak currencies. But the managers of strong currencies saw the problem very differently from the managers of weak currencies. The German idea of symmetry was an EMS in which other member countries shared intervention obligations instead of placing the lion's share on Germany. The Bundesbank was increasingly stressing the inflationary risks to the German economy resulting from the need to provide large amounts of DM for intervention to maintain currency relationships in the snake. The Bundesbank did not want an EMS in which its intervention obligations would be even larger than in the snake. An intervention obligation might also influence countries with weak currencies to change their domestic economic policy in order to strengthen their currency. The non-snake countries had a very different idea of symmetry. They wanted the main burden of intervention to fall on the strong currency, which would normally mean the DM. They knew that when the dollar was weak, as it was at the time, its weakness was likely to exert a stronger upward pressure on the DM than on any of the weaker currencies in the Community. They did not want to be forced to spend their reserves, or to deflate, in order to maintain their parities with a rising DM.

There was here a conflict of interest that could not be resolved. The weaker currencies wanted unlimited support. The strong currency was not willing to give it. The view in Healey's Committee was that there was no more reason why the UK should be compelled to deflate than the Germans to reflate, if the DM and sterling moved outside the permitted margins. It was clear that a form of symmetry of obligations which satisfied both countries did not exist. This was a prime consideration even among 'Europeans' in the Callaghan government. It made them less unhappy with the veto exercised by the anti-Europeans in the Cabinet on any decision not to join the ERM of the EMS. Other non-snake countries, such as France and Italy, faced the same dilemma but came to a different conclusion. When they found that their idea of symmetry of obligations, which they shared with the British, was unobtainable, they nevertheless decided to join, first because they saw the EMS as a step towards monetary union in Europe and secondly because, in the meantime, attachment to the DM would be a discipline in their own battle against inflation.

The Treasury gave its advice to the Committee and to the Cabinet in unmistakable terms.[62] It is worth giving an outline of its advice, first because membership of the EMS continued to be the subject of vigorous controversy in Britain in the 1980s and, secondly, because it throws light on the continuing weaknesses of Britain's economic performance two years after the agreement with the IMF. The Treasury argument began with a survey of experience during the 1970s. World trade had grown by only 16 per cent over the previous four years compared with 31 per cent between 1970 and 1973. Real output in some OECD countries had been virtually stagnant since 1973. Inflation rates had slowed since the early 1970s but were still historically high. Despite a considerable increase in exchange rate flexibility, problems of payments imbalances were not noticeably less acute since the early/mid 1970s. There were still speculative crises in foreign exchange markets. The UK had experienced problems of rising unemployment and high inflation more serious than those of any other major country except Italy. Real output had grown by only 0.25 per cent per annum since 1974 compared with 1.5 per cent or more in Germany and Italy, and over 2.5 per cent in France. Inflation had averaged 18 per cent per annum in Britain over the same period compared with about 10 per cent in most other EEC countries and 5.5 per cent in Germany. More recently, tight incomes policies, a high exchange rate, and falling commodity prices, had combined to bring about a reduction in the rate of inflation to about 7.5 per cent, below France and Italy, but still well above Germany. The gap between the different European countries was now 4:1, and there was no confidence that it could rapidly be reduced.

A successful EMS required a convergence of economic performance among its members. In fact, the divergence of economic performance within the EEC was now greater than when the snake had been originally set up in 1972. The inflation differential between Germany and the other three major countries of the EEC was larger than in the past, the movements of the dollar, the mark, the yen and the Swiss franc exceeded the rates of currency movement in the past, and the funds which could move to affect exchange rates were vastly larger. All the non-snake candidates for membership of the EMS had found it impossible to stay in the snake six years before when the inflation rate gap with Germany was far smaller than it was in 1978. The effective sterling rate was now within 3 per cent of where it had been at the beginning of 1977 but over the last couple of years the UK had lost some international competitiveness. Though up in value against the dollar, it was down against the DM. If sterling had been linked to the DM there would probably have had to be at least two currency step changes to achieve this result.

In the Treasury's view, it was unlikely, despite the increasing contribution from North Sea oil, that sterling could remain in the EMS without successive devaluations, particularly if there was any further expansion of demand. If it did not devalue, Britain would become increasingly uncompetitive. The effects on real GDP would be adverse, by about 1 per cent in 1980, rising to about 3 per cent in 1981, and about 5 per cent in 1982. The current account must be expected to deteriorate sharply. A devaluation of roughly 5 per cent a year might be needed, vis-à-vis all other EEC countries. The necessary exchange rate changes could be achieved more flexibly and quietly through the market outside the system than in an enlarged snake.[63] The movement of the dollar would be very relevant to how successfully an EMS would operate. Left to themselves, the European currencies would respond differently to changes in the value of the dollar. This was particularly true of sterling which traditionally was more influenced by the dollar than other EMS currencies. The EMS would require member currencies to rise or fall together against the dollar. The system would be placed under strain and would require periodic parity changes, as had happened in the snake, if either the dollar continued to fall sharply or if, during 1979 and later, the dollar rebounded. The declared objective of the EMS would be to move towards more fixed exchange rates. It was doubtful whether it would prove workable for long in face of frequent devaluations by a major currency. It was no doubt for this reason that, in his memoirs, Healey comments: 'Far from paying a price to get

Britain in, the other members of the European Community would have paid a lot to keep us out.'[64] He did not, however, think of this possibility at the time.

The Treasury listed other considerations all deterrent to membership. They included scepticism as to whether there would ever be an EMF and whether a satisfactory form of symmetry of obligations within the EMS could ever be found. Then, with the memory of many a sterling crisis in mind, the Treasury advised that the UK would have less flexibility in face of a major attack on sterling. A rigid position could actually invite speculation. It could be exposed to heavy reserve losses, or to increasing the already heavy external debt, with less room for manoeuvre on the exchange rate itself. The government might be compelled to lose reserves in order to prevent appreciation of the DM. Then the UK's less extensive European and more extensive transatlantic trade links put it on the periphery of possible members. Only 37 per cent of UK exports went to the EEC compared with 50 per cent in the case of France and 47 per cent in the case of Italy.

The Cabinet received the Treasury advice under cover of a note from Healey making his own recommendation. He advised against membership of the ERM of the EMS. Britain should, however, participate in the other aspects of the EMS yet to be defined. The notion that the ERM was a mechanism *within* the EMS was a device thought up at the last minute to enable the UK to join the EMS but not the ERM. The EMS could then be launched as a Community project and the UK would have a voice even if sterling was not present in the ERM which was the core of the EMS. Healey wrote that he did not recommend that Britain should stay outside the ERM in order to be free to pursue a policy of sterling devaluation. Reliance on devaluation to compensate for excessive inflation, he asserted, was a soft option which brought no lasting benefit to the economy. Therefore, if the decision was to stay outside the ERM, it would be more than ever necessary to persuade the market that UK policies were right. The Cabinet accepted Healey's advice. Britain did not join the ERM. Healey's retrospective judgement was that the decision to stay out 'was certainly justified in the first four years, when [the EMS] had to accept seven realignments of its currencies'.[65]

The European Commission's 1978 annual report on the activities of the European Communities said of the EMS:

This system will contribute to the convergence of economic development and will give a fresh stimulus to the process of achieving European Union. It must be seen as the kingpin in a comprehensive strategy for achieving sustained growth within a framework of stability, a progressive return to full employment, the harmonization of living standards and the reduction of regional disparities within the Community.[66]

The report also said that

it was understood that within two years from the introduction of the system, the arrangements would be consolidated into their final form, entailing the establishment of the European Monetary Fund and the full utilization of a European monetary unit, the ECU, as reserve asset and instrument of settlement.[67]

By these standards, and by the standards of its own rules, the EMS had been a disappointment even before the crisis of summer 1993. To take a few examples, there was no EMF, the DM not the ECU was at the centre of the system,[68] and unemployment was so high throughout the Community that, in May 1993, Jacques Delors, President of the European Commission, felt it necessary to initiate research into the reasons.[69] It was no matter for regret that Britain did not join at the outset provided that the decision was not taken as just another soft option.

DIMINUENDO

Healey, as he frequently emphasized, was a politician. There was an election to win and he wanted to be leader of his Party. His 1978 Budget was a political Budget designed to help win the election which he expected in the autumn of 1978. He gave 'a full year stimulus to the economy of some £2.5 billion – or about £2 billion in 1978–9'.[70] The PSBR was to be allowed to rise very substantially by about £3 billion to £8.5 billion or 5.25 per cent of GDP.[71]

The market saw exactly what was happening and MLR had to be raised during 1978 and again in January 1979 to sustain a falling pound. The US Administration, supported by Britain, was pressing Germany and Japan to agree to a programme of coordinated economic expansion. At the Bonn summit of the major industrial powers in July 1978, Helmut Schmidt, fearful that there might otherwise be a retrogression to protectionism, promised that Germany would cooperate. In fact nothing was done that the Federal German government had not intended in any case, and what it did do, combined with the 1979 oil price shock, led to accusations against Schmidt that he had put at risk Germany's record of current account surplus and low inflation. Inflation remained the dominant problem in Britain. Healey and Callaghan recommended to the Cabinet an incomes policy limit of 5 per cent at a time when inflation was running at about 8 per cent. 5 per cent was the highest figure consistent with a positive rather than a negative impact on the rate of inflation. On the other hand, trade unionists having rebelled against their leaders, and Jack Jones having been repudiated by his own union, it was no longer possible to negotiate an agreement with the trade unions. The expectation had to be that the policy would have to be enforced by the government itself in the public sector. If it was really to be done, it needed a new government, with a new mandate, not a government facing an election not later than the autumn of 1979. Healey recommended an election in the autumn of 1978. The government had subsisted for eighteen months on the support of the Liberals. In the summer of 1978, the Liberals announced that they would withdraw from the Lib-Lab pact as from the beginning of the new session in November 1978. The government, therefore, would once more lack an overall majority. It could no longer be sure of getting its business through. It was widely believed that there would be a General Election in the autumn of 1978.

Callaghan had, after the resolution of the IMF crisis, proved a good Prime Minister. He was the captain who had weathered the storm and it had been a real storm. He presented an image of calm authority and the public seemed to like him. His prestige stood very high and, by November 1978, Labour, which had long lagged in the polls, was leading. By the time that lead had been revealed, Callaghan had lost his opportunity. He had been advised that Healey's reflationary Budget of April 1978 would be yielding greater political dividends by the spring of 1979 than were to be expected by the autumn of 1978. He announced in September that there was no reason for an election a whole year before it was due. So, with its 5 per cent incomes policy totally rejected by the trade unions, the government advanced blindly into the winter of discontent, and the public, finding vital public services disrupted, turned against Labour and the trade unions. The government lost a vote of confidence in the spring of 1979 and, while the winter of discontent was still fresh in the minds of the electorate, was defeated by Mrs Thatcher and the Conservative Party in the General Election of 3 May 1979. No one can say how Callaghan would have fared had he gone to

447

the people in the autumn of 1978. There was a good chance of Labour emerging as the largest Party. Given the curiosities of the British electoral system, Labour might even have emerged with an overall majority.[72] As it was Labour lost, yet one more sacrifice on the altar of economic forecasting.

The Left resurgent took its revenge on Healey for his outstanding services to the Labour government by denying him the succession to Callaghan as leader of the Labour Party and he had to be content with the deputy leadership under Michael Foot. The Left then succeeded in driving out of the Party some of those leading personalities most likely to command public support. Labour was to experience the frustrations of long years of Opposition. Healey remained a Member of Parliament until 1992 and then went to the Lords. He would tell how, if things had turned out differently, he would be forming his third or fourth government. But he showed no resentment. He knew that there is no gratitude in politics.

FIFTEEN

Sir Geoffrey Howe: the Search for Certainty

ANOTHER LAWYER

Since the war, Conservative Prime Ministers have shown a certain predilection for lawyers as Chancellor and, of these, Geoffrey Howe was probably the most learned. He had had a successful legal career outside politics while making his way in politics. The independence given by a successful career outside politics can be a great reinforcement to independence in government. Lawyers, generally, have a commendable addiction to the rule of law. It was a characteristic that may have led Howe to monetarism which, at one stage, appeared capable of injecting the force of law into economic management. The Prime Minister, herself the product of a legal training, may have found the same comfort and the same certainties in monetarism. Lawyers have a great deal of practice as advisers. There is considerable evidence that Conservative Prime Ministers regard it as the prime function of the Chancellor to advise on economic policy, rather than to decide it. After his retirement as Permanent Secretary to the Treasury, Douglas Wass is reported to have said that Mrs Thatcher was 'much more the First Lord of the Treasury than any previous holder of that office'.[1] While it is perfectly clear that Mrs Thatcher exercised a substantial influence on economic policy during Howe's tenure, his independence of spirit is sufficient to suggest that he was not just a pawn and that he did what he did because he thought it right, not because he was under instruction.

Howe had been surprised when, in 1975 on her election as Leader, Mrs Thatcher appointed him as her shadow Chancellor rather than Keith Joseph. He had not voted for her as Leader. He had been a faithful follower of Heath both before and after the U-turn. Howe had availed himself of the freedom granted to all citizens, and even to politicians, of changing his mind. Though stubborn in the convictions

449

he held at any one time, the convictions were liable to change with experience and with events. All the most prominent people in the Thatcher encampment were converts to monetarism. Howe had converted with the rest and would stay converted at least until he had some experience of economic management.

Mrs Thatcher told him in 1975 that she was appointing him because he and she had the same idea of where it was necessary to go.[2] That meant that, unlike previous postwar Tory governments, they intended really to set the people free. Of previous Tory governments she writes, 'The Tories loosened the corset of socialism; they never removed it.'[3] With particular passion, she rejected the U-turn made by the government of Edward Heath in which she had served. It had 'almost implemented the most radical form of socialism ever contemplated by an elected British Government'. The country had been saved from 'this abomination' only by 'the conservatism and suspicion of the TUC . . .'[4] Now she planned to reverse the whole trend of postwar government, whether Labour or Conservative. In that process, the Treasury, second only to No. 10 Downing Street, would be the most important office of all.

Howe had not had a happy time as shadow Chancellor. As Healey grew in self-confidence reinforced, after the IMF crisis, by the beneficial results of IMF-imposed discipline, he had employed his brutal arts against Howe to savage effect. Howe had no defence against Healey's contemptuous assault and, at one time, had wondered whether he would survive in his shadow appointment, let alone inherit the Treasury if victory ever came. His stubbornness had helped. His survival may also be attributable to Mrs Thatcher's need for a few friends in influential places. There was a notable absence of such friends in her first Cabinet. There was, certainly, Keith Joseph, the spiritual sponsor of the Thatcher revolution and, according to Geoffrey Howe, a great source of 'intellectual stimulus'. But Joseph was emphatically not a safe pair of hands. He was sent to Industry, a department in which he had little to do other than to stop wasteful expenditure, at which he was not particularly good, and provide his officials with reading lists the contents of which he himself ignored in agreeing to a further vast subsidy for British Leyland.[5] Mrs Thatcher herself explains how, in 1980, politics rather than the prospect of commercial viability converted her to a further enormous subsidy of £900 million for British Leyland. Her arguments show a remarkable similarity to those that persuaded the last Wilson government to subsidize both BL and Chrysler UK.[6]

Howe was not yet a Tory grandee. For Mrs Thatcher, it was more important that a friendly and dependent appointment to the Treasury would counterbalance all the grandees she had felt bound to include in her first Cabinet. With that fearlessness that is, no doubt, the Tories' secret weapon, James Prior writes of Howe and his Treasury team, probably encompassing his Prime Minister in the criticism, 'None of them had any experience of running a whelk-stall, let alone a decent-sized company.'[7] British constitutional practice does not require that economic Ministers should have experience of running a whelk-stall or anything else either. Nor is the evidence altogether persuasive that those who have entered the political arena from industrial management can easily transfer their skills to political life. Howe was at the Treasury as a reliable workmanlike figure who owed his advancement to the Prime Minister. He even qualified for membership of Mrs Thatcher's Thursday breakfast prayer meeting, a regular private event at which the Cabinet agenda could be discussed and assessed among friends.[8] Most of the friends who gathered in the early days of the Thatcher government would, in the end, defect. Howe would prove among the most loyal.

MONETARISM – AN OVERVIEW

1. *The Conservative Party and monetarism*

The Conservative Party had been enticed, most unusually, away from the shoals of pragmatism to the clear blue water of dogma. Normally it was only Socialists or Liberals who succumbed to the contagion of dogma. Now the Tories were infected. Their dogma was called monetarism. What was monetarism? For the answer we turn to the most famous political authority on the subject, Nigel Lawson, a trained economist, who became Financial Secretary to the Treasury under Geoffrey Howe in 1979.

In August 1980, Lawson gave the Bow Group the answer in his appropriately entitled lecture, 'The New Conservatism': 'Monetarism is simply a new name for an old maxim, formerly known as the quantity theory of money . . . It consists of two basic propositions. The first is that changes in the quantity of money determines, at the end of the day, changes in the general price level; the second is that government is able to determine the quantity of money.'[9] At this stage it is necessary only to make two comments. Lawson's first proposition is, at the very least, highly contentious. The second proposition is plainly wrong.

However, it was on the basis of these two propositions that Nigel Lawson, perhaps the most knowledgeable political exponent of monetarism, was attempting to renew Conservatism in August 1980.

Politicians, as a class, are wisely chary of categorical assertions. They are normally highly selective in the labelling they will accept. In the case of monetarism there was much justification for any such hesitation. The very word was an offence, a deterrent to sympathy and an encouragement to dissent. Was it sensible to appear to base policy not on evident needs, such as to kill inflation and to bring the trade unions within the law, but on a philosophy baptized 'monetarism'? Some people were bound to be dispossessed of their jobs, in the course of the battle against inflation. Was it sensible to incite them to think that they were the victims not of a pragmatic assessment of national needs but of 'monetarism'? The only explanation of the untypical readiness of some leading Tories to accept the monetarist label is that, for them, monetarism encapsulated a number of intuitions which they believed to be widely shared among the electorate.

The first intuition was that the quantity of money, whatever that means, did have a great deal to do with inflation. It is not surprising that this intuition was widely shared. Ministers of both Parties had made speeches without number proclaiming that inflation had something to do with too much money chasing too few goods. A second intuition was that trade unions had become too powerful. They must therefore not just be disciplined by legislation, they must be deprived of the opportunity to exercise influence on policy. The public had become accustomed to gatherings of trade union leaders at No. 10 Downing Street. The winter of discontent had made such gatherings particularly unappealing to a wide public. If therefore there was another way of reducing inflation, a monetary way which dispensed with incomes policies and with the participation of trade union leaders, that would carry public support. Another intuition was that governments taxed too much, spent too much, and borrowed too much. The idea that governments should leave more money in the pockets of the taxpayer, and that less should be borrowed, was not necessarily monetarist but it fitted in well with other aspects of the monetarist creed. It was on the basis of such intuitions that monetarism became the raw material for skilled political campaigners who wished to break from a past which included the numerous and recent disasters of the 1970s.

2. *Mrs Thatcher's monetarism*

Mrs Thatcher certainly thought she was a monetarist and, indeed, despite all subsequent experience, has remained convinced that she is a monetarist. She was quite clear that 'Inflation was a monetary phenomenon which it would require monetary discipline to curb.'[10] But she never had the educational experience of actually managing monetarism. Ministers in the Treasury were acquiring practical experience which was, nevertheless, difficult to interpret. A monetarist Treasury team was forced to devote hours to persuading a monetarist Prime Minister that they had not fallen into heresy. Lawson concedes her detestation of inflation; but he also found her repeatedly reluctant to embrace his means of fighting it.[11] Sometimes she would dispute his interpretation of monetarism. Sometimes she could reasonably claim that he tended to forget that her government had objectives other than purely economic objectives. One of the most important was to get itself re-elected. Another was to spread home ownership. It was hardly attractive politically to persuade people to buy a home and then reduce its value and increase the burdens of the mortgage by raising base rates or cutting the real value of mortgage interest relief. Governments which have only economic objectives do not set out to encourage home ownership. There is often tension between the tenants of the two Downing Street tied cottages. When Howe or Lawson went to one of their regular meetings in No. 10 they could never be sure whether they would find waiting for them the monetarist or the politician.

3. *Sir Geoffrey Howe's monetarism*

The team Mrs Thatcher appointed to the Treasury was, she believed, monetarist. The fact that Howe was prepared to be described as a monetarist does not imply that there was, to start with, much sophistication in his understanding of economic or monetary phenomena. Monetarism proved much more difficult to implement than Keynesianism had been. Keynesianism had been all about the level of demand. If there was too little demand, the Chancellor ran an increased deficit or a reduced surplus. If there was too much demand, he reduced his deficit or increased his surplus. Monetarism made far greater technical and intellectual demands. What is money? How is it to be measured and how is the quantity to be controlled? Without measurement, there cannot be knowledge. Without knowledge, there cannot be control. There are various measures of the money supply. There was broad money (£M3 later to be broadened to £M4) and narrow money (Mo).[12]

453

In which should they place their trust? Should they put their trust in any of them? It was soon found that none of the measures, singly or in combination, gave Ministers what they wanted, an unambiguous signal of the state of the economy and therefore of what to do next. The simple monetarist intuition – control the money supply and thereby control inflation – proved deceptive.

Howe, who was no economist, found himself submerged in contradictory advice about how to be a successful monetarist and kill inflation. He did not possess the technical qualifications to choose between the different measures of money and the different forms of control offered to him. Probably no one had the necessary qualifications even among those claiming to be expert in the field. All Geoffrey Howe could in the end do was to follow the Treasury's advice, accept what they told him could influence, rather than control, the money supply, and accept also that it would all be much more difficult than he had supposed. His readiness to follow Treasury advice was an example, perhaps, of the Treasury's skill in taking a political slogan and turning it to its own purposes. The methods that Geoffrey Howe adopted included an attempt to reduce the PSBR to a far smaller percentage of GDP than the level which he had inherited and a preparedness to use very high interest rates until a reduced PSBR helped him to bring them down. At a time when the sterling exchange rate was already being elevated by oil self-sufficiency and the 1979 oil price hike, high interest rates raised it further to levels quite inconsistent with the competitiveness of much of British manufacturing industry. The result was much greater unemployment than Mrs Thatcher or Howe had ever anticipated. There was the usual corollary that some of the monetarist advisers began dissociating themselves from a policy which appeared to have such a worrying outcome.

In another context, Howe writes of 'my lawyerly scepticism of economic theorists'.[13] In his 1980 Budget speech he said: 'Monetarism means curbing the excessive expansion of money and credit.'[14] If Howe was right in the meaning he attributed to monetarism, earlier Tory Chancellors had been monetarist. Healey had had similar ambitions. A re-elected Labour government, faced by the breakdown in its relations with the trade unions during the winter of discontent, and confronted by the same need to reduce inflation, would have been as insistent as Howe on the need to curb the expansion of money and credit. Howe's monetarism looked like traditional Treasury policy.

4. *Rules and discretion*

In 1972–3, the Bretton Woods system had collapsed and currencies had floated, thereby depriving economic policy-makers of the exchange rate anchor that had constrained their freedom for 25 years. The Barber boom had demonstrated the risks of leaving too much discretion in the conduct of economic policy to a Prime Minister and a Chancellor of the Exchequer. Howe and Lawson, as monetarist Chancellors, hoped to find in monetarism a system of economic management which would elevate government by rule and reduce government by discretion. They sought in the money supply an anchor to which economic policy could be attached. They then encountered the problem that different measures of the money supply could signal very different messages as to what was happening in the real economy. Thus monetarism appeared not to free them from the difficult problems of judgement that had so often defeated their predecessors. There was still room for too much discretion and too much judgement. Where then should they anchor policy? This search for a single anchor did not attract Nicholas Ridley, for a time Financial Secretary to both Howe and Lawson. He had been a monetarist longer than either of them. He realized that many monetary measures had to be taken into account in deciding policy and, indeed, factors other than the money supply. He accepted that, in the end, policy was a matter of judgement. He annoyed Howe by telling him that he would be well advised to manage the economy by the seat of his pants.[15] Ridley writes of both the Chancellors he served, 'They both hankered after some lodestar, some fixed point, against which to measure progress and to assess the need for policy changes.'[16] Ridley's aristocratic irreverence was not good enough for the two late converts to monetarism, Howe and Lawson.

By the summer of 1981, Lawson, dismayed but persistent, was beginning to look for his unambiguous signal not in measures of the money supply but in the exchange rate. Eventually, as Chancellor, he was to unveil the exchange rate as his desired anchor. Fortuitously the Exchange Rate Mechanism had come into existence shortly before the election of the Thatcher government. At the centre of the ERM stood the DM with its reputation for strength and stability. The ERM could give cover to the adoption of the DM as the anchor for British economic management.[17] If sterling rose or fell against the DM, a Chancellor would know what to do and it would be more difficult for his Prime Minister to forbid it. Policy was to come full circle, from the exchange rate anchor of Bretton Woods to the exchange rate anchor of the ERM.

Lawson would devote much energy to his efforts to argue that, in adopting a DM anchor, he was the true monetarist. He was unable to persuade his Prime Minister who considered him a renegade from the true faith. Monetary discipline, in her view, certainly did not require attachment to a foreign currency, certainly not to a European currency, and least of all to the German currency. Lawson's inability to persuade his Prime Minister did not relate simply to differences in economic theory. The Prime Minister regarded herself as a monetarist but so far from wanting to demote discretion, she was determined to retain it. She did not want to be on automatic pilot. It could generate great political difficulties. Here was another source of perpetual bickering. Her political instincts and her monetarist instincts combined to oppose attachment to the DM. Thus the monetarist experiment ended in dissension within the Thatcher government and in theological disputes about the true nature of monetarism.

THE INHERITANCE

Geoffrey Howe emphasizes his inheritance. He described the outlook as 'almost frighteningly bad', adding 'That was no exaggeration.'[18] The justification he could argue for this assessment was the resurgence of inflation at the end of Healey's reign. Incomes policy had succumbed to the winter of discontent. Healey's 1978 Budget had been intended as an election Budget and followed a long tradition of pre-electoral economic imprudence. It was a tradition from which Geoffrey Howe, in 1983, would not depart. Meanwhile the situation was certainly deeply worrying. Inflation could have become endemic. Nevertheless, if Howe found his inheritance so frightening, it is difficult to imagine what he would have made of his Conservative predecessor's bequest to Healey. Howe came to the Treasury at a good time if his object was prudent management. He had advantages which few of his predecessors had enjoyed. He reports some early difficulties with his Prime Minister. While she was in general sympathy with her Chancellor, she had to ensure that he was not forgetting the politics. She could not be too resolute until the Labour Party had demonstrated its determination to tear itself to pieces, an intention which was finally established by the election of Michael Foot as Leader in November 1980. It would prove to be of inestimable advantage to the government in adopting unpopular policies that Labour was making itself unelectable. For once there was a government that could afford to put the feelings of the electorate farther back in its mind than is typical in a Parliamentary democracy. Labour had provided it with an indemnity against almost any error. In her memoirs Mrs Thatcher does her best to conceal the fact that, in the early days, she herself had doubts, not doubts about the validity of her policies but doubts about the politics of implementation. But, all things considered, Howe had little reason to complain about the support he received from his Prime Minister. Circumstances were, for once, conspiring to ensure united purpose between Nos. 10 and 11 Downing Street.

Howe came to the Treasury with other advantages. The greatest was that he was not the direct inheritor of the Heath regime. The direct consequences of Heath had fallen into Healey's lap and Howe could witness, without responsibility and with freedom to criticize, the twists and turns of Labour policy as Healey struggled against balance of payments deficit, inflation, and unemployment until he, at last, found a comfortable if uncongenial resting place in the arms of the IMF. Healey had started a process that his successor could follow, even though there had been a relapse in the 1978 Budget. That is not to say that Howe and Healey were brothers under their Party skins. Healey had done reluctantly what Howe would do voluntarily and from conviction. Healey's experience had led him to abandon Keynes. Howe was unlikely to raise that particular banner again even if all the economists in the kingdom, and all his Heathite Cabinet colleagues, called for it. Howe's ambition was to create voluntarily a framework for economic policy comparable to that which the IMF had imposed in 1976. That framework would include, as had that imposed by the IMF, control of public expenditure, and caution with the money supply and domestic credit expansion (DCE).

Howe had another advantage – he inherited a subdued Treasury. The chief characteristic of the civil service is its wish for renewal. No department of government has a more frequent need for a fresh start than the Treasury and there was certainly such a need in 1979. It had hardly distinguished itself between 1974 and 1979. That it had been divided and indecisive at a time when, in 1974, all the economic contours had disappeared, was forgivable. But its touch had remained uncertain, and its advice hesitant, even when the pressures for change had become irresistible. Howe informs us that the idea of removing the Keynesian Permanent Secretary, Sir Douglas Wass, was considered and rejected. There was no need. Howe explains: 'I had the impression that he was sceptically eager, along with most of his colleagues, to join in a genuinely fresh and determined onslaught on the "British disease" with which they had grappled so long.'[19] Younger figures in the Treasury were very willing to give less sceptical support, to reject past presumptions, and to assist the new government to make a success of the hunches that the electorate, according to the theory of the mandate, had blessed.

Then there was North Sea oil. By 1979, the long period of waiting for the UK's oil 'bonanza' was over and the country was self-sufficient. Not merely did this afford protection for the balance of payments, provided economic management was prudent, it supplied also a large income for the Exchequer out of the proceeds of Petroleum Revenue Tax (PRT), introduced in 1975, the rates of which had been substantially increased in 1978. With oil tripling in price between the end of 1978 and the end of 1979, the balance of payments and revenue benefits were particularly comforting. When Tory Ministers began to reflect publicly on the success of their economic policies, they seldom placed North Sea oil in the forefront of their explanations. Politically this was understandable. They were in no way responsible either for the presence of oil beneath the North Sea, nor for its discovery, nor for its exploitation, and not even for the enactment of PRT.[20] The benefits were certainly obvious to Tory Ministers, as North Sea oil was subjected to repeated additional imposts when they found themselves incapable of controlling public expenditure. There are signs that, despite its benign effect on inflation, the Chancellor was less than euphoric when the price of oil fell and left him short of revenue.

HOW TO WIN ELECTIONS

Howe felt able, during the 1979 election, to deny an intention to double the rate of VAT. In his memoirs he righteously defends the increase he did make after the election. He points out that the basic rate when he took over was 8 per cent and the weighted average, taking account of the higher rate, was 8.5 per cent. In his first Budget he unified the rate of VAT and raised it to 15 per cent. So, he says, his denial of an intention to double the rate was not 'pedantically misleading' and 'more than technically correct'. He goes on to describe the issue as 'the small change of election campaigning'.[21] Yet the policy of switching the tax burden from income tax to consumption taxes was fundamental to Tory thinking on incentives. It was absolutely right if the absurd level of taxation on high incomes, and the employment it gave to the tax avoidance industry, was to be brought to an end. It was a matter for justification, not denial. Apparently it was felt that it could not be justified to the electorate and that therefore it had better be denied. It is evident that loyalty to one's Party, and to one's own ambitions, can make heavy demands.

This was not the only, or even the most important, respect in which the Conservative campaign had lacked frankness. The implications of Conservative economic policy were not spelled out, and not only because Mrs Thatcher and Howe themselves did not appreciate the full implications. The priority had to be inflation, rising disturbingly once again. They knew that unemployment must rise at least for a time even if they did not know how far it would rise. Though there was bound to be an initial cost in output, future growth depended on the defeat of inflation. Nothing would prove so effective in Howe's successful battle against inflation as his refusal to be deflected by the rise in unemployment. Unemployment stood at 1.4 million just before his first Budget.[22] It would rise and rise. But, in his view, the defeat of inflation had to come first. Yet the electorate was entitled to believe from their campaign that the Tories had the answer to unemployment. During the 1979 election, Mrs Thatcher had referred to Labour as the natural Party of unemployment.[23]

The election campaign took place so soon after the winter of discontent that Tory policy had not caught up with its implications for future policy. There were Tory commitments to dialogue with trade unions. Mrs Thatcher conceded that 'pay policies are . . . extremely important'.[24] The winter of discontent had discredited the unions but the Tory campaign was conducted as though, with some mild reform, they were still to be a power in the land.

Given the priority that it was clearly necessary to give to the defeat of inflation, it was remarkable that, during the election campaign, the Conservative Party announced that it would accept the recommendations of the Clegg Commission on pay comparability. The Clegg Commission had set up by the Labour government in an attempt to conciliate public sector workers during the winter of discontent. Mrs Thatcher was always subject to outbreaks of nerves during an election, even when the probability of victory was far greater even than in 1979. She found it politically necessary to endorse Clegg in advance. In the midst of a General Election, she, too, wished to conciliate public sector workers. Her decision was taken on the advice of James Prior despite some opposition from Howe. Prior claims that the Conservatives could not have won the election without the commitment to Clegg and that the consequences of the commitment were made worse by Howe's unwise increase in the VAT rate in his first Budget.[25] Neither explanation justifies Prior's feeble capitulation to electoral pressures. The election would certainly have been won without the commitment to Clegg. It was unlikely that the Clegg Commission's findings would be helpful in the battle against inflation whatever the rate of VAT and it was clear enough that something significant would be done about the rate of VAT if the Tories won the election. Howe would have to contend with the consequences of Clegg, a self-inflicted wound, as well as of Healey. Perhaps he believed and, more important, Mrs Thatcher believed, that if the government could control the money supply, Clegg's recommendations would not matter.[26]

THE FIRST BUDGET

A Chancellor should not pretend more than he can achieve. Having won power there was no longer a need to pretend. In his first Budget in June 1979, Howe said that 'There is a definite limit to our capacity, as politicians, to influence these things for the better ... The notions of demand management, expanding public spending and "fine tuning" of the economy have now been tested almost to destruction.'[27] Judged by that modest, and appropriate, philosophy, his Budget was both brave and politically farsighted.

If a transformation in economic management is intended, there is no point in delay. The government's majority was large enough to sustain it through a full Parliamentary term. The argument for prompt action was compelling. A key element in the Budget strategy was a reduction in the PSBR. Howe aimed to reduce the PSBR from £9.25 billion in 1978–9, or 5.25 per cent of GDP, to £8.25 billion in 1979–80, or 4.25 per cent of GDP. As the forecast for 1979–80 stood at £10 to £11 billion, this implied tax increases or public expenditure reductions of £2 to £3 billion. It was to be the beginning of a process whereby the PSBR would be reduced to between 1 and 2 per cent of output.[28] Despite the intention to reduce the PSBR, it was considered prudent to increase MLR by 2 per cent to 14 per cent in order apparently to give credibility to an announced reduction in the money supply target that Howe had inherited.

Part of the government's programme was to improve incentives. The Thatcher government believed in supply-side action to improve the performance of the economy. Monetarism, according to Keith Joseph, was not enough. Income tax cuts were regarded as an incentive which could be expected to improve the supply-side, though Lawson considered that the principal justification was a moral one, the enlargement of individual freedom.[29] John Biffen seems to have been alone in believing that the effect of cuts in the higher rates of tax could be more time spent on the golf course rather than in the office. It was as an incentive that Howe reduced the basic rate of income tax to 30p from 33p and the top rate to 60p from 83p. This would cost the revenue £4 billion. Asset sales and a first attack on public expenditure would help. But he would still need a major increase in indirect taxation, including VAT to 15 per cent, if he was to achieve his planned PSBR. The trouble was that the required increase in indirect taxation would have raised that misleading indicator the RPI by almost 4.5 per cent. The Prime Minister feared the reaction of trade union negotiators and that Howe was taking dramatic action too far. She proposed a 12.5 per cent VAT instead of 15 per cent. She was persuaded to accept the 15 per cent, but it proved necessary to compromise with her electoral sensitivities by cancelling the proposed increase in excise duties on tobacco and alcohol. That reduced the increase in the RPI to 3.6 per cent.[30]

An increase in indirect taxes raises the RPI. A reduction in income tax does not reduce the RPI. The nonsenses forced upon both Healey and Howe by this statistical dilemma were legion. Even a Chancellor as economically literate as Lawson justifies his failure to revalorize excise duties in his 1987 pre-election Budget, in which he cut income tax, by fear of the inflationary effect of an RPI increase.[31] It is of course true that a rise in the RPI encourages trade union demands for wage increases which ignore any benefit trade unionists receive from direct tax cuts. In the course of his onslaught on what he regards as the 'monetarist' policies of the government of which he was a member, Ian Gilmour comments that 'most people are fairly well aware that the best way to bring inflation down is not to put prices up . . .'[32] On this argument it would have been impossible ever, in the inflationary UK, to rebalance taxation between direct and indirect taxation. It is one of the costs of high inflation that there is no way forward which does not have damaging side effects. If the balance between direct and indirect taxation was to be changed, and there were strong arguments for changing it, Howe's first Budget was the best time to do it.[33]

Other steps announced in the Budget included the decision to link pension increases simply to price increases rather than, as before, to price or income increases whichever was the higher. This was, according to Lawson, necessary to regain control of public expenditure.[34] It was also decided to allow the prices and incomes legislation to lapse and with it the Price Commission. Three weeks after the election of the 1979 government, James Prior, Secretary of State for Employment, sent Mrs Thatcher a paper on incomes policy which she returned with some rude comments.[35] There were certainly ideological reasons for rejecting anything so interventionist as an incomes policy. The monetarist conviction was that one man's price increase was in no way due to another man's wage increase but was simply a lagged response to an increase in the money supply some time previously. That conviction would probably have prevailed whatever the pragmatic arguments. But the rejection of incomes policy at that time could be argued on purely pragmatic grounds. The Callaghan government had certainly exhausted the usefulness of incomes policy for the time being, if not for ever. A Conservative government could expect to pay a high price for an incomes policy if it expected any cooperation from the trade union movement. The price would certainly include the abandonment of its proposed trade union reforms.

The Price Commission had been first a Tory and then a Labour sop to the trade unions. It was probably more effective in deterring investment than price rises. Its abolition was not a heroic act. Nevertheless its abolition was consistent with the conviction that inflation was a monetary phenomenon and that controlling the money supply, if ways could be found, would be more effective in the battle against inflation than any Price Commission. It would have been more to the point to abolish the Clegg Commission. There were, however, the election promises and, apparently, a curious expectation, doomed to disappointment, that Clegg might be tough on the public sector, tougher than Cabinet Ministers.[36] In fact he showed a 'generosity' to which Mrs Thatcher pays ironic tribute.[37] The Clegg Commission was kept in being until September 1980. Its last report was issued in March 1981, nearly two years after the formation of the government.

The Budget gave Howe an early opportunity to learn the frailty of Treasury forecasting, especially about the PSBR. The PSBR is the difference between the two very large figures of income and expenditure and is therefore very difficult to forecast. In the upshot, the PSBR for 1979–80 was not £8.25 billion but almost £10 billion. To help fund it, and to reduce monetary growth which was increasing far faster than target, MLR was raised, on 15 November 1979, by 3 per cent to 17%, the largest single increase ever announced. Payment of PRT was also advanced by two months. The oil industry was now finding that the Tories were as greedy of their profits as they had expected Labour to be. Howe is engagingly honest about the effect on policy of this overshoot in the PSBR. 'This ... gave an early and non-doctrinaire shove to the privatization process.'[38] On any substantial scale, however, revenues from privatization would take time to extract.[39] The oil industry with its vast fixed investments in the North Sea could not run away and was available for squeezing until the pips squeaked.[40]

In his Budget statement, Howe dwelt on Britain's economic decline as compared with France and Germany. He was surprised that so little notice was taken of his words on so important a topic. But there was nothing new in what he said; it was a comparison of which many had spoken over the years, including Ministers of all Parties. When Ministers spoke of it, it was as advocates of policies that were designed to reverse the relative decline. It sometimes seemed that to mention the decline was sufficient justification for the policy. Selwyn Lloyd had tried planning. Maudling and Barber had attempted a dash for growth. Labour had come in, both in 1964 and 1974, with the same ambition of improving the relative performance of the British economy. The question now was whether a new Conservative government with a new approach to the resolution of economic problems would succeed where its Conservative and Labour predecessors had failed.

CONVERTIBILITY AT LAST — THE ABOLITION OF EXCHANGE CONTROL

On 23 October 1979, with Mrs Thatcher nervously consenting, Howe took the step that at long last made sterling freely convertible. Exchange control was abolished and residents were now permitted to exchange their pounds for foreign currencies at their own discretion in whatever amounts they thought fit. It was a step made easier by the temporary strength arising from the availability and price of North Sea oil. Until the abolition of exchange control, that was a right that had been confined to non-resident holders of sterling. Among the costs was that it was at odds with Howe's attempt to control the domestic money supply. It was an aspect of the decision to abolish exchange control that was not considered at the time. Liberalization, or setting the people free, had been given a higher priority than control over the money supply without the Chancellor realizing it. Mrs Thatcher recalls only the 'personal pleasure' this step gave her rather than the apprehension which her Chancellor detected.[41] Enoch Powell congratulated Howe in the House and expressed his 'envy' that it had fallen to him to have 'the opportunity and the privilege of announcing a step that will strengthen the economy of this country, and help restore our national pride and confidence in our currency'.[42] There is no evidence, unfortunately, that the abolition of exchange control gained for sterling the status of a strong currency.

The Cabinet was not informed in advance and was given no opportunity to object. Peter Walker, Minister of Agriculture, read of the decision in the newspapers.[43] There was, however, nothing new, or necessarily monetarist, in the arguments that led to the decision. Exchange control was far from a universal phenomenon. It was unnecessary where a government could feel confident in its currency and some governments did not operate it because they did not possess the bureaucratic capacity. Many commentators in Britain, including at least one in the Callaghan Cabinet, had speculated on the need to relax or abolish exchange control as the oil came on stream.[44] It would provide some offset to the upward pressure on the exchange rate that the oil might otherwise cause. It would ease outward investment and thereby enable UK companies to build up assets abroad. It would, at least in theory, compel investment in Britain to show a return comparable with that available abroad. The British example was followed by many other countries, not at all monetarist in economic theology, that still had in place comparable controls. Freedom of capital movements would eventually be required within the European Community. In any case it was becoming increasingly difficult to police controls because of the spread of information technology. Governments found the consequences of decontrol greater than they had expected. Vast flows of capital, far exceeding the value of trade, destabilized exchange rates, forced movements in interest rates, and deprived governments of much of their remaining control over their domestic economies. But the process was irreversible.

THE MEDIUM-TERM FINANCIAL STRATEGY

Conservative monetarism was still to make its greatest gesture. It was in Howe's 1980 Budget statement that the Medium-Term Financial Strategy (MTFS) was unveiled. It had been prepared under the supervision of the Financial Secretary to the Treasury, Nigel Lawson. It had the support of the new Chief Economic Adviser, Terry Burns, formerly of the London Business School. It was an idea that had been earlier canvassed at the London Business School by Burns and by Alan Budd, also of the London Business School, who was later to be Burns's successor as Chief Economic Adviser. Howe explains its purpose. 'The important innovation that we proposed with the establishment of the Medium-Term Financial Strategy was to set out our monetary targets for a period of years ahead.'[45] Specifically he wanted the growth in the money supply measured by sterling M3 to decline from 7–11 per cent in 1980–81 to 4–8 per cent by 1983–4, a decline of 1 per cent per annum.[46] The PSBR was to decline from 4 per cent of GDP in 1980–81 to 1.5 per cent in 1983–4. There is an engaging innocence about the way Howe records his account of the origins of the MTFS in his memoirs. He defends himself against charges of naiveté in committing himself to such a programme by pointing to the qualifying passages in his Budget statements, as though the Treasury would ever voluntarily allow a Chancellor to face the slings and arrows of his critics without a due meed of qualifying phraseology. Not just in his Budget statement but in the MTFS itself there was a bevy of conditional clauses intended to qualify the government's actual commitment to specific figures. Such clauses are inserted, often on the advice of Treasury officials, to permit Ministers to defend themselves when the out-turn differs from the promise. Lawson, in his memoirs, defines the objective of the MTFS as being to replace discretion by rules.[47] But he himself refers lavishly to the conditional clauses in his defence of the MTFS. An accumulation of conditional clauses does tend to undermine the value of the whole exercise.[48] The MTFS never in practice succeeded in replacing discretion by rules in economic management.

Gilmour appropriately describes the MTFS as 'a series of signposts without a road'.[49] There was considerable scepticism in and out of the government on whether it was possible to plan so far ahead in an open economy, and to achieve so much. That Wass was sceptical was to be expected. Less expected was the scepticism of John Biffen, Chief Secre-tary to the Treasury, a longstanding monetarist and a devoted follower of Enoch Powell. He found the MTFS inflexible. Inflexibility is the enemy of politics and, with any other Minister, it could have been suspected that he was a politician before he was a monetarist. But no such suspicion could attach to Biffen who had made many sacrifices of ambition in loyalty to his convictions. He saw monetarism being brought into disrepute by high unemployment. To that source of disrepute would now be added targets for the PSBR and the money supply which were unlikely to be met.[50] Biffen was even prepared to allow his dissent to become public. There was also very high monetarist authority for questioning an MTFS which concentrated on the PSBR. Milton Friedman told the Treasury Select Committee, 'The key role assigned to targets for the PSBR. . . seems to me unwise . . . There is no necessary relation between the PSBR and monetary growth.'[51]

There is some conflict of evidence as to the enthusiasm with which Mrs Thatcher endorsed the MTFS. She herself writes of the MTFS as of an idea to which she felt totally committed. 'We announced' the MTFS in the Budget, she writes.[52] Evidently she was a ventriloquist and Howe her dummy. She was certainly committed to the intentions of the MTFS but seems to have had some doubts about its political wisdom. Howe's probably reliable account, confirmed by Lawson, finds her initially dubious about 'graph-paper economics'. Her instincts often provided sound guidance. But, according to Howe, there was one clear merit in the idea which in the end gained her acceptance. It would, he argued, help to discipline the spending ambitions of Cabinet colleagues and get interest rates down.[53] It was yet to be established whether colleagues would allow themselves to be disciplined by graph-paper economics.

The MTFS grossly exaggerated the government's power to control events, but Howe's 'lawyerly scepticism' did not find a target in the MTFS. The reason is probably to be found in the search for an anchor to which to tie economic management. Howe was looking for a British anchor which would do for his economic management what the IMF had done for Healey's. It was an understandable ambition in itself. Nothing is more worrying than the exercise of discretion on matters of importance in the absence of accurate information. The error lay in believing that the MTFS would act as an anchor or, indeed, that policy could rely on one single dependable anchor. Lawson defends the MTFS by comparing it to the discipline exercised on national policy by the

Gold Standard, the Bretton Woods system and the ERM.[54] Lawson himself, over a year after the introduction of the MTFS, concluded that the UK should join the ERM. It was for him a second-best solution. He had decided that the first-best solution, domestic monetary discipline, could not be enforced by rule in the absence of reliable monetary indicators and was, therefore, unlikely to survive the political pressures.[55] Thus was to begin a rift in the government with explosive potential.

From one point of view the MTFS might be defended. If it signalled serious anti-inflationary purpose, then all the other justified criticisms could be disregarded. Mrs Thatcher writes, 'I would not bow to demands to reflate: it was this which turned the MTFS from an ambitious aspiration into the cornerstone of a successful policy.'[56] If, without the MTFS, Thatcher and Howe and Lawson would have surrendered even more readily, even more extravagantly, and even sooner, to political pressures, then an argument for the MTFS can be accepted. One does not have to justify every dot and comma in a religion if it succeeds in keeping people moral. Unfortunately the MTFS did not.

DISSENSION IN CABINET

Geoffrey Howe is surprised to find in retrospect that, from the beginning, he did not carry all his Cabinet colleagues with him in his economic policies. But he did not, at first, notice any hostility. This seems exceedingly odd because Cabinet Ministers live and work close together both in Cabinet and off the corridors of the House of Commons. Gilmour concedes that Howe's critics in the Cabinet were 'mostly silent'.[57] He writes that economic policy was 'not that of the Cabinet but of a secret monetarist clique'.[58] Howe confesses that Gilmour has 'some justification'. Although the MTFS was discussed at Cabinet on 13 March 1980, there was evidently, in these early days, no sustained discussion of economic policy in Cabinet.[59] In November 1979, Wass commented to a private dinner party that there had not been a single economic discussion in Cabinet since the government had come in.[60] But did Ministers of different persuasions never talk together privately? Jim Prior, who was given no advance notice of its contents, has written that the 1979 Budget gave him 'an enormous shock' and did 'much harm'.[61] Ian Gilmour mocks Geoffrey Howe's monetarism, arguing that the money supply was neither controllable nor measurable. In subsequent public debate, the mockers and the critics have had the advantage, at least until the appearance of Lawson's memoirs. Just as the *literati* supported Crosland against Healey, so they supported the Priors and Gilmours against Mrs Thatcher and Howe. Their task has been quite simple. They could accuse economic management of being monetarist and then show that monetarism was both flawed and incapable of implementation due to problems of measurement and control. Or they could show that Mrs Thatcher and Howe professed monetarism but did not abide by it. Or they could do both. They could show the apparent impact of policy on output and employment and insist that there must have been a better way, without carrying the burden of having to define the better way or implement it. They could point to the figures which showed the money supply increasing far beyond forecast but inflation coming down. These penalties were incurred by Mrs Thatcher and Howe because they made the mistake of professing monetarism which, like other economic panaceas, may provide its believers with psychological comfort but only very occasionally, and then usually by accident, with reliable guidance.

Howe was a monetarist, but a naive monetarist. The complexities of monetarism were not for him. It is still true that the monetarist recipe as interpreted by Howe and the Treasury had more to offer in the actual circumstances of 1979 than Keynesianism had in the actual circumstances of 1974 or would have had in the actual circumstances of 1979. Just as it was fortunate that in 1976 Crosland was not Chancellor, now it was fortunate that Howe's critics did not hold the levers of power. If they had, and had acted as they wanted Howe to act, the inflation that threatened would have become endemic. The determination that accompanied Howe's naiveté was invaluable. A less naive Chancellor might have done a great deal less well. Given the inflationary situation in 1979, naive monetarism had found its transient niche in economic history. Certainly nothing his critical colleagues had to offer, if they had anything to offer other than a deep distress that was itself perfectly understandable, would have served as well in bringing inflation down. Howe's problem with his 'wet' colleagues was that no one had told them that the price of monetarism was three million unemployed. They had not been told because, in advance of the experiment, no one knew. Not merely did they not know, they had expected that monetarist policies would bring unemployment down. When Howe's Ministerial colleagues found that the Conservatives had once more become the Party of unemployment, they made feeble attempts to rebel. But they had no means of bringing inflation down that did not involve serious unemployment.

Mrs Thatcher writes, 'There has never been a more devout believer in the virtues of consultation than Geoffrey.'[62] From the language it can be assumed that this was a form of devotion that Mrs Thatcher did not share. Howe believed that he could persuade his ideological opponents in the Cabinet. He concedes that there should have been more opportunity to debate economic policy.[63] It sounds as though Howe wanted more discussion of economic policy in Cabinet but that the Prime Minister was opposed to it. Howe does not seem to have been very insistent on discussion and it was certainly easier to conduct the Thatcher-Howe policy without too much Cabinet intervention than it would have been with it.

There is, generally speaking, little benefit to be derived from discussions of economic policy around the Cabinet table because few Ministers have anything of value to say about economic management. But, in this case, there was the additional difficulty that, if the battle against inflation was to be given priority, there genuinely was no alternative except at the margin. The critics were not talking about marginal differences. They wished to make a wholesale onslaught on a policy that appeared to them to depart in its character from 'one nation' Toryism. The British economy and the world economy had both been deflated by the tripling of oil prices since the beginning of 1979. It was an opportunity for a repeat of the arguments last heard after the oil price hike of the 1970s when the British Keynesians had advocated reflation in one country. They had been too influential with the result that the IMF had, in the end, to be summoned to the rescue.

Geoffrey Howe comments on the failure of his critics to press their doubts about economic policy in Cabinet. They raised them but then allowed them to drop. He says that 'It is hard to see any reason for that but the extreme difficulty, when it came to the point, of deploying any coherent alternatives.'[64] Lay Ministers will always have that difficulty when they lack the support of a department competent to brief them. Nevertheless there was a coherent alternative. It was reflation, a higher PSBR, abandonment of any attempt to control the money supply, a switch in priority from inflation to unemployment. It was an alternative that, in the view of the Prime Minister and the Chancellor, would lead to disaster in the 1980s as it had in the 1970s. There was no possibility of compromise between two points of view which were diametrically opposed. Therefore, although the dissidents could not be prevented from criticizing in Cabinet when opportunity offered, there was little point in deliberately bringing them into the discussion when the two groupings started from premises so different.

How could Mrs Thatcher and Howe persuade the country if they could not persuade their own Cabinet colleagues? Mrs Thatcher appeared to be of the view that there was no need to persuade the country, except at election times, and that if the existing Cabinet refused to be persuaded she would appoint a Cabinet that she did not need to persuade. She had the power, she would proceed remorselessly, and the country would, in due course, acknowledge her wisdom. She would not seek consensus because consensus involved compromise, and compromise would be the death of her policies. When the Cabinet had shed a number of those flattered or disdained by the description 'wets', it became the practice to devote a special Cabinet meeting to a discussion of Budget prospects. But the benefits were primarily spiritual. Ministers could feel they were being consulted though the Chancellor would keep his hands free. The costs were loss of time and they could include compromise with incompatible views. There is no evidence that even the drier Cabinet of 1982 and 1983 had much to offer on these occasions. Those who, in the Prime Minister's or Chancellor's view, did have something of value to contribute could always be brought together in a small, formal or informal group for discussion with the Chancellor.

PROBLEMS GALORE

Howe was soon to find that honesty of purpose and devotion to duty do not command instant success in economic management. Everything was going wrong. Unemployment was rising fast. Inflation peaked at 21.9 per cent in May 1980 and then began to fall back but remained far too high. Interest rates were high enough to deter investment but not to provide a positive return taking account of the rate of inflation. Public expenditure seemed impossible to control and not just because recession was forcing up unemployment. Most embarrassing perhaps was the explosion in the money supply. Howe had decided to abandon the system of special deposits, known as the 'corset', which had been used by Barber and Healey to control the growth in the money supply. It was not a very satisfactory system because it tended to divert lending away from the banks, which were controlled, to other sources, some of them less reputable, which were not controlled. But it had helped. In introducing the MTFS in his 1980 Budget statement Howe had warned that an initial effect of abandoning the corset could be an overshoot in the money supply target. But such was the explosion in the money supply that actually occurred, far outside the MTFS forecast, that his prior warning provided no rescue from embarrassment. It was an example of the way the policy of setting the people free, which was the Tory supply-side policy, could come into conflict with the Tory objective of controlling the money supply.

The explosion in the money supply should have created an opportunity for a sustained attack by the 'wets' on Geoffrey Howe's economic policy. A 'monetarist' Chancellor without control of the money supply is like a ship without a rudder. There was no such attack. The wets excuse themselves by claiming that they did not want to convert themselves into a cabal.[65] There is a simpler and probably more truthful explanation – they did not understand. It is easy for Ministers to employ, and even understand, the language of Keynesian demand management. They can argue that the PSBR should not be reduced in a recession but allowed to grow. They can criticize cuts in public expenditure. But monetary policy and the money supply, and instruments of control of the money supply such as the corset, are very difficult subjects even for many Ministers who have served in the Treasury. On such subjects, Ministers stand in grave danger of making themselves appear foolish. They are well advised to keep their mouths shut.

Among those who were particularly annoyed by this apparent failure in economic management was the Prime Minister. She believed that the Bank of England was at fault but it was both unfair and ignorant to blame the Bank for the consequences of her policy of liberalization. Mrs Thatcher had her own advisers on economic management and among them was the monetarist Alan Walters. He had his ideas on how to control the money supply without high interest rates.[66] The Treasury persuaded Howe to have none of it. Walters's ideas, it argued, could work only at the cost of unpredictable variations in interest rates.[67] As Mrs Thatcher's concern arose from her desire for lower interest rates rather than unpredictable interest rates, it was possible to steer her away from Walters's ideas on this occasion, though she was inclined to return to them whenever interest rates had to rise. Economic management is an area of policy in which outside advisers will always insist that they know better than practitioners. They cannot lose. They can always claim that their advice, even if taken, was implemented in the wrong way, by the wrong instruments, at the wrong time, at the wrong exchange rate,

471

and with the wrong rate of interest. That is the history of monetarism in Britain as told by the monetarists. It did not work because it was not properly implemented, or because it was implemented by a disbelieving Treasury. But it is not just the history of monetarism; it is the history of economic advice. While the credentials of advisers remain impeccable, the person who primarily suffers is the Chancellor who was, in this case, already carrying the burden of an apparent failure, and who was compelled to spend time arguing a case which was right in his judgement but which, by its nature, could not be ultimately compulsive. Nigel Lawson noticed that in the course of the debates on controlling the money supply in No. 10, in 1980, the Prime Minister was sometimes less than courteous to her Chancellor.[68]

Among others less than courteous to this Tory Chancellor in the early days were leading, or at least prominent, businessmen. British self-sufficiency in oil at a time when the price of oil was sometimes touching $40 per barrel, together with high interest rates, still at 16 per cent after a 1 per cent fall in July, had pushed the exchange rate to a level inconsistent with the competitiveness of British manufacturing. In September 1980, the exchange rate reached $2.40. Recession plus lack of competitiveness was having a serious effect on manufacturing production. The decline in manufacturing production meant more unemployment. The August 1980 unemployment figure showed a rise of 200,000. At the CBI's autumn conference, the new Director-General, Terence Beckett, promised a 'bare-knuckle fight' against the government, and Michael Edwardes, the protectionist chairman of British Leyland, which depended on government money for its survival, provided further useful guidance by declaring that if the government could find no other way of living with North Sea oil, it should be left in the ground. But if the oil was left in the ground, where would the government get the revenue from which to subsidize British Leyland?

There were those, not alone in the world of business, who believed that the sterling exchange rate could have been better controlled if Britain had adhered to the ERM. But Howe who, earlier and later, was an advocate of sterling membership of the ERM, did not seem to hold that view at this time. Mrs Thatcher reports a series of meetings on the ERM leading up to one in January 1982 at all of which Howe argued that the time was not right to join the ERM.[69] Indeed, the idea that membership could have been a significant stabilizing force for sterling in the circumstances at that time can be seen to be preposterous in the light of the later experience with the ERM. The Bundesbank did not see it as any part of its responsibilities to ensure the competitiveness of the British economy.[70]

THE LADY IS NOT FOR TURNING

While criticism and unemployment mounted, and there was increasing talk of a U-turn, the Prime Minister remained firm. At the Conservative Party conference in October 1980, she uttered her most famous words. 'You turn if you want to. The lady's not for turning.' It was the ultimate statement that she was different from Heath and all those Tory predecessors who had deceived the country by shaping policy to political clamour and the level of unemployment. They might call it 'one nation Toryism'. For her it was betrayal. Those leading Tories who had believed that 'monetarism' was a passing phase which would be reversed when its effects became apparent, found themselves denied the victory they had expected over what they regarded as dogma. It was their own fault. Their alternative policies would have proved rapidly unviable. They had remained ignorant of the forces operating in the world after Bretton Woods, forces as unsympathetic to Tory sentimentalism as they had proved to Labour sentimentalism.

Howe had the comfort of knowing that on the fundamentals his Prime Minister remained staunch, whatever criticisms of detail she might make, however discontented she might be at the failures in control which she attributed to the weakness of the Treasury and of the Bank rather than to the nature of the agreed policy. If there had been any serious hesitation in No. 10, the policy would have crumbled and the 1981 Budget would have been inconceivable. There are suggestions that Howe himself was weakening around this time owing to the apparent lack of success of his policies thus far. It is suggested that he showed signs of reverting to 'pragmatism' which, in the language of the time, indicates a readiness to abandon ship.[71] Howe himself makes no such admission. He would have been aware that Chancellors are more easily dispensed with than Prime Ministers. It is within the power of a Prime Minister, however committed to a policy, to make the Chancellor the scapegoat for failure. Howe had no future if he admitted failure. Such an admission could not be on his agenda and quite clearly it was not on the agenda at No. 10.

THE 1981 BUDGET

The greatest embarrassment for Howe and the government was their failure to control public expenditure, a failure attributable in part to the recession, in part to promises made at the 1979 election, but in part also to the political impossibility of winding up the welfare state. Howe was being warned by the Treasury that his forecast at the time of his 1980 Budget of a PSBR of £8.5 billion was likely to be exceeded by a very large amount, perhaps £3 billion. In his autumn statement on 24 November 1980, he announced about £2 billion of what was in effect increased taxation accompanied by a reduction of 2 per cent in MLR to 14 per cent. He was increasing taxation at a time of recession. The PSBR was ruling economic policy. His attack on the PSBR represented a marked departure from the theory, still argued in many an academic publication and also by eloquent economic journalists, that it *should* be allowed to rise in a recession. The market, which otherwise might have been impressed by his stubborn commitment to a lower PSBR, would have noticed that public expenditure was out of control and that interest rates were being brought down.

In preparing his 1981 Budget, Howe found himself confronted, as Healey had been before him, with ever-rising Treasury estimates of the PSBR on unchanged policies. Whatever Milton Friedman might argue about the relationship between the PSBR and the money supply, Howe's mind was now concentrating on the PSBR. By November 1980, the PSBR for 1980–81 was being forecast at £11.5 billion as against £6 billion targeted the previous March and implied by the MTFS. It eventually came out at £12.5 billion.[72] An early forecast of the PSBR for 1981–2 put it at £11.5 billion as compared with a figure of £7.5 billion implied by the MTFS. If the PSBR was to be hauled down to the less ambitious target of £10 billion as Howe, ignoring the MTFS, tells us he thought desirable, he would be forced to impose an additional £1.5 billion of taxation. By 10 February 1981, the PSBR forecast had risen to £13 billion. Hardly had that figure been absorbed by shocked Treasury Ministers than a new figure of £13.5 to £13.75 billion emerged from the forecasters. By the end of February, the figure had risen again and the PSBR on unchanged policies actually published on Budget day was £14.5 billion.[73] For the Chancellor there were various options. He could be content with a PSBR of £14.5 billion. Alternatively he could stick with what he says was his original presumption, that the PSBR should not be more than about £10 billion, which would imply an increase in taxes of about £4 billion. Or he could choose an intermediate position. For political reasons, he did not seriously consider Alan Walters's proposal that the PSBR should be £7 billion, implying £7.5 billion of additional taxation.[74] Perhaps, nevertheless, Alan Walters's apparent extremism played a helpful role in gaining the support of Prime Minister and Chancellor for more modest, if still fearsome, intentions.

In the battle of the memoirs, there is some conflict between Mrs Thatcher and Geoffrey Howe as to who can claim most credit for the 1981 Budget. In the view of both, it was the turning-point from which can be dated the revival of the British economy. There is, therefore, credit to be claimed and, given their later disagreements, to be denied. In Howe's memoirs, it was Mrs Thatcher who had to be brought round to the need for a tough deflationary Budget in the midst of a recession. It was he that was insistent on a £10 billion PSBR. The Budget was made in the Treasury, not in No. 10.[75] In Mrs Thatcher's memoirs, Howe would have been content to reduce the PSBR to £11.25 billion and she, advised by Alan Walters, had to bring him round to a tougher stance.[76] Hers is the more detailed account of the exchanges between the two Downing Street residences. Lawson's account supports Howe rather than Mrs Thatcher but he may have got it through Howe.[77] In any case, there is nothing reprehensible about an evolution of opinion. The two were obviously thinking on similar lines and, in the end, it was a political judgement. The more ready she was to be tough, the more readily he could be tough.

The eventual decision, after much debate, was to raise an additional £4 billion in taxes. Excise duties were substantially increased. A once-for-all windfall tax was imposed on the clearing banks which had been enjoying the benefits of Geoffrey Howe's high interest rates. By freezing personal allowances, Howe was able to avoid an increase in the *rate* of income tax. That no doubt gave *political* satisfaction. Taxpayers still had to pay more.

Thus the spectacle on Budget Day would be of a Chancellor raising taxation once more in the midst of a recession and when unemployment, already high, was rising. The Cabinet, meeting on the morning of the Budget, had the usual minimal opportunities to object, though some senior Cabinet Ministers had had the advantage of an earlier meeting with the Chancellor. The majority of the Cabinet was remarkably submissive and accepted that Howe's hand had been forced by bitter necessity. Their reluctant support may have derived in part from an acknowledgement that they had created the problem that the Chancellor was now trying to solve. It was they who had insisted on a level of public expenditure that confronted him with a £14.5 billion PSBR. Even for a Conservative Chancellor, raising taxation may be the only way of educating spendthrift colleagues in the merits of economy.

Howe had done Prior the courtesy of giving him an account of his intentions the day before the Budget Cabinet and statement. 'I told him I thought it was awful ... I couldn't say anything bad enough about it.'[78] At Cabinet, James Prior, Peter Walker and Ian Gilmour were critical.[79] For them the correct reaction to the enlarged PSBR would have been to accept it, and even glory in it, as the harbinger of the reflation that the country so obviously needed. Gilmour, as the intellectual spokesman of the 'wets', is of this school. He writes, 'when a government spends less, it indirectly causes its own income to fall. A government which cuts its spending on goods and services reduces national income and increases unemployment. As a consequence, it has to spend more on unemployment benefit and receives lower income from taxes.'[80] One does not need to be a monetarist to reject Gilmour's faith in an ever-increasing PSBR as a way of increasing national income. Prior writes contemptuously of Thatcher and Howe, 'The idea of pumping money into the economy to reduce unemployment was anathema.'[81] It is a pity perhaps that Prior did not reread the speech of James Callaghan at the 1976 Labour Party conference. If this was the quality of criticism that Mrs Thatcher and Howe had to meet in Cabinet, it is no wonder that she, at least, saw no merit in listening to it.

But, even though Cabinet Ministers may be talking nonsense, they are Cabinet Ministers and they have to be conciliated or sacked. These Cabinet Ministers appear to have been conciliated by an offer from the Prime Minister that in future there would be a Cabinet discussion of economic policy each July and a discussion of Budget strategy each January or February.[82] No doubt as an aid in justifying his decision not to resign, Walker describes this as 'an important constitutional change'.[83] It was certainly not a constitutional change and it is doubtful whether, as Prior confesses, it was even important.[84] By the time of the first scheduled discussion of Budget strategy, 28 January 1982, Gilmour was no longer in the Cabinet and Prior had left the Department of Employment for Northern Ireland. Meanwhile, the wets did not feel that Howe's 1981 Budget took them beyond the limits of tolerance. If the Chancellor stubbornly insisted that, in accordance with what was left of his MTFS, the appropriate way of dealing with the increased PSBR was to raise taxation, the critics were equally firm that it would be a mistake to resign on the issue or attempt to take rebellion to the point of forcing resignation on the Chancellor. They considered that it would be a mistake to deprive the government of their services when it so much needed the counterbalance of their opinions. Prior particularly lists loss of influence as an excuse for not resigning.[85] But as he had no influence on economic policy, it is not clear what he thought he would lose.

Gilmour considers the question why the 'moderates' as he calls them were defeated although 'In one sense the moderates had a majority in Mrs Thatcher's first cabinet.'[86] He rejects the answer that they had no alternative. He defends their failure to advance a worked out alternative on the grounds that the situation was changing and that they would not, in any case, have been allowed to table their alternative policy: 'Mrs Thatcher would not have permitted the flaunting of heresy in a cabinet paper'.[87] This is a feeble excuse. A body of Cabinet Ministers who have an alternative policy to propose can always insist on their paper being tabled on threat of resignation. Gilmour's own explanation of their failure is the 'personal inadequacies of the wets'.[88] He excuses it by what he describes as the 'unprecedented' circumstances. 'Never before had a prime minister and a few close associates embarked upon so disastrous an economic experiment while keeping the cabinet at a distance.'[89] Gilmour is right to accept the personal inadequacies of the wets. Cabinet Ministers who are required to take responsibility for what they regard as a disastrous economic experiment have no honourable alternative but resignation.

But the failure of the wets to honour, by resignation, the ancient convention of Cabinet government, is an incomplete explanation of their defeat. The more probable explanation is that they themselves, while having numerous complaints, did not have sufficient confidence in their alternative to insist on tabling it. Pym asserts that 'The failure of the "non-monetarist" Conservatives is not that we have lacked a realistic alternative, but that we have not articulated it with sufficient vigour and clarity.'[90] Cabinet Ministers with something to propose do not usually lack vigour or clarity and, if they do, it is attributable either to their incompetence, ignorance or to their lack of confidence in their alternative. Their determination to whinge in the background, and in coded messages, was equalled only by their determination to cling to their portfolios and their lack of confidence in their own alternative.

There is another explanation for the failure of the wets which Gilmour does not explore. This is that some senior members of the Cabinet, who might normally be expected to take a one-nation view of Conservative policy, had become convinced that something drastic did need now to be done. They had witnessed the humiliations of the 1970s and the decline in Britain's standing in the world. They saw that inflation was once more mounting to unacceptable levels. They may not have had much understanding of monetarist economics, but they were persuaded that shock therapy was now required. Lord Carrington writes, 'I believed that there was, in fact, probably no alternative.' He confesses to his own doubts and expresses the wish that what was done had been done with greater concern for 'the human side of the process'. But it had become necessary 'to stand firm against a sentimentality which would make things worse tomorrow in return for a little popular easement today'.[91]

364 ECONOMISTS

While the wets in Cabinet were clinging to their portfolios, outside the Cabinet the Budget was greeted with an outburst of hostility of probably unparalleled proportions. It included much of the press, some of which considered that such a Budget must end the career of this particular Chancellor. It included among his own backbenchers, Peter Tapsell, whose City connections gave him some authority to speak on such matters. It included two economists, Francis Cripps and Wynne Godley, who had strongly urged Healey to turn to protectionism at the time of the IMF crisis.[92] In an article in *The Guardian* they declared that it was 'a severely disinflationary Budget that will cause a hyper-slump such as Britain has never seen before', and that they were 'amazed and aghast'.[93] Above all there was the letter in *The Times*, drafted by Frank Hahn and Robert Neild, and signed by 364 economists including five out of the six surviving former chief economic advisers to the government. They wrote that

> There is no basis in economic theory or supporting evidence for the Government's belief that by deflating demand they will bring inflation permanently under control and thereby introduce an automatic recovery in output and employment; Present policies will deepen the depression, erode the industrial base of our economy and threaten its social and political stability; There are alternative policies; The time has come to reject monetarist policies and consider urgently which alternative offers the best hope of sustained economic recovery.[94]

The letter of the 364 economists failed to provide specific policy guidance. Their suggestion that alternatives should be examined to discover where lay the best hope skilfully plastered over the probability that many alternatives would have been on offer, perhaps even 364. Happily deploying conveniently selected figures, Howe, Lawson, and Mrs Thatcher, in their memoirs, laugh at the 364 economists. Howe points out, by way of defence, that it was in the very quarter that he introduced a Budget that was so bitterly condemned as deflationary by so many authorities, that the fall in national output came to an end and that over the following eight years real GDP grew by an average of 3.2 per cent per annum.[95] Lawson makes the same point.[96] Among the disagreements among economists are the questions how to calculate growth rates and what periods it is appropriate to take and are comparable one with another. It is no surprise that politicians and politically committed economists claim more for their policies than they are likely to have achieved and that they show a tendency to select those figures and those periods that prove their successes rather than their failures.[97] For the historian it is better to decide that no periods are comparable one with another and thereby to escape the dilemma of judging policies by growth rates.

Howe's real justification lies in a different direction. It was vital in 1979–81 to direct policy to defeating inflation. The price was high and regrettable but inescapable. For a period, there was bound to be a cost in slow or even negative growth. Unemployment was not the only damage being done to the British economy and society. Christopher Johnson writes, 'The deficiency of supply in the economy in the late 1980s can be traced back to the excessive severity of the 1980–81 recession.'[98] This may be so, though much of the capacity lost in the early 1980s was soon for the scrap heap in any case. There is no evidence that a wiser Chancellor could have more sensitively modulated the severity of his action if he was serious in his attack on inflation. That such methods had to be employed to deal with inflation was a tragedy that had its roots long in the past.

Nothing could bring out more poignantly than this controversy the problems of economic management. Neither Howe nor his critics could *know* that they were right and, in their different ways, neither was. The economists based their condemnation on 'economic theory' and 'supporting evidence'. There is a problem of economic management precisely because there is no agreed and relevant economic theory, because 'evidence' even when it is available can be difficult to interpret, and because, in any event, decisions have to be taken on the basis of evidence that is out of date. Therefore economic management is always a matter of judgement. It always involves the balancing of risks. Quite apart from the monetarism which may have inhabited Howe's mind, there were sound reasons in March 1981 for risking the possibility of further damping economic activity in the interest of further damping inflation. Inflation, though coming down, was still far too high and the rate of descent was being slowed by the falling pound. Howe took the safer, the anti-inflationary, risk. He avoided the error of changing priorities in the midst of the battle against inflation. If he had attempted to change priorities, the market would soon have dragged him back, humiliated, to the battle against inflation. Ironically, he had lacked sufficient confidence in his own MTFS which demanded that he do more, not less. There was nothing specifically monetarist in the 1981 Budget except in the sense that monetarism was being interpreted as toughness in economic management. But toughness does not necessarily need a monetarist inspiration and some monetarists thought he was being too tough and that monetarism would get the blame.

No one denies that growth did recommence, though sluggishly, round about the time of the 1981 Budget. In one sense, history was repeating itself. Healey had had to argue in Cabinet that the 1976 agreement with the IMF was not deflationary. Howe's 1981 Budget would prove not to have been deflationary. But he could not know that, and the recovery for which he claims credit was based in part on a declining exchange rate, not the most convincing indicator that, even yet, he had won market confidence.

OVERKILL?

Though history was repeating itself, there was one lesson from Healey's experience that Howe had overlooked. He had not learned that if the market has lost confidence, there is no alternative to overkill. The legitimate question about Howe's Budget is whether, having failed to control public expenditure, it would not have been better to raise taxation even higher and leave an even smaller borrowing requirement. That suspicion is confirmed by the experience with both the exchange rate and with MLR after the Budget. The exchange rate, $2.37 at the beginning of the year, had fallen by mid-August to a four-year low of $1.75. On 14 September 1981, fearful that it would not be possible to fund the PSBR, and on the advice of Gordon Richardson, Governor of the Bank, Howe reversed the 2 per cent cut in MLR that had been one of the few elements in the 1981 Budget that had been greeted with any pleasure. Given the size of the PSBR, the cut had clearly been a mistake. On 1 October, shortly before the Conservative Party conference, MLR was raised further to 16 per cent. If there had been a smaller PSBR, Howe might well have got away with his interest rate cut. However the 16 per cent MLR seems at last to have converted the market. It was a final sign of virtue. With confidence restored, it was not long, a matter of months, before it proved possible to bring the Base Rate down.[99] The parallels with the autumn of 1976 must have been particularly striking to Richardson, who had lived through both episodes. There was little evidence that, until the 16 per cent MLR, Howe's political courage in raising taxes in a recession had sufficiently impressed the market. In his Budget, he had moved in the right direction but not far enough. He may have judged that politically the overkill option was not available. But there is no evidence that it was seriously considered. It was the preparedness to use interest rates dramatically a few months later that turned the corner for Geoffrey Howe.

PUBLIC EXPENDITURE

The problem which had forced Geoffrey Howe to make such a difficult choice was the continued failure to control public expenditure. The MTFS had not proved to be of much assistance. Controlling public expenditure should be easier for a Conservative than for a Labour government. First, Conservative governments believe in the control of public expenditure whereas, for Labour, devotion to public expenditure is the only aspect of socialism that, in popular appeal, has survived experience with its other aspects. The second reason why control of public expenditure should be easier for a Conservative government is that they are not constrained by the linkage to the public sector trade unions which inhibits a Labour government from a search for greater efficiency. However, despite these advantages, the rise in public expenditure was a problem for Howe, second only to inflation. Conservative Ministers appeared as devoted to the expenditure claims of their departments as any Labour Minister. This might have been expected where 'Tory' issues like defence and police were concerned, but, in fact the enthusiasm for expenditure spread across the spectrum of government activity. For some Ministers the enthusiasm was derived not just from departmental concerns but from a wish to change the whole direction of policy in a reflationary direction. Even Ministers who had served in the Treasury, such as John Biffen, once Chief Secretary, now Secretary of State for Trade, could not be relied on as allies. John Nott, Minister of State at the Treasury during the time of Edward Heath, who was now Secretary of State for Defence, could hardly be expected to bring to the Cabinet table greater concern for public expenditure than he had shown in the 1970s. But Mrs Thatcher had expected it, which was the reason she had replaced Francis Pym at Defence by Nott. He was a grave disappointment.

There was a major row in Cabinet on 23 July 1981 at which harsh words were used about the Chancellor's policies. Very large increases in public expenditure had been proposed and were supported partly as a way out of recession. The Treasury had responded by proposing cuts in the estimates of £5 billion. In the first two years of the government there had been the largest falls in output and in industrial production since 1931.[100] The day before the meeting it had been announced that unemployment now stood at 2.85 million. During the spring and early summer there had been serious riots in Brixton, Liverpool and Manchester which could reasonably be attributed to the rising unemployment. Biffen who, the year before, had forecast 'three years of unparalleled austerity', now argued that enough had been done to cut public expenditure. Heseltine, Secretary of State for the Environment, proposed a pay freeze, a remedy from the days of Heath, and received support from Walker and Lord Soames. Pym argued that the problem was employment, not inflation. Hailsham warned that unemployment could destroy the Conservative Party. Carrington was among the critics. The Treasury team was isolated apart from Joseph and Mrs Thatcher. The meeting concluded without any decisions other than that there should be no public mention of the possibility of a pay freeze. The discussion would continue later on the basis of a further paper from the Chancellor.[101] The Chancellor escaped to fight another day. He had had the satisfaction of the Prime Minister's strong support.[102]

The problem of controlling expenditure, therefore, remained. There were many possible approaches to its solution. One was to rid the Cabinet of the Tory grandees brought up in the Macmillan and Heath traditions, or at least move them from the mainstream departments. By September 1981, Mrs Thatcher had a Cabinet more in her own image. Some of the 'wets' had been despatched. Prior had been re-located in Northern Ireland; he had been resistant not just to the economic policy of the government but also to legislation restricting trade union immunities demanded by Mrs Thatcher and Howe. But public expenditure is insidious – it claims the driest Ministers as its advocates once they have departmental responsibilities.

It was necessary therefore to look for other approaches. One was to free the Exchequer from a major burden by privatization of nationalized industries that required subsidy. The problem was that those nationalized industries requiring subsidy were the most difficult to sell at a good price. Another approach was to privatize profitable nationalized industries. It was an approach with great attraction for Conservative politicians because it enabled them to laud the merits of competitive private industry over uncompetitive public sector industries. That it also brought in money for the Exchequer and thus helped reduce the PSBR was an encouragement, not a deterrent. Another approach was to seek greater efficiency in the delivery of public services. This assumed that there were significant gains to be made and that was not always clear. Other approaches included higher payments by the public for public services, encouraging private individuals who could afford it to make their own provision for medical treatment through insurance, and so on. While all these approaches could be tried the only one which was likely to provide major relief to the PSBR was privatization, and that only as long as the stock of saleable properties lasted. On the other hand, there is no silver lining without its cloud. The availability of money from privatization could lead to softness in the control of public expenditure.

It was necessary, therefore, to examine whether institutional changes could deliver public expenditure economies. Cash allocations to departments and cash limits provided a better control system than the Plowden control by volume, especially in an inflationary era. By March 1982 all future expenditure plans were being expressed only in cash terms, not in volume terms, though the idea that planning could be done in cash terms alone had itself to be abandoned and some account taken of inflation. Whatever its merits for the purpose of control, cash planning still left the question of the totals of public expenditure at which control would be exercised. The Cabinet is not a satisfactory instrument for determining totals. The Prime Minister presides over a body composed of two Ministers, the Chancellor and the Chief Secretary, who have an interest in containing public expenditure, and many more departmental Ministers with an interest in increasing it. It is not surprising that Prime Ministers tend to seek compromises instead of siding unequivocally with their Treasury Ministers. It is less painful that way, at least in the short term. The incentives are poorly designed. Departmental Ministers win their spurs both in their Departments and among the clients of their Departments by winning battles against the Treasury. It is the Chancellor who, as in the 1981 Budget, suffers the consequences. His colleagues win their plaudits. If, as a result of their winning their plaudits he has to raise taxes, or deny a tax reduction, it will be he who has to endure execration by those who are applauding his colleagues, for it is well-known to all client classes that public money would grow on trees if only the Treasury fertilized them properly.

The question for the Prime Minister and the Chancellor was how to get decisions about public expenditure out of Cabinet and into their own hands. In the 1970s, it had been decided that Treasury Ministers could not be overruled in Cabinet committees. But that still left the ultimate decision to Cabinet. In 1982 a Cabinet Committee was established, popularly known as the Star Chamber, to which was referred the resolution of disagreements between the Treasury and departmental Ministers. Until his resignation on health grounds in 1988, the chair was taken by Willie Whitelaw, Deputy Prime Minister.[103] It was not an entirely satisfactory solution because the chairman would still be seeking compromise and there is nothing like compromise for increasing public expenditure totals. The hope was that the terrors of being referred to the Star Chamber would persuade departmental Ministers to settle, as it were, out of court on or near the Treasury's terms. Very often everything would be settled out of court. If one is to judge by the government's record with public expenditure, either the committee lacked the terrors of the Tudor Star Chamber or Treasury Ministers were less ferocious with public expenditure than is reputed.

JUSTIFIED BY SUCCESS

In the manner of Chancellors who have been badly bruised by criticism, Howe had been tempted to cry recovery before it was readily apparent. Before the summer of 1981 was out, he was declaring that the recession had ended. The evidence of recovery *was* gradually accumulating. Once he had emerged from his *annus horribilis*, 1981, Howe could feel himself justified by success. The market had been reconciled by his willingness to repeat the 16 per cent rate of interest, though the decline in the exchange rate was hardly evidence of enthusiasm. His Cabinet colleagues and his Parliamentary Party could feel placated by the beginning, how-ever hesitant, of recovery. The first Budget strategy meeting promised by the Prime Minister to the Cabinet at the time of the 1981 Budget took place on 28 January 1982. Hugo Young describes the meeting as the occasion on which 'the prime minister and the Chancellor found the confidence, for the first time, to open up discussion of the Budget strategy to the whole cabinet'.[104] By that time both Mrs Thatcher and Howe had exhausted their capacity for economic heroism and were having electoral thoughts. In November 1981, Shirley Williams had, at a by-election, won the safe Conservative seat of Crosby for the Social Democratic Party on a swing of 25 per cent. Of the Cabinet of 28 January, Howe writes that it 'turned out to be an unthreatening and useful occasion. It showed very clearly that Cabinet – certainly in its new make-up – was well able to make a balanced and supportive contri-bution to the debate. The test was less severe, no doubt, at a time when some of the worst pressures were beginning to ease.'[105] The pressures that in his view were easing were the economic. The political pressures were increasing. Mrs Thatcher had become a listening Prime Minister, but only when she was fairly sure that she would like what she would have to hear. In March 1982, Roy Jenkins won Hillhead in Glasgow from the Tories. Politics was dictating a retreat from valour. According to the public opinion polls, the government and the Prime Minister were intensely unpopular. While the words remained firm, the time had evidently come when economic management and the control of public expenditure could be more sensitive. It would be to misunderstand Mrs Thatcher and, indeed, Howe, to imagine that they were unaware of the political limits on economic heroism. Those limits had been extended by divisions in the Opposition but they were still there.

Even if his claim of recovery was premature, Howe was entitled to feel more serene. His 1981 Budget achieved his PSBR forecast. His 1982 and 1983 Budgets caused him far less anxiety. Borrowing was now declining as a percentage of GDP faster even than planned. Giving evidence on his 1982 Autumn Statement, Howe admitted the difficulties of monetary control but added, 'The thing that has been most consist-ently put in place has been the manifest determination to reduce the real burden of public borrowing.'[106] Mrs Thatcher's reputation for resol-ution had been established once and for all by the Falklands War. Enoch Powell had told her she was made of genuine metal and he was at least as great an authority on metallurgy as on economics. Having passed the Powell test, she no longer needed to prove her mettle in the field of economic policy and thereby incur political unpopularity. Economic policy was back in the consensus mode. 'I really am the true Keynesian, when I'm taken whole', she told the electorate as the election loomed.[107] In November 1982 she wrote to the local authority associations and to the nationalized industry chairmen encouraging them to increase their capital expenditure. Howe felt able to reward the electorate rather than inflict penalties upon them. Public expenditure was allowed to surge. He relaxed monetary policy. In July 1982, hire purchase controls were abolished, a most potent restorative of consumer demand. He even claimed success for the MTFS as a contributor to economic stability. It was, however, a much devalued and amended MTFS.[108] In 1983, forgetting the cautionary words in his 1979 Budget speech, Howe appeared to claim responsibility for the improved economic prospects. His previous humility succumbed to the imminence of an election campaign. Support for the government began to return even before victory in the Falkland Islands endowed the Prime Minister with heroic stature. Howe now had time to supervise the preparation of the Conservative Party's election manifesto. He also became more deeply involved in the problems of the international economy. He was elected Chairman of the IMF Interim Committee in which position he had the satisfaction of negotiating a 50 per cent increase in IMF quotas, for the benefit principally of the developing world. He could do this confident that no British claim for assistance would sap any part of the IMF's increased resources. Britain's begging bowl had been put away.

Howe had enjoyed great advantages: a divided Opposition, a generally supportive Prime Minister, the revenue benefits of North Sea oil and privatization, the protection provided by North Sea oil to the balance of payments. He had not wasted his advantages. Overseas indebtedness had been halved. Greatly helped by a fall in world commodity prices, inflation was down to 3.7 per cent despite the fact that the increase in money supply had far exceeded that forecast in the first version of the MTFS. Not everything was as intended. The government had planned to make a real cut of 4 per cent in public expenditure in its first four years. In fact there proved to have been a 6 per cent increase.[109] The tax burden had increased between 1979 and 1983 from 34 per cent of GDP to nearly 40 per cent. The cuts in direct taxation were benefiting only the higher paid, and even with a divided Opposition and the Falklands factor to help it, this resolute government still thought it necessary to assist its electoral prospects with a pre-election spending spree. The government was moving back into the mainstream British tradition of inflationary economic management. Yet, when he left the Treasury for the Foreign Office after the Tory victory in the 1983 election, Howe could reasonably claim to be the most successful postwar Chancellor. No previous postwar Chancellor had bequeathed to his successor so few problems that would cause anxiety in the market place.

Yet Howe had set for himself a much more severe criterion of success than that he would be trusted by the market. He certainly did not expect that during his tenure of duty at the Treasury unemployment would reach 3 million.[110] He quotes *The Economist* to the effect that he had achieved the 'neutralization' of unemployment as an electoral issue.[111] This could have been of little comfort to the unemployed. It was not his fault – no alternative policy would have prevented it. The fault lay in the long history of the British economy and in the history of British economic management. On coming into office, he had spoken of the 'British disease' and of the relative decline of the British economy. There was little sign of any reversal despite his fiscal and monetary policies, despite the beginnings of privatization and the much-needed trade union reforms for which he had pressed and which the government had, in stages, introduced. Economic performance was still poor by international standards. Given that his four years at the Treasury would hardly have been enough to secure such a reversal, the point that he had failed in this respect would not be worth making were it not a characteristic of political discourse to make premature and exaggerated claims. If there was to be a dividend from his policies, it would be his successors who cashed it. Given the decline in the exchange rate, he had not yet guaranteed the 'economic stability provided by sound money' that his Prime Minister claimed as her objective.[112] Indeed she herself verged on dampness when, at a CBI dinner shortly before the 1983 election, she took credit for a decline in the exchange rate from $2.45 in October 1980 to £1.54 in April 1983.[113] This was certainly adding to the competitiveness of British exports and therefore contributing to the recovery but it was hardly sound money. If sound money was really her objective, it too would take its time and its tolls. Howe's tenure of the Treasury shows the limits of what a Chancellor can hope to accomplish. As we have seen, there is contradictory evidence on whether he realized those limits. But, whether or not he realized them, he acted, although he did not always speak, as though he did. His task was economic stabilization. The main responsibility for economic transformation then lay, where it had always lain, not with the Treasury, not with government-induced stimuli or incentives, but with the economic actors in the market place. The question now was whether his successor would understand, would build on the progress made during his watch, or undermine it by too much ambition.

THE EXCHANGE RATE MECHANISM OF THE EUROPEAN MONETARY SYSTEM

Among the respects in which Howe himself appears to have thought his achievement incomplete was that there was as yet no adequate anchor to which to tie policy. He had advocated British participation in the ERM of the EMS when it was debated in the House of Commons in November 1978, partly perhaps in that spirit of contradiction that informs so much Opposition activity. He tells us of his belief in German principles of economic management. The Conservatives' 1979 manifesto certainly read as though a Tory government would take sterling into the ERM. When Howe became Chancellor, he decided that the time was not right.[114] He continued to believe that 'membership should remain a medium-term objective'.[115] The question was repeatedly examined during his tenure of the Treasury. During the four years of Howe's Chancellorship, there were seven realignments within the ERM. As sterling was not directly involved, Howe was invited to preside over the long meetings at which the realignments were decided. His experience confirmed him in the view that sterling should in due course join. He seems to have seen it both as an anchor and as a means of securing a high degree of stability between European currencies.[116] His prayer apparently was that sterling should in due course become righteous, but not quite yet.

By 1984–5, he says, even the Treasury, which had so vigorously opposed membership in 1978, was agreed that the time was right for accession. The implication must be that the Treasury also saw a need for an anchor, that the MTFS had failed in that role, and that therefore the anchor had to be provided by the German DM. On any other assumption, it would have been perceived that the argument for joining the ERM had grown weaker with the years, not stronger. The abolition of exchange control would certainly make it more difficult to hold the rate within the required margins. In 1978 there was an argument for joining as a form of discipline. But if a Conservative government could show that the UK could itself bridle its longstanding inflationary excesses, the better course was to continue floating but with tight fiscal and monetary discipline. If, by 1984–5, the Treasury had come to favour

British accession to the ERM, the implication was clear enough. It could only mean that, in its view, even a Conservative government under Mrs Thatcher could not ensure the necessary domestic discipline and that therefore it was the least worst option to tie sterling to the vagaries of German domestic policy. The Treasury would have observed that, though this government was different from its predecessors in some respects, it was no different in its anxiety to win elections, even at the expense of economic discipline. Howe's argument that membership of the ERM would contribute to currency stability ignores the fact that the fiscal and monetary discipline necessary to keep sterling within its ERM margins would, if imposed without the constraint of ERM membership, be quite as effective in that role. All that would be needed would be that the government should be prepared to impose it.

CONCLUSION

After victory in the 1983 General Election, Howe moved to the lesser responsibilities of the Foreign Office. He should have stayed where he was and continued his fight for sanity in economic management. The Exchequer is the second position in government even if the Foreign Secretary wears more finery. Howe's move brought him into even closer working contact with the Prime Minister and their incompatibilities became even more manifest. Contemptuous though she was of the Treasury, she was even more contemptuous of the Foreign Office. The contempt was bound to spread eventually to its political master. Howe was too stubborn to submit his convictions to her instincts. She could not conceal her increasing irritation with a colleague whose character and modes of thought were so different from her own. She said she liked vigorous argument but she could lead only by dominating. Persuasiveness was no part of her equipment. Her problem perhaps was that she had no way of dealing with Ministers who were her intellectual superiors. Their arguments about membership of the ERM and about Europe took place in an atmosphere of increasing exasperation. Even differences on Europe might not have led to the final breach had any mutual sympathy survived between these two pillars of the Thatcher revolution. She did not realize that he had it in him to destroy her, though the only way he could do it was by destroying also his own political career. But he was not a traitor, merely one of the most honest men in politics finally driven to the end of his tether.

SIXTEEN

Nigel Lawson: Thatcher's Inseparable Antagonist

THE MAN AND THE APPOINTMENT

Nigel Lawson was elected to the House of Commons at the age of 42, rather late by the standard of most prominent politicians. But he had behind him a successful career as an economic journalist and editor, which meant that he was better known than most new MPs. The House is seldom impressed by success outside its Chamber, and is inclined to resent excessive publicity for a new Member consequent on his many friendships in the media. Nevertheless, a successful, and well publicized, career outside politics is not, on balance, a disadvantage, the House of Commons' jealousies notwithstanding. In a politician's career, personal publicity means a great deal, especially to an MP who arrives late. Lawson became Chancellor nine years after becoming an MP. Apart from Hugh Gaitskell, it was the most rapid rise to the postwar Chancellorship. From the Prime Minister's point of view, there were many arguments for appointing Lawson. He had no established position in the Party, and was not the leader of any faction. It was unlikely that he would ever be a challenger for No. 10. He would be her creation, and therefore he might feel grateful. She believed their views on economic policy to be much the same. Where they differed, he was likely to do what he was told. His background and intellectual equipment suggested that he would do it well. The omens, at least, were favourable. On appointing him Chancellor, she told him to get his hair cut. He arranged an early appointment with his barber.[1] But his hair grew again along with his self-confidence.[2]

Mrs Thatcher was an unusual Prime Minister in many ways. One of those ways was that, although she felt compelled to make some obeisance to considerations of political balance within her Cabinet, she was prepared to raise people of high ability to senior Cabinet posts irrespective of their standing in the Party. The only conditions other than high ability were her expectation that they should agree with her, feel grateful to her, and not constitute a threat to her. For a person of high ability who lacked standing in the Party, say a Brittan or a Lawson or a Tebbit, there was a strong temptation to agree with her. It was a temptation that extended to some not of high ability who gained her approval simply through personal devotion. In the case of Lawson it was a temptation that diminished as he acquired a status of his own. In retrospect, as Lawson's memoirs frequently demonstrate, he became free of all temptation to agree with her. Though he managed carefully the timing of his disagreements with his Prime Minister and, until the end, was not prepared to press them against her veto to the point of resignation, it remains true that in a government that, in the end, contained too many sycophants, he was not one.

Economic journalism is a much better preparation for the Treasury than Membership of Parliament. Economic journalists have easy access to the actors in the market place and, which is denied even to front bench Opposition spokesmen except just before an election, to Treasury officials. The costs attributable to these privileges include, probably, a long record in print. The views happily and confidently expressed in a long-distant past may not in retrospect look too good, or at least not consistent. Lawson's past is littered with detritus of this kind. That economic journalists change their minds is no more to be criticized than such changes among lesser human beings. This is a minor embarrassment when compared with the benefit that should accrue to a writer whose thinking has moved through a variety of contradictory phases, the benefit of humility. Humility was not, however, among the more obvious qualities that Lawson brought to the Treasury.

Humility apart, Nigel Lawson was certainly, in so far as anyone can be qualified in advance, the best qualified Chancellor of the postwar epoch. His memoirs are an outstanding record of life at the Treasury in the 1980s. He was capable of delivering lectures on economics which economists appeared to take seriously, even to the extent of causing some of them to suffer apoplectic seizures.[3] He had spent over two years as an unusually active and effective Financial Secretary to the Treasury. Howe, as Chancellor, found that Lawson's 'economic thinking was as stimulating as it was (often) dogmatic . . .'[4] While Financial Secretary, his dogmatism seems to have been accompanied by loquacity on such a scale as to distress other Treasury Ministers who felt that they were not getting a fair hearing.[5] In January 1981, Lawson let the Prime

Minister know that he was exceedingly annoyed when Leon Brittan was plucked from the Home Office and appointed to the Cabinet as Chief Secretary over his head. Brittan was a close friend of Howe's and, at the Home Office, had earned the admiration of William Whitelaw, Home Secretary and effectively Deputy Prime Minister. Whitelaw, on the other hand, did not like Lawson and was an obstacle to his promotion until later when, finding Lawson virtually friendless in the Party, he decided to befriend him.[6] It is not inconceivable that Howe would not have wanted the garrulous Lawson as his deputy in the Treasury and his principal coadjutor in the Cabinet. Howe may have suspected that Lawson was insufficiently sensitive to the requirement on all deputies to assist their bosses, not to discomfit them by demonstrating before colleagues their superior knowledge and mental agility. Lawson need not have worried too much about Brittan's preferment. By September 1981, he was in the Cabinet as Secretary of State for Energy and, after the June 1983 election, now with strong backing from Howe, he entered into his inheritance as Chancellor, the appointment to which he may have felt his whole preceding life had prepared him.[7]

Leaving aside any personal deficiencies, there was only one disability of which Lawson could complain in taking on the role of Chancellor. He could not blame his immediate predecessor for any of his problems, at least in public. On the other hand he had many advantages: monetarism, though controversial among economists, had survived the test of a General Election; inflation was relatively low; the economy was recovering; there was a surplus in the current account of the balance of payments; North Sea oil was delivering revenue to the Exchequer as well as protecting the balance of payments; with the exception of the miners, the trade unions were cowed; personal incentives were being provided, if not yet in the full measure that Lawson would introduce; and he had the support of an ideologically sympathetic Cabinet. He also enjoyed the financial benefits of privatization. Privatization was one of the principal achievements of the Thatcher regime. The Treasury was the lead department on privatization. Lawson appears to acknowledge that privatization was carried out in a manner that benefited the Exchequer rather more than the consumer. The revenue won seemed more important to the government than the competition created. This, however, was by no wish of his. He assures us that 'the Treasury was always on the side of introducing competition, and a tough regulatory regime where no competition was practicable, despite the fact that either would reduce proceeds'.[8] The Treasury does not win all its battles but it does not normally enjoy such princely consolation for defeat.

In reviewing his world as he found it in June 1983, there was also the question of his relations with his Prime Minister. He had every reason to expect that they would be good and that he would receive from her the strong support without which a Chancellor cannot succeed. In fact, his dealings with his Prime Minister became increasingly diffi-cult. He portrays Mrs Thatcher as a Prime Minister who lived up to her radical reputation only because of the pressure which he and others repeatedly brought to bear upon her. Other Chancellors have had their battles with No. 10 but probably none worse than Lawson. In the end there was total breakdown in what had become an impossible partner-ship. But it took an exceedingly long time – Lawson's was the longest postwar tenure as Chancellor. There was a contest between the forces that held them together and those that drove them apart. From her point of view he was too good at his job to be sacked but too wrong in his macroeconomic views to be permitted to act on them. They agreed on many things not of the first importance but on nothing that *was* of the first importance. It was no way to manage the British economy. If it had been a marriage, the divorce would have come sooner. A major purpose of their memoirs appears to be to wound, and to settle scores.

A HARD LIFE

Lawson points out justly that the life of a Chancellor is even busier in a government devoted to reform than in a government content with the status quo.[9] The Thatcher government wished to change many things and Lawson was therefore heavily occupied with many matters outside his direct responsibilities for economic management. He was, for example, involved with a rapidly changing cast of departmental Ministers in proposals for reforms in social security, health, education, legal services, broadcasting and local government taxation. Indeed such was the burden he carried that he could be diverted at crucial moments from his own primary responsibilities. Little of this burden was avoidable because very often the reforms proposed had their economic as well as their political implications. Fortunately he had the health and the intel-lect to cope. He did not always win where his view differed from those of the reforming Minister. But, advised by the Treasury, he probably prevented some harm and eliminated some nonsenses that would other-wise have passed through the machinery of a government led by a Prime

Minister of whom it was impossible to tell in advance when she would be impulsive and when cautious, and whose hunches, though frequently sound, were as frequently unsound. His worst failure was to prevent the enactment of the Community Charge or poll tax. He opposed it as 'unworkable and politically catastrophic'. He seems to have concluded despairingly that, though the poll tax was dangerous nonsense, it was not his nonsense.[10]

Apart from the travels that the European Community imposed on Finance Ministers, Lawson spent a great deal of his time in other international fora. There was the IMF, and its Interim Committee charged to supervise the affairs of the IMF in between its annual meetings. There were the annual economic summits of the five leading industrial powers, which became seven when Canada and Italy were added to the USA, France, Germany, Japan and the UK. There were the meetings of the Finance Ministers of the same five, then seven, leading industrial powers, the so-called G5 and G7. These were occasions when attempts were made to reconcile the divergent interests of the separate participant countries in a world no longer held together economically by American hegemony and fixed exchange rates. With Reagan as President, a constant source of anxiety was the large American Budget deficit with its varying effects on the external value of the dollar. Sometimes the dollar was too high and sometimes it was too low. Sometimes the US Administration seemed to be concerned about its external value, sometimes it was treated with benign neglect. The movements of the dollar in either direction tended to affect sterling. Whatever the condition of the UK economy, there was a tendency for sterling to be dragged up when the dollar was rising and down when it was falling. Even the ERM, whatever stability it might afford its members in their trade with each other, left European currencies floating haphazardly against the dollar and the yen. The US Administration would make Keynesian complaints about the difficulties caused by the uncooperative policies of Germany and Japan. The Germans and Japanese would tell the Americans to reduce their Budget deficit. These quarrels, and the gyrations of the dollar dragging sterling with it, helped to persuade Lawson that something more was required than to leave such important matters to the market. But his could not be a decisive voice. Sometimes the divergent interests of the G7 came sufficiently close together for an agreement of some kind to be struck which attempted to take exchange rates out of the exclusive control of the market. At the Plaza and Louvre meetings of 1985 and 1987 respectively, there were agreements intended to achieve exchange rate stability and thereby reduce external imbalances. There would then be temporary relief until once more interests and perceptions moved apart.

From the point of view of the UK, an additional problem was that the decisive economies were those of the USA, Germany and Japan. It was Lawson's constant fear that there would in the end be a G3 from which the UK would be excluded. For a British Chancellor it was important to be present at these gatherings, and have a voice, even if his influence was inevitably small. There were also the annual meetings of Commonwealth Finance Ministers. These Lawson seldom attended. He did not enjoy the perpetual battles between the developed and developing members of the Commonwealth, in which the UK was always the principal target of developing-country anger, and in which not all the developed members were invariably loyal to the cause of good sense as he saw it, usually rightly. He did, however, attend in 1987 when he was gathering support for his scheme of debt relief for those countries in sub-Saharan Africa categorized as 'the poorest of the poor'.[11] It was an occasion on which the UK was likely to be more popular than usual with the poorest developing countries of the Commonwealth and at which complaints would probably be heard only from the richer developing countries that would not benefit. Lawson's initiative did lead in 1988 to some relief for the poorest countries at virtually no cost to the donors who, realistically, had to accept that they would not have been repaid in any case.[12]

THE TASK

As it seemed in June 1983 that the government had regained control over the economy it could now turn its attention to its second major target, improved economic performance. Lawson tells us that on becoming Chancellor he gave priority to dealing with three major problems. The first was how to improve the labour market by supply-side reforms. This he saw as the only lasting way of making inroads into unemployment. The second was the problem of the monetary indicators which were not doing a good job of providing a stable financial framework. The third was to keep public expenditure to the government's chosen path.[13] There was, when he entered No. 11, what he describes as 'a very worrying surge in public expenditure'.[14] It was a formidable programme. Even so, there was not one of his postwar predecessors who would not have wished to exchange his inheritance for Lawson's. He even had time for tax reform. Lawson considered this an essential contribution to the supply side. Many of his predecessors, while by no means denying the importance of tax reform, would have considered it a luxury to be indulged in by Chancellors who did not face more serious problems. There were two Conservative tax-reforming Chancellors in this era, Barber and Lawson. Coincidentally or not, their names are today associated with unsustainable booms.

In view of the importance of public expenditure control, and the emphasis which Lawson gives to the role of tax reform in improving the supply side, it is necessary to say a few words on these two topics before turning to the major controversies that dominated relationships between an opinionated Prime Minister and this opinionated Chancellor.

PUBLIC EXPENDITURE

Those who may have been encouraged by Tory propaganda to think that the Thatcher government had come in pledged to reduce public expenditure would have been disappointed. Such an objective was unrealistic. But clearly some anchor for public expenditure was necessary. If none was found the consequences for taxation and borrowing would be unacceptable. Governments of different Parties may differ on where the anchor should be placed, but they can hardly deny the need for some anchor. In evidence before the Treasury and Civil Service Committee before Christmas 1983, Lawson said that his objective was to hold the level of public spending steady in real terms while the economy grew. He subsequently in his own word 'refined' this by taking as his objective a slower rate of growth for public spending than the sustainable growth rate of the economy as a whole.[15] It was not a refinement but a retreat.

Lawson underlines two achievements. One was to avoid, in the 1986 public expenditure round, a pre-election public spending bonanza. 'The 1987–8 out-turn proved to be virtually identical to the previous year in real terms. This was a remarkable and almost unprecedented result given the electoral calendar.'[16] Lawson thereby praises himself and criticizes all his predecessors. We need have little doubt that the criticism is justified but, though no politician can be denied the privilege of self-praise, for the lack of anyone else ready to take up the banner, it is not at all clear that in this case it is deserved. The government did not need to add to its electoral advantages the promise of good things to come in the field of public expenditure. The Opposition was still badly divided. Lawson had reduced income tax by 2p just before the election after a 1p reduction the previous year. Andrew Britton comments drily, 'A cynic would claim that monetary policy was more relaxed in the latter part of 1986 and in early 1987 than a totally apolitical judgement would have recommended. The blind eye turned to the expansion of credit no doubt helped to keep the consumer boom going.'[17] There was a record of economic recovery, whether or not sustainable, with unemployment and interest rates falling. Nothing more, surely, was necessary to persuade the electorate, though in fairness it has to be admitted that governments, especially governments led by Mrs Thatcher, were subject to the most improbable nightmares in the course of elections they were bound to win. Political courage was not the most obvious characteristic of Thatcher governments at election time. Lawson is certainly scraping the barrel for credit when he claims not to have permitted a spending binge before the election.

His second achievement was to reduce public expenditure as a share of GDP.

> Where previous Conservative governments (with the rather special exception of a few years in the early 1950s, when defence spending was greatly reduced following the end of the Korean War) had merely succeeded in slowing down the seemingly inexorable onward march of the State, the Thatcher Government, by single-minded determination, succeeded in reversing it.[18]

Such claims depend on the careful selection of periods and it is the view of this historian that no periods are comparable and therefore nothing is to be claimed by comparing them, especially when, as in this case, the achievement in the carefully selected period is at best marginal. Moreover one might expect Conservative Chancellors, before flaunting claims regarding public expenditure as a percentage of GDP, to think of the taxpayer. As Lawson acknowledges, the tax burden was certainly not reduced as a percentage of GDP under the Thatcher and Major governments. The excuse, because politics requires that there should always be an excuse, lies in the need to reduce the unsustainably large Budget deficit inherited from Healey.[19] In view of the later history of Budget deficits, this excuse too can be considered a criticism of Lawson's successors. But, his disdain for his successors aside, one would have expected a truly resolute government, after more than ten years in office, to have thrown off the effects of that part of their inheritance. What it achieved on public expenditure could not have made more than the most minimal difference to the performance of the British economy.

TAX REFORM

Lawson makes the modest claim that he left the tax system in less of a mess than he found it.[20] The modesty of his claim arises from recognition that the tax system is always likely to be complex until it is abolished, and it is not likely to be abolished. It was Conservative Party policy to reduce income tax rates partly on the principle that people should be left free to spend their own money as far as possible and partly as a supply-side incentive. Howe had raised VAT in compensation. Political pressures inhibited Lawson from significantly extending the range of VAT, which he would have liked to do in order to provide for further income tax reductions. On the other hand he could continue Howe's policy of reducing the top rate of income tax without too high a revenue cost. The appropriate rate of tax on higher incomes will be judged differently in different parts of the political spectrum. Lawson's 1988 Budget reduced the top rate of income tax from 60 per cent, to which Howe had cut it in 1979, to 40 per cent. In a world of free capital movements, competition for mobile investment is bound to imply that top rates of income tax should not be out of line with those levied in comparable countries. Whether that required a top rate of 40 per cent, as Lawson enacted, or 50 per cent as Mrs Thatcher would have preferred, is a secondary question.[21] A rate of 50 per cent would have been less dramatic, would have suggested greater caution at a time when the state of the economy required caution, and might have provoked marginally less waving of order papers by his backbenchers. A problem now constraining Conservative Chancellors is that the reduction in the *rates* of income tax, whatever the circumstances, has become a shibboleth. If, therefore, there is a need for more revenue, the most difficult method for a Conservative government is to raise income tax rates, even if that is the preferable course.

Lawson's tax-reforming ambitions were of wide scope. But many of his ideas were stamped on by the Prime Minister who feared the opposition they might evoke, and he felt compelled to retreat from others because of warnings from Conservative MPs who had been successfully lobbied by a variety of vested interests. He therefore accomplished in the area of tax reform substantially less than he had hoped. His principal tax-reforming achievement lay in the area of company taxation. His aim was 'neutrality'. He wished, for example, to remove the various incentives to investment and to compensate by a lower rate of Corporation Tax. The incentives were distorting decisions. As he put it, 'We need investment decisions based on future market assessments, not future tax assessments.'[22] Although criticized by the CBI, the move to neutrality was sensible and precisely for the reason Lawson gives. Investment based on a tax assessment will frequently prove to be a poor investment yielding a poor return.

However, even a Chancellor as dedicated to the principle of neutrality as Lawson could not be dissuaded from imposing his own economic judgements on the tax system. Howe had introduced a Business Start-up Scheme which developed into the Business Expansion Scheme (BES). Of the BES Lawson claims that it provided 'tax incentives which have helped substantially to promote new businesses, to the undoubted benefit of the economy as a whole'.[23] He leaves unexplained why the tax system should be employed to encourage new businesses any more than it should be employed to encourage new investment. In fact the BES tax incentives not merely reduced the cost to the investor of his capital outlay in a BES project. It also reduced the incentive to enquire too deeply into the merits of the project in which the investor was being invited to invest. The result was the creation of a large number of badly conceived new businesses which did not survive the subsequent recession and from which the only beneficiary was the sponsor, who gathered in the money for the project and took his commission out of the folly of the investor.

THE MAIS LECTURE

In his Mais Lecture in June 1984, Lawson, according to his own assessment 'challenged what had hitherto been the conventional wisdom head-on . . .'[24] The kernel of what he said was:

> The proper role of [macroeconomic and microeconomic policy] is precisely the opposite of that assigned to it by the conventional postwar wisdom. It is the conquest of inflation, and not the pursuit of growth and employment, which is or should be the objective of macroeconomic policy. And it is the creation of conditions conducive to growth and

employment, and not the suppression of price rises, which is or should be the objective of microeconomic policy.[25]

In his memoirs and in his Budget speeches he qualified this dichotomy to some extent. He writes: 'In reality, the distinction may not always be quite as clear-cut as this. In certain circumstances, which history suggests do not occur very often, macroeconomic policy could also play a role in supporting economic activity.'[26] It might be added, though Lawson does not say this, that where policy has gone badly wrong and inflation is high, microeconomic policy might sometimes be appropriately used in the form of an incomes policy as a junior partner of macroeconomic policy in conquering inflation. The impact of the Mais lecture owes more to Lawson's journalistic training than to any originality. It was the unqualified and paradoxical formulation that won attention rather than any addition he was making to the sum of human wisdom. So far as macroeconomic policy is concerned, James Callaghan had said as much in his 1976 report to the Labour Party conference. As Lawson admits, in many other countries such views would have appeared so obvious as hardly to warrant reiteration. Unfortunately, since the war, economic policy had been conducted in Britain on the assumption that this country had been the site of a superior revelation.

In the opinion of this author, the Mais lecture stated an important truth in a striking fashion. Moral education is, however, not enough. It has to be accompanied by moral fibre. Since 1974, policy-makers in London had been learning. Among them were the policy-makers of the Conservative Party. But how deeply, in the prevailing political and electoral climate, had the lesson really been absorbed? That the Conservative Party had, at least in words, abandoned Keynesian demand management was not news. What remained to be proved was whether the Conservative government was prepared to stick to its principles in face of political pressures. Economic policy in the months before the 1983 election provided little reason for confidence, even though the government had the unprecedented advantage of facing, and continuing to face, a divided Opposition. Where, in the opinion of this author, Lawson went wrong was in his belief that, having rediscovered these ancient and modern truths, it was necessary in addition to join the ERM as a way of 'locking in' the reduced level of inflation achieved by 1984.[27] That he believed that this additional discipline was necessary demonstrated a striking lack of confidence in the government of which he was a Member. Moreover, if that lack of confidence was justified, membership of the ERM would not be a substitute. Indeed the belief that it might be a substitute could actually lessen the determination to follow appropriate domestic macroeconomic policies. It is only by such policies that there is any hope of inflation remaining 'locked in'.

There was an unobserved danger in the formulation in the Mais lecture. This lay in the reference to 'the creation of conditions conducive to growth and employment'. The creation of such conditions is a difficult proposition and, at best, long-term. One of the dangers for this government would be that it would grossly overestimate what it had actually achieved in this area of policy and how rapidly its fruit could be gathered. Exaggeration of its own achievements in this respect led it to tolerate for far too long the re-emergence of an inflationary boom.

LAWSON'S MONETARISM

As Financial Secretary, Lawson the monetarist had become doubtful about monetary indicators. As Chancellor, he continued his search for a monetary indicator that would actually be useful in determining policy. The resources of the Treasury were mustered to assist in the search. To decide policy Lawson was seeking information about Nominal GDP, the total amount of the national income in money terms. The trouble was that direct information about Nominal GDP was late and unreliable. He therefore needed a reliable 'proxy' for Nominal GDP. M3, the 'broad money' measure, had proved unsatisfactory. It was continually overshooting the target set for it. Its relationship with Nominal GDP was 'uncertain and unpredictable'.[28] He could not trust it to give him timely warning. In his Mansion House speech in autumn 1985, Lawson announced the suspension of the sterling M3 target.[29] It was soaring despite high real interest rates. Broad money, M3, having been found unsatisfactory for any purpose known to this monetarist Chancellor, the search for an alternative ended up with 'narrow money' or M0. M0 consists essentially of notes and coins in the hands of the public plus till money in the banks. This seemed a long way from Nominal GDP. Nevertheless M0, according to experience over a number of years, had enjoyed a reliable relationship to Nominal GDP. Lawson therefore valued it as 'a very good proxy' for Nominal GDP.[30] This did not mean that M3 was abandoned. That was impossible because the market knew about M3 and would be worried if the Chancellor forgot about it. Mrs Thatcher would also be very worried because she adhered uncritically to the true faith and had no part in Lawson's treacherous speculations. In his Mansion House speech, Lawson said that he 'would be considering what target to set for £M3 at the time of the next Budget'.[31] But M3 would now stand alongside M0. One problem with different monetary indicators is that they can convey different signals. While Lawson was digesting the signals from M0, the market might be digesting different signals from M3.

If one was searching for a candidate for the Treasury who actually understood monetary metaphysics, the name of Lawson would certainly pop out of the bag. But after all this intellectual striving and Treasury research, did he now have a useful aid to policy formation even on monetarist assumptions? One trouble with M0 was that no one, apart from its advocates, could believe that its composition represented an adequate definition of 'money' and it certainly could not be regarded as the 'money supply'. As Lawson puts it, in retrospect, 'it lacked street credibility . . . The achievement of the M0 target – or even its under-shooting – had no great effect on inflationary expectations.'[32] But one of the purposes of monetary indicators was that their movements should influence inflationary expectations. M0 was not fulfilling an important part of its role. Another, even more important, fault was that, at key moments, it too might fail to give the signals that Lawson felt he needed to guide policy. In explaining his decision to adopt M0, he writes:

> Had there been a monetary aggregate with a clear and predictable causal connection with inflation, I should certainly have used it. The whole problem was that no such aggregate existed. In its absence an accurate and up-to-date indicator of what was happening to Nominal GDP would be invaluable. If such an indicator causes warning bells to ring in time and leads the monetary authorities to take action, such as an increase in interest rates, when danger threatens, then it serves its purpose.[33]

If it neglects to ring the warning bells, such an indicator also provides an explanation of misdeeds, or an excuse. The house burnt down not because a match was put to it but because the fire alarm did not ring.[34] Lawson notes the failure of M0 to give a true picture at one or two crucial points, notably in early 1988.[35] That was when he would have liked M0 to give him early warning of the extent of inflationary pres-sures. It was Professor Charles Goodhart who discovered that the identi-fication of monetary indicators is likely to affect the reliability of the indications provided by them.[36]

A third problem from the point of view of Lawson's reputation was that, in the market, where understanding of the complexities of monetary measurement is hardly less imperfect than it is among the population generally, and where M3 had become a totem to be worshipped, not downgraded, it would not be understood that he was simply doing his heroic best to make sense of monetarism. The market's suspicions would be confirmed by those described by Lawson as 'sectarian monetarists' who had come to distrust Lawson's monetarism.[37] The suspension of the M3 target in 1985 was regarded by them as the 'death of monetarism'. Monetarist Nicholas Ridley articulates the criticism with the moderation due from one colleague to another. 'It is arguable', he writes, 'that the downgrading of M3 in 1985 was Nigel Lawson's first error.'[38] In economics, almost anything is arguable. Lawson's reward for valour in the cause of monetarism would be to be accused in retrospect of launching an unsustainable boom through a reckless abandonment of monetarism. The one defence which Lawson could not use was that monetarism had already been tested to destruction. It would have been inconsistent with his earlier convictions and would have exacerbated his relations with his Prime Minister. In the safety of his memoirs, however, he refers to his 1984 Mansion House speech as his last significant utterance as an unreconstructed parochial monetarist.[39]

Lawson had sought to find a measure of the money supply that was actually useful in guiding policy and influencing conduct. His failure confirmed him in his view that M0, much better than any of them, was an exchange rate anchor. In his 1985 Mansion House speech, having paid his tribute to M0, he added, 'The other good and early guide to changing financial conditions is the exchange rate.'[40]

INTERNATIONAL MONETARY REFORM

Lawson describes international monetary reform as one of his two overriding ambitions as Chancellor.[41] It was an exaggerated, and indeed costly, ambition for a British Chancellor. It replaced an earlier scepticism about the value of encounters with other Finance Ministers. Mrs Thatcher's instincts brought her nearer the truth than Lawson's naive belief in what could be achieved in the 1980s through international economic cooperation. In 1987, he delivered an address at the annual conference of the IMF and World Bank on the basis of an assumption that, following the Louvre agreement of that year, the world was 'already three-quarters of the way' towards 'a new international monetary order'.

He was at the time making one further unsuccessful attempt to persuade Mrs Thatcher into the ERM. It was an address of which his Prime Minister thoroughly disapproved. She had given her assent to British participation in the earlier Plaza agreement of 1985 but later came to the conclusion that this had been a mistake. She comments, 'The Plaza Agreement gave Finance Ministers – Nigel above all perhaps – the mistaken idea that they had it in their power to defy the markets indefinitely. This was to have serious consequences for all of us.'[42] As Lawson has to admit, he was 'much too optimistic' in his 1987 IMF speech. Within a matter of weeks, the Wall Street crash of 19 October 1987 had made such optimism appear naive.[43]

It proved possible, two months later, to secure from the G7 a communiqué reiterating an intention to cooperate in maintaining exchange rate stability.[44] It was obviously sensible where interests and perceptions did converge to work together with one's partners. It was sensible to maintain contact so that opportunities to act in the mutual interest were not overlooked. It is an illusion, however, to imagine that the outcome of such contacts can be regarded as a new international monetary order, to rely too much on exchange rate cooperation, for a country such as Britain to spend large sums of money in its support, or even to neglect the probability that interests will diverge at least as often as they converge. The USA is abnormally insulated against panic about the exchange rate of the dollar because of the size of its economy and its relatively low, though increasing, dependence on international trade. It is impossible for other countries to ignore the value of the dollar, and its ups and downs, some of them rather violent, and yet it is never certain when the US Administration will move from an attitude of benign neglect to one of active concern or, indeed, back again. American attitudes may even be affected by the change from one US Treasury Secretary to another.[45] However much changing attitudes in Washington may affect the British economy, this is not a situation that a British Chancellor can alter. Obviously countries with weak currencies feel themselves more exposed to the hazards of the world economy than countries with strong currencies. They are therefore more ready to seek permanent arrangements that eliminate or reduce such hazards. France had been a consistent advocate of such schemes since the breakdown of Bretton Woods. Lawson's efforts are to that extent understandable. But they were misguided and he exaggerates their outcome.

THE EXCHANGE RATE MECHANISM OF THE EUROPEAN MONETARY SYSTEM

Lawson's experience of the obstacles to international monetary order, and of the effort often required to achieve even momentary cooperation, might have led to a more sceptical approach to the ERM within which the DM was central but where the Bundesbank's monetary decisions were governed by domestic, rather than European, considerations.[46] Yet, having lost confidence in his monetary indicators, it was to the DM that he wished to anchor policy. Lawson was not a European federalist. He believed that the proper constitution of Europe was as an association of nation states. He was strongly opposed to monetary union as inconsistent with the sovereignty of the nation state.[47] His attachment to the ERM, therefore, had nothing in common with the European visions of a Jean Monnet or a Jacques Delors. He explains it with a battery of pragmatic arguments.[48] The first is that thereby he was exploiting for the benefit of Britain the market credibility that attaches to the DM. The monetary authority for the DM was the Bundesbank which was not just non-political but could claim a long record of success in squashing inflation in the German environment. By seeking to attach sterling to the DM, Lawson was apparently hoping to achieve sterling credibility with fewer tears, lower interest rates, and less unemployment. The objective of restoring credibility to sterling was commendable. Given sterling's history over the decades since the war, it would be a difficult task. It was a task that demanded radical changes in British domestic policy. It could not be achieved quickly, or at a small price. The price could not be lessened by gimmicks. France and Italy, the two major countries that sought to exploit the credibility of the DM when the ERM began functioning in 1979, have found, the market being what it is, that they must seek their own credibility and that the task is in no way eased by attaching their currencies to the DM. Indeed the link to the DM can impose tough, and sometimes insoluble, policy dilemmas.

During 1985 there was a series of meetings with the Prime Minister at which entry into the ERM was discussed. Lawson notes that there was at the time increasing support among backbenchers for membership of the ERM. At a bilateral meeting with Mrs Thatcher on 3 February 1985, and at a subsequent seminar at No. 10 attended among others by Foreign Secretary Geoffrey Howe, now reconverted to membership,

Lawson argued that it would be helpful with future controversies about public expenditure and borrowing if backbenchers faced 'a discipline of their own choice'.[49] No doubt he also hoped that his colleagues in the Cabinet would be similarly disciplined. There is a theme running through Lawson's thinking that discipline on public expenditure and borrowing is needed, that it is absent, and that therefore it has to be imposed externally. The MTFS had been intended to impose that discipline. It had failed, so something else had to be tried. In fact there are only two forms of effective discipline. One is the market which, perhaps after some delay, will condemn excess and compel retrenchment. The other is self-discipline. If self-discipline was not available, joining the ERM would not provide it. When the UK did join the ERM in September 1990, it did not prevent a lack of discipline on public spending.[50]

Another argument advanced by Lawson was that within the ERM, companies know that if they fail to control their costs they are unlikely to be saved from bankruptcy by devaluation, and both companies and individuals will lower their inflationary expectations and act accordingly.[51] He claims that entry in November 1985 would have put a dampener both on pay and price increases in the internationally exposed sector of the UK economy.[52] Unfortunately nothing could be further from the truth. The market, the employers, and the trade unions, were always aware that devaluations against the DM within the ERM were not merely permitted but probable. In the early years of the ERM, when Lawson was first advocating membership, there were repeated devaluations. Between 1987 and 1992 there was a period of stability which might have suggested to the innocent observer that devaluations were a thing of the past. Ironically, this period of stability was encouraged by the prospect of monetary union, a project to which Lawson was totally opposed. By 1992 that period of stability had come to an end. A system of exchange rate management which can provide only five years of stability cannot be expected to ensure either the credibility, or the presumption against devaluations, for which Lawson was looking. No Department of government was keener on British entry into the ERM than the Foreign Office. In August 1985, the Foreign Office produced a paper on the ERM which, Lawson tells us, seemed to envisage automatic realignments in order to cope with the different inflation rates in different member states. Lawson comments acidly that such an idea 'rather destroyed the point of joining in the first place'.[53] At any rate the Foreign Office was recognizing certain probabilities.

In November 1985, Lawson was recommending entry to the ERM at DM 3.70 to the pound.[54] There was a realignment of the French franc in April 1986. Lawson accepts that it would have been necessary at the same time, in other words five months after an assumed entry in November 1985, to devalue sterling to DM 3.50.[55] This was no way in which to build confidence in the immutability of the sterling exchange rate. There would almost certainly have had to be at least one further sterling devaluation during 1986. At a meeting on 30 September 1985, Lawson had argued that the extent to which the markets regarded sterling as a petrocurrency had greatly diminished.[56] But this proved not to be the case. During 1986 the oil price collapsed and sterling collapsed with it. By December 1986, the exchange rate was DM 2.85 to the pound largely though not exclusively because of the fall in the oil price. Lawson claims that a second devaluation could perhaps have been avoided by raising interest rates. He traces the later Lawson boom to his failure in 1986 to take sufficiently strong monetary action. He argues that, if sterling had been in the ERM, he would have been forced to take stronger action to maintain its parity even though he did not at the time realize that it was also necessary on domestic monetary grounds. It would have required a very large increase in interest rates to prevent the very substantial further depreciation of sterling that occurred in the latter part of 1986.

Experience shows that within any system of fixed, if adjustable, exchange rates, politics soon becomes a determining factor. Governments fear the humiliation of a devaluation. Experience certainly confirms that British governments have resisted highly visible devaluations to the utmost. If sterling had been within the ERM in 1986, Lawson would certainly, in any arguments with the Prime Minister on interest rates, have derived some assistance from the fear of humiliation. On the other hand, devaluations within the ERM were at that time such a regular feature as to deprive them of much of their horror. The horror of a devaluation within the ERM would certainly have been less than that of the kind of interest rate increase required to prevent it. It is, therefore, much more likely that, if sterling had joined at DM 3.70 in November 1985, there would have been some, ultimately unsuccessful, resistance to a devaluation in April 1986, followed by a further devaluation forced by the market before the end of the year. In short, Lawson's expectation that membership of the ERM would persuade companies to control their costs because they would be unlikely to be saved from bankruptcy by devaluation, defied both the contemporary evidence as well as experience of the effect of fixed exchange rates on inflation in Britain during the Bretton Woods era.

Lawson's final argument is that in a Europe in which the ERM exists, to be absent from it will suggest to the market an intention to devalue which will add a premium to interest rates. But throughout its existence, the ERM has been dogged by the market's perceptive suspicion that its members would be forced to devalue against the DM, even France whose determined attachment to the DM and the ERM was originally a surprise and then a source of admiration. In the end, after a prolonged period of stability, the ERM might have accumulated sufficient credibility for the purposes Lawson had in mind. But he can hardly blame those who had the foresight to see that such a period of stability was unlikely, or excuse his own failures by their resistance to membership of a system which they believed to be fatally flawed. In the modern world the lonely and difficult path to the credibility of a national currency has to be sought through the operations of Lawson's first Mais principle, that the object of macroeconomic policy is the conquest of inflation. In that search, the help to be obtained from linkage to the DM is illusory at best and may be counter-productive.

The decisive meeting on membership of the ERM took place at No. 10 on 13 November 1985. It was an ad hoc meeting of senior Ministers, the Governor, and officials. The discussion was based on a singularly half-hearted and unconvincing Treasury memorandum circulated on Remembrance Day.[57] Lawson's oral presentation must have been more convincing than his memorandum. The meeting was unanimous for joining except for Mrs Thatcher and John Biffen. Even Norman Tebbit was in favour. The Prime Minister had thought she could rely on him. He was then Party Chairman, and was later to be a scourge of all things European. Her Deputy Prime Minister, Willie Whitelaw, who usually made a point of throwing his support her way, supported Lawson.[58] According to Lawson, she then said, 'If you join the EMS, you will have to do so without me.' Howe confirms the strength of her refusal to accept the view of her colleagues. Her own account is that she simply said she had not been convinced.[59] It was a veto. As it was a Prime Ministerial veto, it was effective.[60] Howe comments that to overcome her veto 'we should, I think, have needed to go almost off the constitutional map'.[61] It has been argued that if the question of the ERM had been brought to Cabinet, there would have been an overwhelming majority in favour of joining. Lawson, however, believes this view to be wrong because most Ministers did not have strong feelings on the subject and they would not have wanted to defeat the Prime Minister who might have resigned.[62] Ridley believed that if Howe and Lawson had brought the issue to Cabinet 'they would have found a distinct majority against them . . .'[63] The question was never tested. The decision to stay out and the later decision to join were neither of them Cabinet decisions. It would have been better for Mrs Thatcher's reputation if she had stood fast in September 1990 when at last she did agree to sterling membership. Her difficulty was that, as a way of papering over differences within the government, she had accepted as official policy that Britain would join the ERM when the time was right. In her view, it would never be right. But, in that case, she should not have permitted the fudge.

On 25 November 1988, Lawson made to the Prime Minister a much better proposal than that to join the ERM. He regarded it as to some extent an alternative to membership of the ERM. He had sought in monetarism for rules which would govern monetary policy, and had not found them. He had been refused his alternative, which was membership of the ERM. As there could not be rules, the question that remained was where the exercise of discretion should lie. During the summer of 1988, he decided to recommend independence for the Bank of England. It was an idea borrowed from the successful experience of the Bundesbank in Germany and the Federal Reserve in the USA. He presented Mrs Thatcher with a paper embodying a fully worked-out plan which had been prepared, much to their distress but under his instructions, by Treasury officials. The Bank would by legislation be made responsible for monetary policy with the preservation of the value of the currency as its statutory remit. This would free interest rate decisions from political pressures. Where there had to be discretion, as in monetary policy, it was better that it be exercised by central bankers rather than by politicians. The Bank would have much higher market credibility than any government could command. To ensure a measure of accountability, it could report to a Select Committee of the House of Commons. The Prime Minister brushed the proposal aside. She told him that 'it would be seen as an abdication by the Chancellor when he is at his most vulnerable'. It should be considered, she suggested, only when the government itself could show that it had successfully reversed the rising curve of inflation.[64] But, as Lawson knew, she had no more intention of adopting an independent central bank as government policy than she had of entering sterling into the ERM. His problem was that he was advancing this idea not when his reputation was high, but when it was seeping away against a background of rising inflation and interest rates, and a worrying current account deficit. It was easy enough for Mrs Thatcher to present the proposal as an attempt to escape responsibility rather than as the means to establish long-term anti-inflationary credibility. Lawson did not pursue the subject with her, nor insist on bringing it before Cabinet. He mentioned it in public for the first time during his resignation speech on 31 October 1989. The idea was worthy of a better baptism.[65]

THE 1987 GENERAL ELECTION AND AFTER

The final battle in the war between the Prime Minister and her Chancellor began with the Tory victory in the 1987 General Election. Lawson had had a very good election during which he had successfully demolished Labour's economic policy. He had extracted from Labour leaders admissions regarding the level of taxation implied by their policies that they would have preferred not to make. He believes that Mrs Thatcher resented widespread comment that attributed the Conservative victory to him. Great as was her power and reputation, she was becoming jealous of his success, and he believes that her resentment embittered their relationship. She now thought of him as a rival for her job. Although in no way undervaluing his own role in the election, he regards any such idea as nonsense. He had never had any ambition to be Prime Minister. He considered himself ineligible. So far as he was concerned, he was at the pinnacle of power open to him. Nevertheless, even if that were true, she might consider that a threat from which she was to be rescued only by his ineligibility was a slight on her leadership of the Conservative Party and her exceptional services. In fact, she only had to wait. For him it was now downhill all the way.

The battle between them was fought out at two levels, the political and the intellectual. On the political level, she was supreme. Whatever fears she might entertain of his popularity in the Party, his standing could not rival hers. She now had three election victories behind her. It was true that her overwhelming victories in 1983 and 1987 had been made possible not by persuading the electorate but by the divisions among the Opposition. She was still gaining the suffrage of only about 42 per cent of the voting electorate, little enough considering the quality of the Opposition. But what counted with her Party was the achievement once again of a large majority in the House of Commons. The MPs on her backbenches felt profoundly indebted to her. It would take a great deal to rouse within the Parliamentary Conservative Party doubts about her leadership and her competence. On the intellectual level, it was very different. He was far cleverer than she, and had lived with economic policy all his adult life. She had never held an economic portfolio, she had never been a Treasury Minister. The nearest she had come to any economic responsibility was when she had been an aide to Iain Macleod and to Robert Carr in their roles as Shadow Chancellor in the 1960s and 1970s. Lawson had policies to which he had devoted deep thought and which he had extensively discussed with Treasury officials. She had only instincts. They were powerful instincts but she found it difficult to articulate them as considered policies in discussion with Lawson until she had received from her adviser, Alan Walters, both comfort that she was right in her instincts and arguments to deploy in their support.

Lawson met her regularly to report on his conduct of affairs. This was in addition to the information communicated to her on paper on a daily basis about the government's activities in the markets. In his memoirs he comments with apparent surprise that often she made no criticism even though he was uneasily aware that she in fact disagreed with what he was doing. But her silence on such occasions was not remarkable. She would not wish to expose herself in argument until adequately briefed. She had a parcel of instinctive objectives for economic policy which, in the situation of the UK economy, were often not compatible. She wanted sterling to be strong, inflation and interest rates to be low, the economy to be growing, the reserves to be accumulating. She relied on Alan Walters to reinforce her feelings with arguments which she could then deploy against her self-confident Chancellor. Fundamentally she felt that there was something wrong with a policy that departed from monetarism as she understood it, and was too dependent on international cooperation in the form of intervention on the exchanges intended to buck the market. It led to the purchase by the Bank of England of vast quantities of dollars, $27 billion by the end of 1987, ironically far more than the Bundesbank found it necessary to buy.[66] She thought intervention on such a scale inflationary. He denied it because he was 'sterilizing' the additional sterling by the sale of an equivalent amount of gilts.[67] But whoever was right on 'sterilization', a controversial subject, how could it be sensible for the Bank of England to buy dollars in such quantities to prevent it depreciating? It was a *folie de grandeur* unjustified by the interests of the UK economy.

Mrs Thatcher had assured Lawson that she would be prepared to entertain further discussion of British entry into the ERM after the 1987 General Election. But when he raised the matter in the immediate aftermath of the election, he found that she was unwilling to discuss it and felt that he had been tricked. There were at the time discussions proceeding between Central Bank Governors in an attempt to improve the machinery of the ERM. Lawson believed that a satisfactory outcome of these discussions would provide a suitable occasion to announce British membership. But his expectation illustrates Lawson's curious misunderstanding of the nature of the ERM. When it was set up it was agreed that when two member currencies reached their floor and ceiling against each other, both Central Banks would intervene to ensure that they remained within the permitted margins. In other words cooperative action would be required from the Central Bank with the stronger currency. The task of keeping its currency within the margins would not just be left to the Central Bank with the weaker currency. In this sense the system was supposed to be symmetrical. The problem was that the country with the weaker currency would naturally wish to intervene *before* it reached its floor. Yet there was no provision for these so-called intra-marginal interventions to be supported by the Central Bank with the stronger currency. In practice the problem almost always was that the DM was strong and some other member currency was weak. But there was no obligation on the Bundesbank to assist by buying the weaker currency as it approached its floor. In practice therefore the system was asymmetrical with the intervention obligation falling heavily on the Central Bank with the weaker currency.

Lawson suggests that the architects of the ERM had 'strangely not foreseen' this problem.[68] This is untypically naive although it has to be said that Lawson was generally naive about the prospects of exchange rate cooperation, not just within the European Community but in the wider world. Of course the problem had been foreseen by the architects of the ERM.[69] The Bundesbank had feared that the ERM would impose upon it unacceptable intervention obligations which would be inflationary. Lawson never seemed to understand the Bundesbank's reluctance to create DM for the purpose of buying, and thereby supporting, another country's currency. Yet, as a monetarist, he should have been able to appreciate that a central bank as cautious as the Bundesbank might consider the creation of DM inflationary. As he believed that money created for the purpose of intervention on the foreign exchanges could be 'sterilized', he thought that the Bundesbank's attitude was simply bloody-minded. But the Bundesbank, which had a certain record of success in countering inflation, did not share his view. The Bundesbank had the whip hand in the negotiations to establish the ERM and, in consequence, the system had been designed to limit the Bundesbank's intervention obligations. For the other members, and for France in particular, they had either had to submit to the Bundesbank's conditions or accept that there would not be an ERM.

France's complaints about this asymmetry led to discussions among Central Bank Governors at Basle in 1987 to see whether, after eight years' experience with the ERM, there was any way of achieving real symmetry. In these discussions Britain supported France as it had during the original negotiations in 1978. It was these discussions that Lawson hoped would create the occasion for British membership. The outcome of the discussions at Basle was ratified at a meeting of European Community Finance Ministers at Nyborg in Denmark. The outcome, such as it was, is therefore known as the Basle-Nyborg agreement. Nothing of substance had been achieved. There was talk of greater cooperation between Central Banks, but no legal obligation was placed on the Bundesbank to assist with intra-marginal interventions. The system remained asymmetrical and the French had to like it or lump it. The whole incident simply illustrated a lesson of the postwar world; how difficult it is to force cooperation out of a government or a Central Bank with a strong currency. Those who are strong believe that weakness is the fault of the weak. They feel no moral compulsion to help. They will not accept any legal obligation to help. Rather they believe the weak should help themselves and become strong. They will help only if they see an interest in helping. Action will remain at their discretion.

SHADOWING THE DM

Having met a further veto on joining the ERM, the next source of tension between Lawson and his Prime Minister was his policy of shadowing the DM under a cap of 3 DM to the pound. He explains this policy not primarily as a preparation for membership of the ERM but by his desire to arrest the secular fall in sterling. The decline, he says, had worried him since 1984.[70] It was indeed worrying and hardly a tribute to the success of monetarist policies. Yet, whatever his intentions, the logic for intervention on the exchanges as a method of achieving this objective seems unconvincing. At the time the pressures on sterling were up, not down. The Prime Minister would have preferred to let sterling rise so that interest rates could come down. Lawson was aware that with an emerging current account deficit, the market might well lose confidence and begin to sell sterling rather than to buy it.[71] He writes, 'By resisting *upward* pressure on the pound I sought to create credibility for a commitment to resist *downward* pressure.'[72] Why action to resist upward pressure should give credibility to an intention to resist downward pressure if it re-emerged is unclear. Such an interpretation might have been conceivable at the time of Bretton Woods and fixed exchange rates. It was unlikely to be the interpretation placed upon his actions by the market at a time of floating rates. Given the record of the UK economy, it would be far more likely to confirm suspicion in the market that the UK government was behaving as UK governments had so frequently behaved in the past, that it was selling sterling through fear that the economy was becoming uncompetitive and was still prepared, whatever it might say, to allow sterling to fall to restore competitiveness and payments balance. Lawson himself confesses that he did not wish to put British industry once again under the strains it had experienced during the period of very high exchange rates in the early 1980s.

But the market had an even more compelling reason for refusing the confidence that Lawson was attempting to generate for the existing exchange rate of sterling. He clearly did not have the support of his Prime Minister. In his Mansion House speech in November 1987, he said, 'Nor should there be any doubt about our commitment to maintain a stable exchange rate, with the rate against the Deutschmark being of particular importance. It gives industry most of what it wants, and provides a firm anchor against inflation.'[73] But in an interview with *Financial Times* journalists on 20 November 1987, published on 23 November, Mrs Thatcher emphasized that there was no exchange rate target for the pound. She said that the 'DM at the moment is slightly deflationary. That means that the whole of Europe is geared to a slightly deflationary policy. Now, we have not been so geared and we have had a degree of freedom in relation to both the dollar and the D-mark and I just think that I am grateful for that.'[74] His only reply could be that 'actions speak louder than words', in other words that the market should rely on what he was doing rather than on what she was saying.[75] She claims that she did not know before her *Financial Times* interview that Lawson was setting interest rates in order to shadow the DM at or below DM 3.[76] She was instinctively highly suspicious of any policy that proposed too strong a link to the Germans and their economy. He confirms that there was no meeting at which the DM 3 ceiling was specifically agreed. Nevertheless, he asserts that she did know and, indeed, that she must have known from the flow of information she regularly received about market interventions.[77] Clearly he believes she is attempting to discard responsibility, whereas she wishes it to be understood that she was not responsible for the consequences of his actions. It is not necessary to regard either as untruthful. It is always possible for two interlocutors to assume knowledge in the other and then to be astonished to find the assumption incorrect. In view of her well-known opposition to membership of the ERM, and the reasons for it, and her categorical assertions in retrospect, the probability is that she did not at first know although he thought she did. There was then the question, how far in the circumstances could she press her disagreements. She could stop him on major issues like membership of the ERM. But a relationship of constant bickering between Prime Minister and Chancellor was certainly disagreeable and, in the end, impossible.

She summarizes the situation as follows:

> First, Nigel had pursued a personal economic policy without reference to the rest of the Government. How could I possibly trust him again? Second, our heavy intervention in the exchange markets might well have inflationary consequences. Third, perhaps I had allowed interest rates to be taken too low in order that Nigel's undisclosed policy of keeping the pound below DM 3 should continue.[78]

When Prime Minister and Chancellor disagree on policy to such an extent, they must either sort out their differences or the Chancellor must go. On the other hand she did not feel strong enough to sack him.[79] She may have been asking herself what she should do with a Chancellor with whom she disagreed so violently but whom she could not move, first because of his standing in the Party and the government, and then because there was really no other post, except perhaps her own, to which he would wish to move.[80] For him, everything else would be a step down in power and influence. The logic of the situation was that he should resign. But he was not yet prepared to resign. He brought to his convictions a certainty equal to hers and he thought he might still prevail.

The dangers of international cooperation were illustrated when, in December 1987, there was a concerted European cut in interest rates. UK base rate was reduced by 0.5 per cent at a time when, if British domestic considerations were to be the criterion, interest rates should, if anything, have been raised and certainly not reduced. Lawson says that he agreed only to show that international cooperation was still alive and to meet American terms for active participation in stabilizing the dollar.[81] He should have remembered the example of the Bundesbank. The Bundesbank adheres strictly to the rule that domestic criteria must determine its actions, not the requirements of international cooperation. If they coincide, well and good. But domestic considerations come first. Lawson was putting the requirements of international cooperation ahead of domestic criteria. Not merely was this wrong in principle; it was pretentious to imagine that British cooperation was a condition of international cooperation. If the managers of the dollar, the DM and the yen saw a common interest in cooperation, they would act.

Shadowing the DM led to a variety of complications and absurdities. On 8 December 1987, Lawson decided, with the agreement of the Prime Minister, that all future intervention should be in DM. Both of them felt that they had bought quite enough dollars. Lawson emphasizes her agreement but it was clearly reluctant.[82] In agreeing with his tactics, she was merely approving the least bad method of implementing his policy. In 1991, she told Simon Jenkins that allowing the shadowing of the DM was her 'great mistake'.[83] Having decided to confine interventions to DM, it was then found that, under the EMS, of which the UK was a signatory even though not yet a member of the ERM, the Bank of England was not allowed to buy DM without the permission of the Bundesbank. Karl-Otto Pöhl, President of the Bundesbank, refused permission. He did not want the DM to become a reserve currency. Lawson and his Prime Minister considered Pöhl's refusal unjustified. It was just another example of the way the EMS had been constituted to serve German interests. They decided, against the advice of the Governor of the Bank, to buy DM for the reserves despite the breach of EMS rules. The Governor was then approached by the Governor of the Bank of France. He protested that if the Bank of England bought DM, the DM would rise and it would become more difficult for the French franc to keep pace within the ERM. So, in order to conciliate France, it was decided to buy roughly equal quantities of DM and francs. Thus the UK would be helping to keep the French franc within its ERM margins. But the same consideration applied to all the other currencies in the ERM. So in order to buy DM to keep sterling below DM 3, it became necessary to authorize the Bank to purchase a variety of other ERM currencies and, indeed, Swiss francs and yen.

By the end of December 1987, sterling was still rising and it seemed that intervention would fail and that it would, after all, be necessary to allow sterling to break through the DM 3 ceiling. Just at that moment, Lawson's policy was, for the time being, saved by a reassessment of sterling in the market. The exchange rate for sterling fell slightly and the DM 3 ceiling was preserved for a further two months. However, on 2 February 1988, Lawson raised base rate by 0.5 per cent. On 4 March 1988, a few days before the Budget, when upward pressure on sterling had returned, the Prime Minister insisted at a stormy meeting with Lawson that the pound should be uncapped, and that intervention other than for the purpose of 'smoothing' the pound's path should cease. The pound then passed through the DM 3 ceiling.[84] Lawson felt that he could not resign just before a Budget which would confer benefit that he had long planned. He does, however, comment that the Prime Minister was interested only in stopping intervention and that she at no time suggested that interest rates needed to be higher and monetary policy tighter. In other words she was as ignorant as he of the real nature of the economic conjuncture. He adds, 'The uncapping of the pound in March 1988, coupled with her adamant refusal to contemplate British membership of the exchange rate mechanism of the EMS, removed a major plank of my counter-inflation policy.' The plank was removed, he underlines, when a substantial current account deficit was already looming and, therefore, when sterling was likely to come under severe pressure and the reserves he had acquired in resisting its upward movement would prove very useful in averting a collapse. By way of support for his thesis he turns to David Nickson, then President of the CBI, who claimed that the uncapping of the pound represented a major threat to British industry since it lowered the resistance of his members to high pay awards.[85]

The concern of this Chancellor for the interests of British industry is no doubt commendable. British industry being what it is, a higher pound undoubtedly makes life more difficult. Chancellors, however, have not invariably regarded the views of the CBI as authoritative, often with good reason. It is a little odd that this Chancellor in particular should call the President of the CBI in evidence for a claim that a higher pound makes resistance to wage claims more difficult. The opposite might be thought to be the case. Indeed in a paper prepared by Terry Burns for a meeting at No. 10 on 25 March, ten days after the 1988 Budget, it was explicitly stated that an appreciating exchange rate reduced inflationary expectations.[86] Beyond that, there really is no justification for Lawson's failure to resign if he really considered that his counter-inflation policy had been swept away. There may be argument whether he should have perceived that inflationary pressures were mounting seriously. There will be controversy whether the 1988 Budget, which would make substantial reductions in income tax, including the reduction to 40 per cent of the higher rate of income tax, was the appropriate Budget at that time. It is the view of this author that Lawson was wrong to cap the pound, wrong to wish to join the ERM, and wrong to employ such triumphalist language in his 1988 Budget statement at a time when he knew that a substantial current account deficit was emerging. Even Howe refers to shadowing the DM as an 'unsatisfactory halfway house' and appears to agree with Mrs Thatcher in attributing to it responsibility for the Lawson boom.[87] However that may be, what cannot be doubted is that a Chancellor who finds himself in head-on collision with his Prime Minister must resign. He had been refused two elements that he regarded as crucial to his policy, first membership of the ERM and then the capping of the pound.[88] He had thereby been robbed of what he himself describes as a major plank in his counter-inflationary policy. The British political system depends on Ministerial resignation in such circumstances. At his pre-Budget session with the Queen, Lawson said that he thought his 1988 Budget would be his last because the Prime Minister was making the conduct of policy impossible.[89] That confidential conversation was no substitute for resignation. What did he expect the Queen to do about it? Change her Prime Minister?

On 25 March 1988, there was a meeting at No. 10 to try to establish a concordat between the Prime Minister and her Chancellor. There was an agreement between them that they should pursue a measure of exchange rate stability, supported as necessary by limited intervention within the context of a sound anti-inflation policy, though without commitment to a specific level for sterling.[90] It was a fudge, though one nearer to her position than to his. That it was a fudge was speedily revealed to the public. The pound was rising, encouraged by the content and presentation of the Budget but also by the current account figures. The figures for the first four months of the year as originally presented showed a large deficit but with a declining trend. Later revision revealed a much larger deficit without any evidence of a declining trend.[91] In an interview on 24 April Lawson said that the rise in sterling was 'unsustainable'. It would do 'nobody any good and is damaging for business and industry'.[92] Then, on 12 May, at Prime Minister's

Questions, she was challenged by Neil Kinnock, Leader of the Opposition, to say that she agreed with her Chancellor. She failed to do so categorically, employing instead various circumlocutions which left her attitude to her Chancellor, and his views on the level of sterling, obscure. The following day the pound rose to its highest level since 1985, DM 3.18. Lawson points out the irony of a Prime Minister who always expected her Ministers to agree with her but found it so difficult to express public agreement with her Ministers.[93]

Lawson was already facing multiple difficulties. The pound was rising when he wanted it down. In an attempt to get it down he had already cut interest rates which he did not really want to do.[94] Now the rise was going further because the Prime Minister, by failing to endorse his statement that it was overvalued, still appeared to be prepared to permit the pound to go where it might. Lawson felt he had to extract a categorical public endorsement from the Prime Minister. At Questions on 17 May she used an acceptable formula negotiated between them. This was accompanied by a further cut in interest rates to 7.5 per cent, the lowest ever reached during the Thatcher regime. On the responsibility for this cut, there is total disagreement between them. He says that he was forced to pay for the concordat by agreeing the cut. It was a further cut that, from the point of view of domestic monetary conditions, he did not want. She says that the cut was an idea of his to which she agreed. It was 'the price of tolerable relations with my Chancellor . . . For the whole of this period the interest rate was too low. It should have been a good deal higher, whatever the effect on the level of sterling – or the level of the Chancellor's blood pressure.'[95]

The truth probably is that the official Treasury was recommending a cut but the Chancellor disagreed with the Treasury's advice and refused. No. 10 had, however, been told of the Treasury recommendation and thought that it was also Lawson's recommendation. The cut then took place, both of them reluctant but both of them thinking that it was something the other wanted. Confidence between them had so far broken down that they could no longer talk frankly or even discover the true views of the other. The cut at the height of a boom was, Lawson says, 'subsequently to do considerable damage to my reputation'.[96] It is not, however, easy to extend to him the sympathy for which he appears to be appealing. He had not resigned before the Budget because, he says, it was the culmination of much hard work which he wanted to introduce to the House and the public. The Budget had now been introduced. His relations with his Prime Minister remained impossible.

To achieve any kind of concordat between them, he was being forced to negotiate away his own position. Her refusal to endorse him categorically on 12 May gave him all that he needed by way of justification for resignation.[97] Instead, five days later, he was willing, as he thought, to pay for her endorsement by a cut in interest rates that he recognized as damaging and found in the endorsement an excuse to continue in office.

This final cut in interest rates was rapidly reversed. Between 17 May 1988 and 8 August, Lawson raised base rates in half-point steps from 7.5 per cent to 11 per cent. With the announcement on 25 August of a massive current account deficit in July of £2.2 billion, interest rates were raised by 1 per cent to 12. Thus further justification for remaining in office had become available. He regarded the very poor July current account figures as the turning-point of his Chancellorship. 'It was then that my colleagues realized that I was no longer the miracle worker that some had imagined me to be. It was then that I recognized that there could be no thought of resignation. I owed it to the Government and myself to see the thing through.'[98] Perhaps it was at the same time that he realized that he was not the miracle worker that *he* had imagined himself to be. The conclusion that he should allow someone untainted by past mismanagement to take up the burden did not occur to him. No Chancellor wants to leave under a cloud. Nor did this Prime Minister feel able to make for him the decision that he was unable to make for himself.

In the summer of 1988 when the current account was moving seriously into deficit, Lawson advanced a comforting thesis in a lecture to the Institute of Economic Affairs and in his annual address to the IMF/World Bank conference. The deficit apparently mattered a great deal less than was normally thought. He started by pointing out that in a world with free capital movements, it would be surprising if some countries did not have a net capital inflow. A net capital inflow might arise from a low savings ratio combined with good investment opportunities. If there was a net capital inflow, there was bound to be a current account deficit because the inflow and the deficit necessarily summed to zero. He accepted that in the existing state of affairs in the UK the current deficit was a symptom of an excessively rapid boom. Nevertheless, the implication was that there was a great deal less need to be worried by the deficit figures than commentators were suggesting. He accompanied his thesis by stating the necessary provisos. The first was that the public finances must be in balance. He could claim that the UK public finances were at least in balance which indicated that the current account deficit was attributable to the private, not the public, sector. A second proviso was that the government must be taking any necessary action by raising interest rates to fight inflationary pressure. He could claim to be doing exactly that as well, though by his own admission too little and too late.[99] The third proviso was that the government must not accommodate increases in costs by a depreciation in the exchange rate. This proviso is, of course, much more difficult to satisfy because the market, in its crude way, may always interpret a large current account deficit as evidence of an overvalued exchange rate and start selling the currency concerned. This may have a destabilizing effect that undermines all other policy.

Lawson's economics is, as is usual with economic propositions, controversial.[100] But, even if it were uncontroversial, the question remains to what practical use a Chancellor can put such a highly conditional hypothesis which flies in the face of the practical wisdom of the market place. Its political use is quite clear as is shown by the occasion on which it was advanced, that is when the UK current account had moved seriously into deficit. It was meant to inform the British electorate that Lawson's management of the economy had not, despite all appearances, gone awry. But it had gone awry. The trouble with such a communication to British public opinion was that it operated in a manner directly opposed to what was required. In the summer of 1988 it was necessary to emphasize the seriousness of the situation, not to attempt to temper its gravity with academic theories of little practical utility. In practice Lawson was reacting to the bad trade figures by raising interest rates. He should have been reinforcing the message of those increases, not detracting from it.

THE RESIGNATION

On 26 October 1989 Lawson resigned at the end of a sequence of events without parallel in modern British political history and perhaps in any period of British political history. Certainly there can be no other example in which a Prime Minister, in deep disagreement with the Chancellor, and yet finding it impossible to sack him or reshuffle him, decides to undermine him and his policies with the national currency one of the victims of the dispute. Mrs Thatcher, of course, was accustomed to undermining her Ministers, to acting as leader of the Opposition as well as of the Government, and seemed to have no conscience about making the lives of random members of her Cabinet a misery until she pushed them or they fell away. Lawson, once he had so obviously lost her favour, should have expected no different treatment and should have gone voluntarily long before. Instead he allowed her to play with him until he was left with no other option than resignation. The problem for Lawson, and equally for Howe, was that whereas they regarded themselves as her colleagues, she regarded them as her servants. She was Prime Minister and Lawson was simply her appointee. She had made him and he should do what he was told when she had worked out what to tell him. When, on 3 May 1989, Lawson attempted to discuss with her once more membership of the ERM, she told him, 'I do not want you to raise the subject ever again. I must prevail.'[101]

The story of Lawson's resignation can conveniently begin with the Delors Report on economic and monetary union published in 1989. It was the report of a committee of Central Bank governors and some academics with Jacques Delors, President of the European Commission, in the chair. The committee had been established at the European Council in Hanover the previous year. The British government had expected that central Bank governors, being practical men, would have nothing to do with visionary policies. Lawson had naively put his trust in Karl-Otto Pöhl, President of the Bundesbank, who was known to be sceptical about EMU. His role would be to join with Robin Leigh-Pemberton, Governor of the Bank of England, in securing a report that the British government would not have to repudiate out of hand. But Pöhl proved 'a broken reed' and Leigh-Pemberton was not a man to leave isolated among European Central Bankers if there was any importance to winning the argument.[102] It was innocent in the extreme to believe that Pöhl would publicly associate himself with the UK in opposition to his own government's policy of EMU when, in the end, decisions would be the responsibility of the German government, not the Bundesbank. So the British government faced the embarrassment of a report on EMU to which the Governor of its own Central Bank was fully committed.

The report of the Delors committee recommended a three-stage progress to monetary union. The third stage was monetary union. The second was a preparatory stage in which the necessary institutions to run a monetary union, notably a European Central Bank, would be established. The first stage required the completion of the single market as required by the 1986 Single European Act and membership of the

ERM within its narrow band. Lawson and Howe both wanted for their different reasons to join the ERM. Lawson saw it as his counter-inflationary anchor, other anchors having failed. Howe, having imbibed the European enthusiasms of the Foreign Office, by no means rejected the possibility of monetary union without political union, and regarded a single European currency as 'a desirable medium-term goal'.[103] They could therefore make common cause against Mrs Thatcher on member-ship of the ERM. Mrs Thatcher proved amenable to accepting British participation in the first stage even though it embodied a commitment to membership of the ERM. She strongly favoured completion of the single market, indeed regarded the single market programme as the outcome of her initiative and, after all, the government had long been committed to the ERM when the time was right. It was no burden on her conscience to repeat a commitment which already existed but which she had no intention of honouring at any time if she could possibly avoid it. She would certainly not accept a commitment to monetary union. Monetary union was, for her, far beyond the bounds of what was acceptable. The ultimate mark of sovereignty was the right to issue one's own currency and in her refusal to contemplate the sacrifice she was in entire accord with Lawson.

Howe and Lawson were not deceived by her willingness to accept the repetition of the commitment to the ERM when the time was right. Their problem was how to secure her agreement to the time actually being right in a future rather less distant than the Greek Calends. A European Council meeting at Madrid was due on 26 and 27 June 1989 at which the Delors Report would be discussed. In a joint paper dated 14 June 1989, they attempted to convince their Prime Minister that Britain would have no influence on the follow-up to the Report if she did not give at Madrid a clear 'non-legally binding' commitment to sterling joining the ERM by the end of 1992 providing certain con-ditions were fulfilled. They were content that, at the outset, sterling should be traded within the wider margins of the ERM. Theirs was not a very persuasive argument and she remained unpersuaded that thereby the UK could influence progress to EMU.[104] She regarded their joint action in submitting the paper as 'an ambush'.[105] The use of the word says a great deal about the state to which this government had by then descended. Howe and Lawson asked for a meeting with the Prime Minister because, despite the importance of the issues before the Madrid Council, she had not called a meeting with her Ministerial colleagues. They were 'eventually granted an audience' on 20 June. She was 'uncompromising and resistant'.[106] At a further meeting with her on 25 June, they jointly threatened resignation unless at Madrid she made the forward move on the ERM that they had suggested.[107] She had, meanwhile, been preparing her own plans for Madrid without consultation with her two senior colleagues. At the Madrid Council she listed the conditions which would have to be met before the UK joined the ERM, even though she did not set a date. The UK would join when the single market was complete including a free market in financial services, when all foreign exchange controls had been abolished, when Community competition policy had been strengthened by reducing state aids and when UK inflation had been reduced.[108] This was accepted by the European Council at Madrid as a forward movement by Britain. It was enough for the meeting to be accounted a success and for Howe to decide he had no need to resign. If Howe was not resigning, Lawson was not resigning even though Mrs Thatcher's reference at Madrid to the need to reduce inflation showed that he was in her sights.

Howe then found that in the government reshuffle the following month he was removed as Secretary of State for Foreign and Commonwealth Affairs, the appointment he had held since ceasing to be Chancellor six years before. The Prime Minister would pay a price in increased isolation for thus separating herself publicly from the most senior, and respected, of the original Thatcherites. Evidently she was unaware of it. Or she was aware of it and judged it necessary to pay the price in order to acquire a more robust, or more subservient, Foreign Secretary. As Howe was succeeded by Chief Secretary John Major, it must be assumed that it was the latter rather than the former quality for which she was looking. Howe should have resigned. Instead he allowed himself to be compensated for the loss of the Foreign Office, and of the tied country mansion at Chevening which went with it, by the title of Deputy Prime Minister, the Lord Presidency of the Council, the Leadership of the House, and Lawson's tied but smaller mansion at Dorneywood. The transfer of Dorneywood to Howe was evidently at Mrs Thatcher's insistence. Howe was to be punished by losing the Foreign Office, Lawson by losing Dorneywood.[109] Lawson's reward for his courageous partnership with Howe was to be permitted one final summer holiday at Dorneywood before he was evicted. But he still, of course, had No. 11, a desirable location even if an inconvenient home.[110]

Meanwhile sterling was going through a bad patch. The pound had dropped from DM 3.21 at the beginning of 1989 to DM 3.02 by end-June and from $1.81 to $1.55 over the same period.[111] In an interview with the BBC on 19 May, Mrs Thatcher asserted that the UK had 'picked up our inflation tendency' as a direct result of the intervention in the foreign exchanges necessitated by the shadowing of the DM.[112] It was a direct public rebuke to Lawson. He considered resignation but allowed himself to be deflected by an apology. She claimed not to have intended an attack on him. She had been provoked by the interviewer.[113] He could hardly have believed her apology – he knew perfectly well that she attributed the rise in inflation to his economic management. Her conviction that the rise was attributable to the shadowing of the DM is reflected in her memoirs. There she accuses him of a triple crime. He had kept interest rates too low in order to shadow the DM, with inflationary consequences. He had allowed British inflation to rise because of 'his passionate wish to take sterling into the ERM'. He had undermined confidence in her government.[114] One would have thought that all this amounted to a capital charge. But whereas she was always ready to embarrass him, execution did not appear as yet to be on her mind. Five days after her apology, on 24 May 1989, he raised interest rates to 14 per cent in an attempt to combat the inflationary surge.[115] The concordat between them was being ripped apart. Anything that either of them said in public about economic policy which expressed their genuine convictions, in particular about inflation and the exchange rate, was bound to widen the rift. Both of them were sufficiently honest to find it easier to express views in which they believed than as dictated by a fudged concordat.

From Lawson's point of view there was another trouble. The Prime Minister had been taking private advice from Alan Walters even during the years after 1983 when he was working in the USA. His views on Lawson's conduct of policy were well-known. In May 1989 Mrs Thatcher re-employed him as her economic adviser at No. 10 Downing Street. This in itself was an overt, and considered, rebuke to Lawson. Lawson was now faced at No. 10 not just by a rival for the Prime Minister's attention but by a critic who was feeding her instincts with the raw material for criticism. By end-September sterling stood at DM 3.02 and $1.62. On 5 October 1989, the Bundesbank increased its interest rates by 1 per cent. Lawson, who had warning of the increase, had secured the Prime Minister's reluctant agreement to matching the increase even though the timing was politically inconvenient, just before the Conservative Party conference. Thus interest rates were now at the uncomfortably high level of 15 per cent. The weekend press carried a story that Walters had been opposed to the increase. Lawson had

attempted to persuade Walters to deny the report before it was published but his pleas were unavailing as the report was correct.[116] On
Monday, the pound plunged through DM3.[117] Lawson, so recently a
hero among Chancellors, was subjected to a bitter attack in the *Daily
Mail* which called on the Prime Minister to sack 'this bankrupt Chancellor'. Nevertheless he delivered a highly successful, and much
applauded, speech to the Conservative Party conference in which,
employing political licence well beyond the limits of permissible partisan
rhetoric, he claimed that the Conservative Party was never the Party of
devaluation.[118]

On 18 October 1989, the *Financial Times* published extracts from an
article by Alan Walters in which he referred to the ERM as 'half-baked'
adding that 'my advice has always been for Britain to retain its system
of flexible exchange rates and stay out . . . So far, Mrs Thatcher has
concurred.'[119] He had written the article in 1988 before rejoining No. 10
but it was not an accident that the *Financial Times* had become aware
of it. There was much other evidence that his appointment to No. 10
would not induce him to silent service. Lawson had no option but to
expect that Walters would continue to undermine his policies. It might
not have been important if sterling had been strong but now it was
fragile. On 26 October, Lawson informed Mrs Thatcher that Walters
must go or he would go. She took the view that to dispense with
Walters's services would undermine her authority. There was much in
this as the differences of view between Lawson and the Prime Minister,
and her preference for Walters's advice, were so public. She refused
Lawson's ultimatum and Lawson resigned the same day. Walters then
also resigned. He was persuaded to resign by Brian Griffiths, Head of
Mrs Thatcher's political office, at the insistence of Kenneth Baker,
Chairman of the Party.[120]

Lawson's decision to resign took Mrs Thatcher by surprise. She had
not intended to sack him despite their disagreements and expected that
he would want to soldier on to repair the damage he had done. 'I felt
that since [Lawson] had got us into this inflation, he should face up to
the unpopular requirements for getting us out of it. It would, after all,
be a highly unpalatable prospect for a new, incoming Chancellor.'[121]
This is an odd rationalization for the former Prime Minister to make.
It is more likely that, despite everything that had happened, she did not
feel strong enough to sack him or could not see in her Cabinet a credible
successor.

In a disobliging reference to Karl-Otto Pöhl, President of the Bundesbank, Lawson comments that among his few achievements was knowing when to quit 'just before unification . . . was to throw the German monetary scene into turmoil'.[122] Lawson did not seem to like Pöhl. It is difficult for any British Chancellor of the Exchequer to like the President of the Bundesbank. The Bundesbank has so much more power than any Chancellor of the Exchequer and, annoyingly, it acts on its perception of German, not British, interests. It would be easy to be seduced into being equally disobliging and to say of Lawson that he knew when to quit, when the problems consequent on his failed economic management were apparent and mounting. This is the view taken, for example, by Kenneth Baker.[123] But the truth is that Lawson did not know when to quit.

In his resignation speech on 31 October Lawson said that the key economic issue was whether the exchange rate was 'to be part of the maximum practicable market freedom or . . . a central part of the necessary financial discipline? I recognise that a case can be made for either approach. No case can be made for seeming confusion or for apparent vacillation between these two positions.'[124] This was an untypically clumsy expression of his differences with the Prime Minister. Nowhere in his resignation speech did he mention shadowing the DM or capping the pound at DM 3. It is perfectly possible to treat the exchange rate as a central part of the necessary financial discipline without either shadowing or capping. Yet, if this extract from his speech is to be taken as an adequate expression of his differences with Mrs Thatcher, they had existed at least since November 1985, it was publicly known, and he had nevertheless allowed the damaging confusion to continue. The inevitable inference is that he should have resigned long before. The latest Walters incident gave him a further perfectly justifiable reason for resignation and at last he took it. The situation was intolerable and damaging to the national interest. There is no reason to conclude that he was employing a trivial excuse to escape from problems that he had brought upon himself. He *had* brought the problems on himself by sins of commission and omission but no Chancellor likes resigning with interest rates at 15 per cent and inflation rising to 7.5 per cent and probably beyond. He would have much preferred to continue. But his Prime Minister was making it impossible for him, apparently deliberately, and, at long last, he realized that in the national interest, he must go. He went at the worst possible time for his reputation, and when it was open to his enemies to suggest that he had run away.

THE GILMOUR CRITIQUE

The most intriguing question about the Lawson Chancellorship is why a tenure which began under such favourable auguries ended with the economy out of control and in irreconcilable conflict between Nos. 10 and 11 Downing Street. That this happened is a source of considerable satisfaction to the exiled 'wets'. That does not mean that their own critique has much validity. Gilmour, as the most articulate critic of Lawson's conduct of the Treasury, has a great deal of justifiable, if unoriginal, fun with monetarism. But it is highly questionable whether monetarism of any shape had much to do with Lawson's policies after 1983. More to the point are Gilmour's criticisms of what Lawson actually did than of the theoretical basis upon which he sought to defend what he did. As time went on, Lawson, to some degree inadvertently, conducted a grossly inflationary policy and it would be surprising that many monetarists would wish to defend it. It is certainly true that at this stage in the life of the Thatcher government there were not merely alternative policies but better policies available to a Chancellor less persuaded of his own insights. But what Gilmour has to propose is not among the better policies. His proposal has two key elements. The first is based in a conviction that 'North Sea oil could have been used to finance a massive increase of investment in industry and in the infrastructure . . .'[125] What he calls the 'oil bonanza' could have been 'used to put Britain's industry on a proper footing and to provide for its secure future'.[126] He believes that 'any prudent government would do everything in its power to strengthen its manufacturing base . . .' and he criticizes the fact that 'no attempt was made to devise an industrial strategy'.[127] The need for an industrial strategy is also argued by another exiled 'wet', Francis Pym.[128] Neither Gilmour nor Pym takes his advocacy of an industrial strategy much further than an assertion of the need. But, since the war, successive governments had attempted to devise and implement an industrial strategy. Their attempts have certainly had costs but they have brought few, if any, visible benefits. Despite all the industrial strategies, the competitiveness of the British economy has been maintained, in so far as it has been maintained, only by successive devaluations. Such have been the costs in massive ill-directed public investment, and in the preservation of lame ducks, that it must be all but certain that if British governments had, since the war, abstained

528

from all industrial intervention, the country would now be better off.

It may be that the UK's industrial strategies, implemented by Labour and Conservative governments, have been badly devised and that something better would have made a positive contribution. Gilmour certainly does not outline a more prospective industrial strategy, or how North Sea oil could have been used to fund it, and the suspicion must be that a Gilmour government would not have found a way of using the revenues derived from the North Sea any more productively than the revenues, derived from traditional forms of taxation, which had previously been wasted on industrial policy. In the view of this historian, the government was absolutely right to reject any idea of developing an industrial strategy and it was equally right to ignore the report from a House of Lords Committee in the mid-1980s, chaired by Lord Aldington, which advocated an industrial strategy. But even if Gilmour, or Pym, could have designed a more effective prototype than those that had wasted resources in the past, they ignore a crucial element accepted by all devotees of such policies. Even on the best assumptions, an industrial strategy would take many years to yield significant benefits. The government would not have found in an industrial strategy escape from any of its immediate and worrying dilemmas.

Gilmour's second idea is full membership of the EMS. The EMS was not actually made for Keynesians and therefore not for Gilmour. The EMS would not have provided a protective cover for the Keynesian policies of a Gilmour government. There is strong reason to suspect that behind the monetarist rhetoric with which Mrs Thatcher defended her opposition to full membership of the EMS was her fear that it would eliminate the possibility of suitable Keynesian stimuli to the economy just before an election. Gilmour writes that 'The country would have been saved a great deal of pain had we entered the EMS at the right rate in 1981 (or 1985).'[129] As we have seen, in 1981 Lawson was advocating membership of the EMS because the failure of the monetary indicators was turning his thoughts towards an exchange rate anchor. Gilmour's motives, however, were different. His reference to 'the right rate' must at once evoke a cautionary word. He obviously wanted a sterling devaluation before entry. Exchange rates within the EMS are subject to agreement. There has never been any obvious enthusiasm among our European competitors for encouraging devaluations. They have been accepted reluctantly when the market has left no option. Frequently, agreement has been refused to a devaluation of the size requested. Any idea that the UK would have been allowed in

1981 or 1985 or 1990 to become a full member of the EMS at a significantly devalued exchange rate, is at least questionable. It is equally possible that if, in 1981, sterling had entered at a devalued exchange rate, the market would have soon been pressing it towards and above its upper limit unless, of course, the UK was conducting Keynesian policies in which case no devaluation would ever have been enough. We then find Gilmour welcoming the fact that in 1985 'The government engineered (perhaps lay back and enjoyed) a substantial devaluation or, as the Chancellor preferred to call it, "an exchange rate adjustment"' in the UK's 'overvalued exchange rate'. Members of the EMS were expected to conduct themselves so as to avoid devaluations so far as possible. The deliberate engineering of devaluations was certainly not accepted practice in the EMS. Gilmour's error is to imagine that the UK could become a member of the club and yet make its own rules.

WHAT WENT WRONG?

A more serious analysis of his failures is provided by Lawson himself. He does not attempt to evade all responsibility for the state of the economy as he left it. His confession of mismanagement, as presented in his memoirs, is as honest as can reasonably be expected from a Chancellor whose reputation was, mid-term, *in excelsis*, but whose name is now grouped with predecessors such as Maudling and Barber, all famed only for their unsustainable booms. On the other hand, he does attempt to share his responsibility with his advisers, his forecasters, his independent economic advisers, and his Prime Minister.[130] His advisers, he tells us, whether in the Treasury or the Bank of England, had no more inkling than he that the economy was moving into unsustainable boom. Writing of the Treasury mandarins, he says, 'When we got things right, we got them right together; and when we made mistakes, we made those mistakes together.'[131] They, like him, missed the significance of indicators such as soaring house prices, which were encouraging house owners to believe that they were better off than they were, and a cascading exchange rate. They gave him no warning, fired no shot across his bows. The Bank and the Treasury were indeed reinforcing each other in their misconceptions of where the economy was and where it was going. His team of independent economic advisers performed no better. He makes repeated references to these failures. Lawson thereby reveals how dependent even the most qualified Chancellor is on his advisers. Yet he arrived in the Treasury with his own theories and remedies, with the confident assertion of a monetarist message which he then imposed upon his advisers, many of them sceptical, in the form of the MTFS. He regularly disregarded Treasury caution on income tax reductions.[132] That was his prerogative as Chancellor. However, it hardly seems reasonable in the circumstances that he should then complain about the failure of Treasury mandarins to foresee, and to warn him about, the consequences of his actions, especially as, by the time he made his admitted errors, he was a longstanding Chancellor with considerable experience and a strongly rising reputation which he himself, understandably, was doing a great deal to cultivate. The most that can be said about this line of defence is that it demonstrates that, unlike the Maudling and Barber booms which were intended, Lawson's occurred by inadvertence.

The Prime Minister, in Lawson's view, has to carry her share of the responsibility because of her debilitating resistance to interest rate increases and because she refused to allow him to enter sterling into the ERM. In his eyes, she repeatedly demonstrated the traditional Prime Ministerial reaction to any proposal to move interest rates up. Neither domestic monetary conditions nor the exchange value of the pound ever seemed to her to justify it. He had to drag agreement out of her. Understandably, Mrs Thatcher gives rather a different picture of her attitude to interest rate rises. Certainly she was sensitive to the political implications. Certainly she asked a great many questions before agreeing. But, when he proposed an increase in interest rates, she did in the end agree on virtually every occasion.[133] That he almost always did get agreement is not something he can deny though, equally understandably, he attributes particular importance to those rare occasions.

Yet, even by his account, she seems to have had an intuition that something was going wrong in the economy at a time when the signals were still being ignored by him and his advisers. Thus at a seminar at Chequers on 19 October 1986, she complained that the combination of shrinking savings, high consumer spending, the growing current account deficit and the falling pound, smacked of another Barber boom. Lawson resisted her intuition because many of her facts were wrong. She believed that the trouble was on the fiscal side when, in his view, any trouble was on the monetary side. She told him to *reduce* the PSBR to a figure *higher* than it turned out to be. On 10 December 1986, she refused to countenance a 1 per cent increase in base rate.[134] Lawson is deeply critical of her ignorance of what was going on, of her forgetfulness of what she had been told, and, indeed, she does not seem to have been particularly well briefed. She was perhaps too greatly influenced by commentators who thought the PSBR was spiralling out of control.[135] But even though she may not have recalled or believed the latest Treasury forecast for the PSBR, her instincts do seem to have been sound.[136] In any case, it is surely perverse to criticize her for being badly informed when he, sitting in the Treasury, did not by his own admission know or understand much of what was happening either. Perhaps if Lawson had paid more attention to her hunches and less to her reasoning, his economic management might have been better. But that would have been too much to expect from so cerebral a Chancellor.

Both Lawson and Howe lay a heavy of burden of responsibility on Mrs Thatcher because of her veto on membership of the ERM in 1985. In this veto they both find the key to later failures. She, therefore, emerges as the principal culprit. Howe argues that 'if in 1985 we had buttressed our faltering monetary discipline with that of the Exchange Rate Mechanism, we should have avoided or substantially abated most of our later mistakes of economic policy.'[137] He does not specify who was responsible for the faltering monetary discipline or who made the later mistakes, but the Chancellor was Nigel Lawson. Howe and Lawson, although allies on the ERM, were not close friends and take pleasure, as memorialists, in discharging shafts at each other's economic management. It is unkind of Howe to emphasize his ally's mistakes but they are not to be justified by the failure to join the ERM. Once Lawson had decided not to resign on this issue he retained the responsibility for economic management and certainly was not entitled to extract any excuse for his mistakes from the failure to join the ERM.

It is, in any case, somewhat unjust to blame the Prime Minister for not abandoning monetary indicators as easily as her Chancellor. Lawson had come in brimful of confidence in his monetary indicators. He then came to believe that they had failed him. He had discarded them one by one. In response to the collapse, as he saw it, of classical monetarism, he had invented what he calls his 'exchange-rate monetarism', a name chosen no doubt in an attempt to conciliate those who might otherwise consider him a heretic. But he had not carried the monetarist sect with him. Why, in the circumstances, should she repose her trust in this latest bright idea? Membership of the ERM was contrary to the normal presumptions of a market-oriented government. Her own view, as presented in her memoirs, is that 'if the exchange rate becomes an objective in itself, as opposed to one indicator among others for monetary policy, "monetarism" itself has been abandoned.'[138] It was true that many businessmen supported membership of the ERM. But experience shows that businessmen go in and out of economic principles with as little thought as they go in and out of a swing door. Because they do not carry the responsibility, they can change their minds about economic policy with lightning speed, and as they believe their immediate interests dictate. Lawson could summon in his support increasing numbers of backbench Tory MPs who had adopted membership of the ERM as their panacea of the moment. But they did not carry responsibility either and would be ready to castigate the government if membership turned out badly. If economic management was to be by gut feeling, she preferred hers to his, even if his was dressed in the latest, and most widely received, economic policy fashion.

Next in Lawson's list of culprits is financial deregulation, regarded as one of the government's principal supply-side reforms. In this, there is more substance. How, he asks, was he to know how the deregulated banks and building societies would conduct themselves? He confesses that, with hindsight, he greatly underestimated the demand effect that financial deregulation would have. But, again distributing responsibility, he insists that borrowers and lenders alike also made their mistakes. Building societies went beyond the bounds of prudence in their lending policies in the second half of the 1980s.[139] But the building societies were not as imprudent as the banks. He demands whether the Government is to be regarded as responsible for the banks taking leave of their senses and stimulating a credit binge.[140] As a good free market man he does not criticize the banks and building societies for profit maximization. He criticizes them only for acting against their own commercial interests by excessive lending to weak borrowers. This led to much hardship among borrowers and unprecedented bad debts reported by lenders.[141]

Anyone but a dedicated free market man might have been more cautious in the pace of financial deregulation. There had, after all, been many signs in the 1970s that banks did not always display consummate skill in assessing their lending. Lending to the developing world, admittedly often encouraged by governments with as little foresight as the banks, had left a multitude of non-performing loans as an abiding rebuke to the banks' prudential standards. As for the building societies, everyone knew that they had lived in a cartelized world, had little experience of competition even for mortgages, had virtually no experience of lending other than on mortgage, and that there was grave danger that competition and the power to lend other than on mortgage might lead them into unwise excesses. The government does not appear seriously to have considered whether it should have done more to supervise the freedom it had extended. In the light of previous experience of the banks' behaviour, there was a strong argument for doing so. As the government would suffer the consequences of any improvidence, it certainly had an interest. It was only once the horse had bolted that Lawson attempted to slam the stable doors.

Lawson says that if he had foreseen how excessive lending would become, his only useful weapon would have been to raise interest rates further and faster than he did.[142] In the early summer of 1988, alarmed by the massive increase in lending on mortgage, he did attempt to restrain the building societies and banks. He thought he could exercise a prudential influence on the building societies through the Building Societies Commission but realized that he could only do so if a comparable influence could be exercised on the clearing banks, the building societies' competitors in lending on mortgage. In May 1988, he tried to persuade the Governor of the Bank of England to intervene with the clearing banks. In an exchange reminiscent of Thorneycroft's failure with Cobbold over twenty years before, Robin Leigh-Pemberton refused. He told Lawson that there was no risk to depositors, or to the banking system as a whole, and that mortgage lending was the safest form of lending in which the banks were engaged. Lawson surmises that an unstated reason for the Bank not wishing to intervene was that it might well be ignored. He nevertheless believes that the Bank was wrong to take the stand it did.[143]

The situation is not without its humour. A government of deregulators had evidently done a U-turn, first because it did not trust the commercial judgement of the clearing banks and building societies and, secondly, because it considered that they ought to collaborate against their own judgement in the conduct of government policies. Lawson was astonished to find that the clearing banks were not deterred by the implicit warning of the interest rate increases between May and the end of August 1988. In May 1989, he found that lending had continued to increase at the explosive rate of 23 per cent, undiminished by his attempts beginning a year earlier to cool the economy.[144] He finds that his own misjudgements were enormously compounded by the mistakes of the private sector in general and of the banks in particular.[145] Thus he was the victim of his own supply-side policies. He had allowed freedom to commercial institutions ill-prepared for freedom. He takes comfort from the fact that what Britain went through in the later 1980s following financial deregulation was a once-for-all experience. In other words he feels that the benefits of financial deregulation will in the future far outweigh the costs. He warns other countries that their passage to financial deregulation will have its problems.[146] Perhaps they will learn from his experience how to reduce the costs attributable to the benefits.

One factor in the delay in taking action was the Wall Street crash of 19 October 1987.[147] Lawson's belief, expressed in his Mansion House speech shortly after the crash, was that it 'should reduce any risk of over-heating'.[148] He came under very strong pressure from the press and, inevitably, from the Opposition in the House of Commons, to do something to stave off the slump that was widely feared.[149] He avoided the worst mistakes. For example he did not initiate a programme of emergency measures such as public works. Nor did he raise public expenditure. But he did make the three successive reductions in interest rates, each of 0.5 per cent. As usual he was looking to monetary methods of safeguarding economic activity rather than to fiscal.[150] In fact the Wall Street crash had very little impact on the real economy 'which expanded all too vigorously'.[151] He claims, with justification, that whilst he overreacted to the Wall Street crash, he would have done even worse if he had listened to the advice and criticism that was pouring in from all quarters.[152] This no doubt is true but Chancellors are expected to know what they cannot know and are blamed if their guesses turn out badly. The episode shows how enormously difficult it can be to assess an economic conjuncture. But, in the eyes of colleagues, ignorance of a conjuncture is no more a defence for Chancellors than ignorance of the law is for other citizens.

Yet Lawson's best defence is ignorance. It is always difficult to know what exactly is happening in an economy as open as that of the UK and, in the mid-1980s, it was particularly difficult because of the consequences of financial deregulation. Economic forecasting is always hazardous and now it was even more hazardous. Traditional relationships had been unhinged. How could forecasters forecast without a reliable model of a deregulated world?[153] They underestimated both the growth rate and the consequent current account deficit. Lawson feels that the forecasters let him down badly.[154] Forecasters are a convenient scapegoat for any failed Chancellor – as they can always be relied on to be wrong, they always provide a guaranteed excuse. Some ex-Chancellors could hardly write their memoirs if there were no forecasters to chastise. But Lawson believed the forecasts because they were in line with his own expectations. 'I expected the long upturn of the 1980s to give way to a

535

downturn well before it did and was thus unprepared for the extent of the late 1980s boom.'[155]

An equally fallible group was the team of outside advisers that Lawson had recruited. He dates his errors in the conduct of macroeconomic policy from the time he equipped himself with outside advice.[156] He tells us that his outside advisers were divided in the summer of 1987 on whether the economy was beginning to 'overheat'. Some were dismissive of any such idea.[157] Lawson recalls that, in the autumn of 1987, after the Wall Street crash, one of his outside advisers, Gordon Pepper, a distinguished monetarist, warned of the onset of recession.[158] Outside advisers, enamoured of the opportunity to advise a Chancellor of the Exchequer, may not realize when recruited how great is the burden of responsibility that two or three meetings a year may place upon their shoulders. The Bank of England was as wrong as Lawson's other advisers in its failure to alert him to the inflationary dangers.[159]

Such was Lawson's reputation that he was peculiarly successful in generating what he now condemns as too much optimism. It led to behaviour patterns damaging both to the economy and to individuals. There had been continuing economic growth since 1982. There was excessive optimism due to the sense that personal assets had increased. House prices and pay had both risen substantially. There was therefore greater willingness to borrow.[160] Howe himself confesses that 'we had all been carried away by our own success story . . .' Like others, Howe did not realize how limited those successes had been. Perhaps by way of excuse, he then comments in one of those delicate side-kicks in which these two champions of monetarism engage at each other's expense, 'It is hard to resist the feeling that Nigel's own "animal spirits" had carried him further towards optimism than my own less adventurous instincts might have allowed.'[161] Here too Lawson accepts his share of the responsibility though some has to be allocated to the predecessor Labour government.

> With hindsight . . . I must accept my share of the responsibility for the excessive optimism that characterized the climate of the time. Given the all-pervasive defeatism that was the grimmest aspect of our 1979 inheritance, I regarded the creation of a climate of confidence as a major object of policy and the tone of my speeches tended to reflect this.

Such was the climate of confidence that Lawson created that steps that he now sees to have been necessary would have appeared incongruous at the time. He comments, for example, that his increase in interest rates on 7 August 1987 was regarded as bizarre and that it would have been considered highly eccentric to have conducted a tighter monetary policy than he did.[162] He accepts also the psychological effect of his Budgets, particularly the 1988 Budget, 'which does not invalidate the Budgets, but reinforces the case for more measured speech-making'.[163] The language in which the Budget was presented suggested not an act of considered statesmanship so much as a claim to a personal political triumph by a supreme economic manager to whose deeds tribute was appropriate. He had achieved the hat-trick, higher government spending, lower taxes, and yet a Budget surplus.[164] He took advantage of his surplus to reinstate the doctrine of a balanced Budget.[165] It was yet one more example of his yearning for rules which would outlaw discretion. It was no wonder that the pound soared, persuading him into a series of base rate cuts which he now regards as inappropriate, which even at the time he was reluctant to make, and which had to be rapidly reversed, and more. In other words not merely was his optimism premature. It was, in the not-so-long run, self-defeating. Exaggeration is a temptation to which politicians succumb, enticed by the lure of reputation and the cycle of elections at which claims have to be made and policies offered. It is harmful to the conduct of policy. In the end it is damaging to reputations. Yet more measured speechmaking by politicians is an ideal for which the public will wait in vain.

But behind this attractive concession of error lies a greater truth. There was something more than the fault to which Lawson confesses. It was a depth of conviction that concealed from his eyes the great truth that improvements in economic performance are not achieved easily or quickly. Lawson appeals to the figures of economic growth to demonstrate the superiority of Tory economic management.[166] He is able to show that the rate of growth over the Tory cycle 1979–89 was much greater than that over the largely Labour cycle 1973–9. On the other hand, as Johnson comments, although the economy was growing, the rate was no better than in past periods.[167] Such comparisons are meaningless, first because of the brevity of the periods, secondly because they grossly overestimate the contribution to growth that any Chancellor can make in a tenure even as long as that of Lawson, and thirdly because they ignore both the background circumstances in the UK and the international environment.

That this criticism can be made without partisanship is demonstrated by the fact that in the Labour/Tory cycle of 1964–73 (one Tory balance of payments crisis to another) the rate of economic growth was higher than in the Tory cycle 1979–89. Lawson at once uses the excuse that there was a world economic slowdown after the oil price hike of 1973. That of course is true but it affects the comparison which he so gaily makes to the advantage of his 1979–89 cycle as compared with the mainly Healey cycle of 1973–9. Moreover Healey inherited a vast balance of payments deficit, and an inflationary surge much greater than Howe inherited in 1979. And Howe had the advantage of a strong balance of payments. The worthlessness of such comparisons even for the purpose of Tory propaganda is shown when the Tory 1979–89 cycle is divided between Howe and Lawson, much to the apparent advantage of Lawson. We then find that although Howe's inheritance was so much better than Healey's, the growth rate in the four years of Howe was much lower than in the mainly Healey cycle of 1973–9 and that the Tory performance over the cycle 1979–89 is rescued only by the unsustainable Lawson boom. It is absurd to judge the quality of economic management, or of supply-side policies, by growth rates over such short periods. Lawson's premature confidence in his economic miracle was one reason why the economy ran out of control and why his long tenure was followed by a recession almost as long.

This is in no way to denigrate the supply-side reforms of the Thatcher period such as the trade union legislation, privatization and deregulation. The whole gamut of reforms intended to stimulate the supply-side may have been brilliantly designed. Financial deregulation may have been a great supply-side incentive. The trade union reforms were certainly essential and long overdue. But all of them would take time before they yielded their fruit in better economic performance. And while the supply-side effects would be slow in coming, the demand effects of financial deregulation would appear very rapidly in a deterioration in the balance of payments and in inflation. Lawson clearly thought that the supply-side measures had already yielded their fruit and that the move back to current account deficit presented no special difficulty. Most damaging of all, he began to believe the government's propaganda. It really had transformed the performance of the British economy. Through self-deception and inadvertence, he allowed the development of a boom which his successors had to cool at great political cost. An exaggerated air of prosperity was induced, not just by an unsustainable boom but by a significant increase in the share of national product going to consumption. The share going to investment, and hence to building the economy for the future, fell. Privatization receipts and North Sea oil revenues encouraged the illusion that all was well with the national finances. Lawson did not appear to understand that such transformation as was claimed in Party propaganda was an unlikely outcome of the few years of economic management under Howe and himself.

In a speech at Edinburgh in June 1987 he referred to the 'transformation' of the British economy.[168] Economic growth was high not just because of a recovery from the downturn of 1979–81 or because of a credit binge but because the economy was already performing significantly better.[169] In other words he was not riding an unsustainable boom. Where Maudling and Barber had tried and failed, he had succeeded. As Johnson puts it, the Thatcher government's 'fundamental error was to mistake the short-term 1987 peak for a new high plateau of rapid growth'.[170] Lawson looked upon the future that he had created and it was good. It is this self-deception that is revealed in his speeches, not excessive optimism so much as misplaced conviction. In his speeches, he was taking credit prematurely for being a great economic guru, with achievements soundly based on a range of new insights into economic processes, whom it was an honour even for journalists to know. And many of them believed him. He was encouraged in his self-deception by the hoorays of friendly journalists who welcomed the economic miracle of which they had, for so long, despaired. Why should he be critical of his own performance when commentators were prepared to take him at his own valuation and find in him the prophet so long awaited?

The historian will wish to resist temptation and to be fair to Nigel Lawson. The probability must be that any Chancellor would have been caught out by the particular group of circumstances that confronted him from 1986 onwards. On the other hand, if he had been less of a monetarist; if the lesson he had learnt from its failure had been to value a much wider variety of indicators; if, as a substitute for failed monetarism, he had not become so attached as an anchor to his 'exchange-rate monetarism'; if he had placed less faith in international monetary cooperation, had therefore been guided in his decisions by domestic criteria and not by commitments into which he believed himself to have entered in the Plaza and Louvre agreements; if his instincts had been as sensitive as his intellect was powerful; if he had shown more of the humility which is desirable in any Chancellor; and if, therefore, he had had an earlier sense of his own fallibility; there would have been a greater chance of his noticing the dangers in time and taking precautionary measures. Lawson has an arguable claim to be the best-equipped Chancellor of the postwar epoch and yet, although Howe had left him the best legacy of any Chancellor of that epoch, he ended his tenure with inflation much higher than he had inherited and rising, and with interest rates at 15 per cent.

SEVENTEEN

John Major: in and out of the ERM

THE MAN AND THE APPOINTMENT

Mrs Thatcher tells us that, on Lawson's resignation, she would have preferred Nicholas Ridley as Chancellor of the Exchequer but was deterred by his 'scorn for presentational niceties'.[1] Instead she selected John Major who, three months previously, had been her surprise choice as Foreign Secretary in succession to Geoffrey Howe. In appointing Major to the two high-profile posts of Foreign Secretary and Chancellor, and thereby so obviously favouring him as compared with his Cabinet colleagues, she came as close as is safe for any leader to designating a successor. But she would hardly have sensed any threat to her own position. If she needed any guarantee, she would have found it in his youth and inexperience. She must have felt confident that she could still choose her own date to retire and Major, in the meantime, would have had more than enough time to gain experience.

Under her patronage, Major had achieved a meteoric rise to high office. He had shown himself a very skilled communicator in a number of junior Ministerial posts. He had been in the Cabinet since the 1987 election, first as Chief Secretary to the Treasury and then as Foreign Secretary. For his promotion to Chancellor, he had had to wait only slightly longer than Lawson, having been first elected to Parliament in 1979. Peter Jay writes of Major's 'exceptional aptitude for mastery of a complex subject, for persuasive advocacy and for untiring persistence'.[2] But no one, including Major himself, could suggest that, despite his two years as Chief Secretary, he possessed for the job any of the qualifications, of intellect or experience, that Lawson had brought to it. Lawson reports that Major had at first found his responsibilities as Chief Secretary daunting. He concedes that Major did then take command but of course the tasks of Chief Secretary, difficult as they can be, have in them nothing comparable to the intellectual and judgemental strains put upon the Chancellor. Major, as Chief Secretary, had not attempted to influence the course of economic management outside the field of public expenditure.[3]

After losing so cerebral a Chancellor, it was perhaps a relief to the Prime Minister to nominate a successor who knew even less than she about economic management. It was also, in her view, an advantage that he had no 'personal capital sunk in past policy errors'.[4] It was nevertheless in some ways a curious appointment. She may have believed that John Major was 'one of us' and that he shared her convictions. But it must have been rather difficult at the time to determine from his record what convictions he held sufficiently strongly to fight for them. Certainly she was taking a risk if she thought that she would no longer be harassed by her neighbour in Downing Street about joining the ERM. Major had, after all, served for two years in the Treasury under a dominant Chancellor. Even if he had felt insufficiently equipped to enter into debate on the wider aspects of economic management, it would have been remarkable if he had not absorbed something of his Chancellor's enthusiasm for the ERM, especially as it had the support of Treasury officials. He had then spent three months as Foreign Secretary under the influence of advisers strongly committed to the European project. Admittedly they were three summer months when the minds of members of the diplomatic service are seldom at their most active but some influence would have seeped through. There is also always the danger, when rapid promotion may appear to a wider public to be the result of patronage more than of merit, that the beneficiary may wish to prove that he is not simply a poodle by forcing through a policy of which his benefactor is known to disapprove. If Mrs Thatcher had thought about it, she might have been apprehensive. Yet, having been successful in vetoing entry into the ERM when argued by a Chancellor as powerful as Lawson, she would probably have concluded that she could veto Major if he annoyed her with Treasury arguments on a subject which he did not understand.

HURTING AND WORKING

Major's most famous statement of economic policy was made on his first day in office in a speech at Northampton. 'The harsh truth is that if the policy isn't hurting, it isn't working.' To such a state had Tory economic management brought the country. He pledged himself to 'the reduction and the elimination of rising prices . . .'[5] The statement was inspired by the high and rising inflation and by the credit binge with its effect on the current account of the balance of payments. For almost the whole of Major's tenure of the Treasury, interest rates remained at 15 per cent, the level to which Lawson had raised them shortly before his departure. However, by the time of Major's appointment, over two years of the 1987 Parliament had passed and minds were turning towards the next election. The question was whether, at a time of rapidly declining popularity, mainly attributable to the poll tax, the government would remain firm in hurting the electorate so that its economic policy should once more work. Evidence shortly began to accumulate that the government was becoming less determined in the battle against inflation, and more complacent about rising public expenditure, than Major's words of personal dedication might have suggested.

REINTERPRETING EMU

The Thatcher government, in its last years, was attempting to deflect the European Community from the objective of EMU. In the interpretation of all other member countries, EMU understandably implied a single European currency. Now, signalled by the Delors Report, there seemed to be a serious medium-term thrust to create a single currency, a thrust which derived its strength primarily from France. French governments had long wished to exchange the dominance of the Bundesbank over European monetary policy for a system into which the French government, or at least its monetary authorities, would have some input. A single currency appeared to France to be the only way. In the Single European Act, signed in February 1986, Mrs Thatcher had committed herself and her country to economic and monetary union. As a single currency represented, in her view, an unacceptable surrender of sovereignty, it was now necessary to put upon this commitment to EMU some interpretation that was not a single currency. Lawson had offered the idea of competitive currencies in which the good currencies would drive out the bad, or less good, with, as a possible conclusion, one currency managed by one national Central Bank. This idea had lent itself to parody and caricature and was speedily forgotten. Was a shopkeeper in London's East End, or in the Paris West Bank, to be offered payment in a variety of currencies until the date long hence when one currency drove out the rest? There were certainly some places, for example on the borders between two countries or in major supermarkets, where purchasers could pay in a variety of currencies. Large commercial firms might be able to handle the complexities of a system of competing currencies. But it hardly seemed a viable system for the citizens of Europe generally.[6]

In a speech on 20 June 1990, Major offered the 'hard ecu' as his contribution to the government's attempt to divert Europe from its mistaken ambition of a single currency. The ecu is a 'basket' within which are valued the currencies of the members of the EMS even if not also members of the ERM. Thus sterling was part of the basket even though it was outside the ERM. The weighting of each currency within the basket was reassessed but only at long intervals. As currencies within the EMS were devalued against the DM, the ecu itself was devalued against the DM. The idea of the hard ecu was that when such devaluations occurred, the share of the devalued currency within it would be at once reduced and the ecu would not become weaker. On the contrary it would approximate more and more to the DM and, as a reliable store of value, it could conceivably one day rival the DM. The hard ecu would be a common currency rather than a single currency. National currencies would continue to exist. The idea was both clever and pointless. No European government would take it seriously. Those intent on creating a single currency were not impressed, as an alternative, by the idea of an additional currency. The Bundesbank particularly scorned the idea. The Bundesbank might, reluctantly, be prepared one day to surrender the DM to a single European currency. It certainly did not want to permit a parallel European currency. That, it was sure, would be inflationary. So far as most European governments and Central Banks were concerned, these British ideas merely demonstrated a lack of seriousness. In fact no one was more disparaging of the idea of the hard ecu than the British Prime Minister, even though her Chancellor had proposed it.

JOINING THE ERM

The immediate question was whether the Prime Minister would, at long last, permit sterling to join the ERM. She and Major were discussing the issue regularly from March 1990 onwards. He argued that in addition to its beneficial effect on market sentiment, and on inflation, it would relieve political strains within the government and Party.[7] Improved market sentiment, and the comforting spectacle of a united government and Party, would help to bring interest rates down. Clearly the Prime Minister was listening though she still reached for her Mauser when she heard arguments that appeared to her reminiscent of 'Nigel's cracked record to the effect that you should steer by the exchange rate rather than by the money supply'.[8] Perhaps it had occurred to her that joining the ERM might avoid a damaging challenge to her leadership such as had been launched the previous year by the enthusiastic European, Sir Anthony Meyer. At a meeting with Major on 13 June she said that she would no longer resist joining the ERM. She explains that 'I had too few allies to continue to resist and win the day.' Almost her only ally in the Cabinet was Ridley. She was, nevertheless, still resisting in July when Major wanted to join.[9] That July, she lost Ridley, victim of an interview in the *Spectator* in which he had said what he and she actually believed about the Germans, namely that they were attempting once more to dominate Europe. Ridley looked foolish, but so did she. At last, on Friday 5 October 1990, just before the week of the Conservative Party conference at Bournemouth, it was announced that, the following Monday, 8 October, sterling would join the ERM within the wider 6 per cent band at a central rate against the DM of DM 2.95. Thus the greenhorn Chancellor, Major, had succeeded where Lawson, long in tooth and experience, had failed. The Cabinet had not been told on the Thursday before.[10] The Deputy Prime Minister, Sir Geoffrey Howe, learned of the decision only on 5 October, not from the Prime Minister but from the Queen who asked him his view of the morning's news which he had not yet heard.[11] At the same time as sterling joined the ERM, interest rates were reduced by 1 per cent to 14 per cent. Mrs Thatcher stipulated the wider, 6 per cent, band and the 1 per cent cut in interest rates as her price for accepting defeat. She also claims to have demanded that, so far as the UK was concerned, the ERM was to be regarded as a system of adjustable rates. She would not consent to large scale intervention in the market, or to inappropriate interest rates, in an attempt to buck the market's view of the sterling exchange rate.[12] The unconsulted Howe, exiled from the decision-making process on this most important of decisions, must have felt himself vindicated. A few days later, at a fringe meeting at the Bournemouth Party conference, he exclaimed, 'Depreciation is no longer an option.'[13] He underestimated the wayward fiscal ways of his government and the incredulity of the market.

Seven weeks later, Major was Prime Minister. Mrs Thatcher had finally pushed Geoffrey Howe into resignation. The deep hostility to further European integration which she had displayed in the course of reporting back to the House from the October 1990 Rome meeting of the European Council had been the last straw. Howe's devastating resignation speech on 13 November 1990 provoked a challenge from Michael Heseltine to Mrs Thatcher as leader of the Party. In the first ballot, Conservative MPs denied her the majority she needed under the rules to prevent a second ballot. She was then persuaded by her Cabinet colleagues, and by most of her friends, to stand down on the grounds that humiliation awaited her if she did not withdraw. She was warned that she was likely to poll worse on the second ballot than on the first. Her withdrawal left the leadership to be fought out between Heseltine, Douglas Hurd, the Foreign Secretary, and John Major. On 27 November 1990, Major won with Thatcherite support and became Prime Minister. On 9 April 1992 he gained a further General Election victory for the Tories.

A sterling crisis erupted in the summer of 1992. On 16 September 1992, 'Black Wednesday', the Major government ignominiously suspended sterling from membership of the ERM after swearing on a stack of bibles that it would not devalue, let alone creep away from the ERM itself with its tail between its legs. Major's great act of policy as Chancellor had collapsed. On Black Wednesday, it was not merely the credibility of sterling that was undermined but that of the Major government as well. Lawson had once said, 'I am keenly conscious that few Chancellors of the Exchequer have left office with their reputations enhanced.' He went on to note that the few, except for Howe, had stayed only a short time.[14] Major is unique in that he was already Prime Minister when his credibility as Chancellor was so unmercifully drained. No one seriously expected him to resign as Prime Minister for what he had done as Chancellor. A sacrificial lamb was, after all, available in the form of his friend and successor as Chancellor, Norman Lamont, though he was allowed a short stay of execution before being despatched eighteen months later.

LISTING THE EXCUSES

Following Black Wednesday, all those who over the years had advocated membership of the ERM have attempted to explain why they were right even though their policy failed. One of the Treasury's most utilized and valued assets is a large stock of often contradictory excuses for policy failures of all kinds and, in this case, recourse to it was lavish. The stock was made freely available to anyone who could use it. In this case there was quite a demand.

Mrs Thatcher

The most pathetic example of the self-exculpatory tendency is Mrs Thatcher herself. For political reasons, she had given her reluctant consent to membership against Alan Walters's better judgement. Her real loss from Lawson's resignation was not that of her Chancellor but of her personal economic adviser. In his absence, she had run out of arguments, and had surrendered to the politicians seven weeks before her dismissal from office. Now she had to defend a failed policy which she had never really wanted to adopt. In a passage in her memoirs of pardonable brevity, she attributes the failure of the policy to the rigidity that the drive for EMU had injected into the ERM. The pound's tragedy was all due to 'my successor' who 'went along with the objective of EMU as spelt out in the Maastricht Treaty and made it clear that sterling would enter the narrow band of the ERM . . .'[15] This is nonsense. She knew perfectly well in October 1990 that the EMS was now, more clearly than ever before, the chosen route to EMU. She knew yet she succumbed.

Nigel Lawson

Lawson argues that after promising for years to join when the time was right, the government eventually joined when the time was emphatically not right. There was a world recession, and recessions are seldom ideal times for experiments. The paradoxical consequence of German reunification was that the DM rose against the dollar.[16] In 1978 it had been foreseen, and subsequent experience had confirmed, that a DM strengthening against the dollar would cause strains within the ERM. Other ERM currencies would be dragged up by the DM and their economies would become less competitive. It is true that sterling joined the ERM at a moment of particular difficulty. The occasion could hardly have been worse chosen. But that is not to say that any other time would have been significantly better.

Lawson, writing in 1992, believed that with time sterling would have become 'locked in' within the ERM and would have begun to experience such considerable benefits of membership as to avoid the humiliation of September 1992. The implication is that sterling would have been safe within the ERM if only it had joined earlier than October 1990 as Lawson had recommended. However, one year after the British debacle, even the currencies of countries that had been members from the beginning, and therefore had had plenty of time to become 'locked in' came under attack. In September 1993, to save anything out of the ERM in face of market pressures, it was necessary for its remaining members to agree to operate a 15 per cent margin on the central rate as compared to the 2.25 per cent margin with which the ERM started and the 1 per cent margin of the Bretton Woods system. Though formally the ERM remained in existence, its credibility as a zone of monetary stability was seriously compromised.

Lawson agrees with Mrs Thatcher that a further reason which made October 1990 a problematic moment for membership is that the ERM had become entangled with EMU. This challenged the market to test the ERM and the test destroyed it.[17] There may be something in this argument. But the EMS had, from the beginning, been seen by many of its strongest protagonists as a preliminary to EMU. It is true that with the Delors Report and the Maastricht Treaty, the prospect of EMU had become more serious and imminent. But it is not possible to argue that the French could have been diverted from their drive to EMU or that the German government would have been less willing to concede to French pressure if Britain had been a member of the ERM. For the French and the Germans, British membership of the ERM was a secondary question. If Lawson is right about the dangers of entangling the ERM with EMU, that is just one more argument why sterling should not have joined whether in 1979, 1981, 1985 or 1990.

As is customary with British Chancellors, Lawson attacks the Bundesbank. He finds in it a scapegoat for the failure of British membership of the ERM. The Bundesbank, he writes, was 'guilty not only of irresponsible talk but of a damaging reluctance to fulfil its international obligations – not merely under the Basle-Nyborg agreement but under the rules of the European Monetary System itself'.[18] Irresponsible talk never undermined a strong currency and sterling, after thirteen years of Tory rule, was not a strong currency. It was as likely to be the victim of irresponsible talk as it ever had been under Labour. The Bundesbank has always disliked intervention and dislikes it most of all when it is expected to lose money buying an overvalued currency. Its primary responsibilities are domestic. Subject to that, it supports the policies of the German government. But was it really the policy of the German government to waste money trying to prevent a devaluation of sterling?

The Bundesbank fulfilled what it saw as its obligations to sterling without enthusiasm but equally without profligacy. There is no justifiable complaint to be made against the Bundesbank. Complaint is justifiable only against those who advocated membership and took sterling into the ERM ignorant of the role and attitudes of the Bundesbank.

The Keynesians

Some advocates of British membership of the ERM have argued that sterling joined at too high an exchange rate.[19] The Bundesbank is reputed to have warned Major that DM 2.95 was an unsustainable exchange rate for sterling within the ERM. The Bundesbank had reason for anxiety because it foresaw that it might be facing a bill of some magnitude for the costs of keeping sterling at this parity. After Lawson's resignation, sterling had been down to DM 2.70 before recovering to just under DM 3 by July 1990. There might have been an option to join at a lower exchange rate than DM 2.95. On the other hand, to propose an exchange rate lower than the current exchange rate might have caused difficulties with Britain's prospective partners within the ERM who might have resisted Britain's being granted the additional competitiveness. In any event, this is not an argument that can easily be advanced by those who advocated membership as an anti-inflationary discipline. To commence life within the ERM with a devaluation would hardly have given evidence of the strong counter-inflationary intention to which Major, supposedly, was dedicated. It is the Keynesian advocates of membership who have mainly argued that there should have been a lower entry exchange rate and they always misunderstood the nature of the system. They thought it would confer market credibility on Keynesian policies. Nothing could have been farther from the truth.

CONCLUSION

There is another reason why October 1990 was a bad time to join the ERM. It was within two years of a General Election. The decision to join smelt of political calculation rather than counter-inflationary zeal. The 6 per cent margin hardly demonstrated wholehearted commitment. Political calculation was signalled by the immediate 1 per cent reduction in interest rates, just before the Conservative Party conference. The Treasury and the Bank had opposed the reduction but were overruled by the Prime Minister.[20] Major himself had employed political arguments –

the unity of the government and the Party – rather than economic arguments. Certainly he was better equipped to use political, rather than economic, arguments. As time passed, electoral pressures led to a relaxation of control over public expenditure and to the acceptance of ever-larger PSBRs. Lawson notes that under Lamont there was a worrying discretionary relaxation of public spending control.[21] He had advocated membership of the ERM in part because it would impose government by rule rather than by discretion. In fact it was still government by discretion, a discretion directed to buying back the support of a disillusioned electorate. The market tolerated such conduct until the Conservatives under John Major had won a further election victory. It then struck, and no words of the Prime Minister or his Chancellor, after the election, could save sterling from devaluation. Because of the timing of entry into the ERM, there never was a serious intention to conduct the strict policies that might have enabled sterling to avoid devaluation.

It has been argued that, even if only as a temporary expedient against inflation, it was right to join the ERM. This view enjoys the support of one of the actors in the fiasco, Robin Leigh-Pemberton, Governor of the Bank of England. A few days after Black Wednesday, on the second anniversary of membership, the Governor let it be known that 'the decision to join the ERM two years ago was right in the circumstances; that, having joined, we were right to endeavour to stick it out; and that, in the circumstances which evolved, we were also right to withdraw'.[22] In such ways does the Bank of England put its reputation at risk. Inflation did fall after sterling joined the ERM. But the fall is to be attributed to a year of 15 per cent interest rates, and to a year of 13 per cent before that, as well as to the onset of recession, rather than to membership of the ERM.

Thus forty-five years after sterling was linked to the fixed exchange rate system of Bretton Woods, and eighteen years after it had floated away while the Bretton Woods regime crumbled, it was committed by Mrs Thatcher and John Major to a regional fixed rate system somewhat less tight than Bretton Woods but nevertheless too tight for the British economy. But, as the outcome was cruelly to demonstrate, no postwar Prime Minister, no government, and no Chancellor, had yet found either the recipe that would transform the performance of the British economy or even, as a lesser and more practical objective, how to manage it without repeated disasters and humiliations.

CONCLUSION

THE PROCESSION OF CHANCELLORS did not end in 1990. And the world which had changed dramatically over the 45 years visited by this book, has continued to change. Does change rule out learning from the past? What stands out in this history is the way this country, a rich country by most standards, has repeatedly made itself contemptible through its inability to manage its own affairs. There is the continuous depreciation of the currency. There is the begging bowl regularly extended in the direction of the IMF, the USA and other Central Banks. There are the threats that if our partners would not stretch out a helping hand on our terms, we would renege on our international obligations, for example to the defence of Europe. There is the preaching tendency, the repeated demands that the major countries of the world should act to relieve the stresses on sterling by conducting expansionist policies in accordance with a Keynesian recipe which their governments considered grossly inflationary. The criterion determining *their* conduct should be *our* interests. This message, wherever addressed, has repeatedly met the same response. 'Yours is the stumbling economy, not ours. It is you who must change, not we.' But when the response came, British governments did not appear to be listening. Britain had lost an empire and had not found an economic policy.

It did not help that this country suffered for 18 of these 45 years from two frivolous Prime Ministers, Harold Macmillan and Harold Wilson, and from one, Edward Heath, whose performance in office defies rational explanation. It did not help that governments convicted the Treasury of responsibility for what, almost invariably, were their own failures. It did not help that key elements of economic policy, particularly the control of public expenditure, were delegated to a Cabinet which by its nature was unlikely to accept Treasury arguments when they were unfriendly to departmental expenditures. It did not help that the Treasury was frequently too sensitive politically, and refrained from strong advice when it was clearly needed. It did not help that the

551

Treasury has lost confidence in itself. The Treasury has almost through-out been a beleaguered department, its scepticism found unattractive and unhelpful by Ministers who brought their own enthusiasms to the conduct of economic policy. Given the nature of those enthusiasms, scepticism was the only rational reaction but the Treasury, having lost confidence in itself, has proved an inadequate defender of the public interest against the whimsies of successive governments. Finally, it did not help that the quality of public commentary on economic management has frequently encouraged governments in folly.

Since the IMF crisis of autumn 1976, there has, in one important respect, been a change. The begging bowl has been put away. That must be accounted a great and beneficial advance. In other respects, life has gone on as before or, where there have been changes, they have not been for the better. The experiment with monetarism, the extraordinary attempt to replace discretion by rule in the conduct of economic man-agement, has revealed dogmatism at its worst and the country undoubtedly suffered. Although Lawson's shadowing of the DM was ill-advised, at least he showed concern about the exchange rate. But concern was clearly not enough. The exchange rate has continued to depreciate, floating but sinking. Prime Ministers and Chancellors have, since 1976, proved as susceptible to the temptations of electoral politics as any of their predecessors. Britain has been exposed to the quite unnecessary humiliation arising from the decision to embrace the ERM. The preaching tendency has continued, with the Bundesbank increas-ingly the villain of the piece, though it has done no more than act according to its well-established principles and in the interests as it sees them of its principal client, the people of Germany. Indeed the sugges-tion that the Bundesbank should have poured out even more DM in September 1992 to support sterling, indicates that in this respect the statement that the begging bowl has been put away requires qualifica-tion. Above all, despite premature claims to the contrary, there has been no improvement in economic performance greater than would be extrapolated from previous history. Policy intended to stimulate econ-omic growth has often been counter-productive. The Lawson boom and its subsequent collapse did not inspire confidence in the hearts of the entrepreneurs and investors in whose hands it lies to make the real decisions that influence economic growth. Despite this record there has been no lack of premature political boasts, the most extravagant being the suggestion by former Chancellor, John Major, shortly before 'Black

Wednesday', that sterling was becoming a threat to the DM's pre-eminence.*

British governments have learned few lessons from the history of economic management and the evidence indicates that the same is true of Oppositions. Political Parties continue to promise what they cannot deliver. Perhaps the most comforting thought at the end of this review of 45 years comes from Adam Smith. It is that there is a great deal of ruin in a nation.

* *Effect* 186.

Chancellors of the Exchequer 1945–1990

HUGH DALTON	July 1945 – November 1947
SIR STAFFORD CRIPPS	November 1947 – October 1950
HUGH GAITSKELL	October 1950 – October 1951
RICHARD AUSTEN BUTLER	October 1951 – December 1955
HAROLD MACMILLAN	December 1955 – January 1957
PETER THORNEYCROFT	January 1957 – January 1958
DERICK HEATHCOAT AMORY	January 1958 – July 1960
SELWYN LLOYD	July 1960 – July 1962
REGINALD MAUDLING	July 1962 – October 1964
JAMES CALLAGHAN	October 1964 – November 1967
ROY JENKINS	November 1967 – June 1970
IAIN MACLEOD	June 1970 – July 1970
ANTHONY BARBER	July 1970 – March 1974
DENIS HEALEY	March 1974 – May 1979
SIR GEOFFREY HOWE	May 1979 – June 1983
NIGEL LAWSON	June 1983 – October 1989
JOHN MAJOR	October 1989 – November 1990

Table of Approximate Equivalents

NOTE

The sums in pounds sterling given in the text are in money of the day. The following table enables the reader to calculate an approximate equivalent in 1995 money.

YEAR	MULTIPLY BY
1945	20
1950	16
1955	12.5
1960	11
1965	9
1970	7.5
1975	4
1980	2
1985	1.5
1990	1.1

NOTE

This table is derived from the Retail Price Index. To put the resulting figures in context, it should be remembered that the *standard* of living in the UK rose about three times between 1945 and 1990.

Notes

INTRODUCTION

1. For the origins and development of the office of Chancellor of the Exchequer see David Kynaston and Henry Roseveare.
2. Bridges 2nd ed. 162.
3. The Chief Secretary, the Parliamentary Secretary (Chief Whip), Financial Secretary and Economic Secretary, rank as Secretaries of the Treasury Board but are not members of it.
4. The Chief Secretary was not a member of the Cabinet for the first four years of the Wilson Administration in the 1960s, for the first three years of the Wilson/Callaghan Administrations in the 1970s or during the Heath government.
5. C. A. R. Crosland, *The transition from capitalism*, in ed. Crossman, *New Fabian Essays*, 39–40.
6. The Bretton Woods system is named after the town in the USA where it had been negotiated in the latter days of the war, mainly between the American Administration and Britain represented by John Maynard Keynes. As the resources available to the IMF and World Bank were insufficient for the needs of European recovery in the immediate postwar years, the Bretton Woods system could not operate fully until Marshall Aid had done its work.
7. Cairncross (1992), 17.

CHAPTER ONE · DALTON UNDER KEYNES

1. Third Reading of the Trade Disputes and Trade Union Bill, Apr. 1946.
2. Donoughue and Jones 367.
3. Dalton 52.
4. Harrod 619, in a letter to Halifax, 1 Jan. 1946.
5. Pimlott, *Dalton*, 508–9.
6. Donoughue and Jones 344. Morrison was also Leader of the House.
7. John Wheeler-Bennett, *King George VI*, 636–8 quoted by Dalton 9.
8. In 1939, a Central Economic Information Service was established in the Cabinet Office. In 1941 it was split into two parts, the Economic Section and the Central Statistical Office.
9. Dalton 12 quoting Attlee in an article in the *Observer*, 23 Aug. 1959. Dalton 237 refers to Attlee making this point to him in Apr. 1947 when changes in the government were being considered. Morgan (1984) 50 prefers this interpretation. So does Jay (1980) 129 who adds that Sir Edward Bridges advised Attlee in this sense.

10. Pimlott, *Dalton*, 411.
11. Donoughue and Jones 345.
12. Pimlott, *Dalton*, 411–17.
13. Hennessy (1992) 212. Dalton's book was *Principles of Public Finance*, Routledge, 1922.
14. Pimlott, *Dalton*, 465.
15. Dalton 4.
16. Dalton 4–5.
17. Dalton complained about Tory exploitation of this phrase, employed in his Budget of 9 Apr. 1946, about expenditure in the development areas. Dalton 110n.
18. Sales of investments abroad exceeded £1000 million. Cairncross (1992) 49.
19. C. Barnett (1995) 168–9.
20. T 267/3 and 4. At the end of the war the UK's short term liabilities to foreign banks and official holders were nearly £3,500 million against gold and dollar reserves of just over £600 million. Cairncross (1992) 47. 'And this distortion was deliberately worsened by Lend-Lease itself. We deliberately forced down our exports to the bare minimum. Why? To make munitions . . . to man the Navy, the Army and the Air Force.' Dalton, HC Debs. 12 Dec. 1945, col. 423.
21. T 267/3 and 4.
22. Attlee estimated the UK's foreign income in 1945 as perhaps £800 million and its outgoings as about £2,000 million, leaving a gap of £1,200 million. HC Debs. vol. 413 col. 956 quoted Cairncross (1992) 48. In 1947, the UK was taking 42.5 per cent of its imports from the New World but only 14 per cent of its exports had the New World as their destination. Morgan (1984) 341.
23. CAB 129/1.
24. Cairncross (1985) 4.
25. And despite assurances given by Roosevelt to Churchill at the Quebec Conference in 1944. Cairncross (1992), 48. Balfour 812.
26. Statement published on 24 August 1945 by Leo T. Crowley, the US Foreign Economic Administrator, on the Termination of Lend-Lease, FO 371/45699.
27. Alan P. Dobson, *The Export White Paper, 10 September 1941*, Economic History Review, Second Series, Vol. XXXIX, No. 1, Feb. 1986.
28. Cmd. 6321.
29. Harrod 587.
30. Dalton 73.
31. Balfour 809.
32. Fforde 71.
33. Harrod 606. Harrod attributes this story to the actual negotiations. But it is more likely to have been at the meeting with Clayton because when the negotiations began, Keynes conceded the point.
34. Balfour 810–11.
35. Balfour 821.
36. Plowden 30.
37. Bridges, 2nd ed., 74. Subsequently the Finance Division was divided into Home and Overseas Finance (OF).
38. Fforde 63.
39. Clarke, Document 7.
40. Minute from Keynes to Sir Wilfrid Eady, 9 July 1945. Clarke, *Anglo-American*, 58 and 134. Eady was Clarke's boss.
41. Balfour 821.
42. Bullock 121.
43. Fforde 63.
44. Fforde 67.
45. Dalton's experience of American wartime economic diplomacy is described in Dobson 40–1, 47.

46. Pimlott, *Dalton*, 432.
47. GEN 89/1, 12 Sep. 1945 Cabinet, Proposals for financial arrangements in the sterling area and between the US and UK to follow after Lend-Lease, Prepared by Lord Keynes, FO 371/45699.
48. Later Chief Justice of the US Supreme Court. Keynes told Dalton that Vinson's most conspicuous gift was the accuracy with which he could spit into a distant spittoon. Dalton 75n.
49. Clarke has commented, 'with Vinson unquestionably the key American in the negotiation . . . it is by no means obvious to me that Keynes was the right leader for the delegation'. Clarke 63.
50. *Hall Diaries*, 11 Nov. 1952.
51. Skidelsky, *Keynes*, volume 2, says of Keynes 'He wanted to decentralise and devolve only down to the level of Top People. Keynes's anti-market, anti-democratic bias was driven by a belief in scientific expertise and personal disinterestedness which now seems alarmingly naive.'
52. Clarke 56.
53. Diary, 22 Apr. 1946, Clarke 71.
54. Balfour 814.
55. HL Debs. 18 Dec. 1945, col. 781.
56. Dalton 74.
57. Balfour 821. Fforde 72–3.
58. Fforde 81–2.
59. Dalton 78.
60. 2 Nov. 1945, Telegram No. 7329 from Halifax to Prime Minister.
61. FO 371/45699.
62. The Americans had offered a low interest loan to help with reconversion as early as May 1943. Dobson 64.
63. HC Debs. 12 Dec. 1945, cols. 446 and 445.
64. Dalton 84.
65. Harrod 613.
66. Dalton 84.
67. Fforde 85.
68. Balfour 819–20.
69. John Snyder, Treasury Secretary, appears to have been less than enthusiastic about it. Dow 26n.
70. The UK had estimated the UK dollar deficit over the next three years at $4.87 billion. The US Treasury estimated the deficit at $3.3 billion. Balfour 815.
71. HL Debs. 18 Dec. 1945, cols. 783–4.
72. HC Debs. 12 Dec. 1945, col. 426.
73. HL Debs. 18 Dec. 1945, col. 787.
74. HL Debs. 18 Dec. 1945, cols. 784–5.
75. HL Debs. 18 Dec. 1945, col. 788.
76. Fforde 97–101. $5 billion at the current rate of exchange was £1.250 billion. To this figure has to be added $650 million on account of pipeline goods. Dalton told the House that if it rejected the agreement 'this would mean a grave embarrassment to our friends in Canada, who look to their earnings from the sterling area to cover their deficit from their trade with the United States'. HC Debs. 12 Dec. 1945, col. 443.
77. Hogan 50.
78. Dalton 82.
79. HL Debs. 18 Dec. 1945, cols. 782–3.
80. HC Debs. 12 Dec. 1945, col. 425.
81. HC Debs. 12 Dec. 1945, col. 429.
82. See especially Montagu Norman's minute to Richard Hopkins (Treasury) dated 11 Mar. 1943 quoted Fforde 47.
83. Fforde 33.
84. Dalton 84.
85. HC Debs. 12 Dec. 1945, cols. 438 and 439.

86. HC Debs. 12 Dec. 1945, col. 439.
87. Pimlott, *Dalton*, 431.
88. Harrod 606.
89. HC Debs. 12 Dec. 1945, col. 454.
90. HC Debs. 12 Dec. 1945, col. 424.
91. HL Debs. 18 Dec. 1945, col. 789.
92. HL Debs. 18 Dec. 1945, cols. 788–9. Keynes's reference was to Clause 10 of the Agreement entitled *Accumulated Sterling Balances* which embodied a statement in general terms of Britain's intentions regarding the sterling balances.
93. Paper by Keynes, 'Overseas Assets and Liabilities of the UK', 12 Sep. 1945, FO 371/45699.
94. Dalton 83.
95. HC Debs. 12 Dec. 1945, col. 429.
96. Fforde 86.
97. Fforde 76–7.
98. HC Debs. 12 Dec. 1945, col. 430.
99. Dalton 83.
100. T267/3 and 4. Fforde 114.
101. Dalton 73. Fforde 101–3 explains that Australia and New Zealand preferred to make gifts rather than to agree formal write-downs of their sterling balances. The UK wanted a formal write-down as an example to India and Egypt.
102. Fforde 103–8.
103. Harrod 615.
104. HC Debs. 12 Dec. 1945, col. 432.
105. HC Debs. 12 Dec. 1945, cols. 431–2.
106. HL Debs. 18 Dec. 1945, col. 779.
107. HL Debs. 18 Dec. 1945, col. 783.
108. HL Debs. 18 Dec. 1945, col. 794.
109. *Times*, 12 Dec. 1945. There was also a letter from Thomas Balogh.
110. Fforde 31, 83.
111. Fforde 83.
112. Fforde 85.
113. HL Debs. 18 Dec. 1945, col. 790.
114. HL Debs. 18 Dec. 1945, col. 790.
115. HC Debs. 12 Dec. 1945, cols. 442–3.
116. Dalton 84–5.
117. Dalton 233.
118. HC Debs. 12 Dec. 1945, cols. 467–8.
119. Quoted Pimlott, *Dalton*, 436.
120. Quoted Pimlott, *Dalton*, 436.
121. HL Debs. 18 Dec. 1945, col. 779.
122. HC Debs. 12 Dec. 1945, cols. 442–3.
123. HL Debs. 18 Dec. 1945, col. 779.
124. GEN 89/2 Cabinet – Commercial Policy and the Lend-Lease Negotiations in Washington, Memorandum by President of the Board of Trade, FO 371/45699.
125. HC Debs. 12 Dec. 1945, col. 482.
126. HC Debs. 12 Dec. 1945, col. 503.
127. HC Debs. 12 Dec. 1945, col. 497.
128. HC Debs. 12 Dec. 1945, cols. 494–5.
129. HC Debs. 12 Dec. 1945, col. 482.
130. HC Debs. 12 Dec. 1945, cols. 489–90.
131. HC Debs. 12 Dec. 1945, col. 490. This had already been emphasized by Attlee in his statement in the House on the conclusion of the loan negotiations on 6 Dec. 1945.
132. HC Debs. 12 Dec. 1945, cols. 492–3. All this was a rerun of the Mutual Aid Agreement of 23 February 1942. Dobson 34.
133. HC Debs. 12 Dec. 1945, col. 492–3.
134. Hennessy (1992) 214.
135. Fforde 60.
136. Though Philip Snowdon, Labour's Chancellor in the MacDonald governments, had favoured the return to gold. Skidelsky 189.

137. *The Collected Writings of John Maynard Keynes*, xix, 223–4, quoted Skidelsky 204–5.

138. HC Debs. 12 Dec. 1945, cols. 485–6.

139. Finlay Lecture, Dublin, April 1933 quoted Skidelsky 477. In a Treasury paper of 8 September 1941, Keynes wrote that 'It would be madness on our part to deprive ourselves of the possibility of action along . . . [autarkic] lines until we have an equally satisfactory solution of a different kind.' T247/116, quoted Dobson 50.

140. Harrod 609.

141. Stein 77. In 1978, Congress, under the influence of Hubert Humphrey, did pass a Full Employment Act. It has been a dead letter.

142. Skidelsky Vol. 2, 207, argues that in retrospect the strongest criticism of the return to gold in 1925 was that it was not part of a concerted move back to a fixed exchange rate system with the parities and rules of the game agreed in advance. Bretton Woods was such a system. But those characteristics of it were less central than Skidelsky argues.

143. HL Debs. 18 Dec. 1945, col. 792.

144. HC Debs. 12 Dec. 1945, col. 440.

145. HC Debs. 12 Dec. 1945, col. 468. Boothby says that Keynes was listening in the gallery. This cannot be the case. Boothby 207.

146. HC Debs. 12 Dec. 1945, col. 456.

147. HC Debs. 12 Dec. 1945, col. 460.

148. HC Debs. 12 Dec. 1945, cols. 463–4.

149. HC Debs. 12 Dec. 1945, col. 463.

150. HC Debs. 12 Dec. 1945, col. 466.

151. HC Debs. 12 Dec. 1945, col. 463.

152. HC Debs. 12 Dec. 1945, col. 469.

153. HC Debs. 12 Dec. 1945, col. 467.

154. Dalton explained the origins of the sterling area dollar pool. 'When war came, we and the rest of the sterling area enforced, for the first time, a complete system of exchange control . . . All members of the sterling area were free to spend sterling anywhere within the area or outside it, for any purpose approved by their own control; but . . . we asked the other members of the sterling area to cut to a minimum their demands on our reserves of gold and dollars, since these were the central reserves for the whole area. That was the origin of what is now called "the sterling area dollar pool".' HC Debs. 12 Dec. 1945, col. 425.

155. HC Debs. 12 Dec. 1945, col. 465.

156. Boothby would not agree. In Boothby (1978) 203, he quotes Nicholas Davenport: 'Boothby was always ahead of his time, and always right.' Boothby adds, 'From this conclusion I cannot dissent.'

157. Clarke 57.

158. The $5 billion, or £1.250 billion loans were intended to cover deficits foreseen for the period 1946–8 of £750 million, £250 million and £250 million. In fact, taking the three years together, the deficit was only £750 million. But the scale of assistance made no provision for the strain of convertibility nor, according to Dow 18n, for financing any of the deficit of the overseas sterling area. But see Keynes's speech to the House of Lords, 18 Dec. 1945.

159. At the Wheat Talks in September 1941, the US had insisted on high prices for their wheat and a

controlled market, contrary to their normal advocacy of freer trade and decontrol. Alan P. Dobson, *The Export White Paper, 10 September 194*, Economic History Review, Second Series, Vol. XXXIX, No. 1, Feb. 1986.

160. Dalton 221. See also T 267/3 and 4.
161. See, for example, Dalton 171.
162. Dalton 255.
163. Harrod 620.
164. Clarke 70.
165. Dalton 89.

CHAPTER TWO · DALTON: *ANNUS MIRABILIS* AND *ANNUS HORRENDUS*

1. Keynes to Dalton 28 Oct. 1945, Dalton 76–7.
2. Pimlott, *Dalton*, 440.
3. HC Debs. 12 Dec. 1945, col. 443–4.
4. Fforde 85–6.
5. Pimlott, *Dalton*, 452.
6. Beveridge, Chapter XV. For Churchill's broadcast see Beveridge 326.
7. A White Paper, *Housing Policy*, Cmd. 6609, March 1945, had committed all three parties to a minimum target of 3–4 million houses in the first 10 or 12 years of peace. This was raised by the Labour Manifesto to 4–5 million. C. Barnett (1995) 153; Morgan (1984) 163 ff.
8. Beveridge (1953) 310. Beveridge indicates that his proposed long transition was part of a deal with Keynes.
9. By 1951–2, the National Insurance Fund was generating a surplus greater than the entire cost of the National Health Service. Cairncross (1992) 5–6.
10. Cairncross (1992) 62 and 80.
11. Dalton 224.
12. Cairncross (1992) 59–60.
13. MS. Attlee dep. 29.
14. Dalton 220.
15. Cairncross (1985) 33.
16. Cairncross (1992) 80.
17. Cairncross (1985) 10.
18. Hennessy (1992) 268.
19. In *Note of a Difference of Opinion*, Dalton 197.
20. C. Barnett (1995) 72–3.
21. C. Barnett (1995) 76.
22. Dalton 196.
23. Dalton 194–8.
24. The British had accepted the Ruhr as its zone of occupation at a time when the Morgenthau Plan was still seriously in contemplation. Britain would shoulder the unpleasantness of deindustrializing Germany but could expect the benefit of inheriting Germany's export markets. The abandonment of the Morgenthau Plan meant that Britain faced the costs of occupation without any compensating benefit. Dobson 69.
25. C. Barnett (1995) 168.
26. C. Barnett (1995) 396 shows that even by 1950, exports by value were only 97.5 per cent of 1913.
27. Cairncross (1985) 36.
28. Cairncross (1985) 35.
29. Herbert Morrison, *Government and Parliament*, 1954, 20, quoted Dow 13n.
30. *Let us face the future* (Labour Party election manifesto, 1945, 4) quoted Dow 11.
31. In *Why this socialism?*, 1934, 82, quoted Dow 12n.
32. Cairncross (1992) 71 indicates the considerable success of import controls in improving the balance

of payments and in switching supplies from dollar sources.

33. Dalton 236.
34. Dalton 18.
35. Bridges 2nd ed. 89.
36. Cairncross (1985) 20.
37. Dalton 138.
38. Cairncross (1992) 78.
39. 'Young Guard on the Back Benches'. A favourite phrase. Dalton 100.
40. Dalton 34–5.
41. Fforde 4. The reference is to Montagu Norman, Governor of the Bank for 20 years up to 1944.
42. For the role of XYZ and of Davenport and his City friends, see Hennessy (1992) 203–4.
43. Pimlott, *Dalton*, 458.
44. Pimlott, *Dalton*, 459.
45. Dalton 212.
46. Two Labour sympathizers, Robin Brook and George Wansbrough, were appointed to the first Court of the nationalized Bank as well as George Gibson, Chairman of the TUC.
47. Fforde 15.
48. Fforde 27.
49. Fforde 5.
50. The section in question is S. 4(3).
51. Cairncross and Watts 214.
52. Dow 224.
53. See Dow 224n2 quoting Sir John Anderson and Oliver Stanley. The Opposition modified its support as criticism gathered.
54. Dow 21. There were those in the Bank who believed that monetary policy should be flexible 'up and down' but this view was not strenuously argued by the Governor with the Chancellor. Fforde 323–7. In the summer of 1944, Sir John Anderson had issued a 1950 maturity at par at 1.75% and commended it to the House as commanding the lowest yield offered by the Government during the war on any Stock Exchange Security. Fforde 331–2.
55. Bank Rate was briefly raised at the outbreak of war.
56. Dalton 160–1, 178–84.
57. Fforde 338–55.
58. In 1945 an internal Committee chaired by Sir Edward Bridges, and dominated by Keynes, argued in favour of the maintenance of low interest rates, long and short, far beyond the transitional period. The Economic Section (Meade and Robbins) was in general agreement but added a note of scepticism as to the practicalities. The Committee, however, warned that any attempt to force down long-term interest rates would be premature. Cairncross and Watts 210–12.
59. Dalton 231.
60. Dalton 183.
61. Cairncross (1992) 73. Otto Niemeyer, Executive Director at the Bank, in the course of an internal note strongly criticizing the Treasury's National Debt Enquiry Report, expressed the view that interest rates had little effect on investment. Fforde 335–7.
62. Speech at Lord Mayor's Banquet for the Bankers and Merchants of the City of London on 16 October 1946, Dalton, *High Tide*, 165.
63. Dalton 51–2.
64. Investment cuts, intended to amount to £200 million, were announced in October 1947. It proved easier to announce them than to implement them.
65. Dalton 238.
66. Dalton 221.
67. Fforde 147.
68. Dalton 222. While the fusion of the

American and British Zone was finalized, the cost of food for the American Zone was also temporarily being covered by Britain. These outgoings were to be reimbursed.

69. Dalton, *Principles of Public Finance* (1954 edition), 244, quoted Dalton 255.

70. Fforde 142–4. But 161–2, Fforde seems to revise this view and concludes that an approach would have caused trouble with Washington without any helpful outcome.

71. Fforde 144–6.

72. Dalton 256.

73. Hennessy (1992) 290.

74. Hennessy (1992) 299 ff. on Otto Clarke's paper T 229/136 of 17 July 1947. Sir Harry Lintott told Hennessy that Clarke's paper 'was largely intended to make Ministers' flesh creep'. Hennessy doubts that.

75. MS. Attlee dep. 59/1.

76. MS. Attlee dep. 59/2.

77. MS. Attlee dep. 59/1.

78. MS. Attlee dep. 59/1.

79. MS. Attlee dep. 59/1.

80. MS. Attlee dep. 59/2.

81. Dow 24.

82. Dow 24.

83. Of which the net drawings of the independent Commonwealth amounted to $1,100 million. Cairncross (1992) 56.

84. Morgan (1984) 340.

85. Fforde 96. Eady had learnt his negotiating skills at the Ministry of Labour.

86. Minute of 29 Oct. 1947 from Sir W. Eady to Gorell Barnes. MS Attlee dep. 62.

87. Fforde 150.

88. Donoughue and Jones 412.

89. Before the coal crisis broke, Attlee put Dalton in the chair of a Cabinet Coal Committee. It had little effect.

90. Dalton 257.

91. Fforde 160.

92. HC Debs. 8 July 1947, col. 2158.

93. Dalton 257.

94. Pimlott, *Dalton*, 489.

95. Dalton 272.

96. Plowden 15.

97. *Hall Diaries*, 13 Nov. 1947.

98. Cairncross (1992) 72.

99. For example Pimlott, *Dalton*, 540.

100. Dalton 239–41.

101. Dalton 278.

102. Pimlott, *Dalton*, 544, argues that Attlee may have felt gratitude to Cripps for some financial assistance sixteen years earlier, and was therefore more prepared to forgive.

103. Dow 29.

CHAPTER THREE · THE UNCERTAIN AUSTERITY OF SIR STAFFORD CRIPPS

1. Franz-Josef Strauss said that he was perfectly happy to have Helmut Kohl, as Chancellor of the Federal German Republic, serving under him.

2. Dalton 246.

3. MS Attlee dep. 60.

4. Shinwell became Minister of War outside the Cabinet. He never forgave Gaitskell.

5. MS Attlee dep. 61.

6. Plowden 19.

7. Estorick 367.

8. Dalton 210.

9. Plowden 22.

10. Dalton 239.

11. *Hall Diaries*, 12 and 24 Sep. 1947.

12. Plowden 19–21.

13. Dalton 237.

14. HC Debs. 18 Apr. 1950, col. 52.
15. *Gaitskell Diary* 187.
16. Milward (1984) 437.
17. According to *The Marshall Plan and the Future of US-European Relations* (German Information Centre, New York, 1972), quoted C. Barnett (1975) 473, of the $13 billion total of Marshall Aid roughly $3.1 billion went to Britain, $2.7 billion to France, $1.5 billion to Italy and just under $1.5 billion to West Germany.
18. Cairncross (1992) 57.
19. Cairncross (1992) 76.
20. CAB 134/224, EPC (50) 18th, item 1, 13 July 1950, quoted C. Barnett 397.
21. The government's White Paper, *Statement on Personal Incomes, Costs and Prices*, CMD 7321, was published in February 1948 and overwhelmingly endorsed by the TUC at a special conference with provisos relating to low pay and the maintenance of differentials. The White Paper also called for a freeze on incomes from profit, rent or other like sources. There was a parallel agreement with the FBI on voluntary dividend limitation. There were exceptions for undermanned industries or for increased productivity.
22. Cairncross (1992) 63.
23. Cairncross (1992) 63.
24. An overinflated tyre could be disinflated but it should not be punctured and thus deflated. HC Debs. 5 July 1948, col. 46, quoted Dow 36n.
25. *Hall Diaries*, March 1948.
26. Cairncross (1992) 7.
27. Speech January 1949 quoted in *The Economist*, 22 Jan. 1949, 130, quoted by Plowden 36.
28. The thirteen became fourteen when Western Germany became a member in October 1949.
29. *Hall Dairies*, 17 June 1948.
30. CP (48) 61.
31. Milward (1984) 100, and Plowden 41–3.
32. Plowden 4.
33. Plowden 46.
34. Clarke Diary, quoted by Hennessy (1992) 291.
35. Later such plans were required under the ERP.
36. *Hall Diaries*, 8 Apr. 1948. Cairncross comments that what Plowden said at the dinner may have been true in peacetime but that the 1941 Budget is generally regarded as the first attempt to set the Budget in the context of the economic situation as a whole.
37. Plowden 78.
38. Plowden 78–9.
39. Bridges, 1st ed. 199. The first edition was signed off by Bridges in Aug. 1963 and published in 1964. The same words appear in the 2nd ed. of 1966.
40. HC Debs. 18 Apr. 1948, col. 39, quoted Cairncross (1992) 65.
41. HC Debs. 15 Apr. 1950, col. 52. Quoted Bridges 2nd ed. 93.
42. Fforde 371.
43. Plowden 56.
44. HC Debs. 6 April 1949, cols. 2091–2, quoted Dow 40.
45. HC Debs. 6 Apr. 1949, col. 2093, quoted Dow 40.
46. Draft brief for Bevin and Cripps visit to Washington, *Gaitskell Diary* 139.
47. 'Unrequited' exports were exports that earned nothing because they merely cancelled part of the sterling balances. The Bank of England questioned the whole concept of unrequited exports on the ground that such exports

'mopped up' excess sterling in foreign hands and thereby limited opportunities for creating 'cheap sterling'. Fforde 229.

48. Hennessy (1991) 484.
49. Fforde 279.
50. Plowden, 52–3.
51. Milward, *Western Europe*, 287–8.
52. Fforde 281.
53. Plowden, 58.
54. Hennessy (1991) 489.
55. Plowden 53, and *Hall Diaries*, 18 Mar. 1949. Plowden told Gaitskell that he had been in favour of devaluation since Feb. 1949. *Gaitskell Diary* 128.
56. Plowden 53.
57. For example in *The Economist* of 7 May 1949, quoted Dow 42n.
58. *Hall Diaries*, 7 June 1949.
59. Hennessy (1991) 485. This comment is somewhat qualified on 486.
60. *Hall Diaries*, 15 Feb. 1950.
61. Fforde 291.
62. Cairncross and Watts 216.
63. Plowden 56–7.
64. Williams 200.
65. Pimlott, *Dalton*, 570.
66. Donoughue and Jones 439.
67. Pimlott, *Dalton*, 570–1.
68. Ed. Cairncross, *Hall Diaries* entry for June 2 1948.
69. CAB 134/220, EPC (49) 24th meeting quoted Hennessy, *Never Again*, 372.
70. Cobbold, Governor of the Bank of England, subsequently told Attlee that in his discussions with Cripps before he left England, Cripps was talking of the need to associate devaluation with strong action against inflationary pressure at home and to deal with the weight of the sterling balances. Morgan, *Labour in Power*, 282–3.
71. Milward (1984) 289.

72. Plowden, 58.
73. *Gaitskell Diary* 130.
74. *Hall Diaries*, 8 July 1949.
75. *Hall Diaries*, 13 July 1949.
76. Williams 198.
77. *Hall Diaries*, 11 July 1949.
78. Jay (1980) 185, See also Hennessy (1991) 499.
79. *Gaitskell Diary* 130. c) apparently reflects Jay's view, influenced by Edgar Whitehead, Finance Minister of Southern Rhodesia, who produced evidence at the Commonwealth Economic Conference that British exports were uncompetitive in price. Plowden 59.
80. *Hall Diaries*, 21 July 1949.
81. Hennessy (1991) 492. Wilson sacked Jay as President of the Board of Trade in August 1967.
82. Milward, *Western Europe*, 290.
83. Plowden, 59–60.
84. Donoughue and Jones 410–11.
85. PREM 8/1178 Part 1, Attlee to Cripps, 5 Aug. 1949 quoted Plowden 60–1.
86. *Gaitskell Diary* 137.
87. MS Attlee dep. 87 and *Gaitskell Diary* 151–4.
88. *Gaitskell Diary* 126.
89. Fforde 296–7.
90. MS Attlee dep. 87 and *Gaitskell Diary* 143–50.
91. Fforde 297–8. Plowden 63. HC Debs. 27 Sep. 1949, col. 12.
92. Plowden 63.
93. Plowden 64.
94. Plowden 63–4.
95. George F. Kennan 458.
96. Milward (1984) 292.
97. Williams 203.
98. Cairncross (1992) 55.
99. Churchill made a strong attack on Cripps which included '[He] stands woefully weakened in

reputation . . .' HC Debs. 28 Sept. 1949, cols. 167–8

100. *Gaitskell Diary* 141.
101. *Gaitskell Diary* 135 and Pimlott, *Dalton*, 573.
102. *Gaitskell Diary* 155.
103. Plowden 66–7. Williams 204.
104. Plowden 67–8.
105. At the end of 1951, the UK's obligations would increase by some $200 million a year in the form of repayments of the American loan.
106. Plowden, 69–70, 78, 79.
107. Cairncross, *British Economy since 1945*, 12.
108. The IMF's Agreement required that the Fund should be given 72 hours notice where a proposed change in par value exceeded 20 per cent. The British devaluation was of 30.5 per cent. The IMF in fact gave its immediate agreement.
109. Nevertheless all sterling area countries, with the exception of Pakistan, moved with sterling.
110. Young (1984) 125.
111. Milward (1984) 296–7.
112. Young (1984) 310.
113. Milward (1984) 303–4.
114. T 232/183.
115. Milward (1984) 455.
116. Williams, *Gaitskell*, 207. But see *Gaitskell Diary* 161.
117. *Gaitskell Diary* 192. Cripps returned to London for a special defence debate for which the House was recalled mid-September 1950.
118. Plowden 64–5.

CHAPTER FOUR · HUGH GAITSKELL: REARMAMENT AND CIVIL WAR

1. Dalton 352.
2. Donoughue and Jones 465–6. Plowden 105.
3. Foot 238. At a meeting on 4 July 1948, Bevan had said of the Tory Party that 'So far as I am concerned they are lower than vermin.'
4. Morgan (1984) 442 says Cripps preferred Bevan. This seems doubtful. See *Gaitskell Diary* 215. See also 309 where Gaitskell records that Bevan had 'frequently asserted that Stafford promised that he would be Chancellor.'
5. *Gaitskell Diary* 215.
6. Williams 238.
7. *Gaitskell Diary* 174.
8. *Gaitskell Diary* 193. Foot 294. Williams 214.
9. M. Foot 294–7.
10. Gaitskell had been joint head of the economics department at University College, London, with Paul Rosenstein-Rodan before the war.
11. *Hall Diaries*, 9 Aug. 1949.
12. Plowden 106.
13. Butler (1971) 154.
14. Brittan (1971) 180–1.
15. Cairncross (1992) 4.
16. *Gaitskell Diary* 116.
17. *Gaitskell Diary* 127.
18. Williams 218–19.
19. Williams 219.
20. *Gaitskell Diary* 172 and 191.
21. *Gaitskell Diary* 179–81. Gaitskell claimed that Belgium, Switzerland and West Germany had put themselves on a dollar standard and therefore the UK had to discriminate against them.
22. *Gaitskell Diary* 193
23. Williams 218. Gutt was Belgian

Minister of Finance 1939–45 and stabilized the Belgian currency after the war.

24. Cairncross and Watts 216.
25. See *Gaitskell Diary* 227 re advice from the Governor.
26. Fforde 388.
27. Fforde 392.
28. Fforde 394. An increase in interest rates had costs. For example, it would increase the cost of government debt and of the sterling balances.
29. Mitchell 213.
30. Williams 223.
31. Fforde 209–10.
32. A thought expressed by Nigel Lawson in his first speech in the House as Chancellor, 29 June 1983, Lawson 271.
33. Cairncross (1992) 55.
34. Williams 246.
35. Plowden 111.
36. *Hall Diaries*, 30 April 1951.
37. Cairncross (1992) 55 says 'over $2.5 billion in grants and loans'.
38. *Gaitskell Diary* 204–6.
39. *Gaitskell Diary* 194–6 and 206–11 which discusses the situation as it existed in October 1950 during Gaitskell's visit to Washington.
40. *Gaitskell Diary* 221.
41. *Gaitskell Diary* 201–4.
42. *Gaitskell Diary* 232.
43. *Gaitskell Diary* 229.
44. *Gaitskell Diary* 229.
45. Bevan had been offered the Colonial Office after the February 1950 election but had turned it down. But, according to Philip Williams, Bevan wanted it but was not offered it. *Gaitskell Diary* 174n.
46. The Ministry of Health was split, with housing and local government going to the Ministry of Local Government and Planning.

47. For example in the devaluation debate in 1949.
48. *Gaitskell Diary* 237.
49. *Gaitskell Diary* 238.
50. Williams 240.
51. *Gaitskell Diary* 175.
52. Williams 255. Children were exempt and so were the poor and the sick.
53. Williams 252.
54. *Gaitskell Diary* 245.
55. Morgan (1984) 449.
56. Williams 253.
57. *Gaitskell Diary* 248.
58. Williams 258.
59. Under pressure from the TUC and some Labour MPs, Gaitskell subsequently agreed to some further small improvements in the pension arrangements. Williams 262. Although pensions were increased, there were provisions to discourage early retirement.
60. Morgan (1984) 453.
61. Quoted Morgan (1984) 453.
62. *Hall Diaries*, 11 Dec. 1951.
63. Williams 248n.
64. Morgan (1984) 457.
65. Williams 260.
66. *Gaitskell Diary* 281.
67. *Economic Survey for* 1952, par. 11.
68. Dow 71.
69. *Gaitskell Diary* 266.
70. *Gaitskell Diary* 267.
71. Mitchell 224.
72. For example by Morgan (1984) 459.
73. Morgan (1984) 479.
74. Plowden 131–2 records how the report of the NATO 'Three Wise Men' exercise, on which he was the British member, eased British ability to reduce its defence programme.
75. *Gaitskell Diary* 266.
76. Butler (1971) 163.
77. *Gaitskell Diary* 254.
78. *Gaitskell Diary* 258–9.

79. *Gaitskell Diary* 267.
80. *Gaitskell Dairy* 268.
81. Williams 264.
82. Harris 486–7.
83. Quoted Williams 266.
84. *Gaitskell Diary* 257.

CHAPTER FIVE · BUTLER AND
THE LIBERATION OF STERLING

1. Butler (1971) 156.
2. Dow 71.
3. There was a general impression, shared by politicians, that the distinction between above and below the line referred to the accounting distinction between current and capital expenditure. This was not true. The line did not divide government expenditure according to its economic character, but according to the nature of the government's borrowing powers. For below-the-line payments the government had specific powers to borrow. But it could also borrow for above-the-line expenditure under general borrowing powers. In other words the line had significance for Parliamentary procedures but none for the impact of the Budget on the economy. Nevertheless Butler's instinctive reaction against an above-the-line deficit was not simply folly. The system of presenting government accounts was reformed in the 1960s.
4. Salter 216.
5. J. W. Wheeler-Bennett, *John Anderson, Viscount Waverley*, London, 1962, 352. Quoted Macmillan (1969) 485n.
6. Plowden 141. 'Before the "Korean" price rise in 1951–2 an annual increase in wages was far less general ... By 1953 it was clear that wage inflation was to be a continuing problem, not just a problem of the immediate transition from the war.' Dow 99nl.
7. I am grateful to Robert Taylor of the *Financial Times* for this information.
8. Butler (1982) 137.
9. Butler (1971) 154–5.
10. Macmillan (1969) 375. MacDougall reports, 103, an unsuccessful attempt by Butler to get the housing programme cut.
11. *Gaitskell Diary* 307.
12. Butler (1971) 157.
13. Lyttelton, after some discussion, was appointed Colonial Secretary.
14. Lyttelton 343.
15. £360 million in November, £150 million in January, and £100 million in March.
16. Fforde 404.
17. Procter 33–4.
18. Procter 31–5.
19. T 236/3240. Par. 46 of the paper of 8 Feb. 1952.
20. Fforde 398–400.
21. T 236/3240.
22. *Hall Diaries*, 27 Nov. 1952.
23. *Hall Diaries*, 27 Nov. 1952.
24. T 236/3240.
25. Dow 72.
26. Fforde 424–5.
27. Bolton had begun to consider a new approach to exchange rate policy immediately after the election of a Conservative government. Procter 36.
28. Hall on Rowan: 'It is a dreadful thing to have our overseas finances in the hands of an emotional man with a stomach ulcer ... He is at present completely in Otto Clarke's hands.' *Hall Diaries*, 27 Mar. 1952. Rowan is 'really nothing but [Otto's] creature now'. *Hall Diaries*, 24 Feb. 1953.

29. T236/3240.
30. American and Canadian account sterling was already convertible.
31. Arrangements had been made under Labour to regulate drawings on the sterling balances by agreement with their owners.
32. T 236/3241.
33. T 236/3240, 13 Feb. 1952.
34. Procter 36.
35. *Septuagesima Plus*, 12 Feb. 1952, T236/3240.
36. Fforde 425–6.
37. T236/3240.
38. Oliver Lyttelton to PM 26 Feb. 1952, copied to Butler, Woolton, Maxwell Fyfe, James Stuart and Cherwell, T 236/3241.
39. Fforde 437–8.
40. RWBC/4926 of 26 Feb. 1952, T 236/3241. Author's emphasis.
41. Draft Memorandum by Chancellor of the Exchequer, 26 Feb. 1952, T 236/3241. Author's emphasis.
42. Salter 222.
43. Fforde 167.
44. T 236/3240.
45. T 236/3241, RWBC/4926 of 26 Feb. 1952.
46. T 236/3241.
47. Note by Professor Lionel Robbins undated but obviously written after the Budget though carrying the words 'Feb./Mar. 52'. T 236/3241.
48. Note by Hall drawn up on 4 March, T 236/3245.
49. Plowden 148 regarding Hall's retrospective thoughts.
50. T 236/3241.
51. Note by Professor Lionel Robbins undated but obviously written after the Budget. T 236/3241.
52. 1 July 1952, T 236/3244.
53. Draft Memorandum by Chancellor of the Exchequer, 26 Feb. 1952 (Third draft), T 236/3241.
54. RWBC/4950 to Rowan, 11 Mar. 1952 entitled 'Robot rides again', T 236/3241.
55. T 236/3241.
56. T 236/3241, RWBC/4926 of 26 Feb. 1952.
57. Letter from Hall to Plowden (in Lisbon), 22 Feb. 1952 and Robert Hall Memorandum on 'External Action', 23 Feb. 1952, T 236/3240.
58. T 236/3241, RWBC/4926 of 26 Feb. 1952.
59. T 236/3241.
60. Robert Hall Memorandum on 'External Action', 23 Feb. 1952, T 236/3240.
61. Notes of a talk with Professor Robbins, 27 Feb. 1952, and Note by Professor Lionel Robbins undated but obviously written after the Budget, T 236/3241.
62. T 236/3241. The 'B-plan' was, of course, the Bank's plan.
63. Salter 220–1.
64. Record of the Cabinet's three discussions on external sterling on 28 and 29 Feb., T 236/3242.
65. *Hall Diaries*, 4 Mar. 1952.
66. Gradually a somewhat distorted view of what had happened within the government in 1952 got through to Gaitskell and he learnt that Plowden had opposed Robot. Gaitskell told Plowden, 'I wish you had not advised [Eden] that way. If they had been so foolish as to go for convertibility, we might now be back in power, or at least have a much better prospect of getting there.' *Gaitskell Diary* 316.
67. *Hall Diaries*, 4 Mar. 1952 and 25 Mar. 1952.
68. *Hall Diaries*, 4 Mar. 1952.
69. Butler encouraged Plowden to accept the offer of the job as Secretary General of NATO.

Oliver Franks had turned it down.
Hall Diaries, 7 Mar. 1952.

70. *Hall Diaries*, 12 Aug. 1954.
71. Dow 73.
72. Cairncross and Watts 216.
73. Dow 73.
74. Dow 91.
75. T 326/3244.
76. T 326/3244. Butler to Hall, 27 June 1952.
77. T 326/3244.
78. Salter 222.
79. Butler (1971) 158.
80. Butler (1971) 160. The offending journalist was Norman Macrae. The word was resented by both Butler and Gaitskell.
81. *Hall Diaries*, 30 Dec. 1953.
82. Cairncross (1985) 270n.
83. Salter 224.
84. Fforde 482.
85. *Hall Diaries*, 18 Mar. 1953.
86. Fforde 482–92.
87. MacDougall 108.
88. Cairncross (1985) 270.
89. Plowden 157.
90. Brittan (1971) 200.
91. Roll (1995) 28.
92. I do not include Copleston in this group.
93. Paper by Robert Hall 24/25 Mar. 1952 entitled 'The Future of Sterling', T 236/3242.
94. Plowden 154.
95. See J. A. Jukes to Rowan 10 Apr. 1952 covering paper by Economic Section entitled 'Prices under a two world system: Note by the Economic Section' and Rowan to Clarke 24 Apr. 1952 re Economic Section paper 'Prices under a two world system'. 'This seems to me the most fluffy and inadequate paper that I have come across for some time.' In T 236/3243.
96. 'The Future of Sterling' – O.F.

Comments on Hall's paper, 27 Mar. 1952, T 236/3242.
97. RWBC/4978 to Rowan 26 Mar. 1952 entitled 'Dollar Shortage', T 236/3242.
98. Cairncross (1985) 268.
99. *Hall Diaries*, 18 Mar. 1952; 1 Oct. 1954.
100. Butler (1971) 177.
101. Howard (1987) 188.
102. T 326/3244. Flett to Rowan, 26 June 1952.
103. William Armstrong 'confirmed that the Chancellor is now much more doubtful about Robot, and he has lost confidence in Leslie Rowan's judgement. He says that the Chancellor is "perplexed and distressed" and does not feel that he gets any really good advice.' *Hall Diaries*, 15 May 1952.
104. Butler (1971) 157.
105. Cairncross and Watts 263.
106. Butler (1971) 157. This tribute is at odds with Hall's appreciation of Butler's final attitude to Plowden. *Hall Diaries*, 25 June 1953. But it was Hall's view that Plowden's departure from the Treasury was a misfortune. *Hall Diaries*, 27 June 1956.
107. *Hall Diaries*, 20 Jan. 1953. See also *Hall Diaries*, 28 Oct. 1954.
108. Hall was even beginning to appreciate Rowan despite his tendency to stomach ulcers and bad temper. *Hall Diaries*, 7 Dec. 1955. The decision was also opposed by Cherwell, now out of government.
109. *Hall Diaries*, 3 Mar. 1955. *Hall Diaries*, 26 May 1955 and 18 July 1955. Another factor was that dollars were now more plentiful. *Hall Diaries*, 2 Dec. 1955.
110. Cairncross (1992) 92.
111. Cairncross and Watts 269.

112. In the Budget debate Tony Crosland argued that the Chancellor should have increased taxation rather than reduced it.
113. Cairncross and Watts 217–21.
114. *Hall Diaries*, 5 Apr. and 21 June 1956.
115. Fforde 631–2.
116. Dow 78.
117. Fforde 641.
118. Cairncross and Watts 271.
119. HC Debs. 26 July 1955, col. 1027.
120. Dow 90.
121. Butler (1971) 180.
122. Butler (1971) 180.
123. Letter from Leslie Rowan to Bridges from Istanbul 18 Sep. 1955, T 171/468.
124. Cairncross and Watts 272.
125. Howard (1987) 216. 'I could not get my way and, no doubt, should have resigned.' (Undated diary note apparently written in Dec. 1955.)
126. Harry Crookshank. Butler (1971) 182, Howard (1987) 221.
127. Butler (1971) 180.
128. Howard (1987) 219.
129. Rhodes James (1987) 410. Butler (1971) 180–1.
130. This was also Macmillan's perception. Macmillan (1969) 696.
131. Howard (1987) 199 reports on the precautions taken to prevent Butler's succession if Churchill should prove incapable of carrying on while Eden was still undergoing treatment in the USA. See also Macmillan (1969) 517.

CHAPTER SIX · HAROLD MACMILLAN: PROMISE UNPERFORMED

1. Macmillan (1969) 692.
2. Macmillan (1969) 693.
3. Howard (1987) 221.
4. Horne (1990) 389.
5. Macmillan (1969) 692.
6. Macmillan (1971) 29.
7. Macmillan (1971) 3.
8. Horne (1990) 386.
9. Cairncross and Watts 273.
10. Heathcoat Amory was Minister of Agriculture, Thorneycroft was President of the Board of Trade.
11. The story is told in Macmillan (1971) 12–14.
12. *Hall Diaries*, 20 Feb. 1956.
13. Horne (1990) 387.
14. Cairncross and Watts 274.
15. Macmillan (1971) 30.
16. Cairncross and Watts 274. *Hall Diaries*, 28 Mar. 1956.
17. Macmillan (1971) 30.
18. Macmillan (1971) 31.
19. See *Hall Diaries*, 3 May and 21 June 1956. By the end of the year cuts of £93 million had been secured, half in defence. Macmillan (1971) 50–1.
20. Dow 94n has some comments on this declaration.
21. Macmillan (1971) 42.
22. Cairncross and Watts 274.
23. Dow 384.
24. Macmillan (1971) 5.
25. Cmd. 9725, 1956, par. 25. Quoted Bridges, 2nd ed. 93. The White Paper was being prepared, and could have been issued, while Butler was still Chancellor, but he held it up.
26. Macmillan (1971) 16.
27. Macmillan (1971) 56.
28. Quoted Horne (1990) 391.
29. Cairncross, *British Economy since*

1945, 113. The story is also told in *Hall Diaries*, 30 Aug. 1956.

30. Horne (1990) 423.
31. Macmillan (1971) 6.
32. Macmillan (1971) 7–8.
33. Macmillan (1971) 12.
34. To the Northern Conservative Club of 25 May 1956. Macmillan (1971) 56.
35. Macmillan (1971) 16. HC Debs. 20 Feb. 1956.
36. Macmillan (1971) 7.
37. Macmillan (1971) 199.
38. Macmillan (1969) 468. The Foreign Office was commenting on a proposal for the complete union of the Schuman Plan countries.
39. These problems are discussed in *Hall Diaries*, 7 Dec. 1955. One problem was Rowan's uncertain health and temper.
40. Macmillan (1971) 2.
41. *Hall Diaries*, 27 June 1956.
42. Makins was 'joint' with Sir Norman Brook. Makins headed the economic side, Brook the civil service management side of the Treasury.
43. Horne (1990) 429.
44. Horne (1990) 430.
45. Macmillan (1971) 157.
46. Horne 423.
47. Fforde 553.
48. Fforde 555.
49. Fforde 553n.
50. Horne (1990) 422.
51. Horne (1990) 438–9, 442.
52. Horne (1990) 439.
53. Horne (1990) 442.
54. Horne (1990) 445.
55. *Hall Diaries*, 29 Nov. 1956.
56. Fforde 557.
57. Kyle 465.
58. Macmillan (1971) 53.
59. Horne (1990) 389.
60. Macmillan (1971) 164.
61. Fforde 544.

62. Macmillan (1971) 164.
63. Macmillan (1971) 167.
64. Macmillan (1971) 167.
65. Dow 96. The IMF drawing was of $561 million and there was also a standby, which was not used, of $739 million. These figures represented 100% of quota and totalled more than the whole of the IMF's lending hitherto. The EXIM Bank credit was $500 million.
66. Macmillan (1971) 177.
67. Macmillan (1971) 166.
68. Eden 557.
69. A further factor alienating French opinion was the British defence cuts in Europe. After Macmillan had become Prime Minister, Duncan Sandys, as Minister of Defence, proposed a reduction of British forces in Europe from 80,000 to 50,000. After French and German opposition, the agreed cut was from 77,000 to 64,000. Macmillan (1971) 246–7, 264.
70. Horne (1990) 452.

CHAPTER SEVEN · PETER THORNENCROFF: A CHANCELLOR BETRAYED

1. Macmillan (1971) 78.
2. Another similarity was that both Macmillan and Thorneycroft had been defeated in the July 1945 General Election in their constituencies of Stockton and Stafford respectively and had been returned at early by-elections, Thorneycroft for Monmouth, Macmillan for Bromley.
3. Fforde 562.
4. Macmillan (1971) 342–3.
5. Cairncross and Watts 276. In fact the surplus for 1957 turned out to

be £211 million. HC Debs. 23 Jan.
1958, col. 1271. The Treasury
suggested a figure of £450 million
to the Radcliffe Commitee.

6. Macmillan (1971) 344.
7. *Hall Diaries*, 7 Mar. 1957.
8. Dow 95.
9. Macmillan (1971) 347–8. The
reductions in taxes included income
tax, surtax, purchase tax and
entertainment tax. Dow 96. Horne
Vol. 2, 62 is of interest.
10. Fforde 674.
11. Macmillan (1971) 349.
12. Fforde 674.
13. See, for example, *Hall Diaries*, 1
April 1957.
14. Cairncross and Watts, 227.
15. Dow 96.
16. Fforde 572.
17. Dow 96.
18. French exports received a 20 per
cent subsidy and French imports,
other than essential raw materials,
were charged a 20 per cent tax.
Dow 97nl.
19. Dow 97.
20. Fforde 570.
21. Fforde 573–5.
22. *Hall Diaries*, 19 Aug. 1957.
23. Dow 97n4.
24. Dow 101nl.
25. Macmillan (1971) 211, diary 15
Mar. 1957.
26. Macmillan (1971) 255.
27. Quoted Horne Vol. 2, 64.
28. Macmillan (1971) 350–1.
29. Macmillan (1973) 38–9.
30. The three were Lord Cohen, Sir
Harold Howitt and Sir Dennis
Robertson. Hall comments 'I was
somewhat doubtful about whether
[Robertson] would accept as he is
not too strong and in any case
thinks we ought to deflate more
and have more unemployment.'
Hall Diaries, 19 Aug. 1957.

31. Macmillan (1971) 352.
32. HC Debs. 25 July 1957, Col. 645.
33. *Hall Diaries*, 31 July 1957.
34. Fforde 673.
35. Dow 100–1.
36. Cairncross and Watts 227.
37. Dow 240.
38. Fforde 12–13, 20, 26–7, 680–7.
See also *Hall Diaries*, 29 Oct. 1957.
That the powers of direction to the
banks could only be used if the
Bank thought it in the public
interest was made clear by Dalton
on Second Reading of the
Nationalization Bill. It was
reiterated by Lord Chancellor
Jowett in the Lords.
39. Macmillan (1971) 356–7. Butler
and Hailsham subsequently told
Hall privately that they disagreed
with the policy of 19 September
because production was being held
back instead of expanded.
Maudling seems to have expressed
similar views to Hall privately: *Hall
Diaries*, 30 Jan. 1958. An alleged
leak about the increase in Bank Rate
led, under pressure from the
Shadow Chancellor, Harold
Wilson, to the Bank Rate Tribunal.
40. Macmillan (1971) 357–8.
41. Macmillan (1971) 359.
42. Dow 101.
43. Macmillan (1971) 356–7.
44. Dow 97n4.
45. *Hall Diaries*, 22 Oct. 1957.
46. Cairncross (1992) 110 says
Thorneycroft's strategy was 'not
well considered'.
47. *Hall Diaries*, 22 Oct. 1957.
48. HC Debs. 29 Oct. 1957, cols. 57–
8, quoted Dow 101 and 101n5.
49. *Hall Diaries*, 29 Oct. 1957.
50. *Hall Diaries* (1992), 122.
51. *Hall Diaries*, 29 Oct. 1957.
52. Fforde 687.
53. Allen 177.

54. The Duncan Sandys Defence White Paper published on 4 April 1957 had proposed cuts amounting to £78 million in the first year. National Service was to end after the end of 1960. By end 1962, armed forces were to consist exclusively of regular voluntary recruits. The total, still in 1957 690,000, would be reduced by 1962 to 375,000.
55. Macmillan (1971) 363.
56. In the spring of 1957, Macmillan feared a General Strike; see Macmillan (1971) 346. As shown in his memoirs, he kept a close eye on public opinion polls. See, for example, Macmillan (1971) 358.
57. Macmillan (1971) 368–9.
58. Dow comments that Thorneycroft thought it was a crisis of internal inflation. 'In retrospect the external factors seem of far greater importance.' Dow 97.
59. Cairncross and Watts 228.
60. 'During the next three years disinflation caused us to lag behind other European countries, where expansion continued rapidly – as it did in the United States till the further recession of 1958. Taking the world as a whole, the rapid upsurge in industrial production in 1955 decelerated gradually; was reversed in 1958; and was resumed in 1959.' Dow 92.
61. Brittan (1971) 212.
62. Brittan (1971) 215. Macmillan (1971) 360.
63. Macmillan (1971) 355. *Hall Diaries*, 28 Aug. 1957. Cairncross and Watts 229.
64. *Hall Diaries*, 30 Dec. 1957.
65. *Hall Diaries*, 8 Jan. 1958.
66. *Hall Diaries*, 8 Jan. 1958.
67. Horne, Vol. 2, 75.

68. Morgan (1990) 174 quoting CAB 128/32, pt. 1.
69. Horne Vol. 2, 71 quotes Macmillan's diary for 6 January 1958 which emphasizes that, at the Cabinet on 3 January, Thorneycroft was so rude that 'I had difficulty in preventing some of the Cabinet bursting out in their indignation . . .' John Boyd-Carpenter, Minister of Pensions, who was attending Cabinet, and himself threatening to resign, tells how on 3 January 1958, Thorneycroft absented himself from Cabinet and sent Lord Chancellor Kilmuir to negotiate with the Cabinet on his behalf. Macmillan instructed Thorneycroft to attend. Boyd-Carpenter 137–9.
70. Lord Randolph Churchill and C. T. Ritchie.
71. Horne, Vol. 2, 77.
72. Morgan, *People's Peace*, 172–3. According to Horne Vol. 2, 389, Amory was Eden's first choice for No. 11.
73. Macmillan (1971) 372.
74. Macmillan (1971) 365.
75. Macmillan (1971) 366.
76. Macmillan (1971) 372.
77. HC Debs. 23 Jan. 1958, cols. 1295–6.
78. Thatcher 150 and 152.
79. Macmillan (1971) 374.
80. Horne Vol. 2, 78.

CHAPTER EIGHT · DERICK HEATHCOAT AMORY: HIS MASTER'S VOICE

1. Macmillan (1971) 702–3.
2. Horne, Vol. 2, 140. Interview with Lord Amory.
3. Callaghan 178.

4. Maudling 67.
5. Allen 177.
6. Allen 17.
7. Allen 66.
8. Butler (1971) 143.
9. Allen 171.
10. Thorpe 244 and 250; Morgan (1990) 151, 154.
11. Macmillan (1971) 709.
12. HC Debs. 7 Apr. 1958, col. 50. Quoted Dow 104.
13. HC Debs. 7 Apr. 1958, col. 54. Quoted Dow 104.
14. Cairncross (1992) 120.
15. Cairncross (1992) 114.
16. *Hall Diaries*, 12 May 1958.
17. Fforde 576–7.
18. Fforde 577–8.
19. HC Debs. 15 Apr. 1958, cols. 51–3. Quoted Dow 106–7.
20. HC Debs. 23 Jan. 1958, col. 1329.
21. Macmillan (1971) 498.
22. Fforde 589.
23. Fforde 587–8.
24. Fforde 590–1.
25. Fforde 591.
26. *Hall Diaries*, 14 Aug. 1958.
27. Dow 104. Cairncross (1992) 119, for the Treasury's 1958 balance of payments target surplus.
28. *Hall Diaries*, 30 Dec. 1958.
29. *Hall Diaries*, 31 Mar. 1958.
30. Fforde 532.
31. *Hall Diaries*, 8 Jan. 1959. *Hall Diaries*, 19 Feb. 1959.
32. Fforde 536–7.
33. *Hall Diaries*, 31 Mar. 1958.
34. Macmillan (1971) 723.
35. Macmillan (1971) 723.
36. Macmillan (1971) 726.
37. Macmillan (1971) 728. See also Burke Trend's minute to Macmillan, 4 Dec. 1958, PREM 11/2973 quoted Lamb 54.
38. Macmillan (1971) 728.
39. *Hall Diaries*, 5 Mar. 1959.
40. HC Debs. 7 Apr. 1959, cols. 44–8. Quoted Dow.
41. Cairncross (1992) 95.
42. At one point, a shilling reduction was considered on the recommendation of the Inland Revenue. *Hall Diaries*, 5 Mar. 1959.
43. Fisher 133. Hall describes it as a huge drop: *Hall Diaries*, 7 Apr. 1959.
44. Fisher 134.
45. *Hall Diaries*, 7 Apr. 1959.
46. *Hall Diaries*, 22 June 1959.
47. *Hall Diaries*, 7 Apr. 1959.
48. Dow, 106.
49. Horne Vol. 2, 143. Amory discussed his worries several times with Hall who assured him that there was no danger at present. *Hall Diaries*, 22 June and 21 July 1959.
50. *The Report of the Committee on the Working of the Monetary System*, Cmd. 827.
51. Quotations from Dow 108.
52. HC Debs. 26 Nov. 1959, col. 576.
53. Macmillan (1972) 162–3. But the Bank said it was due to the internal situation. *Hall Diaries*, 5 Feb. 1960.
54. Brittan (1971) 232.
55. Brittan (1971) 229.
56. Quoted Lamb 66.
57. Lamb 66.
58. Macmillan (1972) 224. Diary 25 Mar. 1960.
59. HC Debs. 4 Apr. 1960, cols. 39–40.
60. HC Debs. 4 Apr. 1960, cols. 40, 45. Quoted Dow 110–1.
61. Macmillan (1971) 703.
62. Morgan (1990) 176.
63. Macmillan (1972) 226. Diary 27 Apr. 1960.
64. These were compulsory deposits made by the banks with the Bank of England. The effect was to reduce the banks' power to lend. This first use required the banks to

deposit £70 million. Dow 111 and 111n3. Fforde 670–1.

65. Brittan (1971) 230.
66. Horne, Vol. 2 143. Interview with Lord Amory.
67. The Rt Hon. the Viscount Amory KG PC GCMG TD DL, *The Service of Youth*, The 12th Basil Henriques Memorial Lecture 1975.

CHAPTER NINE · SELWYN LLOYD: SCAPEGOAT

1. Thorpe 309.
2. Thorpe 312.
3. *Hall Diaries*, 29 July 1960.
4. Thorpe 310. Alderman 255.
5. Thorpe 308.
6. Thorpe 311.
7. *Hall Diaries*, note to entry for 27 Oct. 1954. The note was written in Feb. 1957.
8. Macmillan (1972) 371, Diary 5 Mar. 1961.
9. HC Debs. 17 Apr. 1961, col. 792.
10. HC Debs. 17 Apr. 1961, col. 801.
11. HC Debs. 17 Apr. 1961, col. 810 and 822.
12. *Cairncross Diaries*, Preface and 17 June 1961.
13. HC Debs. 9 Apr. 1962, col. 971.
14. HC Debs. 17 Apr. 1961, col. 793.
15. HC Debs. 17 Apr. 1961, col. 796.
16. HC Debs. 17 Apr. 1961, col. 797.
17. HC Debs. 17 Apr. 1961, col. 800.
18. One problem with the regulator was that it included drink and tobacco. So, if purchase tax was reduced, the reduction had to include drink and tobacco.
19. Lamb 70–1.
20. *Cairncross Diaries*, 17 June 1961. There was also the problem that it had not yet been enacted.
21. *Cairncross Diaries*, 16 Sep. 1961.

22. Macmillan (1973) 49.
23. *Hall Diaries*, 20 Nov. 1960.
24. *Hall Diaries*, 2 Apr. 1961.
25. The hot money inflow was stimulated by doubts about the dollar ahead of a Presidential election in the USA and by barriers imposed by Germany and Switzerland against the inflow of short-term funds. See Brittan (1971) 252.
26. Brittan (1971) 253.
27. *Cairncross Diaries*, 16 Sep. 1961.
28. Brittan (1971) 254. Because Cairncross had only just joined the Treasury when the July 1961 measures were announced, there were those in the Labour Party who blamed him for the deflation and the pay pause.
29. PREM 11/3757 quoted Lamb 75.
30. Macmillan (1973) 36, quoting his Diary of 9 Aug. 1961. The introduction of the pay pause was assisted by the arrival as Permanent Secretary at the Ministry of Labour of Sir Laurence Helsby, a former economics don, who did not believe the Ministry could simply conciliate whatever the cost to the economy. The Minister, John Hare, was also a personal friend of Selwyn Lloyd. See Brittan (1971) 260.
31. Morgan (1990) 211.
32. Macmillan (1973) 57–8, 63. Horne vol. 2, 336.
33. Macmillan (1972) 376, Diary 23 July 1961.
34. Plowden 23.
35. HC Debs. 25 July 1961, col. 220.
36. HC Debs. 26 July 1961, col. 439.
37. Brittan (1971) 242.
38. These phenomena are discussed by Brittan 230–1.
39. See, for example, *Cairncross Diaries*, 15 July 1962.

40. *Cairncross Diaries*, explanatory note before 14 May 1962.
41. HC Debs. 9 Apr. 1962, col. 968.
42. HC Debs. 9 Apr. 1962, col. 969.
43. Brittan draws attention to the fact that the Kennedy Administration had set a target over ten years of 50 per cent growth for the West at meetings of the OECD. Brittan (1971) 263, Callaghan 164.
44. Thorpe 318.
45. HC Debs. 9 Apr. 1962, cols. 978–9.
46. Macmillan (1973) 37, 'To Selwyn Lloyd, supported by his advisers in the Treasury, belongs the credit for this forward-looking scheme.'
47. Macmillan (1972) 375, Diary 15 July 1961.
48. Macmillan (1973) 50.
49. Macmillan (1973) 49.
50. Macmillan (1973) 36.
51. Macmillan (1973) 52.
52. *Incomes Policy: The Next Step*, Cmnd. 1626.
53. Macmillan (1973) 52–3. White Paper *Incomes Policy: The Next Step*, Cmnd. 1626.
54. Macmillan (1973) 53.
55. HC Debs. 9 Apr. 1962, col. 968.
56. HC Debs. 9 Apr. 1962, col. 990.
57. HC Debs. 9 Apr. 1962, cols. 962–3.
58. HC Debs. 9 Apr. 1962, cols. 963–4.
59. HC Debs. 9 Apr. 1962, col. 965.
60. Brittan (1971) 265.
61. HC Debs. 9 Apr. 1962, cols. 1020–1.
62. Brittan (1971) 240.
63. HC Debs. 11 Apr. 1962, col. 1405.
64. HC Debs. 11 Apr. 1962, col. 1408.
65. PREM 11/3930.
66. Macmillan (1972) 360.
67. Macmillan (1973) 35–6.
68. Macmillan (1973) 70.
69. Macmillan (1973) 68–70.
70. Macmillan (1973) 72.
71. Macmillan (1973) 86–7. The Consumers' Council was not actually created until 1976.
72. Macmillan (1973) 88.
73. Macmillan (1973) 89, Diary entry for 21 June 1962. Butler says he was first brought into consultation about government changes on 6 July. Butler 233.
74. Horne Vol. 2, 341–2.
75. Macmillan (1973) 89.
76. Macmillan (1973) 90, Diary 6 July 1962.
77. Alderman 247.
78. Macmillan (1973) 92.
79. Despite his leak, Butler still managed to be critical of Macmillan's handling of the reshuffle. Horne Vol. 2, 350.
80. Alderman 248.
81. The various, and often conflicting, explanations of Macmillan's action are discussed by Alderman, *passim*.
82. Thorpe 356.
83. Bridges 207.

CHAPTER TEN · REGINALD MAUDLING AND THE DASH FOR GROWTH

1. Jay (1980) 324.
2. *Economist*, 19 Oct. 1963.
3. Frank Lee, *Cairncross Diaries*, 16 Oct. 1963.
4. Maudling 27. Armstrong became Permanent Secretary on 30 July 1962.
5. Maudling 19.
6. Maudling 102. Thorpe 359.
7. See, for example, Thorpe 308–9.
8. If the international economy expanded too rapidly commodity prices would rise. That might be fine for the sterling area, but not for Britain.

9. Maudling 103. The Concise Oxford Dictionary tells us that the shell of the cowrie, a small gastropod of the Indian Ocean, was used as money in Africa and South Asia.

10. See, for example, *Hall Diaries*, 19 Feb. 1958.

11. Macmillan (1972) 327–8.

12. Macmillan (1973) 385.

13. See Macmillan (1972) 365 and Macmillan (1973) 381.

14. Maudling 105 and Callaghan 157.

15. Maudling 105–6. The principal author was Lucius Thompson McCausland of the Bank.

16. Maudling 106.

17. Wilson (1971) 265.

18. *Economist*, 22 Sep. 1962.

19. *Cairncross Diaries*, explanatory note before entry for 23 Jan. 1963.

20. Implemented in the 1963 Finance Act. See HC Debs. 3 Apr. 1963, cols. 487–8.

21. *Economist*, 10 Nov. 1962. The other two were Amory in 1959 and Dalton in 1945.

22. *Economist*, 6 Oct. 1962.

23. HC Debs. 3 Apr. 1963, col. 458. The January figure had been about 800,000.

24. HC Debs. 3 Apr. 1963, col. 455.

25. HC Debs. 3 Apr. 1963, col. 469.

26. Maudling 112.

27. HC Debs. 3 Apr. 1963, col. 454.

28. Maudling's Budget judgement given in HC Debs. 3 Apr. 1963, col. 472 was for tax concessions of 'about £250 million'.

29. HC Debs. 3 Apr. 1963, col. 475.

30. Macmillan (1973) 399.

31. Maudling 111. Brittan (1971) 244.

32. MacDougall 142–3.

33. HC Debs. 3 Apr. 1963, col. 476.

34. HC Debs. 4 Apr. 1963, col. 642.

35. HC Debs. 4 Apr. 1963, col. 646.

36. HC Debs. 4 Apr. 1963, col. 697.

37. HC Debs. 8 Apr. 1963, col. 1004.

38. *Cairncross Diaries*, 15 May 1963.

39. See, for example, Roy Jenkins, HC Debs. 8 Apr. 1963, cols. 999–1000.

40. HC Debs. 3 Apr. 1963, col. 470.

41. Macmillan (1973) 407 quoting Annual Register. *Cairncross Diaries*, explanatory note before entry for 8 May 1963.

42. Macmillan (1973) 399.

43. HC Debs. 3 Apr. 1963, col. 493. There were remissions of £186 million in 1963–4 and £240 million in a full year of which 42% would accrue to those earning less than £1000 p.a. and 50% to those earning between £1000 and £2000 p.a. HC Debs. 3 Apr. 1963, col. 491.

44. Brittan (1971) 280.

45. Wilson, HC Debs. 3 Apr. 1963, col. 513. Callaghan, HC Debs. 4 Apr. 1963, col. 649.

46. Brittan (1971) 280.

47. *Cairncross Diaries*, 11 Dec. 1963, particularly regarding the railway dispute.

48. HC Debs. 3 Apr. 1963, col. 471. Emphasis added.

49. Wilson (1971) 33.

50. *Cairncross Diaries*, 10 Oct. 1965, (sic).

51. Maudling 116.

52. Brittan (1971) 282. Author's emphasis.

53. Callaghan in HC Debs. 4 Apr. 1963, col. 639.

54. MacDougall 140.

55. PREM 11/4202 and 11/4209 quoted by Lamb 94, 96. Lamb 100 appears to believe that there was an *agreement* between Macmillan and Maudling that import controls and floating were to be used as ways of staving off a balance of payments crisis if it erupted before the election. If so, it shows

extraordinary naiveté on both their parts.

56. *Cairncross Diaries*, explanatory note before entry for 15 July 1962.
57. Benn (1987) 70.
58. Maudling 118. *Cairncross Diaries*, 26 Nov. 1963.
59. *Cairncross Diaries*, 6 Jan. 1964.
60. *Cairncross Diaries*, 23 Feb. 1964.
61. HC Debs. 14 Apr. 1964, col. 239. See also Maudling 116.
62. HC Debs. 14 Apr. 1964, col. 239.
63. HC Debs. 14 Apr. 1964, col. 261.
64. Cromer to Maudling, 24 July 1964, PREM 11/4771.
65. HC Debs. 14 Apr. 1964, cols. 239–40.
66. *Cairncross Diaries*, explanatory note before entry for 14 Dec. 1963.
67. HC Debs. 14 Apr. 1964, cols. 228–9.
68. Wilson, HC Debs. 14 Apr. 1964, col. 285. Callaghan, HC Debs. 15 Apr. 1964, col. 431.
69. HC Debs. 14 Apr. 1964, col. 287.
70. Cairncross later came to think that even £200 million would not have been enough to prevent an exchange crisis. *Cairncross Diaries*, 25 Dec. 1965.
71. Jenkins (1991) 291.
72. Maudling 119. After my own maiden speech in the House of Commons on 4 Nov. 1964, Maudling asked me, as a former ICI executive, why exports had responded so sluggishly to his measures. I was surprised at the question.
73. Maudling 119.
74. Maudling 119.
75. Maudling 120.
76. Maudling 116.
77. *Cairncross Diaries*, explanatory note before entry for 15 July 1962.
78. Maudling 115.
79. Brittan (1971) 85. Callaghan 163.

CHAPTER ELEVEN · JAMES CALLAGHAN: DEVALUATION DEFIED

1. Pimlott (1993) 333.
2. Callaghan 160–1.
3. For examples of his colleagues' attitudes to Callaghan as Chancellor, see Crossman (1975) *passim*.
4. Roll (1985) 149. *Cairncross Diaries*, 7 Sep. 1963.
5. *Cairncross Diaries*, 23 Oct. 1963. Leo Pliatzky was present at the lunch.
6. Jay (1980) 295, 297–9; Callaghan 164–5.
7. Brown 96 and 113.
8. cf. Wilson (1971) 5 with Callaghan 165–6.
9. Callaghan 165–6.
10. Brown 95.
11. Brown 97.
12. Eric Roll, moved from his Washington post, appears to have been none too happy to be with George Brown either; Roll (1985) 150. *Cairncross Diaries*, 16 Nov. 1964.
13. It was indicative that John Diamond, the Chief Secretary, was not a member of the Cabinet and did not become so until 1968, after devaluation. Wilson had so filled his Cabinet with new departments clamouring for representation that there was no room for the custodian of public expenditure. Successive Chief Secretaries were excluded from membership of the Cabinet throughout Heath's government. Joel Barnett, appointed Chief Secretary in 1974 by Wilson, did not join the Cabinet until 1977 after the IMF crisis.
14. See Tony Crosland, HC Debs. 4 Apr. 1963, col. 699.

15. The incentive was in the form of a remission on exports of various indirect taxes such as purchase tax notionally calculated.
16. See Roll (1985) 157-8.
17. MacDougall 152.
18. In his Budget statement on 6 Apr. 1965, Callaghan said: 'The deficit amounted to £745 million and would have been over £800 million if we had not been relieved from payments of interest and capital on our North American loan.' IIC Debs. 6 Apr. 1965, col. 244. The *current* deficit is now calculated at £362 million. Overseas investment, much of it by oil companies, accounted for about a further £300 million.
19. Callaghan 163. Brown says the decision was taken at Chequers with officials. Brown 100. Brown is wrong.
20. See for example Callaghan's response to Maudling's 1963 Budget statement. HC Debs. 4 Apr. 1963, cols. 647-8. See repeated statements to this effect quoted by Paul Foot, 138-40.
21. Callaghan 154.
22. Callaghan 159-60.
23. Wilson (1971) 6.
24. Jay (1980) 298.
25. Jenkins (1991) 157.
26. Callaghan 160.
27. Wilson (1971) 6.
28. The Soviet Union had had Bulganin and Kruschev.
29. Pimlott (1993) 352. *Cairncross Diaries*, 25 Nov. 1964. This is also MacDougall's view. MacDougall 153.
30. Ziegler 190 based on Susan Crosland. Pimlott says that by July 1966, even Balogh had decided in favour of floating. He had in fact changed his view on the exchange rate long before. Pimlott (1993) 421.
31. Ziegler 190 quoting Kellner and Hitchens, *Callaghan*, 47.
32. Callaghan 164.
33. Brown 113-5.
34. Ziegler 191.
35. Ziegler 191.
36. Pimlott (1993) 349.
37. Wilson (1991) 444. Wilson's emphasis.
38. See also Wilson (1971) 6 and Pimlott (1993) 350 quoting Brian Lapping, *The Labour Government, 1964-70*, 34.
39. Callaghan 170.
40. Callaghan 171 and HC Debs. 20 Nov. 1967, cols. 946-7. Cairncross presents evidence that the Swiss also favoured devaluation of sterling. *Cairncross Diaries*, 10 and 14 Dec. 1964.
41. Callaghan 160 uses this argument.
42. Callaghan 160 uses this argument.
43. Callaghan 160.
44. Wilson (1971) 4.
45. Neild's official title was Economic Adviser to HM Treasury.
46. *Cairncross Diaries*, 25 Nov. 1964.
47. Pimlott (1993) 354.
48. The White Paper, *The Economic Situation*, announced an intention to cancel the Anglo-French Concorde aircraft. Jenkins explains how the brusque nature of the announcement probably saved a project which the French were probably quite ready to cancel. Jenkins (1991) 166.
49. An export rebate had been recommended to Selwyn Lloyd by Treasury advisers in July 1961. *Cairncross Diaries*, entry for 14 July 1961. There is nothing new under the Treasury's sun.
50. Roll (1985) 159-60. Callaghan said that no one was consulted. HC

Debs. 24 Nov. 1964, col. 1092. Walter Padley made clear that Washington was given more notice than EFTA. HC Debs. 14 Dec. 1964, cols. 25–7.

51. Jay (1980) 298.

52. Callaghan 170.

53. Canada had imposed an import surcharge in 1962. There was, therefore a precedent. GATT disliked it but Canada did not suffer the embarrassment of dealing with EFTA.

54. The EFTA countries had exactly the same margin of preference as before over other *foreign* competitors but were placed at a disadvantage in the UK market as compared with UK suppliers.

55. Paragraph 7. For Opposition exploitation of this sentence, see for example Heath, HC Debs. 1 Mar. 1966, col. 1132.

56. 1% unemployment was equal to about 250,000.

57. HC Debs, 7 Dec. 1964, col. 1263.

58. Jay (1980) 313.

59. The Treasury itself had, a week earlier, opposed the increase as reflecting on the Budget.

60. Callaghan 173; Wilson (1971) 36. *Cairncross Diaries*, 24 Nov. 1964. Johnson had argued for coordination of interest rate movements before the Bank Rate increase of 27 Feb. 1964.

61. Wilson (1971) 35.

62. Announced by Callaghan, HC Debs. 22 Feb. 1965, cols. 31–4.

63. Wilson (1971) 37.

64. Wilson (1971) 37. Callaghan 174–6.

65. Ziegler 194 quoting Castle Diaries, 58.

66. Ziegler 194 quoting Michael Stewart, *The Jekyll and Hyde Years*, 35.

67. Wilson (1971) 32.

68. Wilson (1971) 31.

69. *Cairncross Diaries*, 25 Nov. 1964.

70. *Cairncross Diaries*, 27 Dec. 1964.

71. HC Debs. 6 Apr. 1965, col. 244. The method of reducing net capital outflow was primarily through the new Corporation Tax and changes in exchange control. See HC Debs. 6 Apr. 1965, cols. 261–73. Capital outflow was, of course, encouraged by an overvalued exchange rate.

72. HC Debs. 6 Apr. 1965, col. 244.

73. There was a call for special deposits on 29 April. On advice of the Governor, there was a cut in Bank Rate on 27 May, intended to demonstrate the government's confidence in its policies, partly compensated by tougher hire purchase restrictions announced at the same time. The Governor's advice was almost certainly mistaken.

74. *Cairncross Diaries*, 6 and 29 April, 22 May and 25 June 1965.

75. HC Debs. 27 July 1965, cols. 228–32.

76. *Cairncross Diaries*, 25 and 29 July 1965.

77. HC Debs. 27 July 1965, col. 230.

78. Ziegler 204–5.

79. *Cairncross Diaries*, 15 Mar. 1966.

80. Wilson (1971) 131–3 tells the story. Date from Callaghan 190. Brittan (1971) 310 gives the date as 8 September.

81. MacDougall 161 refers to pressure from the USA, in August 1965, for a tightening-up of prices and incomes policy.

82. Callaghan 190.

83. MacDougall 159 describes some last-minute hesitations on the part of the CBI.

84. MacDougall 156–7.

85. Cairncross (1992) 15.
86. Callaghan 182–4.
87. Pliatzky (1982) 64. Pliatzky comments ironically on the word 'limit'.
88. For the story of the IRC, see Dell (1973) Chapter 3.
89. Wilson (1971) 202.
90. Brittan (1971) 322–3.
91. HC Debs. 7 Feb. 1966, cols. 31–2.
92. HC Debs. 8 Feb. 1966, col. 216. The NIESR was making less confident noises about the balance of payments. Brittan (1971) 323.
93. HC Debs. 1 Mar. 1966, col. 1114.
94. HC Debs. 1 Mar. 1966, col. 1116.
95. Callaghan 193. Wilson (1971) 201.
96. *Cairncross Diaries*, 13, 22 and 23 Mar. 1966.
97. *Cairncross Diaries*, 3 and 13 Apr. 1966.
98. Callaghan 193.
99. HC Debs. 3 May 1966, col. 1460.
100. Callaghan 196.
101. Callaghan 196.
102. The circumstances of the admitted discourtesy are described in Wilson (1971) 249.
103. Callaghan 197.
104. Callaghan 197.
105. Pimlott (1993) 414–5. Jenkins (1991) 191 and 193.
106. Pimlott (1993) 421.
107. Pimlott (1993) 417–19 reviews this story.
108. HC Debs. 14 July 1966, cols. 1733–5.
109. Wilson (1971) 257.
110. Callaghan 199 lists the supporters and opponents of devaluation. According to Callaghan, one future Chancellor, Roy Jenkins, supported it. Another, Denis Healey, opposed it. The alleged identity between the devaluationists and the pro-Europeans seems somewhat overdone. Some anti-Europeans, such as Crossman, supported devaluation. According to Pimlott (1993) 424–5, Jenkins was in July 1966 not clearly for devaluation. It appears that the subject may have been considered on its merits rather than as a by-product of other commitments.
111. Callaghan 200.
112. HC Debs. 20 July 1966, col. 627.
113. HC Debs. 20 July 1966, col. 628.
114. HC Debs. 20 July 1966, col. 636–7.
115. Prices and Incomes Act 1966, Public General Acts and Measures of 1966, chapter 33. The powers were contained in Part IV of the new Bill.
116. Callaghan 202.
117. Callaghan 203–4 tells how he threatened resignation in order to secure from Wilson a sensible division of responsibilities between the Treasury and the DEA. He did not get it but in any case it was much less necessary. With the departure of Brown, the DEA had in any case lost status.
118. Pimlott (1993) 438.
119. Brittan (1971) 349.
120. Brown 118.
121. HC Debs. 27 July 1966, col. 1849.
122. HC Debs. 27 July 1966, col. 1850.
123. HC Debs. 27 July 1966, col. 1848.
124. Callaghan 205–6. ASSET was the Association of Supervisory Staffs, Executives and Technicians. The General Secretary was Clive Jenkins.
125. Unemployment reached 515,000 in the first quarter of 1967. Pimlott (1993) 430.

126. MacDougall 171 explains why REP involved no real economic costs to the economy.

127. HC Debs. 11 Apr. 1967, col. 976.

128. HC Debs. 11 Apr. 1967, col. 975.

129. See Dell (1991) for my conversation with Callaghan at Nuffield College in early 1967.

130. Brittan (1971) 340.

131. HC Debs. 11 Apr. 1967, col. 994.

132. HC Debs. 11 Apr. 1967, col. 993-4.

133. HC Debs. 11 Apr. 1967, col. 994.

134. HC Debs. 11 Apr. 1967, col. 1010.

135. Callaghan 210.

136. HC Debs. 17 Apr. 1967, col. 92-3.

137. Brittan 350.

138. The borrowing requirement was at one stage estimated at £1,400 million but eventually calculated in the Budget statement as nearly £1 billion. HC Debs. 11 Apr. 1967, col. 997 and 1010.

139. *Cairncross Diaries*, 20 and 28 Feb. and 27 Mar. 1967.

140. Callaghan 209-10.

141. HC Debs. 11 Apr. 1967, col. 977. The Group of Ten supplemented the work of the IMF.

142. SDRs were a form of IMF 'gold'.

143. Callaghan 211.

144. Wilson (1991) 400.

145. Brittan 349.

146. The author was a DEA Minister.

147. Brittan 352-3.

148. Brittan 354. Actually there was a deficit of £700 million.

149. Brittan 355. Wilson (1971) 443.

150. Wilson (1991) 444.

151. In announcing the government's intention to probe the possibility of entry into the EEC, Wilson said that 'it is vital that we should enter only when we have secured a healthy economy and a strong

balance of payments, with the £ standing no less firm and high than it is today.' HC Debs. 10 Nov. 1966, col. 1540.

152. Crossman Vol. 2 567.

153. Wilson (1971) 448.

154. Wilson (1971) 452, 454.

155. Wilson (1971) 453, 455.

156. George Brown as Foreign Secretary was now less enthusiastic about devaluation than he had been as Secretary of State for Economic Affairs. Wilson (1971) 452.

157. Jenkins (1991) 282.

158. Wilson (1971) 455-6 does not explain why he abandoned his earlier preference for floating.

159. HC Debs. 16 Nov. 1967, cols. 632-5.

160. Jenkins (1991) 213.

161. Jenkins (1991) 213 says that Sheldon *was* asked to withdraw the PNQ. Sheldon informs me that this is not correct.

162. Wilson (1991) 400.

163. Callaghan 217.

164. HC Debs. 20 Nov. 1967, cols. 935-9. The government's statement on 18 November is at HC Debs. 20 Nov. 1967, cols. 951-2.

165. Wilson (1971) 464.

166. Wilson (1971) 467.

CHAPTER TWELVE · ROY JENKINS: MASTERY IN RETROSPECT

1. Jenkins (1991) 220.

2. Jenkins (1991) 221.

3. HC Debs. 5 Dec. 1967, col. 1152.

4. HC Debs. 5 Dec. 1967, col. 1199.

5. Jenkins (1991) 222.

6. Callaghan 221.

7. Crossman (1976) 613-53 *passim*;

Castle (1984) 348-59 *passim*; Benn (1988) 1-17 *passim*. See also Crosland (1982) 193-4.

8. Wilson (1971) 483.
9. Jenkins (1991) 230.
10. Jenkins (1991) 282.
11. The expansion in 1968 was £1,900 million. HC Debs. 14 Apr. 1970, col. 1223.
12. Cairncross draft.
13. Wilson (1971) 583. Jenkins (1991) 264-5.
14. Crosland announced a tightening in hire purchase controls on 1 Nov. 1968. HC Debs. 1 Nov. 1968, cols. 345-54.
15. HC Debs. 22 Nov. 1968 cols. 1790-7. Ceilings were relaxed in September 1969 but over calendar year 1969 restricted lending by the banking system as a whole fell by about £40 million. HC Debs. 14 Apr. 1970, col. 1222.
16. HC Debs. 14 Apr. 1970, col. 1223.
17. About £600 million in 1969-70, a turnaround of about £2,250 million over two years.
18. Jenkins (1991) 249.
19. Jenkins (1991) 249.
20. Ziegler 299.
21. Castle, *Diaries*, 15 Dec. 1968. Castle omits the sleeping presence of Jenkins. The author was also present as he was staying the night at Chequers. He was a silent witness of the proceedings.
22. HC Debs. 15 Apr. 1969, cols. 1003-6.
23. Jenkins (1991) 287.
24. Wilson (1971) 643.
25. Jenkins (1991) 290.
26. Ziegler 312.
27. Callaghan 277. Wilson discusses the concessions that were made by the TUC in Wilson 649 ff.
28. HC Debs. 14 Apr. 1970, col. 1214.
29. HC Debs. 14 Apr. 1970, cols. 1214-15
30. HC Debs. 14 Apr. 1970, col. 1215.
31. HC Debs. 14 Apr. 1970, col. 1215.
32. HC Debs. 14 Apr. 1970, col. 1216.
33. HC Debs. 14 Apr. 1970, cols. 1216-21.
34. HC Debs. 14 Apr. 1970, cols. 1224-5.
35. Brittan (1971) 407.
36. HC Debs. 14 Apr. 1970, cols. 1231 and 1251.
37. Jenkins (1991) 292.
38. MacDougall 178.
39. HC Debs. 22 Mar. 1972, col. 1526.
40. Brittan (1971) 408.
41. Wilson (1971) 790.

CHAPTER THIRTEEN · ANTHONY BARBER, CHANCELLOR IN OFFICE BUT NOT IN POWER

1. Butler (1982) 110.
2. Walker 53.
3. Shepherd 534.
4. HC Debs. 7 July 1970, col. 504. He said that between 1958-64 there was an annual rate of price increase of 2.2%; between 1964-7, 3.7%, in 1968 and 1969 5% and in the three months to May 1970, 5.5%.
5. HC Debs. 7 July 1970, col. 511.
6. Even working in a merchant bank, which Heath had done, was not evidence.
7. 'The Heath Government', ed. Michael David Kandiah, *Contemporary Record*, Volume 9, Summer 1995, Number 1204.
8. Blackstone and Plowden 77.
9. The First Report of the PAC, Session 1972-3, *North Sea Oil and Gas*, was published on 1 Mar. 1973. See also Edmund Dell, 'Origins of Petroleum Revenue Tax',

Contemporary Record, Volume 7, Number 2, Autumn 1993.

10. HC Debs. 27 Oct. 1970, cols. 37–51.
11. HC Debs. 2 Nov. 1970, col. 668.
12. HC Debs. 30 Mar. 1971, cols. 1358–9.
13. HC Debs. 30 Mar. 1971, col. 1360.
14. HC Debs. 30 Mar. 1971, col. 1369.
15. HC Debs. 30 Mar. 1971, col. 1361.
16. HC Debs. 30 Mar. 1971, col. 1361.
17. HC Debs. 30 Mar. 1971, col. 1363.
18. HC Debs. 30 Mar. 1971, col. 1362.
19. HC Debs. 30 Mar. 1971, col. 1371.
20. HC Debs. 30 Mar. 1971, col. 1370.
21. HC Debs. 30 Mar. 1971, col. 1374.
22. HC Debs. 28 June 1971, cols. 54–5.
23. HC Debs. 19 July 1971, cols. 1035–41.
24. HC Debs. 30 Mar. 1971, col. 1396.
25. HC Debs. 2 Nov. 1971, col. 5.
26. MacDougall 190.
27. Burk and Cairncross 198.
28. MacDougall 190.
29. MacDougall 188–9.
30. HC Debs. 20 Dec. 1971, cols. 1115–18.
31. HC Debs. 23 Nov. 1971, col. 1259.
32. HC Debs. 21 Mar. 1971, col. 1354.
33. HC Debs. 21 Mar. 1972, col. 1343.
34. HC Debs. 21 Mar. 1972, cols. 1345–6.
35. HC Debs. 21 Mar. 1972, col. 1351.
36. HC Debs. 21 Mar. 1972, col. 1353.
37. HC Debs. 21 Mar. 1972, col. 1366.
38. HC Debs. 21 Mar. 1972, cols. 1366–9.
39. HC Debs. 21 Mar. 1972, cols. 1389–90.
40. In his 1973 Budget, Barber thought it would prove to be about £500 million less than his estimate the year before. HC Debs. 6 Mar. 1973, col. 252.
41. HC Debs. 21 Mar. 1972, col. 1347.
42. HC Debs. 21 Mar. 1972, col. 1390.
43. HC Debs. 21 Mar. 1972, col. 1390.
44. HC Debs. 22 Mar. 1972, col. 1528.
45. Dell (1973) 22.
46. HC Debs. 21 Mar. 1972, col. 1354.
47. HC Debs. 21 Mar. 1972, col. 1354.
48. HC Debs. 23 June 1972, cols. 877–9.
49. HC Debs. 6 Nov. 1972, cols. 626–7.
50. HC Debs. 6 Nov. 1972, cols. 631–2.
51. Keegan and Pennant-Rea 27.
52. *NIER*, Feb. 1973, 5–6.
53. HC Debs. 6 Mar. 1973, col. 248.
54. HC Debs. 6 Mar. 1973, cols. 253–4.
55. HC Debs. 21 May 1973, cols. 38–43. The £500 million is at 1972 prices.
56. *NIER*, May 1973, 5.
57. Sterling rose against the devalued dollar by 4%.
58. *NIER*, Feb. 1973, 57.
59. *NIER*, Nov. 1973, 3–5.
60. Quoted by Denis Healey, HC Debs. 11 Mar. 1976, col. 746.
61. Castle 29.
62. *NIER*, May 1973, 5, 6.
63. HC Debs. 6 Feb. 1974, col. 1227.
64. HC Debs. 17 Dec. 1973, cols. 952–66.
65. Campbell 583 makes this point in his excellent biography of Edward Heath.
66. HC Debs. 6 Feb. 1974, col. 1242.

CHAPTER FOURTEEN · THE THREE HEALEYS

1. Wilson (1979) 17.
2. *Institutional Investor*, June 1987, 66.
3. Dryden wrote a poem, *Absalom and Achitophel*, in which he brilliantly characterized the politicians of his age.
4. MacDougall 208.

5. HC Debs. 6 Feb. 1974, col. 1230.
6. Garritsen de Vries (1985) 199.
7. At the time of his March 1974 Budget, Healey was able to announce a $2.5 billion loan for ten years and that the inter-central bank swap arrangement was being raised from $2.5 billion to $3 billion. HC Debs. 26 Mar. 1974, col. 286.
8. Healey 422–3.
9. HC Debs. 26 Mar. 1974, col. 294.
10. His deputy was this author.
11. Various tax reductions and subsidies, at a cost of some £340 million to the PSBR, were designed to have a direct impact on retail prices calculated at 1.5% within the following three months. HC Debs. 22 July 1974, cols. 1048–53.
12. HC Debs. 12 Nov. 1974, col. 279.
13. See Dell (1991) 112, 126.
14. HC Debs. 15 Apr. 1975, col. 281.
15. HC Debs. 15 Apr. 1975, cols. 285–6.
16. HC Debs. 15 Apr. 1975, col. 319.
17. HC Debs. 15 Apr. 1975, cols. 279, 287.
18. HC Debs. 15 Apr. 1975, col. 284.
19. Healey 378–9.
20. Britton 299 asserts that the form of the 1975 incomes policy caused inflation to be *higher* than it would have been under free collective bargaining.
21. Burk and Cairncross 189, Table 9.
22. Donoughue 83–4.
23. Castle (1980) 548–9.
24. Cmnd. 6393.
25. Cmnd. 5879.
26. Garritsen de Vries (1985) 465–6.
27. Dell (1991) 195.
28. *NIER*, Feb. 1976, 3, 13–14, 70.
29. MLR may be regarded as another name for Bank Rate.
30. *Bank of England Quarterly Bulletin* for June 1976.
31. Traders with sterling who were going to need foreign currency bought it early. Those who were going to need sterling waited as long as possible before buying it in the expectation that it might be cheaper. This combination is known as 'leads and lags'.
32. HC Debs. 6 Apr. 1976, col. 245.
33. HC Debs. 6 Apr. 1976, col. 280.
34. The PSBR for 1975–6 was of the order of £40 billion in 1988 money or about £60 billion in current money. See Lawson's 1988 Budget statement and Lawson 811.
35. HC Debs. 6 Apr. 1976, cols. 236, 281.
36. How far Zijlstra was unique in his perception of the need for a stand-by is discussed in Burk and Cairncross 39–41.
37. Healey 419–20.
38. Burk and Cairncross 47–8.
39. HC Debs. 22 July 1976, col. 2019.
40. Quoted by Pliatzky (1989) 123. See also Healey 383.
41. Callaghan 426–7.
42. Barnett J. 101.
43. It seems that Callaghan had suggested that Jenkins might return to the Treasury in due course Jenkins (1991) 441.
44. Dell (1991) 239–41.
45. Pliatzky (1982) 153.
46. Lever's visit to Washington is covered in Burk and Cairncross 76–82.
47. Dell (1991) 251.
48. Pliatzky (1982) 53.
49. Crosland 377–8.
50. *Panorama* on 25 October.
51. Benn (1989) 670–1.
52. Crosland 381–2.
53. HC Debs. 15 Dec. 1976, col. 1525.
54. Barnett J. 110, 115–16.
55. The previous system of control by

'volume' involved automatic adjustment as prices rose.

56. Burk and Cairncross 190.
57. Burk and Cairncross, Chapter 4, gives a full account of the discussions leading up to the January 1977 agreement on the sterling balances.
58. Callaghan 446.
59. For a detailed account of Britain's role in the origins of the EMS, see Edmund Dell, 'Britain and the Origins of the European Monetary System', *Contemporary European History*, Volume 3, Part 1, March 1994.
60. Healey 438. On the other hand this was not the view of the Bundesbank. Otmar Emminger, President of the Bundesbank, asserted that 'we in Germany do not consider the EMS as an arrangement for artificially holding the exchange rate of the Dmark down (as has often been imputed to us by foreign observers).' Financial Times Conference, Frankfurt, 14 and 15 Feb. 1979, 20.
61. Healey 439.
62. For a more detailed account of the Treasury's advice, see Edmund Dell, 'Britain and the Origins of the European Monetary System', *Contemporary European History*, Volume 3, Part 1, March 1994.
63. Barber had given it as one of his conditions for sterling's participation in a common float that 'each member must have an unimpaired right to change its central rate after consultation with the Council of Ministers.' HC Debs. 6 Mar. 1973, col. 244.
64. Healey 439.
65. Healey 439.
66. Twelfth General Report on the Activities of the European Communities, Feb. 1979, 19.
67. Twelfth General Report on the Activities of the European Communities, Feb. 1979, 76.
68. At Frankfurt on 29 June 1993, Helmut Schlesinger, President of the Bundesbank, said that 75% of transactions in ERM currencies in 1992 were in DM. *Financial Times*, 30 June 1993.
69. According to OECD, the French since 1975 have had the worst unemployment record of any major industrialized country.
70. HC Debs. 11 Apr. 1978, col. 1194.
71. HC Debs. 11 Apr. 1978, col. 1194.
72. Even on 3 May 1979, after the winter of discontent, Labour's vote was higher than in October 1974.

CHAPTER FIFTEEN · SIR GEOFFREY HOWE: THE SEARCH FOR CERTAINTY

1. Young (1989) 146.
2. Howe 94.
3. Thatcher 7.
4. Thatcher 7.
5. Howe 98, 255. In this he had the support of Mrs Thatcher. See Thatcher 114 ff.
6. Thatcher 114 ff. See Edmund Dell, 'The Chrysler UK Rescue', *Contemporary Record*, Volume 6, Number 1, Summer 1992.
7. Prior 122.
8. Howe 147–8.
9. Lawson 1042. The whole text of the talk is given as Annex 1. See also Lawson 69–70.
10. Thatcher 33.
11. A theme to which he returns repeatedly. See Lawson 11, 478, 668, 686.
12. £M3 is cash plus bank deposits.

£M4 is £M3 plus building society deposits. £Mo is cash. The £ signifies that these are measures of sterling and that they exclude foreign currencies.

13. Howe 157.
14. Quoted Johnson 38.
15. Ridley 184.
16. Ridley 189.
17. Thatcher noticed that, in 1981, Lawson took a different view from other Treasury Ministers on membership of the ERM. Thatcher 693. Ridley 183 believed that Howe also was beginning to believe that it was impossible 'to rely entirely on mercurial and unreliable monetary indicators' and that he was therefore turning his gaze towards the ERM.
18. Howe 145.
19. Howe 126.
20. See Edmund Dell, 'The Origins of Petroleum Revenue Tax', *Contemporary Record*, Volume 7, Number 2, Autumn 1993.
21. Howe 116.
22. Unemployment was falling until the end of 1979.
23. Gilmour 60.
24. Young (1989) 129.
25. Prior 120–1.
26. Britton 45.
27. Quoted Johnson 6.
28. 1979 Budget speech.
29. Lawson 693.
30. Howe 130–1, Thatcher 42–3.
31. Lawson 687.
32. Gilmour 22.
33. A new index, the Tax and Prices Index (TPI) was produced in August 1979 to deal with this irrationality but has had little success in that respect. Lawson 48.
34. Lawson 37.
35. Gilmour 38n.
36. Thatcher 44–5.
37. Thatcher 50.
38. Howe 128.
39. It is right to record at this point that Lawson denies that revenue was any part of the motivation for privatization. He claims the support of Sir Leo Pliatzky but Pliatzky was less categorical.
40. Lawson admits that the Tories overdid it. Lawson 187–90.
41. Howe 142, Thatcher 44.
42. Howe 143.
43. Walker 161; Young (1989) 202.
44. This author. Lord Lever supported the abolition of exchange control in the House of Lords.
45. Howe 162.
46. Sterling M3, often written as £M3, is the so-called 'broad' definition of the sterling money stock favoured at the time in the Treasury. There are other narrower and also broader definitions. All are difficult to measure and impossible to control.
47. Lawson 1021.
48. Lawson Chapter 7.
49. Gilmour 27.
50. Young (1989) 203.
51. Quoted Johnson 41.
52. Thatcher 96.
53. Howe 163, Lawson 71.
54. Lawson 67.
55. Lawson 111–13, 138.
56. Thatcher 97.
57. Gilmour 41.
58. Gilmour 26.
59. Howe 169.
60. Young (1989) 157.
61. Prior 119.
62. Thatcher 281.
63. Howe 149.
64. Howe 169–70.
65. Young (1989) 204.
66. It was called monetary base control.
67. Howe 184–7, Lawson 78–82.
68. Lawson 85, Howe 186.

69. Thatcher 691–3. Howe 274–5.
70. Britton 308 and Lawson 63 believe that membership of the ERM *might* have enabled the top to be shaved off the sterling rate at the end of 1980 and the beginning of 1981.
71. Young (1989) 206.
72. Lawson 88.
73. Howe 202.
74. Howe 203.
75. Howe 203.
76. Thatcher 136.
77. Lawson 94–5, 98.
78. Prior 140.
79. Walker 159–60. Prior 140.
80. Gilmour 29.
81. Prior 119.
82. Lawson 96.
83. Walker 160.
84. Prior 141.
85. Prior 141.
86. Gilmour 41.
87. Gilmour 38.
88. Gilmour 38.
89. Gilmour 38.
90. Pym 147.
91. Carrington 309–10. Lawson 108.
92. Cripps was an adviser to Tony Benn.
93. *Guardian*, 16 Mar. 1981.
94. *Times*, 30 Mar. 1981. Reprinted in Lawson 97. The former chief economic advisers who signed were Robert Hall, Alec Cairncross, Bryan Hopkin, Kenneth Berrill and Fred Atkinson. Donald MacDougall did not sign.
95. Britton 56–7; Howe 209.
96. Lawson 98.
97. Johnson 11–14 assembles a variety of more or less relevant comparisons.
98. Johnson 25.
99. MLR had been abolished in August 1981 and replaced by Base Rate which, for our purposes, is the same thing.
100. Young (1989) 232–3.
101. Young (1989) 218–19.
102. Howe 222–3, Thatcher 148–9.
103. Whitelaw 252–3.
104. Young (1989) 246.
105. Howe 240.
106. Quoted Johnson 48.
107. Young (1989) 322.
108. See Lawson 449 for his judgement of the target actually hit by Howe!
109. Johnson 86.
110. Definitions of unemployment have varied over the period. Conservative politicians of the 1980s tend to use definitions that lower the figures. On any definition unemployment was getting on for three times its level in May 1979.
111. Howe 298.
112. Thatcher 14.
113. Thatcher 272.
114. Howe 110–12.
115. Howe 274.
116. Howe 276.

CHAPTER SIXTEEN · NIGEL LAWSON: THATCHER'S INSEPARABLE ANTAGONIST

1. Lawson 250.
2. Lawson 702.
3. Baker 310 comments, however, that Lawson 'was not someone to listen to when it came to investing the family legacy'.
4. Howe 112.
5. Howe 168.
6. Young (1989) 333–4. Whitelaw 252.
7. Lawson 248, 255.
8. Lawson 207, 215–16. See also Walker 189–90 on Lawson's objection to the way in which British Gas was privatized.
9. Lawson 586.

10. Peter Walker appears to feel let-down by Lawson in the battle against the poll tax. Walker 186, 225.
11. Lawson 742.
12. The Toronto terms. Lawson 742–4.
13. Lawson 282.
14. Lawson 282.
15. Lawson 305–6.
16. Lawson 315.
17. Britton 80.
18. Lawson 300.
19. Lawson 339.
20. Lawson 345.
21. Lawson 816–17.
22. Lawson 351.
23. Lawson 344.
24. Lawson 414.
25. Lawson 414–15.
26. Lawson 415. Lawson also considers the exceptional situations which might arise if there are shocks such as the collapse of the American banking system in 1931. Lawson 421.
27. Lawson 416.
28. Lawson 460.
29. Lawson 447–8.
30. Lawson 454. See Britton 268 Table 17.
31. Lawson 481.
32. Lawson 457.
33. Lawson 454.
34. Actually the analogy is imperfect. MO was a proxy for a fire alarm, not itself the fire alarm.
35. Lawson 455, 807, 938.
36. Lawson 646, 807. Goodhart's law derives ultimately from the Heisenberg uncertainty principle.
37. Lawson 482.
38. Ridley 189. See also Ridley 193.
39. Lawson 464.
40. Lawson 481.
41. Lawson 814. The other was tax reform.
42. Thatcher 694.
43. Lawson 738.
44. Lawson 756.
45. Lawson 860, 944.
46. Lawson 455 comments that in 1988 the Bundesbank switched from equivalent of Mo to M3 'to the considerable discomfort of other ERM members'.
47. Lawson 892–4.
48. Lawson 419–20.
49. Lawson 488. Thatcher 695.
50. Lawson 584 refers to the 'gradual loosening of public expenditure control' between October 1989 and the 1992 election.
51. Lawson 498, 420.
52. Lawson 504.
53. Lawson 491.
54. Lawson 503. In private meetings, the Germans had suggested DM 3.50 to 3.75. See Lawson 501.
55. Lawson 503, 653.
56. Lawson 495.
57. Lawson gives the full text of this memorandum as Annex 2. The fact that it was Remembrance Day would have stirred all Mrs Thatcher's anti-German predilections.
58. Howe 450. Lawson 499.
59. Lawson 499. Thatcher 697–8. Howe 450.
60. She uses the word 'veto'. Thatcher 701.
61. Howe 450.
62. In answer to a question at an ICBH seminar on 9 Mar. 1994. See *Contemporary Record*, 8/3, Winter 1994.
63. Ridley 207.
64. Thatcher 706.
65. Lawson 867–73. The text of his memorandum to the Prime Minister is given as Annex 3.
66. Lawson 788, 790.
67. Lawson 788. Lawson 801–3

discusses whether sterilized intervention is inflationary and whether it is effective. He believes that it can be effective and that it is certainly not inflationary. The Bundesbank believes it can be inflationary. Mrs Thatcher, advised by Alan Walters, believed that it could be inflationary because the large inflow of capital, even if sterilized, enabled the Chancellor to justify lower interest rates than would otherwise be necessary. Thatcher 694, 702.

68. Lawson 734.
69. Edmund Dell, 'Britain and the Origins of the European Monetary System', *Contemporary European History*, Volume 3, Part 1, March 1994.
70. Lawson 783.
71. Lawson 785.
72. Lawson 785, 796.
73. Lawson 788.
74. Lawson 785–6. *Financial Times* 23 Nov. 1987.
75. Lawson 786.
76. Thatcher 701.
77. Lawson 739.
78. Thatcher 701–2.
79. Baker 419.
80. Thatcher 703. She explains why she did not sack Lawson though 'fully justified in doing so'.
81. Lawson 750, 786–7.
82. Lawson 789.
83. Lawson 789.
84. Lawson 795. Thatcher 702–3.
85. Lawson 796.
86. Lawson 831. The Treasury, in an assessment of policy at Lawson's request a year later, concluded that the DM should have been shadowed at DM 3.30 rather than DM 3, and that it had excusably overlooked both the unprecedented investment boom and the unprecedented fall in the savings ratio. Lawson 799–800. Lawson suggests that the Treasury might also have referred to the effects of financial deregulation.
87. Howe 451.
88. Yet in his resignation speech on 31 October 1989 Lawson was to describe membership of the ERM as 'not indispensable'. Lawson 1063.
89. Lawson 799.
90. Lawson 830–3.
91. Lawson 846. The deficit for the first four months as originally stated was £2.4 billion. Later revision showed it to be £4 billion.
92. Lawson 833.
93. Lawson 836.
94. Lawson 830, 832.
95. Thatcher 705.
96. Lawson 837. Thatcher's account is in Thatcher 704–5.
97. Lawson 860 tells us that his wife was advising him to resign.
98. Lawson 846.
99. Lawson 870.
100. The distinguished economist, William Cline, wrote an article 'Managing International Debt', in *The Economist* of 18 February 1995: 'The current Mexican crisis reflects a policy error in one specific area: excessive reliance on the "exchange-rate anchor" strategy to fight inflation, with a resultingly overvalued exchange rate and an excessive current-account deficit. This experience should retire once and for all Nigel Lawson's thesis in the late 1980s that large current-account deficits are not a problem if they are not caused by a large fiscal deficit.'
101. Lawson 918.
102. Lawson 908.
103. Howe 534.

104. Thatcher 709, 711. Howe 578.
105. Thatcher 710.
106. Howe 579.
107. Howe 580. Lawson 933.
108. Alan Walters had helped her to list her conditions. Thatcher 709. Howe 582.
109. Howe 587, 594.
110. Howe 586–7.
111. Lawson 949.
112. Lawson 919.
113. Lawson 920.
114. Thatcher 690, 691, 697.
115. Lawson 847–8, 921.
116. Thatcher 707.
117. Lawson 950–2.
118. Lawson 466, 654, 954.
119. Quoted Lawson 955.
120. Baker 308.
121. Thatcher 715.
122. Lawson 662.
123. Baker 311–12.
124. Lawson 970 and Annex 4.
125. Gilmour 56.
126. Gilmour 68.
127. Gilmour 6, 74.
128. Pym 144–7.
129. Gilmour 62.
130. Lawson 638.
131. Lawson 478.
132. As at the time of his 1987 Budget. Lawson 477, 686. Lawson 478 refers to Treasury wish to get borrowing down which would help with interest rates and to its 'austere quasi-moral disapproval' of any significant reduction in tax rates.
133. Thatcher 698–9.
134. Lawson 660–1, 666–7.
135. Lawson 685.
136. Johnson 25 believes that fiscal action rather than monetary action was required because increases in interest rates did not help the supply side.
137. Howe 451.

138. Thatcher 690.
139. Lawson 629.
140. Lawson 630.
141. Lawson 628.
142. Lawson 630.
143. Lawson 839–41.
144. Lawson 848. See also Lawson 851–2.
145. Lawson 852.
146. Lawson 631.
147. Lawson 639.
148. Lawson 747.
149. Lawson 750–1.
150. Lawson 749–50.
151. Lawson 748.
152. Lawson 751.
153. Lawson 643, 687, 806.
154. Lawson 806–7.
155. Lawson 390.
156. Lawson 390.
157. Lawson 804.
158. Lawson 390, 806.
159. Lawson 805–7.
160. Lawson 631–2.
161. Howe 606.
162. Lawson 639, 645, 732.
163. Lawson 632.
164. Lawson 829.
165. Lawson 811–13.
166. Lawson 976–7.
167. Johnson 11.
168. Lawson 804.
169. Lawson 805.
170. Johnson 13.

CHAPTER SEVENTEEN · JOHN MAJOR: IN AND OUT OF THE ERM

1. Thatcher 717.
2. *Effect*, 183.
3. Lawson 719–20.
4. Thatcher 719.
5. *Effect* 204 n. 11.
6. The idea of competing currencies would become more practical with the arrival of electronic money.

7. Baker 369 reports a conversation in which Major emphasized inflation as a prime reason for joining the ERM.
8. Thatcher 719.
9. Thatcher 722–3.
10. Baker 368.
11. Howe 639.
12. Thatcher 719. This is confirmed by Baker 370.
13. Howe 639.
14. In his first speech in the House as Chancellor, 29 June 1983, Lawson 271.
15. Thatcher 723.
16. Lawson 1009–10.
17. Lawson 1010–11.
18. Lawson 1024.
19. See, for example, Roll (1995) 68.
20. Thatcher 724.
21. Lawson 1015.
22. In a speech to the CBI Eastern Region Annual Dinner on 8 October 1992, quoted by Peter Jay in *Effect* 185.

Select Bibliography

PUBLIC RECORD OFFICE FILES, PARLIAMENTARY DEBATES, AND
PRIVATE COLLECTIONS

As indicated in notes

BOOKS AND ARTICLES

Alderman, Keith, 'Harold Macmillan's Night of the Long Knives' in
  Contemporary Record, Vol. 6, No. 2, Autumn 1992.
Allen, W. Gore, *The Reluctant Politician: Derick Heathcoat Amory*, Christopher
  Johnson, London, 1958.
Attlee, C. R., *As It Happened*, Odhams, London, undated.
Baker, Kenneth, *The Turbulent Years: My Life in Politics*, Faber & Faber,
  London, 1993.
Balfour, Corinna, *The Anglo-American Loan Negotiations – The US viewpoint*,
  Appendix C to Fforde, John, *The Bank of England and Public Policy, 1941–
  58*, Cambridge University Press, Cambridge, 1992.
Bank of England, *The Development and Operation of Monetary Policy, 1960–
  1983*, Clarendon Press, Oxford, 1984.
Barnett, Correlli, *The Audit of War: The Illusion and Reality of Britain as a
  Great Nation*, Papermac, London, 1991.
  The Lost Victory: British Dreams, British Realities 1945–1950, Macmillan,
  London, 1995.
Barnett, Joel, *Inside the Treasury*, André Deutsch, London, 1982.
ed. Beckerman, Wilfred, *The Labour Government's Economic Record, 1964–
  1970*, Gerald Duckworth, London, 1972.
Benn, Tony, *Out of the Wilderness, Diaries 1963–67*, Hutchinson, London,
  1987.
  Office without Power, Diaries 1968–72, Hutchinson, London, 1988.
  Against the Tide, Diaries 1973–76, Hutchinson, London, 1989.
  Conflicts of Interest, Diaries 1977–80, Hutchinson, London, 1990.
Beveridge, Lord, *Power and Influence, An Autobiography*, Hodder & Stoughton,
  London, 1953.
Birkenhead, Lord, *The Prof in Two Worlds*, Collins, London, 1961.
  Walter Monckton, Weidenfeld & Nicolson, London, 1969.

Blackstone, Tessa, and Plowden, William, *Inside the Think Tank: Advising the Cabinet 1971–1983*, William Heinemann, 1988.

Boothby, Robert, *Recollections of a Rebel*, Hutchinson, London, 1978.

Boyd-Carpenter, John, (Lord Boyd-Carpenter), *Way of Life: Memoirs*, Sidgwick & Jackson, London, 1980.

Bridges, Lord [Edward], *The Treasury*, 2nd edition, George Allen & Unwin, London, 1966.

Brittan, Samuel, *Steering the Economy*, Penguin Books, London, 1971.
The Role and Limits of Government: Essays in Political Economy, Temple Smith, London, 1983.

Britton, Andrew, *Macroeconomic Policy in Britain*, 1974–87, Cambridge University Press, Cambridge, 1991.

Brown, George, *In my way: The political memoirs of Lord George-Brown*, Gollancz, London, 1971.

Budge, Ian, 'Relative decline as a Political Issue: Ideological Motivations of the Politico-Economic Debate in Post-War Britain', in *Contemporary Record*, Vol. 7, No. 1, Summer 1993.

Bullock, Alan, *Ernest Bevin, Foreign Secretary 1945–51*, Oxford University Press; Oxford, 1983.

Burk, Kathleen, and Cairncross, Alec, '*Goodbye, Great Britain*', *The 1976 IMF Crisis*, Yale University Press, London and New Haven, 1992.

Butler, David, and Freeman, Jennie, *British Political Facts 1900–1960*, Macmillan, London, 1964.

Butler, R. A. (Lord Butler), *The Art of the Possible*, *The Memoirs of Lord Butler*, Hamish Hamilton, London, 1971.
The Art of Memory, *Friends in Perspective*, Hodder & Stoughton, London, 1982.

ed. Butler, Lawrence, and Jones, Harriet, *Britain in the Twentieth Century*, Vol. II, Institute of Contemporary British History and Heinemann, London and Oxford, 1995.

Cairncross, Alec, *The British Economy since 1945: Economic Policy and Performance*, *1945–1990*, Blackwell for the Institute of Contemporary British History, Oxford and London, 1992.
Years of Recovery, *British Economic Policy 1945–51*, Methuen, London, 1985.

Cairncross, Alec, and Eichengreen, Barry, *Sterling in decline: the devaluations of 1931, 1949 and 1967*, Blackwell, Oxford, 1983.
and Watts, N., *The Economic Section 1939–61: a study in economic advising*, Routledge, London, 1989.

Callaghan, James, (Lord Callaghan), *Time and Chance*, Collins, London, 1987.

Campbell, John, *Edward Heath*, Jonathan Cape, London, 1993.

Carrington, Lord, *Reflect on Things Past: The Memoirs of Lord Carrington*, Collins, London, 1988.

Castle, Barbara, (Lady Castle), *The Castle Diaries, 1964–70*, Weidenfeld & Nicolson, London, 1984.

Castle, Barbara, (Lady Castle), *The Castle Diaries, 1974–76*, Weidenfeld & Nicolson, London, 1980.

Clarke, Sir Richard, ed. Cairncross, Alec, *Anglo-American economic collaboration in war and peace, 1942–49*, Clarendon Press, Oxford, 1982.

Cooke, Colin, *The Life of Richard Stafford Cripps*, Hodder & Stoughton, London, 1957.

Coopey, Richard, 'The Ministry of Technology 1974–76 (Witness Seminar Transcript)' in *Contemporary Record*, Vol. 5, No. 1, Summer 1991.
'The White Heat of Scientific Revolution' in *Contemporary Record*, Vol. 5, No. 1, Summer 1991.

ed. Crafts, N.F.R., and Woodward, Nicholas, *The British Economy since 1945*, Clarendon Press, Oxford, 1991.

Crosland, Susan, *Tony Crosland*, Jonathan Cape, London, 1982.

ed. Crossman, Richard, *New Fabian Essays*, Turnstile Press, London, 1952.

Crossman, Richard, *The Diaries of a Cabinet Minister*, Vol. 1, Hamish Hamilton and Jonathan Cape, London, 1975.
The Diaries of a Cabinet Minister, Vol 2, Hamish Hamilton and Jonathan Cape, London, 1976.

Dalton, Hugh, (Lord Dalton), *High Tide and After: Memoirs, 1945–1960*, Frederick Muller, London, 1962.
Papers at the British Library of Political and Economic Science.

Danchev, Alex, *Oliver Franks, Founding Father*, Clarendon Press, Oxford, 1993.

Dell, Edmund, *Political Responsibility and Industry*, George Allen & Unwin, London, 1973.
'The Politics of Economic Interdependence', Fifth Rita Hinden Memorial Lecture, February 1977.
The Politics of Economic Interdependence, Macmillan, London, and St Martin's, New York, 1987.
A Hard Pounding, Politics and Economic Crisis, 1974–6, Oxford University Press, Oxford, 1991.
'The Origins of Petroleum Revenue Tax', *Contemporary Record*, Vol. 7, No. 2, Autumn 1993.
'Britain and the Origins of the European Monetary System', *Contemporary European History*, Vol. 3, Part 1, March 1994.

Dell, Sidney, *International Development Studies*, Duke University Press, 1991.

Delors Report, see *Report on economic and monetary union in the European Community*.

Dobson, Alan P., *The Politics of the Anglo-American Economic Special Relationship*, Wheatsheaf Books Limited, Brighton, 1988.

Donoughue, Bernard, and Jones, George, *Herbert Morrison, Portrait of a Politician*, Weidenfeld & Nicolson, London, 1973.

Donoughue, Bernard, *Prime Minister: The Conduct of Policy under Harold Wilson and James Callaghan*, Jonathan Cape, London, 1987.

Dow, J. C. R., *The Management of the British Economy, 1945–60*, Cambridge University Press, Cambridge, 1964.

Dow, J. C. R., and Saville, I.D., *A critique of monetary policy*, Oxford University Press, Oxford, 1990.

Durbin, E. F. M., *Problems of Economic Planning*, Routledge and Kegan Paul, London, 1949.

Economic Survey, 1947, Cmd. 7046, HMSO, London.

Economic Trends, published for the Central Statistical Office by HMSO, various dates.

Eden, Anthony, *Full Circle, the Memoirs of Sir Anthony Eden, KG, PC, MC*, Cassell, London, 1960.

Estorick, Eric, *Stafford Cripps*, William Heinemann, London, 1949.

Fay, Stephen, and Young, Hugo, *The day the £ nearly died, Sunday Times*, 14, 21, and 28 May 1978.

Fforde, John, *The Bank of England and Public Policy, 1941–58*, Cambridge University Press, Cambridge, 1992.

Fisher, Nigel, *Iain Macleod*, André Deutsch, London, 1973.

Foot, Michael, *Aneurin Bevan, 1945–1960*, Davis Poynter, London, 1973.

Foot, Paul, *The Politics of Harold Wilson*, Penguin Books, Harmondsworth, 1968.

Gaitskell, Hugh, *The Diary of Hugh Gaitskell, 1945–1956*, ed. Philip Williams, Jonathan Cape, London, 1983.

Gardner, Nick, *Decade of Discontent: The Changing British Economy since 1973*, Basil Blackwell Ltd, Oxford, 1987.

Gardner, R., *Sterling-Dollar Diplomacy*, Oxford University Press, Oxford, 1956.

Garritsen de Vries, Margaret, *The International Monetary Fund, 1972–78: Cooperation on trial*, Vols. I, II, III, Washington, International Monetary Fund, 1985.
The IMF in a Changing World, 1945–85, Washington, International Monetary Fund, 1986.

Gillingham, John, *Coal, steel and the rebirth of Europe, 1945–1955: The Germans and French from Ruhr conflict to economic community*, Cambridge University Press, Cambridge, 1991.

Gilmour, Ian, (Lord Gilmour), *Dancing with Dogma: Britain under Thatcherism*, Simon & Schuster, London, 1992.

Haines, Joe, *The Politics of Power*, Jonathan Cape, London, 1977.

Hall, Robert, (Lord Roberthall), *The Robert Hall Diaries, 1947–53*, ed. Alec Cairncross, Unwin Hyman, London, 1991.
The Robert Hall Diaries, 1954–61, ed. Alec Cairncross, Unwin Hyman, London, 1992.

Harris, Kenneth, *Attlee*, Weidenfeld & Nicolson, London, 1982.

Harrod, Roy, *The Life of John Maynard Keynes*, Macmillan, London, 1951.

Hatfield, Michael, *The House the Left Built, Inside Labour Policy-Making, 1970–75*, Gollancz, 1978.

Healey, Denis, (Lord Healey), *The Time of My Life*, Michael Joseph, London, 1989.

Heclo, Hugh, and Wildavsky, Aaron, *The private government of public money*, Macmillan, London, 1974.

ed. Helm, Dieter, *The Economic Borders of the State*, Oxford University Press, Oxford, 1989.

Hennessy, Peter, and Arends, Andrew, *Mr Attlee's Engine Room: Cabinet Committee Structure and the Labour Government 1945–51*, Strathclyde Papers on Government and Politics, 1983.

ed. Hennessy, Peter, and Seldon, Anthony, *Ruling Performance, British Governments from Attlee to Thatcher*, Basil Blackwell, Oxford, 1987.

Hennessy, Peter, '1949 Devaluation' (Transcription of a Witness Seminar on 4 October 1989) in *Contemporary Record*, Vol. 5, No. 3, Winter 1991.
Never Again: Britain 1945–1951, Jonathan Cape, London, 1992.

Hogan, Michael J., *The Marshall Plan: America, Britain, and the reconstruction of Western Europe, 1947–1952*, Cambridge University Press, Cambridge, 1987.

Horne, Alistair, *Macmillan*, Vol. 1, Macmillan, London, 1988.
Macmillan, Vol. 2, Macmillan, London, 1989.

House of Commons, *Official Report*.

Howard, Anthony, *RAB, The Life of R. A. Butler*, Jonathan Cape, London 1987.
Crossman, The Pursuit of Power, Jonathan Cape, London, 1990.

Howe, Geoffrey, (Lord Howe), *Conflict of Loyalty*, Macmillan, London, 1994.

Jay, Douglas, (Lord Jay), *Change and Fortune, A Political Record*, Hutchinson, London, 1980.
Sterling, Oxford University Press, Oxford, 1986.

Jenkins, Peter, *Mrs Thatcher's Revolution, The Ending of the Socialist Era*, Jonathan Cape, London, 1987.

Jenkins, Roy, (Lord Jenkins), *Essays and Speeches*, Collins, London, 1967.
European Diary, 1977–1981, Collins, London, 1989.
A Life at the Centre, Macmillan, London, 1991.

Johnson, Christopher, *The Economy Under Mrs Thatcher, 1979–90*, Penguin Books, Harmondsworth, 1991.

Jones, Jack, *Union Man – An Autobiography of Jack Jones*, Collins, London, 1986.

Jones, Tudor, 'Labour Revisionism and Public Ownership' in *Contemporary Record*, Vol. 5, No. 3, Winter 1991.

Kavanagh, Denis, *Thatcherism and British Politics: The End of Consensus?*, Oxford University Press, Oxford, 1990.

ed. Kavanagh, Denis and Seldon, Anthony, *The Major Effect*, Papermac, London, 1994.

Keegan, William, and Pennant-Rea, Rupert, *Who Runs the Economy, Control and Influence in British Economic Policy*, Maurice Temple Smith, 1979.

Keir, D. Lindsay, *The constitutional history of Modern Britain, 1485–1937*, Adam & Charles Black, London, 1947.

ed. Kenen, Peter B., *Managing the World Economy: Fifty Years after Bretton Woods*, Institute for International Economics, Washington, 1994.

Kennan, George F., *Memoirs 1925–1950*, Hutchinson, London, 1968.

Keynes, John Maynard, (Lord Keynes), *The General Theory of Employment, Interest and Money*, Macmillan, London, 1947.

King, Cecil, *The Cecil King Diary, 1965–1970*, Jonathan Cape, London, 1972.

Kyle, Keith, *Suez*, Weidenfeld & Nicolson, London, 1992.

Kynaston, David, *The Chancellor of the Exchequer*, Terence Dalton Limited, Lavenham, Suffolk, 1980.

Lamb, Richard, *The Macmillan Years 1957–1963: The Emerging Truth*, John Murray, London, 1995.

Lawson, Nigel, *The View from No. 11: Memoirs of a Tory Radical*, Corgi Books, London, 1993.

Likierman, Andrew, *Public Expenditure, The Public Spending Process*, Penguin Books, London, 1988.

Lyttelton, Oliver, Viscount Chandos, *Memoirs*, The Bodley Head, London, 1962.

MacDougall, Donald, *Don and Mandarin: Memoirs of an Economist*, John Murray, London, 1987.

ed. McKie, David, and Cook, Chris, *The Decade of Disillusion: British Politics in the Sixties*, Macmillan and St Martin's Press, London, 1972.

Macmillan, Harold, (Lord Stockton), *The Blast of War, 1945–55*, Macmillan, London, 1967.
  Tides of Fortune, 1945–55, Macmillan, London, 1969.
  Riding the Storm, 1956–59, Macmillan, London, 1971.
  Pointing the Way, 1959–61, Macmillan, London, 1972.
  At the End of the Day, 1961–63, Macmillan, London, 1973.

Maitland, F. W., *The constitutional history of England*, Cambridge University Press, Cambridge, 1931.

Marjolin, Robert, *Architect of European Unity: Memoirs 1911–1986*, Weidenfeld & Nicolson, London, 1989.

Marquand, David, *Sir Stafford Cripps*, in Michael Sissons and Philip French (eds.), *The Age of Austerity*, Hodder & Stoughton, London, 1963.

Martin, Paul, *The London Diaries, 1975–79*, University of Ottawa Press, 1988.

Maudling, Reginald, *Memoirs*, Sidgwick & Jackson, London, 1978.

Meade, James, *The Collected Papers of James Meade*, Volume IV, *The Cabinet Office Diary 1944–6*, ed. Susan Howson and Donald Mogridge, Unwin Hyman, London, 1990.

Milward, Alan S., *The Reconstruction of Western Europe. 1945–51*, Methuen & Co. Ltd, London, 1984.
  The European Rescue of the Nation-State, Routledge, London, 1992.

Mitchell, Joan, *Crisis in Britain 1951*, Secker & Warburg, London in association with the University of Nottingham, 1963.

Monnet, Jean, *Memoirs*, London, Collins, 1978 (Translated by Richard Mayne).

Morgan, Kenneth O., *Labour in Power 1945–1951*, Clarendon Press, Oxford, 1984.
　The People's Peace, British History 1945–1989, Oxford University Press, Oxford, 1990.
National Institute Economic Review.
Part, Antony, *The Making of a Mandarin*, André Deutsch, London, 1990.
Pimlott, Ben, *Hugh Dalton*, Jonathan Cape, London, 1985.
ed. Pimlott, Ben, *The Political Diary of Hugh Dalton*, Jonathan Cape, London, 1986.
Pimlott, Ben, *Harold Wilson*, HarperCollins, London, 1993.
Pliatzky, Leo, *Getting and Spending: Public Expenditure, Employment and Inflation*, Basil Blackwell, Oxford, 1982.
　Paying and Choosing: The Intelligent Person's Guide to the Mixed Economy, Basil Blackwell, Oxford, 1985.
　The Treasury under Mrs Thatcher, Basil Blackwell, Oxford, 1989.
Plowden, Edwin, (Lord Plowden), *An Industrialist in the Treasury: The Postwar Years*, André Deutsch, London, 1989.
Prior, Jim, (Lord Prior), *A Balance of Power*, Hamish Hamilton, London, 1986.
Procter, Stephen J., 'Floating Convertibility: The Emergence of the Robot Plan, 1951–52' in *Contemporary Record*, Vol. 7, No. 1, Summer 1993.
Public Expenditure White Papers, London, HMSO, various dates.
Pym, Francis, (Lord Pym), *The Politics of Consent*, Hamish Hamilton, London, 1984.
Report on economic and monetary union in the European Community (Delors Report), Office for Official Publications of the European Communities, Luxembourg, 1989.
Rhodes James, Robert, *Ambitions and Realities: British Politics 1964–1970*, Weidenfeld & Nicolson, London, 1972.
　Anthony Eden, Papermac, London, 1987.
　Bob Boothby, A Portrait, Hodder & Stoughton, London, 1991.
Riddell, Peter, *The Thatcher Government*, Martin Robertson, Oxford, 1983.
Ridley, Nicholas, (Lord Ridley), *'My Style of Government'*, *The Thatcher Years*, Hutchinson, London, 1991.
Roll, Eric, (Lord Roll), *Crowded Hours*, Faber & Faber, London, 1985.
　Where Did We Go Wrong? From the Gold Standard to Europe, Faber & Faber, London, 1995.
Roseveare, Henry, *The Treasury: The Evolution of a British Institution*, Allen Lane, The Penguin Press, 1969.
Salter, Arthur, (Lord Salter), *Slave of the Lamp, a public servant's notebook*, Weidenfeld & Nicolson, London, 1967.
Schenk, Catherine R, 'The Sterling Area and British Policy Alternatives in the 1950s' in *Contemporary Record*, Vol. 6, No. 2, Autumn 1992.
Shepherd, Robert, *Iain Macleod*, Hutchinson, London, 1994.
ed. Sissons, Michael, and French, Philip, *Age of Austerity*, Hodder & Stoughton, 1963.

Skidelsky, Robert, (Lord Skidelsky), *John Maynard Keynes*, Vol. 2, *The Economist as Saviour, 1920–1937*, Macmillan, London, 1992.

Smith, Adam, *The Wealth of Nations*, Dent 'Everyman', London, 1947.

Smith, David, *The Rise and Fall of Monetarism: The theory and politics of an economic experiment*, Penguin Books, Harmondsworth, Middlesex, 1987.

Stein, Herbert, *Presidential Economics: The Making of Economic Policy from Roosevelt to Reagan and Beyond*, Simon & Schuster Inc., New York, 1985.

Stephenson, Hugh, *Mrs Thatcher's First Year*, Jill Norman, London, 1980.

Stewart, Michael, (Lord Stewart), *Life and Labour, An Autobiography*, Sidgwick & Jackson, London, 1980.

Thatcher, Margaret, *The Downing Street Years*, HarperCollins, London, 1993.

Thirlwall, Anthony P., *Nicholas Kaldor*, Wheatsheaf Books, Brighton, 1987.

Thorpe, D. R., *Selwyn Lloyd*, Jonathan Cape, London, 1989.

Walker, Peter, (Lord Walker), *Staying Power*, Bloomsbury, London, 1991.

Whitelaw, William, (Lord Whitelaw), *The Whitelaw Memoirs*, Aurum Press, London, 1989.

Williams, Geoffrey, and Reed, Bruce, *Denis Healey and the Policies of Power*, Sidgwick & Jackson, London, 1971.

Williams, Philip, *Hugh Gaitskell, A Political Biography*, Jonathan Cape, London, 1979.

Wilson, Harold, (Lord Wilson), *The Labour Government 1964–1970: a Personal Record*, Weidenfeld & Nicolson and Michael Joseph, London, 1971.
The Governance of Britain, Weidenfeld & Nicolson and Michael Joseph, London, 1976.
Final Term: The Labour Government, 1974–76, Weidenfeld & Nicolson and Michael Joseph, London, 1979.

Wright, John F., *Britain in the Age of Economic Management*, Oxford University Press, Oxford, 1979.

Young, David, (Lord Young of Graffham), *The Enterprise Years: A Businessman in the Cabinet*, Headline, London, 1991.

Young, Hugo, *One of Us, A Biography of Margaret Thatcher*, Macmillan, London, 1989.

Young, John W., *Britain, France and the Unity of Europe 1945–1951*, Leicester University Press Leicester, 1984.

Ziegler, Philip, *Harold Wilson, The Authorised Life*, Weidenfeld & Nicholson, London, 1993.

Index

NOTE   British politicians and civil servants tend to change their names during the course of their careers moving up through knighthoods to peerages. The name used in this index is the one by which they were best known during their careers.